Social Software and the Evolution of User Expertise:

Future Trends in Knowledge Creation and Dissemination

Tatjana Takševa
Saint Mary's University, Canada

Information Science
REFERENCE

Managing Director: Lindsay Johnston
Editorial Director: Joel Gamon
Book Production Manager: Jennifer Romanchak
Publishing Systems Analyst: Adrienne Freeland
Assistant Acquisitions Editor: Kayla Wolfe
Typesetter: Lisandro Gonzalez
Cover Design: Nick Newcomer

Published in the United States of America by
        Information Science Reference (an imprint of IGI Global)
        701 E. Chocolate Avenue
        Hershey PA 17033
        Tel: 717-533-8845
        Fax: 717-533-8661
        E-mail: cust@igi-global.com
        Web site: http://www.igi-global.com

                Library of Congress Cataloging-in-Publication Data

Social software and the evolution of user expertise: future trends in knowledge creation and dissemination / Tatjana Takseva,
editor.
    p. cm.
 Includes bibliographical references and index.
 Summary: "This book examines the vital role that social software applications play in regards to the cultural definitions by
experts and challenges the reader to consider how recent changes in this area influence how we create and distribute
knowledge"-- Provided by publisher.
 ISBN 978-1-4666-2178-7 (hardcover) -- ISBN 978-1-4666-2179-4 (ebook) -- ISBN 978-1-4666-2180-0 (print & perpetual
access) 1. Social sciences--Research--Methodology. 2. Online social networks. 3. Web 2.0 I. Takseva, Tatjana, 1970-
 H62.S72471817 2013
 001.0285'6754--dc23
                        2012019283

British Cataloguing in Publication Data
A Cataloguing in Publication record for this book is available from the British Library.

Table of Contents

Section 1
Expertise and the Changing Nature of Knowledge Creation and
Dissemination in the Web 2.0 Environment

Section 2
Changing Expert Environments in the University and in the
Areas of Research and Scholarship

Section 3
Reimagining Pedagogical Expertise

Section 4
Case Studies of Collective or Decentralized Expertise

Detailed Table of Contents

Section 1
Expertise and the Changing Nature of Knowledge Creation and
Dissemination in the Web 2.0 Environment

The chapters in this section investigate in broad and sometimes philosophical terms the changing contexts of knowledge creation and dissemination in relation to expertise and social software. Collectively, they provide a framework for considering the evolution of expertise from its traditional bases to more recent developments under the influence of social media. The chapters re-conceptualize expertise in ways that account for the often serious and valid contributions amateurs now make to the process of knowledge production and dissemination, suggesting that new definitions of expertise need to include collective or decentralized forms of expertise, originating from the community or the collective rather than only from individual traditionally-accredited experts(Mitra; Sweet; Watts). The authors also draw attention to the need for more systematic approaches to evaluating the validity of knowledge thus produced, and for a more thoughtful engagement with the new means of knowledge production (Pure, et al.; Watts).

A fundamental epistemological question that has been the focus of much deliberation over time is: how do we know what we know? One of the answers to this question has been found in the theories of narrative asserting that humans learn through stories, ranging from religious epics to personal anecdotes. The social media phenomenon offers a unique form of narration that utilizes "narbs," narrative bits that tell the stories of specific individuals who may be, but often are not, traditional experts. Yet, as a collection, these narbs could become the authoritative narrative about a particular issue where expertise is located in the collective. This chapter examines the theoretical basis of knowledge creation through narrative, and how the narbs of social media users are creating dynamic bodies of information. The chapter offers a lexicon for categorizing narbs and provides an analytical frame for examining them. The overall aim of this chapter is to demonstrate that interaction and new modes of gathering and disseminating information and knowledge in the digital environment require different and emergent expertise in narrative construction and interpretation.

The Free Online Encyclopedia, as Wikipedia calls itself, is a radical departure from traditional encyclopedias and traditional methods of knowledge creation. This chapter is an examination of how a community of amateurs on Wikipedia has challenged notions of expertise in the 21st century. It does so by first looking at the roots of Wikipedia in a phenomenon known as the "wisdom of the crowds" and in the open source software movement. The reliability of Wikipedia is examined as are the claims made by major critics of the project. Throughout, epistemological questions raised by Wikipedia are addressed.

Chapter 3

Recent technological changes have created a radically different information environment from the one that existed even a few decades ago. Rather than coming from a small number of sources, each with a substantial investment in the information production and delivery processes, information is increasingly provided by a wide range of sources, many of which can readily provide and deliver information to large audiences worldwide. One consequence of this evolution in information production is an almost incomprehensibly vast information repository in the form of the Web and other online resources. A variety of social media have extended this information and source fecundity even further by connecting individuals to one another and by providing significant opportunities to share myriad types of information generated by users themselves. This shift in information dissemination challenges longstanding models of the provision of credible information by suggesting circumstances under which sources that are not understood as "experts" in the traditional sense are in fact in the best position to provide the most credible information.

Social software forms new kinds of collectives and expands the means of producing and disseminating knowledge. Yet the combination of persistent connection and fragmented communication can undermine intentionality. Philosophies of technology that privilege data over users exacerbate this danger; more humanistic approaches to software design are now required. Through personal observation and an examination of recent literature (largely drawn from the popular press), the author examines the philosophies that underlie social software designs, explores ways they affect interaction, describes potential pitfalls, and theorizes a reimagining of expertise in this context—complementing, rather than replacing, the scholarly traditions of the academy.

Section 2
Changing Expert Environments in the University and in the Areas of Research and Scholarship

The chapters in Section 2 consider from various disciplinary perspectives the impact of new models of knowledge creation and dissemination on higher education and universities as cultural institutions (Scolari et al.; Phipps, Friend Wyse and Amundsen), including academic libraries within universities (Cassella and Calvi). Authors consider not only the changing role of universities, faculty members, and librarians in view of the changes urged by social media and the speed and ease of access to information and knowledge, but also the nature of scholarly communication and research as it is affected by various social software applications and their implications for academic expertise (Beaulieu, van Dalen-Oskam and Zundert; Landes; van Dijck). One of the chapters in particular critically examines a social software application that acts as a search engine but also as an implicit ranking system that through its operation participates in the creation of scholarly knowledge and its dissemination (van Dijck).

Chapter 5

Carlos A. Scolari, Universitat Pompeu Fabra, Spain
Cristóbal Cobo Romani, Oxford Internet Institute, UK
Hugo Pardo Kuklinski, Universidat de Barcelona, Spain

Disintermediation based on digital technology has transformed different environments, including banking, commerce, media, education, and knowledge management. The spread of social software applications and digital media in general has given rise to new models of knowledge production and distribution in higher education. This chapter redefines higher education institutions and academic experts based on these changes. The chapter discusses the diffusion of disintermediation practices in higher education and proposes new categories, such as knowledge brokering, knowledge networking, and knowledge translation, to map a new environment that promotes disintermediation, innovation, and openness. Beyond the prophecies announcing the "death of the university," the authors suggest new agents, actions, and transactions that are useful for envisaging the higher education institutions of the new century.

Chapter 6

Laurie Craig Phipps, Simon Fraser University, Canada
& Kwantlen Polytechnic University, Canada
Alyssa Friend Wise, Simon Fraser University, Canada
Cheryl Amundsen, Simon Fraser University, Canada

Discussion of changing notions of faculty expertise and the role of technology within the educational enterprise is nothing new. However, the current demand for change in teaching and learning practices is particularly strong, in part due to the pressures arising from emerging technologies and the shifting nature of faculty expertise. Web 2.0 technologies enable social connectivity, academic interactivity, and content co-creation. Thus, they change the ways of interacting with information and can support collaborative and constructivist approaches in higher education. This both inspires and requires a corresponding expansion in faculty's role: from imparter of knowledge to orchestrator of learning experiences. Within the general metaphor of orchestration, other specific roles and functions will also be required; for example, scripting, translating, introducing, and co-exploring. As educators attempt to reimagine an educational paradigm in this context, the integration of new technologies must be grounded in how they can support educational experiences and outcomes that are focused on learning.

Chapter 7

Anne Beaulieu, University of Groningen, The Netherlands
Karina van Dalen-Oskam, Huygens Institute for the History of the Netherlands, The Netherlands
Joris van Zundert, Huygens Institute for the History of the Netherlands, The Netherlands

Web 2.0 is characterized by values of openness of participation (unrestricted by traditional markers of expertise), collaboration across and beyond institutions, increased value of resources through distributed participation, dynamic content and context, and self-organization and scalability. These values seem to offer new possibilities for knowledge creation. They also contrast in important ways with traditional forms of knowledge creation, where expertise, institutional affiliation, and restrictions on access and circulation have been important. Yet, rather than seeing a dichotomy between Web 2.0 and non-Web 2.0 modes of working in digital humanities, the authors observe the rise of hybrid forms that combine elements of these two modes. In this chapter, the authors reflect on the reasons for such hybrids, specifically through an exploration of eLaborate. As a virtual research environment, eLaborate targets both professional scholars and volunteers working with textual resources. The environment offers tools to transcribe textual sources, to annotate these transcriptions, and to publish them as digital scholarly editions. The majority of content currently comprises texts from the cultural heritage of Dutch history and literary history, although eLaborate does not put limits on the kind of text or language. Nor does the system impose limits on the openness of contribution to any edition project. Levels of openness and access are solely determined by the groups of users working on specific texts or editions. This Web 2.0 technology-based software is now used by several groups of teachers and students, and by scholarly, educated, and interested volunteers.

Chapter 8

José van Dijck, University of Amsterdam, The Netherlands

Search engines in general, and Google Scholar in particular, are co-producers of academic knowledge. They have a profound impact on the way knowledge is generated, transmitted, and distributed. This chapter first explores how Google Scholar works as a human-technological system in order to analyze the site's technology in combination with its inscribed usage and its actual use and users. The chapter then scrutinize the complex power relationships of digital networks with Google at its epicenter. Following Manuel Castells's proposal to "unwire" the construction of academic knowledge through the coded dynamics of search engines, the author examines the larger legal and political-economic implications of the platform's architecture and organized structure. Combining these two layers of analysis should inform an enriched type of information literacy.

Chapter 9

Lilian Landes, Bavarian State Library, Germany

With digitalization increasing, scholars' reading habits and communication methods are also changing, thus affecting the field of traditional reviewing in the humanities. The expert formulating a comprehensive review of a recently published work, will, in the medium term, see a scholarly community working together. In the age of Web 2.0, the disadvantages of a traditional book review, which usually does not allow for a reply or an open discussion, become apparent. This chapter describes (the preconditions for) these changes, as well as other issues in the current field of reviewing, that will eventually not only increase the speed of reviewing new publications in general, but will also, in compliance with the nature of this field, make it more focused on process and detail, more interdisciplinary, more flexible, and more international, thus adapting the model of "live" reviewing procedures as already established in the commercial book market.

Chapter 10

Maria Cassella, University of Torino, Italy
Licia Calvi, NHTV University of Breda, The Netherlands

This chapter presents the results of a survey of Dutch and Italian academic libraries conducted to identify how academic libraries deal with the growing adoption of social media for professional purposes, and how they consider this adoption as the only possible way for them to reposition themselves among an audience that is more and more involved with social media. The results, surprisingly, show that although the interest and the need for such an adoption are felt rather strongly, the complete conversion to a library 2.0 is still not in reach. Many respondents, especially in the Dutch context, were interested in the outcome of this study to help them decide which direction they should take.

Section 3
Reimagining Pedagogical Expertise

The chapters that follow engage closely with the implications of social software applications and social media on how students acquire information and conduct research, as well as their behavior in the classroom. The authors investigate the extent to which pedagogical expertise has changed and still needs to change in order to adapt to the changes in communication and social networking practices encouraged by the new media and favored by most students (Fitzgibbons; Beuschel; Broussard, et al.). Two of the chapters propose adopting social software applications such as Twitter and text-messaging into the classroom as explicit strategies to teach writing and composition, thus capitalizing on a skill and a form of expertise that most students already possess (Grant; Girardi).

Chapter 11

Megan Fitzgibbons, McGill University, Canada

The advent of social media necessitates new pedagogical approaches in the field of political science, specifically in relation to undergraduate students' critical thinking and information evaluation skills. Instead of seeking out traditional static pools of knowledge, researchers and researchers-in-training now interact with information in an amorphous stream of production and consumption. Socially created information is now firmly integrated in the basic subject matter of political science, as manifested in primary sources in the field, scholars' communication practices, and the emergence of collective and distributed expertise. Existing models of information evaluation competencies do not address these realities of participatory authorship and decentralized distribution of information. Thus, in order to educate "information-literate" students in political science, educators must foster an understanding of how information is produced and how to critically evaluate individual information sources in the context of academic tasks.

This chapter uses a methodological approach to investigate research and design knowledge acquisition in the context of social software applications, an area cluttered by an ever-growing number of applications and high expectations about the capabilities of a new generation of young users, the Net Generation. Its objectives are twofold: to provide a rational point of departure for developing a research and design framework and to exemplify it for the use of social software in higher education. The chapter scrutinizes popular assumptions about the Net Generation, basing the framework on the interdependency of user audience and technology. The results of a longitudinal exploratory study for the area of social software use in higher education are presented. The final part of the chapter discusses implications for the design of learning environments and a number of ideas for further research on knowledge acquisition within the social software context.

Social media applications like wikis, blogs, and comments on online news feeds emphasize user participation, encouraging ongoing revision by volunteer expertise. Surveying undergraduate students and teaching faculty at two small liberal arts institutions enabled the researchers to examine how both students and faculty view this new expertise, and how appropriate each group sees this expertise for completing undergraduate research. The results show that students are using social media extensively for preliminary research and educational videos, with Wikipedia and YouTube being the most popular sites for this purpose. Students and faculty continue to value advanced degrees, publications, and experience as the most important indicators of expertise. Students and faculty agree that users must always question the accuracy of information on social media sites, but faculties are not satisfied with students' ability to evaluate such information.

Text messaging has many similarities to poetry or short prose writing. Instructors typically discount text messaging as a distraction in the classroom, but this chapter includes a review of the positive aspects of implementing the genre of text messaging in the composition classroom as a means of teaching writing. Using a community of practice approach, this chapter looks at the technologically savvy generation of college students in today's classrooms and attempts to capitalize, educationally, on the writing skills that students already possess. Next, it explores both the theoretical and practical implementations of this genre into the composition classroom with careful consideration of the positive and negative impacts of this, before examining the transition from student text messaging to the writing of other, longer genres. Although this chapter's focus is on the teaching of writing, the information can be considered to be interdisciplinary.

Chapter 15

Twitter represents a virtual, global classroom of collective intelligence and an epistemological shift in which the "experts" in the exchange are not necessarily the traditional teachers. The experts on Twitter are those who share information of value and do so often, a definition that could and should include students engaging the medium for academic purposes. As an academic tool, Twitter offers students the opportunity to engage in a wider discourse than the classroom environment and to gain confidence in their knowledge and potential "expert" status. Furthermore, the nature of Twitter closely aligns with Tapscott's (2009) identified norms for the Net Generation, which includes current high school and college-aged students. The eight norms—freedom, customization, scrutiny, integrity, collaboration, entertainment, speed, and innovation—provide an appropriate theoretical framework for a curriculum-related question such as: What is the value of implementing Twitter into classroom instruction?

Section 4
Case Studies of Collective or Decentralized Expertise

The chapters in Section 4 provide specific examples drawn from different contexts in which collective or decentralized expertise has already changed and possibly replaced traditional notions of expertise. From the ways in which professional ICT knowledge and expertise is acquired and maintained (Truyen and Buekens), the decentralized nature of technical support in community forums related to technology hardware and software (Ovadia), and team expertise involved in making a 3-D movie online (Karasavvidis), to the changed nature of archiving and archival expertise (Clark), these chapters demonstrate the ways in which the idea of expertise has evolved to incorporate the valuable and often expert contributions of those who have been traditionally considered lay-persons or amateurs and excluded from the process of knowledge creation and dissemination.

Chapter 16

Several co-evolving trends have impacted expectations of professional workers' quality of knowledge. The abundance of information shared through the Internet, the ever-increasing specialization of tasks, the possibility of immediately accessible information through social networks, the participation of stakeholders in the social web, and the increased requirements for separation of duty in a corporate context have contributed to a situation where the current 'knowledge worker' is not expected to have the same level of readily available knowledge as before. This chapter describes this phenomenon in detail with a case study from ICT-expert jobs. It shows that an ICT manager can no longer overlook the work of collaborators, just by virtue of being the smartest employee around. He/she will increasingly rely on organizational procedures and professional standards to assess whether the right people - with the right competencies for the job – are at his/her disposal. After describing the specifics of professional knowledge for ICT experts and the role of social software plays in this, the chapter focuses on the epistemological aspects of ICT expertise. The authors discuss current strands of reliabilistic accounts for knowledge in relation to expertise. They show that besides reliability, it is accuracy that is needed in order to perform as an expert.

This chapter discusses the authority structures found within the community support forums of open and closed source operating systems (Linux, Windows, and OS X), demonstrating how, because of these forums, technical expertise is shifting away from the organizations responsible for creating these systems and into the community using them. One might expect this kind of migration within Linux communities, where in theory anyone can contribute to the code of the project, but it is also being seen in closed source projects, where only certain people, usually employees, have access to the underlying code that controls the operating system. In these situations, expertise is becoming decentralized despite the fact that members of the support community sometimes lack access to the code behind these operating systems.

Chapter 18

In the world of archives, Web 2.0 means more than wider and easier access to digital surrogates of archival objects. Newly developing Web 2.0 applications provide multiple possibilities for contextualizing archival objects through the contributions of many users, rather than a few established experts, marking a shift in archival practice and the role of the expert archivist. For many archival objects with origins in collaborative and popular cultural traditions, a context for online access that invites collaboration and challenges the authority of the expert is particularly conducive to helping users make sense of the archival objects. While this may lead to tensions between innovation and tradition in archival practice, user-contributed knowledge and multiple interpretations of documents can be incorporated as a complement to institutional records, rather than a replacement for traditional methods of description and classification. The purpose of this chapter is to describe recent developments in interactive and collaborative online archives that challenge and enhance traditional ideas about archival expertise. For one Appalachian folk song collection in particular, a community of expertise, ownership, and collaboration may help to keep unique recordings in continued use as part of a living, and still-evolving, musical tradition.

Chapter 19

Social software facilitates the linking of people in unprecedented ways and leads to new knowledge creation and application practices. Even though expertise remains an important constituent of these practices, there is a knowledge gap in the literature regarding its role. This chapter was written with the aim of filling this gap by using Project Durian as a case study. Project Durian presented a unique opportunity to study expertise as mediated by social software because it involved both social software and various layers, forms, and configurations of expertise. In this chapter, data from Project Durian are used to examine the outsourcing of tasks and the role that social software played in that outsourcing. Data analysis indicated that, in the hybrid practice that was established, expertise was spatio-temporally distributed, involved individuals with a broad range of skills, facilitated the crossing of disciplinary boundaries, and was renegotiated. The implications of these findings for expertise in the Web 2.0 era are discussed.

Preface

The term Web 2.0 technologies, also known as *social software,* was coined by Rohit Parikh in a paper that appeared in *Synthese* in 2002. At the time, Parikh did not provide a precise definition of the term, but rather attempted to suggest what it means through a series of provocative examples demonstrating procedures that structure social realities in a very broad sense. The term caught on and began to refer to a second generation of Internet technologies and a new generation of Web applications providing an infrastructure for more dynamic user participation, social interaction and collaboration. Thanks to the applications of this software, as well as open source software-- which makes source code available to the general public with minimal copyright restrictions and with resulting participation and interaction-- a variety of facts and content previously in the possession of experts traditionally seen as the only legitimate sources of knowledge can be created, accessed and shared almost instantly by any user with an Internet connection. Among applications of this kind of software are blogs, Wikis, MySpace, Twitter, Vkontakte, Facebook, Flickr, Odeo, Google Video, Google docs, Partyflock, Wasabi, YouTube, and other communication tools such as social bookmaking, peer-to-peer social networking, instant messaging, podcasting, etc. While computer scientists like to point out the differences between social software and open source software, this collection assumes a conceptual area of overlap between the two terms, as well as 'open source' as a philosophy, referring to computer mediated platforms enabling and encouraging forms of user participation, modification and interaction.

Web 2.0 technologies make it easy for members of the public previously considered readers or audience to contribute ideas and content to the public sphere of discourse and thus enlarge the existing body of knowledge in various ways. These technologies are bringing about a change in the production and definition of knowledge as well as affecting the direction of future knowledge creation and dissemination. The phenomenon of *mass amateurization* of knowledge-- the emergence and increasing availability of so called user-generated online content enabled through the rise of Web 2.0 technologies and its associated applications-- carries broad implications for future concepts of expertise.

The new forms of collective intelligence powered by the digital media invite redefinition of expertise traditionally defined as mastery of facts and content of a certain subject. They encourage collaboration, ongoing revision, interdisciplinarity, and a new understanding of knowledge as a process of inquiry, rather than simply its product. This aim of this collection is to present preliminary findings and generate a discussion on how older models of expertise are adapting to the new cultural and media-driven environment and on the emerging forms of expertise shaped by digital media.

To be an expert traditionally means to know a lot of content and to have a great deal of prepositional knowledge *that...* (such and such is the case). Accreditation by public or reputable private institutions continues to be the dominant way of distinguishing experts from non-experts. However, degree granting structures and the narrow disciplinary orientation of most graduate programs, where professional values are most firmly shaped, have encouraged a narrow view of knowledge and expertise. In 1990, Ernest Boyer, the president of the Carnegie Foundation for the Advancement of Teaching, pointed out that the doctoral dissertation, thought of as original research, is usually written on an increasingly isolated, narrow topic disconnected from the concerns of the world beyond the university or often even other disciplines, in a language understood by a limited number of equally narrowly specialized readers; consequential assertions made in the dissertation are often footnoted, and creative, integrative thinking often discouraged (Boyer, p. 68).

Boyer's statements echo the criticism of narrow specialization made by the Nobel laureate physicist, Philip Anderson who said, "the more the elementary particle physicists tell us about the nature of the fundamental laws, the less relevance they seem to have to the very real problems of the rest of science, much less to those of society" (Anderson, 1972). More recently, Lauglin and Pines (2000) note, referring to the Theory of Everything (in use at the particle level in physics): "we have succeeded in reducing all of ordinary physical behavior to a simple, correct Theory of Everything only to discover that it has revealed exactly nothing about many things of great importance" (pp. 28-31).

Some aspects of this situation have changed over the last couple of decades as the number of interdisciplinary programs at universities and colleges has expanded globally, seeking to approach various topics of inquiry from a wider set of perspectives. The increasing appreciation of interdisciplinarity has been influenced in part by the rapid spread of ubiquitous computing and global connectivity, both of which make visible the complex interdependence and simultaneity of most research questions. However, the results of the orientation toward narrow specialty are still embedded in dominant cultural notions of what constitutes expertise.

The largely subject-based conception of knowledge, as a body of information and ideas to be transmitted from expert to laypersons, rests on the widely-held belief that to be an expert means to know a lot of content and to have a great deal of prepositional or factual knowledge within a narrow area of specialization. This definition of expertise conceives of knowledge as a product of inquiry processes rather than a process in relation to the products. Experts traditionally belong to small, exclusive groups that make up the social structures of authority when it comes to producing and distributing knowledge, information, and opinion. The concept of knowledge in this paradigm has been understood implicitly as a more or less closed or exclusive set of ideas or facts relating to different subject areas, and *meaning* was seen as a set of predetermined nuggets of particular knowledge transferred from experts to the laity. These views gained a cultural stronghold partly because they imply that there is something tangible and quantifiable that distinguishes expert from non-expert, which justifies the experts' position and privilege. The assumptions on which this conception of expertise rest is that knowledge is something that one "receives, holds, and then releases in highly controlled environments, with the underlying message that knowledge is preexisting and that the world is more or less static and unchanging (also Takseva Chorney, 2010).

That things have begun to change is indicated by a number of factors. Last year, for example, the Modern Language Association (MLA), the main professional US association with international scope for academic scholars, professors, and graduate students who teach and study languages and literatures, started considering radical changes in the dissertation, the dominant model of scholarship required from graduate students granted a Ph.D. The association found that the traditional model of producing a several-hundred-page analysis based on a linear argument that still dominates language doctoral programs is overused and frequently ineffective, governed by out-of-date conventions, and leading to the production of "proto-books" that may do little to promote scholarship, and may not even be advancing the careers of graduate students. It was pointed out that the nature of scholarship in the 21st century is changing and that degree granting institutions need to reexamine the criteria on which their credentialing is based (also Jaschick, 2012).

Key global trends concerning higher education and the nature of the student body point to the fact that interaction and collaboration are becoming increasingly relevant in the context of teaching and learning. This is not surprising given that most students belong to the so-called Net Generation, those who have never known life without digital media. It has been said that they tend to gravitate toward group activities that promote social interaction, and they prefer to learn and work in teams; they value connectivity and interactivity, learn better through inductive discovery than by being told, often find peers more credible than teachers, and are more likely to use the Internet for research than the library. In many cases, often resulting from the combination between increasingly cross-cultural contexts of instruction and the instantaneous access the digital media provide to a staggering amount of resources and information, expert teachers find themselves in a position where their students have knowledge that they may not.

What is perhaps more surprising is that faculty members in all disciplines are increasingly relying on Web 2.0 technologies both in and outside the classroom. A recent study of 940,000 college professors conducted by Pearson Learning Solutions indicates that 91% of college professor use social media, such as Youtube, Facebook, blogs, Linkedin, Wikis, Twitter, and Flickr (in that ranking) for professional development and as teaching aids (Knight, 2011). A series of recent focus groups conducted by the Canadian Research Network at a number of Canadian universities, mine included, aimed at assessing the impact of digital content on research and scholarship across different disciplines, revealed that the way research is conducted and scholarship in general is profoundly influenced by digital networking technologies in a number of ways. The most significant changes noted were ease of access to a variety of materials, reduced travel, a more rigorous interdisciplinarity, the ease of creating networks as well as other forms of collaboration. While collaboration among scholars has always been part of academic life, the ease and speed of access to resources and colleagues enabled by the new technologies has brought this dimension of scholarship to the forefront of scholarly interaction.

The implications of social software for knowledge creation, dissemination and expertise within academic institutions are especially great due to the fact that it is academic institutions that are the 'producers' of future experts. One of the most significant changes to scholarship now is the combination between ease of access to a variety of materials that previously required extensive time and travel, and the consequent speed of producing scholarship. These developments raise important questions about the nature of scholarship in the future: if a scholar finds accurate and verifiable data needed to build his/her argument very quickly and easily though Google and Wikipedia, does that by default diminish the quality of his or her scholarship? Does quality in traditionally-understood scholarship depend on where and how the data was obtained, or does it depend on the skill of argument, or a combination of both? These and other related issues challenge the traditional academic notion that good scholarship should and does take much time and effort, thus also suggesting that, perhaps, the scholar's set of skills is also changing under the influence of digital technologies.

These are only some indicators that the impact of digital media and social software on the process and shape of traditional scholarship and scholarly activity within academic institutions is significant and ongoing. The proliferation of user-generated content combined with open-access content models is changing the way academics think about scholarship and publication, and highlights the emergence of collective wisdom and knowledge creation as a social activity with much greater speed and scope than before. Some academic journals and magazines use shared editing tools such as *Google Docs* and wikis to create online books that allow readers to comment sometimes even at the paragraph level, opening up the process of writing to ongoing collaboration between experts and non-experts. Many hobbyists and amateur scholars are engaged in data collection and field studies that make a significant contribution to many areas, and whose work is available on blogs and photostreams.

It is developments such as these that have led Glen Reynolds, law professor, founder of the American political blog "Instapundit," and author of *The Army of Davids,* to claim that we are on the brink of the amateur century, where technology confers upon every individual the power traditionally available only to "nation-states, superheroes, or gods" (Reynolds, 2006, p. 237). While this near –mythical prophecy is not completely self-evident, it seems clear that in different ways and differing degrees Web 2.0 technologies tend to blur the lines between expert and amateur; that they change the structures of authority for producing and distributing knowledge, information and opinion (Lemann, 2006), and so challenge traditional notions of expertise. The creation and dissemination of knowledge is no longer exclusively controlled by a relative minority who acted as its gatekeepers.

The participatory, open, and socially-constructed models of knowledge creation and dissemination encouraged by Web 2.0 highlight the need for responsiveness to an active and constantly changing landscape of knowledge in which amateur contributions in many areas cannot be discounted. These new paradigms are influencing a number of important areas of public life, effecting a change in how knowledge, information and opinion is produced and distributed.

There are several representative examples. The paradigms underlying journalism and newspaper publishing are changing under the influence of social software. News "is evolving from a lecture into a conversation" (Gillmor, 2009, p. 5). The traditional model is being extended into a two-way communication, where readers can re-broadcast the "editorials and articles by superimposing their viewpoints and observations along with the original" (Babu, 2007), as well as publish news independent of the traditional media outlets. This shift in the creation and distribution of news has been referred to as "democratization" of the media. Professional journalists and editors, who have traditionally been the gatekeepers of the profession by providing a necessary or desirable social function, were also the ones controlling that function; that is, they were the ones deciding what is and is not newsworthy (also Shirkey, 2008, pp. 63-65). The mass amateurization of publishing undoes the limitations that were inherent in having a small number of traditional press outlets (Shirkey, 2008, p. 65). Control over the media and over decisions of what constitutes news is now less completely in the hands of expert journalists and editors. Even though the change is often decried as evidence that amateur journalism will replace professional journalism, the reality is probably closer to what Dan Gillmor, a journalist and a blogger, calls the "diversification of the journalist ecosystem," not professionals vs. amateurs, not one or the other, but rather, a world of one and the other" (Gillmor, 2009, p. 5).

In the area of economics and business, recent research regards it important for new media companies to find ways of making profit with the help of Web 2.0, suggesting that the economy of the "new web" depends on collaboration. The Internet-based economy has been termed "Wikinomics" and is based on principles of openness, peering, sharing and acting globally (Tapscott and Williams, 2006). In this business model, companies relinquish traditional ideas of expert knowledge by "designing and assembling products with their customers, and in some cases customers can do the majority of the value creation" (p. 89). Employees, business partners, and even competitors "co-create value in the absence of direct managerial control, demonstrating the nature of interdependence in the business world" (p. 55). In this case, traditionally passive buyers and those on the margins of the decision process become equal partners in product value creation. Wikinomics illustrates that "peer to peer models and seeping into an industry where conventional wisdom favors the lone super star stock advisor" (p. 24).

Social software, for example, also increasingly plays a role in the area of social work. Community organizers use interactive Web technologies to identify services in traditionally disadvantaged neighborhoods, and social workers use chat programs to provide real-time online therapy. More significantly, however, social software allows for self-directed treatment through web-based modules (see Singer, 2009). Self-directed treatment places patients in the position of 'expert' as it allows them to develop their own resources, acquire control over crucial aspects of their own treatment and so become their own therapist. The design and implementation of self-directed treatment with the help of social software compels social workers, counselors and therapists to redefine and rethink their position of expert in important ways.

More generally, wiki projects, built on collaborative computer software used to create collaborative websites, are a good example of Web 2.0 applications "comprising of the perpetual collective work of many authors" and allowing "anyone to delete or modify content that has been placed in the website using a browser interface" (Webpoedia). For an increasing number of digital users, Wikipedia provides answers to a wide range of questions formerly associated with encyclopedic or expert knowledge, and is cited as a credible source of encyclopedic knowledge in many scholarly publications (one of which is the *Cambridge Handbook of Expertise and Expert Performance*, 2006).

Wikibooks and Wikiuniversity, provide examples of social software in the service of education. Wikibooks, established in 2003, hosts collections of open-content textbooks written collaboratively by students, teachers, and interested members of the public. The site is described as a community for collaborative writing of textbooks and manuals, and uniquely suited for use in classroom collaborative projects. The Wikiuniversity, built on the open source software model, was officially begun in 2006 with the aim of creating and hosting a range of collaboratively-created free content, multilingual learning materials and resources for all age groups in all languages. These developments challenge some models of expertise understood in a traditional sense, and raise the question as to how will expertise and knowledge be redefined in an age where important facts and informed opinions are easily accessible from a variety of sources often created collaboratively by experts and non-experts alike?

While the answers to these questions are still imprecise, the articles in this collection suggest that some trends are becoming visible. On the whole, they suggest that the challenge to some models of expertise does mean that we will be able to dispense with experts in general. What the challenge means, rather, is that experts in many fields such as medicine, law and academia, need to rethink their roles vis-à-vis a changing media landscape, reexamine how new technologies enable new ways of doing their work, and redefine the manner in which they think about and act on their expertise. While it is unlikely that the experts' "epistemic leadership role" (Sanger, 2009, p. 60), will be made obsolete, it is likely, and probably inevitable, that the ways in which they conduct that leadership role will change. For example, rather than relying on the collection and management of information and knowledge as the basis of their credibility and expertise--something that is now very efficiently done by many non-experts-- the new kinds of expert leadership will be concerned with "what information ought to be collected, reported and highlighted" (Sanger, 2009, p. 60), as well as in what ways it might be brought together into meaningful narratives.

One of the main implications of the mass amateurization of knowledge or the "aggregation of public opinion" (Sanger, 2007, par. 2) driven by technological networks is that it compels us to reevaluate the nature of expertise itself. While prevalent definitions of expertise traditionally default to the expert's factual knowledge within a narrow area of specialization, it is less frequently acknowledged that experts regularly perform process-oriented tasks based on mastery of cognitive, critical, and theoretical skills that can be said to constitute the hidden, tacit aspects of expertise, harder to articulate and impossible to quantify. The performance of expertise always depended on the relationship between factual knowledge and process-based cognitive tasks. In other words, prepositional or content-based knowledge on the one hand, and forms of critical thinking and judgment involved in identifying main problems, classifying, evaluating, and making relevant connections on the other, were always interdependent aspects of expertise. Knowing the "what" always went along with knowing "how" in any line of expertise.

The so called rise of the amateur, and the instant and almost ubiquitous access to seemingly infinite specialized information and relevant facts relating to any form of existing knowledge, are redefining expertise in that they challenge the relationship between content based knowledge and the cognitive, process based skills involved in expertise. That is, since the expert no longer has exclusive control and mastery over content-based knowledge and information, it may suggest that the new forms of expertise will gradually become less associated with mastery of facts and content, the "what," and more with "how," that is, those tacit aspects of expertise having to do with the performance of complex cognitive tasks that assume knowledge of content but cannot be equated with it.

This redefinition of expertise does not minimize the valuable contributions that many well informed and knowledgeable amateurs make to any field; to the contrary. It is useful to recall that an expert is someone "who is very skillful and well-informed in some special field" (*Webster's New World Dictionary*, 1968, p. 168), as well as someone who is "widely recognized as a reliable source of knowledge technique or skill whose judgment is accorded authority and status by the public or his or her peers. Experts have prolonged or intense experience through practice and education in a particular field" (*Wikipedia)*. By not making accreditation the primary or only criteria for establishing expertise, these two definitions point to the great conceptual and practical overlaps that may exist between the traditional expert and the knowledgeable amateur. Furthermore, while in some domains, such as chess, the medical profession, and musical performance, there are objective criteria for finding experts who are consistently able to exhibit superior performance for representative tasks in their respective domain, in other areas it is difficult to identify experts without relying on peer-nominations by professionals in the same domain, and even then, they are no better than novices when it comes to some essential tasks (Anders Ericsson, 2006, par. 3). Examples of these would include selecting stocks with superior performance, the treatment of psychotherapy patients, forecasts, or expert auditors' assessments, which have been found to differ more from each other, than the assessments of less experienced auditors (Anders Ericsson, 2006, par. 3).

2.0 technologies encourage forms of interdisciplinary inquiry, ongoing epistemological revisionism and a new approach to knowledge and expertise in the widest sense. Instant access also means access to various relevant bodies of knowledge across disciplines, which thus enables and indeed encourages the pursuit of any line of inquiry without extensive travel. As Manuel Castells (2004) points out, the key dimension of social organization and social practice has become the network, as in his concept of the network society. While networks are an old form of human organization, digital networking technologies characteristic of the Information era are powering social and organizational networks into endless expansion and reconfiguration, and thus overcoming the traditional limitations of networks to manage complexity beyond a certain size (Castells, 2004).

Emphasizing interconnectedness, interdependence, and collaboration, the new forms of knowledge creation and dissemination are dynamic and dialectical, rather than static and uncontested, and as such they suggest that the boundaries of specialization itself may become elastic and permeable. In an interconnected, complex world, wired for instantaneous access to information and interaction, divisions between disciplines appear to loosen, showing that only interdisciplinary approaches can effectively tackle complex issues. Revisionism and fluidity of approach become traits of the new expert, who is able to revise and quickly but accurately evaluate current findings in light of new information. The environment fostered by the new technology encourages a horizontal or generalist, rather than only a vertical or specialist approach in so far as the generalist is inclined to detect systemic patterns across various subject areas. Deep knowledge of issues is still required; however, in this new paradigm, knowledge is moving away from being a product, to becoming an ongoing and a rather fast paced process of inquiry inviting participation, interaction, and ongoing evaluation.

What this means is not that expertise will become obsolete, but rather that it will adapt from being a relatively closed system to a more open one. Since facts on any subject now likely exist somewhere in the public domain and are being refined and augmented as we speak, in addition to being easy to find and access, the new expert will be the one who does have content-based knowledge as well as good research skills, but who combines them with a skill that is increasingly gaining relevance: that is the monitoring of and bringing together of information from other disciplines and sectors, as needed and as they relate to the project at hand. The new climate of knowledge creation and dissemination demands that experts be able to seek out relevant knowledge from a wide variety of sometimes disparate and seemingly unrelated sources and disciplines, and perceive how parts of new information combine to illustrate a new aspect of a given subject. They thus need to have the ability to place their own specialties into a larger context, interpreting data in a revealing way and fitting them into a larger pattern (also Boyer, pp. 18-19). In a climate where data and opinions abound, knowledge of systems and their functioning become increasingly valuable, which means that synthesis and integration may be at the heart of newly redefined forms of expertise. Through this process of purposeful integration the new experts would also facilitate and organize the process of turning information into knowledge. In a world where we often speak of the overload of information, the ability to sort, select, evaluate, and provide a coherent view is one of the faces of future expertise.

Similarly, the new form of specialization may increasingly become functional specialization, specialization arising from a close, purposeful and detailed engagement with a changing subject matter upon which the expert would bring to bear all of her or his tacit forms of expertise related to the successful performance of cognitive tasks. In this new environment, experts will be more likely to enter into collaborative relationships with non-experts, and to engage in public discourse as their findings will be placed within a larger context, relevant to a broader spectrum of people, not just a small group of other experts.

The 19 chapters in the present volume address the changes in the production and definition of knowledge powered by digital technologies and the direction of future knowledge creation and dissemination. They investigate the implications that the emergence and increasing availability of user-generated online content enabled through the rise of Web 2.0 technologies and its associated applications have for the notions of expert and expertise, now and in the future. The aim of the volume is not to suggest that the issues here considered are comprehensive and cover all possible areas of inquiry; rather, it is to begin a conversation on the issue of how expertise is being redefined, and lay some of the groundwork for future consideration of this important topic.

The authors of the chapters bring to the discussion a unique international blend of perspectives on the issue of expertise. Their backgrounds vary greatly, from philosophy, archival studies, and communication and media studies, to library science, business management, research science, as well as those who are knowledgeable field practitioners. The chapters reflect both qualitative and quantitative approaches in addressing the topic. To the extent that the authors' approach to the subject matter is informed by their diverse disciplinary backgrounds, the essays in the collection approach the subject in an interdisciplinary way. At the same time, however, the collective outcome of their contributions as well as the approach of many of individual contributions can more accurately be described as transdisciplinary in orientation.

Transdisciplinary research tries to overcome the mismatch between knowledge production in academia and demands for knowledge to contribute to real-world engagement, and participatory constructive problem solving with importance to real social issues in a way that destabilizes disciplinary boundaries and responds to the needs of the knowledge society in the 21st century (Hirsch Hadorn et.al., 2008). Thus many authors in this volume explicitly engage not only with academic sources but also with materials from the popular press and their own experience in an attempt to investigate the subject of expertise in a context wider than academia. Others base their findings on interviews with field practitioners as well as personal experiences with the issues they analyze. And while the chapters look at the issue of changing expertise with respect to many different issues and contexts, there is a thread common to all. All authors are in agreement that there are changes in the nature of expertise brought about by recent technological developments; that our cultural expectations from experts and expertise are changing; and that forms of "collective," "distributed," or "interactional" expertise are becoming a reality in many professional arenas.

Although there are conceptual overlaps among many of the chapters, based on their dominant context of inquiry, the volume is divided into 4 sections. The 4 chapters in Section 1 provide a broad theoretical framework against which to explore expertise and the changing nature of knowledge creation and dissemination in the context of social software applications and the Web 2.0 environment. In "Collective Narrative Expertise and the Narbs of Social Media," Ananda Mitra engages the fundamental epistemological question, *how do we know what we know?* and locates some of the answers in theories of narrative. More specifically, his chapter proposes that social software applications and social media in general, offer opportunities for unique forms of narration that utilizes *narbs,* a term he coins to describe narrative bits that collectively could and do sometimes form into a grand narrative about a particular issue and where expertise is located in the collective. The chapter offers a lexicon for categorizing narbs and provides an analytical framework for examining them. Mitra demonstrates that since as users we live at the confluence of the real and virtual, we are immersed in different knowledge paradigms requiring different and emergent expertise of narrative construction and interpretation.

In "Wikipedia's Success and the Rise of the Amateur Expert," Christopher Sweet adopts a conceptual approach to the investigation of Wikipedia, whose short but successful history encapsulates many of the benefits and some of the drawbacks of Web 2.0 technologies, as well as the changing attitudes toward expertise and knowledge creation in the context of encyclopedic knowledge. The chapter examines some of the empirical research regarding Wikipedia's accuracy and reliability. It also discusses the issue of who creates knowledge on Wikipedia, the major problems associated with this online encyclopedia, as well as the implications for objectivity, open source scholarship and the rise of the amateur expert.

In "Understanding and Evaluating Source Expertise in an Evolving Media Environment," Rebekah A. Pure, Alexander R. Markov, J. Michael Mangus, Miriam J. Metzger, Andrew J. Flanagin, and Ethan H. Hartsell, provide a conceptual framework for examining the origin of information created through social software applications, where the quality and veracity of that information is sometimes unclear. The authors contend that under conditions where knowledge is diffused among many individuals and depends on a situational understanding, it is often the case that the most reliable information is not found in a traditional source, but rather from a diversity of individuals lacking the traditional markers of expertise. They propose new forms of expertise rooted in the experience of individuals rather than based on their formal credentials, and put forward several approaches to judging and conceptualizing expertise that attempt to address the challenges and opportunities presented Web 2.0 technologies.

In the final chapter of Section 1, "Connection, Fragmentation, and Intentionality: Social Software and the Changing Nature of Expertise, "Christopher Watts examines the philosophies underlying social software design, arguing that they facilitate an environment where it is data itself, rather than people, that makes connections across other data and assumes a theoretical primacy. Watts identifies features in the current set of social software applications and the forms of collective intelligence they encourage that tend to fragment and decontextualize information in a way that undermine intentionality, weakening the connection between the individual and the content he or she creates. Watts examines the way in which social software designs affect human interaction and the relationship to knowledge and its production and consumption, and advocates a human-centered technology design, reminding that the relationship between information and knowledge is very complex. The chapter also reimagines expertise as not being replaced by new models of knowledge creation and dissemination but complemented and enhanced by them.

The 6 chapters that make up Section 2 of the collection deal with changing expert environments in the university and in the areas of research and scholarship. The opening chapter, "Should we Take Disintermediation in Higher Education Seriously? Expertise, Knowledge Brokering, and Knowledge Translation in the Age of Disintermediation," by Carlos A. Scolari, Cristobal Cobo Romani, and Hugo Pardo Kuklinski, identifies knowledge production and knowledge distribution as the two areas of academic work that have been affected the most by the new models of information exchange and knowledge sharing, and that are challenging traditional academic practice and the role of experts in education. The authors analyze the appearance of disintermediation practices in higher education, defining the term to mean "cutting out the middleman," a process that threatens to make highly specialized professionals obsolete. The main objective of the chapter is to explore how disintermediation is reshaping the role of faculty and administrative mechanisms that support higher education in the 21st century. The authors propose knowledge brokering and knowledge translation as categories that can help map a new territory promoting disintermediation, innovation, and openness in higher education settings, and help redefine the traditional role of faculty.

Laurie Craig Phipps, Alyssa Friend Wise, and Cheryl Amundsen, the authors of "The University in Transition: Reconsidering Faculty Roles and Expertise in a Web 2.0 World," explore the potential of Web 2.0 technologies to support dialogue as a core activity for learning in higher education in relation to the changing role of faculty members as their expertise shifts from "teller" to that of a "guide." Conceiving of this metaphor as encompassing activities such as scripting, translating, introducing, and co-exploring, the authors propose technology-based methods of reimagining an educational paradigm in this context, thus responding to the need for collaborative and constructivist practices in teaching and learning that may be enabled by various social software applications. One of this chapter's main informing contexts is the investigation of a transitional period of unprecedented scope and impact affecting the university as an institution as it is repositioning its place in an environment of emerging information and communication technologies, ubiquitous access to information and increased social connectivity.

In "Between Tradition and Web 2.0: E-Laborate as a Social Experiment in Humanities Scholarship,"Anne Beaulieu, Karina van Dalen-Oskam, and Joris van Zundert consider the contrast between the values of openness of participation with regard to traditional markers of expertise associated with Web 2.0 technologies, and traditional forms of knowledge creation in academic contexts, where expertise, institutional affiliation, and restriction on access and circulation have been important. Rather than seeing this contrast as a dichotomy, they investigate the rise of hybrid forms of scholarly collaboration and participation that combine the two models. The chapter explores in some detail one such hybrid form, "e-Laborate," a virtual research environment targeting both professional scholars and volunteers and offering tools to transcribe, annotate, and publish scholarly editions. By investigating the changes in the digital humanities resulting from the intermediate models between academic exclusiveness and Web 2.0 openness, the authors demonstrate that hybrid forms are powerful agents of change.

In "Google Scholar as the Co-Producer of Scholarly Knowledge," Jose van Dijck argues that Google Scholar, as a search engine but also a social software application whose efficacy depends on the activity of its users, is not a neutral tool for research and a mediator of knowledge, but in fact a significant co-producer of scholarly knowledge. Unlike library search engines, in Google Scholar, sources are ranked on the basis of *popularity* rather than truth-value or relevance, and there is no clear peer-review system or citation analysis system that publicly lays out its ranking principles. The author points out that the engine takes into account not just peer-reviewed scholarly papers, but also working papers, unpublished material, documents in preprint repositories, power-point presentations published on university websites, and lecture notes, and that ranking academic sources through Google Scholar is like ranking celebrities: you get what most people voted for, or rather, clicked for. The chapter considers the implications of this process for the dissemination of scholarly knowledge, the issue of quality and relevance, as well as cultural ideas of expertise, and argues for an enriched kind of information literacy that would include an understanding of the economic, political and socio-cultural dimensions of search engines.

Lilian Landes in "Reviewing in the Age of Web 2.0: What Does Web Culture Have to Offer to Scholarly Communication?" considers the scholarly book review, a genre she argues is inherently suited for online publication due to the benefits of speed, flexibility, and detectability. She investigates the potential of review models based on the concept of Web 2.0 technologies, and discusses in detail one such model, recensio.net, a European project whose aim is to increase the speed with which reviewing happens, facilitate rating and commenting, and enable commenting functions so as to encourage interdisciplinary reviewing of scholarly work even in its pre-publication phases. The chapter explores the concept of collaborative reviewing enabled by the platform recensio.net in light of a general confidence in collective intelligence and the ability of the masses of users with varying degrees of traditional subject expertise to exchange recommendations and provide constructive criticism.

In "The Effect of Social Software on Academic Libraries," Maria Cassella and Licia Calvi present the results of a study conducted in Italian and Dutch academic libraries. The study aims at assessing how libraries reposition themselves and their traditional expertise in a more complex informational context, increasing number of remote users, and widespread adoption of social software applications for professional use. The authors focus on the adoption rate and Facebook use-patterns in academic libraries, as a social tool for attracting new users, for advertising library services and events and for facilitating research. The study also considers the level of expertise of librarians in terms of using Facebook for professional purposes, and identifies some of the challenges associated with the adoption of a social networking tool such as Facebook in this context.

Section 3 of the volume is comprised of 5 chapters that reimagine pedagogical expertise in light of recent technological affordances and examine some of the pros and cons of bringing social software applications into the classroom, as well as the new demands for media literacy. In "Teaching Political Science Students to Find and Evaluate Information in the Social Media Flow," Megan Fitzgibbons argues that the advent of social media applications necessitates new pedagogical approaches in the field of political science, a discipline where both primary and secondary materials are now found in increasing abundance, ranging from politicians tweets to blogs and organizations like Wikileaks, as well as pundits' blogs. She asserts that students of political science must understand how information and knowledge is produced and disseminated as a part of their study of international power structures, government and local politics, and extend their awareness of the relationship between social media and civic participation. The chapter focuses on ways in which educators in political science can facilitate students' skills for evaluating information that in the flow of social media has become an iterative, constant process, and teach the competencies required for finding information produced through social conduits.

In "The Net Generation and Changes in Knowledge Acquisition," Werner Beuschel traces a methodological approach to knowledge production and acquisition among undergraduates in the context of social software applications. Beginning with the assessment of recent literature that presents various visions about the aptitudes and capabilities of the so-called Net Generation and their strategies for coping with information challenges, Beuschel provides the results of a longitudinal, exploratory study conducted over two years in a German university on what kinds of social media students actually use and in what way. Based on this empirical framework, Beuschel puts forward a tentative model of how students collect, assemble and disseminate knowledge, as well as the changes in expertise acquisition and competency that may be expected in the future.

Mary J. Snyder Broussard, Rebecca A. Wilson, Janet McNeil Hurlbert, and Alison S. Gregory's research in "Faculty and Undergraduate Perceptions of Expertise within Social Media" is based on the results of two surveys administered by the authors to faculty and undergraduate students in the sciences, social sciences, fine arts, and humanities at two small liberal arts institutions. In the context of the new generation of Web applications allowing for user participation, instant collaboration and ongoing revisionism by volunteer experts, one of the surveys assesses how students view these new forms of expertise, how they define expertise in terms of writing college papers, and whether they perceive a difference in the information offered via various social networking sources. The other survey, addressed to faculty members, aimed at identifying faculty views on the new forms of expertise and their suitability for use in research as well as teaching.

Highlighting the pros of using instant text messaging in the composition classroom, in "Textperts: Utilizing Students' Skills in the Teaching of Writing" Abigail Grant identifies text messaging as a unique genre whose character limitations and other physical limitations in some respects make it similar to the writing of poetry or short prose. Considering through a number of examples the pros of implementing text messaging into the composition classroom, Grant argues for the adoption of this form of writing mediated through technology as a way to motivate students to practice and experiment with writing by utilizing a skill and an aptitude for which they may already be considered "experts." The chapter explores the theoretical and practical implementation of this genre into the classroom, including a careful consideration of the potentially negative aspects relating to the adoption of this strategy and tool, as well as a discussion of how text messaging thus employed may provide a useful transition to writing longer genres.

In "Working toward Expert Status: Love to Hear Students Go 'Tweet, Tweet, Tweet," Tamara Girardi sees Twitter as a type of classroom of collective intelligence that represents an epistemological shift in which the "experts" in the exchange are not traditional teachers. In the chapter, she argues that this social software application may be used as an academic tool of instruction that offers students the opportunity to engage in a discourse related to their subject of study beyond the traditional classroom, and to acquire the status of "expert" by gaining confidence in their knowledge and gaining influence they may not have gained in the narrower context of the traditional classroom. The chapter considers issues such as knowledge sharing, and building/maintaining a reputation as an expert through consideration of audience. The author presents an overview of the use of Twitter in academic contexts, and situates its potential for instruction in its capacity to act as an outlet for a more dynamic classroom discussion, encouraging educators to consider in more innovative ways how the social and cultural contexts of Twitter may suit their instructional goals.

The final section of the collection, Section 4, presents 4 case studies of collective or decentralized expertise at work in the context of ICT, technical support community forums, a music archive, and the creation of a 3D movie. In "Professional ICT Knowledge, Epistemic Standards, and Social Epistemology," Frederik Truyen and Filip Beukens demonstrate within a philosophical framework that the knowledge required to perform professional tasks related to expertise in the ICT profession has become a dynamic network of insights spread over a network of sources and other experts. They argue that, on the one hand, an ICT manager increasingly needs to rely on organizational procedures and professional standards to assess that he has the right people with the right competencies for the job. On the other hand, the ICT expert increasingly relies on pools of collective intelligence in the ICT area to establish and maintain his expertise. The chapter shows how ICT professionals perform their work as experts in the context of the ICT community's innovative ways of sharing knowledge collaboratively, using social software and other technologies.

Steven Ovadia's chapter "Decentralized Expertise: The Evolution of Community Forums in Technical Support"examines open source applications such as community forums in technical support, and their implications for the changing nature of expertise. It investigates Linux support forums to illustrate the decentralized nature of authority structures within them, contrasting them to the more hierarchical technical support systems seen in closed-source operating systems, like Microsoft's Windows and Apple's OS X. The chapter demonstrates that users now have access to technical support communities beyond whatever is offered by the entities responsible for the production of the operating systems and that expertise and authority now rest within these communities.

Emily Clark considers the new possibilities offered by newly developed Web 2.0 content management software for contextualizing archival objects though the contribution of many users, rather than a few established experts in her "Interaction and Expertise in an Appalachian Music Archive." Clark documents the development of her MSIS thesis project based on designing a Web exhibit for a collection of North Carolina folk songs—the Bascom Lamar Lunsford Collection—that utilizes the user-contribution capabilities afforded by the new technologies with the purpose of reflecting the populist values of the North Carolina musical tradition. Clark shows the ways in which the Lunsford Collection Web exhibit not only displays the songs collected over the course of the musician's life, but relies on user-contribution to contextualize the songs as part of a living and still evolving populist tradition. She argues that the site facilitates the creation of community expertise that calls into question the role of the expert in a traditional archive.

Last but not least, in "Rethinking Expertise in the Web 2.0 Era: Lessons Learned from Project Durian," Ilias Karasavvidis focuses on project Durian, and the creation of Sintel, a 3D open content movie, to address the new notions and practices of expertise defined by new technologies. Karasavvidis analyses all instances where the Durian artistic team enlisted community feedback and support. He draws on multiple sources to discuss how Web 2.0 technologies facilitate a spatial and temporal distribution of expertise, and the consequent pooling of expertise from among interested members of the community, many of whom have no formal kind of expertise related to this work. The chapter shows that the pooling of expertise from experts in many different domains also facilitated interdisciplinary and transdisciplinary types of collaboration that resulted in questioning and re-negotiating expertise.

In its scope and orientation, this volume will be of interest not only to members of the international academic community, but also to professionals, administrators, and managers in many fields. One of the questions that remain to be answered by future research is whether emergent paradigms in relation to expertise can be effectively described or assessed based on criteria that predate them. The point relevant to expertise in general is that sometimes the expert outlook can become a disadvantage, "preventing the very people who have the most at stake—the experts themselves—from understanding major changes in the structure of their professions" (Shirkey, 2008, p. 58). In that sense, the authors in this collection stand at the forefront of a new kind of thinking about expertise, one that is based on understanding of the major changes in many professions and important areas of our social and cultural lives, and a willingness to examine what those changes may mean for the future. The collection thus hopes to provide a starting point for further inquiries into this subject.

Tatjana Takševa
Saint Mary's University, Canada

REFERENCES

Anders Ericsson, K. (2006). An introduction to the Cambridge handbook of expertise and expert performance: Its development, organization and content. In N. Charness, R. R. Hoffman, & P. Feltovich (Eds.), *Cambridge handbook of expertise and expert performance*. Cambridge, UK: The Cambridge University Press. Retrieved from: http://lib.mylibrary.com.library.smu.ca:2048?ID=56761

Anderson, P. (1972). More is different. *Science, 177*, 393–396. doi:10.1126/science.177.4047.393

Babu, M. (2007). The changing paradigms of newspaper publishing. *Ubiquity, 8*(1). Retrieved from http://www.acm.org/ubiquity/views/v8i31_mohan.html

Boyer, E. (1990). *Scholarship reconsidered: Priorities of the professoriate. Report for the Carnegie Foundation for the Advancement of Teaching*. San Francisco, CA: Jossey-Bass Publishers.

Castells, M. (2004). *Rise of the network society*. Blackwell Publishing.

Gillmor, D. (2009). Introduction: Toward a (new) media literacy in a media saturated world. In Papacharissi, Z. (Ed.), *Journalism and citizenship: New agendas in communication* (pp. 1–11). New York, NY: Routledge.

Hirsch Hadorn, G., Hoffmann-Riem, H., Biber-Klemm, S., Grossenbacher-Mansuy, W., Joye, D., & Pohl, C. … Zemp, E. (Eds.). (2008). *Handbook of transdisciplinary research*. Springer Science: Business Media B. V.

Jaschick, S. (2012, January 9). Dissing the dissertation. *Inside Higher Education*. Retrieved from http://www.insidehighered.com/news/2012/01/09/mla-considers-radical-changes-dissertation

Knight, C. (April 14, 2011). Top 7 social media sites, ranked by professors: Special report. *Education Tech News*. Retrieved from www.educationtechnews.com

Laughlin, R. B., & Pines, D. (2000). The theory of everything. *Proceedings of the National Academy of Sciences of the United States of America, 97*, 28–31. doi:10.1073/pnas.97.1.28

Lemann, N. (2006, August 7, 14). Amateur hour: Journalism without journalism. *The New Yorker*.

Parikh, R. (2002). Social software. *Synthese, 132*, 187–211. doi:10.1023/A:1020391420768

Reynolds, G. (2006). *The Army of Davids: How markets and technology empower ordinary people to beat big media, big government and other Goliaths*. Nelson.

Sanger, L. (2007). Who says we know? On the new politics of knowledge. *Edge: The Third Culture*. Retrieved from http://www.edge.org/3rd_culture/sanger07/sanger07_index.html

Sanger, L. (2009). The fate of expertise after Wikipedia. *Episteme*, 52–69. doi:10.3366/E1742360008000543

Shirkey, C. (2008). *Here comes everybody: The power of organizing without organizations*. New York, NY: The Penguin Press.

Singer, J. (2009). The role and regulations for technology in social work practice and e-therapy: Social work 2.0. In Roberts, R. A. (Ed.), *Social workers' desk reference* (2nd ed.). New York, NY: Oxford University Press.

Takseva Chorney, T. (2010). Knowledge and expertise redefined: *Consensus sapientia* in the digital era and reframing the modalities of teaching and learning. *TRANS: Internet Journal for Cultural Studies, 17*(7). Retrieved from http://www.inst.at/trans/17Nr/7-9/7-9_chorney7.htm

Tapscott, D., & Williams, A. D. (2007). *Wikinomics: How mass collaboration changes everything*. New York, NY: Penguin.

Acknowledgment

I would like to acknowledge the generous financial support provided by the Social Sciences and Humanities Research Council of Canada that allowed me to work on the present collection. To the members of the Editorial Advisory Board, Bill Badke, Tatyana Dumova, Stylianos Hatzipanagos, Niki Lambropoulos, Karl Stolley, and Kirk St. Amant, I am very grateful for your diligent work on this project. My sincere thanks also go to José van Dijck, Anne Beaulieu, Ilias Karasavvidis, Christopher Sweet, Fred Truyen, Christopher Watts, and Kate Lyons for their willingness to serve as reviewers. The collective expertise of these two groups of scholars was invaluable to how knowledge was constructed in this volume. My thanks to Leslie Cameron for her help with copy-editing; it was a pleasure working with her. To my husband, Steven Tucker, I am deeply grateful for his unfailing support and honest criticism of my work. This book is dedicated to my children, Nikolai, Sofia and Milena, members of the future generation whose ideas about knowledge and expertise are developing in a very different environment from the one in which my views on the subject were formed.

Section 1
Expertise and the Changing Nature of Knowledge Creation and Dissemination in the Web 2.0 Environment

Chapter 1
Collective Narrative Expertise and the Narbs of Social Media

Ananda Mitra
Wake Forest University, USA

ABSTRACT

A fundamental epistemological question that has been the focus of much deliberation over time is: how do we know what we know? One of the answers to this question has been found in the theories of narrative asserting that humans learn through stories, ranging from religious epics to personal anecdotes. The social media phenomenon offers a unique form of narration that utilizes "narbs," narrative bits that tell the stories of specific individuals who may be, but often are not, traditional experts. Yet, as a collection, these narbs could become the authoritative narrative about a particular issue where expertise is located in the collective. This chapter examines the theoretical basis of knowledge creation through narrative, and how the narbs of social media users are creating dynamic bodies of information. The chapter offers a lexicon for categorizing narbs and provides an analytical frame for examining them. The overall aim of this chapter is to demonstrate that interaction and new modes of gathering and disseminating information and knowledge in the digital environment require different and emergent expertise in narrative construction and interpretation.

INTRODUCTION

One of the most important facets of most communities is the designation of an expert who adopts the role of a leader in the community by virtue of acquiring a specialized and esoteric knowledge about something. Ancient civilizations relied upon religious leaders as the source of information for moral issues; later, expertise moved into the

hands of those who could provide evidence for their knowledge by showing careful examination of a body of work. However, once a person or an institution has demonstrated expertise, it has been traditionally the case that it is then formally and institutionally credited; for an individual it could be the conferring of an academic degree—for instance, a doctoral degree recognizes and acknowledges expertise. Thereafter, what the individual states and does is traditionally considered trustworthy, authentic, and a source

DOI: 10.4018/978-1-4666-2178-7.ch001

of knowledge by non-experts because the status of expert has been established. For institutions, the accreditation could be earned through peer recognition where, for instance, one media outlet is considered to be the expert source of information because other experts have conferred that status on the particular outlet. Once the experts become available, having access to them becomes critical to the development and sustenance of communities and social systems because experts are expected to create and disseminate knowledge so that the amateur gains a portion of the knowledge and gets to "know" something. A child going to school is a quintessential traditional example of the interplay between expertise, creation, and dissemination of information. A child could say, "I know this because my teacher told me so," and in such a statement expertise is located in a trustworthy individual whose information is necessarily considered authentic. This system worked well because there were often few alternatives to what the expert disseminated as correct and trustworthy information. In this chapter, I call into question the sanguineness of this information and the power of traditional expertise as more people gain access to information delivered digitally.

Here I consider the question "How do we know what we know?" in the age of instantaneous access to information, with nearly 500 million people actively using a digital tool. The question, however, is not at all new, and an entire branch of philosophy—epistemology—focuses on the question of knowledge, how it is acquired, and how its authenticity is established. The purpose of this chapter is to consider how new digital processes are calling into question some of the accepted ways of knowing and gathering knowledge while complicating the ability to judge the reliability of the information that is considered to be knowledge. I aim to show that emerging knowledge sources could have an impact on the ways in which things are known. In particular, I focus on the ways in which micro-narratives, or narrative bits—abbreviated as "narbs"—can be

combined to create narratives that can serve as the mode that we now know, and that now coexist with the narratives offered by traditional expert individuals and institutions. The primary argument of this essay is that narbs begin to challenge expertise that has been established and acknowledged a priori. Narbs do not originate from people who have already been established as experts within the norms of a social and cultural system, yet by their very nature, as explained in this essay, they could call into question the normative experts— individuals and institutions—producing a crisis of expertise and eventually an epistemological concern. First, it is useful to briefly consider the question of epistemology and consider one accepted way of knowing.

MODES OF KNOWING AND TRADITIONAL EXPERTISE

In the traditional mode of producing, collating, and distributing information, expertise was often based on an epistemic capital, where the expert held a certain epistemic superiority that made his/her knowledge somehow better than other knowledge. This relationship between expertise and epistemology can be traced to the very meaning of epistemology. After it was introduced as a named area of study by Ferrier in the mid-1800s, the question of epistemology became connected with the notion of modernity where the objective of knowing was increasingly connected with the pursuit of a singular and unambiguous truth about any matter. Much of the endeavor of epistemology has been to consider the ways in which truth, belief, and justification work together in relation to any phenomenon so that eventually an approximate true knowledge is obtained about a phenomenon. It is the expert, in enthusiastic pursuit of the truth, who then becomes the keeper and disseminator of the knowledge, earning the epistemic capital because s/he followed an accepted mode of gathering the knowledge. Indeed, the process of training to be an expert is eventually an apprenticeship in learning how to learn. A scientist working within a positivist perspective is taught to think of the scientific method as the supreme source of knowledge; a humanist working within the tradition of literary interpretation would learn that aesthetic and historical knowledge is the pathway to uncovering knowledge about an artifact or the history of ideas. Each would remain true to their chosen methods of gathering knowledge and both would claim expertise in their field.

Often, the recognition of expertise does not lie only in the knowledge that the expert produces but in the way that the expert gathered the knowledge. In the case of media institutions, for example, one particular news source could be considered the expert source because it utilizes the best practices of news gathering, as explicated within the norms of journalism, and the news or knowledge that the source produces receives an ipso facto value. The propagation of expertise is also tied to the reproduction of the modes of knowledge gathering; a scientist trains other scientists; a linguist trains other linguists; and via such processes the expert way of knowing is propagated and normalized. Because expertise is thus tied to the normative methods of gathering knowledge there is debate over the mechanism that is used to obtain the true knowledge.

The epistemological debate takes on a pragmatic value as individuals and collectives have to answer the question regarding the way in which a particular knowledge was acquired and whether the knowledge can be considered to be true and justifiable. In the absence of the assumption of truth, knowledge becomes tenuous and decisions made on the basis of the acquired knowledge could lead to different levels of error. Consider, for instance, a situation where the mode of acquiring knowledge—circumstantial evidence—creates morally incorrect decisions when people are punished for a crime that they did not commit (see, for example, Thompson-Canino, 2009). Such examples are especially telling because they pitch

two modes of knowledge acquisition against each other. Many "criminals" have been acquitted when evidence in the form of data such as DNA matching unequivocally demonstrates that the crime could not have been committed by the accused. Such "hard" evidence then calls into question the initial basis of the decision when circumstantial evidence and the testimony of witnesses and other people become the primary basis for decision making and an assumed truth. We could say that such situations that exist outside digital media and predate it can produce series of crises that call into question the nature of expertise itself and the way experts produce knowledge. Yet these crises are built into the very fabric of the democratic legal system and do not seriously undermine the validity of circumstantial evidence as a method of obtaining the truth. Witness narratives are still considered a potentially trustworthy way of acquiring and disseminating particular knowledge. Narratives and storytelling are a prevalent mode of generating knowledge where the credentials of the narrator traditionally determine the validity or trustworthiness of the particular narrative.

THE TRADITIONAL EXPERT AS A LICENSED STORYTELLER

While storytelling has not necessarily been examined from the perspective of accreditable expertise, stories have played a significant role in defining the moral fabric of societies, and, through narratives and parables, the preferred moral path or the correct or accepted worldview. With the adoption of the technologies of mass production the volume of stories proliferated as societies adopted the tools of mass media; storytelling has become an industry that ranges from the traditional print industry to television and film and digital media. Specific institutions, including the news industry, have developed to specialize in certain forms of narration. Specific styles of storytelling have evolved that are intelligible to the listener, and much of the process of making sense of the world is dependent on the stories that are told of the world. I use the term "stories" to denote narrative forms of knowledge dissemination in the widest sense (including reporting and the news, literature, and scientific and religious narratives aimed at explaining aspects of the world, as well as narratives that provide us with answers or solutions to our questions and problems) as the knowledge through which we see the world and understand our place in it.

Within this narrative worldview the truth often lies in both the story itself and also the expertise of the storyteller. This is an expertise that is not necessarily built on diligent and dispassionate adherence to trusted methods of uncovering the truth. Indeed, expertise in some cases is based largely on the eloquence of storytelling. As traditional Greek scholars of rhetoric such as Aristotle remind us, the truth of a text or discourse remains tied to its logical strength (*logos*), its emotional appeal (*pathos*), and the way in which the audience judges the character of the storyteller (*ethos*). As such, a storyteller who can tell a good tale with all the trappings of attractive discourse can adopt the role of expert who disseminates information so that other learn and know.

The dependence on the ad hoc belief in the ethos of the storyteller creates a condition whereby many of the most important tales have traditionally been produced and distributed by institutions that always and already possess the trust of the listener. Consider, for instance, the way in which, even with thousands of news sources available on the Internet, a large portion of news consumers turn to "trusted" names such as the BBC or CNN to find news stories. Expertise in this case is directly and closely associated with the "name" of the storyteller that vouchsafes the excellence with which the story is told. This reliance on institutional voices produces a set of standardized narratives and those narratives allow all to make decisions about the world in which they dwell.

This tendency to look at the world through stories also connects directly with the narrative

paradigm proposed by Fisher (1984) who argues that a key epistemological process is one that is built around the fact that all humans are storytellers. The way people make sense of the world is by telling stories and listening to stories, and via that combination the epistemological question is answered. We know what we know because we have heard stories about it. As stated earlier, such an argument places the onus of truth and justification of knowledge on the quality of the story and the characteristics of the storyteller. Much like the ancient rhetoricians, Fisher stresses that the quality of the story is based on its coherence, and this kind of fidelity becomes the primary metric for judging the authenticity of the story. A story that makes logical sense, and is thus internally coherent, is more likely to be considered true. In a similar way, when a story mimics the worldview of the listener, s/he is more likely to consider the story to be true. As a corollary to Fisher's arguments, Foucault has suggested that stories that come from those in power are often considered to be true, which helps to explain the centrality of trusted news sources as the primary providers in a society. Much of the aim of cultural studies scholars like Stuart Hall and others has been to carefully examine the content and structure of signs to peek into the underlying ideological systems within which cultural narratives have been produced (see, for example, Hall, 1997). Consequently, the analysis of news on television can offer insights into the way in which a specific cultural system chooses to interpret specific events just as specific representations of nations and groups produce images of people and places within ideological systems that are the substrate for the production and circulation of stories. These experts who tell the eloquent stories become the definers of the ideological worldview of a cultural system. Expertise then becomes the property of the institution or individual who can tell the most compelling story with which most of the amateurs agree.

Most of the stories that have attracted attention are products of specific institutions—governments, corporations, universities—that act as experts or that provide accreditation to individuals within a social system. What is important to note is that these stories have been produced by those who are always and already empowered to speak. Foucault calls these "the authoritarian voice" that in its extreme form could become a tool for repression, silencing not only the voices of all non-experts, but also the voices of other experts. Thus the stories of the authority become the dominant, natural, and conventional representation of the world. Such a condition necessarily silences powerless groups, and individuals lose the opportunity or space to find a voice for themselves to tell their story. In such a system no one other than those in power can claim expertise and produce and disseminate their information encoded in their set of symbols. In such cases the heterologlossia—made up of many languages and voices—as suggested by Bakhtin (1980) disappears and a set of preferred voices and their narratives become central. Such a condition has been possible partly because the expert "voice" has remained aligned with existing regimes of political/social/economic power.

The ability to establish expertise is also largely dependent on many different kinds of capital that the expert and institution must possess in order to create and circulate the narratives. The notion of capital refers to specific powers that the expert has been awarded by the cultures and societies within which the authors and institutions operate. The notion of capital is not very different from the way in which experts are accredited by other experts and peers. Such capital extends beyond the technological (which is intimately linked to financial) but enters the regime of social and political capital. For instance, a politician agreeing to appear for a personal interview on a television station offers it a political capital that transforms into a recognition of expertise for the specific channel. At a more granular level, the specific television reporter who is selected to conduct the interview automatically gains the status of expertise because the individual becomes the principal

teller of the story that emerges from the interview. These people then become the expert voices and storytellers who have the ability to create normative knowledge at any moment in time, precisely and only through their stories. These powers are usually not obtained by coercion but by agreement where a hegemonic system offers some the authoritative voice and allows some discourses from a selected set of voices to become dominant and powerful (see, for example, Gramsci, 1980). In such conditions, to have a voice requires a set of powers, and it is correspondingly assumed that only those who are powerful have a voice. A significant component of this power relates to the financial and technological capital possessed by the powerful and that offers the powerful the opportunity to have the expert voice. In totalitarian systems the capital is available to the state which becomes the expert at creating specific national narratives; in free societies, corporations that can establish the industries of mass media take on the voice and become the experts responsible for telling the stories. Much of the history of the development of radio and television describes the component of these industries where major institutions such as the BBC, ABC, CNN, and others, with their vast financial and technological strengths, dominate the realm of storytelling. This produces a sense of expertise that marginalizes all other experts who might not possess the capitals wielded by the institutional experts.

THE EMPOWERMENT OF INDIVIDUAL VOICES VIA SOCIAL NETWORKS

Every individual has a narrative to tell and such narratives could demonstrate a level of expertise that could be as valuable as the expertise that is drawn from the institutions (Mitra & Watts, 2002). One principal barrier to such a condition traditionally has been the cost of "voicing." The situation changed somewhat with the development of digital tools that allowed individual access to a large global network. This dates back to the early days of the development of the Internet when individuals were able to create their personal narratives and place them on the World Wide Web for mass consumption. The key to this process was the fact that it required very little capital, other than a network-connected tool and knowledge of the appropriate computer languages, to create a "home page" for an individual. This process began to change the way in which narratives could be produced and distributed. The individual voice could now be empowered and potentially heard by many and those who were silenced could gain the possibility of developing a new voice and speaking in it. An individual could, at a fraction of the cost that traditional institutional experts paid, create a voice that eloquently distributed information that was available to the individual. The availability of tools to create digital social networks that produce narratives in cybernetic space becomes most visible in the contemporary social media services such as MySpace and Facebook. It is also here that new answers to the question "How we know what we know?" begin to emerge as a new construct of expertise manifests itself in the digital social networks. It is useful now to consider the ways in which individuals become connected with such networks.

Social network systems such as Facebook, Orkut, Twitter, Hi5, and MySpace were made possible by two major developments in the technological sphere: the availability of powerful digital machines and the widespread penetration of high-speed data connections. The first component of the change refers to the proliferation of digital tools, from computers to smart cell phones that can rapidly process the large amounts of data produced by the digitization of audio and image information. These are tools that have become commonplace with instruments like the widely used iPhone. The second component of the change refers to the way in which the digital tools can connect to a central repository of data files that can store extremely large amounts of data that can be rapidly transmitted from a centralized location to a digital tool. This has become possible with high-speed Internet connections and through systems such as the 3G cell phone systems, which transmit data at a very fast rate. What is important to note is that these two changes are primarily technological and do not refer to any fundamental shifts in the way in which people would want to interact with each other. The people who might have been members of real-life or virtual communities can now use the social networking tools to create (more) technologically efficient connections with other people. Yet, the technological shift to social networking technology does lead to some major shifts in the way in which people tell stories.

The shift to the new technologies for creating communities became noticeable around 2005 when users discovered sites such as MySpace and Facebook—which quickly came to be known as social network sites (SNS)—and migrated from their existing virtual communities to the SNS forums because they offered a greater degree of technological sophistication in terms of the way in which users interact with other members of the SNS. Boyd and Ellison (2007) point out that numerous SNS forums came and went in the latter 1990s and the early 2000s, with different SNS providing different kinds of functionality and attracting different levels of following among users.[1] The development of SNS was relatively uneven in the early days, but by 2010, participation in SNS had become commonplace for a large number of people worldwide (Lenhart, 2009).

One notable component of the adoption of SNS was the change in the scale of the networks to which people could be connected. Within the large connections the real person was replaced by a discursive construction of the person. The replacement of the real person by the virtually available discourse created a condition where the discourse became the primary mode of creating a presence and narrative of the person. This identity narrative was removed from the real because it might have been impossible to ever have a clear understanding of the real entity since the entity was always produced by discourses that are available in cyberspace.[2]

Within this system, the discourse that emerges is made up of tiny stories that constantly update the knowledge available to, and possessed and distributed by, an individual. These are the narbs that become the source of information within cybernetic space. The only person who is an expert in creating the narbs is the individual who is telling personal stories through the narbs. Social networks and social software application encourage a process whereby expertise that is based in storytelling can potentially be wrenched from the institution as more and more individuals produce narbs. This situation results in forms of communal or collective expertise that can be located in the confluence of the narbs. It is useful to examine the idea of the narb carefully.

NARBS AND COLLECTIVE EXPERTISE

Narbs offer a counterpoint to most existing modes of expertise. Because they encapsulate the individual bits of knowledge and information of millions of people on social software applications, there needs to be an acknowledgment of their open-ended potential to be part of a new form of expertise that could supplement or contradict the existing norms of expertise. Keeping in mind that normative expertise becomes critical to judging the authenticity of knowledge, there could easily come a point where the vast number of narbs on a specific knowledge area could, by the weight of sheer numbers, acquire the status of expertise. Consider, for instance, the story of the death of technology pioneer Steve Jobs in 2011. That knowledge was already distributed via narbs as authentic and true information just as the normative experts were beginning to present the story through the traditional means of knowledge distribution.

Another recent example was the disruption in air travel due to volcanic ash in the atmosphere in the spring of 2010. At that time, thousands of people used social networks to tell individual stories about the event that offered a body of information that can be synthesized into knowledge about managing similar situations in the future. Such events make it important to examine narbs for the opportunities that such narrative bits offer for recasting the idea of expertise.

As suggested earlier, narbs operate as tiny bits of information that a member of an SNS chooses to share with others who are connected to the individual or who have access to this information. In the summation of narbs, which can be updated in a regular fashion, it is possible to know about an individual, community, or institution that participates in the process of creating narbs. Indeed, narbs become the starting point of participation in an SNS where a user is required to create a specific "profile" that serves as the starting point of the identity narrative of a person. Consequently, most digital social networking systems make an assumption that members would be interested in creating specific identity narratives about themselves and subjects that are of interest to them.

Digital social networking systems also allow members to constantly change the narbs. These changes could be in the form of updating personal information, adding new information, or reporting on the status of a person at any time. These make up different kinds of narbs but all add to the overall set of information that is available to the observer who is trying to put together the composite, albeit constantly changing, narrative of a person, group, or institution. The narb becomes a completely new source of information and a new epistemology can be built around the different kinds of narbs that are available in the digital regime. These narbs can be further categorized into different types, each offering specific kinds of information. They can be placed into different categories based on their content. The content-based categorization offers a way to understand the different kinds of information that is made available to the world. The primary content-based categories are:

- **Text Narb:** The kind of narb that only has a certain amount of words associated with it as in the case of status updates in Facebook or Twitter. This kind of information contains only textual content such as, for example, a statement that a person is doing an activity, or a short bit of news on any subject.
- **Picture Narb:** The kind of narb that includes a digital still image, ranging from a photograph to a piece of clip art. For an institution like a university, this could simply be a set of pictures of the campus.
- **Video Narb:** The kind of narb that includes a digital moving image with or without sound. For a specific group this could be, for example, the recording of a specific event performed by the group.
- **Audio Narb:** The kind of narb that includes an audio signal such as music or voice. An individual might produce an audio narb by providing a link to a piece of music that the person likes.

These content-based categories are certainly not meant to be mutually exclusive and often work together in a single narb—for example, a video narb may include a certain amount of text and an audio component. However, the categorization scheme offers the opportunity to parse a narb into its building blocks and show how often each different content category shows up in constructing a specific composite story, providing a new kind of information that is a direct product of a new technological phenomenon.

The content-based categorization has to be coupled with the functional categorization where narbs of all kinds can also be considered based on the specific function they perform in telling a story. The functional categorization process can be approached through a simple set of yardsticks

that have been central in considering any kind of narratives. The first set of functional categories would deal with the "spatial narb" that offers specific information about the real-life spatial location or spatial attributes of an entity. These are the narbs that answer the "where" question related to a story. The second functional category can be referred to as a "temporal narb" that offers specific chronological information. This kind of information can allow an observer to get a better sense of the flow of information as narbs are updated as well as answer the "when" question related to a narrative. A third functional category would be the "causal narb" that offers information about the fundamental attitudes and opinions of a person that shape the identity narrative of that person. This category would be especially important in understanding what motivates an entity to do things that become a part of the information about an entity by answering the "why" question related to a story. The fourth functional category focuses on specific activities and is called the "activity narb." Examining this category of narbs would allow an observer to create a narrative identity that is made up of the specific things that could be considered to be the central activities for a person, group, or institution, eventually answering the "what" question related to a story.

Digital social network systems are built around narbs. To any user of these systems, the core activity is updating information regularly to keep others informed. The kind of information shared varies, from mere personal updates to specific facts, behaviors, and opinions, all of which could have a greater social impact than a personal narrative. When such individual narbs on a specific issue are combined, the abundance of narbs could take on the authenticity that has been traditionally connected with expertise. The narbs thus become the new way of telling stories and offering information. As a corollary, for those seeking to answer the question "How should information be sought?" a completely new source of information becomes available as narbs rapidly multiply and are distributed to more and more observers. It is useful to consider how this new epistemological phenomenon can become a new source of information and how this information must be contextualized to yield most value for both the creator and the user of the information.

This system could completely upset and eventually redefine a culture of expertise that has remained with institutions where those in power or those with access to capital can claim expertise. Now individuals with no formal expertise are assuming the role of an expert. For instance, the spatial narb allows access to information that the individual expert can immediately make available to the world. Examples of such happenings are available across numerous recent moments in history as individual experts have offered information that created a composite picture of an event, one that could be quite different from what the institution represents. An early example from the digital realm was offered at the beginning of the second war in Iraq when the coalition forces began the attack on Baghdad. That night, while expert sources such as news networks across the world offered live coverage of the attack, someone was writing and distributing a Web-based log (blog) of the events from the perspective of what appeared to be a resident of Baghdad. Those reading the blog obtained a different sense of the story of the attack compared to those relying on the conventional media experts. In such cases, the locus of expertise is immediately called into question when the observer seeking "expert" information is faced with a crisis of authenticity. Which is more believable: what CNN is saying about an event or what hundreds of narbs are saying about an event? To be sure, this crisis would have to be dealt with as more experts—individual and collective—acquire the ability to produce and distribute information using narbs.

Given the rapid adoption of social media systems and the increasing number of narbs that are available on the systems, an important change is happening in terms of the source of the informa-tion available to those seeking information. The traditional modes of collecting information relied heavily on institutions that made it their business to provide information. Expert institutions such as mass media agencies would offer news of the world, expert book publishers would carefully select information and place them in encyclo-pedias, government and state institutions would offer critical information about specific facts about a phenomenon, and other authoritative voices would become the source of valid information. The narbs challenge such sources of information by offering an alternative set of experts who offer an alternative way of knowing the world. Through narbs the institutional experts offering informa-tion is supplemented by individuals whose narbs become yet another way in which it is possible to answer this chapter's critical question: "How do we know what we know?" Now it is possible to know of specific events by examining the narbs of individuals and then looking at a collection of narbs, and considering the way in which the individual agents, usually unfettered by institu-tional restraints, can offer a new way of knowing about an event. This is specially the case within a worldview where narratives are given the spe-cific importance they deserve in the process of creating knowledge. Twitter offers examples of narbs in the form of micro-narratives, or "tweets," providing information about political events, natural disasters, and other public events. In the "Twittersphere" private agents have become the source of information. By acknowledging narbs as a way of knowing, it becomes important to begin to analyze them in a systematic manner to gather the information from them and build a body of information that supplements other sources of information.

Such a move not only demands a re-thinking of epistemological traditions and the ways of knowing but also calls into question the notion of expertise based on the traditional epistemo-logical perspective that argued that people knew what they knew because the experts told them so. In the new scenario expertise is atomized and knowledge must be produced through a summative process of gathering the information from numerous narbs, and then collating it into a new authentic narrative. This is a trend that is already visible in certain areas of knowledge production. The internationally popular meteorological television channel along with its Internet presence, The Weather Channel (TWC), has been offering an option called "social" where individuals facing specific weather conditions can produce narbs. The narbs offer information that the TWC experts can never produce simply because they are not there to see events unfold as a tornado tears through the heart of a community, for example.

CONCLUSION

The argument presented here, and some of the examples provided, suggests that a new form of expertise and knowledge creation is unfolding that could make the traditional expert less central in an epistemological sense. If the traditional expert is superseded by new forms of expertise, the way knowledge is created and distributed changes radically. And at that moment of change, the judging of the value of information shifts to the one who seeks the information. With the reduced reliance on the traditional sources of expert authority, exemplified by the likes of CNN and the BBC, the new seeker of information must be able to judge the information carefully from the perspectives of a narrative paradigm of the world. The narbs are stories that the reader/user must analyze carefully before considering the authenticity of the story. Thus, within this new form of collective expertise, the reader/user needs to take on additional responsibilities. New forms of expertise will also produce a new reader/audience.

Future research also needs to continue to examine the relationship between the traditional experts and the emergent experts. There could well be a point of inflection where the stories offered by the

traditional experts are ignored in the face of the collective narbs of the new experts. Such shifts could indicate changes in ideology, as exemplified by the 2011 events in the Arab world where the narbs of individuals created an alternative structure of political reality in countries such as Tunisia and Egypt. In examining the events of the revolution in Tunisia and Egypt, which have been collectively named the events of the Arab Spring, it has been argued that social media played a role in the way in which a specific and alternative political reality was being constructed by the people participating in the protest and uprising. Although narbs and social media might not have been central to the role, the Egyptian government felt it necessary to shut down Internet services in order to slow down the impact of social media in the uprising (see, for example, Kanalley, 2011; Ray, 2011; Rosen, 2011). While there will be continuing debates about the role of narbs in the Arab Spring, or other such political movements, it remains the case that the new forms of collective expertise enabled by digital media call into question the narratives that the traditional experts insist upon. It will have to be seen how this interaction plays out, and if indeed it is possible to find a negotiated space for different kinds of expertise.

REFERENCES

Bakhtin, M. M. (1981). *The dialogic imagination: Four essays* (Holquist, M., Trans.). Austin, TX: University of Texas Press.

Boyd, D., & Ellison, N. (2007). Social network sites: Definition, history, and scholarship. *Journal of Computer-Mediated Communication*, *13*(1). Retrieved from http://jcmc.indiana.edu/vol13/issue1/boyd.ellison.html. doi:10.1111/j.1083-6101.2007.00393.x

Fisher, W. R. (1984). Narration as human communication paradigm: The case of public moral argument. *Communication Monographs, 51,* 1–22. doi:10.1080/03637758409390180

Hall, S. (1992). Cultural identity and diaspora. In Rutherford, J. (Ed.), *Identity: Community, culture, difference.* London, UK: Sage.

Hyde, M., & Mitra, A. (2000). On the ethics of creating a face in cyberspace: The case of a university. In Berdayes, V., & Murphy, J. (Eds.), *Computers, human interaction and organizations* (pp. 161–188). New York, NY: Praeger.

Kanalley, C. (January 27, 2011). Egypt's Internet shut down, according to reports. *The Huffington Post.* Retrieved from http://www.huffingtonpost.com/2011/01/27/egypt-internet-goes-down-_n_815156.html

Lenhart, A. (January 14, 2009). Social networks grow: Friending Mom and Dad. *Pew Internet & American Life Project.* Retrieved from http://pewresearch.org/pubs/1079/social-networks-grow

Mitra, A. (2002). Trust, authenticity and discursive power in cyberspace. *Communications of the ACM, 45*(3), 27–29. doi:10.1145/504729.504748

Mitra, A., & Schwartz, R. L. (2001). From cyber space to cybernetic space: Rethinking the relationship between real and virtual spaces. *Journal of Computer-Mediated Communication, 7*(1). Retrieved from http://jcmc.indiana.edu/vol7/issue1/mitra.html.

Rosen, R. R. (September 3, 2011). So, was Facebook responsible for the Arab Spring after all? *The Atlantic Online.* Retrieved from http://www.theatlantic.com/technology/archive/2011/09/so-was-facebook-responsible-for-the-arab-spring-after-all/244314/

Thompson-Canino, J., Cotton, R., & Torneo, E. (2009). *Picking cotton: Our memoir of injustice and redemption.* New York, NY: St. Martin's Press.

ADDITIONAL READING

Barnes, J. (1954). Class and committees in a Norwegian island parish. *Human Relations, 7,* 39–58. doi:10.1177/001872675400700102

Baym, N. K. (2000). *Tune in, log on: Soaps, fandom, and online community.* Newbury Park, CA: Sage Publications.

Chyi, H. I. (2009). Information surplus and news consumption in the digital age: Impact and implications. In Papacharissi, Z. (Ed.), *Journalism and citizenship: New agendas* (pp. 91–107). New York, NY: Taylor & Francis.

Didi, A. L. R. (2006). Getting hooked on news: Uses and gratifications and the formation of news habits among college students in an Internet environment. *Journal of Broadcasting & Electronic Media, 50*(2), 193–210. doi:10.1207/s15506878jobem5002_2

Jones, S. (1994). *CyberSociety: Computer-mediated communication and community.* Newbury Park, CA: Sage Publications.

Jones, S. (1997). *Virtual culture: Identity and communication in cybersociety.* Newbury Park, CA: Sage Publications.

Mitra, A. (1996). Nations and the Internet: The case of a national newsgroup, "soc.cult.indian. *Convergence: The Journal of Research into New Media, 2*(1), 44–75. doi:10.1177/135485659600200106

Mitra, A. (1997). Virtual commonality: Looking for India on the Internet. In Jones, S. (Ed.), *Virtual culture.* Newbury Park, CA: Sage.

Mitra, A. (2010). *Alien technology: Coping with modern mysteries.* Newbury Park, CA: Sage Publications.

Mitra, A., & Watts, E. (2002). Theorizing cyberspace: The idea of voice applied to the Internet discourse. *New Media & Society, 4*(4), 479–298. doi:10.1177/14614440232146678

Rakow, L. F. (1988). Women and the telephone: The gendering of a communications technology. In Kramarae, C. (Ed.), *Technology and women's voices: Keeping in touch* (pp. 226–236). New York, NY: Routledge & Kegan Paul.

Ray, T. (2011). The "story" of digital excess in revolutions of the Arab Spring. *Journal of Media Practice, 12*(2), 189–196. doi:10.1386/jmpr.12.2.189_1

Wu, H. D., & Bechtel, A. (2002). Web site use and news topic and type. *Journalism & Mass Communication Quarterly, 79*(1), 73–86. doi:10.1177/107769900207900106

KEY TERMS AND DEFINITIONS

Cultural Capital: A relational concept that exists alongside other forms of capital (economic, social) and whose possession or lack thereof constitutes social advantage or disadvantage. Its transmission and accumulation often perpetuate social inequalities.

Cybernetic Space: The interaction between real and virtual spaces produces this synthetic space in which we live.

Epistemology: A branch of philosophy concerned with the study of knowledge and justified belief. It investigates the nature of knowledge and its acquisition.

Expertise: A condition that allows a person or an institution to have authority on a body of information.

Narb: An item of personal information posted online, particularly as it contributes, often unwittingly, to a personal narrative that an individual is creating online. Short for "narrative bit."

Narrative Paradigm: The way people make sense of the world by telling stories and listening to stories.

Social Media: The digital system that connects the narbs of many individuals in one single digital space.

ENDNOTES

[1] For instance, MySpace was an open site that was popular among a large cross-section of users since it provided unrestricted access to the SNS, and the creators of MySpace stayed well in touch with the users to provide specific features that the users demanded. Conversely, the early version of Facebook was restricted to young people in academic institutions, most of the users of Facebook had a priori connections with each other, and the SNS was an extension of the real-life connection as compared to MySpace that facilitated a connection between people who might not have known each other in real life. Other SNS were restricted to specific parts of the world, as in the case of Bebo which had a large following in Europe but not in the rest of the world, and Orkut that had an initial following in Brazil, and later in India.

[2] This phenomenon produced specific issues related to the authenticity of the entity that would be available in a discursive way (Mitra, 2002). It would be impossible to be sure that what was being presented in a discursive form was indeed what the entity was. This phenomenon extends to all entities that have a digital presence—from a person to an institution—and the presence is often the careful construction of a "face" that is visible to the world (Hyde & Mitra, 2000). The user of the information must decide if the presence is authentic and trustworthy so that the observer can make specific attributions about the real entity that is depicted online.

Chapter 2
Wikipedia's Success and the Rise of the Amateur–Expert

Christopher Sweet
Illinois Wesleyan University, USA

ABSTRACT

The Free Online Encyclopedia, as Wikipedia calls itself, is a radical departure from traditional encyclopedias and traditional methods of knowledge creation. This chapter is an examination of how a community of amateurs on Wikipedia has challenged notions of expertise in the 21st century. It does so by first looking at the roots of Wikipedia in a phenomenon known as the "wisdom of the crowds" and in the open source software movement. The reliability of Wikipedia is examined as are the claims made by major critics of the project. Throughout, epistemological questions raised by Wikipedia are addressed.

INTRODUCTION

"Because the world is radically new, the ideal encyclopedia should be radical too. It should stop being safe—in politics, in philosophy, in science" (Encyclopedia Britannica editor, Charles Van Doren, 1962).

For most of the 20th century, having a print encyclopedia set on your home bookshelf was a hallmark of learning and education. While tradi-

tional encyclopedias are undoubtedly a valuable and authoritative reference source, the process of their creation from beginning to end is imbued with a certain level of elitism. Individual articles are written only by carefully selected experts, publication is tightly controlled by major printing houses, and access is limited to academic institutions, libraries, and those who can afford to purchase a set. In 2011, the 32 volumes of the *Encyclopedia Britannica* cost $1,395, putting it far out of reach for the vast majority of individuals (BritannicaStore.com, 2010).

DOI: 10.4018/978-1-4666-2178-7.ch002

Well before the advent of the Internet, one of the most successful strategies for selling encyclopedias was through door-to-door salesmen. While unimaginable in the digital age, encyclopedia publishers found that it often required that intimate level of human interaction to convince customers to make such a substantial book purchase. In *The Great EB: The story of the Encyclopedia Britannica,* Herman Kogan recounts the heyday of the door-to-door encyclopedia salesman:

On any day or night of any week there is an Encyclopedia Britannica salesman sitting or standing in a living room, a kitchen, a study, a den, an office or in some less conventional place, with material from his sales kit spread before him as he "tells the story" to a potential customer. (Kogan, 1958: 299)

Salesmen were trained in the psychology of selling, they had to serve an apprenticeship under an experienced salesman, and they even went so far as to scour newspapers for the names of recent graduates to contact for a potential sale (Kogan, 1958). One evening in 1969, the Wales family of Huntsville, Alabama, was convinced to purchase a set of *World Book Encyclopedias* from one of these door-to-door salesmen (Schiff, 2006). Three years prior to that evening, the Wales family had welcomed a son, Jimmy Wales. Jimmy was educated in the private Montessori-influenced school where his mother taught. During this time Jimmy "spent lots of hours pouring over the *Britannicas* and *World Book Encyclopedias*" (Lamb, 2005). Drawing in part on these early childhood experiences, in 2001 Jimmy Wales helped to found Wikipedia, The Free Encyclopedia. Wikipedia quickly became more radical than anything Charles Van Doren could have dreamed of in 1962.

As of 2011, Wikipedia is the sixth-most-visited US website, falling not far behind giants such as Google and Facebook (Top Sites in the United States. 2011). The scale of Wikipedia is astounding. Its English language version currently has more than 3.6 million articles; worldwide, it has 17 million articles in 270 different languages (Statistics, 2011). As an entity that both creates and disseminates knowledge, Wikipedia has no peer. Its articles frequently appear among the first few links returned by a Google search, so its reach and impact factor are enormous. As an encyclopedia, Wikipedia is certainly radical in that the site is freely accessible to anyone with an Internet connection. What the average Wikipedia user often does not realize is that the site has been operated as a not-for-profit from the very beginning. The site does not sell any advertising and is not beholden to any outside interests. According to Wales, the goal of Wikipedia is nothing short of creating "a world in which every single person is given free access to the sum of all human knowledge" (Lih, 2009: xv). The radical freedom of Wikipedia extends well beyond free access. The use of its content is governed by both a Creative Commons License and the GNU Free Documentation License, ensuring that all users of Wikipedia can copy, modify, and redistribute anything in Wikipedia that is not otherwise protected. Wikipedia is also radically egalitarian in its approach to the creation of knowledge. All 17 million Wikipedia articles have been created by uncompensated, anonymous users. In stark contrast to the traditional encyclopedia model, Wikipedia does not require that one be a credentialed expert to write on a subject. With a few exceptions, anyone can create a new article or edit an existing one. Of this radical facet of Wikipedia, Wales has said, "To me, the key thing is getting it right. I don't care if they're a high-school kid or a Harvard professor" (Schiff, 2006: 5). In practice, this does not mean Wikipedia is an "anything goes" sort of place. On the contrary, the Discussion Pages that accompany each Wikipedia article often reveal the nitty-gritty details of the process of knowledge creation, detailing, long, impassioned battles over various elements of the article. Over the long term, this radical openness helps to mitigate authorial bias that often plagues single-authored works.

BACKGROUND

The encyclopedic impulse—to collect and codify human knowledge—is nearly as old as writing itself. Wikipedia is the most recent in a long line of attempts to document what we collectively "know." The word *encyclopedia* is derived from the Greek *enkyklios paideia*, meaning "a general or all-around education." One of the earliest surviving works that has many similarities to modern encyclopedias is the 37-volume *Naturalis Historia* written in the first century AD by the Roman Pliny the Elder. Denis Diderot's French *Encyclopédie* written in 1751 was the first to introduce an organizational structure that resembles that of current encyclopedias. *Encyclopedia Britannica* is the oldest (1768) and best-known English-language encyclopedia (Blair, 2010). For a more detailed history of early encyclopedias and dictionaries, Ann Blair's *Too Much to Know: Managing scholarly information before the modern age* is a valuable resource (2010).

Wales's comment about not caring if Wikipedia authors are high school kids or Harvard professors cuts to the heart of the vigorous debates that surround Wikipedia. In an interconnected, online environment, who are the experts and on what grounds are they claiming expertise? The *Oxford English Dictionary* defines an expert as "One whose special knowledge or skill causes him to be regarded as an authority; a specialist" (Expert, 2011). Interestingly, the authoritative *Cambridge Handbook of Expertise and Expert Performance* chooses to cite a 2005 definition of "expert" from Wikipedia:

[S]omeone widely recognized as a reliable source of knowledge, technique, or skill whose judgment is accorded authority and status by the public or his or her peers. Experts have prolonged or intense experience through practice and education in a particular field. (Ericsson, Charness, Feltovich, & Hoffman, 2006)

Michelene Chi describes seven ways in which experts excel and seven ways in which they fall short. The list of ways in which they excel are generating the best solution, their detection/recognition abilities, conducting qualitative analyses, self-monitoring, choosing appropriate strategies, seizing opportunities, and cognitive effort. Acknowledging the ways in which experts fall short is essential to understanding the arguments presented in this chapter. Chi lists the following seven ways in which experts fall short: expertise is domain-limited, overly confident, context dependent, inflexible; experts sometimes tend to gloss over important aspects, which may lead to inaccurate prediction; they are judgmental, and show bias and functional fixedness (Ericsson et al., 2006: 24-27). The issue of expert bias in particular has provided one of the footholds for Wikipedia. In a very short period of time, Wikipedia has mounted a major challenge to expert control over knowledge creation and dissemination as traditionally understood. The success of Wikipedia is derived from the tireless efforts of tens of thousands of amateur-experts: people who have gained a great deal of specialized knowledge through study or practice, but who lack traditional academic or professional credentials.

The primary objective of this chapter is to take a closer look at the ways in which amateur-experts are creating knowledge on Wikipedia while subverting traditional notions of expertise. The chapter will explore the roots of Wikipedia in both the encyclopedic tradition and the open source software movement. The concept of epistemic egalitarianism will be defined along with its implications for Wikipedia. Crowdsourcing has enabled Wikipedia to fully utilize its vast community of amateur-experts. Another objective of this chapter is to ask whether crowdsourcing can yield reliable knowledge. The accuracy and reliability of Wikipedia articles has been hotly debated since its inception. I will look at both sides of this argument as well as empirical research done in this area. This chapter also addresses some of the arguments of major critics of Wikipedia. I close with some thoughts on knowledge creation, evolving notions of expertise, and possible implications for Web 3.0.

ROOTS IN THE OPEN SOURCE MOVEMENT

Wikipedia has been able to overcome some of the limitations of traditional encyclopedias such as cost and scale by leveraging the potential of the Internet, and, specifically, lessons learned from the open source software movement. To understand why Wikipedia works successfully without traditional experts, it is important to have a basic understanding of its roots within open source software. Open source is defined as software whose underlying code is made freely available for anyone to improve, modify, or re-use. Open source also requires free redistribution rights (Open Source Software, 2011). The earliest example of open source software is the UNIX operating system released in 1971. Later open source software projects that built on the success of UNIX include the widely used Linux operating system (1991) and the Mozilla Firefox Web browser (2003).

In 1997, open source advocate Eric Raymond wrote a seminal essay about the open source movement titled "The Cathedral and the Bazaar." In the essay (later developed into a book with the same title), Raymond likens the traditional corporate model of software development to a cathedral that was "carefully crafted, by individual wizards or small bands of mages (magicians) working in splendid isolation." The open source community, on the other hand, "seemed to resemble a great babbling bazaar of differing agendas and approaches ... out of which a coherent and stable system could seemingly emerge only by a succession of miracles" (Raymond, 1999: 24). Much to Raymond's (and nearly everyone else's surprise),

open source software design worked quite well in many cases. One of the reasons it works is that it utilizes and simplifies mass collaboration. Raymond has summarized this concept in what has become a maxim for the open source movement: "Given enough eyeballs, all bugs are shallow," meaning that if you get enough people working on a problem, someone will come up with a solution (29). Raymond's essay was very influential in shaping Wales's vision for Wikipedia: "It [*The Cathedral and the Bazaar*] opened my eyes to the possibility of mass collaboration" (Schiff, 2006).

Significantly, many champions of the open source movement take pains to distinguish Wikipedia from traditional open source projects. Jeff Bates, a vice president of the Open Source Technology Group, oversees a website that hosts 80,000 open source projects. In a 2006 *New York Times* article he said, "It makes me grind my teeth to hear Wikipedia compared to open source," and that every open source project has its "benevolent dictator," someone who takes responsibility, even though the code has been contributed by many (Stross, 2006). Throughout its relatively short existence Wikipedia has struggled with just this issue: should the site remain completely open and treat every user as equal or are benevolent dictators in the shape of editors and administrators required to keep the site from devolving into chaos? This debate is ongoing and continues to shape how knowledge is created on Wikipedia. In any case, lessons learned from the open source movement have been critical to Wikipedia's success. It is significant to the arguments put forth in this chapter that the open source movement has always extended an open invitation to anyone who is interested in working on the software. It is not limited to only expert programmers. Many of the most productive open source contributors are often hackers, gamers, and hobbyists—in other words, amateur-expert programmers—working well outside the corporate world and lacking academic credentials.

CROWDSOURCING

The kind of mass collaboration open source software relies upon is referred to as crowdsourcing. Two recent books have explored crowdsourcing not just within open source software design, but also within many business and everyday life contexts: *The Wisdom of the Crowds* (2004) by James Suroweicki and *Crowdsourcing: Why the power of the crowd is driving the future of business* (2008) by Jeff Howe. Howe's book specifically addresses Wikipedia and provides a blueprint for successful crowdsourced projects. Surowiecki's book is perhaps the more interesting read as he provides many examples of how crowdsourcing plays out in everyday life. Both books demonstrate how in many situations the wisdom of a crowd of amateurs surpasses the best efforts of traditional experts. Howe defines crowdsourcing as "the act of taking a job traditionally performed by a designated agent (usually an employee) and outsourcing it to an undefined, generally large group of people in the form of an open call" (Howe, 2006). The genius of Wikipedia is that it managed to successfully crowdsource the substantial work of creating an encyclopedia.

Although the term crowdsourcing is new, the phenomenon is not. *Vox populi* is a Latin phrase that means "voice of the people." *Vox Populi* was also the title chosen by Sir Francis Galton for an article he published in the journal *Nature* in 1907. The article recounts an experiment that Galton designed to test the wisdom of the crowds. At a regional fair in England a competition was set up where participants had to guess the weight of a slaughtered ox. The contestants numbered about 800, and most of them, Galton observed, had no expertise in judging cattle. The result of the experiment was that the average guess—the wisdom of the crowd—was only 9 pounds (less than 1%) off the actual weight of 1,207 pounds. Surprised by the accuracy of the crowd, Galton concluded: "This result is, I think, more creditable

to the trustworthiness of a democratic judgement than might have been expected" (Galton, 1907).

Almost 100 years later, NASA came up with an experiment that they dubbed "Clickworkers." The basis of the experiment was to find out whether "public volunteers, each working for a few minutes here and there can do some routine science analysis that would normally be done by a scientist or graduate student working for months on end" (Benkler, 2006: 69). The task at hand was to classify craters on maps of Mars. In the first six months of the project 85,000 volunteers made more than 1.9 million different entries. Regarding the question of expertise and quality, NASA researchers concluded that "the automatically-computed consensus of a large number of clickworkers is virtually indistinguishable from the inputs of a geologist with years of experience in identifying Mars craters" (Benkler, 2006: 69). The crowdsourcing model has proved to be not only effective in distributing a large task, but also highly accurate and reliable in its results.

Surowiecki provides one more compelling contemporary example of the wisdom of the crowd again bettering the experts. The popular game show *Who Wants to Be a Millionaire?* asked contestants a series of increasingly difficult trivia questions for the chance to win a million dollars. If the contestants were stumped along the way, they had a few "lifelines" that included phoning a friend (the expert) or polling the studio audience. Surowiecki recounts the results of this ad hoc experiment:

[T]he "experts" did okay, offering the right answer—under pressure—almost 65 percent of the time. But they paled in comparison to the audiences. Those random crowds of people with nothing better to do on a weekday afternoon than sit in a TV studio picked the right answer 91 percent of the time. (2004: 4)

Surowiecki summarizes the power of crowdsourcing as follows:

Under the right circumstances, groups are remarkably intelligent, and are often smarter than the smartest people in them. Groups do not need to be dominated by exceptionally intelligent people in order to be smart. Even if most people within a group are not especially well-informed or rational, it can still reach a collectively wise decision. (Surowiecki, 2004: xiii)

This feature of the wisdom of the crowds is precisely why Wikipedia articles are as a whole quite reliable.

BRIEF HISTORY OF WIKIPEDIA

The historical evolution of encyclopedias, the open source software movement, and the power of crowdsourcing all paved the way for Wikipedia. Rather fittingly, Wikipedia itself provides one of the better histories and general overviews of the site. Of particular interest are the entries "About Wikipedia," "Wikipedia History," "Wikipedia: Five Pillars," and "Wikipedia: Contributing to Wikipedia." One of the most thorough books covering the history of Wikipedia and its internal workings is *How Wikipedia Works and How You Can Be a Part of It* (Ayers, Matthews, & Yates, 2008). A more concise overview is provided by *The Wikipedia Revolution: How a bunch of nobodies created the world's greatest encyclopedia* (Lih, 2009).

Jimmy Wales was earlier introduced as one of the founders of Wikipedia, but a general understanding of how Wikipedia came to be and how it works today is critical to understanding how Wikipedia is challenging our understanding of knowledge creation and expertise. Wikipedia was not Wales's first attempt at creating a free online encyclopedia. By 1999, Wales was a retired options trader and successful Web entrepreneur. He had an idea to create a free, online encyclopedia created by volunteers. To help accomplish his vision he hired Larry Sanger. Sanger had a PhD

in philosophy; his specific area of interest was epistemology—the theory and understanding of knowledge. Wales and Sanger named their first encyclopedia effort Nupedia. Nupedia was launched in 2000, and was free and written by volunteers, but unlike Wikipedia, the volunteers were expert scholars with PhDs in their field of study and the articles went through an extensive peer review process. Basically, Wales and Sanger were trying to re-create a traditional encyclopedia on the Web—for free. Not surprisingly, the endeavor failed by 2003. By the time the site went offline it had amassed a grand total of 24 completed articles. Apparently the community of expert scholars was unwilling to contribute to a free encyclopedia without compensation (Lih, 2009; Nupedia, 2011).

In 2001, Sanger had dinner with a friend who told him about a new website called WikiWikiWeb. WikiWikiWeb was created by a programmer named Ward Cunningham who borrowed the Hawaiian word *wiki* which means "quick." Quickness and ease of use were the genius behind the wiki platform. On a wiki any user can quickly edit a webpage without logging on and without any expert programming knowledge. It also archives all edits and also allows easy rollback to an earlier version of the page—something that was important to its eventual use as the platform for Wikipedia. Essentially the connectivity and critical mass of the Internet coupled with the unique features of the wiki platform greatly simplified the potential for crowdsourcing large projects.

Not long after Sanger heard about the wiki platform he created a wiki which he hoped would serve as a feeder site for Nupedia. The Nupedia experts did not like letting amateurs fiddle with their work so, on January 15, 2001, Sanger moved the wiki to its own URL and gave it a new name: Wikipedia. Less than two weeks later, 224 different people had visited Wikipedia and it had nearly 5,000 page views on a single day (Lih, 2009: 65). From then on, more and more time was devoted to Wikipedia as Nupedia foundered and was finally taken offline in 2003.

PHILOSOPHY OF WIKIPEDIA

The philosophical foundations of Wikipedia were shaped by both Wales and Sanger, but it was Sanger's philosophical background in epistemology that most likely had the strongest impact. Undoubtedly, some of the most erudite explorations of the evolving nature of knowledge and expertise in an online environment (not just as it relates to Wikipedia) have come from Sanger. Three of his essays should be required reading for anyone interested in a philosophical inquiry into knowledge and expertise: "Why Make Room for Experts in Web 2.0?" (2006), "Who Says We Know?: On the new politics of knowledge" (2007), and "The Fate of Expertise after Wikipedia" (2009). In "Who Says We Know?: On the new politics of knowledge," Sanger discusses one of the core principles of Wikipedia: *epistemic egalitarianism.*

According to epistemic egalitarianism, we are all fundamentally equal in our authority or rights to articulate what should pass for knowledge; the only grounds on which a claim can compete against other claims are to be found in the content of the claim itself, never in who makes it. (Sanger, 2007)

Herein lies the root of what makes so many people uncomfortable with Wikipedia. Traditionally expertise was clearly defined by academic coursework culminating with the conferring of a degree or by serving an apprenticeship under an established expert. Epistemic egalitarianism completely subverts that model by giving anyone the right to create knowledge. Under this model, individual efforts will be judged solely on the content without regard to the qualifications of the creator.

Wikipedia Principles

Wikipedia operates on just five fundamental principles, known as the five pillars:

1. Wikipedia is an online encyclopedia.
2. Wikipedia has a neutral point of view.
3. Wikipedia is free content.
4. Wikipedians should interact in a respectful and civil manner.
5. Wikipedia does not have firm rules. (Five Pillars, 2011)

Of these, "Wikipedia has a neutral point of view" has the most impact on how Wikipedia is changing the nature of expertise and knowledge creation. This pillar sets Wikipedia in stark contrast to traditional encyclopedias. Most traditional encyclopedia articles are written by a single author and then reviewed and edited by only a couple other people. Wikipedia specifically guards against single-authored articles. For example, you are not supposed to create a biography of yourself on Wikipedia because by definition that would not be a neutral point of view.

One of the major flaws of the traditional model of expertise is that it allows—even encourages—authorial bias and sometimes fails to take into account dissenting and alternative views. Knowledge is created on Wikipedia by specifically encouraging all dissenting views. Two pieces of the wiki platform that enable this exchange are the discussion (or "talk") pages and the history pages. Each and every Wikipedia article has a separate tab for discussion about that article as well as a history tab that documents each and every edit. Author and journalist Cory Doctorow explains the significance of these features of Wikipedia:

[I]f you want to really navigate the truth via Wikipedia, you have to dig into those "history" and "discuss" pages hanging off of every entry. That's where the real action is, the tidily organized palimpsest of the flamewar that lurks beneath any definition of "truth." (2006)

Wikipedia is a grand experiment in determining the nature of truth. You, the user, have to decide if truth is a specific product of expertise or whether it can also arise from a democratic process of debating, compromising, and eventually settling on a consensus.

ISSUES, CONTROVERSIES, AND PROBLEMS

Wikipedia has become very widely used, very quickly: the site received 400 million unique visitors during March 2011 (About, 2011). Wikipedia has also been widely criticized. Many of the general criticisms stem from the tension between experts and amateurs as well as the radical ways in which Wikipedia creates and disseminates knowledge. While far from a comprehensive analysis of the criticisms against Wikipedia, the following section will address both some of the major issues and some of the major critics themselves. Major issues that will be examined are reliability/accuracy, and problems surrounding bureaucracy on the site. Larry Sanger was instrumental in creating Wikipedia, but by 2002 he had become disillusioned with the project and was then laid off by Wales during a budget crunch. Sanger's criticisms of Wikipedia get to the heart of the expert/amateur debate and merit close examination. Two other outspoken critics whose claims will be examined are Jaron Lanier (*Digital Maoism* [2006] and *You Are Not a Gadget* [2010]) and Andrew Keen (*The Cult of the Amateur* [2007]).

Death by Wikipedia

January 20, 2009, was the date of President Barack Obama's inauguration. At a post-inauguration luncheon a great tragedy befell the US political community when both the ailing Senator Edward (Ted) Kennedy and the aging Senator Robert Byrd passed away. According to Kennedy's Wikipedia biography from that day, "Kennedy suffered a seizure at a luncheon following the Barack Obama Presidential inauguration … He was removed in a wheelchair and died shortly after" (Pershing,

2009). Byrd's entry had a death date added, but only noted that he had collapsed during the same luncheon. The speed of this reporting was exceptional, occurring shortly after the actual luncheon. The reliability of the information, however, left much to be desired since neither Senator actually died on January 20, 2009. Both Senators lived for at least a few months after having been killed off on Wikipedia. Kennedy and Byrd are just two of the high-profile examples of a phenomenon that became so common that it had its own name: "Death by Wikipedia." This Death by Wikipedia anecdote serves as the perfect introduction into the single most controversial issue surrounding Wikipedia: reliability.

Reliability

The defining characteristic of traditional encyclopedias has always been reliability. Schoolchildren are taught to cite encyclopedia articles because they are reliable and written by authoritative experts. Indisputable facts spelled out by encyclopedia articles have been the ultimate arbitrator for bar bets the world over. With that in mind, how has Wikipedia become so successful? Writing in the *New York Times*, Randall Stross distills the entire reliability controversy as follows: "Wikipedia raises a single nagging epistemological question: Can an article be judged as credible without knowing its author?" (2006). Restating his question within the context of this chapter we can ask: Can a diverse group of anonymous amateur-experts consistently create reliable knowledge? To begin exploring these questions the following section will detail some of the studies that have been conducted to test the reliability of Wikipedia and the implications for expertise in a Web 2.0 context.

What do we really mean when we call something reliable? The *Oxford English Dictionary* defines "reliable" as "Of a person, information, etc.: able to be trusted; in which reliance or confidence may be placed; trustworthy, safe, sure"

(2011). Larry Sanger draws on his background in epistemology to add nuance to the concept of reliability:

Reliability is a comparative quality; something doesn't have to be perfectly reliable in order to be reliable. So, to say that an encyclopedia is reliable is to say that it contains an unusually high proportion of truth versus error, compared to other publications. (Sanger, 2007)

Encyclopedia Britannica is the oldest and best-known English-language encyclopedia; therefore, comparisons with Wikipedia were inevitable. The first edition of *Encyclopedia Britannica* was printed in 1768 and Wikipedia first appeared online in 2001. In terms of size, the current (2010) print version of the *Encyclopedia Britannica* contains 65,000 articles and the online version 120,000 (Britannica, 2011). The English language Wikipedia currently has 3.6 million articles. Everyone who has used Wikipedia with any degree of regularity will have encountered vast differences in quality between articles. Some articles are fully developed, well written, and well documented. Other articles (usually on lesser-known topics) are barely coherent and almost devoid of documentation. This common experience has led many people to ask, "How reliable is Wikipedia anyway?"

BRITANNICA VS. WIKIPEDIA

In a 2005 issue of the journal *Nature,* Jim Giles reported on a study that attempted to compare the reliability and accuracy of Wikipedia and *Britannica* science articles. While far from comprehensive and widely criticized (particularly by *Britannica*), the study results made national headlines and have since been frequently cited by Wikipedia supporters. *Nature* engaged a panel of experts to review 42 entries on scientific topics for errors. The conclusion of the study was that "[t]he exercise revealed numerous errors in both

encyclopedias, but among 42 entries tested, the difference in accuracy was not particularly great: the average science entry in Wikipedia contained around four inaccuracies; Britannica, about three" (Giles, 2005). While these results can certainly not be applied to Wikipedia as a whole, the fact that articles written by unpaid amateurs were found to be nearly as reliable as those in the best encyclopedia was certainly mind-opening to many.

One of the undisputed advantages of an online encyclopedia is the ability to instantly correct a problem or edit an article based on a new event or finding. The traditional print encyclopedia is less flexible in this respect. The only way to correct a problem is to issue a new print supplement or wait for the next printing. Wikipedia capitalizes on this shortcoming of print encyclopedias by pointing out nearly 30 pages of "Errors in the Encyclopaedia Britannica that have been corrected in Wikipedia" (Errors ..., 2011). In all fairness, the new online versions of *Encyclopedia Britannica* allow editors the same flexibility in fixing errors and updating articles, but this privilege is reserved only for expert editors.

While reporting on Wikipedia for the *New Yorker,* Stacy Schiff asked Jorge Cauz, the president of *Britannica* for an analogy comparing the two resources. He replied, "Wikipedia is to *Britannica* as 'American Idol' is to the Julliard School" (Schiff, 2006). Jimmy Wales quickly responded with his own analogy: "Wikipedia is to *Britannica* as rock and roll is to easy listening. It may not be as smooth, but it scares the parents and is a lot smarter in the end" (Schiff, 2006). One can easily substitute "experts" or "publishers" for "parents" in Wales's analogy and it would still hold true. Wikipedia has played such a crucial role in the quickly evolving nature of new forms of collective expertise because it has been so successful and prolific in such a short period of time. Sanger again spells out the implications for traditional expertise: "In a world in which so many people are consulting an encyclopedia 'anyone can edit' for answers, the conventional wisdom, the accepted knowledge, seems less tethered to experts, exclusive institutions, and publications with professional gatekeepers" (Sanger, 2007).

While the *Nature* study received the most attention from the press, many other lesser-known studies have also tried to tackle the reliability question. One of the most comprehensive lists of Wikipedia reliability studies is on Wikipedia itself under the article "Reliability of Wikipedia." A small sample of these studies is summarized below.

The majority of studies that have examined article reliability on Wikipedia have done so by analyzing or monitoring individual articles. During the 1st Workshop on Social Media Analytics, Sara Javanmardi and Cristina Lopes (2010) presented a paper discussing how they developed "an automated measure to estimate the quality of article revisions throughout the entire English Wikipedia." Their analysis of article "quality" relied heavily upon the reputation of a given editor. Their findings include "that non-featured articles tend to have high-quality content 74% of the time, while featured articles average 86%" (Javanmardi & Lopes, 2010). The authors note that the quality of articles changes over time, but more importantly, this study "showed that the average article quality increases as it goes through edits" (Javanmardi & Lopes, 2010). This study lends weight to the assertion that a crowdsourced project like Wikipedia will increase in quality over time as more and more participants contribute to the project.

Lucy Holman Rector, a librarian at Harford Community College, Maryland, conducted an article-by-article reliability study similar to that conducted by *Nature*. Instead of just comparing the articles to *Britannica,* Rector also included two additional standard information reference sources: the *Dictionary of American History* and *American National Biography Online*. The findings of her study were similar to those published by *Nature*: "Overall, Wikipedia's accuracy rate was 80 percent compared with 95–96 percent accuracy within the other sources" (Rector, 2008).

While this accuracy rate for Wikipedia articles is not bad, Rector also uncovered unattributed quotes in eight out of nine articles and five possible cases of plagiarism.

One final, informal study is significant not so much for its findings, but for what it tells us about behind-the-scenes editing at Wikipedia. In 2008, P.D. Magnus anonymously inserted 36 short, fake statements into Wikipedia articles about notable, deceased philosophers. He then monitored the articles for 48 hours to see if the false statements were corrected. Magnus found that "[o]f 36 fibs, 15 were removed within 48 hours. Three others were not removed, but were marked as needing citation" (2008). As the author realized, some of the speedy corrections were due to "guilt by association." Even anonymous edits are identified by a unique IP address. Wikipedia also tracks recent changes, which volunteer editors monitor closely. In this case, an editor discovered the vandalism to one article and checked to see what other changes were made by the same user.

No traditional information reference source (encyclopedia, dictionary, almanac, etc.) written by experts is entirely free from error. Moreover, many of these traditional resources are much more prone to author bias than Wikipedia. Wikipedia articles certainly vary greatly in quality and accuracy, but if we use Sanger's definition of reliability from above ("contains an *unusually high* proportion of truth versus error, compared to other publications") then Wikipedia can be said to be reliable in general. Cory Doctorow neatly summarizes the reliability issue:

So Wikipedia gets it wrong. Britannica gets it wrong, too. The important thing about systems isn't how they work, it's how they fail. Fixing a Wikipedia article is simple. Participating in the brawl takes more effort, but then, that's the price you pay for truth, and it's still cheaper than starting up your own Britannica. (Doctorow, 2006)

WIKIPEDIA BUREAUCRACY

For all of its radical openness, Wikipedia has not done away that cornerstone of encyclopedias: the editor. Without editors, Wikipedia would quickly devolve into chaos and flame wars between various factions. Editors do serve as a sort of expert on Wikipedia, but the process of becoming an editor remains egalitarian. Many editors are identified only by their username and traditional academic credentials play no role in becoming an editor: "An expert has the same privileges as any other editor: Expertise must manifest itself through the editing and discussion process" (Ayers: 54). In one sense everyone is an editor on Wikipedia. Unregistered users still account for the majority of edits on Wikipedia, but they have not been able to create entirely new articles since 2005. Those who do choose to create an account (as opposed to unregistered, anonymous editing) are given additional editing privileges and tools. According to internal Wikipedia statistics, as of January 2012 there were 16 million of these "named accounts" worldwide. "About 300,000 editors have edited Wikipedia more than 10 times. Approximately the same number, 300,000 editors, edit Wikipedia every month; of those, about 50,000 make more than five edits, and 5,000 make more than 100" (Wikipedians, 2012).

In 2009, researchers from the Augmented Social Cognition Research branch of Xerox's Palo Alto Research Center analyzed 200 million edits from the English language Wikipedia and discovered that [i]n Wikipedia, the population of editors follows a power law distribution (also known as the long tail distribution). That is, relatively few highly prolific users account for a large percentage of the overall editing activity. A large population (the long tail) of less prolific editors contribute the rest of the content. (Suh, Covertino, Chi, & Pirolli, 2009)

A 2006 *New Yorker* article echoed this analysis, finding that, "There are two hundred thousand registered users on the English-language site, of whom about thirty-three hundred—fewer than two percent—are responsible for seventy per cent of the work" (Schiff, 2006). Not only is article creation and editing skewed toward a relatively small minority, the demographics of Wikipedia editors are also unbalanced. A 2010 survey of more than 50,000 Wikipedia contributors worldwide found that 87% were male and the average age was 25 (Glott, Schmidt, & Ghosh, 2010).

Above the category of registered editors, Wikipedia has gradually added a few additional levels of bureaucracy, starting with administrators, bureaucrats, and then stewards. In 2012, there were 1,500 administrators for the English language Wikipedia. Admins "can protect, delete and restore pages, move pages over redirects, hide and delete page revisions, edit protected pages, and block other editors" (Administrators, 2012). To "protect" a page means to restrict the ability of anyone to edit the page content to some degree. There are varying levels of protection ranging from "Full" (only admins can edit) to "Pending Changes" (edits are checked by a reviewer before going live). Restricting the editing of articles in this manner is decidedly anti-egalitarian since it puts special powers in the hands of administrators. Much to the dismay of the purists, these sorts of controls were found to be a necessary evil as Wikipedia evolved. Without the ability to protect articles, some edit wars on controversial topics would go on indefinitely. Prior to being protected, some articles for political candidates were vandalized so frequently that editors could not make corrections fast enough. To some, protecting articles and establishing a bureaucratic hierarchy undermines the entire egalitarian spirit that Wikipedia was founded on. A 2009 *Wall Street Journal* article observed that "as it matures, Wikipedia, one of the world's largest crowdsourcing initiatives, is becoming less freewheeling and more like the organizations it set out to replace" (Angwin & Fowler, 2009). Still, the process of entering and ascending the Wikipedia bureaucracy remains egalitarian and democratic. Credentials count for nothing while a demonstrated history of quality editing is of utmost importance. Administrators, bureaucrats, and stewards are all elected by others in the Wikipedia bureaucracy. Regular editors and administrators can—and often do—challenge the top levels of Wikipedia bureaucracy. It was challenges such as these, coupled with philosophical differences in the structure of Wikipedia, which eventually caused Larry Sanger to leave in the early days of the project.

SANGER'S DEFECTION AND BOMIS

As one of the key architects of both the original Nupedia project and then Wikipedia, and a traditional expert with a doctorate degree in philosophy, Sanger was impressed by Wikipedia's quick success, but he never wholly bought into the idea of a completely egalitarian encyclopedia. Sanger always held onto the idea that Wikipedia would be better and more reliable if experts were granted some level of authority over the amateur editors. This concept of authority and expertise was, of course, very much at odds with Wikipedia's radically open and egalitarian model. Writing for *The Atlantic,* Marshall Poe captured Sanger's conflict over the project:

After forging a revolutionary mode of knowledge building, he came to realize—albeit dimly at first—that it was not to his liking. He found that he was not heading a disciplined crew of qualified writers and editors collaborating on authoritative statements (the Nupedia ideal), but trying to control an ill-disciplined crowd of volunteers fighting over ever-shifting articles. (Poe, 2006)

These philosophical differences with regard to the role of experts on Wikipedia came to a head for Sanger in a public battle with a Wikipedia editor nicknamed Cunctator (Latin for procrastinator). Cunctator argued for a radically open Wikipedia with no internal hierarchy and few limitations on

contributions. He began an edit war (repeatedly undoing deletions or edits) with Sanger. Eventually Sanger appealed to the Wikipedia editors on the internal listserv: "I need to be granted fairly broad authority by the community—by you dear reader—if I am going to do my job effectively" (Poe, 2006). This appeal to authority and expertise struck a sour note not just with Cunctator, but with many of the Wikipedians who believed in the decentralized, open source ideals of Wikipedia. Sanger's struggles with the Wikipedia community coincided with the big dot-com crisis of the early 2000s. Bomis, Wales's other Internet company that actually paid Sanger's salary, was struggling. Due to financial problems at Bomis and Sanger's increasing philosophical differences with Wikipedia, Wales laid off Sanger in early 2002 (Lih, 2009).

For his part, Wales freely admits to being extremely nonconfrontational as a manager. Recognizing the need to encourage amateurs and limit authority, Wales has repeatedly demonstrated an astounding reluctance to use his power, even when the community has begged him to. He wouldn't exile trolls or erase offensive material, much less settle on rules for how things should or should not be done (Poe, 2006). Due in part to its radical openness and commitment to encouraging amateur-experts, Wikipedia has continued to grow successfully.

Not yet ready to completely abandon the idea of a free, universal encyclopedia edited by volunteers, Sanger founded Citizendium in 2007. Quite similar to the original Nupedia concept, Citizendium is explicit in distinguishing itself from Wikipedia:

The project aims to improve on the Wikipedia model by providing "reliable" and high-quality content; it plans to achieve that goal by requiring all contributors to use their real names, by strictly moderating the project for unprofessional behaviors, and by providing what it calls "gentle expert oversight" of everyday contributors. (Citizendium.com, 2011)

The roots of Sanger's dissatisfaction with Wikipedia and its attitudes toward traditional experts are clear in the vision he laid out for Citizendium. As of 2011, Citizendium had 15,000 articles in various stages of development, but only 156 articles that were fully approved by experts (Citizendium.com, 2011).

The Nupedia and Citizendium projects would be classified as failures, while Wikipedia stands as an example of how the Internet can harness mass collaboration for the general good of society. In general, the Citizendium model is quite reasonable and should yield high-quality articles that are free for anyone to access and use. Why have so few people embraced it? First, at this point, Wikipedia has a near-monopoly in the area of free, online encyclopedias. People who were amenable to the idea of freely contributing to an online encyclopedia are already committed to the Wikipedia model. Second, potential contributors are probably put off by the idea of expert editors changing or not using their contributions. Why contribute if you have no assurance that your efforts are even going to be used? Third, the deeply egalitarian nature of Wikipedia has struck a chord with many people. They seized the opportunity to contribute in some small way to an idealistic project that opened up the world's knowledge (as agreed upon by the masses) to everyone with an Internet connection. Nupedia and Citizendium fell just short of this lofty ideal and were never able to achieve any sort of critical mass.

JARON LANIER AND DIGITAL MAOISM

External critics of Wikipedia have attacked the project on more fronts than just reliability issues. Two notable writers have leveled criticisms against Wikipedia that pertain to expertise and knowledge creation. Jaron Lanier's widely read essay "Digital Maoism: The hazards of the new online collectivism" (2006) questions some of the basic premises

of Web 2.0 and Wikipedia in particular. Andrew Keen's book *The Cult of the Amateur: How today's Internet is killing our culture* (2007) also broadly condemns the contributions of amateurs within a Web 2.0 context. The following sections examine these critics' arguments against amateurs and Wikipedia.

Jaron Lanier is known as a computer scientist, composer, visual artist, and author. He was an early pioneer in the field of virtual reality and was named one of the 100 most influential people in the world by *Time* magazine in 2010 (Lanier, n.d.). Lanier writes frequently about various aspects of digital culture, and his 2006 essay, "Digital Maoism: The hazards of the new online collectivism," written for the online magazine *Edge*, is perhaps his best-known work. The essay is a broad critique of Web 2.0. According to Lanier, Web 2.0 has in many instances led to a bland, amateur-derived online collectivism which he calls the "hive mind" that has smothered the unique and creative voices of individuals. He cites Wikipedia as one example of the dangers surrounding online collectivism:

[T]he problem is in the way the Wikipedia has come to be regarded and used; how it's been elevated to such importance so quickly. And that is part of the larger pattern of the appeal of a new online collectivism that is nothing less than a resurgence of the idea that the collective is all-wise, that it is desirable to have influence concentrated in a bottleneck that can channel the collective with the most verity and force. (Lanier, 2006)

Lanier questions the "wisdom of the crowds" encouraged by Web 2.0 applications, and illustrates the problems of collectivism by citing the television show American Idol as a prime example:

As with the Wikipedia, there's nothing wrong with it. The problem is its centrality. More people appear to vote in this pop competition than in presidential elections ... The collective is flattered and it responds. The winners are likable, almost by definition. But John Lennon wouldn't have won. He wouldn't have made it to the finals ... The same could be said about Jimi Hendrix, Elvis, Joni Mitchell, Duke Ellington, David Byrne, Grandmaster Flash, Bob Dylan (please!), and almost anyone else who has been vastly influential in creating pop music. (2006)

Again, the argument here is that the collectivism excludes, or smothers, unique voices in favor of those that appeal to the masses.

If we look closely at the way Wikipedia articles evolve over time, does the process even fit Lanier's definition of an "online collective"? In *Here Comes Everybody: The power of organizing without organizations* (2008), Clay Shirkey argues that Wikipedia is not a collective at all:

The people most enamored of describing Wikipedia as the product of a free-form hive mind don't understand how Wikipedia actually works. It is the product not of collectivism, but of unending argumentation. The articles grow not from harmonious thought, but from constant scrutiny and emendation. (Shirkey, 2009: 139)

Lanier's criticisms did not escape the attention of Jimmy Wales. In one response, he actually agrees with one of Lanier's main points, but disagrees that it constitutes a problem for Wikipedia:

One aspect of Jaron Lanier's criticism had to do with the passionate, unique, individual voice he prefers, rather than this sort of bland, royal-we voice of Wikipedia ... To that, I'd say "yes, we plead guilty quite happily." We're an encyclopedia. (Read, 2006)

"Digital Maoism" attracted many critical responses and Lanier seems to have weighed these opinions and softened his stance toward Wikipedia in his later book, *You Are Not a Gadget* (2010):

While I've run across quite a few incomprehensible, terribly written passages in Wikipedia articles, on the whole there's a consistency of style. This can be either a benefit or a loss, depending on the topic and what you are after. Some topics need the human touch and a sense of context and personal voice more than others. (Lanier, 2006: 143).

In regards to Wikipedia, Lanier's whole concept of digital Maoism is misapplied. While Maoism as an ideology did try to promote an egalitarian, classless, society it is perhaps best known for Chairman Mao's Cultural Revolution. Maoism as it was implemented through the Cultural Revolution is the furthest thing from the open, knowledge-creating community fostered by Wikipedia. The Cultural Revolution tried to create a single, nationalistic vision of China that adhered to Mao's ideology. Mao wanted to foster a revolution that derived from the people, but he used a top-down model to make it happen. Wikipedia, on the other hand, is egalitarian and democratic to a fault. Every article on Wikipedia is the result of the mixing and combining of many voices and opinions. There is no central dictator (or editor as the case may be) that tells people what to write or how to go about it.

One of the things Lanier gets right about Wikipedia is the dilemma of its meteoric rise and vast popularity: "the problem is in the way the Wikipedia has come to be regarded and used; how it's been elevated to such importance so quickly" (Lanier, 2006). Wikipedia's ease of access and place at the top of many Google search results has resulted in an increased lack of critical reading on the Web. A single example will suffice to demonstrate the dangers of not reading critically on the Web. French composer and conductor Maurice Jarre died in 2009. As an experiment, Shane Fitzgerald, a sociology student at Dublin University, quickly inserted a false, undocumented quote into Jarre's Wikipedia bio. Despite being a recent, undocumented addition, multiple large newspapers and websites took the quote at face value and used it in their coverage of Jarre's death. Speaking about the experiment, Fitzgerald said,

I am 100 percent convinced that if I hadn't come forward, that quote would have gone down in history as something Maurice Jarre said, instead of something I made up. It would have become another example where, once anything is printed enough times in the media without challenge, it becomes fact. (Pogatchnik, 2009)

Lack of critical reading can certainly be a great danger within the context of an online collectivism. The problem, though, resides within the collective, not within Wikipedia. What should worry us is how the collective chooses to make use of Wikipedia and other information on the Web.

In response to Lanier's assertions about the dangers of an online collectivism and Wikipedia specifically, Jimmy Wales was on to something. An encyclopedia article is certainly not the place to encourage unique, creative writing. The great advantage of Wikipedia over traditional reference information sources lies in the fact that it is a compilation of many voices. The Web is vast and has many outlets for individual creative expression. Expression and knowledge creation on the Web is not an "either the collective/or the individual" proposition. Both can—and do—coexist quite comfortably.

CULT OF THE AMATEUR

One of the most prominent critics of the amateur-driven Web 2.0 culture in general, and of Wikipedia specifically, is Andrew Keen, author of the 2007 book *The Cult of the Amateur: How today's Internet is killing our culture*. Keen is also concerned about an online collectivism—although he does not use that term—but unlike Lanier he is less concerned about creativity and individualism than he is with the debate surrounding amateurs and

experts. In the book, Keen defines an "amateur" as "a hobbyist, knowledgeable or otherwise, someone who does not make a living from his or her field of interest, a layperson, lacking credentials, a dabbler" (Keen, 2007: 36). Keen contends that the Internet (and specifically newer Web 2.0 applications) has elevated the shoddy work of amateurs at the expense of the experts:

The cult of the amateur has made it increasingly difficult to determine the difference between the reader and writer, between artist and spin doctor, between art and advertisement, between amateur and expert. The result? The decline of the quality and reliability of the information we receive" (Keen, 2007: 27).

At no point does Keen consider the possibility of middle ground between amateur and expert.

However, he does identify a very real problem with today's Internet culture and our ability to filter out information and opinions that are different than our own:

Wittingly or not, we seek out information that mirrors back our own biases and opinions and conforms with our distorted versions of reality. We lose that common conversation or informed debate over our mutually-agreed upon facts. Rather, we perpetuate one anothers' biases. (Keen, 2007: 83)

What Keen describes is certainly occurring and even encouraged by today's Internet (think about RSS feeds, YouTube Channels, companies and organizations you "like" on Facebook). What Keen misses is that Wikipedia is one of the few examples of a Web 2.0 application that embraces informed debate and detests bias. Recall that one of the Five Pillars that Wikipedia is founded on is "Neutral point of view." Neutral point of view is only achieved through the vigorous debates that occur on the discussion pages attached to each Wikipedia article.

Keen goes on to criticize the work of amateurs when it comes to knowledge creation:

Without editors, fact-checkers, administrators, or regulators to monitor what is being posted, we have no one to vouch for the reliability or credibility of the content we read ... There are no gatekeepers to filter truth from fiction, genuine content from advertising, legitimate information from errors or outright deceit. (Keen, 2007: 64-65)

The "gatekeepers" Keen is referring to are the traditional, credentialed experts, but why should we trust the gatekeepers? One of the first principles of research that librarians and professors try to instill in students is to critically assess all sources of information. The gatekeepers—the experts—often have strong biases in the way they interpret information. These biases are laid bare in the book *Information Liberation: Challenging the corruptions of information power* by Brian Martin. Martin's arguments concerning the "corruptions of expert knowledge" are relevant here:

[Once] a group of experts has established itself as having exclusive control over a body of knowledge, it is to their advantage to exclude nonexperts ... Most experts are full-time professionals. Those who might like to make an occasional contribution are not made welcome. Finally, many experts are arrogant, displaying contempt or hostility to amateur interlopers. (Martin, 1998: 135).

Martin demonstrates that the politics and economics of research reinforce disciplinary expertise to the extent that it creates a system that is essentially closed to outsiders. Moreover, the expert gatekeepers that Keen puts so much stock in have been shown to be more biased than non-experts (Ericsson et al., 2006: 26-27). Academics (experts) make a career out of carving out their own niche within a profession which they lay claim to through research and publication. The openness of Wikipedia and the article review process go

a long way in eliminating expert bias. What we need to encourage is not necessarily more expert gatekeepers, but rather critical consumers of information from all sources whether it be Wikipedia, *Encyclopedia Britannica*, or Fox News.

One final assertion by Keen merits some discussion because it illuminates the role that amateurs can play in knowledge creation:

Today, the OED [Oxford English Dictionary] and the Encyclopedia Britannica, two trusted reference volumes upon which we have long relied for information, are being replaced by Wikipedia and other user-generated resources ... Unlike the OED, which was crafted by a carefully vetted and selected team of experienced professionals, Wikipedia ... allows anyone to add and edit entries on its website. (Keen, 2007: 37).

The origins of the *OED* are actually much closer to the Wikipedia model than the *Britannica* model. To understand why this is, one needs to understand the basic history of how the *OED* was created. The *OED* was—and still is—one of the most ambitious works of scholarship and knowledge creation ever conceived. Rather than simply defining words, the idea behind the *OED* was to create a comprehensive dictionary of the English language that provided not only definitions, but also the etymological evolution of every word over time. Changing meanings of words were to be documented through direct quotations from the earliest original sources. Richard Trench first proposed this radically ambitious project in a paper he delivered to the Philological Society of England in 1857. His speech, "On Some Deficiencies in Our English Dictionaries," outlined the problems with current dictionaries and his vision for a new comprehensive English dictionary. The most radical aspect of his proposal is that most of English literature would have to be culled to determine the earliest usages of each word. For this immense task the Philological Society (mostly composed of amateur philologists) hoped that "many besides its own members would gladly divide with them the toil and honour of such an undertaking. An entire army would join hand in hand till it covered the whole breadth of the island … this drawing a sweep-net over the whole extent of English Literature." (Winchester, 2003: 44)

This was certainly a radical departure from the way earlier dictionaries and encyclopedias had been compiled. The democratic nature of the project appealed to the members of the Philological Society "by involving in the making of the lexicon the very people who spoke and read the language, the project would be *of the people*, a scheme that, quite literally, would be classically *democratic*" (Winchester, 2003: 44). By now the similarities with Wikipedia should be apparent. In the end, the *OED* was the first large, successfully crowdsourced reference book. When the first edition of the *OED* was finally completed in 1928, it defined 415,000 words with 1.8 million quotations. The great majority of these quotations were culled from the 6 million slips of paper sent in by volunteer amateur readers (Winchester, 1998:109). The names of many of these volunteers are enshrined in the preface to each edition of the *OED* "Without regard to class or standing, qualification or creed, and certainly disregarding gender" (Winchester, 2003: 188). Nor is this reliance on amateur volunteer readers some quaint historical artifact. One can still volunteer to read for the *OED* today.

As with Wikipedia, it should be noted that the amateur volunteers who created the *OED* were not just random people off the street contributing for the heck of it. Rather, they exemplified the ethos of the amateur-expert. *OED* volunteers read in areas of literature for which they had specific interests. Likewise, Wikipedia contributors do not write and edit articles randomly; rather they focus on areas of knowledge in which they have some experience or interest. The end result, in both cases, has been the creation of two of the most significant compilations of knowledge in the English language.

The Rise of the Amateur-Expert

Does the rise of the amateur-expert entail the decline and fall of the traditional expert? Not necessarily. Web 2.0 and amateur-experts are certainly challenging some of the roles of experts in our society but there are limitations to the reach of these challenges. Amateur-experts have had great success in leveraging the crowdsourcing model to create a massive encyclopedia and write excellent free software. Experts must cede some control over basic knowledge creation to amateur-experts. Traditional expertise will persist in some form because knowledge creation is really only a starting point. Experts are those who can take an existing body of knowledge and interpret it, synthesize it, and apply it to various contexts. For example, Wikipedia provides you with a wealth of information but it does not teach you how to actually conduct research—librarians and educators at various levels of schooling will always be needed for that task. There is an overabundance of health information on the Web, but people still trust doctors to make sense of it all and to apply that knowledge to them specifically. State and federal laws are easily accessible on the Internet, but to actually apply any knowledge of those laws in a court of law requires a level of expertise well beyond that of the amateur-expert.

WIKIPEDIA AND ACADEMIA

From its earliest days Wikipedia and much of academia have been at odds. Academia represents one of the traditional strongholds of expertise. Expertise in academia is closely linked to the level of degree achieved (Masters, PhD, MD, etc.) and to scholarly publications. The authority of scholarly publication rests with the credentials of the author and publication coupled with a peer review process. Wikipedia's threat to this model of expertise is obvious—all its articles are anonymous and peer review is an informal process. Furthermore, the content of Wikipedia can be freely borrowed and reused, a system that is anathema to the rigid rules that govern modern author and publisher agreements. Still, Wikipedia has tremendous potential as a pedagogical tool. Using Wikipedia articles to teach students the research process is an obvious example. Some instructors have also used Wikipedia to teach disciplinary knowledge by having students analyze and then improve specific articles. At this point, Wikipedia is not going away. If the experts still see problems with the reliability and accuracy of Wikipedia articles within their field of expertise, the best course of action is to work actively to improve them.

Wikipedia and other Web 2.0 applications have also forced universities and federal granting agencies to reconsider the traditional publishing model wherein they subsidize writing and research but then have to buy back the results of those efforts from publishers. The open access movement has gained a good deal of traction between 2006 and 2011, both in the United States and internationally. As of 2008, the published results of all research funded by the National Institutes of Health (NIH) must be made freely available in the PubMed Central Database within 12 months of publication. Various prominent universities including Harvard, Stanford, and MIT are either wholly or partially committed to open access (Open Access Directory, 2011).

Experts have also adopted some aspects of the Wikipedia model to create open access text books. The best known of these is the freely available Stanford Encyclopedia of Philosophy, which actually predates Wikipedia by about five years. This work was created and maintained entirely by experts, but is a perfect example of how experts can work collaboratively on a reference work that is not limited to libraries and individuals who can afford it. While writing about Wikipedia for *The Journal of American History*, Roy Rosenzweig summarizes this tension between the expert writers and publishers:

Why are so many of our scholarly journals locked away behind subscription gates? What about American National Biography Online—written by professional historians, sponsored by our scholarly societies, and supported by millions of dollars in foundation and government grants? Why is it available only to libraries that often pay thousands of dollars per year rather than to everyone on the Web as Wikipedia is? Shouldn't professional historians join in the massive democratization of access to knowledge reflected by Wikipedia and the Web in general? American National Biography Online may be a significantly better historical resource than Wikipedia, but its impact is much smaller because it is available to so few people. (Rosenzweig, 2006: 137-138)

Rosenzweig goes on to propose a "collaborative U.S. history textbook that would be free to all of our students" (Rosenzweig, 2006: 145). The Encyclopedia of Life (EOL) is a Wikipedia-like online project whose "goal is to make freely available to anyone knowledge about all the world's organisms" (Help Build EOL, 2011). This online encyclopedia strikes a balance between Wikipedia and The Stanford Encyclopedia of Philosophy. Anyone—expert or amateur—can contribute to the EOL, but all submissions are reviewed by "expert curators" before going live on the site. One of the lasting legacies of Wikipedia will be the way it challenged traditional publishing and its role in forcing the world to consider the potential of open access publishing.

Whither Web 3.0?

Web 3.0 is the supposed successor to Web 2.0 that is generally characterized by user-centered design and open participation. Librarian Steven Harris assesses Web 2.0 in the context of knowledge creation:

That is the real purpose behind the Web 2.0 movement: to make data discoverable and usable (or re-usable) by people. The synthesis of information is what expands human knowledge. Collective endeavors like Wikipedia give all individuals an opportunity to participate in that process. (Johnson, 2007: 49)

Web 3.0 is currently an abstraction with no universally agreed-upon characteristics. Many believe that one element of Web 3.0 will be the "Semantic Web" wherein computers and networks can understand and apply information. In regards to the roles of amateurs and experts, Web entrepreneur Jason Calacanis believes,

The wisdom of the crowds has peaked. Web 3.0 is taking what we've built in Web 2.0—the wisdom of the crowds—and putting an editorial layer on it of truly talented, compensated people to make the product more trusted and refined. (Dokoupil, 2008)

Andrew Keen shares Calacanis's belief that Web 3.0 will be defined—in part—by a resurgence of the experts: "The future of the Internet is the combination of the traditional media expertise of Web 1.0 media with the user-generated democracy of the Web 2.0 revolution" (Keen, 2008). Perhaps another lasting legacy of Web 2.0, as exemplified by the success of Wikipedia, will be a general acknowledgement that the wisdom of the crowds is a very real and powerful phenomenon. Possibly the experts will soften their stance toward the amateurs and find more productive ways to collaborate.

CONCLUSION

What is knowledge? How do we know that we know? What is truth?

The radical nature of Wikipedia lies in how it has answered these epistemological questions. Wikipedia has been a major player in redefining knowledge and expertise in the 21st century. To borrow an example from linguistics, we know a

tree is a tree because that is the commonly agreed-upon term in English. Wikipedia has shown us that knowledge need not come only from experts. The wisdom of the crowds has created an ever-changing base of collective knowledge in the form of Wikipedia. Larry Sanger again best addresses these epistemological questions:

Wikipedia is a global project. Its special feature is that no one is privileged, and over time, the views of thousands of people are weighed and mixed in. Such an open, welcoming, unfettered institution has a better claim than any other to represent the consensus of Humanity. (Sanger, 2009: 58)

Although Sanger does not say it explicitly, the "consensus of humanity" could be one definition of truth. Truth on Wikipedia is a never-ending process of argument and compromise.

The wisdom of the crowds as exemplified by Wikipedia appears to be a new form of expertise. In reality, the wisdom of the crowds is as old as humanity. It is part of the reason that people have always formed communities. For most of history, the wisdom of the crowds was limited to those with close physical proximity. The *Oxford English Dictionary* was the first major information source to successfully tap the wisdom of the crowds over a large geographical area. The Internet and Web 2.0 applications such as the wiki have removed geographical barriers and greatly simplified the process of crowdsourcing. In our global society, the wisdom of the crowds will continue to be a major source of knowledge creation.

In Europe during the Middle Ages, the Church and its "experts" tightly controlled accepted knowledge. Championing science and reason, the Enlightenment challenged and usurped the Church as the universal source of knowledge. Following the Enlightenment, expert knowledge has been controlled and meted out by universities and professional organizations. For the last 300 years or so, there have not been any significant challenges to expertise. Neither radio nor television posed a major threat. In an incredibly short time, the Internet, and specifically Web 2.0 applications such as Wikipedia, have forced a radical rethinking of expertise.

REFERENCES

About. (2011). From Wikipedia. Retrieved July 06, 2011, from http://en.Wikipedia.org/w/index.php?title=Wikipedia:About&oldid=437810305

Administrators. (2012). From Wikipedia. Retrieved January 26, 2012, from http://en.wikipedia.org/wiki/Wikipedia:Administrators

Angwin, J., & Fowler, G. A. (2009). Volunteers log off as Wikipedia ages. *Wall Street Journal—Eastern Edition, 254*(123), A1-A17. Retrieved from http://search.ebscohost.com.proxy.iwu.edu/login.aspx?direct=true&db=nfh&AN=45358947&site=eds-live&scope=site

Ayers, P., Matthews, C., & Yates, B. (2008). *How Wikipedia works: And how you can be a part of it*. San Francisco, CA: No Starch Press.

Benkler, Y. (2006). *The wealth of networks: How social production transforms markets and freedom*. New Haven, CT: Yale University Press.

Blair, A. (2010). *Too much to know: Managing scholarly information before the modern age*. New Haven, CT: Yale University Press.

Bomis. (2011). Retrieved July 06, 2011, from http://en.Bomis.org/wiki?title=Bomis&oldid=100773755

BritannicaStore.com. (2010). Retrieved July 06, 2011, from http://www.britannicastore.com/The-Encyclopaedia-Britannica-2010-Copyright/invt/printset10

Contributing to Wikipedia. (2011). From Wikipedia. Retrieved June 14, 2011, from http://en.Wikipedia.org/wiki/Wikipedia:Contributing_to_Wikipedia

Doctorow, C. (2006). *On "Digital Maoism: The hazards of the new online collectivism" by Jaron Lanier*. Retrieved June 14, 2011, from http://www.edge.org/discourse/digital_maoism.html

Dokoupil, T. (2008). *Revenge of the experts*. Retrieved June 06, 2011, from http://www.newsweek.com/2008/03/05/revenge-of-the-experts.html

Encyclopedia of Life. (2011). *Help build EOL*. Retrieved July 06, 2011, from http://www.eol.org/content/page/help_build_eol

Ericsson, K. A. (2006). *The Cambridge handbook of expertise and expert performance*. Cambridge, UK: Cambridge University Press. doi:10.1017/CBO9780511816796

Errors in the Encyclopedia Britannica that Have Been Corrected in Wikipedia. (2011). From Wikipedia. Retrieved July 6, 2011, from http://en.Wikipedia.org/wiki/Wikipedia:Errors_in_the_Encyclop%C3%A6dia_Britannica_that_have_been_corrected_in_Wikipedia

Expert. (2011). In the *Oxford English Dictionary Online*. Retrieved September 19, 2011, from http://www.oed.com/view/Entry/66551?rskey=hpFQT6&result=1

Five Pillars. (2011). From Wikipedia. Retrieved July 06, 2011, from http://en.Wikipedia.org/w/index.php?title=Wikipedia:Five_pillars&oldid=437188511

Galton, F. (1907). Vox populi. *Nature, 75,* •••. Retrieved from http://search.ebscohost.com.proxy.iwu.edu/login.aspx?direct=true&db=edsref&AN=HFAFDCIG&site=eds-live&scope=site doi:10.1038/075450a0

Giles, J. (2005). Internet encyclopaedias go head to head. *Nature, 438*(7070), 900–901. Retrieved from http://search.ebscohost.com.proxy.iwu.edu/login.aspx?direct=true&db=cmedm&AN=16355180&site=eds-live&scope=site doi:10.1038/438900a

Glott, R., Schmidt, P., & Ghosh, R. (2010). *Wikipedia survey: Overview of results.* United Nations University. Retrieved from http://www.wikipediastudy.org/docs/Wikipedia_Overview_15March2010-FINAL.pdf

History of Wikipedia. (2011). From Wikipedia. Retrieved June 14, 2011, from http://en.Wikipedia.org/wiki/History_of_Wikipedia

Howe, J. (2006). *Crowdsourcing: A definition.* Retrieved July 06, 2011, from http://crowdsourcing.typepad.com/cs/2006/06/crowdsourcing_a.html

Howe, J. (2008). *Crowdsourcing: Why the future of the crowd is driving the future of business.* New York, NY: Crown Business Publishing.

Javanmardi, S., & Lopes, C. (2010). Statistical measure of quality in Wikipedia. *Proceedings of the First Workshop on Social Media Analytics,* Washington, DC (p. 132). doi:10.1145/1964858.1964876

Johnson, K. (2007). Collectivism vs. individualism in a wiki world: Librarians respond to Jaron Lanier's essay "Digital Maoism: The hazards of the new online collectivism.". *Serials Review, 33*(1), 45–53. doi:10.1016/j.serrev.2006.11.002

Keen, A. (2007). *Cult of the amateur: How today's Internet is killing our culture and assaulting our economy.* Great Britain: Doubleday/Currency.

Keen, A. (2008). *Web 1.0 + web 2.0 = web 3.0.* Retrieved July 6, 2011, from http://andrewkeen.typepad.com/the_great_seduction/2008/04/web-10-web-20-w.html

Kogan, H. (1958). *The great EB: The story of the Encyclopaedia Britannica.* University of Chicago Press.

Lamb, B. (2005). *C-SPAN Q&A, Jimmy Wales.* Retrieved June 20, 2011, from http://www.q-and-a.org/Transcript/?ProgramID=1042

Lanier, J. (2006). *Digital Maoism: The hazards of the new online collectivism.* Retrieved July 6, 2011, from http://www.edge.org/3rd_culture/lanier06/lanier06_index.html

Lanier, J. (2010). *You are not a gadget.* New York, NY: Knopf.

Lih, A. (2009). *The Wikipedia revolution: How a bunch of nobodies created the world's greatest encyclopedia.* New York, NY: Hyperion.

Magnus, P. D. (2008). Early response to false claims in Wikipedia. *First Monday, 13*(9). Retrieved from http://search.ebscohost.com.proxy.iwu.edu/login.aspx?direct=true&db=edsref&AN=IDBEEJCC&site=eds-live&scope=site

Martin, B. (1998). *Information liberation: Challenging the corruptions of information power.* London, UK: Freedom Press.

Nupedia. (2011). From Wikipedia. Retrieved 06/07, 2011, from http://en.Wikipedia.org/w/index.php?title=Nupedia&oldid=434451549

Open Access Directory. (2011). Retrieved July 06, 2011, from http://oad.simmons.edu/oadwiki/Main_Page

Open Source Software. (2011). From Wikipedia. Retrieved July 06, 2011, from http://en.Wikipedia.org/w/index.php?title=Open_source&oldid=438039561

Pershing, B. (2009). *Kennedy, Byrd the latest victims of Wikipedia errors.* Retrieved June 27, 2011, from http://voices.washingtonpost.com/capitol-briefing/2009/01/kennedy_the_latest_victim_of_w.html

Poe, M. (2006). The hive. *Atlantic Monthly, 298*(2), 86. Retrieved from http://search.ebscohost.com.proxy.iwu.edu/login.aspx?direct=true&db=aph&AN=21796182&site=eds-live&scope=site

Pogatchnik, S. (2009). Student hoaxes world's media on Wikipedia. Retrieved June 29, 2011, from http://www.msnbc.msn.com/id/30699302/ns/technology_and_science-tech_and_gadgets/t/student-hoaxes-worlds-media-Wikipedia/

Raymond, E. (1999). The cathedral and the bazaar. *Knowledge, Technology & Policy, 12*(3), 23. Retrieved from http://search.ebscohost.com.proxy.iwu.edu/login.aspx?direct=true&db=ehh&AN=6128761&site=eds-live&scope=site doi:10.1007/s12130-999-1026-0

Read, B. (2006). Can Wikipedia ever make the grade? *The Chronicle of Higher Education, 53*(10), A31–A36. Retrieved from http://search.ebscohost.com.proxy.iwu.edu/login.aspx?direct=true&db=ehh&AN=22984124&site=eds-live&scope=site

Rector, L. H. (2008). Comparison of Wikipedia and other encyclopedias for accuracy, breadth, and depth in historical articles. *RSR. Reference Services Review, 36*(1), 7. Retrieved from http://search.ebscohost.com.proxy.iwu.edu/login.aspx?direct=true&db=eda&AN=32895218&site=eds-live&scope=site doi:10.1108/00907320810851998

Sanger, L. M. (2006). *Why make room for experts in Web 2.0?* Retrieved June 14, 2011, from http://www.Bomis.org/roomforexperts.html

Sanger, L. M. (2007). *Who says we know? On the new politics of knowledge.* Retrieved June 14, 2011, from http://edge.org/conversation/who-says-we-know-on-the-new-politics-of-knowledge

Sanger, L. M. (2009). The fate of expertise after "Wikipedia." *Episteme: A Journal of Social Epistemology, 6*(1), 52-73. Retrieved from http://search.ebscohost.com.proxy.iwu.edu/login.aspx?direct=true&db=phl&AN=PHL2133300&site=eds-live&scope=site

Schiff, S. (2006). Know it all: Can Wikipedia conquer expertise? *New Yorker (New York, N.Y.), 82*(23), 36–43. Retrieved from http://search.ebscohost.com.proxy.iwu.edu/login.aspx?direct=true&db=mzh&AN=2006534151&site=eds-live&scope=site

Shirky, C. (2009). *Here comes everybody: The power of organizing without organizations.* New York, NY: Penguin Books.

Statistics. (2011). From Wikipedia. Retrieved 07/06, 2011, from http://en.Wikipedia.org/wiki/Special:Statistics

Stross, R. (2006). Anonymous source is not the same as open source. *New York Times (Late City Edition), 155,* 5. Retrieved from http://search.ebscohost.com.proxy.iwu.edu/login.aspx?direct=true&db=eda&AN=20642306&site=eds-live&scope=site

Suh, B., Convertino, G., Chi, E., & Pirolli, P. (2009). The singularity is not near: Slowing growth of Wikipedia. *WikiSym '09 Proceedings of the 5th International Symposium on Wikis and Open Collaboration,* Orlando, Florida. doi:10.1145/1641309.1641322

Surowiecki, J. (2004). *The wisdom of crowds: Why the many are smarter than the few and how collective wisdom shapes business, economies, societies, and nations* (1st ed.). New York, NY: Doubleday.

Top Sites in the United States. (2011). From Alexa. Retrieved June 20, 2011, from http://www.alexa.com/topsites/countries/US

Van Doren, C. (1962). The idea of an encyclopedia. *The American Behavioral Scientist, 6*(1), 23. Retrieved from http://search.ebscohost.com.proxy.iwu.edu/login.aspx?direct=true&db=eda&AN=53228037&site=eds-live&scope=site doi:10.1177/000276426200600105

Wikipedians. (2012). From Wikipedia. Retrieved January 26, 2012, from http://en.wikipedia.org/wiki/Wikipedia:Wikipedians#cite_note-0

Winchester, S. (1998). *The professor and the madman: A tale of murder, insanity, and the making of the Oxford English Dictionary* (1st ed.). New York, NY: HarperCollins.

Winchester, S. (2003). *The meaning of everything: The story of the Oxford English Dictionary*. New York, NY: Oxford University Press.

ADDITIONAL READING

Arup, C., & van Caenegem, W. (Eds.). (2009). *Intellectual property policy reform: Fostering innovation and development*. Northampton, MA: Elgar.

Badke, W. (2008). What to do with Wikipedia. *Online, 32*(2), 48-50. Retrieved from http://search.ebscohost.com.proxy.iwu.edu/login.aspx?direct=true&db=c9h&AN=31131975&site=eds-live&scope=site

Baytiyeh, H., & Pfaffman, J. (2010). Volunteers in Wikipedia: Why the community matters. *Journal of Educational Technology & Society, 13*(2), 128–140. Retrieved from http://search.ebscohost.com.proxy.iwu.edu/login.aspx?direct=true&db=eric&AN=EJ895662&site=eds-live&scope=site and http://www.ifets.info/others/

Bennett, D. (2011). Ten years of remarkable detail: Wikipedia. *Bloomberg Businessweek,* (4212), 57-61. Retrieved from http://search.ebscohost.com.proxy.iwu.edu/login.aspx?direct=true&db=bsh&AN=57248007&site=eds-live&scope=site

Broughton, J. (2008). *Wikipedia: The missing manual* (1st ed.). Beijing, China: O'Reilly.

Chandler, C. J., & Gregory, A. S. (2010). Sleeping with the enemy: Wikipedia in the college classroom. *The History Teacher, 43*(2), 247–257. Retrieved from http://search.ebscohost.com.proxy.iwu.edu/login.aspx?direct=true&db=eric&AN=EJ893816&site=eds-live&scope=site

Dalby, A. (2009). *The world and Wikipedia: How we are editing reality*. Somerset, UK: Siduri.

Fallis, D. (2009). Introduction: The epistemology of mass collaboration. *Episteme: A Journal of Social Epistemology, 6*(1), 1-7. Retrieved from http://search.ebscohost.com.proxy.iwu.edu/login.aspx?direct=true&db=phl&AN=PHL2133296&site=eds-live&scope=site

Forte, A., & Bruckman, A. (2005). *Why do people write for Wikipedia? Incentives to contribute to open content publishing*. Paper presented at the 41st Annual Hawaii Intenational Conference on System Sciences, Sanibel Island, FL. Retrieved from http://search.ebscohost.com.proxy.iwu.edu/login.aspx?direct=true&db=edsref&AN=DAHICSSSIF.BJJE&site=eds-live&scope=site

Forte, A., Larco, V., & Bruckman, A. (2009). Decentralization in Wikipedia governance. *Journal of Management Information Systems, 26*(1), 49–72. Retrieved from http://search.ebscohost.com.proxy.iwu.edu/login.aspx?direct=true&db=bsh&AN=43590686&site=eds-live&scope=site doi:10.2753/MIS0742-1222260103

Garfinkel, S. L. (2008). Wikipedia and the meaning of truth. *Technology Review, 111*(6), 84–86. Retrieved from http://search.ebscohost.com.proxy.iwu.edu/login.aspx?direct=true&db=mth&AN=35342513&site=eds-live&scope=site

Grathwhol, C. (2011). Wikipedia comes of age. *The Chronicle of Higher Education, 57*(20), B2. Retrieved from http://search.ebscohost.com.proxy.iwu.edu/login.aspx?direct=true&db=ehh&AN=57722392&site=eds-live&scope=site

Head, A. J., & Eisenberg, M. B. (2010). How today's college students use Wikipedia for course-related research. *First Monday, 15*(3). Retrieved from http://search.ebscohost.com.proxy.iwu.edu/login.aspx?direct=true&db=edsref&AN=IDJJDFCC&site=eds-live&scope=site

Kittur, A., & Kraut, R. E. (2008). Harnessing the wisdom of crowds in Wikipedia: Quality through coordination. *ACM 2008 Conference on Computer Supported Cooperative Work,* (pp. 37-46). Retrieved from http://search.ebscohost.com.proxy.iwu.edu/login.aspx?direct=true&db=edsref&AN=ABCCSCW.BJJH.CG&site=eds-live&scope=site

Lamb, G. M. (2006). Online Wikipedia is not Britannica—but it's close. *Christian Science Monitor, 98*(28), 13-17. Retrieved from http://search.ebscohost.com.proxy.iwu.edu/login.aspx?direct=true&db=nfh&AN=19333880&site=eds-live&scope=site

Magnus, P. D. (2006). *Epistemology and the Wikipedia.* Paper presented at the North American Computing and Philosophy Conference. Retrieved from http://search.ebscohost.com.proxy.iwu.edu/login.aspx?direct=true&db=edsref&AN=NACPC.BJJF&site=eds-live&scope=site

Magnus, P. D. (2009). On trusting Wikipedia. *Episteme: A Journal of Social Epistemology, 6*(1), 74-90. Retrieved from http://search.ebscohost.com.proxy.iwu.edu/login.aspx?direct=true&db=phl&AN=PHL2133301&site=eds-live&scope=site

Olleros, F. X. (2008). Learning to trust the crowd: Some lessons from Wikipedia. *International MCETECH Conference on e-Technologies,* Montreal, Canada, (pp. 212-218). Retrieved from http://search.ebscohost.com.proxy.iwu.edu/login.aspx?direct=true&db=edsref&AN=BIMCCEHMCBJ.BJJH.BAB&site=eds-live&scope=site

Raymond, E. S. (2001). *The cathedral and the bazaar: Musings on Linux and open source by an accidental revolutionary* (Rev. ed.). Cambridge, MA: O'Reilly.

Reagle, J. M. (2010). *Good faith collaboration: The culture of Wikipedia.* Cambridge, MA: The MIT Press.

Rosenzweig, R. (2006). Can history be open source? Wikipedia and the future of the past. *The Journal of American History, 93*(1), 117–146. Retrieved from http://search.ebscohost.com.proxy.iwu.edu/login.aspx?direct=true&db=aph&AN=21254262&site=eds-live&scope=site doi:10.2307/4486062

Zickuhr, K., & Rainie, L. (2011). *Wikipedia, past and present.* Retrieved from http://www.pewinternet.org/Reports/2011/Wikipedia/Report.aspx

KEY TERMS AND DEFINITIONS

Amateur: A non-professional who engages in an area of study as an unpaid hobby or pastime.

Amateur-Expert: Someone who has gained a great deal of specialized knowledge through study or practice, but lacks traditional academic or professional credentials.

Crowdsourcing: Outsourcing a task or project to a large, undefined, group of people.

Egalitarianism: A social philosophy that advocates for a classless society and equal rights for all.

Epistemology: The philosophical study of knowledge and the theory of knowledge.

Expert: A person who has obtained academic or professional credentials and a comprehensive and authoritative knowledge in a particular area.

Reliability: A comparative, rather than absolute, quality indicating a consistently high degree of accuracy versus error.

Web 2.0: The second generation of web Web services characterized by a focus on user participation, collaboration, and interaction.

Chapter 3

Understanding and Evaluating Source Expertise in an Evolving Media Environment

Rebekah A. Pure
University of California, USA

Miriam J. Metzger
University of California, USA

Alexander R. Markov
University of California, USA

Andrew J. Flanagin
University of California, USA

J. Michael Mangus
University of California, USA

Ethan H. Hartsell
University of California, USA

ABSTRACT

Recent technological changes have created a radically different information environment from the one that existed even a few decades ago. Rather than coming from a small number of sources, each with a substantial investment in the information production and delivery processes, information is increasingly provided by a wide range of sources, many of which can readily provide and deliver information to large audiences worldwide. One consequence of this evolution in information production is an almost incomprehensibly vast information repository in the form of the Web and other online resources. A variety of social media have extended this information and source fecundity even further by connecting individuals to one another and by providing significant opportunities to share myriad types of information generated by users themselves. This shift in information dissemination challenges longstanding models of the provision of credible information by suggesting circumstances under which sources that are not understood as "experts" in the traditional sense are in fact in the best position to provide the most credible information.

DOI: 10.4018/978-1-4666-2178-7.ch003

INTRODUCTION

Recent technological changes have created a radically different information environment from the one that existed as recently as a few decades ago. As digital network technologies have reduced the cost and complexity of producing and disseminating information, the nature of information providers has shifted. Rather than relying on only a few sources, each with a substantial investment in the information production and delivery processes, information is increasingly provided by a wide range of sources, many of whom can readily create and deliver information to large audiences worldwide. One consequence of this evolution in information production is an almost incomprehensibly vast information repository in the form of the Web and other online resources. A variety of social software applications has extended this information and source fecundity even further by connecting individuals directly to one another and by providing significant opportunities to share myriad types of information that are generated by users themselves.

While this explosion of information has created tremendous opportunities, it has also been accompanied by significant challenges. The traditional media environment typically had a limited number of sources and had barriers in place to control the public dissemination of information. In such an environment of information scarcity, the gatekeepers can produce and filter much of the information available, and also have an incentive to uphold quality standards. Gatekeepers, in turn, were widely regarded as experts and were relied upon for credible information. The Internet and related tools, however, present a very different environment—one of information abundance—which makes traditional models of gatekeeper oversight untenable due to the sheer volume of information to be vetted. In light of this, the origin of information, and thus its quality and veracity, are in many cases less clear than before. This has created a revolution in locating and identify-

ing expertise, and in discerning information and source credibility.

This shift in information dissemination challenges longstanding models of information provision by suggesting circumstances under which sources that are not understood as "experts" in the traditional sense are in fact in the best position to provide the most credible information. Under conditions where knowledge is esoteric, diffused among many individuals, and dependent on specific, situational understanding, it is often the case that the most reliable information is gleaned not from a traditional source that has been imbued with authority by virtue of position or status, but rather from a diversity of individuals lacking special training, credentials, or established reputation. Indeed, not only are such circumstances common, but given the power of social software, they are increasingly supported by precisely the kinds of tools required to harness the power of those with the most relevant, timely, and important information. These shifts in the provision of information suggest both new kinds of expertise as well as new ways to determine and identify it. New forms of expertise, in turn, suggest updated notions about the location and evaluation of what information is most credible.

To examine these issues, we reconsider traditional, top-down models of information authority in order to account for the more diffuse methods of information provision and dissemination supported by the Web and social software. We begin with an analysis of how social software complicates and shifts conceptualizations of source expertise by facilitating direct access to information compiled by a multitude of potentially lay authors. We then propose new forms of expertise rooted in the experience of individuals rather than based on their formal credentials, and consider several approaches to judging and conceptualizing expertise that attempt to address the challenges and opportunities presented by the contemporary online environment. We conclude by evaluating the advantages and risks posed by these new forms of expertise and by considering how these are likely to evolve over time.

The Evolution of Source Expertise

Source expertise has long been established in the literature as a primary dimension of credibility (Hovland, Janis, & Kelley, 1953; Hovland & Weiss, 1951). The link between source expertise and a consumer's evaluation of a media message can be understood through the notion of "credibility transfer" (Schweiger, 2000), whereby credibility judgments transfer between various units of information provision: the credibility of a source both influences and is influenced by the credibility attributed to its message, just as the credibility of a specific media outlet influences and is influenced by the credibility of the medium as a whole. In other words, the credibility attributed to a source serves as an evaluative criterion for the credibility of the information provided by that source, such that sources with more expertise have traditionally been judged to provide higher-quality information than sources with less expertise. However, evaluations of expertise specifically, perhaps even more so than other dimensions of credibility, are undergoing significant transformations as the notion of expertise itself is problematized by emerging media technologies and applications.

Expertise has traditionally been indicated by the existence of a small set of commonly understood features such as formal job position, relevant experience, and specific training or education, which are signaled by markers such as credentials, job title, or, less commonly and even less reliably, by popularity. The relative inaccessibility of these features has ensured that the number of experts in most domains is small, and the difficulty in obtaining the requisite skills, training, and positions has maintained a system of elite expertise that has been perpetuated and has endured over time. For example, one way in which traditional information venues ensure credibility is by drawing on the credentials and reputations of the sources producing the content: credentialed experts presumably produce credible information (Warnick, 2004). Professional journalists, for instance, receive training through college programs, are united under a code of ethics, and have their articles vetted by editors, all of which helps to ensure information accuracy (Usher, 2010). In this manner, expertise has for the most part been the domain of a rather exclusive subset of individuals.

Although this exclusive system of recognized expertise endures today in a number of domains, the evolution of networked information-sharing tools has significantly altered conceptualizations of expertise in many cases. A host of Internet-based tools currently in use complicate the concept of expertise by calling into question several of the indicators on which people have commonly relied to signal expertise. For instance, in contrast to traditional news sources, on most news blogs the author's role is less significant because these blogs typically operate in a culture of linking to and borrowing from other sources, rather than generating original content (Asaravala, 2004; Hanrahan, 2007).

Moreover, people now have at their disposal a range of information options that they can choose from, representing a range of expertise models. Online, information consumers can consult newspaper articles written by credentialed journalists, or they can choose to read blogs instead, which are often self-regulated and largely independent from editors (Sweetser, 2007). Similarly, people with medical questions can choose to consult their physician, or they can go to a website that contains information about a health-related issue that may or may not be written by doctors. Perhaps the most visible example of this trend toward diverse information providers is Wikipedia, which relies on largely anonymous contributions from a variety of users, both expert and non-expert, to generate its articles (Kittur, Chi, Pendleton, Suh, & Mytkowicz, 2007).

To examine how Internet-based tools complicate traditional notions of expertise, we propose three specific ways in which contemporary techno-logical tools obfuscate longstanding conceptions of source expertise. The aspects of how information is produced, disseminated, and consumed on the Web that we consider have proven particularly salient in scholarly analyses of online credibility.

First, the Web facilitates low-cost, non-hier-archical information production, and therefore increases information accessibility. Traditionally, a limited number of often professionally trained gatekeepers acted as intermediaries that directed consumers to content that they vetted based on established criteria for determining information quality. Internet-based communication technolo-gies like the Web and social software, however, have substantially lowered the barriers to infor-mation production and dissemination, thereby increasing the number of information producers and, subsequently, the sheer amount of unfiltered information available directly to information con-sumers. Benkler (2006) describes this as a shift away from an "industrial information economy" and toward a "networked information economy." As a consequence, Internet users need not rely on expert intermediaries to filter information (Eysenbach, 2008). Instead, users can access continuously updated information directly from a variety of sources, including other users. This, of course, has several implications. For example, contributions from traditionally expert sources may be more difficult to locate in this highly clut-tered information landscape, in which control of the resources that drive a networked information economy are "radically decentralized, collabora-tive, and nonproprietary" (Benkler, 2006: 60).

Second, online sources are not merely multiple but are often not well known to information con-sumers, either personally or even by reputation. Moreover, in many cases users cannot easily verify who contributed what information, since online source information is sometimes unavailable, masked, or even entirely missing from a website, chat group, blog, wiki, and so on. These techno-logical features create a kind of "context deficit"

for digital information, where information seekers can easily lose track of the original information source or may not perceive the increasingly blurry line between advertising and informational content (Eysenbach, 2008). The hyperlinked structure of the Web contributes to this deficit by making it psychologically challenging for users to follow and evaluate various sources as they move from site to site, as evidenced by research showing that source and message information can become confused or disassociated in users' minds almost immediately after performing searches (Eysenbach & Kohler, 2002). Various levels of source anonymity are also problematic since under conditions of ambiguous authorship information sources' motivations are often unclear to users. The persuasive intent of messages has been shown to be a key element in people's evaluations of information credibility (Flanagin & Metzger, 2000, 2007).

Third, the hypertext environment often elides authorship. Because sites on the Web link together information from multiple authors, they com-plicate traditional ideas about origin and intent. For example, even when source information is provided, it is often difficult to interpret, such as when information is coproduced or repurposed from one site, channel, or application to another; or when information aggregators display information from multiple sources in a centralized location that may itself be perceived as the source. As Barthes (2006) notes, while a work is inseparable from its originator, evoking authorial trustworthiness and expertise, text is an organic network that eschews authorial filiation. The Web is an instance of text insofar as it is an intertextual milieu of linking and borrowing; sites often reference a multiplicity of interlinked sources rather than an individual original author (Warnick, 2004). Web technology also allows sites to easily aggregate user-generated data, while publicly available application pro-gramming interfaces (APIs) facilitate mash-ups that combine data from multiple sites (O'Reilly, 2005). Moreover, social software enables users to transcend their role as information consumers and become cocreators of online content (Klein, 2008). Wikipedia, for instance, is the seventh-most trafficked website in the world (Alexa, n.d.), and its more than 3.2 million articles are authored and maintained solely by its many user-contributors.

Taken together, the tremendous amount of information and relative anonymity and opacity of authorship on the Web complicates traditional authoritative approaches to source expertise in overlapping and interlocking ways. Changes in information generation from single and identifiable authors to multiple and opaque authors, and reliance on readily available but less well-known sources, have changed the way information consumers gauge source expertise and credibility. For example, judgments of source expertise online are often circular because they draw on information from other Web sources. Moreover, by denying the primacy of any particular author, social software and networked hypertext thwart credibility assessments grounded in isolated, material traits of the source itself (Warnick, 2004). The structure of the Web itself reinforces this tendency by using search engines and hyperlinks that encourage the cross-validation of information across multiple sources in a way that de-emphasizes the notion of expertise as being invested in a single entity and opens up the possibility of credibility being derived from information aggregation. Information consumers may no longer need to consult expert intermediaries to access information as information can easily be located and navigated using search engines.

The problem of finding credible information online thus involves deciding which sources to believe: official, credentialed experts, or other, often unidentified sources on the Web (Lankes, 2008), who may or may not be in a superior position to provide the most accurate information depending on the circumstances (Flanagin & Metzger, 2008). This new reality prompts a need to reconceive source expertise in a way that accommodates the many means of information provision available today, which we endeavor to do next.

RECONCEPTUALIZING EXPERTISE IN THE CONTEMPORARY MEDIA ENVIRONMENT

Expertise typically hinges on the possession of a specialized knowledge base and an externally recognized mastery of a particular topic, usually denoted by some official document or position. We refer to this type of expertise as *credentialed expertise*. Credentialed expertise serves as a backbone for information consumption, by providing people with a relatively reliable indicator of information quality and credibility.

However, while credentialed expertise can grant the competence to provide credible information about certain, specialized topics, one approach to expertise that is prominent in the expertise literature assumes that experts can be defined relative to novices on a continuum such that novices can themselves achieve expertise (Chi, 2006). According to this approach, experts are people who have acquired more knowledge in a domain than others have (Ericsson & Smith, 1991). As people can be competent to report on their personal experiences, they may be considered experts in the domains in which they have personal experience. Moreover, people can acquire and establish their expert status without being sanctioned by official credentials (e.g., self-taught computer programmers). In such circumstances, these people may be recognized as "cognitive authorities in the sphere of their own experience, on matters they have been in a position to observe or undergo" (Wilson, 1983: 15). In other words, these sources are experts in certain domains while lacking any official demarcations of expertise. A person's firsthand experience may serve as the basis of their expertise because it imbues them with what may be called *experiential authority*.

Although experiential authorities have always existed, Internet-based tools have dramatically enhanced their ability to reach others in ways that aggregate their experiences, boost their collective expertise, and influence information seekers.

Indeed, Internet users often turn to Web-based social software applications for experience-derived information, including user-generated ratings, reviews, information, and testimonials, to name only a few options. Accordingly, absolute (Chi, 2006), or credentialed, expertise stands to be challenged by vast, unfiltered access to information, as well as the ability "to aggregate individuals' experiences or opinions, pool their information, and identify the expertise of 'non-experts' based on specific or situated knowledge" (Metzger, Flanagin, & Medders, 2010: 436) that the Internet and its social applications afford.

As an example of one situation in which credentialed expertise may be less important to users than experiential authority, consider the residents of a city in the throes of a natural disaster such as a fast-spreading wildfire. In such a crisis, it is likely that residents would turn to the mainstream media for information, receiving periodic updates about fire-fighting efforts, evacuation plans, and other critical information from television broadcasts, radio programming, and the websites of both television and radio stations. This information would likely originate from a small number of highly credentialed sources, such as fire, police, and relief agencies, and a handful of news reporters in the field. Information obtained through these channels is likely to be accurate and highly credible. However, given the quite limited number of reliable sources and camera crews reporting information about the quickly unfolding disaster in real time, it is also likely to be limited in its scope and currency.

Information on the same event that originates from a diversity of individuals reporting on their own observations of the fire, even though none may be expert in the traditional sense, has the potential to be superior in the context of such a crisis for a number of reasons. Using social software—such as individual and community blogs and microblogging, photo-sharing sites, social network sites, or the Google Maps API—people could provide specific experiential information in

real time to large forums, including information such as the specific location (down to the street or address level) and direction of the fire at any given moment, and this information can be easily aggregated and shared with anyone. In such instances, each individual has the potential to be not only a consumer but also an "expert" provider of information, and the net effect is that each citizen becomes a sensor in a vast information network. In such systems, even unreliable information is likely to be effaced by more prevalent, up-to-date, and eyewitness reports.

Indeed, knowledge that is collectively generated on the Web may be more likely to be complete, because each individual author in a group can fill a gap in another group member's knowledge (Chi, Pirolli, & Lam, 2007). Under these circumstances, each individual's specific expertise is aggregated to provide an information repository that is significantly more powerful than any small number of experts could provide. According to Shirky (2008), a core principle of collaborative knowledge production is the rejection of credentials in favor of the public performance of competence. Moreover, in this type of collective endeavor anyone can authorize themselves to comment in a thread on an email discussion or update Wikipedia, but they risk seeing their contribution dismissed or aggressively challenged if it is deemed not credible (Shirky, 2008). Thus, as Shirky argues, expertise is no longer embodied in a person, but in the process of aggregating many points of view. Moreover, the information produced from the collective is likely to be highly relevant, comprehensive, timely, and reliable (Surowiecki, 2004). When faced with the imminent, localized threat of a fast-moving fire, it is reasonable to expect users to highly value exactly these dimensions of information quality where social software excels.

The rise of user-generated content online can be seen as a movement away from authority being vested exclusively in traditional institutions to a more bottom-up conception of information credibility that capitalizes on the experiences and opinions of many (Madden & Fox, 2006). Thus, in the social media environment, credentialed expertise is complemented by other forms of authority, including experiential authority, which gains credence due to the unique features of social software. In addition, not only do social software tools facilitate experiential authority, they also serve to change the very notion of expertise, by extending the range of voices that can supply relevant and credible information on a diversity of topics. For example, social software in the form of wikis, rating systems, and blogs can make the voice of the uncredentialed individual equivalent in many ways to that of the trained and renowned expert. Indeed, studies investigating the accuracy of information on Wikipedia show that the difference between information produced in Wikipedia and information produced by topical experts or well-known information authorities such as *Encyclopedia Britannica* is not particularly great (Chesney, 2006; Giles, 2005).

Yueng, Noll, Meinel, Gibbens, and Shadbolt (2011) also discuss the changing nature of expertise in the context of online communities in which users collect and share items of interest (e.g., books, photos, Web bookmarks), and optionally choose to describe them using keywords to aid in their organization and future retrieval. The authors argue that an expert user is not only one who has a large collection of high-quality items (those judged as interesting or relevant by others), but also one who is more likely to find and disseminate this high-quality information before anyone else does. Neither criterion discriminates between users whose expertise is grounded in traditional, credentialed authority and those with more experiential expertise.

Of course, in some cases, the untrained individual may in fact *be* more expert, particularly on certain types of issues and under specific circumstances. For example, Denecke and Nejdl (2009) found that user-contributed medical Q&A sites, such as Yedda.com, are a good source of information for those searching for information about health and medical topics, because highly relevant information is produced by other site visitors who are motivated to provide specific, experience-based information about a wide variety of conditions and treatments. Conversely, Scanfeld, Scanfeld, and Larson (2010) identified hundreds of tweets disseminating inaccurate information about antibiotics. The contrast in these findings accords with the notion that different users seeking different types of information may be best served to attend to different types of cues. For health information, online communities of other patients may offer extensive experiential authority about the day-to-day experience of coping with a condition, but a credentialed expert is likely to provide more credible information about the medical science involved in treating it. In a crisis like an ongoing natural disaster, the timeliness and specificity of information may take high priority, even if it has not been vetted by a credentialed authority, whereas when predicting the future path of a hurricane it seems more reasonable to trust a meteorologist. The critical issue for credibility assessment online is therefore how people determine which sources from among the many possibilities provide the most relevant expertise for their unique situation. A crucial point of this chapter is that this calculus has grown more complex due to digital networked technologies.

Determinants of Expertise

There are several possible strategies for making credibility decisions in the contemporary media environment where traditional source expertise cues may no longer be so clearly defined. First, since messages are frequently uncoupled from their authors, users must often rely predominantly on *message* rather than *source* characteristics to evaluate expertise and information credibility. Second, rather than focusing on traditional notions of source authority as the basis of credibility evaluations, users can instead utilize an approach that emphasizes the reliability of a source over time, and/or the reliability of information across multiple sources to overcome the deficit of context in determining the expertise of a source or information. Finally, while this environment sometimes lacks the intermediaries that facilitated traditional source-based credibility assessment, social software empowers users to rely on "apomediaries" that can assist them in evaluating digital information of questionable quality. Each of these strategies for coping with the problems of determining expertise that arise from digital networked information technologies is elaborated next.

REPLACING SOURCE CUES WITH MESSAGE CUES

In an environment where messages can be untethered from their source, credibility evaluations are often made based on the characteristics of the message itself rather than on source characteristics (Warnick, 2004). Message characteristics have even been shown to affect evaluations of credibility generally, as well as people's perceptions of source credibility and expertise (Agichtein, Castillo, Donato, Gionis, & Mishne, 2008; Roberts, 2010). Message factors such as professionalism, accuracy, currency, and comprehensiveness have been shown to positively affect online credibility judgments, including judgments of a source's expertise and trustworthiness (Fogg et al., 2001). For example, Fogg and his colleagues found that the degree to which a website looks professionally designed increases perceptions of the site's credibility, and indications of amateur website design, such as typographical errors and broken links, negatively impact credibility evaluations. Additionally, aspects of message content such as specificity and plausibility of information have been shown to signal source expertise online (Metzger, Flanagin, Eyal, Lemus, & McCann, 2003; Rieh & Belkin, 1998), as has the presence

of quotes, statistics, and references within the message (Hong, 2006; Rains & Karmikel, 2009).

Message cues have similarly been shown to be useful in credibility evaluations that take place in social software environments. For example, high-quality answers on Yahoo!Answers can be distinguished from low-quality answers based on message features such as the number of typos and grammatical errors (Agichtein et al., 2008). User characteristics have also been shown to interact with message features, such that the degree to which message content is salient to users increases their perceptions of information credibility (Flanagin & Metzger, 2007), and the extent to which the persuasive intent of a message is subtle or transparent impacts credibility assessments, with more obviously persuasive messages seen as less credible due to fears of source bias (Flanagin & Metzger, 2000; O'Keefe, 2002).

Thus, in the absence of information about an author's identity, training, and credentials, users rely on message cues to gauge an author's expertise. The presence of typographical errors and inaccuracies negatively impact perceptions of expertise, while a well-designed website positively impacts perceptions of its credibility. Given the importance of assessing the trustworthiness of a message, especially when the issue is salient or consequential to the information seeker, it is not surprising that information consumers will shift their focus to the information itself rather than to its origin when evaluating credibility and expertise online, particularly when source information is ambiguous.

In the context of social software in particular, information providers are often anonymous or pseudo-anonymous, and thus the reliance on message characteristics to assess the expertise of the contributors may be greater. For example, research suggests that when contributing online reviews for commercial products, reviewers are careful to establish their expertise through deliberate use of proper and appropriate language, including the use of specialized terminology (Mackiewicz, 2007), because it is unlikely that information seekers will know the reviewer personally and thus must rely on message content such as language as a proxy to evaluate the reviewer's expertise. In circumstances where experiential expertise is highly valued, no further qualification may be required beyond effective language use. For example, it is reasonable to think that the owner of a product is an authority on his or her experience using the product. However, while appropriate language may be necessary to establish expertise in this case, in circumstances where firsthand experience is less important, language cues alone may be insufficient. For example, a simple heuristic such as appropriate language may be a poor guide to judging source expertise on technical aspects of the product: while a layperson can accurately report their experience *using* the product, they may not be able to accurately report *why* or *how* it works. Other forms of evaluating expertise, including technical training or credentials, would aid in these types of circumstances.

Reliability across Time and Source

While traditional single-source models of credibility evaluation emphasize source authority and credentials as the critical basis of expertise (Hovland et al., 1953), as discussed earlier, with Web-based information and social software applications it is sometimes not possible to know who contributes information, and thus whether the contributors are credentialed experts (i.e., authorities) or not. In such situations, credibility decisions must be made based on factors other than source expertise, including message characteristics as just described, or by cross-validating information. Lankes (2008) asserts that in these circumstances *reliability* rather than *authority* becomes the predominant credibility cue.

According to Lankes, a reliable information source is one that consistently yields accurate information. So, a source may prove itself to be reliable, and by extension credible and possessing

expertise, if it contributes information deemed to be accurate over time. As Shirky (2008) notes, social software applications do not necessarily recognize expertise; deference is manifested through surviving edits. Indeed, research on Wikipedia finds that a good proxy for information quality (quality of contributed information) is the longevity of the original text (Adler & de Alfaro, 2006). The idea is that the expertise of Wikipedia contributors correlates with how long their original text persists over time, especially when there are a lot of editors. Thus, a source that contributes information through social software may be judged credible based on how long the information appears, or has appeared, on the site (Adler & de Alfaro, 2006; Adler, de Alfaro, Pye, & Raman, 2008).

Extending this logic, a source may also be considered reliable if the information it provides is consistent with information provided by other sources on the Internet. Indeed, research finds that cross-validation, or seeking convergence in information across multiple sources, is an important way for information consumers to establish the credibility (i.e., expertise and trustworthiness) of sources and messages in online contexts (Metzger et al., 2010). Social software streamlines the process of cross-validation by aggregating and presenting information from a variety of other sources on the Web in one location, either through search engines and their results, or through aggregated user data, such as commercial product ratings or testimonials. Furthermore, social software encourages connection and collaboration between users, thereby enhancing conversations regarding the credibility of information and facilitating continuing evaluations of information and its source(s). In turn, this helps to create an environment in which evaluations of source expertise and message quality are dynamic and ongoing processes. Also as a result, a community, rather than an individual, helps to determine the expertise of an information source on the Web.

THE SHIFT FROM INTERMEDIARIES TO APOMEDIARIES

As noted earlier, the rise of direct access to information online offers Internet users a greater opportunity to bypass traditional intermediaries and thus to retrieve more unfiltered information (Eysenbach & Jadad, 2001). Some have argued that this has led to the decline of expert information intermediaries. In the context of medicine, for example, Eysenbach (2008) says that the role of health intermediaries, such as doctors and nurses who mediate the transfer of health information to patients, may be diminishing because of the convenience, low expense, and availability of Web-based medical information. Eysenbach uses the term *apomediaries* to describe the agents that replace the traditional expert intermediaries. Apomediaries do not stand *between* the consumer and the information (as in *inter-*), but instead stand *by* the consumer, directing them to relevant and high-quality information online. The presence of apomediaries can be seen not only in health and medical domains, but across many information genres, both online and off.

Apomediaries may be experts, parents, teachers, and peers, who lend their expertise to help an information consumer vet some information or source online. Apomediaries may also be strangers who are not personally known to an information seeker. In all cases, apomediaries contribute valuable information by producing opinion- and user-generated content such as user ratings and reviews, social bookmarks, and wikis that help users navigate through the onslaught of information in the contemporary media environment by giving additional credibility cues and supplying meta-information. Eysenbach (2008) notes that choosing an apomediary to *help* information seekers evaluate the credibility of a message or expertise of a source, rather than a professional intermediary who filters information *for* information seekers, encourages autonomy and empowers information consumers. However, relying on apomediaries rather than expert intermediaries adds an extra layer of complexity to the credibility assessment, as information consumers must first make an evaluation of the credibility and usefulness of the apomediaries themselves, and then evaluate the source or message about which the apomediaries provide information.

Myriad websites use social software to provide users with opportunities for apomediation. One example is Amazon.com, where users are allowed to write reviews of the available products, and where other users are given the opportunity to rate the helpfulness of these reviews, on a scale of one to five stars. The aggregate rating of the product review (i.e., the helpfulness of the reviews) therefore functions as an instance of apomediation: it helps online shoppers evaluate the expertise of product reviewers by providing metadata about the utility of the information these reviewers provide. Research suggests that this information is useful, finding that review quality (as rated by apomediaries) and purchase intent are positively correlated (Cheung & Thadani, 2010). Interestingly, ecommerce and health information are two domains where professional recommendations could easily be biased by financial interests. In these cases, the added expertise provided by apomediaries may be perceived as more neutral than that of professional intermediaries, and thus as a more credible and preferable means of determining whether to trust a piece of information.

CONCLUSION

Evaluating New Approaches to Determining Expertise

Increased reliance on message rather than source cues, reliability rather than authority approaches to credibility assessment, and greater apomediation rather than intermediation techniques are all useful means to help discern expertise in a time when both the meaning and identification of information sources has become more difficult and complex. Yet, while each of these approaches to determining expertise in online environments offers tremendous promise, each also presents considerable risk in helping consumers locate credible information.

The promise of experiential authority shared through social software applications is great. As people share more information with an increasingly large audience through increasingly sophisticated social software tools, the utility of this type of information sharing increases in value and precision. Social software can harness the collective intelligence of users to construct a data source that grows richer the more people use it, thus providing a credible source of information that takes advantage of considerable experiential authority to help users locate and identify expertise in the contemporary media environment. This can reduce the considerable costs of source evaluation in information-rich environments (Taraborelli, 2008).

Groups of people may also be able to generate more complete, accurate information than individual experts can (Sunstein, 2006). Moreover, groups that contain both experts and non-experts have been shown to outperform groups that contain only experts, because non-experts offer unique problem-solving solutions that experts in a certain field might not be able to come up with on their own (Surowiecki, 2004). These are, of course, precisely the conditions that typically define the masses of people collaborating formally or loosely via social software today. Indeed, harnessing the "wisdom of crowds" is best when there is a diversity of opinion in the group—individuals contribute knowledge independently, the group is decentralized, and there is a tool for aggregating the information (Surowiecki, 2004). Social software facilitates all four of these requirements by providing oftentimes fun and easy-to-use tools to a wide range of geographically dispersed and diverse individuals to contribute information and opinions.

However, the risks of relying on experiential authority are also great. For instance, although message cues have been demonstrated to be a major factor to which people attend in their evaluation of the credibility of websites, research has shown that reliance on them is at times problematic, since these cues can lead to assessments based on surface indicators that are not necessarily indicative of deeper information quality (Flanagin & Metzger, 2007). Similarly, although seeking reliability between and within sources over time can boost the chances of accurately discerning the quality of information, reliability does not necessarily imply validity. Indeed, information and sources can be consistent (i.e., reliable) but inaccurate. Furthermore, in the contemporary media environment there may be a risk of equating popularity with expertise or credibility, as research has demonstrated that people often rely on the endorsement of others when evaluating a particular piece of information without engaging in independent or more systematic evaluation of the information (Hilligoss & Rieh, 2008; Metzger et al., 2010).

Finally, the value of apomediation ultimately relies on considerable skill on the part of information consumers, who need to correctly interpret cues from sometimes remote others that are at times complex, contested, or ambiguous. Research that looks at how successful people are when they rely on various heuristic cues finds that relying on these simple decision rules often leads to predictable errors (for a review, see Kahneman, Slovic, & Tversky, 1982). Thus, evaluating the credibility of information online by attending to cues generated by apomediaries may lead to suboptimal credibility decisions. For instance, even simple aggregated commercial ratings can be misinterpreted by information consumers who have been shown to rely heavily on the average "star" rating to the exclusion of critical complementary information regarding the number of ratings provided (Flanagin, Metzger, Pure, & Markov, 2011). Additionally, it is likely that when relying on aggregation to evaluate information credibility and source expertise, the user-generated origins of the apomediated information are overlooked or misunderstood, and therefore there is the risk of a collection of opinions being inappropriately elevated to the level of fact (Eysenbach, 2008).

Thus, the considerable value of user-generated content and new forms of expertise prompted by the use of social software must be weighed and assessed in light of related risks to information consumers today. In the end, however, credentialed expertise and experiential authority coexist in an environment saturated with technologies that both promote and impinge on users' capacity to take appropriate advantage of each.

In sum, social software facilitates an environment of information abundance, while complicating the traditional conceptualizations of source expertise. New forms of expertise are arising, rooted in the experience of individuals rather than based on their formal credentials. Users adapt to this environment by attending to message cues, evaluating the reliability of message content over time and across sources, and by relying on apomediaries to help them assess the quality of the information. While these strategies of evaluating information offer substantial promise, such promise must be considered along with the risks associated with such forms of information provision and evaluation.

REFERENCES

Adler, B. T., & de Alfaro, L. (2006). *A content-driven reputation system for the Wikipedia* (Technical Report No. ucsv-06-18). Santa Cruz, CA: University of California, Santa Cruz. Retrieved from http://works.bepress.com/luca_de_alfaro/3

Adler, B. T., de Alfaro, L., Pye, I., & Raman, V. (2008). *Measuring author contributions to the Wikipedia* (Technical Report No. UCSC-SOE-08-08). Santa Cruz, CA: University of California, Santa Cruz.

Agichtein, E., Castillo, C., Donato, D., Gionis, A., & Mishne, G. (2008). Finding high-quality content in social media. *WSDM '08 Proceedings of the International Conference on Web Search and Web Data Mining.*

Alexa. (n.d.). *Alexa top 500 global sites.* Retrieved from http://www.alexa.com/topsites

Asaravala, A. (2004). *Warnings: Blogs can be infectious.* Wired News.

Barthes, R. (2006). From work to text. In Hale, D. J. (Ed.), *The novel: An anthology of criticism and theory, 1900-2000* (pp. 235–241). Malden, MA: Blackwell.

Benkler, Y. (2006). *The wealth of networks: How social production transforms markets and freedom.* New Haven, CT: Yale University Press.

Chesney, T. (2006). An empirical examination of Wikipedia's credibility. *First Monday, 11*(11).

Cheung, C. M. K., & Thadani, D. R., (2010). The state of electronic word-of-mouth research: A literature analysis. *PACIS 2010 Proceedings, Paper 151.*

Chi, E. H., Pirolli, P., & Lam, S. K. (2007). Aspects of augmented social cognition: Social information foraging and social search. *Proceedings of the 2nd International Conference on Online Communities and Social Computing* (pp. 60-69). Beijing, China: Springer-Verlag.

Chi, M. T. H. (2006). Two approaches to the study of experts' characteristics. In Ericsson, A. K., Charness, N., Feltovich, P. J., & Hoffman, R. R. (Eds.), *The Cambridge handbook of expertise and expert performance* (pp. 21–30). New York, NY: Cambridge University Press. doi:10.1017/CBO9780511816796.002

Denecke, K., & Nejdl, W. (2009). How valuable is medical social media data? Content analysis of the medical web. *Information Sciences, 179,* 1870–1880. doi:10.1016/j.ins.2009.01.025

Ericsson, K., & Smith, J. (1991). *Toward a general theory of expertise: Prospects and limits.* New York, NY: Cambridge University Press.

Eysenbach, G. (2008). Credibility of health information and digital media: New perspectives and implications for youth. In Metzger, M. J., & Flanagin, A. J. (Eds.), *Digital media, youth, and credibility* (pp. 123–154). Cambridge, MA: The MIT Press.

Eysenbach, G., & Jadad, A. (2001). Evidence-based patient choice and consumer health informatics in the internet age. *Journal of Medical Internet Research, 3*(2). doi:10.2196/jmir.3.2.e19

Eysenbach, G., & Köhler, C. (2002). How do consumers search for and appraise health information on the world wide web? Qualitative study using focus groups, usability tests, and in-depth interviews. *British Medical Journal, 324*(7337), 573–577. doi:10.1136/bmj.324.7337.573

Flanagin, A. J., & Metzger, M. J. (2000). Perceptions of Internet information credibility. *Journalism & Mass Communication Quarterly, 77*(3), 515–540. doi:10.1177/107769900007700304

Flanagin, A. J., & Metzger, M. J. (2007). The role of site features, user attributes, and information verification behaviors on the perceived credibility of web-based information. *New Media & Society, 9*(2), 319–342. doi:10.1177/1461444807075015

Flanagin, A. J., & Metzger, M. J. (2008). The credibility of volunteered geographic information. *GeoJournal, 72*(3), 137–148. doi:10.1007/s10708-008-9188-y

Flanagin, A. J., Metzger, M. J., Pure, R., & Markov, A. (2011). User-generated ratings and the evaluation of credibility and product quality in ecommerce transactions. *Proceedings of the 44th Hawaii International Conference on Systems Science.*

Fogg, B. J., Marshall, J., Laraki, O., Osipovich, A., Varma, C., & Fang, N. … Treinen, M. (2001). What makes Web sites credible? A report on a large quantitative study. *Proceedings of the SIGCHI Conference on Human Factors in Computing Systems* (pp. 61-68). Seattle, WA: ACM.

Giles, J. (2005). Internet encyclopaedias go head to head. *Nature, 438,* 900–901. doi:10.1038/438900a

Hanrahan, M. (2007). Plagiarism, instruction, blogs. In Roberts, T. (Ed.), *Student plagiarism in an online world: Problems and solutions* (pp. 183–193). Hershey, PA: IGI. doi:10.4018/978-1-59904-801-7.ch012

Hilligoss, B., & Rieh, S. Y. (2008). Developing a unifying framework of credibility assessment: Construct, heuristics, and interaction in context. *Information Processing & Management, 44*(4), 1467–1484. doi:10.1016/j.ipm.2007.10.001

Hong, T. (2006). The influence of structural and message features on Web site credibility. *Journal of the American Society for Information Science and Technology, 57*(1), 114–127. doi:10.1002/asi.20258

Hovland, C. I., Janis, I. L., & Kelley, J. J. (1953). *Communication and persuasion.* New Haven, CT: Yale University Press.

Hovland, C. I., & Weiss, W. (1951). The influence of source credibility on communication effectiveness. *Public Opinion Quarterly, 15,* 635–650. doi:10.1086/266350

Kahneman, D., Slovic, P., & Tversky, A. (Eds.). (1982). *Judgment under uncertainty: Heuristics and biases.* Cambridge, UK: Cambridge University Press.

Kittur, A., Chi, E. H., Pendleton, B. A., Suh, B., & Mytkowicz, T. (2007). Power of the few vs. wisdom of the crowd: Wikipedia and the rise of the bourgeoisie. *Proceedings of the 25th International Conference on Human Factors in Computing Systems.*

Klein, K. E. (2008). *Demystifying Web 2.0: Richard J. Goossen shows how entrepreneurs can make the most of Web 2.0.* Retrieved from http://www.businessweek.com/smallbiz/content/jun2008/sb20080616_188170.htm

Lankes, R. D. (2008). Trusting the Internet: New approaches to credibility tools. In Metzger, M. J., & Flanagin, A. J. (Eds.), *Digital media, youth, and credibility* (pp. 101–122). Cambridge, MA: The MIT Press.

Mackiewicz, J. (2007). *Reviewer bias and credibility in online reviews.* Paper presented at the Association for Business Communication Annual Convention.

Madden, M., & Fox, S. (2006). *Riding the waves of "Web 2.0."* Retrieved from http://pewresearch.org/pubs/71/riding-the-waves-of-web-20

Metzger, M. J., Flanagin, A. J., Eyal, K., Lemus, D. R., & McCann, R. (2003). Bringing the concept of credibility into the 21st century: Integrating perspectives on source, message, and media credibility in the contemporary media environment. *Communication Yearbook, 27,* 293–335. doi:10.1207/s15567419cy2701_10

Metzger, M. J., Flanagin, A. J., & Medders, R. (2010). Social and heuristic approaches to credibility evaluation online. *The Journal of Communication, 60*(3), 413–439. doi:10.1111/j.1460-2466.2010.01488.x

O'Keefe, D. J. (2002). *Persuasion: Theory & research.* Thousand Oaks, CA: Sage Publications, Inc.

O'Reilly, T. (2005). *What is Web 2.0: Design patterns and business models for the next generation of software.* Retrieved from http://oreilly.com/web2/archive/what-is-web-20.html

Rains, S. A., & Karmikel, C. D. (2009). Health information-seeking and perceptions of website credibility: Examining Web-use orientation, message characteristics, and structural features of websites. *Computers in Human Behavior, 25*(2), 544–553. doi:10.1016/j.chb.2008.11.005

Rieh, S. Y., & Belkin, N. J. (1998). Understanding judgment of information quality and cognitive authority in the WWW. *Proceedings of the 61st Annual Meeting of the American Society for Information Science* (Vol. 35, pp. 279-289).

Roberts, C. (2010). Correlations among variables in message and messenger credibility scales. *The American Behavioral Scientist, 54*(1), 43–56. doi:10.1177/0002764210376310

Scanfeld, D., Scanfeld, V., & Larson, E. L. (2010). Dissemination of health information through social networks: Twitter and antibiotics. *American Journal of Infection Control, 38,* 182–188. doi:10.1016/j.ajic.2009.11.004

Schweiger, W. (2000). Experience or image? A survey on the credibility of the world wide web in Germany in comparison to other media. *European Journal of Communication, 15,* 37–59. doi:10.1177/0267323100015001002

Shirky, C. (2008). *Here comes everybody: The power of organizing without organizations.* New York, NY: Penguin Books.

Sunstein, C. R. (2006). *Infotopia: How many minds produce knowledge.* New York, NY: Oxford University Press.

Surowiecki, J. (2004). *The wisdom of crowds.* New York, NY: Anchor Books.

Sweetser, K. D. (2007). Blog bias: Reports, inferences, and judgments of credentialed bloggers at the 2004 nominating conventions. *Public Relations Review, 33*(4), 424–428. doi:10.1016/j.pubrev.2007.08.012

Taraborelli, D. (2008). How the Web is changing the way we trust. *Proceeding of the 2008 Conference on Current Issues in Computing and Philosophy* (pp. 194-204). IOS Press.

Usher, N. (2010). Goodbye to the news: How out-of-work journalists assess enduring news values and the new media landscape. *New Media & Society, 12*(6), 911–928. doi:10.1177/1461444809350899

Warnick, B. (2004). Online ethos: Source credibility in an "authorless" environment. *The American Behavioral Scientist, 48*(2), 256–265. doi:10.1177/0002764204267273

Wilson, P. (1983). *Second-hand knowledge: An inquiry into cognitive authority*. Westport, CT: Greenwood Press.

Yueng, C. A., Noll, M. G., Meinel, C., Gibbens, N., & Shadbolt, N. (2011). Measuring expertise in online communities. *Intelligent Systems, IEEE, 26*(1), 26–32. doi:10.1109/MIS.2011.18

ADDITIONAL READING

Ericsson, K., Charness, N., Feltovich, P., & Hoffman, R. (Eds.). (2006). *The Cambridge handbook of expertise and expert performance*. New York, NY: Cambridge University Press. doi:10.1017/CBO9780511816796

Jessen, J., & Jørgensen, A. H. (2012). Aggregated trustworthiness: Redefining online credibility through social validation. *First Monday, 17*(1). doi:10.5210/fm.v17i1.3731

Metzger, M., & Flanagin, A. (2008). *Digital media, youth, and credibility*. Cambridge, MA: The MIT Press.

KEY TERMS AND DEFINITIONS

Apomediaries: People or sources that stand *by*, offering you the Internet information you seek. They may have developed an expertise that is not formally credentialed in any particular way, but can be valuable.

Apomediation: Apomediation describes the fact that when you access information on the Internet, you cut out the gatekeepers or any middlemen (like your own doctor or an insurance salesman), which allows you to go directly to the source of information, even if it is not a (previously considered) "expert" source. The expert "stands by" you.

Cognitive Authorities: Those who are deemed to "know what they are talking about."

Credentialed Expertise: Expertise that hinges on the possession of a specialized knowledge base and an externally recognized mastery of a particular topic, usually denoted by some official document or position.

Experiential Authority: Sources who are considered experts based on firsthand experiences, but who may lack official demarcations of expertise.

Experiential Expertise: Expertise that hinges on firsthand experiences.

Intermediaries: Sources that stand *between* the consumer and the information, directing consumers to content vetted according to established criteria for determining information quality.

Source Expertise: The extent to which a communicator is perceived to be capable of providing credible information.

Chapter 4
Connection, Fragmentation, and Intentionality:
Social Software and the Changing Nature of Expertise

Christopher Watts
St. Lawrence University, USA

ABSTRACT

Social software forms new kinds of collectives and expands the means of producing and disseminating knowledge. Yet the combination of persistent connection and fragmented communication can undermine intentionality. Philosophies of technology that privilege data over users exacerbate this danger; more humanistic approaches to software design are now required. Through personal observation and an examination of recent literature (largely drawn from the popular press), the author examines the philosophies that underlie social software designs, explores ways they affect interaction, describes potential pitfalls, and theorizes a reimagining of expertise in this context—complementing, rather than replacing, the scholarly traditions of the academy.

INTRODUCTION

The use of social software in almost every aspect of daily living has exploded in recent years in a way that the earliest adopters of the Web could never have anticipated. It has changed how human beings interact with one another in ways both positive and negative. Perhaps the chief benefit of social software is most succinctly described by Shirky (2008): organizing without organizations. Social software allows users to send and receive information in targeted ways, and can potentially be a powerful way of creating and organizing new knowledge. In higher education, the realization of the epistemological function of digital media technologies (including social software) has been somewhat slow. That is, it would seem that many college professors have been reluctant to see such

DOI: 10.4018/978-1-4666-2178-7.ch004

technologies not only as means of disseminating knowledge, but also as sites of knowledge creation. Making a short video about topic *x*, for example, is not simply a means of showing someone else what one has learned about that topic; making the video is also a *way of knowing* about the topic. Uploading that video to a video-sharing site and participating in an online dialogue about it furthers both the creation and dissemination of knowledge about topic *x*. For a student, this experience can also help to make the concept of joining an ongoing scholarly conversation more concrete—something that does not always happen when the end product is a paper that only a professor will read.

What do educational institutions know about the intersection of relatively new social software and the age-old academy? Some of the benefits are clear enough. The most coordinated ways in which academic institutions have adopted social software, it seems, have been related to admissions and public relations. "Some colleges are treading the new territory with specific strategies—to recruit students or engage alumni—while others are showing up and feeling their way" (Lipka, 2009: para. 7). Social software has crept into the classroom in a more decentralized manner. (The same trend may now be seen with mobile computing; see Keller, 2011.) Many instructors have experimented with using popular social software platforms in place of institutional learning management systems to coordinate communication and resources for class members. There are many different ways to do this, and many different reasons why it might be done. Social software is conducive to ad hoc activities by design, and perhaps there is no need to coordinate such activities in broad ways. However, it is, of course, extremely useful to share best practices, and some organizations, such as the New Media Consortium and EDUCAUSE, are doing so (New Media Consortium and EDUCAUSE Learning Initiative, 2007, 2008).

As with any relatively new technology, the current crop of social software has been the target of some criticism, much of which has been dismissed as Luddite whining. In truth, a number of very smart, thoughtful, and technologically sophisticated individuals have offered serious, considered criticism, and their arguments are well worth considering by technology enthusiasts and Luddites alike.

In the last few years, there has been a great deal of writing about technology in general, and social software in particular, by technology luminaries from across the disciplines (using the quaint technology of the book). The questions raised in this chapter have now become relevant for a general readership. Interestingly, much of the material that I have found most relevant appears in the popular press, and it is from the popular press, then, that I will draw most of the context for this chapter. In 2010 alone, a number of compelling and contradictory books were published that have profoundly affected my thinking. I am indebted to several recent books in particular that have helped shape my ideas: Kelly's *What technology wants* (2010), Lanier's *You are not a gadget* (2010b), Rushkoff's *Program or be programmed* (2010), Siegel's *Against the machine* (2008), and Turkle's *Alone together* (2011).

The objectives of this chapter are fourfold: (a) to examine briefly some of the philosophies that underlie social software designs; (b) to explore the ways that these designs subsequently affect interaction among individuals and groups; (c) to describe pitfalls of this arrangement that are particularly relevant to higher education; and, finally, (d) to call for a reimagining of expertise in a way that builds on (rather than replaces) the scholarly tradition of the academy.

BACKGROUND

Philosophies of technology—of both the highly developed and the vague varieties—influence social software in important and very direct ways. As a consequence, they are worth examining.

Enlightenment Thought in the Age of LED Bulbs

The 18th-century playwright, historian, and philosopher Friedrich Schiller gave humanists a snappy, well-loved quote: "Live with your century, but do not be its creature" (1794/2004: 54). It appears, for example, in Saul Bellow's novel *Ravelstein* (2001: 82). Schiller's quote resonates with Bellow's character (and with so many people) because of its implicit suggestion that those things that are timely are seldom also timeless. It also seems to imply nobler times in the past, in the future, or maybe even both. I find myself wondering if it is at all possible to live in the current times without being *of* the current times. Kelly (2010) writes that humans have reached a tipping point in the history of technology, and that "the technium's ability to alter us exceeds our ability to alter the technium" (197). On this point, I believe Kelly is absolutely correct. How, then, can anyone hope to follow Schiller's advice?

Interestingly, the second half of Schiller's oft-quoted sentence is less often seen: "Live with your century, but do not be its creature; render to your contemporaries what they need, not what they praise" (Schiller, 1794/2004: 54). In the first decades of the 21st century, perhaps this second piece of advice is of more potential use than the first. How might educators render the needed things to their contemporaries? Within the sphere of social software, I believe that preserving intentionality is truly one of the most-needed things. As Rushkoff (2010) bluntly puts it, "you will either create the software or you will be the software" (7). This may seem overly dramatic to some, but I think the drama is well warranted. Siegel (2008) writes, "Anyone who thinks technological innovation is bad in and of itself is an unimaginative crank … But anyone who denies that technology has the potential to damage us if it is not put to good use is either cunning or naïve" (18). Users must not be so busy celebrating what they are doing with social software that they neglect to ask hard questions about what it is doing to them.

Influence Trumps Argument in Technology Design

If, as Kelly (2010) argues, the complex system of technology has slipped beyond human control, is this a justification for nihilism? Kelly contends that the trajectory of technological development contains a great deal of inevitability. This does not mean, however, that the *details* are inevitable. Kelly would argue, for example, that social software was inevitable in the early years of the 21st century, but that specific implementations such as Facebook, LinkedIn, Twitter, Tumblr, YouTube, Flickr, Delicious (del.icio.us), etc., were not. And the details do matter; educators ought to pay more attention to them if they want to influence the future direction of the ways in which knowledge is created and disseminated.

In order to use a technology successfully, users must adapt their workflow to match the expectations of the people who designed that technology. This changes the way that people work and, more importantly, changes what kinds of work people are likely to do. A technology that makes some things easier likely makes other things more difficult. A technology that serves one constituency very well may not serve another constituency well at all. Because technology evolves at such a rapid pace, design decisions are often made by a very small group of people (or a single person) and without the benefit of historical perspective or even time to think through the ramifications of adopting a particular design. Design decisions may be made for reasons that are philosophical, purely pragmatic, or even arbitrary. However, users may remain oblivious to the reasons for such decisions and to their effects. Lanier (2010b) points out that technology designers do not persuade indirectly through argument, but directly through the design of the tools people use. "We make up extensions to your being … These become the structures by which you connect to the world and other people. These structures in turn can change how you conceive of yourself and the world" (5-6). Such implicit arguments underlie social software designs; users owe it to themselves and one another to examine those arguments as they employ those technologies. Rushkoff (2010) argues that learning about programming is the best strategy for avoiding the negative impacts of technologies' biases. Writing as computers were first beginning to become a part of everyday life, Turkle (1984) said, "On the eve of a new era we, by definition, do not know where we are" (65). At the beginning of *this* new era, people have smartphones and tablets with GPS location services—and can check in on Foursquare—but still do not really know where they stand. Failure to fix a position and chart a course for the future, with purpose and a critical eye, is a failure humans can ill afford.

GENERALIZING WEB 2.0 DESIGN

For the purpose of fixing a current position, what general statements can be made that apply to the broad array of social software designs of the last 10 years called Web 2.0? The following is an attempt to generalize.

- **The focus is on connectivity, loosely defined:** The fundamental idea of social software is connection with others. This can take various forms, and the terms "friend" and "connection" are used in many different ways to name the relationships among participants. In any given social software space, a user may be connected to many, many others—ranging from family members and intimate friends to work associates, acquaintances, and complete strangers.
- **Communication tends to be fragmentary:** Fragments are the preferred means of communication because they are fast and

convenient, and can work either synchronously or asynchronously. Context and nuance are easily lost, however, and users must be careful in this regard.

- **User presence in social software spaces is persistent:** In a typical multiuser virtual environment or game, the user moves through and interacts in virtual space via an avatar. When the user logs out, the avatar disappears. In contrast, social software is always on: profile pages, walls, comment threads, tagged photographs, etc., remain when the user is disconnected. If user presence is a performance of identity, how the user "performs" while absent is worth considering.
- **Advertising is the economic engine driving social software platforms:** The economic model of social software resembles that of broadcast media in many respects. Most or all costs are incurred by advertisers rather than users. The major difference, of course, is the precise targeting of advertisements in social software spaces that is not possible with broadcast media. Under this model, complex demographic information becomes increasingly valuable while also becoming easier to obtain.
- **Cloud-based strategies make physical location largely irrelevant:** As users interact with data and with other people on an increasing number of devices and in a variety of places, cloud-based strategies become more useful and more ubiquitous. This means, of course, that user data move to third-party storage facilities.
- **Content creation tends to be form- and template-based:** In the earliest days of the Web, online content was coded "by hand" in HTML, with form and content intertwined. Software companies then developed programs that made this process resemble word processing or page layout. Online content is now typically coded in

a complex combination of languages: HTML, CSS, PHP, Javascript, Ajax, etc. Most content is generated by users who lack the technical knowledge to do this, and who are contributing content from a wide variety of devices; it makes sense, then, that designs tend to be controlled by templates and content generated via forms.

Some list items pertain to some types of social software more than others (or to some specific instances more than others). Facebook, for example, may be seen to embody all of these elements to some degree. The same may be said of a typical blog, though many blogs do not employ advertising. Wikipedia does not depend on advertising, and it suppresses user presence in articles but not in the corresponding discussion pages.

The items in the list above, taken together, have the potential to perform a homogenizing function on content and, by extension, on users. In the sections that follow, I will focus on the first two items in the list—connectivity and fragmentation—followed by a section that explores the potential dangers of combining these two elements in a social software design.

CONNECTION

Ted Nelson has a remarkable penchant for coining new words that are instantly understandable and somehow more satisfying than the existing words they elide. In *Computer Lib/Dream Machines* he wrote quite simply: "Everything is deeply intertwingled" (Nelson, 1974/1987: 68). Indeed, people's lives are intertwingled in the sense that relationships with other people and the world at large form a crucial part of who each person is. As connections to other people and the world are increasingly made and maintained via social software, it is not at all surprising that the designs of social software will impact the kinds of interactions in which one participates. As the

quantity of interactions increases, questions arise about what happens to the quality of those interactions. As interactions with other people become increasingly mediated by technology, users may find that other people begin to seem less "real." As interactions take place in social spaces where users are anonymous (or virtually anonymous), they may find that actions begin to seem divorced from their consequences. It is for these reasons that users might do well to avoid the trap of connecting solely for the sake of connecting.

A few years ago, a coworker of mine had exactly 200 friends on Facebook (while some users have substantially more, the average among all users is approximately 130 friends; see Facebook, 2011). One morning, he logged in to discover that he had 199 friends. He was both curious and a little upset. Who had dropped him, and why? He spent some time poring over his list of friends, trying to figure out who was missing, but could not. This raises the question: Was this connection meaningful in any way?

Social software users do, of course, have many meaningful interactions on a regular basis, or there would be little reason to participate. Yet meaningless connections can have a negative impact on the meaningful ones, like interference on a phone call. Social software is incredibly powerful, but only when used purposefully. Using social software does not constitute a purpose for using social software.

Users Are Not Customers

Messages, status updates, links, photographs, videos, tags, mentions, retweets, and trackbacks are the currency of social software. Less often, in many cases, do people actually see the faces of other users in real time and, rarer still, in real space. Communications are heavily mediated, and this sometimes allows (or causes?) each user to see others as less than a person. Empathy can atrophy. Social software platforms are usually designed to serve two masters: users and advertisers.

Advertisers pay the bills, and they gladly do so in exchange for precisely targeted ads. Because of this arrangement, social software designs are often data-centric rather than user-centric (Lanier, 2010b). In the traditional software model, value comes from proprietary code and the functionality it provides—the software is the product, and the user is the customer. In the new model, the functionality (if not the code) is given away for free, and value comes from users—user data are the product and the advertiser is the customer. This puts the proprietors of social software services in a potentially awkward position. They need data for advertisers in order to generate revenue, and they need users in order to generate data in the first place. Keeping both groups happy can be a delicate balance, but a business has to put its paying customers first.

The way that Facebook manages privacy settings for its users can serve as an example. When Facebook decides to change its default privacy settings, it does so not only for new users but also for existing users. An example of this occurred in June 2011, when Facebook automatically enabled facial recognition software that prompts users' friends to tag them in photos (Cluley, 2011). At issue is not that Facebook deployed this software, but that when it does such a thing it changes users' privacy settings automatically—always requiring them to opt out—no matter how many times they previously may have opted for more privacy. Is this an indication that the proprietors of Facebook value data more than people? At the moment they have little to lose: everyone is on Facebook, because everyone is on Facebook (tautological, but still true).

What it means for users is a different problem: a data-centric model makes content more important than the user who produces it, and weakens the connection between the individual and the content he or she produces. This plays out most plainly in the serial (viral) reposting of fragments, which causes a loss of provenance and context. When users are not being careful, the voices of individuals are lost and their content exploited. People become less real to one another.

Trolls

It is easy to imagine that connecting with people in ways that do not include face-to-face exchanges could result in a deterioration of civility. The level to which interactions are mediated can certainly make a difference in how the consequences of actions are perceived. When this situation occurs in an environment that is largely anonymous, it is conducive to a descent into very nasty behavior. The caustic comment threads on YouTube[1] or the edit wars on Wikipedia[2] are examples of what can happen when users feel neither any personal connection with one another, nor any sense of responsibility for the consequences of their actions. This combination of remoteness and immunity can bring out the worst in people, and also has the potential to turn groups into mobs (Siegel, 2008; see also Lanier, 2010b).

However, the capability for anonymity is fundamental to the design of the Internet as it currently exists, and there are certainly instances when anonymity can be necessary for personal safety. Fortunately, most of the time, for most people there is no need to hide. Public discourse is more likely to be meaningful when people take direct responsibility for their own words and actions, while also having a sense of the other real people who are participating in the discussion.

The Posthuman Condition and Collective Intelligence

Among technology thinkers and philosophers, the concept of the posthuman has been fertile ground for many years. The posthuman condition is one in which the boundaries between human and machine are no longer readily discernible. Ever since Alan Turing proposed his seminal thought experiment in 1950 (the Turing test; see Turing, 1950), the concept of disembodiment has been central in philosophies of technology. Turing "made the crucial move of distinguishing between the enacted body, present in the flesh … and the represented body, produced through the verbal and semiotic markers constituting it in an electronic environment" (Hayles, 1999: xiii). Hayles argues that, since the enacted body and represented body come together only via connecting technologies, the subject is a cyborg by definition. "By the late twentieth century … we are all chimeras, theorized and fabricated hybrids of machine and organism; in short, we are all cyborgs" (Haraway, 1991: 150). No need to wait for strong artificial intelligence or the monstrous cyborgs of science fiction[3]—the question is already relevant. Where does person stop and technology begin? Personal identity has crossed that boundary, but the ramifications remain unclear. What does it mean for identity, for example, that in a social networking environment the "represented body" persists even when the "enacted body" is disconnected?

Likewise, in the age of social software, the individual is seen as a component part of a meta-organism, composed of human minds and the machines that connect them (Kelly, 2010). Much store is subsequently placed in the wisdom of crowds. Lanier (2010b) cautions that, while there are many types of decisions that are best made via broad consensus (systems such as democracy and markets, for example), there are other types of decisions that are better made by small groups or individuals (individual court cases are not decided by referendum, for example). A balance between the influence of individuals and collectives is key in establishing a culture that is both productive and stable. Along these same lines, Lanier expresses a concern that communication is increasingly experienced at a level that looms above the individual, and that this might reduce expectations about what an individual person can accomplish. If this is true, there is deep irony in the idea that a shift from broadcast to narrowcast media produces effects exactly opposite to those intended.

Taken together, the blurring boundaries between human and machine and a dogmatic belief that large groups always make the best decisions suggest a world in which the individual loses his or her voice. How might this be reconciled with the frequent complaint that the current society is the most self-involved in history? Turkle (2011) argues that social software enables self-involved behavior, as people use social software to perform their privacy and package themselves as products. Authors of a recent study that analyzed the lyric content of popular songs found that songs about the individual have replaced songs about togetherness over the last three decades, and concluded (controversially) that this should be read as evidence of an increase in narcissism (DeWall, Pond, Campbell, & Twenge, as cited in Tierney, 2011). Is it possible for the members of a society to lose individual agency while simultaneously becoming more convinced of their own self-importance? Siegel (2008) suggests that social software's metric for success—popularity uncoupled from merit—is responsible for these simultaneous trends. Turkle writes that people use technology to satisfy the desire for relationships while simultaneously using it to shield themselves from the attendant risks and disappointments. Does this take the work out of relationships?

Siegel (2008) surmises that a tendency to connect mostly with like-minded people via social software may contribute to a sense of self-importance—constantly reaffirming the user's values and opinions without challenging them. If people are using social software to connect only with others who think as they do, and do most of their connecting via social software, there are fewer chances to have genuine conversations with those who think differently. People become less tolerant of difference and less capable of engaging with it productively. If that is indeed the direction in which things are headed, we should be very worried. Connecting for the sake of connecting is useless, but what Siegel and Turkle suggest may well turn out to be connecting for the sake of disconnecting. "Digital connections … may offer the illusion of companionship without the demands of friendship" (Turkle, 2011: 1). This is a stark possibility, and it is well worth the effort of making sure things do not turn out this way.

FRAGMENTATION

The broad, interconnected world of social software is fast-paced, and the preferred forms of communication in such an environment are correspondingly brief. This style of communication, while convenient, also has the potential to strip the context and subtlety from a conversation. This is not the only aspect of social software designs with such potential. Automatic aggregation of fragments, template-based content, and even the sheer volume and constant stream of messages each person receives make it easier for the forest to disappear among the trees. The trick is to make use of—and sense of—the ocean of fragments without becoming fragmented.

Weinberger (2007) is one of many authors in recent years to write about the fundamental differences between traditional means of organization in the physical world (categorical, hierarchical) and new means possible in the digital world (associative, polyvalent). Weinberger rightly extols the value of user-generated metadata (a Web 2.0 staple) in maximizing the ways in which a user might find what they seek in the ocean of fragments. He further argues that applying traditional means of organization to the digital world is not merely insufficient, but ultimately a waste of effort. Many librarians are not willing to concede this last point. Without some means of classification and shared vocabulary, there is less opportunity to encounter competing points of view (Badke, 2008). Personalized search terms are a great place to start, but may create a bubble. (This is distinct from any "filter bubble" created by the search engine's personalization; see Pariser, 2011.) In a social network, users can create their own bubbles;

in a search, a bubble can emerge from personalized metadata and search terms. Assembling fragments to make meaning must not be celebrated as a simple task in the new order.

Digital Tools Are Fundamentally Different from Physical Tools

Digital tools are not the software equivalents of hand tools. The difference is programming (Rushkoff, 2010). A hand tool is designed to be used in certain ways, but has no means of guiding itself along the path toward those uses. (There is an old joke that the hammer is the world's most widely used screwdriver.) Twitter is not like a hammer, because it is not only designed but also programmed. In a sense, Twitter "wants" to be used in certain ways, and guides its users toward those uses. The singular aspect of Twitter is its well-known 140-character limit on each tweet. Social software prefers fragmentary communication because of its speed and convenience. Twitter goes a step further by *requiring* fragments: "Don't let the small size fool you—you can share a lot with a little space" (Twitter, 2011: para. 2).

While fragments are indeed fast and convenient—and a service like Twitter makes users feel present with one another—this fragmentary, one-to-many style of communication has its downsides. Tweets and status updates—continuously delivered to and from tiny devices that seldom leave users' hands—connect people to the world but only provide small pieces of the story. Frequent, brief interactions tend to be fragmentary, and fragmentation can very easily lead to reductionism. Complex issues may be reduced to simple binaries, and complex arguments stripped of nuance and context. Life can become a series of fragments, driving questions to which the answers must be yes or no, right or wrong, them or us. It is difficult to see things any other way when the stream never pauses. This is not reason enough to abandon social software, by any means, but it brings an urgency to careful and ongoing reflection.

Digital Representations of Reality Are Not Real

Human interaction is increasingly mediated by digital technologies. Yet while digital systems represent experience as strings of discrete events, humans experience the world as continuous and rooted in time (Lanier, 2010b). "Our computers live in the ticks of the clock. We live in the big spaces between those ticks, when the time actually passes" (Rushkoff, 2010: 34). In order to make these mediated interactions easier, people often pretend that digital representation and reality are interchangeable. One example of this pretending is the anthropomorphizing of machines. Turkle (2011) describes the many ways in which people attribute human characteristics to robots (especially robotic toys). IBM's chess-playing and Jeopardy-playing computers, Deep Blue and Watson, were built for the purpose of advancing AI research (and probably for raising IBM's profile), but inevitably are presented to the public in ways that make them seem sentient. People often talk of a computer system's processing and data storage in terms of what the system "thinks" and what it "knows." Computers may think and know someday, but not yet.

Pretending that the digital representation of experience and experience itself are functionally equivalent is convenient, but it requires a reduction. Such a reduction is useful for the purpose of making models to test; but when people are careless, the model can be substituted for the real thing. Some users of a social networking site like Facebook or a microblogging service like Twitter, for example, may begin to define their identities through fragmentary status updates or tweets; effectively shifting the emphasis of their existence to the ticks of the clock rather than the spaces between.[4]

This is not solely a technology issue, then, but also a relationship issue. However, the effect of software design on the relationships that develop through and around the software is so significant that it simply cannot be ignored. While social software tools do indeed put the world's information within reach, the continuous barrage of fragments can make it extremely difficult for users to direct their thoughts and actions in the service of their chosen purposes; in other words, there is a danger of losing one's intentionality.

INTENTIONALITY

In the study of philosophy, *intentionality* is a technical term and a source of much debate—particularly in the context of the work of John Searle (1983) and the many responses to it in the intervening years (see also Lepore & Van Gulick, 1991; Lyons, 1995). I am not using the word in that technical sense here. Rather, I am using it in a more commonplace sense—to mean something like purposefulness or mindfulness, though those are not quite right, either. Intentionality might be conceived in relation to delayed gratification—that is, as a child grows up he or she must learn to make choices in the present for the future benefit of some chosen purpose. Intentionality is more than this, however, because it also involves the ongoing choosing of those purposes (something that necessitates a certain degree of self-reflection). Furthermore, there is a feedback loop in the sense that one's choices can affect one's purposes, just as one's purposes affect one's choices. Persistent connection and fragmentation mean that each person receives more information, but that information is incomplete, and there is little time to step back and assess choices reflexively. Intentionality can start to slip.

A Conflation of Artificial and Collective Intelligences

One of the most unusual ideas that technology thinkers have embraced in recent years lies at the intersection of collective intelligence and evolution. Having largely abandoned the dream of strong AI[5]—a self-contained machine entity with superhuman intelligence—many have looked to networked collectives (what Lanier calls "computer-plus-crowd constructions," 2010b: 34) instead, so that the concepts of machine intelligence and collective intelligence become largely inseparable. Just as biological organisms evolved into increasingly complex forms, the concept of evolution is extended such that a metaorganism comprised of networked computers and people represents the next step in the evolution of life (Kelly, 2010). Just as the human mind somehow arises from the brain, the noosphere (the sphere of human thought) is believed to be a "brain" from which a superhuman mind will arise. Opinions vary as to what this might mean for individual autonomy.

Kelly (2010) argues that such a mutualism will serve to increase human autonomy, and that the primary benefit humans reap from technology is choice—that quality of life increases as choice increases. According to Rushkoff (2010), digital technologies are biased toward discrete options and away from nuance, contradiction, and compromise. This leads to a problem: choice for the sake of choice does not necessarily increase quality of life, and may, in fact, do the opposite. In March 2011, *Newsweek* science reporter Sharon Begley brought a cover story to the mainstream press on information overload and decision making. She describes the work of a group of neuroscientists and information systems experts studying cognitive overload. When the volume of information becomes overwhelming, the researchers found, the part of the brain primarily responsible for decision making—the dorsolateral prefrontal cortex—essentially shuts down (Dimoka, Adomavicius,

Gupta, & Pavlou, as cited in Begley, 2011). In other words, making an informed decision benefits from more information—but only up to a certain point; then decision-making ability actually gets worse. Digital technologies are biased toward discrete options, and yet there seems to be a point at which increasing options results in information overload and ceases to be useful. Perhaps the quality of life increases with choice, as Kelly argues, but to what extent is this subject to a law of diminishing returns? In a posthuman world, some will advocate turning complex decision making over to machines as a potential solution; people already use digital storage extensively as an aid to memory, so why not digital decision making? Others will find this idea horrifying.

This is complicated further when the machine brain is the noosphere, and people are the neurons. What does it mean to be a worker bee in the metaorganism of collective intelligence? Does being part of something superhuman eventually require becoming a drone with little or no first-person experience? This seems far-fetched to me, but "what do you do when the techies are crazier than the Luddites?" (Lanier, 2010b: 24). In William Gibson's novel *Neuromancer* (1984)—the novel that first popularized the concept of cyberspace—there is a scene in which one of the antagonists, 3Jane, explains her late mother Marie-France's philosophy:

"She dreamed of a state involving very little in the way of consciousness," 3Jane was saying ... "Animal bliss. I think she viewed the evolution of the forebrain as a sort of sidestep." ... "Only in certain heightened modes would an individual—a clan member—suffer the more painful aspects of self-awareness." (Gibson, 1984: 217)

Marie-France viewed symbiosis with AI technology as a means to escape the burden of consciousness while also achieving a kind of immortality. In the novel, however, her plans have not come to pass, and instead the family has turned inward in a way that is isolated from the world, morally bankrupt, and utterly devoid of purpose. Is either one of Gibson's scenarios possible in the future? Hopefully not, but many people seem to share the antihumanistic view that Gibson glimpsed almost 30 years ago.

Furthermore, thinking about technology as being alive, especially in the context of network-enabled collective intelligence, easily fosters a worldview that makes information seem more important than people—information becomes, for some, the very stuff from which the universe was made. Every phenomenon becomes reducible to an informational transaction of one kind or another. In the context of social software, however, the concept of "pure information" is absurd; if an information tree falls in the social software forest, and no one is around to hear it, does it make a sound? No. Avoiding this antihumanistic conception of collective intelligence in social software is imperative (Lanier, 2010b; Rushkoff, 2010; Siegel, 2008).

Human-Centered Technology Design

Data are phenomenally useful. The scientific method is perhaps the single most useful thing humans have conceived to understand the world. It is, however, a process and not a religion. The idea that scientists pursue "truth" while scholars in other fields pursue "a perspective" is stupid. Everyone pursues truth, and everyone instead finds a perspective. In a technology-obsessed culture, people have begun to fetishize quantitative data at the expense of more qualitative measures—and indeed anything that proves difficult to measure objectively. The pendulum has swung too far. The crisis of the humanities today is nothing less than a call for those working in the humanities to justify the existence of their fields.

Indeed, technology creates the future. But it is not enough to create the future. We also need to organize it, as the social sciences enable us to do. We need to make sense of it, as the humani-

ties enable us to do. (Deresiewicz, 2011: section 4, para. 7)

A strictly utilitarian view of the pursuit of knowledge is no more useful than the antiscience view displayed by some religious fundamentalists. (Paulson, 2011, compares the faith-science tensions keenly felt by some Muslims and Christians.) A balance is needed between what can and cannot be measured, and this is as true in computer science and other technology fields as anywhere. This balance is a core part of what makes people human.

Casting technological development in economic and biological terms skirts issues of morals and ethics almost entirely (Morozov, 2011). If market forces and evolutionary processes make the world the way it is, and if the harm is outweighed by the good (Kelly, 2010), then there is little cause for concern. Admittedly, in a pluralistic society it can be difficult to address moral and ethical issues directly without wading into the murky waters of religion. Ironically, viewing technology as a living force that lifts human society ever out of the darkness resembles a religion in many respects (Lanier, 2010b), albeit an amoral religion. People are to place their trust and hope for salvation not in the supernatural or in humanity, but in technology.

Is there a more human-centered way to approach technology—and social software in particular, since it is the defining technology of the time? There have always been people working in computer science fields whose focus has remained on the human users of computers—for example, Douglas Englebart, Ted Nelson, Alan Kay, and Jaron Lanier. Networked technologies, and most especially social software, have become so central to daily life—and their influence so great on the habits of the mind—that the responsibility for constantly questioning and critiquing these technologies must now rest on each user. Yet the educational system, focused as it is only on those quantities that can be easily measured (test scores, grades, certifications, etc.) and despite having eyes for the ways in which people might use technology, is blind to the ways they might be used by technology. Educators must prepare students to ask the hard questions.

New technologies change people, and that has always been true. When it begins to happen, there are always those who decry it. That is not what I am doing here. Rather, I am urging that users not allow themselves to be changed *unknowingly* by new social software technologies, and that designs for such technologies be based on principles that value the human beings over the bits. "There is absolutely no inevitability as long as there is a willingness to contemplate what is happening" (McLuhan & Fiore, 1967/2005: 25).

Valuing Curricula over Courses in Higher Education

A discussion of intentionality in the context of connection and fragmentation would be incomplete without some mention of curricula in higher education. I have described ways in which connection and fragmentation may undermine intentionality, and this also affects the way that students conceive of a curriculum. While flexibility and mobility have increased in many higher education programs in largely positive ways, it seems to me that a side effect of these developments has been a shift of emphasis from the curriculum to the course. While there probably has always been such a thing as a transfer student in higher education, it is now possible for students to pursue a buffet-style higher education without ever really having an alma mater. I am neither interested in being sentimental about this, nor ignorant of the fact that this arrangement increases access for many kinds of students; rather, my concern is that higher education becomes simply about taking the correct number of courses. This promotes credentialism and decreases intentionality. (The Spellings Commission seemed especially blind to this problem; see The Secretary of Education's Commission on the Future of Higher Education, 2006.) "Curriculum" means "race course" after all, which is

supposed to evoke a sense of unity and direction. When each course is seen as a self-contained unit, practically hermetically sealed and effectively interchangeable, then courses become nothing more than the currency with which students buy a diploma. If education is merely a commodity, then it likely serves no purpose beyond landing a particular job. The long-term aims of education at a societal level evaporate. No wonder the humanities are getting squeezed.

EXPERTISE, RE-IMAGINED

The broader themes of connection, fragmentation, and intentionality form a context for the changing nature of expertise, and a changing conception of the ways in which knowledge might be created and disseminated. The traditional conception of expertise, embodied in the archetype of the scholar, is undoubtedly weakening as the age of machine intelligence, collective intelligence, and crowdsourcing begins.

The Gatekeepers Meet the Gatecrashers

One of the traditional roles of the expert has been that of gatekeeper. It is no longer necessary to go through an expert to get information about a topic. Information is not the same thing as knowledge, however, and the knowledge of crowds does not directly replace the knowledge of experts any more than television directly replaced radio or email directly replaced the postal service. These relationships are always more complex, and oversimplifying them is a mistake. Conceiving a direct shift in the locus of expertise from the individual to the collective would be just such an oversimplification.

It is also important to remember the fundamental ways in which individuals and collectives are different. An individual expert has a unique voice and, one hopes, a coherent point of view on the topic of their expertise. This coherence comes from digesting and reflecting on information and placing it in context—and participating in a meaningful, ongoing scholarly conversation. In contrast, there is no reason to assume that a collective functions with a single voice or a coherent view of the world. Possessing the relevant data is necessary but seldom sufficient (although Anderson, 2008, strongly disagrees on this point, as I will describe later). Examining the work and views of a small number of individual experts on a topic—*especially* if they disagree—is likely in many cases to be much more useful than looking only at the results of a collective effort on the same topic. In the latter case, much of the voice, nuance, and context often blurs or disappears in the process. That is the nature of building consensus. It is important to think about when consensus is the most important criterion, versus when nuance is truly needed. Sometimes groups make the best decisions, but sometimes they do not. This is why the phrase "design by committee" remains pejorative, even in the age of crowdsourcing and open source software.

It remains undeniable, nevertheless, that the concept of expertise *is* shifting, and educators must think carefully about what expertise will mean for the future of higher education. In this context, then, the role of the "traditional" expert is less about information and more about synthesis. The expert's viewpoint—based on a deep familiarity with the relevant facts and with all the attendant context and nuance—remains highly valuable, even as the expert no longer controls the gate that grants access to that information. A person searching for a single obscure fact may very well have no need for an expert. However, complex decisions do not often turn on a single obscure fact. The wisdom of crowds is not a new phenomenon by any means, but social software's remarkable benefit is that it allows this resource to be tapped so readily. The trick lies in knowing when and how to tap it—something society is still working out.

Antihumanistic Reimaginings of Expertise

Several ideas about the changing nature of expertise have arisen from the antihumanistic view of technology I described earlier, and which other authors have described at length and from other perspectives (Lanier, 2010b; Rushkoff, 2010; Siegel, 2008; Turkle, 2011). Lanier cites two of the best examples I have encountered, including the idea that individual authors are obsolete. The Internet enables all of the world's books to become one book, and one book that contains everything is far superior to millions of books that contain a few things. Fragmentation and decontextualization, along with the divorce of content from its authors, are seen as a trivial price to pay for such a resource. How trivial is it? The question of whether sought-after information appears on a screen or a physical page is mostly irrelevant; the question of who wrote it (and in what context it appears) is critical. There is no reason why the reader must trade one question for the other, unless the design of the search tool requires such a trade. Google Books, for example, maintains the separateness of each book and author (but returns fragmentary results because the texts are copyrighted). This could easily change if such distinctions are no longer deemed economically valuable (or if publishers lose their remaining leverage against Google).

Another example that arises from this same antihumanistic view focuses on the processing power of machines rather than the collective. The idea is that laboratory scientists should abandon testable hypotheses, because the world is so full of data that correlation is now sufficient and causation unimportant. "View data mathematically first and establish a context for it later" (Anderson, 2008: para. 5; see also Lanier, 2010b). Theoretical models are counterproductive in this view; questions of "why" are irrelevant; the only question worth asking is "what." Disciplinary methodologies are summarily replaced with algorithms, and intentionality is abandoned as obsolete. The idea that technology knows better than people do is implicit in Anderson's argument, as is the notion that rejecting this view is either sentimental or whiny. The machine knows best, because only data matter—and only the machine can parse the data.

A Third Way

The expert must change as the world changes. While the ideal of the scholar as the individual embodiment of expertise is weakening, and the conception of expertise that resides in a collective is on the rise, I argue a case for a new kind of scholar in higher education—one that does not replace, but instead complements, the traditional scholar. The traditional scholar spends a lifetime deepening his or her knowledge in a very specific field. The new kind of scholar develops deep knowledge but is ever branching out as well; searching out connections across the work of many "experts" of both the individual and collective varieties. This kind of scholar possesses an expertise that is rooted in deep knowledge, but flowers in its breadth. This kind of scholar cares deeply—and broadly—about the big picture.

This conception of what it means to be an expert already exists, of course. There are already such people "in the field," and they make the colleges and universities in which they work better in ways that stretch well beyond the walls of their own classrooms and offices—and campuses. Such people also fill myriad other roles in business, government, the professions, the arts, and just about everywhere else. These people are called "liberally educated persons." The ideal of liberal education is not to produce a generalist so much as it is to produce a different kind of specialist. Liberal education strives to produce graduates who possess both a broad, well-rounded education and a depth of knowledge in at least one specific field (Association of American Colleges and Universities, 2002). Armed with this dual perspective, the liberally educated person is poised to provide a

different and much-needed kind of expertise: one that engages meaningful connections productively, mitigates the downsides of fragmentation, and preserves a human-centered intentionality. This is a tall order, but I see reason to be optimistic.[6]

EDUCAUSE is a broad organization whose members come from all types of higher-education institutions, and no one is likely to accuse it of being overly sensitive to the liberal arts philosophy. Still, a recent article in *EDUCAUSE Review* seems to be making the case for liberal education quite accidentally:

We believe that in the future, it will be less important to have skills in or experience with particular technologies and more important to be able to evolve with technology to contribute in a meaningful way… The focus will no longer be on the technology, in itself. The focus will be on the relationship between the evolving technology and the user. (Tamarkin & The EDUCAUSE Evolving Technologies Committee, 2010: 43)

To my mind, this encapsulates the mission of a 21st-century liberal education as it relates to technology. I hope that liberal arts institutions and programs will take on the challenge of human-machine relationships as a core part of what they do in preparing the next generation for a life that will be largely defined by the answer to this challenge. The liberal arts are not going to save the world, but they can guide things in the right direction.

CONCLUSION

Perhaps, then, there are three different models for expertise that can coexist in the age of social software: *the traditional expert:* possessing a depth of knowledge and privileged with the time and capacity for reflection; *the collective:* possessing the ability to tap collective knowledge quickly and achieve broad consensus; *and the new expert:*

possessing an ever-branching nature coupled with the ability to step back and look at the big picture with a critical eye, guiding collective efforts to increase and disseminate knowledge in ways that continue to value people over bits.

Technology is about people. It extends the individual and connects each person to the larger world in profound ways. Social software has increased the potential for the latter by many orders of magnitude, but users must take care that no corresponding decrease occurs in the former. While Web 2.0 designs have tended toward increasing numbers of connections and greater fragmentation, the resulting threat to intentionality can and must be resisted. As the nature of expertise shifts, human-centric practices will help ensure that people are not changed in unintended ways by the more tightly integrated relationship with technology now developing. The traditional notion of the scholar can coexist with collective intelligence, and be balanced by a new conception of expertise that not only digs down but also branches out. Expertise can play out in multiple, mutually reinforcing ways.

The central role that social software, and technology writ large, will play going forward is clear. My hope is that the role of the humanities, in balance with science and technology, is also apparent. Achieving some sort of healthy balance in this regard is not easy, and requires a large number of people engaging with the big questions about what it means to be human in the age of social software. As new tools for creating and disseminating knowledge develop, they do not directly replace the old ones. Instead, they change the context of human endeavors. Balancing the objectivity of data with the murkier values that also define what it is to be human—the quantifiable with the unquantifiable—is one of the great tasks that contemporary society must undertake. Of achieving this balance, Lanier wrote, "The trick is being ambidextrous, holding one hand to the heart while counting on the digits of the

other" (2010a: MM32). If social software is indeed redefining what it means to be human, I hope that humanity goes forward with its head up and eyes open; becoming different by becoming what it wishes to be, and not by some accident or because of a misguided view of the relationship between people and technology.

REFERENCES

Anderson, C. (2008, June 23). The end of theory: The data deluge makes the scientific method obsolete. *Wired*. Retrieved June 25, 2011, from http://www.wired.com/science/discoveries/magazine/16-07/pb_theory

Association of American Colleges and Universities. (2002). *Greater expectations: A new vision for learning as a nation goes to college*. Washington, DC: Author. Retrieved July 2, 2007, from http://www.greaterexpectations.org

Badke, W. (2008, January). If everything is miscellaneous. *Online, 32*(1), 48–50.

Baum, E. B. (2004). *What is thought?* Cambridge, MA: The MIT Press.

Begley, S. (2011, March 7). I can't think! *Newsweek, 157*(10), 28-33.

Bellow, S. (2001). *Ravelstein*. New York, NY: Penguin.

Bukatman, S. (1993). *Terminal identity: The virtual subject in postmodern science fiction*. Durham, NC: Duke University Press.

Cluley, G. (2011, June 7). Facebook changes privacy settings for millions of users: Facial recognition is enabled. *Naked Security*. Retrieved June 25, 2011, from http://nakedsecurity.sophos.com/2011/06/07/facebook-privacy-settings-facial-recognition-enabled

Deresiewicz, W. (2011, May 23). Faulty towers: The crisis in higher education. *The Nation*. Retrieved June 24, 2011, from http://www.thenation.com/article/160410/faulty-towers-crisis-higher-education

Facebook. (2011). *Statistics|Facebook*. Retrieved June 11, 2011, from http://www.facebook.com/press/info.php?statistics

Gibson, W. (1984). *Neuromancer*. New York, NY: Ace Books.

Haraway, D. J. (1991). *Simians, cyborgs, and women: The reinvention of nature*. New York, NY: Routledge.

Hayles, N. K. (1999). *How we became posthuman: Virtual bodies in cybernetics, literature, and informatics*. Chicago, IL: The University of Chicago Press.

Keller, J. (2011, January 23). Colleges search for their place in the booming mobile web. *The Chronicle of Higher Education*. Retrieved June 26, 2011, from http://chronicle.com/article/colleges-search-for-their/126016

Kelly, K. (2010). *What technology wants*. New York, NY: Viking.

Lanier, J. (2010a, September 15). Does the digital classroom enfeeble the mind? *The New York Times*, p. MM32.

Lanier, J. (2010b). *You are not a gadget: A manifesto*. New York, NY: Alfred A. Knopf.

Lepore, E., & Van Gulick, R. (Eds.). (1991). *John Searle and his critics*. Oxford, UK: Blackwell.

Lipka, S. (2009, May 1). Colleges using technology to recruit students try to hang on to the conversation. *The Chronicle of Higher Education*. Retrieved June 1, 2011, from http://chronicle.com/article/colleges-using-technology-to/117193

Lyons, W. (1995). *Approaches to intentionality*. Oxford, UK: Clarendon Press.

McLuhan, M., & Fiore, Q. (2005). *The medium is the massage*. Berkeley, CA: Gingko Press. (Original work published 1967)

Morozov, E. (2011, March 24). E-salvation. *New Republic (New York, N.Y.)*, *242*(4), 28–31.

Nelson, T. (1987). *Computer lib/Dream machines* (Rev. ed.). Redmond, WA: Tempus Books of Microsoft Press. (Original work published 1974)

New Media Consortium & EDUCAUSE Learning Initiative. (2007). *The horizon report: 2007 edition*. Austin, TX: The New Media Consortium.

New Media Consortium & EDUCAUSE Learning Initiative. (2008). *The horizon report: 2008 edition*. Austin, TX: The New Media Consortium.

Pariser, E. (2011). *The filter bubble: What the Internet is hiding from you*. New York, NY: Penguin.

Paulson, S. (2011, June 19). Does Islam stand against science? *The Chronicle of Higher Education*. Retrieved June 27, 2011, from http://chronicle.com/article/does-Islam-stand-against/127924

Qderth. (2011, June 10). *Rebecca Black: Friday* (official video). Retrieved June 27, 2011, from http://www.youtube.com/watch?v=9u9-AdPAOy0

Rushkoff, D. (2010). *Program or be programmed: Ten commands for a digital age*. New York, NY: OR Books.

Searle, J. (1983). *Intentionality: An essay in the philosophy of mind*. Cambridge, UK: Cambridge University Press. doi:10.1017/CBO9781139173452

Secretary of Education's Commission on the Future of Higher Education. (2006). *A test of leadership: Charting the future of U.S. higher education*. Washington, DC: U.S. Department of Education, Education Publications Center.

Shirky, C. (2008). *Here comes everybody: The power of organizing without organizations.* New York, NY: Penguin.

Siegel, L. (2008). *Against the machine: Being human in the age of the electronic mob.* New York, NY: Spiegel and Grau.

Tamarkin, M. & The 2010 EDUCAUSE Evolving Technologies Committee. (2010, November). December). You 3.0: The most important evolving technology. *EDUCAUSE Review, 45*(6), 30–44.

Tierney, J. (2011, April 26). A generation's vanity, heard through lyrics. *The New York Times,* p. D1.

Turing, A. M. (1950). Computing machinery and intelligence. *Mind, 59*(236), 433–460. doi:10.1093/mind/LIX.236.433

Turkle, S. (1984). *The second self: Computers and the human spirit.* New York, NY: Simon and Schuster. doi:10.1177/089443938600400229

Turkle, S. (2011). *Alone together: Why we expect more from technology and less from each other.* New York, NY: Basic Books.

Twitter. (2011). *Twitter is the best way to discover what's new in your world.* Retrieved June 23, 2011, from http://www.twitter.com/about

von Schiller, J. C. F. (2004). *On the aesthetical education of man* (R. Snell, Trans.). New York, NY: Dover. (Republication of Schiller, F. (1954). *On the aesthetical education of man* (R. Snell, Trans.). New Haven: Yale University Press. (Original work published in 1794-1795)

Weinberger, D. (2007). *Everything is miscellaneous: The power of the new digital disorder.* New York, NY: Times Books.

Weiner, R. (2011, June 6). Fight brews over Sarah Palin on Paul Revere Wikipedia page. *The Washington Post.* Retrieved June 27, 2011, from http://www.washingtonpost.com/blogs/the-fix/post/sarah-palin-fans-fight-over-paul-revere-wikipedia-page/2011/06/06/AGxtzHKH_blog.html

ADDITIONAL READING

Alexander, B. (2011, April). This visible college. *EDUCAUSE Quarterly, 34*(2). Retrieved June 27, 2011, from http://www.educause.edu/EDUCAUSE+Quarterly/EDUCAUSEQuarterlyMagazineVolum/ThisVisibleCollege/230536

Bolter, J. D., & Grusin, R. (1999). *Remediation: Understanding new media.* Cambridge, MA: The MIT Press.

Boyer, E. L. (1990). *Scholarship reconsidered: Priorities of the professorate.* San Francisco, CA: The Carnegie Foundation for the Advancement of Teaching.

Brooks, D. (2011, March 8). The new humanism. *The New York Times,* p. A27.

Brooks, D. (2011). *The social animal.* New York, NY: Random House.

Copeland, B. J. (Ed.). (2004). *The essential Turing: Seminal writings in computing, logic, philosophy, artificial intelligence, and artificial life, plus the secrets of Enigma.* New York, NY: Oxford University Press.

Englebart, D. (2003). Augmenting human intellect: A conceptual framework. In Wardrip-Fruin, N., & Montfort, N. (Eds.), *The new media reader* (pp. 95–108). Cambridge, MA: The MIT Press. (Original work published 1962)

Gerson, M. (2007, October 5). With friends like these. *The Washington Post,* p. A21.

Gleick, J. (2011). *The information: A history, a theory, a flood.* New York, NY: Pantheon. doi:10.1109/TIT.2011.2162990

Hansen, M. B. N. (2004). *New philosophy for new media.* Cambridge, MA: The MIT Press.

Healey, S. (2006, September). Adventus internetus and the anaerobic soul. *Academic Commons.* Retrieved March 9, 2011, from http://www.academiccommons.org/commons/essay/Healey-adventus-internetus

Kaplan, D. M. (Ed.). (2004). *Readings in the philosophy of technology.* Lanham, MD: Rowman & Littlefield.

Kay, A., & Goldberg, A. (2003). Personal dynamic media. In Wardrip-Fruin, N., & Montfort, N. (Eds.), *The new media reader* (pp. 391–403). Cambridge, MA: The MIT Press. (Original work published 1977)

Kurzweil, R. (1999). *The age of spiritual machines: When computers exceed human intelligence.* New York, NY: Viking.

Kurzweil, R. (2006). *The singularity is near: When humans transcend biology.* New York, NY: Penguin.

Manovich, L. (2001). *The language of new media.* Cambridge, MA: The MIT Press.

McLuhan, M. (1994). *Understanding media: The extensions of man (Thirtieth anniversary edition).* Cambridge, MA: The MIT Press. (Original work published 1964)

Nye, D. E. (2006). *Technology matters: Questions to live with.* Cambridge, MA: The MIT Press.

Olsen, J. B., & Selinger, E. (Eds.). (2007). *Philosophy of technology: Five questions.* Automatic Press/VIP.

Postman, N. (1985). *Amusing ourselves to death: Public discourse in the age of show business.* New York, NY: Penguin.

Postman, N. (1992). *Technopoly: The surrender of culture to technology.* New York, NY: Knopf.

Rheingold, H. (2002). *Smart mobs: The next social revolution.* Cambridge, MA: Perseus.

Shirky, C. (2010). *Cognitive surplus: Creativity and generosity in a connected age.* New York, NY: Penguin.

Slayton, J. (2002). Collaboration as media. *Leonardo, 35*(3), 231–232. doi:10.1162/002409402760105172

Strate, L. (2008). Studying media as media: McLuhan and the media ecology approach. *MediaTropes, 1,* 127–142.

Weinberger, D. (2002). *Small pieces loosely joined: A unified theory of the web.* Cambridge, MA: Perseus.

Weng, J. (2006). Computational thinking. *Communications of the ACM, 49*(3), 33–35. doi:10.1145/1118178.1118215

Weng, J. (2010, January). *Computational thinking.* Paper presented at the Annual Meeting of the EDUCAUSE Learning Initiative, Austin, TX.

Williams, P. J. (2007). Valid knowledge: The economy and the academy. *Higher Education, 54,* 511–523. doi:10.1007/s10734-007-9051-y

KEY TERMS AND DEFINITIONS

Anthropomorphism: Attribution of human characteristics to an animal, object, or machine.

Disembodiment: The concept that content can exist apart from form. This concept is implicit in the way that many authors define information, and pivotal in discussions of posthumanism.

Epistemological: Relating to the nature of and/or sources of knowledge.

Metaorganism: A group of organisms that collectively display the behavior of a complex, living system. The metaorganism exhibits behaviors that are not observed on the level of the individual organisms.

Noosphere: Conceptual entity in which the machines connected to the Internet and their human users become the components of a larger mind.

Posthuman: Condition in which the distinctions between human intelligence and machine intelligence are no longer clear. This is a contested term, but for the purposes of this chapter the view of the posthuman condition expounded by N. Katherine Hayles is used (see Hayles, 1999).

Strong AI: An artificial intelligence possessing a self-contained personality and will; a machine that is "alive"; see also Turing Test.

Technium: The term coined by Kevin Kelly to encompass all products of the mind that function within the vast, interconnected scope of technology. This includes everything from electronics hardware and tools to software, laws, and medicine.

Turing Test: Famous thought experiment posed by Alan Turing in 1950. In this scenario, the subject interacts with two entities via computer terminals, and must determine which entity is a person and which is a machine. If a machine can "trick" the subject into thinking it is a person, is the machine alive?

ENDNOTES

[1] The comment threads on YouTube can be particularly mean-spirited; a great example being the comments on the music video for the song "Friday" by Rebecca Black. After hundreds of millions of views and thousands of disparaging comments, the video was taken down. A copy of the video has been reposted by another YouTube user, and the vitriol continues (see Qderth, 2011).

[2] Editing and re-editing of Wikipedia entries can sometimes be fierce and even petty. In June 2011, after Sarah Palin made erroneous statements about Paul Revere's historic ride, Palin supporters began editing the Wikipedia entry on Revere to include an account of events that matched Palin's misstatements. Other Wikipedia users deleted the changes as quickly as they appeared, and Wikipedia was forced to lock the entry (see Weiner, 2011). A phenomenon like this makes Wikipedia resemble Orwell's Ministry of Truth in a bizarre way.

[3] Bukatman (1993) makes the intriguing claim that cyborg characters in postmodern science fiction retain their subjectivity only because of their continued connection to the flesh. Translation to a fully electronic existence changes the subject into an object.

[4] PostSecret is a blog to which viewers mail anonymous postcards conveying a secret, and images of selected cards appear on the site. In February 2011, an image of a card appeared on the site that depicted the Twitter interface. In the space for composing a tweet, the card's maker typed, "I think I'm starting to constantly think in 140 characters." The cards change each week, but the site does not maintain a public archive. A copy of the image is available from the author.

[5] The dream of strong AI is certainly not dead among AI researchers, and computationalism as a theory of mind continues to hold enormous sway. This view of the world is beautifully explicated in Baum (2004).

[6] This will necessitate that the tenure and promotion process (or what is left of it) adjust more quickly to accommodate forms of scholarly work that are generous in scope and diverse in form. Books, journal articles, and grants are not the only products of contemporary scholarship, and yet they are still often the only ones that "count."

Section 2
Changing Expert Environments in the University and in the Areas of Research and Scholarship

Chapter 5
Should we Take Disintermediation in Higher Education Seriously?
Expertise, Knowledge Brokering, and Knowledge Translation in the Age of Disintermediation

Carlos A. Scolari
Universitat Pompeu Fabra, Spain

Cristóbal Cobo Romaní
Oxford Internet Institute, UK

Hugo Pardo Kuklinski
Universitat de Barcelona, Spain

ABSTRACT

Disintermediation based on digital technology has transformed different environments, including banking, commerce, media, education, and knowledge management. The spread of social software applications and digital media in general has given rise to new models of knowledge production and distribution in higher education. This chapter redefines higher education institutions and academic experts based on these changes. The chapter discusses the diffusion of disintermediation practices in higher education and proposes new categories, such as knowledge brokering, knowledge networking, and knowledge translation, to map a new environment that promotes disintermediation, innovation, and openness. Beyond the prophecies announcing the "death of the university," the authors suggest new agents, actions, and transactions that are useful for envisaging the higher education institutions of the new century.

DOI: 10.4018/978-1-4666-2178-7.ch005

INTRODUCTION

The spread of digital technology and the emergence of a network society (Castells, 1996) have changed the role of the institutions that have traditionally been considered the unique providers of "legitimate" knowledge. The diffusion of the World Wide Web has greatly expanded the generation of new models of knowledge production and distribution. Two of the main dimensions that have affected the transformations of knowledge can be labeled as new models of:

1. **Knowledge Production:** E-science, online education, distributed R&D, open innovation, peer-based production, online encyclopedias, user-generated contents, etc.
2. **Knowledge Distribution:** Digital print on demand, e-journals, open repositories, Creative Commons licenses, academic podcasting initiatives, etc.

These new means of knowledge production and distribution are challenging the traditional intermediated academic practices and even the role of those considered to be the "experts" in education (professors, researchers, and education managers). As Jarvis (2009, p. 215) states, "if students could take courses from anywhere, a marketplace of instruction would emerge that should lead the best to rise: the aggregated university."

In this context it is important to analyze the appearance of *disintermediation* practices in higher education. Disintermediation is essentially "cutting out the middleman" in the production/distribution/consumption chain. Traditional professions like real estate agents, publishers, and journalists, as well as service providers in areas like travel agencies and video rental, have already faced this dilemma. Now the role of education experts (teachers, professors, researchers, education managers, etc.) is being directly affected by disintermediation. It is not important whether we consider "expertise" to be a characteristic of individuals or a socially constructed institutional process. At first glance, disintermediation seems to make highly specialized professionals obsolete. Those who once held the position of renowned expert are currently witnessing a change in their hierarchy; now they need to flatter, reshape, or share their privileges with other agents or entities.

In this chapter we explore questions such as:

*   Is it possible to imagine a radical disintermediation of educational processes—that is, the disappearance of mediating higher education institutions?
*   How is the redefinition of *knowledge production* and *knowledge distribution* affecting the role of higher education institutions and experts?
*   Will the rapid evolution of digital technologies lead to a crisis for Higher Education institutions? How have the roles of the formal education actors (educators, students, researchers, managers, etc.) been modified?
*   How can new categories such as *knowledge brokering* or *knowledge translation* help us to map a new territory full of proposals that promote disintermediation, innovation, and openness in higher education?

The issues raised in this chapter are taken from the experience of Western universities, particularly the "Latin" and "Anglo-Saxon" institutional models. There are significant differences between these two models in terms of hierarchy, tradition, funding sources, methodology, and level of internationalization; however, it is interesting to observe that the disintermediation phenomenon is observed in both of them. Rather than exploring the differences or similarities between these kinds of universities, the aim of this work is to explore and better understand how disintermediation is reshaping the role of the agents and mechanisms that support higher education in the 21st century.

THE DEATH AND RESURRECTION OF A CAR SALESMAN: DISINTERMEDIATION IN A BROADER SOCIAL CONTEXT

Disintermediation

The main objective of disintermediation is to decrease the final cost of the product and speed up the whole economic process. According to Tucker (2010), disintermediation is a process in which a "middle player poised between service or product providers and their consumers is weakened or removed from the value chain"; the resources removed from the chain are recuperated in order to provide the consumer with a lower cost and/or better value from the provider (Tucker, 2010). By bypassing the middlemen like wholesalers, retailers, brokers, agents, etc., the consumer can establish a direct relationship with manufacturers and increase the transparency of the system.

Although the term was introduced in the 1960s in the banking industry, the concept of disintermediation only became prevalent in the 1990s with the expansion of the World Wide Web. At that time the candidates to be disintermediated were real estate agents; the recorded music, car, computer, book, and video rental industries; and the construction trade sector, hotel reservation sector, and capital markets. In 1995 the *Journal of Computer-Mediated Communication* published a special issue called *Electronic Commerce*. At that time the potential of the Web as a distribution channel and a medium for marketing communications was evident for most professionals. Considered as a distribution channel, the Web potentially offered providers the opportunity to participate in a market in which distribution costs or cost of sales shrank to zero, especially in certain sectors like publishing, information services, and digital product categories. Introducing the appropriate information technology allowed the manufacturer to leap over all intermediaries and so reduce the cost of the entire process (Benjamin & Wigand,

1995; Hoffman, Novak, & Chatterjee, 1995). One of the benefits for producers, Michalski (1995) notes, is that "digital products can be delivered immediately, hence such businesses may encounter massive disintermediation or even the eventual elimination of the middleman" (). According to Sarkar, Butler, and Steinfield (1995), reducing costs and internalizing activities are the main arguments for cutting out intermediaries. On the Web, buyers and sellers can find and contact each other directly, thus eliminating some of the marketing costs and constraints imposed on such interactions in the real world.

Disintermediation soon reached the popular cybercultural discourses (Scolari, 2008, 2009; Silver, 2000). In 1997 Nicholas Negroponte (1997) wrote in his classic column in *Wired* magazine that

The new story of disintermediation is an old bits-and-atoms classic. The complex process of "things" has created a food chain of middlemen and wholesalers who import, export, warehouse, and redistribute physical items. For this reason, when you buy tomatoes for US$1.57 per pound, the grower gets less than 35 cents, while the rest goes to all the people in the middle (in the case of tomatoes, up to seven intermediaries may be involved). If you could buy direct, it would be a no brainer to split the difference with the farmer, which would no doubt please the both of you.

Disintermediation and other concepts like *end-user empowerment, outsourcing,* and *reintermediation* (see below) became the buzzwords of the 1990s (Fourie, 1999). *End-user empowerment* refers to end users having both access to information and the necessary skills to retrieve their own information according to their own needs; in other words, they can do it on their own. With empowerment, users should be less dependent on information specialists. However, this does not necessarily mean that the information specialist as an intermediary will become obsolete: not all end users will have the time or the interest to make their own searches. Disintermediation was one of the basic (and utopian) components of the cybercultural discourse in the mid-1990s. Managers included disintermediation in their digital wish list, scholars transformed these processes into one of their favorite research objects, and journalists fed the discursive machine with utopian visions of a new economy without car salesmen.

Reintermediation and Cyberintermediation

Are intermediaries doomed to extinction? How can they survive in the new digital ecosystem? Negroponte (1997) recommended that, if threatened, the intermediary should "reintermediate by adding a new dimension of value. Typically, this is a service with some flavor of added personalization" (). As early as 1995, in the middle of the debate about disintermediation, some scholars warned about the limits of these processes. For example, Sarkar, Butler, and Steinfield (1995) disagreed that the radical restructuring of the manufacturer-consumer relationship would cause intermediaries to disappear. These researchers suggested that we should expand our view of the functions of intermediaries to include providing search and product evaluation services (quality control, consumer reports, etc.), helping customers determine their needs, reducing consumer uncertainty, improving product communication, informing consumers about the existence and characteristics of products, enhancing the packaging and distribution of goods, and influencing consumers' purchasing behavior as well as providing information about these consumers. Their analysis—based on the nature of consumer needs, particularly in a computer-mediated environment—suggests that both traditional and new types of intermediaries still have a role to play. They even introduce a new figure: the *cyberintermediator.*

In this new context the cyberintermediator was conceived as a new network-based intermediary that replaced former direct linkages. These new actors would apply technology to reduce the *producer-to-intermediary* or *intermediary-to-consumer* transaction costs. The existence of cyberintermediaries was considered consistent with traditional marketing theory, which views intermediaries as organizations that support exchanges between producers and consumers, increasing the efficiency of the exchange process by aggregating transactions to create economies of scale and scope. Cyberintermediaries were simply intermediaries that took advantage of the technology to create these economies of scale and scope. Distribution service firms such as Federal Express are a good example of how information technology started to make it economical to offer services that were historically provided by retail intermediaries.

In a scale economy, the digital technology allowed transaction services provided by intermediaries to be offered at a very low cost. The expansion of e-commerce also triggered a *reintermediation* process in the form of huge portals like Amazon and eBay. The traditional middleman was substituted by a buying-selling interface based on algorithms, databases, fulfillment of data centers around the world, and, last but not least, the information provided by millions of user interactions. In this context the original disintermediation proposal—based on the so called "killer-car salesman" idea—grew into a mixed clicks-and-bricks economy.

Disintermediation beyond Economy

The discussion about disintermediation went beyond the field of economy and emerged in the media and education environments. Schools and mass media should be considered the most important social reproduction devices of industrial societies. Traditionally the school has taught a combination of knowledge, ideology, and discipline (Althusser, 1970). In the second half of the 20th century the media system joined the school in providing social reproduction functions. Disintermediation is now challenging both the mass media and educational institutions.

In the media, the discussion about the possible disintermediation of information processes arrived with the spread of blogging and other social media at the beginning of the 21st century. The arrival of the collaborative Web (Cobo Romaní & Pardo Kuklinski, 2007; O'Reilly, 2005) and the expansion of social networking have raised new questions in the digital landscape (Pardo Kuklinski, 2010). If information is produced and distributed in collaborative environments, will information professionals end up like the car salesmen of the 1990s? Is there any future for professional journalists in the digital world of social networks? The debate about citizen journalism (Gant, 2007; Gilmour, 2004) is a remarkable example of this kind of discussion about disintermediation in the media field. According to Gilmour (2004), "tomorrow's news reporting and production will be more of a conversation, or a seminar. The lines will blur between producers and consumers, changing the role of both in ways we're only beginning to grasp now." In this context the communication network itself "will be a medium for everyone's voice, not just the few who can afford to buy multimillion-dollar printing presses" (p. xiii).

Shirky (2008) believes that the organizational forms perfected for industrial production have to be replaced with structures that are optimized for digital data. At this point we need to ask whether the educational institutions—an organizational form that, like journalism, was "designed" for the industrial mass society—have to be replaced with new structures and processes adapted to digital knowledge production and distribution. As early as 1996, researchers like Homan (1996) introduced the concept of disintermediation into the educational discourse. The questions were always the same: Will educational intermediaries be disintermediated? Will this enhance their role? How can the profession continue to add value in an age of information access for all? Is disintermediation just the latest buzzword and marketing hype of the Internet circuit or should education experts be concerned?

DISINTERMEDIATION IN HIGHER EDUCATION

The rapid development of information and communication technologies (ICTs) is facilitating unprecedented forms of production, distribution, and management of old and new knowledge. Over the last two decades we have witnessed a proliferation of information resources. Schools, books, and teachers are no longer the only and exclusive knowledge production/distribution sources. By providing access to an ever wider range of social and informational resources "new technologies are expanding our notion of where

'learning' happens across the physical-virtual map of a student's life at the same time that they are setting up new challenges for how to integrate across these highly distributed experiences" (Rhoten, Racine, & Wang, 2009, p. 1). Rhoten, Racine, and Wang's (2009) conception of learning in the 21st century is defined in Table 1.

Information and communication technologies facilitate all these processes, from exploring large databases to stimulating intellectual curiosity. Peer-based practices also find in ICT a powerful platform for promoting the expansion and exportation of knowledge to new audiences and contexts. Rhoten, Racine, and Wang considered that "there is a critical need to bridge non-formal learning by linking with classroom instruction through the use of technology and media" (2009, p. 3).

The practices of interest-driven, socially situated learning, like gaming, sports, or music, have long been part of the informal learning tradition; however, they have generally been differentiated from the classroom teaching practices in formal education establishments. In this context we can talk about *complementary* or *integrated* learning that mixes school and non-school activities in a new environment mediated by digital network technology (Cobo Romaní & Moravec, 2011).

Table 1. Learning in the 21st century

Self-directed	Learning is largely self-directed and the outcomes emerge through exploration and investigation.
Interest-driven	Learning can be motivated by personal avocation, professional vocation, social/political/cultural concern or cause, individual/identity development, or intellectual curiosity.
Peer-based	Young people can learn from "experts" at the same time that they teach, mentor, and coach less experienced "peers" (learning/teaching cycle).
Practice-focused	Learning is also about the integration of practice and the performance of real-world tasks that demonstrate their meaningful application.
Mastery-oriented	When a learner perceives that certain knowledge or skills are useful to the pursuit of or participation in an interest, he or she is drawn to master the knowledge or skills. The experience of having "mastered" skills in one arena creates the disposition of an expert and an understanding of knowledge structure that transfers to learning in other areas.

Source: Rhoten, Racine, & Wang (2009)

Knowledge Production and Distribution

The transformations, expressed as new practices and systems, in knowledge production and knowledge distribution are affecting the traditional role of higher education institutions. Benkler (2006) explains that a *radical decentralizati*on is shaping the current network society. According to Benkler, the radical decentralization of intelligence in our communications network and the centrality of information, knowledge, culture, and ideas in advanced economic activity are

leading to a new stage of the information economy—the networked information economy. In this new stage, we can harness many more of the diverse paths and mechanisms for cultural transmission that were muted by the economies of scale that led to the rise of the concentrated, controlled form of mass media, whether commercial or state-run. The most important aspect of the networked information economy is the possibility it opens for reversing the control focus of the industrial information economy. (2006, p. 32)

From an institutional perspective this radical decentralization is articulated by new agents, actions, and transactions. What is happening in higher education? Like the car salesman in the 1990s, the educational institutions are going

through a disintermediation process that affects their knowledge production and distribution circuits. These new educational attitudes and conceptions are addressed in Table 2.

From an ecological and holistic perspective we can say that universities are now being forced to change and adapt if they want to survive in the new knowledge economy. It is in this context that many researchers propose redefining higher education institutions and redesigning the skills and functions of experts (see Boyer, 1990; Cobo Romaní & Moravec, 2011; Gibbons et al., 1994; Johnston, 1998: Pardo Kuklinski, 2010).

The Expanded Role of the University

Boyer (1990) developed a model to explain the expanded role of the university in contemporary society. Although this theoretical model was elaborated before the expansion of the World Wide Web, it still contains valuable ideas for discussing the university's position of *knowledge broker* institution in a networked society. Boyer's model stated that the four key functions of the university are discovery, teaching, application, and integration of knowledge. Johnston (1998) summarizes Boyer's model as follows:

- *Teaching* is not simply a matter of transferring contents but rather a scholarship of transforming and extending knowledge by

Table 2. Traditional intermediated closed practices/New disintermediated open practices

Education	Traditional intermediated practices: Closed practices[1]	New disintermediated practices: Open practices[2]
Pedagogical conception	The student is an empty container to be filled by the knowledge supplied by the teacher (Freire's *banking conception*) (Freire, 1980). Content-based learning.	The student is a node of an educational network. Project-based learning. Problem solving–based learning.
	Learning by listening/copying.	Learning by doing/playing.
Communication	Monologue.	Polyphony.
Media (info source)	Monomedia (book, PowerPoint).	Transmedia (Wiki).
Space	Physical space: classroom, library, school labs, special learning rooms, etc.	Cyberspace: virtual classrooms, Skype, Elluminate and other videoconference systems, social networks, Second Life, satellite television channels, etc. Blended learning: combination of face-to-face and technology-mediated instruction. Disruptive spaces. Mixing playful experiences with academic activities. Any place is good to teach and learn.
Textual production	Mostly written.	Multimedia.
Knowledge production/ consumption	The teacher is an intermediary (the knowledge is in the book). The student is a passive consumer of contents produced by specialists.	Collaborative production and distribution of contents. Student as a co-developer of contents. Cognitive surplus (free time as a source of creative acts) (Shirky, 2010). Reversing the traditional model: work in class, learn at home (Kahn Academy).
Knowledge management format	Books, notebooks, personal notes.	eBooks, digital documents, portable devices (notebooks, tablets, smartphones, etc.), social networks, cloud computing tools (Google Docs), etc.
Evaluation	Written/oral exams. Periodic.	Multimedia production/portfolios. Continuous.
Institutional legitimation	Top-down. Hierarchical ("degrees"). Centralized recognition systems. Big university brands.	Bottom-up. Social and digital visibility. Virality. Page rank/Google Scholar. Digital identity (digital footprint).
Expertise	Individual. Professional.	Social/distributed. Professional/amateur.

classroom debate and by continually examining and challenging both the content and pedagogy. Teaching fosters the active, critical, and continuously updated process of learning.

- *Discovery*, or research, is a pervasive process of intellectual excitement rather than a simple concern for outcomes in the form of new knowledge. It includes producing new knowledge by resolving problems.

- The scholarship of *application* is defined as professional activity in practice and service, which must be subjected to the same rigor of evaluation and accountability as teaching and research. It facilitates applying theoretical and empirical knowledge.

- The scholarship of *integration* is the process of making connections between knowledge and models from different disciplines and within a wider context. It promotes combining disciplines inside and outside the academic environment.

Using this model as his foundation, Johnston (1998) stated that the university has lost its "monopoly" over the production and distribution of knowledge. He explained that the university is no longer unique with regard to the scholarship of teaching, discovery, application, and integration. These functions are increasingly shared with "non-university institutes, research centers, government agencies, industrial laboratories, think-tanks [and] consultancies." As Gibbons et al. (1994) envisioned, "[t]he university must enlarge its view of its role in knowledge production from that of being a monopoly supplier to becoming a partner in both national and international contexts" (p. 156). Nowotny, Scott, and Gibbons (2003) also suggested that it is necessary to "enlarge the role of the university" and purposed a new academic paradigm of knowledge generation (also called "Mode 2"[3]) that is socially distributed, application oriented, transdisciplinary, and subject to multiple accountabilities. Nowotny et al. and Jacobson, Butterill, and Goering (2004) highlighted that the university needs to "extend" its role, and emphasized aspects like the communication between the producers of knowledge and the users of knowledge, the brokering and negotiation of knowledge translation arrangements, and the delivery of knowledge.

If we apply Boyer's categories to the new disintermediated educational environment, we can identify a significant number of practices and platforms—situated on the institutional frontier of the university or even far beyond it—that challenge the traditional role of higher education experts.

In order to fulfill the aims of this study, a mixed "purposeful sample" of websites was included to "purposefully inform an understanding of the research problem and central phenomenon in the study" (Creswell, 2007, p. 125). The platforms included in this analysis meet the following criteria: 1) they fit into one or more of the categories described in Boyer's model, and 2) they provide mechanisms of Mode 2 production or distribution of knowledge. However, the sample is indicative and clearly not representative of all the platforms and practices adopted in higher education today.

REINTERMEDIATION IN HIGHER EDUCATION: NEW EXPERTISE, KNOWLEDGE BROKERING, AND KNOWLEDGE TRANSLATION

Earlier we asked, "What is happening in higher education?" We answered that educational institutions are going through a disintermediation process, and now we can expand the answer and state that *we are witnessing the diffusion of new educational platforms and practices that play a role as reintermediaries*. The debate on disintermediation in the media field introduced new concepts like *citizen journalism;* likewise, for analyzing disintermediation in the education field we need to create a new glossary of concepts and analytical categories. In this context we can retrieve the concept of *cyberintermediation* developed in the 1990s. We already defined the cyberintermediator as a network-based intermediary that reduced the transaction costs and increased the efficiency of the exchange process. Many of the new educational platforms and practices introduced in the second section of this chapter can also be considered as cyberintermediators.

In a network-based system the information is distributed and the production of new knowledge is the result of the interactions between actors. The knowledge is no longer located in a specific place or object—the book, the school—or interpreted by an exclusive expert—the teacher, the lecturer, the professor. In this context we can talk about the emergence of a new era of *collaborative* or *distributed expertise*.

How can traditional experts survive in a knowledge economy dominated by new social networks, open databases, and open source tools

Table 3. Applying Boyer's categories to disintermediated platforms and practices in higher education

Boyer's model categories	Disintermediatory platforms and practices in higher education
Teaching	OpenCourseWare Consortium (MIT) (http://www.ocwconsortium.org/) iTunesU (http://www.apple.com/education/itunes-u/) Open Learning Initiative (OLI) (http://oli.web.cmu.edu/openlearning/) Academic Earth (http://academicearth.org/) Polimedia (http://polimedia.blogs.upv.es/) OpenLearn (http://openlearn.open.ac.uk/) P2P University (http://p2pu.org/) The Khan Academy (http://www.khanacademy.org/) OER Commons (http://www.oercommons.org/) Shibuka University Network (http://www.shibuya-univ.net/english/) Flat World Knowledge (www.flatworldknowledge.com)
Discovery	Academia.edu (http://www.academia.edu/) iCamp (http://www.icamp.eu/) ResearchGate (http://www.researchgate.net/) Public Library of Science/PLOS (http://www.plos.org/) SciVee (http://www.scivee.tv/) Google Scholar (http://scholar.google.com/) Scientific search-engines and databases (http://www.online-college-blog.com/index.php/features/100-useful-tips-and-tools-to-research-the-deep-web/)
Application (Experimentation)	iLabs Project (http://icampus.mit.edu/projects/iLabs.shtml) Directory of Open Access Journals (DOAJ) (http://www.doaj.org/) Edufire (http://edufire.com) School Factory (http://www.schoolfactory.org) Open Living Labs (http://www.openlivinglabs.eu/) Innocentive (http://www.innocentive.com/)
Integration (Trandisciplinarity)	Joint Computer Science and Philosophy Degree (http://www.comlab.ox.ac.uk/admissions/ugrad/Computer_Science_and_Philosophy) The Bank of Common Knowledge (http://www.bancocomun.org/) Wikipedia (http://www.wikipedia.org) Hyper Island Master Class (http://masterclass.hyperisland.se) Knowmad School (http://www.knowmads.nl) Bookcamps Social Networking

such as Wikipedia? Will teachers, professors, and other experts become extinct? How can they survive? We need new concepts and categories in order to start answering these questions. In the next section, we outline two concepts: *knowledge brokering, knowledge networking*, and *knowledge translation*.

What do we Understand by Knowledge Brokering and Knowledge Networking?

What or who is a *knowledge broker*? The concept of *knowledge brokering* was introduced by Hargadon and Sutton (2000) and should be considered the natural evolution of the term *knowledge worker* coined by Drucker (1959). A broker is a person or a certain kind of organization that arranges or negotiates with an intermediary. From the perspective of the knowledge economy, this figure is an emerging human resource profile that facilitates the connections between information, people, and context. A fundamental skill of a knowledge broker is the capability to make proficient use of digital technologies to bridge the gap between different stakeholders or communities (Straus, Tetroe, & Graham, 2009). According to Pawlowski and Robey (2004), brokering practices include gaining permission to cross organizational boundaries, facilitating the transfer of knowledge

Figure 1. Applying Boyer's categories to disintermediated platforms and practices in higher education

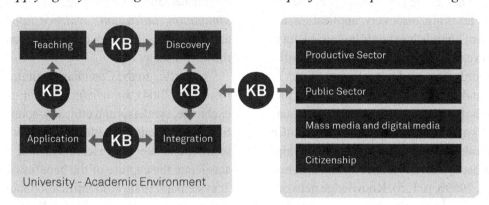

among organizational units, and contributing to organizational learning. For instance, a knowledge broker provides decision makers and researchers with a better understanding of each other's field of expertise or interest. According to Dobbins et al. (2009), the knowledge broker "facilitates knowledge exchange, builds rapport with target audiences, forges new connections across domains" (p. 2).

A knowledge broker can be identified in different socio-cultural contexts. In the specific case of higher education institutions it is more appropriate to refer to the knowledge networker because this concept is embedded in what has been said about the knowledge broker, but it also stresses the importance of working through networks of collaboration between different agents and within different contexts. In other words, the broker becomes a networker when she or he is capable of creating connections, recognizing patterns, and making sense across decentralized knowledge sources, nodes, and communities that are strategic for the educational institutions. These agents facilitate connecting and bridging different activities of knowledge production and distribution either within the university or outside it. The networking activity can vary significantly depending on the link (see arrows) and the stakeholders or context. Higher education institutions need to include the figure of the *knowledge networker* in their organizations. The knowledge networker

could be an individual or a group of professionals who act as an interface between the different internal and external actors of the educational process.

The knowledge networker mediates between researchers and user communities and must understand both the research process and the users' decision-making processes (Jacobson, Butterill, & Goering, 2003). Jacobson et al. (2003) explain that knowledge brokers mediate between researchers and user communities and must understand both the research process and the users' decision-making processes. From an educational perspective, teachers and other educators need to develop the skills of a knowledge broker in order to better connect (and update) the knowledge that has been created with what is taught and learned by students. There is no single action for promoting the *brokering* approach; instead there is a set of strategies. Educators need to understand that it is vital to stimulate the development of research skills across disciplines, institutions, and regions. It is also important to promote collaboration with non-academic partners as an essential part of the openness and remix principles that trigger the creation of new inter- or multidisciplinary knowledge. This approach fosters the adoption of new dynamics that consolidate the interactions between distributed communities that produce, disseminate, and consume knowledge in different times and spaces.

Coming back to the key functions of the university, the teaching, discovery, application, and integration of knowledge should be carried out by people who can understand and adopt this profile. In other words, knowledge brokering "links researchers and decision makers, facilitating their interaction so that they are able to better understand each other's goals and professional culture, influence each other's work, forge new partnerships, and use research-based evidence" (Straus, Tetroe, & Graham, 2009b, p. 125). Knowledge networkers promote the interaction between researchers and end users, contribute to establishing a mutual understanding of goals and cultures, and facilitate the identification, access, assessment, interpretation, and translation of research results into local policy and practice (Dobbins et al., 2009).

We would now like to analyze the concept of *knowledge translation*. From our perspective this term can provide a useful conceptual framework for fostering the visibility and connectivity of academic knowledge in a variety of contexts.

What do we Understand by Knowledge Translation?

The terminology in this complex area is by no means standard. *Knowledge translation* is a relatively new term, also described as a "frontier concept"; it has been borrowed from medicine, public health, and health care policy development. However, today the term is used in a broader spectrum of disciplines. Knowledge translation refers to a number of fairly synonymous terms—*knowledge utilization, knowledge exchange, research transfer*, and *research utilization*—and phrases—including *translating research into practice, getting research into practice, knowledge use, knowledge dissemination, knowledge transfer, evidence translation, research uptake,* and *evidence uptake* (Jacobson et al., 2003; Lang, Wyer, & Haynes, 2007). Armstrong, Waters, Roberts, Oliver, and Popay (2006) stated that the principles of knowledge translation are well established and have long been described as *dissemination, utilization, evidence into practice,* and *knowledge transfer* both inside and outside the health sector.

According to the Canadian Institute of Health Research (2004), *knowledge transfer* means "the exchange, synthesis and ethically-sound application of knowledge—within a complex system of interactions among researchers and users—to accelerate the capture of the benefits of research ... systematic review, identification, aggregation and practical application" (p. 28). For instance, in medicine, strategies for knowledge translation may vary according to the target audience (e.g., researchers, clinicians, policy makers, the public) and the type of knowledge being translated (i.e., clinical, biomedical, or policy related) (Straus et al., 2009b).

Pawlowski and Robey (2004) explained that knowledge transfer can also create new ideas by: 1) rearranging information already in use, and 2) incorporating information that has been previously neglected. For them, the translation process involves framing the elements of one community's world view in terms of another community's world view. In order to make academic knowledge comprehensible to another community of knowing, its meaning must be translated or transformed in terms of not only words, but also channels, formats, devices, mechanisms, etc. Thus, translation becomes a critical function of knowledge networking because it allows members of two communities to understand each other's language. The transfer of knowledge within an organization may be arduous, partly because much of what must be transferred is tacit rather than explicit.

The ability to translate certain knowledge implies having a clear understanding of the context and the environment of the community of interest. There is no one-size-fits-all translation; on the contrary, a basic requisite of this process is adaptability and flexibility. As knowledge creation, distillation, and dissemination are not enough to ensure that knowledge will be taken into consideration (i.e., by the institution, decision makers, or mass media) (Straus et al., 2009a, 2009b), a detailed strategy for translating the knowledge is required. According to Armstrong et al. (2006), knowledge translation can be seen as an acceleration of the knowledge cycle, which implies an acceleration of the natural transformation of knowledge into use.

Knowledge management is necessary, but it does not ensure effective knowledge translation (Straus et al., 2009a, 2009b). Actually, the translation process has more to do with language, extension, format, frequency, accessibility, usability (user-friendliness), etc. Armstrong et al. (2006) suggest that a deep understanding of the users' contexts provides strategic insight that can be used for effective knowledge translation, which means having an in-depth knowledge of the profile, environment, and interests of the target group. Knowledge translation provides useful clues for how to put knowledge into action; in this context this means moving the knowledge in the right direction, with the right intensity, and at the right time to the right stakeholder (either a person or an institution). The knowledge is then adapted to match the context of interest.

The next step is to assess the barriers and facilitators related to the knowledge to be adopted, the potential adopters, and the context or setting in which the knowledge is to be used. This information is then used to develop and execute the plan and strategies for facilitating and promoting awareness and implementation of the knowledge. Once the plan has been developed and executed, the next stage is to monitor knowledge use or application according to the *types of knowledge use identified* (conceptual use, involving changes in levels of knowledge, understanding, or attitudes; instrumental use, involving changes in behavior or practice; or strategic use, involving the manipulation of knowledge to attain specific power or profit goals) (Sudsawad, 2007). As we mentioned above, the interest in and strategies for

implementing knowledge translation may vary depending on the discipline. For instance, while a pharmaceutical chemist may need to make his or her scientific discoveries relevant for a certain laboratory, a social scientist may try to adapt his or her research to make it meaningful for a certain group of policy makers. Sudsawad (2007) explains that the concept of *knowledge translation* is a complex and multidimensional category that requires a comprehensive understanding of its mechanisms, methods, and measurements, as well as of its influencing factors at the individual and contextual levels and the interaction between both of these levels.

Knowledge translation describes any activity or process that facilitates transferring high-quality research evidence into effective changes in certain policies, practices, or products (Lang et al., 2007). Knowledge translation aims to address the interests of relevant stakeholders of a certain field; therefore, a basic condition for effective translation is selecting the right stakeholder(s). It is also important to mention that for certain disciplines stakeholders could be policy makers, while for others they could be citizens, entrepreneurs, consumers, or a certain elite group of experts. However, in all cases the translation process aims to increase the stakeholders' awareness of knowledge products or the specific and discrete strategies and dissemination mechanisms used to promulgate knowledge products (Graham et al., 2006).

There is a variety of actions to implement in order to apply knowledge translation in higher education institutions. The applicability of the knowledge translation will differ depending on aspects such as the kind of knowledge, the target communities, the relationships between institutions, and the accessibility and removability of the knowledge. At least two driving factors are considered in this translation process: the "institutional" and the "individual." Institutions may foster knowledge translation by (re)creating extension services departments. In addition, the management of "intellectual property" is usually an area that requires new practices and more flexible licensing policies. The "individual practices" will be based on promoting and developing "new" digital and informational skills, not only to disseminate academic production into new contexts more effectively but also to facilitate the transfer of knowledge into new languages, formats, and communities.

Summarizing, Armstrong et al. (2006) explain that knowledge translation has been defined in various ways but has generally focused on the *application* of knowledge—in other words, turning knowledge into action encompassing both knowledge creation and knowledge appliance (Graham et al., 2006). The idea of *knowledge-to-action* (KTA) also assigns special importance to the connection and use of knowledge. Graham et al. (2006) highlight "the importance of understanding (1) the complete KTA process, (2) the range of stakeholders involved beyond the practitioners, and (3) conceptual frameworks that may be useful for facilitating the use of research in practice settings."

COEXISTING WITH DISINTERMEDIATION

The emergence of a globalized and hyperconnected society is reshaping the traditional role of higher education within society. This process is considered an incremental (not radical), complex, and gradual transformation in which institutions and experts need to redefine their roles and learn how to coexist with other practices and actors. Homan (1996) writes that the process of disintermediation in education has made it necessary to become "more proactive in identifying information needs; managing the end user; new retrieval methods, sources and dissemination techniques; improving efficiency and cost-effectiveness; and adding value" (p. 589). During the last decade universities all around the world have begun to

explore more flexible strategies for teaching and carrying out scientific research. This diversification of strategies can be understood as gradual hybrid transformations that have been adopted in educational institutions in different ways: top-down and bottom-up initiatives, free or paid content, and the creation of formal and/or informal learning environments, etc. To provide some examples of tools and relevant trends that describe the disintermediation process, Figure 2 illustrates:

- Different possibilities of combining knowledge production and knowledge distribution, which can be open practices or closed practices.
- A revisitation of Boyer's model taking into account new instruments and platforms that reconceptualize and expand this model.

Reorganizing Knowledge Production/Knowledge Distribution Strategies

In Figure 2 we propose a reorganization of the different educational experiences presented above. This organization is based on 1) knowledge production/knowledge distribution (horizontal axis) and 2) the open/closed philosophy of educational practice (see Mode-1 and Mode-2 of Gibbons et al., 1994, and Nowotny et al., 2003) (vertical axis).

This Cartesian figure illustrates four possible combinations:

- **Closed production of knowledge/Closed circulation and distribution of knowledge:** The knowledge is produced within the academic context and is traditionally recognized as "valid knowledge." In this case, the produced knowledge is communicated through traditional mediums such as academic papers, academic books, posters in a congress, lectures, etc. Example: high-impact scientific journals.

Figure 2. Knowledge production/Knowledge distribution strategies

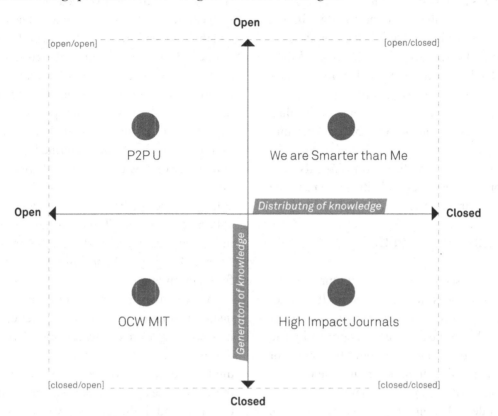

- **Closed production of knowledge/Open circulation and distribution of knowledge:** The knowledge is produced within the academic context and is traditionally recognized as "valid knowledge." In this case, the knowledge is broadcast and openly distributed on the Internet. There is no major interaction between producers (broadcasters) and users (consumers). Example: OpenCourseWare (MIT).
- **Open production of knowledge/Open circulation and distribution of knowledge:** Open resources in higher education. The opposite of closed resources, the meta-structure of these platforms is based on the network design and prioritizes the openness of platforms. It breaks with two main axes of the organizational culture of universities: exclusivity of own contents for in-house students, and centralized con-

trol and management of the educational process and strict rules governing the relationship between experts and students according to the taxonomies designed by institutions.
- This Open/Open combination does not rely exclusively on the accessibility and commoditization of information or resources, as the Creative Commons license states. Open architectures facilitate combining knowledge and stimulate the creation of new knowledge. The milestone of the open principle is the idea that individuals and communities can learn from their peers (and not only from experts or academic institutions) (Cobo Romaní & Moravec, 2011). Example: Peer 2 Peer University.
- **Open production of knowledge/Closed circulation and distribution of knowledge**: In this case the production of knowl-

edge is based on open and collective structures of collaboration and the distribution of the produced knowledge (product or service) is closed. Example: Barry Libert and John Spector's book, *We Are Smarter than Me*, began with an open call in a wiki, contains contributions from more than 4,000 people, and is available on Amazon.[4]

This basic map can be used to identify new educational experiences and situate them in the context of learning practices.

Open Educational Initiatives

Figure 3 is a second map that summarizes the concepts and ideas discussed above. It is noteworthy that what has been denominated "disintermediatory" is proposed as a collection of hybrid mechanisms of change that could be useful for envisaging possible futures for higher education institutions. After exploring some of the combinations described in the previous sections we give some examples and relevant cases that show how the process of disintermediation is acquiring increasing relevance in higher education.

Interestingly, most of the examples that we present fulfill more than one of the key functions described by Boyer (teaching, discovery, integration, application), which is why it is important to revisit Boyer's model.

CONCLUSION: DISINTERMEDIATION, EXPERTISE, AND REINTERMEDIATION

In pre-digital times the intermediary had expertise that facilitated the exchange of commodities between producers and consumers (the car salesman), or the exchange of information between "reality" and the citizen (the journalist). In this pre-digital context, teachers were the intermediaries between the knowledge archived in books/libraries and the

students. Over the last two decades the dichotomy between producers and consumers has changed, and the limits of the two roles are no longer well defined. The introduction of the concept of the *prosumer* by Toffler (1980) 30 years ago was a good sign of times to come. The diffusion of digital networks and the rapid spread of an online culture in the 1990s accelerated the transformation of the role of former intermediaries and the emergence of new cyberintermediation systems. Society seems to be moving from individual/institutional intermediators to collective/distributed cyberintermediators. Today the expertise is also in the network, distributed in the collective intelligence (Levy, 1997) and just a few clicks away from any Internet user.

As we have seen in this brief description of disintermediation processes in higher education, it is not easy to map this territory. Every week new practices, concepts, and experiences join our digital and discursive networks. To understand these processes we need new categories and taxonomies, and in this chapter we have attempted to reorganize the field and introduce concepts to map these practices. However, we consider that old intermediaries (car salesmen, teachers, journalists) must reinvent themselves and learn how to move within a new environment where the expertise is distributed and networked. In this context the network is not a flat, transparent territory; the Web also has knowledge concentrations (like mountains) and hierarchies (15 followers on Twitter cannot compare with 150,000). Expertise is still needed and necessary, but for experts to survive they need to learn how to develop their professional skills in a networked ecosystem.

From our perspective, an increasingly connected society demands that the higher education institutions and their communities can:

1. Design and exploit new channels and strategies for knowledge production and distribution. The channels adopted can be traditional media but also digital media and social networks.

Figure 3. Applying Boyer's categories to open/closed educational experiences

2. Develop partnerships with other organizations and sectors of society (e.g., production sector, government, mass media) so that the generated knowledge is better known, discussed, and in certain contexts adopted or transformed.

3. Incorporate new internal professional profiles and skills—like the knowledge broker—and new practices—like knowledge translation—to expand and feed the knowledge network.

Should We Take Disintermediation in Higher Education Seriously? Although the traditional role of the university as an intermediation institution is being challenged, this does not mean the death of formal education or the extinction of its experts, but rather their coexistence with new institutional actors (from non-governmental organizations that operate in the educational field to social platforms and anti-institutional initiatives like the edupunk movement) (Downes, 2008). These new actors sometimes "compete" with the university by proposing disintermediated educational practices or creating new collaborative cyberintermediations.

A deeper reflection on the disintermediation of higher education should include issues like the role of the university as a social elevator and the crisis this institution as a unique source of knowledge legitimation is facing. We need a new and creative articulation of the now continual reformation and transformation of the higher education landscape. More than being a threat to traditional institutions, disintermediation is a great opportunity for upgrading an institution that was born almost a millennium ago.

REFERENCES

Althusser, L. (1970). Ideology and ideological state apparatuses. In L. Althusser (Ed.), *Lenin and philosophy and other essays*. Retrieved from http://www.marxists.org/reference/archive/althusser/1970/ideology.htm

Armstrong, R., Waters, E., Roberts, H., Oliver, S., & Popay, J. (2006). The role and theoretical evolution of knowledge translation and exchange in public health. *Journal of Public Health, 28*(4), 384–389. doi:10.1093/pubmed/fdl072

Benjamin, R., & Wigand, R. (1995). Electronic markets and virtual value chains on the information highway. *Sloan Management Review*, (Winter): 62–72.

Benkler, Y. (2006). *The wealth of networks: How social production transforms markets and freedom*. New Haven, CT: Yale University Press.

Boyer, E. L. (1990). *Scholarship reconsidered*. Princeton, NJ: Carnegie Foundation for the Advancement of Teaching.

Canadian Institute for Health Research. (2004). *Knowledge translation strategy: Niche and focus 2005– 2009*. Ottawa, Canada: Canadian Institute of Health Research.

Castells, M. (1996). *The rise of the network society: The information age: Economy, society and culture (Vol. I)*. Cambridge, MA; Oxford, UK: Blackwell.

Cobo Romaní, C., & Moravec, J. W. (2011). *Aprendizaje invisible. Hacia una nueva ecología de la educación*. Barcelona, Spain: Col·lecció Transmedia XXI. Laboratori de Mitjans Interactius/Publicacions i Edicions de la Universitat de Barcelona.

Cobo Romaní, C., & Pardo Kuklinski, H. (2007). *Planeta Web 2.0. Inteligencia colectiva o medios fast food*. Barcelona, Spain: GRID, Universitat de Vic/Flacso México.

Creswell, J. W. (2007). *Qualitative inquiry & research design: Choosing among five approaches*. Thousand Oaks, CA: Sage Publications.

Dobbins, M., Robeson, P., Ciliska, D., Hanna, S., Cameron, R., & O'Mara, L. (2009). A description of a knowledge broker role implemented as part of a randomized controlled trial evaluating three knowledge translation strategies. *Implementation Science; IS, 4*(1), 23. doi:10.1186/1748-5908-4-23

Downes, S. (2008). *Introducing edupunk*. Retrieved from http://www.downes.ca/cgi-bin/page.cgi?post=44760

Drucker, P. F. (1959). *Landmarks of tomorrow*. New York, NY: Harper.

Fourie, I. (1999). Should we take disintermediation seriously? *The Electronic Library, 17*(1), 9–16. doi:10.1108/02640479910329400

Freire, P. (1970). *Pedagogy of the oppressed*. New York, NY: Continuum.

Gant, S. (2007). *We're all journalists now: The transformation of the press and reshaping of the law in the Internet age*. New York, NY: Free Press.

Gibbons, M., Limoges, C., Nowotny, H., Schwartzman, S., Scott, P., & Trow, M. (1994). *The new production of knowledge: The dynamics of science and research in contemporary societies.* London, UK: Sage.

Gilmour, D. (2004). *We the media: Grassroots journalism by the people, for the people.* Sebastopol, CA: O'Reilly Media.

Graham, I. D., Logan, J., Harrison, M., Straus, S., Tetroe, J., Caswell, W., & Robinson, N. (2006). Lost in knowledge translation: Time for a map? *The Journal of Continuing Education in the Health Professions, 26,* 13–24. doi:10.1002/chp.47

Hargadon, A., & Sutton, R. I. (2000). Building an innovation factory. *Harvard Business Review, 78*(3), 157–166.

Hoffman, D., Novak, T., & Chatterjee, P. (1995). Commercial scenarios for the Web: Opportunities and challenges. *Journal of Computer-Mediated Communication, 1*(3). Retrieved from http://jcmc.indiana.edu/vol1/issue3/hoffman.html

Homan, J. M. (1996). Disintermediation and education. *Bulletin of the Medical Library Association, 84*(4), 589–590.

Jacobson, N., Butterill, D., & Goering, P. (2003). Development of a framework for knowledge translation: Understanding user context. *Journal of Health Services Research & Policy, 8,* 94–99. doi:10.1258/135581903321466067

Jacobson, N., Butterill, D., & Goering, P. (2004). Organizational factors that influence university-based researchers' engagement in knowledge transfer activities. *Science Communication, 25*(3), 246. doi:10.1177/1075547003262038

Jarvis, J. (2009). *What would Google do?* New York, NY: Collins Business.

Johnston, R. (1998). The university of the future: Boyer revisited. *Higher Education, 36,* 253–272. doi:10.1023/A:1003264528930

Lang, E., Wyer, P., & Haynes, R. Brian. (2007). Knowledge translation: Closing the evidence-to-practice gap. *Annals of Emergency Medicine, 49*(3), 355–363. doi:10.1016/j.annemergmed.2006.08.022

Levy, P. (1997). *Collective intelligence: Mankind's emerging world in cyberspace.* New York, NY: Basic Books.

Michalski, J. (1995). People are the killer app. *Forbes ASAP*, June 5, 120-122.

Negroponte, N. (1997). Re-intermediated. *Wired,* 5.09.

Nowotny, H., Scott, P., & Gibbons, M. (2003). Introduction: Mode 2' revisited: The new production of knowledge. *Minerva, 41*(3), 179–194. doi:10.1023/A:1025505528250

O'Reilly, T. (2005). *What is Web 2.0: Design patterns and business models for the next generation of software.* Retrieved from http://www.oreillynet.com/pub/a/oreilly/tim/news/2005/09/30/what-is-web-20.html

Pardo Kuklinski, H. (2010). *Geekonomia. Un radar para producir en el postdigitalismo.* Barcelona, Spain: LMI/Publicacions i Edicions de la Universitat de Barcelona.

Pawlowski, S., & Robey, D. (2004). Bridging user organizations: Knowledge brokering and the work of information technology professionals. *Management Information Systems Quarterly, 28,* 645–672.

Rhoten, D., Racine, L., & Wang, P. (2009). *Designing for learning in the 21st century* (Working paper). Retrieved from http://startl.org/about/the-future-of-learning/

Sarkar, M. B., Butler, B., & Steinfield, C. (1995). Intermediaries and cybermediaries: A continuing role for mediating players in the electronic marketplace. *Journal of Computer-Mediated Communication, 1*(3). Retrieved from http://jcmc.indiana.edu/vol1/issue3/sarkar.html

Scolari, C. A. (2008). *Hipermediaciones. Elementos para una teoría de la comunicación digital interactiva.* Barcelona, Spain: Gedisa.

Scolari, C. A. (2009). Mapping conversations about new media: The theoretical field of digital communication. *New Media & Society, 11,* 943–964. doi:10.1177/1461444809336513

Shirky, C. (2008, March 17). Newspapers and thinking the unthinkable. *Edge: The Third Culture.* Retrieved from http://www.edge.org/3rd_culture/shirky09/shirky09_index.html

Shirky, C. (2010). *Cognitive surplus: Creativity and generosity in a connected age.* New York, NY: Penguin.

Silver, D. (2000). Looking backwards, looking forward: Cyberculture studies 1990-2000. In D. Gauntlett, D. (Ed.), *Web studies: Rewiring media studies for the digital age* (1st ed.). London, UK: Arnold. Retrieved from http://www.com.washington.edu/rccs/intro.asp

Straus, S., Tetroe, J., & Graham, I. (2009a). Defining knowledge translation. *Canadian Medical Association Journal, 181,* 165–168. doi:10.1503/cmaj.081229

Straus, S., Tetroe, J., & Graham, I. (2009b). *Knowledge translation in health care: Moving from evidence to practice.* Chichester, UK: John Wiley and Sons. doi:10.1002/9781444311747

Sudsawad, P. (2007). *Knowledge translation: Introduction to models, strategies and measures.* Austin, TX: Southwest Educational Development Laboratory, National Center for the Dissemination of Disability Research.

Toffler, A. (1980). *The third wave: Democratization in the late twentieth century.* New York, NY: Bantam Books.

Tucker, R. (2010, May 27). Disintermediation: The disruption to come for Education 2.0. *Reading About Leading.* Retrieved from http://www.readingaboutleading.com/?p=767

ADDITIONAL READING

Agarwal, P. (2008). *Privatization and internationalization of higher education in the countries of South Asia: An empirical analysis.* New Delhi, India: Indian Council for Research on International Economic Relations.

Barrera-Osorio, F., & Linden, L. (2009). *The use and misuse of computers in education: Evidence from a randomized experiment in Colombia.* (Policy Research Working Paper, 4836. Impact Evaluation Series, n° 29.) The World Bank, Human Development Network.

Bjornavold, J. (2000–2001). Making learning visible: Identification, assessment and recognition of non-formal learning in Europe. *Vocational Training European Journal, 22,* January-April, 24-32. Luxemburgo, Cedefop. Retrieved February 10, 2011, from http://www.cedefop.europa.eu/EN/publications/13370.aspx

Brown, P., Lauder, H., & Ashton, D. (2008). Education, globalisation and the knowledge economy: A commentary by the Teaching and Learning Research Programme. Retrieved February 10, 2011, from http://www.tlrp.org/pub/documents/globalisationcomm.pdf

CEDEFOP. (2008). *Terminology of European education and training policy: A selection of 100 key terms.* Belgium: Office for Official Publications of the European Communities. Retrieved February 10, 2011, from http://www.cedefop.europa.eu/etv/Upload/Information_resources/Bookshop/369/4064_en.pdf

Colardyn, D., & Bjornavold, J. (2004). Validation of formal, non-formal and informal learning: Policy and practices in EU Member States. *European Journal of Education, 39*(1), 69–89. doi:10.1111/j.0141-8211.2004.00167.x

Contreras, M. E. (2005). Aprender a desaprender en la búsqueda de un aprendizaje transformativo: Apuntes sobre la capacitación de gerentes sociales. *Serie de Documentos de Trabajo I-54. Banco Interamericano de Desarrollo.* Retrieved February 10, 2011, from: http://www.udlap.mx/rsu/pdf/1/DocumentosdeTrabajodelINDES.pdf

Cope, B., & Kalantzis, M. (2009). *Ubiquitous learning. Exploring the anywhere/anytime possibilities for learning in the age of digital media.* Urbana, IL: University of Illinois Press.

Council of the European Union. (2004). *Draft conclusions of the Council and of the representatives of the Governments of the Member States meeting within the Council on Common European Principles for the identification and validation of non-formal and informal learning.* (9175/04 EDUC 101 SOC 220). Retrieved February 10, 2011, from http://ec.europa.eu/%E2%80%A6lifelong-learning-olicy/doc/informal/validation2004_en.pdf

Council of the European Union. (2009). Council conclusions of 12 May 2009 on a strategic framework for European cooperation in education and training ("ET 2020"). *Official Journal of the European Union*, 2009/C 119/02. Retrieved February 10, 2011, from: http://eurlex.europa.eu/LexUriServ/LexUriServ.do?uri=OJ:C:2009:119:0002:0010:EN:PDF

D'Antoni, S. (5 Aprile 2003). *The virtual university.* Retrieved May 15, 2008, from http://www.unesco.org/iiep/virtualuniversity

European Commission. (2007). *Key competences for lifelong learning: European reference framework.* Brussels, Belgium: Commission of the European Communities. Retrieved February 10, 2011, from: http://ec.europa.eu/dgs/education_culture/publ/pdf/ll-learning/keycomp_en.pdf

European Commission. (2008). *The use of ICT to support innovation and lifelong learning for all: A report on progress.* Retrieved February 10, 2011, from http://ec.europa.eu/education/lifelong-learning-programme/doc/sec2629.pdf

Friedman, T. (2005). *The world is flat: A brief history of the twenty-first century.* New York, NY: Farrar, Straus & Giroux.

Garcia, I., et al. (2010). *Informe horizon: Edición iberoamericana.* New Media Consortium and la Universitat Oberta de Catalunya. Retrieved April 15, 2011, from http://www.nmc.org/pdf/2010-Horizon-Report-ib.pdf

Hofheinz, P. (2009). *EU 2020: Why skills are key for Europe's future.* Brussels, Belgium: The Lisbon Council. Retrieved April 15, 2011, from http://www.lisboncouncil.net/publication/publication/54-skillseuropesfuture.html

Illich, I. (1971). *Deschooling society.* New York, NY: Harper & Row.

Jantsch, E., & OCDE. (1967). *Technological forecasting in perspective: A framework for technological forecasting, its technique and organisation; a description of activities and an annotated bibliography.* Paris, France: Organisation for Economic Co-operation and Development.

Kamenetz, A. (2009). *DIY U: Edupunks, edupreneurs, and the coming transformation of higher education.* White River Junction, VT: Chelsea Green.

Kerka, S. (2000). Incidental learning. *Trends and Issues Alert, 18.* Retrieved April 15, 2011, from http://calpro-online.org/eric/textonly/docgen.asp?tbl=tia&ID=140

Miller, R., Shapiro, H., & Hilding-Hamann, K. E. (Eds.). (2008). *School's over: Learning spaces in Europe in 2020: An imagining exercise on the future of learning.* Seville, Spain: Joint Research Centre, Institute for Prospective Technological Studies. Retrieved April 15, 2011, from ftp://ftp.jrc.es/pub/EURdoc/JRC47412.pdf

OECD. (2008). New millennium learners. Initial findings on the effects of digital technologies on school-age learners. OECD/CERI International Conference Learning in the 21st Century: Research, Innovation and Policy. Paris, France: Organisation for Economic Co-operation and Development. Retrieved April 15, 2011, from http://www.oecd.org/dataoecd/39/51/40554230.pdf

UNESCO. (2010). *United Nations Educational 2010: The current status of science around the world.* Paris, France: UNESCO.

KEY TERMS AND DEFINITIONS

Collaborative (Distributed) Expertise: Set of skills or knowledge not situated in a specific environment or community but distributed in a digital network of users.

Cyberintermediator: Digital network-based intermediary that occupies a middle position in a social, economic, or cultural process. The intermediation functions are performed by an autonomous system or by the user interactions within the system.

Disintermediation: The reduction of the role of intermediaries until they eventually become obsolete in a social, economic, or cultural process. The objectives of disintermediation include dropping the final cost of products or services, speeding up processes, consolidating direct relationships between the different components, and/or increasing the transparency of a system.

Intermediary: Any agent, institution, or platform that occupies a middle position in a social, economic, or cultural process.

Knowledge-based Economy: Advanced economies with a greater and growing dependence on knowledge, information, and high skill levels, in which it becomes increasingly necessary for the business and public sectors to have ready access to all of these.

Knowledge Translation: The exchange, synthesis, and application of knowledge within a complex system of interactions between researchers and users to accelerate obtaining the benefits of research.

Literacy: Capacity to apply knowledge and skills in key areas to analyze, communicate effectively, and solve problems in different situations.

ENDNOTES

[1]   *Closed* refers to those initiatives of knowledge production or distribution developed exclusively by the so-called "educational experts."

[2]   *Open* refers to those initiatives of knowledge production or distribution developed *collectively* by people with different profiles and who are not necessarily "education experts" (parents, Internet-savvy people, artists, anonymous collaborators, etc.)

[3]   Mode 1 is considered closed, isolated, objective, decontextualized, restricted to scientific communities, and discipline based, while Mode 2 is defined as open, interconnected, socially robust, context dependent, not restricted to scientific communities, and transdisciplinary (Gibbons et al., 1994; Nowotny et al., 2003).

[4]   www.wearesmarter.org

Chapter 6

The University in Transition:
Reconsidering Faculty Roles and Expertise in a Web 2.0 World

Laurie Craig Phipps
Simon Fraser University, Canada & Kwantlen Polytechnic University, Canada

Alyssa Friend Wise
Simon Fraser University, Canada

Cheryl Amundsen
Simon Fraser University, Canada

ABSTRACT

Discussion of changing notions of faculty expertise and the role of technology within the educational enterprise is nothing new. However, the current demand for change in teaching and learning practices is particularly strong, in part due to the pressures arising from emerging technologies and the shifting nature of faculty expertise. Web 2.0 technologies enable social connectivity, academic interactivity, and content co-creation. Thus, they change the ways of interacting with information and can support collaborative and constructivist approaches in higher education. This both inspires and requires a corresponding expansion in faculty's role: from imparter of knowledge to orchestrator of learning experiences. Within the general metaphor of orchestration, other specific roles and functions will also be required; for example, scripting, translating, introducing, and co-exploring. As educators attempt to reimagine an educational paradigm in this context, the integration of new technologies must be grounded in how they can support educational experiences and outcomes that are focused on learning.

INTRODUCTION

The discussion of changing notions of faculty expertise and the role of technology within the educational enterprise is nothing new. While historically teaching was expected to be the imparting of knowledge from faculty to student, over the last 40 years this approach has been heavily critiqued as ineffective in preparing engaged citizens and skilled professionals, and thus not successful as a singular approach (Laurillard, 2002). Specifically, when the goals of learning involve higher-order thinking and preparation for transfer to future situations, interactive methods are generally considered more effective (Amundsen, Winer, &

DOI: 10.4018/978-1-4666-2178-7.ch006

Gandell, 2004; Wise & O'Neill, 2009). Molenda (1997) has suggested that the sense of inadequacy around the imparting knowledge paradigm and the challenge for universities to push toward deeper understanding occurred in tandem with the rise of a more constructivist philosophy in education. Together, these changes have broadened the framing of the faculty role from that of an imparter of knowledge to a mediator of learning.

In this new role, the faculty member is often seen as a facilitator, whose expertise is valued not simply for the wealth of information at their disposal, but their ability to help students "acquire knowledge of someone else's way of experiencing the world" (Laurillard, 2002: 24). Of course, this conceptual change in thinking about learning does not always translate into changes in teaching actions and learning activities. It does, however, raise questions about current teaching practices and what new ones can be imagined. Web 2.0 technologies present an opportunity to support and extend the desire for change in higher education through the ways in which they make "constructivist, collaborative knowledge-making more natural" (Moore, 2007: 181). At the same time, the use of these technologies outside the classroom also puts pressure on the university as they change our relationship with information. Thus, Web 2.0 technologies both provide a call for, and can help enable, more collaborative and constructivist practices in teaching and learning in higher education.

This chapter begins by positioning the university as undergoing a transitional period that may be unprecedented in scope and impact (Amirault & Visser, 2009). The combination of emerging information and communication technologies that move beyond ubiquitous information access (Web 1.0) to enhance social connectivity, academic interactivity, and "sharing, creation, and participation" (Downes, 2006: 1) has been termed learning 2.0 or e-learning 2.0 (Downes, 2006; Ravenscroft, 2011). Web 2.0 technologies are at the center of a transitional pressure on universities that arises

from the ways in which they change how we interact with information and thus the characterization and value of experts and expertise. Specifically, the emergence of these Internet-based technologies has made information—its dissemination and its creation—broadly available and no longer mainly the preserve of universities. This has required a corresponding shift for university faculty as they attempt to reconceptualize their role and expertise in the learning endeavor, and as they come to understand and exploit the learning potential of these digital technologies.

Another source of pressure arises from the current generation of students. Much has been written about the millennial generation and their presumed comfort with and preference for digital technologies (Prensky, 2001). This literature implies that for universities to survive, they need to move their technological profile to match the expectations of a "new" kind of student (Amirault & Visser, 2009). While there is little empirical evidence to support a homogeneous group of "digital natives" with well-defined characteristics (Bennet, Maton & Kervin, 2008), Web 2.0 technology does affect the amount and kind of information readily available to all students and thus, perhaps, their perceptions of the relevance of the teaching and learning processes in which they are expected to engage. The question to be asked, then, is not whether the current wave of Web 2.0 digital technologies must be integrated into higher education based on new students' demand for these technologies. Instead, we must look at how the affordances of this group of technologies is already affecting relationships in teaching, learning, information, and knowledge in the university and the ways in which they can increase the educational potential for learning within higher education. In other words, as educators we need to move beyond simplistic stereotypes of current students and focus on the more complex challenges of developing appropriate educational uses of these technologies (Bullen, Morgan, & Qayyum, 2011).

THE UNIVERSITY IN TRANSITION AND WEB 2.0: PRESSURE FOR CHANGE

The university has proven itself to be a remarkably adaptable institution. Over the course of its history, it has had to respond to a wide variety of intellectual and political as well as technological challenges in order to remain relevant (Amirault & Visser, 2009). However, in spite of its successful history, the question remains whether the university can adapt to today's challenges, which may be "greater than any it has faced in any previous historical epoch" (Amirault & Visser, 2009: 64). Within the short span of several decades, the university's relationship to knowledge creation has changed and its mission has been redefined from that of educating society's elite to being responsible for universal access to higher education (Laurillard, 2002). Internet technologies have also diminished each institution's geographic monopoly and increased competitive pressure from other institutions that are expanding their virtual presence. Finally, the university has been challenged to alter its approach to teaching by becoming more student-centered and incorporating emerging information and communication technologies (Garcia & Roblin, 2008).

In this context, the intellectual challenge that universities face can be characterized as the juggling of pre-modern, modern, and post-modern characteristics attempting to coexist (Bloland, 2005). Some stakeholders still hold the pre-modern perspective of the university as a repository of knowledge, and thus see its role as presenting a stable set of facts as delivered truth. From a modernist perspective, the university's role is to disseminate knowledge in its current state while working to produce new knowledge; this leads to an emphasis on research and a rigorous process of challenging existing ideas. Finally, a post-modern perspective suggests that knowledge production and distribution "have moved far beyond the boundaries of the university, seriously challenging … higher education's control of knowledge" (Bloland, 2005: 133). The result, it can be argued, is that universities are no longer clear on their mission or what societal functions they will be able to and ought to perform in the future (Bloland, 2005).

Intellectual challenges are also evident for faculty. Information and communication technologies have enabled faculty to connect as easily with colleagues around the world as with those at the same geographic location. This has supported a trend toward increasingly specialized disciplinary expertise and a corresponding disciplinary fragmentation (Bloland, 2005). At the same time, there has been a blurring of disciplinary boundaries as new specialties combine perspectives across disciplines. These changes have implications for faculty expertise as they require faculty to not only develop knowledge of their own discipline, but also understand how their discipline overlaps with and can be informed by the perspectives of other disciplines, as well as emerging fields within the disciplines. This in turn creates teaching challenges as faculty strive to help learners build an understanding of foundational principles without becoming lost in the multiple perspectives and challenges made public through the Internet.

The political challenges for universities arise from the state's social project of universal access to higher education for its citizens in exchange for greater financial support (Bloland, 2005). The goal of universal access began with more physical campus space and expansion of the university system (including community colleges and similar institutions) to accommodate local students, but now includes accommodation of students farther afield through distance education programs. Distance education courses and programs have become more central players on and off campus as Web-based technologies facilitate both the distribution of content and more interactive modes of learning. Open Universities in particular were created to enable participation regardless of an individual's distance from an existing university campus. The resulting increase in the diversity of students' political, social, and cultural backgrounds adds yet another layer of challenge for teaching.

These challenges faced by universities are magnified by the opportunities presented by Web-based digital technologies. The adoption of Web-based technologies into all areas of our daily life has increased the desire for greater technological innovation and adoption in university classrooms. Specifically, the development of interactive Web 2.0 technologies has altered the education landscape away from earlier Web 1.0 technologies that mainly "pushed" content at learners, and toward the development of interactive learning environments. In a narrow sense, this shift toward more active learning is an extension of the dissatisfaction with the traditional "imparting knowledge" approach and a move toward a more constructivist, learner-centered paradigm. In a broader sense, a more learner-driven model challenges the link between the provision of courses and programs and the certification of those courses and programs of study (Johnson & Liber, 2008). The proliferation of Web-based courses implies that learners may well want to pick and choose those that interest them from among the thousands available regardless of the institutional provider. Brown and Duguid (2002) have described this as an "unplug and pay" (215) model of education. Learners will still want their program certified and thus put pressure on institutions to enable transfer of credits, to some extent decoupling university programming from university credentials.

Universities are also challenged to optimize education for students who, some claim, are different from students of previous times. However, as mentioned above, there is little if any clear evidence to support the notion of "digital natives" or the broader implication that there is a generation of learners who are homogeneous in terms of learning and technology needs. It is also not clear whether this is an important or meaningful distinction for education. The basis of arguments for a difference in students characterized as digital natives requires two assumptions. First, that growing up exposed to digital technologies has embedded "sophisticated knowledge and skills" in learners, and, second, that this is manifested in different ways of learning (Bennet et al., 2008: 777). The research findings to support these assumptions are mixed at best. A study by Jones, Ramanau, Cross, and Healing (2010) found some age-related differences in technology uses, but they conclude that there is as much difference within groups as between generations. Other research concludes that the so-called "new students" may not match the imagined stereotype and may not "have the characteristics of epitomic global, connected, socially-networked technologically fluent 'digital natives'" (Margaryan, Littlejohn, & Vojt, 2011: 439). Ironically, despite their out-of-class behaviours, students appear to prefer more passive forms of learning in the classroom. When digital technologies are integrated into teaching, students favor conventional classroom practices rather than any transformation of practices (Margaryan et al., 2011). In summary, there is little empirical support to argue for institutions to undertake significant educational reorganization and adopt pedagogies that incorporate technologies based on the argument that today's students learn differently or that they are frequent and sophisticated users of certain technologies.

Given these findings, what are the implications or opportunities presented by today's students' use of interactive technologies? One argument is that the dissonance between the technologies used in higher education and those used by students in their everyday lives may increase students' dissatisfaction with current university approaches to education (Amirault & Visser, 2009). While they are careful to avoid the suggestion that this argument should necessarily lead to using these technologies for instruction, Amirault and Visser do suggest the importance of understanding that "for today's learners, these technologies are arguably becoming the defining attributes of their world" (65). South (2010), a self-described millennial, makes the intriguing suggestion that the greater integration and greater ease with which students use interactive technologies highlights the potential for having a broad-based exchange of ideas as part of the learning process. Millennials, she claims, are open to and even hungry for the possibility of using technology-enabled interaction to support dialogue that is purposeful to the intended learning, and involves a willingness to listen in the search for understanding. The result could be exciting opportunities for new pedagogical models that move away from information transmission to engage more active learners in developing knowledge through technology-enhanced interactions with peers and experts both inside and outside of universities. This transition from passive to active pedagogical models parallels the transition from Web 1.0 technologies that provide access to abundant resources (Weller, 2011) toward Web 2.0 technologies that foster collaborative and interactive opportunities. In other words, the pedagogical opportunities mirror the shift in focus "from access to information toward access to other people" (Brown & Adler, 2008: 18).

Web 2.0 and the University

Web 2.0 is an umbrella term that includes a broad array of electronic interchanges (Conole & Culver, 2010; Hughes & Narayan, 2009) that connect users. More importantly, these technologies represent a suite of "social software" (Dron, 2007) that create networks linking people together and allowing them to share information and perspectives (Pidduck, 2010). These social technologies include a range of digital tools from tagging and photo-sharing systems to collections of wikis and blogs (Dron, 2007). Laouris, Underwood, Laouri, and Christakis (2010) also include "podcasts, talk-

ing characters, and virtual environments with 3-D avatars "living" almost normal lives" (154–155) as Web 2.0 technologies. More recently, microblogging (using tools such as Twitter) has joined the Web 2.0 collection of technologies (Rinaldo, Tapp, & Laverie, 2011) and new types of tools are sure to follow. More important than the current set of specific tools is the kinds of activities they afford. From this perspective, Web 2.0 encompasses all technologies that are social, interactive, and enable user-created content (Moore, 2007). The implication here may be that Web 2.0 cannot have a single contained definition. Instead, many of the scholars listed above offer a set of characteristics and tools that, for them, are consistent with the potential of Web 2.0. One important distinction that these applications share compared to previous information and communication technologies is the ability to scale. While earlier forms of interactive media, such as chat rooms, newsgroups, and discussion forums, tend to become overwhelming as numbers rise, the emerging social software "scales very well, gaining strength from large numbers" (Dron, 2007: 62).

The power of Web 2.0 technologies is the combining of access to information (Web 1.0) with enabling learners to interact with each other and work collaboratively in the creation and negotiation of content (Moore, 2007). In other words, a core affordance of these technologies is how they connect people, creating spaces and opportunities for dialogue. In the same way that Web 1.0 made access to information independent of physical locations such as libraries (Weller, 2011), Web 2.0 makes interaction, collaboration, and learning dialogues independent from physical locations such as universities. Thus, the challenge to universities is how the affordances of these technologies can be harnessed within higher education to inform teaching and learning practices. In other words, how can faculty exploit the potential of Web 2.0 technologies in a way that goes beyond simply providing more efficient access to greater amounts of information?

Information vs. Knowledge

The transition toward Web 2.0 is a movement away from individual information access and toward collaborative information exchange and construction. But this distinction makes no claim regarding knowledge. The labels *information* and *knowledge* are often used interchangeably and are considered to share a common characteristic as a "self-contained substance" (Brown & Duguid, 2002: 120). However, Costa and Silva (2010) offer an important and useful distinction between information and knowledge. In their view, information is foundational as "basic material" (402), a point of beginning. Knowledge extends this foundation by adding context, understanding, or meaningfulness within particular circumstances. This distinction is useful when considering the nature of expertise. The National Research Council (2000) describes experts as those who are able to activate and conditionalize their knowledge in response to a particular situation. Thus, while information can be considered as an independent entity, knowledge is deeply connected to someone doing the knowing (Brown & Duguid, 2002). In addition, while information is inert, knowledge "implies the evolving state of meaning of an active knower" (Wise & Duffy, 2008: 182) which is in constant motion as circumstances change and situations differ.

The distinction between information and knowledge offers a way to shift our perspective on Web 2.0 and suggests a future role for universities in how technologies are used. Information is accessible through the Web from universities, research organisations, corporations, professional associations, and informed amateurs. While the production and elaboration of information remains a key initiative of universities, its role as a repository of information may be shifting to that of a repository of expertise. Thus, the focus shifts to how information is used and combined to understand current problems and develop new knowledge. In this view expertise is no longer focused on what faculty can transmit to students but rather how they can shape and contextualize the ways in which students interact with the vast amount of information available. That is, a central faculty role is helping students cope with abundance (Weller, 2011) as they evaluate the massive amount of information available to them. The emphasis for student learning is placed not on the information they can access and acquire but what they are able to do with and through that information. In other words, faculty expertise helps students avoid simply collecting a large amount of inert information and instead develop robust knowledge that can be activated and conditionalized in relevant situations. Thus, two central questions for a value proposition for universities today are: in what specific ways can faculty expertise bridge information and knowledge and how can Web 2.0 technologies support university faculty in this role?

REIMAGINING THE EDUCATIONAL PARADIGM

Change is difficult. Hennessy, Ruthven, and Brindley (2005), in research conducted with teachers at the secondary education level, indicated that enthusiasm for new technologies was tempered with caution. Its use was perceived as inevitable, but the actual integration of technology was approached more as an extension of current pedagogical practice than as a departure point for change. This mixture of caution and enthusiasm is also evident in the higher education literature. Web 2.0 technologies in particular are described as presenting challenges for educators when they disrupt current practices of teaching (Laouris, Underwood, Laouri, & Christakis, 2010). In response, some faculty have taken a "conservative approach" (Hennesy, Ruthven, & Brindley, 2005: 185) by simply grafting blogs, wikis, Twitter, and social networks into existing courses. Added-on Web 2.0 technologies can coexist easily with current teaching methods; for example, lectures that are delivered or available for review via podcasting or YouTube. However, research has shown that bringing new technologies into a course without a strong rationale and tight connection to the intended learning is unlikely to be successful (Ravenscroft, 2011).

The perceived potential to support learning is what draws many educators to emerging technologies. But to capitalize on that potential, educators need to use these technologies as a starting point for adapting and reimagining their current teaching and learning practices. Web 2.0 technologies are inherently interactive and participatory (Conole & Culver, 2010) and connect learners through the Internet to an abundance of both information and people (Weller, 2011). They therefore require pedagogies that take advantage of these properties. The nature of interactive technologies aligns with pedagogical moves toward more student-centered learning implied in a constructivist philosophy that sees learning as being constructed by learners through personal experiences and interactive negotiation of meaning. Specifically, the collaborative and interactive nature of Web 2.0 technologies offers a foundation for dialogue and dialogic processes in higher education (Ravenscroft, 2011). These technologies present the opportunity to help realize the potential of initiating interactions with others and with ourselves, learning through and with each other, long thought to be valuable in education (Kazepides, 2010). However, to be successful in this endeavor, Web 2.0 technologies must be intentionally learningful, specifically designed to encourage and support genuine dialogue, and lead to a relevant knowledge-building enterprise (Ravenscroft, 2011).

The literature seems reluctant to settle on one descriptive term for "dialogue." The terms "dialogue," "discussion," and "conversation" are used largely interchangeably, often with qualifiers such as "meaningful" or "genuine." We think it is useful to begin with a tighter definition of the term "dialogue." Kazepides (2010) makes

a distinction among these terms, first between conversation and dialogue, and finally with genuine dialogue. Conversation, he suggests, is a broad description and is contextual in meaning; it includes all interactions, sad, serious, humorous, or nonsense. Dialogue, however, is always purposeful. In addition, dialogue is not a path to a particular predefined position; rather it is a search for understanding that requires reason and argumentation. Genuine dialogue is more than just a process. Genuine dialogue requires "respect, trust, open-mindedness, and a willingness to listen and risk one's own preconceptions, fixed beliefs, biases, and prejudices in the pursuit of truth" (Kazepides, 2010: 92).

Creating Dialogic Spaces with Web 2.0 Technologies

Learning through dialogue and dialogic spaces occurs when there is purpose in the interactions and tasks required of the learners. It is precisely this purposefulness associated with higher education learning that opens the door for the dialectic dimension of dialogue. A dialectic approach highlights critical analysis and reasoned logic by which learners can develop a deeper conceptual understanding of a particular discipline. This conceptual foundation will open up learners to multiple perspectives and dialogue that encompasses "new or conflicting ideas that we are encouraged to explore and understand rather than reject or attack" (Ravenscroft, 2011: 145). Learning in this case means confronting alternative and conflicting perspectives, questioning one's own belief, and changing one's mind. Below we describe the specific affordances of several currently common Web 2.0 technologies to support these processes.

A wiki is a Web-borne space that enables "mass collaborative authoring," (Laouris et. al., 2010). Beyond the ability for individual authors to add or delete or edit existing content posted to the wiki site, the wiki internally documents each change. That is, each change made in the document can be traced back to its particular author. As well, a history of the evolution of the site is created so that any earlier incarnation of the site can be retrieved. Thus, wikis enable a collaborative process whereby a heterogeneous group can collaboratively construct knowledge through the combining, clarifying, and refining of ideas in a shared space. In particular, the "talk" or "discussion" page generally associated with each wiki document provides a venue for explicit coordination and negotiation as part of these activities (Viégas, Wattenberg, Kriss & van Ham, 2007). This can constitute a dialogic space as individuals present their perspectives, question the perspectives of others, and then clarify their own perspectives. They discuss emerging positions to negotiate collaboratively toward an agreed-upon understanding. The benefit here is that none of the discussion is lost and can be recalled, revisited, reinterpreted, or returned to at any point in the process.

Blogging (Web-logging) can offer students a forum to discuss their existing perspectives and to reflect on those perspectives. Blogs present the most recent iteration of an individual's thinking but also enable an unfolding online conversation to be visible through the sequence of posts and comments ordered from most recent to oldest (Paulus, Payne, & Jahns, 2009). While blogs are often perceived as records of individual journeys, comment sections and inter-linking from one individual's blog to another's have the potential to create a dialogic space. Initial research in higher education suggests that blogs encourage reflection, collaboration, and critical thinking (Paulus et al., 2009).

Alternatively, dialogic space can be created through social networks. The literature describes using external social network sites such as Facebook or MySpace (Nardi, Whittaker, & Schwartz, 2002) or developing a purposely designed educational social network that supports social interchanges as well as task-oriented ones (Cho, Gay, Davidson, & Ingraffea, 2007). Using either

approach can result in educational exchanges that have been described simultaneously as "conversation, collaboration, and social" (Cho et al., 2007: 312). Learners' previous experience with social networks can increase their willingness to accomplish a particular task within such an environment (Nardi et al., 2002). Familiarity with social networks and social network communication styles therefore provide a foundation upon which learners can more quickly build new social learning networks (Cho et al., 2007). There is encouraging evidence that social networks can have a "tangible impact on individual performance" (Cho et. al., 2007: 324). However, there is the potential that learners with strong pre-existing social ties or pre-existing friendships with others in their collaborative learning group will experience negative consequences of these ties as they can "restrict one's ability to renew his/her existing [social] capital by confining the social actor to pre-determined social circles" (Cho et al., 2007: 323).

Twitter is a more recent interactive microblogging technology. Used during class, it can be a real-time way of engaging learners in experiential learning. Twitter provides direct communication that can generate further discussion and create interest in the course and course topics. It can also engage students in their own learning through the application of content, through observations on the content, and through reflection about the content. Twitter also provides an opportunity for learners to connect with authentic members of a disciplinary community by "following" them, and possibly responding to their comments. This can be a platform for expanding learning beyond the classroom walls and supporting learners in testing their understandings through "tweets" sent out to the class or the world (Rinaldo et al., 2011). Twitter can be used dialogically if it enables interactive engagement among individuals. It can act as a way of interjecting questions or requests for concept clarification during presentations. It allows multiple perspectives to emerge as different individuals experience the same event and provide a platform to discuss diverse perspectives toward a common understanding.

Actualizing the potential of these and other Web 2.0 technologies to meet the requirements of dialogue and genuine dialogue may require a change in faculty roles. In this new model, the learner is truly at the center of the process and the faculty is just one of multiple connections to the world of information. Importantly, however, they are a connection that is steeped in a disciplinary perspective. Thus, dialogue provides the interactive mechanism by which learners can merge personal experiences with the diverse information and expertise available on the Web. The role of faculty is to bring content and disciplinary expertise to manage the information and shape the dialogue toward an intentional educational outcome. Faculty expertise is also required to help learners develop dialogic skills, to manage the relationships fostered by the social technologies, and to support learners' use of technologies to accomplish purposeful academic goals. In doing so, faculty members must begin to take on new roles in the learning process. We consider the broad role of *orchestrating* the total learning experience with several more specific roles embedded within it: scripting, translating, introducing, and co-exploring. Each of these roles will require expertise in teaching and learning beyond, but inclusive of, disciplinary knowledge.

Shifting Faculty Roles in the Support of Learning

Orchestrating Learning

One way to conceptualize the new role of faculty within an interactive technologies environment is as that of an *orchestrator* (Dillenbourg & Jermann, 2010): one who coordinates a variety of elements to create a learning experience for students. There is an important distinction to make between the term "guide" or "facilitator" and that conveyed through the orchestration metaphor. While the former are often used to represent the move of an instructor from a "sage on the stage" to a "guide on the side," in orchestration the instructor directs the learning process. This musically themed metaphor relates to the coordination of the various elements of the learning environment to work together harmoniously as a whole. At the same time, unlike a conductor working with a stable score, learning environments are dynamic, shifting with the contributions and interactions among learners and with faculty. The faculty, as orchestrator, alters the activities and modifies the process as learning outcomes require (Dillenbourg & Jermann, 2010).

While the process is dynamic with the shape of the learning process co-emergent, the activity design is both planful and goal-oriented. Thus, in an orchestration model, faculty play a central role in the learning process, from leading the process, to creating activities to supporting learners as they confront alternate and unfamiliar perspectives, to assessing final outcomes (Dillenbourg & Jermann, 2010). In some sense then, orchestration focuses more on the design of the activities that promote the learning than directly on the information or knowledge base that is the target of the learning. The challenge in design is to balance the freedom inherent in Web 2.0 technologies with the formal requirements of higher education (Laouris et al., 2010).

For example, the freedom of the Web is illustrated in the abundance of information available (Weller, 2011), but formal academic education requires evaluating and validating information. We can imagine how a faculty member might orchestrate a purposeful learning activity that navigates this tension; for example, a history professor in a large, entry-level class who creates an assignment focused on a current event such as the Arab Spring uprisings. Students could first be asked to gather different sources of information about the event (e.g., official government or political movement websites, online news articles from different publications/countries, individuals' blogs, etc.). The class would compile these via a particular tag on a social bookmarking site (such as de.lic.ious). Once the contributions had been collected, the professor could introduce the idea of evaluating the sources and the kinds of characteristics that might be attributed to them (e.g., Western media, local youth perspective, reputable organization, opinion piece, etc.), which in turn could serve as the foundation for a second phase of tagging. With this annotated body of sources at their disposal, students could then dive into projects dealing with the issue of neutrality in reporting, or distinctions in interpretation depending on source location.

In a real-world example, Ching and Hsu (2011) describe the use of a specifically designed Web 2.0 application to support a collaborative concept mapping activity. The construction required 37 learners in an online course in a Master's program in Instructional Design to collaborate in self-created groups of three or four people to create "sophisticated graphic representations of the instructional design process" (787). Each group discussed initial impressions, negotiated an understanding, and presented their group's collective subject knowledge in a graphical format. The Web 2.0 technology enabled interaction, collaboration, and an externalization of individual process (Ching & Hsu, 2011). There was also evidence of gains in generic skills such as communication and collaboration skills. The authors highlight that "the activity and [the] assessment of Web 2.0 practices are inseparable parts of quality learning experiences" (794). In this example, the faculty member provided feedback at both the formative and summative levels to guide or orchestrate the learning through the collaborative activity.

Following from this, as part of the orchestration of activities for purpose and relevance, there also needs to be a shift in the broader perspective of learning from the more traditional competitive assessment model to one that is more socially collaborative (Ruth & Houghten, 2009). For example, wikis can be used to initiate a community of inquiry (Garrison & Vaughn, 2009) that shifts the role of faculty from teaching "things" to participating in community knowledge building. Within this community, the wiki disrupts the usual hierarchy in information sources between teacher and learner, thus supporting a continuous dialogue. Knowledge and learning arise through the active process of learning rather than in any final course document (Ruth & Houghton, 2009). For example, a professor of Economics working with a class in International Trade might use a wiki to connect two classes located in different countries. Students would be divided into small groups of five to eight people and paired with a group in the other country. The task could be to create an international trade agreement between the two countries. Students would use the wiki to set out starting positions and industry exclusions and then work toward accommodating stated needs in each country while negotiating an agreement that promotes the goal of mutual economic growth. The faculty in each country would take on expert consultant roles in helping each group recognize potential problems and inconsistencies.

Collaborative Scripting

Within the general metaphor of orchestration, there are several more specific roles that the use of Web 2.0 technologies in teaching and learning may require. One such role, in an example of a specific learningful orchestrated design, is *collaborative scripting*. Collaboration scripts aid collaboration by providing "a sequence of actions where each actor has a specific part to play and pre-specified actions to take" (King, 2007: 15). In this way, scripts impose structure on a process of collaborative interaction "to foster systematic and efficient communication, coordination, and collaboration" (Haake & Pfister, 2010: 192) and "support the sort of meaning making that corresponds to learning" (Ravenscroft, 2011: 155). The importance of scaffolding dialogue with the use of collaborative scripting is explained by recognizing that in its absence, there is an unwarranted presumption that learners will automatically share, exchange, and engage in meaningful dialogue.

Learners arrive in courses with a diversity of backgrounds and previous experiences and supporting these diverse learners is necessary "to support seamless participation among networked learners" (Cho et al., 2007: 325). Genuine learning dialogue requires taking into account both the diverse characteristics of the learners and the affordances of the technologies in use. Even where learners have a familiarity and comfort with social networking and interactive technologies, it is unlikely they will be experienced with the approaches of formal academic study combined with and articulated through these technologies.

Collaborative scripts can coordinate the learning process, enable more efficient interactions, and enhance the benefit of collaboration (Haake & Pfister, 2010). Collaboration scripts can be designed and enacted at multiple levels of granularity; for example, a micro-level with the focus on individual roles or actions (Weinberger, Ertl, Fischer, & Mandl, 2005), or a macro-level focusing on the learning task and the overall process (Dillenbourg & Hong, 2008). Scripts can also be integrative, including both individual and collective actions (Dillenbourg & Jermann, 2007). An example of an integrative approach in collaborative scripting is provided as a Structured Dialogic Design or SDD (Laouris et al., 2010). In the first phase, the learners' role is to share personal knowledge and perspectives. The intent here is to expose "contributions from learners ... with divergent prior knowledge and with diverse backgrounds and perspectives" (Laouris et al., 2010: 155). Once each of these initial views is shared, a learner's role is to move though questioning and clarification, comparing and contrasting perspectives, and finally negotiating toward a new or modified understanding. The final phase of dialogue as described by SDD is the negotiated construction of new knowledge. This entire

cycle of dialogue represents a "spiral of learning" (Laouris et al., 2010: 167).

One example of a situation in which SDD might be useful to support university work using Web 2.0 tools is with an upper-level seminar in political science. If the topic of learning is constitutional frameworks, students could be asked to consider the design of such a framework for an emerging democracy such as Libya. Small groups made up of North American and Libyan students could work in a wiki to elaborate on and dialogue around the issues involved. The first phase would involve gathering individual framing principles from each group member. In the second phase, students would identify similar and contrasting principles and begin to write a framework that identifies common ground and negotiates conflicts. This would clarify differences in perspectives and present an illustration of perspectives as they relate to cultural background and experiences. The third and final stage would be a final document outlining their constitutional framework.

Translating

Another specific role within the orchestration metaphor relates to the difference between information and knowledge discussed earlier. Faculty can use their expertise to help students *translate*, understand, and interpret the mountain of information available. In this role, faculty can aid students "learning to 'see' or 'decode' from the perspective of a discipline" (Wise & Duffy, 2008: 183) thus adding value to the process. The result is that faculty support students in the creation of knowledge (rather than only the accumulation of information) and the ability to apply that knowledge to current and future situations.

Imagining the translator role in action, a professor in a large lower-level Archeology class might connect on-campus students with experts and advanced students on an actual archeological dig site. A daily or weekly blog created at the dig site would become the source documentation for the on-campus group. Students would be asked to follow the blog on their own for homework; in class, the professor could help the students make sense of the significance of the different kinds of actions, observations, and findings that the archeologists record. This in turn would help them interpret the blog on their own in the following week. The comments function within the blog could also be used to enable interactive discussion. For example, on-campus students could engage with on-site students to ask questions and create a dialogue linking their studies to authentic practice in the field.

In a smaller course, blogs could also be used to enable faculty to "see" student's thinking in terms of the course material. Course students could be asked to create their own blogs about their growing understanding of archeology. This would be supported by specific blogging instructions with ongoing faculty prompts and facilitation to create a greater likelihood of cognitive engagement with course content (Halic, Lee, Paulus, & Spence, 2010). The student blog posts would provide faculty with insight into the aspects of course material where misunderstanding occurs, and they could then use this feedback as a basis to redesign learning activities to help students better "decode" the material (Halic et al., 2010).

Introducing

Faculty may also take on a role as *introducers* both in the narrow sense of drawing students into alternative experiences and perspectives, and more broadly as connecting students with other authentic members of a disciplinary community. Faculty may, in fact, perform this role simultaneously with the translating role as they introduce information and perspectives and aid in the decoding of that information. In addition, interactive Web 2.0 technologies make possible learning relationships with individuals not co-located with students (Penny & Bolton, 2010).

In some cases, these interactive relationships can be characterized as mentoring or, with a nod to technology, telementoring. One such application that has been conducted at the secondary level involves student groups working with research telementors (O'Neill, Asgari, & Dong, 2011). In this example, groups of students in a high school history class were each connected with telementors who had expertise in historical research related to students' chosen perspective on a particular event. The intention was to have students learn about history and historical research by actually doing it in a supported environment. A similar approach could be imagined at the university level working in a small seminar course. However, one important challenge identified by O'Neill, Asgari, and Dong was how to sufficiently articulate and communicate the purpose of the interactions (dialogues) and the role of the mentor so that the intended learning outcomes were accomplished. This is an important factor in generating learning experiences rather than only interesting experiences.

Social networking sites provide another forum for introducing students to the expertise of individuals or organizations. One way of realizing this scenario might be to create a design whereby social policy positions are argued within a social network where organizations such as those working in homelessness, literacy, or social justice issues are introduced and connected to the network site. Students would be expected to produce documents or blogs that describe their thought journey and a portfolio of their own learning produced in a website or blog form.

Co-Exploring

One perspective on learning in the digital age places the learner at the center of the learning process as the central agent of the learning that occurs through their own experiences (Hase & Kenyon, 2007). Thus, learners are *co-explorers* with faculty. While learners are expected to become more self-directed and independent (Ashton

& Newman, 2006), the faculty role becomes a "deep partnership" (Ashton & Newman, 2006: 837) in supporting learning about and within a disciplinary community. As a partner, faculty becomes engaged as part of the dialogue, not proffering solutions or answers but pushing for deeper analysis and connecting disciplinary concepts and approaches to the discussion. In a sense this is an expanded version of the "guide-on-the-side" role often associated with constructivist practices; but the space to be explored is unconstrained and is one that the faculty member may or may not have explored before. This role may be most appropriate in small upper-level or graduate seminars or in the context of a supervisory relationship, where students are ready to be in control and the instructor can devote attention to each individual. A more relaxed version of this role might involve co-exploration with a small group.

As an example, faculty might work with small groups of graduate students who are developing research plans for the completion of their degree programs. Each student would create a blog as a way of working through their own thinking and their possible research approaches. Faculty and other students would engage in dialogue through the comments function within the blog and each subsequent blog entry would synthesize the student's own thinking with the comments received. Students and faculty may find their own thinking pushed to deeper levels and may recognize insights that might not have occurred to them otherwise. In this case, both students and faculty have the opportunity to learn. The final student outcome would be a workable research proposal.

Students' Shifting Role for Learning

Just as we consider the need for a shift in the roles of faculty, we must also realize that students have prior experiences that shape the way they approach learning in the university environment. Students arrive with past habits, strategies, skills, and a belief about what it takes to be successful, refined over their time already spent in a formal learning environment. They arrive with expectations of what the university environment should be and of their own learning capacity. Despite the fact that the majority of students are familiar with and use a wide variety of technologies, as we have discussed, they may not have experience using them in a formal learning environment or be familiar with anything other than traditional pedagogical approaches.

As technologies change and new technologies emerge, the ease of adoption has, and will continue to have, a significant impact on student learning.

Learning that uses this technology requires new—or at least more highly developed—skills. They are skills in searching the wide variety of information sources; skills in sorting and sieving the infinite volume of information available; skills in synthesizing from multiple sources of information—all a long way from traditional skills needed to assimilate "validated" sources of knowledge like that found in textbooks or a professor's lectures. (Moore, 2007: 180)

Collins and Halverson (2009) echo this change both in the digital availability of information and in the necessity of acquiring new learning skills. Laouris et al. (2010) found that using a wiki developed a number of more generic skills such as using Web 2.0 technologies generally, developing collaboration skills, and broader organizational skills toward achieving the learning task. Moore's (2007) description of advanced skills in searching, sorting, synthesizing, and validating information is also part of the more generic skills arising from course work. It is important to reinforce, however, that information and knowledge are not necessarily the same thing. Any increased ability of students to find information and use interactive—that is, Web 2.0—technologies is not to suggest that such comfort automatically transfers into either more active or more capable approaches to learning.

CONCLUSION

As faculty attempt to reimagine teaching and their roles as teachers and students are asked to embrace different ways of learning in the era of Web 2.0, the focus must continue to be on learning with and through new technologies. We are reminded that "educators need to explore new ways of teaching … by capitalizing upon the multi-faceted nature of new media, rather than by simply translating existing face-to-face techniques into the new media" (Laouris et al., 2010: 170).

But if, as we have noted, the call for changed practice is nothing new (Laurillard, 2002), why should we expect a different outcome from that experienced in the past? Simply continuing to call for change in higher education is not enough to actualize that change. A change in teaching practice and student learning will require scaffolding. A bridge must be built that can enable faculty to move from an imparting knowledge paradigm—faculty transmitting their expertise to learners—to one where learning is orchestrated (Dillenbourg & Jermann, 2010). This is a move to a paradigm where faculty act as designers and conductors of the learning process, taking on a variety of roles to translate, introduce, co-explore, and collaborate on scripts (Laurillard, 2002; Wise & Duffy, 2008).

In order for this to occur, faculty must reimagine their own approach to teaching and higher education institutions must enable that reimagination. This will require clear guidance to translate the potential of new technologies into instructional practice and ongoing support throughout this transition. There must be examples of sound practice and time to tailor such examples to one's own teaching practice. It is important to recognize, however, that many of the challenges that confront educators with these new emerging technologies are similar to those they encountered in incorporating previous technologies. The mere use of technologies in learning—whether Web 1.0, Web 2.0, or whatever comes next—will not

be sufficient. Most technologies can be integrated into current teaching practice without altering the essential form that teaching takes. A blog, after all, could simply be a textual form of a lecture. The affordances of Web 2.0 technologies are their interactivity, the capacity to connect individuals, information, and expertise across space and time. To capitalize on the potential they offer, we need to reimagine current teaching and learning practices and faculty roles.

The use of dialogue and the creation of dialogic spaces within academic courses offer a way to take full advantage of interactive Web 2.0 technologies and expand knowledge creation through user-created content. Faculty need to take on the role of orchestrating learning, designing and managing the learning activities and processes that will achieve the learning outcomes intended for the course. But the process of learning is dynamic and the learning is co-emergent with the learning activities. The result is that faculty need to adopt other roles as they become necessary to the learning process. Faculty cannot presume that learners arrive with skills in argumentation or synthesis and may have to become adept at scaffolding these skills—for example, through collaborative scripting that structures a dialogic process and students' roles in it. Faculty must also take on the role of translator requiring them to gain and become experts at helping students search for information, evaluate the information, and contextualize the information in order to understand a specific problem or problem set within a disciplinary or multidisciplinary perspective. Faculty must help students understand, interpret, and decode the abundant information available on the Web and, through meaningful learning experiences, develop knowledge. Faculty may also take on the role of co-explorer, not just mediating interactions for learning but actually engaging with learners in creating new knowledge. In this role, faculty become co-learners as much as course leaders. Finally, faculty must be introducers, drawing students into alternative experiences and perspectives and connecting students to the larger disciplinary community. By considering the new faculty roles both enabled and required by Web 2.0 technologies, we can collectively begin to reimagine higher education teaching and learning.

REFERENCES

Amirault, R. J., & Visser, Y. L. (2009). The university in periods of technological change: A historically grounded perspective. *Journal of Computing in Higher Education, 21*(1), 62–79. doi:10.1007/s12528-009-9016-5

Amundsen, C., Winer, L., & Gandell, T. (2004). Designing teaching for student learning. In Saroyan, A., & Amundsen, C. (Eds.), *Rethinking teaching in higher education: From a course design workshop to a faculty development framework* (pp. 71–93). Sterling, VA: Stylus Publishing, LLC.

Ashton, J., & Newman, L. (2006). An unfinished symphony: 21st century teacher education using knowledge creating heutagogies. *British Journal of Educational Technology, 37*(6), 825–840. doi:10.1111/j.1467-8535.2006.00662.x

Bennet, S., Maton, K., & Kervin, L. (2008). The 'digital natives' debate: A critical review of the evidence. *British Journal of Educational Technology, 39*(5), 775–786. doi:10.1111/j.1467-8535.2007.00793.x

Bloland, H. G. (2005). Whatever happened to post-modernism in higher education? No requiem in the new millennium. *The Journal of Higher Education, 76*(2), 121–150. doi:10.1353/jhe.2005.0010

Brown, J. S., & Adler, R. P. (2008). Minds on fire: Open education, the long tail, and learning 2.0. *EDUCAUSE Review, 43*(1), 17–32.

Brown, J. S., & Duguid, P. (2002). *The social life of information*. Boston, MA: Harvard Business School Press.

Bullen, M., Morgan, T., & Qayyum, A. (2011). Digital learners in higher education: Generation is not the issue. *Canadian Journal of Learning and Technology, 37*(1), 1–24.

Ching, Y.-H., & Hsu, Y.-C. (2011). Design-grounded assessment: A framework and a case study of Web 2.0 practices in higher education. *Australasian Journal of Educational Technology, 27*(5), 781–797.

Cho, H., Gay, G., Davidson, B., & Ingraffea, A. (2007). Social networks, communication styles, and learning performance in a CSCL community. *Computers & Education, 49*, 309–329. doi:10.1016/j.compedu.2005.07.003

Collins, A., & Halverson, R. (2009). *Rethinking education in the age of technology: The digital revolution and schooling in America*. New York, NY: Teachers College Press.

Conole, G., & Culver, J. (2010). The design of cloudworks: Applying social networking practice to foster the exchange of learning and teaching ideas and designs. *Computers & Education, 54*(3), 679–692. doi:10.1016/j.compedu.2009.09.013

Costa, G. J. M., & Silva, N. S. A. (2010). Knowledge versus content in e-learning: A philosophical discussion. *Information Systems Frontiers, 12*(4), 399–413. doi:10.1007/s10796-009-9200-1

Dillenbourg, P., & Hong, F. (2008). The mechanics of CSCL macro scripts. *International Journal of Computer-Supported Collaborative Learning, 3*(1), 5–23. doi:10.1007/s11412-007-9033-1

Dillenbourg, P., & Jermann, P. (2007). Designing integrative scripts. In F. Fischer, H. Mandl, J. Haake, & I. Kollar (Eds.), *Scripting computer-supported collaborative learning – Cognitive, computational, and educational perspectives*, (pp. 275-301), Computer-Supported Collaborative Learning Series. New York, NY: Springer.

Dillenbourg, P., & Jermann, P. (2010). Technology for classroom orchestration. In M. S. Kline & I. M. Saleh (Eds.), *New science of learning: Cognition, computers, and collaboration in education* (pp. 525-552). New York, NY: Springer Science+Business Media.

Downes, S. (2006). *Learning networks and connective knowledge.* Retrieved from http://it.coe. uga.edu/itforum/paper92/paper92.htlm

Dron, J. (2007). Designing the undesignable: Social software and control. *Journal of Educational Technology & Society, 10*(3), 60–71.

Garcia, L. M., & Roblin, N. P. (2008). Innovation, research, and professional development in higher education: Learning from our own experience. *Teaching and Teacher Education, 24*, 104–116. doi:10.1016/j.tate.2007.03.007

Garrison, D. R., & Vaughan, N. D. (2009). *Blended learning in higher education: Framework, principles, and guidelines.* San Fransisco, CA: Jossey-Bass.

Haake, J. M., & Pfister, H.-R. (2010). Scripting a distance-learning university course: Do students benefit from net-based scripted collaboration? *International Journal of Computer-Supported Collaborative Learning, 5*(2), 191–210. doi:10.1007/s11412-010-9083-7

Halic, O., Lee, D., Paulus, T., & Spence, M. (2010). To blog or not to blog: Student perceptions of blog effectiveness for learning in a college-level course. *The Internet and Higher Education, 13*(4), 206–213. doi:10.1016/j.iheduc.2010.04.001

Hase, S., & Kenyon, C. (2007). Heutagogy: A child of complexity theory. *Complexity: An International Journal of Complexity and Education, 4*, 111-118. Retrieved October 15, 2011, from http://issuu.com/gfbertini/docs/heutagogy_-_a_child_of_complexity_theory.

Hennessy, S., Ruthven, K., & Brindley, S. (2005). Teacher perspectives on integrating ICT into subject teaching: Commitment, constraints, caution, and change. *Journal of Curriculum Studies, 37*(2), 155–192. doi:10.1080/0022027032000276961

Hughes, J. E., & Narayan, R. (2009). Collaboration and learning with Wikis in higher classrooms. *Journal of Interactive Online Learning, 8*(1), 63–77.

Johnson, M., & Liber, O. (2008). The personal learning environment and the human condition: From theory to teaching practice. *Interactive Learning Environments, 16*(1), 3–15. doi:10.1080/10494820701772652

Jones, C., Ramanau, R., Cross, S., & Healing, G. (2010). Net generation or digital natives: Is there a distinct new generation entering university? *Computers & Education, 54*(3), 722–732. doi:10.1016/j.compedu.2009.09.022

Kazepides, T. (2010). *Education as dialogue: Its prerequisites and its elements.* Montreal, Canada: McGill-Queens University Press.

King, A. (2007). Scripting collaborative learning processes: A cognitive perspective. In Fischer, F., Kollar, I., Mandl, H., & Haake, J. M. (Eds.), *Scripting computer-supported collaborative learning* (pp. 13–37). New York, NY: Springer. doi:10.1007/978-0-387-36949-5_2

Laouris, Y., Underwood, G., Laouri, R., & Christakis, A. (2010). Structured dialogue embedded within emerging technologies. In G. Veletsianos (Ed.), *Emerging technologies in distance education* (pp. 153-173). Athabasca, Canada: Athabasca University Press. Retrieved February 28, 2011, from http://www.aupress.ca/index.php/books/120177

Laurillard, D. (2002). *Rethinking university teaching: A conversational framework for the effective use of learning technologies.* New York, NY: RoutledgeFalmer. doi:10.4324/9780203304846

Margaryan, A., Littlejohn, A., & Vojt, G. (2011). Are digital natives a myth or reality? University students' use of digital technologies. *Computers & Education*, *56*(2), 429–440. doi:10.1016/j.compedu.2010.09.004

Molenda, M. (1997). Historical and philosophical foundations of instructional design: A North American view. In Tennyson, R., Schott, F., Seel, N., & Dijkstra, S. (Eds.), *Instructional design: International perspectives* (pp. 41–53). Lawrence Erlbaum Associates.

Moore, M. G. (2007). Web 2.0: Does it really matter? *American Journal of Distance Education*, *21*(4), 177–183. doi:10.1080/08923640701595183

Nardi, B., Whittaker, S., & Schwartz, H. (2002). NetWorks and their activity in intensional networks. *Computer Supported Cooperative Work*, *11*(1), 205–242. doi:10.1023/A:1015241914483

National Research Council. (2000). *How people learn: Brain, mind, experience, and school*. Washington, DC: National Academy Press.

O'Neill, D. K., Asgari, M., & Dong, Y. R. (2011). Trade-offs between perceptions of success and planned outcomes in an online mentoring program. *Mentoring & Tutoring: Partnership in Learning*, *19*(1), 45–63. doi:10.1080/13611267.2011.543570

Paulus, T. M., Payne, R. L., & Jahns, L. (2009). "Am I making sense here?": What blogging reveals about undergraduate student understanding. *Journal of Interactive Online Learning*, *8*(1), 1–22.

Penny, C., & Bolton, D. (2010). Evaluating the outcomes of an eMentoring program. *Journal of Educational Technology Systems*, *39*(1), 17–30. doi:10.2190/ET.39.1.c

Pidduck, A. B. (2010). Electronic social networks, teaching, and learning. In W. A. Wright, M. Wilson, & D. MacIssac (Eds.), *Collected essays on learning and teaching, Volume III* (pp. 106-111). STHLE Society for Teaching and Learning in Higher Education/SAPES Société pour l'avancement de la pédogie dans l'enseignement superior. Retrieved February 4, 2011, from http://apps.medialab.uwindsor.ca/ctl/CELT/vol3/CELT18.pdf.

Prensky, M. (2001). Digital natives, digital immigrants. *Horizon*, *9*(5), 1–6. doi:10.1108/10748120110424816

Ravenscroft, A. (2011). Dialogue and connectivism: A new approach to understanding and promoting dialogue-rich networked learning. *International Review of Research in Open and Distance Learning*, *12*(3), 139–160.

Rinaldo, S. B., Tapp, S., & Laverie, D. A. (2011). Learning by Tweeting: Using Twitter as a pedagogical tool. *Journal of Marketing Education*, *33*(2), 193–203. doi:10.1177/0273475311410852

Ruth, A., & Houghton, L. (2009). The wiki way of learning. *Australasian Journal of Educational Technology*, *25*(2), 135–152.

South, S. R. (2010). Making the move from shouting to listening to public action: A student perspective on millennials and dialogue. *Journal of Public Deliberation*, *6*(1), 1–10.

Viégas, F. B., Wattenberg, M., Kriss, J., & van Ham, F. (2007). Talk before you type: Coordination in Wikipedia. *Proceedings of the 40th Annual Hawaii International Conference on System Sciences* (HICSS'07), (p. 78a). doi/10.1109/HICSS.2007.511

Weinberger, A., Ertl, B., Fischer, F., & Mandl, H. (2005). Epistemic and social scripts in computer-supported collaborative learning. *Instructional Science*, *33*(1), 1–30. doi:10.1007/s11251-004-2322-4

Weller, M. (2011). A pedagogy of abundance. *Spanish Journal of Pedagogy, 249,* 223–236.

Wise, A., & Duffy, T. M. (2008). Designing online conversations to engage local practice: Implications of a knowledge-building framework. In R. Luppicini (Ed.), *Handbook of conversation design for instructional applications* (pp. 177-200). Hershey, PA: Information Science Reference (Idea Group Inc.).

Wise, A. F., & O'Neill, D. K. (2009). Beyond "more" versus "less": A reframing of the debate on instructional guidance. In Tobias, S., & Duffy, T. M. (Eds.), *Constructivist instruction: Success or failure?* (pp. 82–105). New York, NY: Routledge, Taylor and Francis.

ADDITIONAL READING

Anderson, P. (2007). What is Web 2.0? Ideas, technologies, and implications for education. *JISC Technology & Standards Watch.* Retrieved from http://www.jisc.ac.uk/publications/reports/2007/twweb2.aspx

Bonk, C. J. (2009). *The world is open: How web technology is revolutionizing education.* San Francisco, CA: Jossey-Bass.

Collison, G., Elbaum, B., Haavind, S., & Tinker, R. (2000). *Facilitating online learning: Effective strategies for moderators.* Madison, WI: Atwood Publishing.

Conole, G., & Alevizou, P. (2010). A literature review of the use of Web 2.0 tools in higher education. *The Higher Education Academy.* Milton Keynes, UK: The Open University. Retrieved from http://www.heacademy.ac.uk/assets/EvidenceNet/Conole_Alevizou_2010.pdf

Ebner, M., & Nagler, W. (2010). Has Web 2.0 reached the educated top? In *Proceedings of the World Conference on Educational Multimedia, Hypermedia, and Telecommunications 2010* (pp. 4001-4010), Chesapeake, VA: AACE.

Ellison, N. B., Steinfield, C., & Lampe, C. (2007). The benefits of Facebook "friends": Social capital and college students' use of online social network sites. *Journal of Computer-Mediated Communication, 12,* 1143–1168. doi:10.1111/j.1083-6101.2007.00367.x

Glassman, M., & Kang, M. J. (2011). The logic of wikis: The possibilities of the Web 2.0 classroom. *International Journal of Computer-Supported Collaborative Learning, 6*(1), 93–112. doi:10.1007/s11412-011-9107-y

Johnson, L., Smith, R., Willis, H., Levine, A., & Haywood, K. (2011). *The 2011 horizon report.* Austin, TX: The New Media Consortium.

Kennewell, S., Tanner, H., Jones, S., & Beauchamp, G. (2008). Analysing the use of interactive technology to implement interactive teaching. *Journal of Computer Assisted Learning, 24*(1), 61–73. doi:10.1111/j.1365-2729.2007.00244.x

Lai, Y. C., & Ng, E. M. W. (2011). Using wikis to develop student teachers' learning, teaching, and assessment capabilities. *The Internet and Higher Education, 14*(1), 15–26. doi:10.1016/j.iheduc.2010.06.001

Larreamendy-Joerns, J., & Leinhardt, G. (2006). Going the distance with online education. *Review of Educational Research, 76*(4), 567–605. doi:10.3102/00346543076004567

Laru, J., Näykki, P., & Järvelä, S. (in press). Supporting small-group learning using multiple Web 2.0 tools: A case study in the higher education context. *The Internet and Higher Education.*

Peters, V. L., & Slotta, J. D. (2010). Scaffolding knowledge communities in the classroom: New opportunities in the Web 2.0 era. In Jacobson, M. J., & Reimann, P. (Eds.), *Designs for learning environments of the future* (pp. 205–232). New York, NY: Springer. doi:10.1007/978-0-387-88279-6_8

Ravenscroft, A. (2009). Social software, Web 2.0, and learning: Status and implications of an evolving paradigm. *Journal of Computer Assisted Learning, 25*, 1–5. doi:10.1111/j.1365-2729.2008.00308.x

Ravenscroft, A., Wegerif, R. B., & Hartley, J. R. (2007). Reclaiming thinking: Dialectic, dialogic and learning in the digital age. In Underwood, J., & Dockrell, J. (Eds.), *British Journal of Educational Psychology Monograph Series II: Part 5, Learning through Digital Technologies* (pp. 39–57). British Psychological Society.

Salmon, G. (2003). *E-moderating: The key to teaching & learning online* (2nd ed.). London, UK: RoutledgeFalmer.

Wegerif, R. (2007). *Dialogic education and technology: Expanding the space of learning.* New York, NY: Springer. doi:10.1007/978-0-387-71142-3

KEY TERMS AND DEFINITIONS

Constructivism: A philosophical perspective that suggests that knowledge is not acquired from an external, objective reality, but is "constructed" by each individual in their interaction with the social and material world, and represents an internal mediation of one's experience of this world.

Knowledge: While information is external and can be traded among individuals, knowledge relates to the contextualized understanding of a knower that is constantly evolving and cannot be directly shared with others.

Millennials or Digital Natives: These terms are often used interchangeably to describe individuals who have grown up with digital technologies—generally those born beginning in the 1980s.

Modern Perspective of the University: The university's role is research: the creation of new knowledge, the questioning of existing ideas, and the dissemination of current knowledge.

Post-Modern Perspective of the University: The university is only one element of the knowledge creation process, along with external agencies and organizations and informed amateurs.

Pre-Modern Perspective of the University: The university is the repository of knowledge, a stable set of facts as delivered truth.

Web 1.0: A first generation of Internet applications/use that enabled ubiquitous access to documents, Web pages, and materials geographically remote from users, but without widespread opportunity for interaction.

Web 2.0: A second generation of Internet applications/use that is characterized by more social, participative, sharing, and collaborative interactions, including dialectic and dialogic processes and documents, Web pages, and materials that can be jointly created, edited, and reconstructed.

Chapter 7
Between Tradition and Web 2.0:
eLaborate as a Social Experiment in Humanities Scholarship

Anne Beaulieu
University of Groningen, The Netherlands

Karina van Dalen-Oskam
Huygens Institute for the History of the Netherlands, The Netherlands

Joris van Zundert
Huygens Institute for the History of The Netherlands, The Netherlands

ABSTRACT

Web 2.0 is characterized by values of openness of participation (unrestricted by traditional markers of expertise), collaboration across and beyond institutions, increased value of resources through distributed participation, dynamic content and context, and self-organization and scalability. These values seem to offer new possibilities for knowledge creation. They also contrast in important ways with traditional forms of knowledge creation, where expertise, institutional affiliation, and restrictions on access and circulation have been important. Yet, rather than seeing a dichotomy between Web 2.0 and non-Web 2.0 modes of working in digital humanities, the authors observe the rise of hybrid forms that combine elements of these two modes. In this chapter, the authors reflect on the reasons for such hybrids, specifically through an exploration of eLaborate. As a virtual research environment, eLaborate targets both professional scholars and volunteers working with textual resources. The environment offers tools to transcribe textual sources, to annotate these transcriptions, and to publish them as digital scholarly editions. The majority of content currently comprises texts from the cultural heritage of Dutch history and literary history, although eLaborate does not put limits on the kind of text or language. Nor does the system impose limits on the openness of contribution to any edition project. Levels of openness and access are solely determined by the groups of users working on specific texts or editions. This Web 2.0 technology-based software is now used by several groups of teachers and students, and by scholarly, educated, and interested volunteers. We conducted interviews with coordinators of and participants in

DOI: 10.4018/978-1-4666-2178-7.ch007

different editorial groups, and we evaluate their experiences from the point of view of the described values of Web 2.0. We investigate changes in digital humanities resulting from intermediate forms between traditional academic practices and Web 2.0 modes. Rather than claim a revolution, we show how hybrid forms can actually be very powerful sites for change, through their inclusive rather than oppositional setup in relation to traditional practices.

INTRODUCTION

When technologies are hailed as "new" or "groundbreaking," they invite attention that tends to focus on either the promises or the threats they present. Social software for scholarly research is no exception. However, rather than address the potential, positive or negative, of these new technologies here, we seek to understand how practices are transformed and how the experience of users changes in relation to new tools. In this chapter we trace the development of a particular platform, eLaborate, and analyze user experiences in order to understand how scholarly work is developing in the context of social software.

The developments we discuss in this chapter are in an area that is most commonly labeled "digital humanities," a field of research intersecting humanities and the use of digital technologies. This label addresses the use of a range of digital technologies and has a broader scope than "humanities computing," which tends to focus on data processing. Digital humanities is also posited as a scholarly enterprise, and is often explicitly contrasted with "digitization" as a technical or procedural endeavor of mediation (Schreibman & Siemens, 2001).

eLaborate: A User-Driven Innovation

eLaborate (http://www.e-laborate.nl/en/) is an online work environment for textual scholars working alone or in a group on a text edition. Textual scholars are humanities researchers who make scholarly editions. These kinds of editions have been made for centuries: they provide a trustworthy transcription of, for example, a medieval,

handwritten manuscript in a form that can be used and understood by modern readers, or of printed material from the 16th century, annotated with all kinds of information and with printing errors explained and corrected. Modern material needs editions as well, such as handwritten letters (edited in correspondence editions) or novels that have been published in so many print runs that errors have crept in and now need to be weeded out by the scholarly editors.

Until quite recently, scholarly editors mostly worked alone, or occasionally in a very small group, and they published their editions in the form of books printed on paper. For the past decades, this often involved submitting digital files prepared in Word or WordPerfect to their publisher. Text editing is demanding, time-consuming work that requires a lot of expertise and knowledge of the material. Often, scholars announced the publication of a text edition they were preparing years and even decades in advance, thus explicitly claiming the edition as theirs and keeping the research community waiting for that edition—sometimes in vain.

With the rise of the Internet, a number of scholars from the Royal Netherlands Academy of Arts and Sciences thought that a Web-based work environment for textual scholars would have several advantages. First, the transcriptions could be made from a digital scan of the material—for example, of a medieval manuscript, with zooming and panning tools that the traditional photographs or original manuscripts did not have. Second, editors could work with larger groups, sharing their knowledge in a Web-based discussion forum linked to their digital edition; this larger group need not be confined to academic participants but could also include volunteers from outside academia with experience in this type of humanities task. These ideas went as far as investigating the possibility of pursuing the work collaboratively, with different people using the Web for the first stages of the transcription—what today we would refer to as "crowdsourcing." In such an approach, the first step of keying in the text from digital facsimile to produce digitized copies of textual content would be outsourced to volunteers over an open Web-based work environment. Third, the whole process of making an edition was expected to go much faster when more people could easily work on (parts of) the same edition at the same time. Fourth, working in a Web-based environment would help scholars to think about the possibilities of digital text editions and to theorize about how Web-based digital editions require a different implementation of the traditional editorial ideas than paper print editions. And fifth, working in a Web environment, text editions would automatically result in a digital file that could be used for new kinds of analysis, unlike print editions which would first have to be digitized for this.

The expectations about the potential of such tools were very much rekindled with the rise of Web 2.0 tools. These seemed to offer the textual scholar the opportunity to create and use resources on the Web, and looked as though they might be of major importance for the innovation of scholarly text editing in the Web-based digital world. eLaborate, however, was not built with such innovation per se in mind. The specific drive for the development of eLaborate was the possibility of shared Web-based editing of the same text and Web-based discussions in a forum. A social Web 2.0 approach would allow collaboration between large groups on the same Web-based text edition, which, being visible to all the scholars involved, was expected to speed up work and innovation in the whole field of textual scholarship.

During the development of eLaborate, small groups of test users played a major role in shaping the direction of its functionalities. The project leaders made sure that the principles underpinning eLaborate were followed: a clean, simple-to-use, collaborative way of entering and annotating text on the Web, with a capacity for capturing discussion and notes on the ongoing work. Agile development methodology was used to ensure the software was built with the needs of the user at its core. However, the project leaders did not give the test users complete freedom of choice. In their view, the wishes of the (traditionally schooled) users would lead to the development of an online version of Word or <oXygen/> (an integrated "hard core" XML editor). In prioritizing the functionality to be developed, they chose to focus on those items that the test users marked as having the most added value, but they also gently guided features that they judged to be mere print-on-paper, text-processing "copy-cat" features to the bottom of their "to-do" lists. This type of prioritization in a user-centric approach enabled the users to actually (have to) experience the new possibilities. This in turn seemed to inspire the users to express far more innovative wishes for functionality. However, the project leaders found that scholarly text editors could not always be pushed in the directions that they thought most useful. In eLaborate, the Web 2.0 openness actually had to be limited to keep the textual scholars interested in using the new tool. The scholars did not want infinite openness and access, and opted instead for a carefully selected part of Web 2.0 abilities. This resulted in a hybrid form of Web 2.0 tools which ended up being very popular among textual scholars.

Based on these years of interactions with users, and on recent interviews with members of two different eLaborate edition projects, we will show how users evaluated the different Web 2.0 elements in eLaborate. We will also illustrate why a hybrid form proved to be the much-needed intermediate step toward the innovation of the discipline of textual scholarship—while full Web 2.0 implementations would actually have kept scholars from doing anything at all with the tool.

eLaborate: An Innovative Technical Platform

Researchers and developers at the Huygens Institute for the History of the Netherlands (Huygens, 2011) released eLaborate[1] for the first time in 2005. It was envisaged as being a broad, collaborative, Web-based research environment for the humanities and social sciences. What truly attracted users, however, was its literary research component, the core of which could be described as a digital scriptorium: a Web tool for transcribing and annotating digital facsimiles of manuscript and early print sources. This was built as an extension of an open source content management system[2] that provided additional standard functionality for creating and publishing Web content, communication by mail-in forms, downloading and uploading of files, full text search, rights management, etc.

The original motivation to create a state-of-the-art transcription and annotation tool was not as straightforward as one might imagine. The Web-based collaboratory was aimed at transcribing textual sources into a digital format. This was useful where early print copies and manuscript sources defied automated computer transcription by optical character recognition. The researchers involved needed large amounts of digital text data for computational analysis. They soon acknowledged that they would not be able to produce these amounts of data by themselves. Thus, the creators of eLaborate at the time were looking for a way to provide literary researchers and editors with instruments that would prove useful to them and would, at the same time, multiply the production of digitally available resources for computational analysis in literary history.

Around 2004, most of the available transcription tools relied on verbatim TEI-XML transcription and annotation of textual sources. This meant that literary researchers had to write XML tags (e.g., "<l>a line of verse</l>") into their textual sources and had to structure their texts according to the Text Encoding Initiative schema for encoding text. This XML explicit approach to text modeling, however, seemed to alienate the majority of textual scholars from using XML (tools) at all. Therefore, eLaborate was developed to be a *text*-editor as much as possible, rather than an *XML*-editor. Various technical and usability reasons—no installation requirements, version integrity, ease of maintenance, ease of support—led to the choice of a Web-based tool. eLaborate became a Web-only approach, which was unique at the time within the field.

The recognition that textual scholars wanted to work with text rather than with XML shaped the very approach of the development of eLaborate: user-centric. The research and development team wanted to balance two issues. On the one hand, the tool would have to be far less obtrusive to the research practice of the users than editors using explicit XML. On the other hand, it needed to forcefully move away from commercial word processors that mostly capture layout digitally and do not capture a text's structure, something that is crucial to literary analysis. The balance was found in modeling a concept that is highly recognizable from the practice of textual scholars into the core of eLaborate: the trifecta of facsimile, transcription and annotation. Expressing these concepts in software allowed the software to capture the essential structures of the text and a graphical user interface, with which the textual scholars were familiar, could be offered. Creating a close link with existing practices, concepts, and workflow of targeted users was a key aspect in the development of eLaborate.

Another key aspect of eLaborate was its principled orientation toward an open approach to collaboration. eLaborate was designed to support openness of data and contribution. A project owner in eLaborate can keep any digital object completely private, make it publicly available, or partially disclose it as necessary (e.g., have it both viewable and writeable for an editor, but only viewable for a registered user). This option is used in very specific ways in the field.

Another feature of eLaborate that users seem to value very much is the clarity it offers in relation to the progress of a project. No matter how many people are working on a transcription, annotation, or project, they all have the same real-time view of the information. Although a more extended version management system was foreseen, the advantage of this simpler model seems to be that it offers a more efficient method of working on materials that are still "in flux." It has accelerated the production process quite considerably. For instance, the time-consuming version integration of various document sources is not necessary in this model.

eLaborate was built in a succession of project phases. Starting in 2003, and supported by KNAW (Royal Netherlands Academy of Arts and Sciences), the aim was to develop a content management system for research that required the sharing and exchanging of texts and data sets. One project leader (van Dalen) and representatives from different disciplines (including social sciences, literary history, history, and digital philology) were involved. In a second phase, the project was pursued under the heading of "text enrichment in virtual communities," and funded by a national body, SURF (SURF, 2011), whose mission is to support the pioneering of tools for scholars. In this phase, an annotation function was added to the transcription tool. From this point on, efforts were directed to the needs of scholars who study texts, and the plan to include historical data sets was abandoned. The third stage of eLaborate's development was also supported by KNAW, this time under the heading of Edition Machine). In this phase, the existing functionalities were improved. Between 2009 and 2011, under the name TextLab, eLaborate was further developed using a different data model

and a new service-oriented architecture. New functionalities were added, in particular those for more user-friendly support for adding metadata, and a find and replace function as opposed to the original find only option. Throughout this period, different user groups adopted eLaborate. At the time of writing, the new version is almost ready for release; our research focused on the use of the first two phases of the software.

eLaborate and the Currents of Web 2.0 Dynamics

Looking back on these developments analytically, it is clear that the context in which eLaborate was developed was shaped by two dynamics that are of growing importance in digital humanities. One of these was a strong modernist policy trend that aims to introduce efficiency and acceleration to interpretative scholarly traditions, positing that technology can have such effects (Wouters, 2006). Such policy interventions are often used somewhat instrumentally by researchers since they also offer opportunities for funding (Beaulieu, 2009). Such top-down operations can also intersect with bottom-up initiatives (Hayles, 2012; Presner, 2011). When overly technology-driven, such initiatives result in a "parade of prototypes" (Wouters, 2007). This means that a demonstrator with limited functionality is built into the framework of a specific project in order to show the potential of applying a particular digital tool to a research project. These demonstrators are usually short-lived, being too simple or insufficiently robust to be of use in research and with relatively little adoption by users beyond the beta-phase (i.e., the period or phase in which the tool is released as a prototype).

For eLaborate, and several other cases described in this volume, a second dynamic is also relevant. Beyond highly specialized research tools, a range of new digital environments and practices evolved during the same time period as eLaborate was being built. This led to a wealth of easily accessible, low-threshold Web-based applications that have at their core the exchange of information and insight, the collaborative building of databases (see, for example, Procter et al., 2010). Despite their huge diversity, these developments are collectively labeled Web 2.0. Definitions vary, but Anderson articulates a common vision of Web 2.0:

Web 2.0 encompasses a variety of different meanings that include an increased emphasis on user-generated content, data and content sharing and collaborative effort, together with the use of various kinds of social software, new ways of interacting with Web-based applications, and the use of the Web as a platform for generating, re-purposing and consuming content. (Anderson, 2007)

Such developments have not left academic users unchanged, and we can speak of "Web 2.0 in scholarship" as an intersection of two trends. We propose to consider the role of eLaborate as a crucial hybrid form that joins traditional scholarly practices and new possibilities for scholarship in a digital and networked setting.

As a virtual research environment, eLaborate targets both professional scholars and lay experts (Epstein, 1996), volunteers who dedicate time and effort to contributing to new editions. It offers tools to transcribe, annotate, and publish digital scholarly editions. The majority of content currently comprises texts from Dutch history and literary history, but eLaborate can be used with any language or any type of text and does not impose limits on the openness of contribution to any edition project. Levels of openness and access are largely determined by the communities formed around specific texts or editions—although, of course, some design and implementation decisions and strategies shape the possibilities. eLaborate is now used by several groups of teachers and students, and by scholarly, educated, and interested volunteers.

In order to understand how the promise of new digital support works in practice, we looked at how users experience the platform. This approach enabled us to consider whether, and how, users feel supported in using the platform. Rather than celebrate Web 2.0 as a liberatory manifesto that will lead the way to an ideal form of knowledge production, we opted for a close analysis of practices. We posit that

[g]iven discussions of new forms of cultural production that tend to posit these developments as largely uniform or as convergent (Jenkins, 2006; Bruns, 2008), we feel it is crucial to show the plurality and diversity of these configurations. Instead of either uncritically welcoming these developments as breaking the barriers of traditional power relations in a knowledge-stratified society, or—the reverse argument—criticizing them as incapable of being truly democratic or as leading to mediocre science, we offer a more contextual argument that highlights the constitutive tension between socio-technical reproduction and innovation. (Beaulieu, de Rijcke, & van Heur, 2012)

Furthermore, rather than seeing a dichotomy between Web 2.0 and non-Web 2.0 modes of working in digital humanities, we see the rise of hybrid forms that combine elements of these two modes. If Web 2.0 is characterized by values such as openness of participation (especially without regard for traditional markers of expertise), collaboration across and beyond institutions, increased value of resources through distributed participation, dynamic content and context, and self-organization and scalability, then it is not surprising that it is hailed as potentially leading to quite different forms of knowledge production. In order to understand how this potential might be realized, it is important to consider the actual practices of scholars that shape the use and diffusion of platforms such as eLaborate. We know from earlier work that even if platforms seem to offer new possibilities for knowledge creation, they may be rejected or need to be adapted when they also contrast in important ways with traditional forms of knowledge creation, where expertise, institutional affiliation, and restrictions on access and circulation have traditionally been key (Beaulieu, 2012) or when they require different approaches to formalization (van Zundert et al., 2011). In this, we are in agreement with a recent survey that states that

[o]verall, there is little evidence to suggest that Web 2.0 will prompt the kinds of radical changes in scholarly communications advocated by the open science community in the short or medium term: a wholesale "Web 2.0 revolution" is not imminent. We are, instead, in the initial stage of a process of "social learning," surrounding the development and use of Web 2.0 in research. (Procter et al., 2010: 4052)

If so, it is even more important to look closely at such social learning and how it is experienced. Based on years of feedback from users during the development of eLaborate, we gained some insight into users' views and experience. In order to further document user experiences and confront our perceptions with those expressed by users, we contacted users directly to interview them.

At the time of writing, around 20 different groups of textual scholars were actively working on an edition with eLaborate. The groups differed in their backgrounds and aims. Several projects were set up by university teachers who wanted to instruct a group of students in a limited amount of time in textual scholarship by using eLaborate. Other groups consisted of volunteers outside academia (but with an academic background) collaborating with representatives from academia. And yet other groups consisted of scholars working on their edition project alone or with one or two collaborators at most. For this chapter, we wanted to focus on the first two groups: teachers and students in an academic setting, and volunteers from outside academia.

We interviewed one university lecturer (in her forties) and two of her students (in their early twenties). From a group of around 25 volunteers, we interviewed the moderator (also a volunteer) and one member of the group she monitored. These two interviewees—like most of the others in their group—were in their sixties. We interviewed each person individually and the interviews were taped and transcribed for further analysis. Our questions were aimed at finding out more about the skills required to become a competent user and how these are acquired, about the social relations among users involved in a joint project, and about users' perceptions of eLaborate in the context of changing scholarship and digital humanities.

Because two of the three authors of this chapter were involved in the eLaborate projects, our direct experience with the users and user groups also provided insights for our discussion. Some of our roles in the projects over the years were developer, project leader (deciding priorities in the development based on user feedback), teaching the use of eLaborate in training sessions, giving front-line support through email and occasionally by telephone, answering questions from users about all kinds of technical and methodological aspects.

The analysis that follows was also spurred by ongoing work in Alfalab (Alfalab, 2011), in which the practices of platform and tool development for the humanities was supported by InterfaceLab in which all three authors were participants, albeit with different roles (Antonijevic, 2010). The role of InterfaceLab was to make explicit how the development of tools was shaping use and expectations, and, through being aware of assumptions being built into the tools, to improve the process of tool development. The insights presented here were developed on the basis of this ongoing interaction and mutual interrogation, as well as the interviews conducted specially for this chapter.

NEW PRACTICES AROUND ELABORATE

We present here the three main dynamics whereby the hybrid character of eLaborate comes especially to the fore. From interviews conducted with participants from different editorial groups, we focus on three instances of change in their experience of their scholarly work: integration, shifts in temporality, and collaboration. For each of these changing practices, we consider how it relates to Web 2.0 values and consider its significance for scholarship.

eLaborate for Integration: "It's All Right there, All in One Place"

From the interviews with users that we analyzed, the function of integration came very strongly to the fore as marking a change in users' practices. Using language emphasizing spatial metaphors and evoking a sense of place, users spoke of the platform as a "new site of knowledge production" (Beaulieu, de Rijcke, 2012). Specifically, this was achieved through the way the platform enabled the integration of the required multiple sources of information, the contiguity of text and image, and the possibility of closely associating the "source" and one's creative work around it. Here, the digital character of the platform was especially stressed by users, and their accounts depicted the platform as an "environment" rather than as a tool, a reference, or a source of data. The possibility of interactions was stressed—interaction with what had been, in the users' experience, disparate sources. This convergence of different material into a single environment is an important effect of digital mediation, and a typical element of Web 2.0 applications. (The meaning of "sources" changes, of course, when transferred to digital settings [Hayles, 2002; de Rijcke, 2011], but we focus here on the accounts of users' practices.)

However, it is important to note that it was the platform as a site of manipulation of texts, of a particular kind of textual labor, that was stressed, and not so much the values of Web 2.0 associated with a different kind of sociality or social relations. This was confirmed when we asked respondents to compare the platform to other applications—it was then compared to other "work" tools, such as Microsoft Word, or to applications such as a Web browser, rather than to any kind of social software. As such, we can see that with eLaborate there are shifts in the way we can access, manipulate, and enrich empirical materials. Change at this level is significant since it reshapes a core activity of knowledge production, namely, the relation to the empirical material (Wouters, 2006).

Shift in Temporality: Changing Pace or Setting the Pace with eLaborate

Working with eLaborate not only changes how people perceive and interact with the various sources and material they use, it also changes how they experience the temporality of their work practices.

We also noted a contrast between users who work with eLaborate in the framework of a project in which they are lay experts (volunteers) and users who are students using eLaborate as part of their coursework. For the first group, using eLaborate felt like an investment in time, slowing down their work while they learned to use the platform, but eventually leading to a better outcome. Students and teachers felt that using eLaborate accelerated their work. We explain this difference through the emphasis placed in each context on keeping track of what had been done and by whom. The importance of monitoring completion (keeping track of what has been done) was therefore different in the two contexts. For the coursework, doing the work, but mostly being seen to have done the work, "monitoring" was important, a task well supported by eLaborate. For volunteers, this was not felt to really be a gain (other than by the coordinator who found the project easier to manage).

Speeding up work and increasing efficiency are well-known promises of eScience and of the distributed nature of Web 2.0 research. We found that eLaborate does shift one's perceived efficiency, largely in relation to the changes described in the last section. Because all the material is in one place, using eLaborate feels like a more efficient approach for some users. Users then speak of acceleration in the pace of their work, and of greater efficiency. Both "regular" users and editors praise this aspect of using eLaborate. The immediacy provided by having the various elements side by side was especially noted. For example:

"En verder vind ik het zelf bijzonder prettig werken met zo'n plaatje en daaronder een vak waar je meteen in kan transcriberen." (interview with moderator) And what's more, I personally find it wonderfully convenient to work with the image and underneath, a box into which I can transcribe immediately.

Yet, there are other changes with regards to the temporality of work, due to the contiguity of different users and of their work. In eLaborate, the work "is all in one place," as we learned above. But a corollary of this contiguity is that the work of different users can be examined from a panopticon approach, where the editor/moderator can survey what is happening. Another possibility is that of mutual surveillance of the users, who can see each other's progress. As a result of this potential for overview, the overall progress of the project becomes much easier to assess and eventually manage for the project leaders. This enables moderators to deal with deadlines very differently, even in a proactive kind of way. A moderator is expected by the participants to direct the workflow, and adjust the workload if needed. For example, if the moderator sees that one user is not going to meet a deadline, he or she can simply change assignations in eLaborate. A text that has been assigned to a user who, because of his or her rate of progress, seems unlikely to get

to that text, can be freed up so that another user can work on it.

The pressure of deadlines is also experienced differently when users have insight into the progress of others. Students especially reported that they did not have to rely on the "talk" of others to know how far along they were. A student described the situation pre-eLaborate as

"Ja, je hoort wel natuurlijk mensen praten over... maar dan weet je nooit of het echt zo zit, natuurlijk." (student #1) Sure, you hear people talking about it ... but then again, you never know how far along they really are, of course. (Student 1)

eLaborate means everyone can see how everyone else is progressing.

Another related effect we noted in relation to the use of eLaborate is that it becomes possible to intervene at different points in the work process, because it makes ongoing work visible, which introduces the possibility of steering, or correcting:

"En in Word zie je het eindresultaat pas op het moment dat ze het inleveren." And [when using] Word you get to see the end result only at the point in time where they send it [their work] to you.

Moderators can modulate the work as it develops. Furthermore, since all the work also happens in a standardized environment, there is a big difference in terms of the time moderators have to spend reconciling all the Word versions of submitted texts.

While this account of eLaborate does support the shift in efficiency claimed by some champions of increased use of technology, it also signals a deeper reorganization and reconfiguration of work. As we saw, the changing temporality (faster/slower) is not uniform in its effect, and cannot be attributed solely to the technological platform. Furthermore, the shifts in the timing or visibility of work, and the potential for ongoing surveillance also changes how scholars work, and the manner and time in which their work is evaluated. Ongoing surveillance by colleagues (or even just the awareness of potential surveillance), or the shifting of deadlines and workload by a moderator, changes how users feel about their pace and their obligations. Beyond a potential gain in efficiency, our analysis of work performed through eLaborate points to new forms of accountability for scholars.

Collaboration: eLaborate for All, All for eLaborate

The flow of work changes when using eLaborate. This is where the hybridity of the platform comes most strongly to the fore. Technically, it is possible for all users to see and change the work. This means that one user can improve on the annotations of another, or change a transcription. But we found that this does not happen in practice. It appears that this aspect of textual work is heavily shaped by the tradition in the field—despite the role of the moderator and the expectations being made explicit to the users. For example, in one user group, users are asked to correct the texts of other users—but this only happens once the work has been explicitly "signed off" by its "author." The other users refrain from correcting the text of another author until the author of that text explicitly says that it is completed. In another group of users we interviewed, some users were not even aware of the possibility of seeing or commenting on/changing the work of anyone else. We are therefore confronted with the same platform giving rise to different expectations and different levels of awareness. Yet, among all the users, we found no attempt to really open up work to everyone or to make the work fully collaborative and interactive across the entire process. Interaction remains strictly limited and only occurs in explicitly stated situations.

At most, users told us, they could look at others' work, but not change it. Suggestions are sent by email, in writing, but not directly implemented in what is considered to be someone else's text. Indeed, this possibility was described as "messing around with someone else's work." As one user recounted, any changes were made as follows:

"En we hadden afgesproken dat we enkel in onze eigen gedichten gingen werken, en de verbeteringen die maakten we dan wel ofwel met de hand ofwel in een Worddocument, zodat we niet in de andere zijn tekst gingen rommelen" (student #2) And we agreed that we would only work on our own poems, and the corrections we would make by hand or in a Word document, so that we wouldn't be messing with someone else's text. *(Student 2)*

While we can therefore speak of collaboration in the course of these projects, the platform is used in very specific, limited ways to facilitate collaboration. Any interaction in terms of improving the output that does take place does so via means that are parallel to the platform: putting the text in Word and then changing it, or writing up suggestions for improvement in an email. This indicates that there are limits to the changes that scholars will embrace, no matter what the technology makes possible. The extent to which scholars will embrace new practices is not well defined (Jankowski, 2009). Training certainly plays a role, but so do the context of research, the support available, and the degree of freedom from extreme pressures to produce output so that scholars are at liberty to explore and play. Conventions about ownership of one's work and responsibility for its state shape how scholarly interaction proceeds, and at which points in the workflow collaboration can occur.

This is an interesting finding in that it qualifies other studies that associate collaboration and Web 2.0. Procter, for example, finds that those who collaborate are more likely to use Web 2.0 (Procter et al., 2010). While the accounts of our users do not contradict this correlation, they do draw attention (1) to the need to qualify what counts as collaboration (since it may be said that our users contribute to a common textual text, but do so by working in parallel) and (2) to a strong warning against taking for granted that using Web 2.0 means collaborating. By taking a close look at work practices, we see that collaboration is a highly variable activity, even around a single platform.

Next Steps for eLaborate and the Future of Web 2.0 Scholarship

As developers of eLaborate and scholars who have been committed to engaging various fields in a critical and productive practice using digital tools, this analysis leads us to a number of conclusions about eLaborate. It reinforces our conviction that certain values can only be enhanced through a combination of interventions in eLaborate's design and interaction with user groups.

eLaborate is a platform that accommodates a range of practices, and makes adaptation rather than revolution a winning strategy for the scholars who have been experimenting with it. While, as we have already stated, we do not believe that the tool alone will lead to innovation, the significance of offering a new platform should not be underestimated either. As Hand (2008) has shown, the sense of newness felt and expressed by participants is empirically important. Introducing a new tool can create a window of opportunity for adapting or reflecting on practices.

With regard to eLaborate, we noted a number of transformations in research practices that are also relevant to other digital platforms (without wanting to claim that these are generic changes!). First, we note an atomization of work as a result of using a digital platform. With eLaborate, we see that work gets broken down into "chunks" to be assigned, or into steps to be taken to complete the work. This means separating the work into texts or units of work, which are then distributed among the participants. Such a step relies on and further reinforces a process of formalization. Furthermore, there is a delegation of some parts

of the work to technology and of other parts to humans. The interviews with users show that this picture contrasts with a non-eLaborate-based, holistic pursuit of tasks (of course, this work can also be seen to be parceled out and organized, but we are stressing here the contrast between, not the essence of, the tasks). This results in a different division of labor, between people in a team but also between "expert" tasks and "support" work, for example. The pace of work, keeping track of the work done, and sharing resources are all activities that become much more external to the individual scholar in the context of eLaborate. As such, they can be relatively more easily shared among team members or delegated to research assistants or project managers.

From what users tell us, eLaborate also changes the awareness of the process of work. For example, users become aware of *how* they work to a greater extent, because the platform and the coordination with other team members draw attention to this. For example, their work might become more iterative, so that the tasks of transcribing, annotating and checking might contrast with a more linear process in which one goes through a text from beginning to end. Or there may be changes in the timing when scholars interact with the coordinator and with others as an ongoing part of the work, rather than once a piece is completed. This could mean shifting from a "reviewing" interaction, where one scholar checks the work of another, to a "consulting" interaction, where one draws on others' expertise in the course of doing the work. Such a change has consequences for key components of scholarly work, such as how we define an "editor" or what is means to have literary insights. These may be shifting from a single expert whose life is dedicated to a topic, toward configuration where editions are undertaken as a discrete project with a fixed time frame and pursued as a distributed team-based effort.

Another contrast is in the *view* of the task at hand that becomes possible with eLaborate. If we use optical metaphors, we might say that eLaborate works as a magnifying glass, focusing attention on the specificities of texts, enabling users to work in precise, consistent ways, getting close to the image and lines of the text. However, other textual tasks, such as checking annotations, are currently less well supported. This means that to get a "view" of the texts, to have a more global view, users tend to print out their work. In other words, eLaborate is a platform that is designed for contiguity, not overview.

These changes, though small, are far from trivial. They go to the heart of scholarly work and shape our relationship to the empirical material. eLaborate itself actually hints at how profound these changes may be. Using eLaborate as a means of production, Dr. Mariken Teeuwen published a digital edition of the oldest gloss tradition on Martianus Capella's *De nuptiis Philologiae et Mercurii* (Teeuwen, 2010). The ninth-century manuscript shows scholarly tradition in a striking manner: the base text has been commented on, glossed by, annotated by, and marked by several hands, in several interdependent layers.[3] What we see here is a witness to the scholarly practice of collation and annotation that has remained relatively unchanged for at least 2,000 years. The digital facsimile of the ninth-century manuscript shows how little the act of annotating and commenting has changed in essence over the centuries. Though typography changed over time, the basic model was stable: a base text printed or written on a page with typographical distinct annotations "in margin"; gradually the bottom of the page became the conventional container for such critical apparatus. Basically this scholarly technology has been in use since classical times, and ancient scholars would most probably have little trouble grasping the layout conventions of the majority of modern day scholarly printed works. But the same example (the columns on the right-hand side of the interface are labeled "Transcription" and "Annotations") shows how very different the "materiality" of text and annotations may become from the conventional print-based medium. An-

notations may float in ways that are as interesting as they are unexpected over the graphical Web interface of a digital edition. Progressing along these lines the very fabric of editions may change over time due to Web 2.0 technologies, as editions may become visualizations of distributed sets of data rather than print-like integrated texts (van Zundert & Boot, 2011).[4]

Such changes, though deceptively small indeed, can have profound influence on scholarly workflow and practice. We could say that technology change, or medium change, can provoke a 90-degree turn in one's perception of what it is to work with text on a scholarly level. For example, facilitated collaboration via the Web in the case of eLaborate has already led to further specialization of contributors in parts of the workflow: the one who is good at solving Latin abbreviations focuses on that aspect of a text, another who is versed in using all kinds of dictionaries focuses on adding annotations about word meanings with references to the right sources, for example. This type of specialization could ultimately bring about a great change in publication practices. Currently, humanities scholars are (in general) expected to give large and bold narrative overviews, and to tell well-polished stories. But hyper-specialization may result in publications becoming narrower in scope and focused on more detailed aspects of texts. This would constitute a significant change as it is still unusual in the humanities to compile knowledge by publishing small articles that build on each other, as is more common in the natural or life sciences.

Currently there is also debate about what it means for reading practices and the materiality of text to be transmigrated into a virtual realm (see, for example, McGann, 2001; Kaltenbrunner, 2010). It appears that eLaborate has managed to create—through its particular conceptualization of the scholarly workflow for transcribing and annotating—interesting new insights into scholarly practice for its users. But it has also created some feelings of disconnection from the traditional, print-on-paper modes of verification and control, as expressed through the need expressed by various users for a print function to be able to experience more overview of the textual data contained in eLaborate. By understanding the consequences of eLaborate's reconfiguration of research practices, we come to understand more precisely how deeply Web 2.0 tools can change our approach to knowledge production. We also gain an insight into the dynamics of such change and come to value incremental transformation of practices, rather than bet on revolutionary change through technology alone.

FUTURE DIRECTIONS

We have shown that changes in digital humanities can benefit from intermediate forms, such as eLaborate, which can be situated at different points in relation to Web 2.0 scholarship, depending on how it is used. eLaborate makes it possible for groups of users to adopt different approaches, ranging between academic exclusiveness and Web 2.0 openness, and to reflect on and reorganize their work practices. What is clear, however, is that the technological potential for radical openness and shared expertise does not determine the practices of users.

The developers of eLaborate got two things right. They succeeded in migrating some essential concepts for scholarly workflow from literary studies into the digital realm—"succeeded" insofar as literary researchers found the tool useful and beneficial enough to test-drive it, and to apply it in actual research. They also took eLaborate to a stage where it offered possibilities—although they took no explicit stance on how those possibilities should be used—for experimenting with (Web 2.0) openness. Researchers were welcome to keep their work completely private and under full control; or they could opt to crowdsource their transcriptions in relatively more transparent and

public ways, allowing users to step forward and engage in transcription work via the Web.

In the case of eLaborate, users from the literary research domain valued the way their methodological concepts were modeled into the tool so that they remained recognizable. They also appreciated the opportunities to formalize their workflow. Web 2.0 technologies played a crucial enabling role here, not as objectives in themselves, but rather as enablers of a convenient Web-based workflow support that very much adhered to existing off line practices. eLaborate's use of these new technologies offered a number of benefits that researchers were keen to pick up—mainly enhanced efficiency of production, simple version management, and workflow control.

Many lessons about Web 2.0 approaches in scholarly settings were learned in the context of Alfalab (van Zundert et al., 2011) and eLaborate. One of the key lessons is that capturing and integrating existing scholarly methodology into a new technological environment is difficult—very difficult indeed—but that it is essential to technological innovation within a field. Technology by itself does not constitute methodology, nor methodological innovation. However, methodologies and formalizations are often very much implicit, embedded in a research domain and therefore invisible. Often methodological knowledge and experience is also tacit knowledge, and only rarely expressed in a field where researchers experience such methods as second nature or common sense—acquired through training that develops a sensibility and judgment, and through a long apprenticeship, rather than by following protocols. But precisely by capturing existing methodology and formalizations, and by offering explicit, tangible ways to take up new practices, new technologies may actually prove useful for scholars at large. Technologies by themselves constitute no innovation, merely the potential for it when taken up by researchers to develop new practices.

We should therefore be careful not to see the advent of Web 2.0 technologies, social software, crowdsourcing approaches—or whatever label we want to put on the technologies that promise dynamics of openness—as an ipso facto trend that must permeate the scholarly arena as well. eLaborate in this perspective provides us with an interesting insight into how new technologies may be shaped into supportive tools for existing methodologies, and how they may enhance certain aspects of such existing methodologies.

CONCLUSION

Which of these lessons could be useful for other projects? And how can these lessons be useful for thinking about Web 2.0 and about social software in relation to scholarship? Rather than claim a revolution, we have shown how hybrid forms can actually be very powerful sites for change, through their inclusive rather than oppositional setups. In eLaborate, we see that the early phases of the development of this platform were shaped by high expectations of cross-institutional and cross-disciplinary work, a phenomenon we have also observed in the development of other infrastructures for knowledge production (Beaulieu, de Rijcke, & van Heur, 2012). Institutional factors are therefore important for the growth and uptake of such platforms. But as we have seen, the way groups of users take up eLaborate is also shaped by how participants are rewarded (as students or volunteers) and the way trust in the materials produced is established. How participants experience the platforms, including any tensions between expectations or traditions in the field, is therefore a key component in the deployment of Web 2.0 strategies in scholarly work. This is something that cannot be taken for granted, given recent findings (RIN, 2010) that show that researchers feel neither sufficiently (technically) supported nor stimulated to explore new and challenging ways of researching and disseminating their work. This

means that working closely with research communities (van Zundert et al., 2009) is a winning strategy if this is to be overcome.

REFERENCES

Alfalab. (2011). Retrieved July 13, 2011, from http://alfalab.ehumanities.nl/

Anderson, P. (2007). What is Web 2.0? Ideas, technologies and implications for education. *JISC Technology and Standards Watch*. Bristol, UK: JISC. Retrieved July 13, 2011, from http://www.jisc.ac.uk/media/documents/techwatch/tsw0701b.pdf

Antonijevic, S., & Beaulieu, A. (2010). *Crossing the unexpected: Benefits and challenges of scholarly collaboration in a humanities lab*. HASTAC 2010: Grand Challenges and Global Innovations Conference, April 15, 2010. Retrieved October 10, 2011, from http://www.ichass.illinois.edu/hastac2010/HASTAC_2010/Presentations/Entries/2010/4/15_Crossing_the_Unexpected__Benefits_and_Challenges_of_Scholarly_Collaboration_in_a_Humanities_Labs.html

Beaulieu, A., de Rijcke, S., & van Heur, B. (2012). Authority and expertise in new sites of knowledge production. In Wouters, P., Beaulieu, A., Scharnhorst, A., & Wyatt, S. (Eds.), *Virtual knowledge*. Cambridge, MA: The MIT Press.

Beaulieu, A., & Wouters, P. (2009). E-research as intervention. In Jankowski, N. (Ed.), *e-Research: Transformations in scholarly practice* (pp. 54–69). New York, NY: Routledge.

Bruns, A. (2008). *Blogs, Wikipedia, Second Life, and beyond: From production to produsage*. Peter Lang Publishing.

de Rijcke, S., & Beaulieu, A. (2011). Image as interface: Consequences for users of museum knowledge. *Library Trends, Special Issue on Involving Users in the Co-Construction of Digital Knowledge in Libraries, Archives, and Museums, 59*(3), 664–685.

Epstein, S. (1996). *Impure science: AIDS, activism, and the politics of knowledge.* Berkeley, CA: University of California Press.

Hand, M. (2008). *Making digital cultures: Access, interactivity and authenticity.* Aldershot, UK: Ashgate.

Hayles, N. K. (2002). Material metaphors, technotexts, and media-specific analysis. In Hayles, N. K. (Ed.), *Writing machines* (pp. 18–33). Cambridge, MA: Mediawork, The MIT Press.

Hayles, N. K. (2012). How we think: Transforming power and digital technologies. In Berry, D. (Ed.), *Understanding the digital humanities* (pp. 42-66). London, UK: Palgrave.

Huygens. (2011). Retrieved July 13, 2011, from http://www.huygens.knaw.nl

Jankowski, N. (Ed.). (2009). *e-Research: Transformations in scholarly practice.* New York, NY: Routledge.

Jenkins, H. (2006). *Convergence culture: Where old and new media collide.* New York, NY: New York University Press.

Kaltenbrunner, W., & Wouters, P. (2010). E-research and methodological innovation in Dutch literary studies. *First Monday, 15*(6). Retrieved July 13, 2011, from http://firstmonday.org/htbin/cgiwrap/bin/ojs/index.php/fm/article/view/3078

McGann, J. J. (2001). *Radiant textuality: Literature after the World Wide Web.* New York, NY: Palgrave.

Presner, T. (2010). *Digital humanities 2.0: A report on knowledge.* Retrieved July 13, 2011, from http://cnx.org/content/m34246/latest/

Procter, R., Williams, R., Stewart, J., Poschen, M., & Snee, H. Voss, A., & Asgari-Tarhi, M. (2010). Adoption and use of Web 2.0 in scholarly communications. *Philosophical Transactions of the Royal Society A, Theme Issue: e-Science: Past. Present and Future II, 368*(1926), 4039–4056. doi:10.1098/rsta.2010.0155

RIN (Research Information Network). (2010). *If you build it, will they come? How researchers perceive and use Web 2.0.* Retrieved July 13, 2011, from http://www.rin.ac.uk/our-work/communicating-and-disseminating-research/use-and-relevance-Web-20-researchers

Schreibman, S., Siemens, R., & Unsworth, J. (2001). *A companion to digital humanities.* London, UK: Blackwell.

SURF. (2011). Retrieved July 13, 2011, from http://www.surf.nl

Teeuwen, M. in collaboration with Brouwer, T., Stancefield Eastwood, B., Garrison, M., Guillaumin, J., Lozovsky, N., … Sroczynski, A. (2010). *Carolingian scholarship and Martianus Capella: The oldest commentary tradition.* Retrieved July 13, 2011, from http://martianus.huygensinstituut.knaw.nl

van Zundert, J., Antonijevic, S., Beaulieu, A., van Dalen-Oskam, K., Zeldenrust, D., & Andrews, T. (2012). Cultures of formalization: Towards an encounter between humanities and computing. In Berry, D. (Ed.), *Understanding the digital humanities* (pp. 279-294). London, UK: Palgrave.

van Zundert, J., & Boot, P. (2011). The digital edition 2.0: Services, not resources. *Bibliothek und Wissenschaft, 44*(2011), 141-152.

van Zundert, J., Zeldenrust, D., & Beaulieu, A. (2009). Alfalab. Construction and deconstruction of a digital humanities experiment. *Proceeding of the IEEE e-Science Conference*, December 9-11, 2009 (pp. 1-5). Oxford, UK. Retrieved October 8, 2011, from http://alfalablog.huygensinstituut.nl/wp-content/bestanden/2010/10/Alfalab-paper-Oxford-2009.pdf

Wouters, P., & Beaulieu, A. (2006). Imagining e-science beyond computation. In Hine, C. (Ed.), *New infrastructures for knowledge production: Understanding e-science* (pp. 48–70). Hershey, PA: Idea Group. doi:10.4018/978-1-59140-717-1.ch003

Wouters, P., & Beaulieu, A. (2007). Critical accountability: Dilemmas for interventionist studies of e-science. *Journal of Computer-Mediated Communication, 12*(2). doi:10.1111/j.1083-6101.2007.00339.x

ADDITIONAL READING

Berry, D. M. (Ed.). (2012). *Understanding digital humanities*. London, UK: Palgrave Macmillan. doi:10.1057/9780230371934

Buzzetti, D. (2009). Digital editions and text processing. In Deegan, M., & Sutherland, K. (Eds.), *Text editing, print, and the digital world* (pp. 45–62). Aldershot, UK: Ashgate.

Buzzetti, D., & McGann, J. (2006). Critical editing in a digital horizon. In L. Burnard, K. O'Brien O'Keeffe, & J. Unsworth (Eds.), *Electronic textual editing* (pp. 53-73). New York, NY: MLA. Retrieved July 13, 2011, from http://www.tei-c.org/About/Archive_new/ETE/Preview/mcgann.xml

Davidson, C. N., & Goldberg, D. T. (2004). A manifesto for the humanities in a technological age. Retrieved November 15, 2011, from http://www.jhfc.duke.edu/resources/manifesto.php

Dormans, S., & Kok, J. (2010). An alternative approach to large historical databases: Exploring best practices with collaboratories. *Historical Methods, 43*(3), 97–107. doi:10.1080/01615440.2010.496443

Moretti, F. (2005). *Graphs, maps, trees: Abstract models for a literary history*. London, UK: Verso.

Renear, A. H. (2004). Text encoding. In S. Schreibman Siemens & J. Unsworth (Eds.), *A companion to digital humanities* (pp. 218-239). Oxford, UK: Blackwell. Retrieved July 13, 2011, from http://www.digitalhumanities.org/companion/

Robinson, P. (2004). Making electronic editions and the fascination of what is difficult. *Linguistica Computazionale, 20-21*, 415–438.

Schmidt, D. (2010). The inadequacy of embedded markup for cultural heritage texts. *Literary and Linguistic Computing, 25*(3), 337–356. doi:10.1093/llc/fqq007

Schneider, S., Foot, K., & Wouters, P. (2009). Taking Web archiving seriously. In Jankowski, N. (Ed.), *e-research: Transformation in scholarly practice* (pp. 205–221). London, UK: Routledge.

Schreibman, S. (2007). Re-envisioning versioning: A scholar's toolkit. In A. Ciula & F. Stella (Eds.), *Digital philology and medieval text* (pp. 93-102). Pisa, Italy: Pacini editore.

VKS. (2008). Messy shapes of knowledge—STS explores informatization, new media, and academic work. The virtual knowledge studio. In E. J. Hackett Amsterdamska, O., Lynch, M., & J. Wajcman (Eds.), *The handbook of science and technology studies* (pp. 319-335). Cambridge, MA: The MIT Press. Retrieved July 13, 2011, from http://www.virtualknowledgestudio.nl/documents/handbook-messyshapes.pdf

Wouters, P., Beaulieu, A., Scharnhorst, A., & Wyatt, S. (Eds.). (2012). *Virtual knowledge*. Cambridge, MA: MIT Press.

KEY TERMS AND DEFINITIONS

Annotation: A note or comment that is made while editing a text, and that may end up in a final publication of the text. It provides additional information for the reader about meaning, formal aspects, or context relevant to an aspect of a text.

Collation: In textual criticism and bibliography, collation is the process of determining the differences between two or more texts, or the comparison of the physical makeup of different versions or copies of a text.

Digital Humanities: Sometimes called humanities computing, an area of study, research, teaching, and invention concerned with the intersection of a wealth of digital technologies and the disciplines of the humanities. It can be contrasted with computational humanities, which has a more narrow focus on computation and the use of computers as data-processing machines.

Editor: In the context of the humanities an editor is a textual scholar who produces an edition (i.e., a representative specimen) of a text based on all the relevant scholarly knowledge that is available about that work, its author(s), and current or contemporary use. Somewhat confusingly in the context of digital humanities, an editor can also indicate an application that enables copy editing of a text in a digital environment.

Formalization: A process that attempts to define attributes, categories, and steps in actions, often with the goal of standardizing, mechanizing, or regulating interactions, operations, and behaviors. Formalization can take different shapes, depending the goals it is meant to achieve and on the demands of organizations or technologies for which formalization is being pursued. Formalization can make relationships and elements more visible and explicit, but can also reduce their complexity and hide their contextual and interdependent nature.

Gloss: A specific type of brief annotation about the meaning of a word or wording in a text. It may be in the language of the text, or in the reader's language if that is different.

Humanities Scholarship: The humanities is a label assigned to a group of disciplines. Often, these include the study of languages, literature, philosophy, history, music and theater, though there is variation between national and institutional traditions. According to Cathy Davidson and David Goldberg, Humanities Scholarship "Engages three broad sets of questions: those of meaning, value, and significance. Meaning concerns interpretation of data, evidence, and texts. Value ranges over the entire field of cultural, esthetic, social, and scientific investments. Significance, implicating both the former two, raises questions of representation, in the sense of accounting for (explanation) and of capturing, in the sense both of offering a faithful rendition (description) and of making broad claims (generalization)".

Scholarly (Text) Edition: The outcome of editing a state-of-the-art version of a text. See Editor.

Textual Scholarship: The investigation of texts. Textual scholars attempt to understand how texts have come to be as they are and, in order to achieve this, they examine different sources of a text, some of which are considered primary. There are several different schools of thought and practice within the discipline. Whereas some scholars emphasize authorial intention, others seek to understand the emergence of texts as collaborative products. Textual scholarship usually involves producing editions of the texts that have been studied. (cf. http://www.textualscholarship.org/). See Collation, Editor, Scholarly (text) edition.

Transcription: The production of formalized, often typed or digitized, text from a (handwritten) manuscript, printed text, or facsimile. See also Formalisation.

Web 2.0: A label that became popular around 2004, when the term was prominently used by Tim O'Reilly, at the O'Reilly Media Web 2.0 conference. It has had an important role in rebranding the Web, in the aftermath of the dotcom crash of 2001. The term is often associated with Web applications that facilitate participatory information sharing and creative uses of the Web, rather than purportedly passive consumption.

ENDNOTES

1   See eLaborate: http://www.e-laborate.nl/en/

2   See: http://Web.archive.org/Web/20050204165838/http://www.i-tor.org/en/

3   Cf. an example of one folio at http://martianus.huygensinstituut.knaw.nl/path/facsimile/leiden_vossianus_48/book_3_grammatica/folio_20v.

4   Note that in order to indicate just one such major shift, typography in the case of Martianus Capella made a 90-degree rotation. The bottom half of the conventional paper page became a column in a basically vertical divided layout. This does happen in print-based publications as well, but it is by no means an established convention in scholarly publishing.

Chapter 8
Google Scholar as the Co–Producer of Scholarly Knowledge

José van Dijck
University of Amsterdam, The Netherlands

ABSTRACT

Search engines in general, and Google Scholar in particular, are co-producers of academic knowledge. They have a profound impact on the way knowledge is generated, transmitted, and distributed. This chapter first explores how Google Scholar works as a human-technological system in order to analyze the site's technology in combination with its inscribed usage and its actual use and users. The chapter then scrutinize the complex power relationships of digital networks with Google at its epicenter. Following Manuel Castells's (2009) proposal to "unwire" the construction of academic knowledge through the coded dynamics of search engines, the author examines the larger legal and political-economic implications of the platform's architecture and organized structure. Combining these two layers of analysis should inform an enriched type of information literacy.

INTRODUCTION

Digitized searching has changed the way we learn and read, and it might well be argued that the production of scholarly knowledge has never been easier because we now have more access to more sources than ever before (Carr, 2008a). A college student assigned to write a paper or thesis these days is likely to start with Google Search, Google Scholar, or Wikipedia. When you ask students how they researched their topic, their likely answer is that they "Googled" it, meaning they clicked on the 10 top-ranked results.[1] The role of libraries and librarians has changed dramatically—from being mediators in the process of searching to being facilitators of digital processes, and from being managers of *collections* to being managers of *connections*. One reason students appreciate the university library these days is LibraryLink, a Google service that, coupled with the library's online journal subscriptions, provides convenient access to full-text downloads. As information

DOI: 10.4018/978-1-4666-2178-7.ch008

specialist Stephanie Taylor (2007) points out, many students think of library services as "an add-on to the Google Scholar service, rather than the other way around" (p. 5). Search engines are commonly regarded as neutral tools for information gathering. In this chapter I argue that Google Scholar, in particular, is a co-producer of academic knowledge because it has a profound impact on the way knowledge is generated, transmitted, and distributed.

Production of knowledge, as we have learned since Foucault (1980), is intricately intertwined with the *technologization of power* and the *mechanisms of power distribution*. Search engines play an important role in organizing the world's information (Segev, 2008). In order to identify how knowledge is produced through search engines, I will first explore how Google Scholar works as a human-technological system, meaning that we need to analyze the site's technology—its ranking systems and profiling systems—in combination with its inscribed usage and its actual use and users. Google Scholar is in fact a piece of *social* software whose value is highly defined by the activity of millions of users whose click-activities result in automated click-aggregation. Socially based methods of information retrieval, such as search engine optimization, augment the so-called "filter bubble" phenomenon in which the information gatekeepers are Web-based services like Google.

The second level of investigation examines the mechanisms underlying the complex power relationships of knowledge production sites, with Google at its epicenter. Whereas academic libraries, publishers, and journals conventionally dominated the public dissemination of academic knowledge, Google Scholar brought a new set of values to academic-oriented search and database technologies. How do values like popularity ratings and reputational rankings relate to traditional library values like neutrality, confidentiality, and relevance? I follow Manuel Castells's (2009) proposal to "unwire" the construction of academic knowledge through the coded dynamics of search

engines, thus examining the larger legal and political-economic implications of the platform's architecture and organized structure.

Combining these two layers of analysis should help spark a critical discussion of digital knowledge production. Society needs students and scholars who are not only competent users of search engines, but who can also reflect critically on the principles underlying knowledge formation. Teaching information literacy, including the strengths and weaknesses of various proprietary and public search tools, may partly remedy the growing influence of Web search engines. Therefore, I suggest in the conclusion to expand information literacy to include reflective skills on the social construction of knowledge and thus to account for the political and ideological dimensions of automated search.

GOOGLE SCHOLAR AS A HUMAN-TECHNOLOGICAL SYSTEM

For decades, library information and reference systems have relied on transparent yet complex systems for indexing. As a student, finding your way through the giant numbers of academic sources often required the help of professional librarians trained in the coded structure of the reference labyrinth. The Dewey system, which relies on appropriate labeling of keywords, never was the easiest system to use, and even if electronic library services (Web of Science, Metalib, Project Muse, etc.) made searching faster and more efficient, users' dependence on keywords applied by reference librarians and publishers restricted retrieval and slowed down access. Electronic library services are less well known than search engines.[2] University libraries serve academic interest by filtering, ordering, and ranking quality materials on the basis of their evaluated academic weight. They have always been public service institutions, relying on traditional library values, such as usefulness and reliability, neutrality and transparency, independence and respecting the right to privacy and confidentiality of their users (Caufield, 2005). In contrast to search engines, electronic library systems offer filtered sources that are carefully selected, indexed, and described by specialists; their function as gatekeepers in the process of knowledge formation is based on criteria such as quality assessment, weighed evaluation, and transparency in listed source databases. These values are profound to the constitution of scientific knowledge. The obvious question thus arises: how does Google Scholar compare to these library values firmly rooted in the public domain?

Since Google Scholar's arrival in 2004, academics and librarians have extensively discussed the engine's effectiveness and usefulness, deliberated its reliability and relevance, and evaluated its merits and shortcomings vis-à-vis library-based Web tools. As far as usefulness is concerned, it appears that the proprietary engine is extremely effective in finding precise quotes, citations, or specific authors. Library scientist Bruce White agrees that Google Scholar "works best for very tightly-defined searches, those for which conventional database searches produce few or no results" (White, 2007, p. 22). Especially now that full-text copies of articles are increasingly accessible on the Internet—although some remain locked behind a publisher's paid access portal—it has become easier to trace exact quotations and references back to their original publication. While the beta versions of Google Scholar suffered from overblown citation counts on their result pages—for instance, bogus author names such as "F. Password" resulted in thousands of ranked hits—these retrieval problems have been more or less addressed in recent versions of the engine (Jacso, 2008). Over the six years of its development, Google Scholar has improved its functionality when it comes to tracking well-defined, precise scientific sources.

When Google Scholar arrived in 2004, it was applauded as a system that was better in terms of accessibility and comprehensiveness than most

existing library systems combined—an electronic aid that would soon replace many traditional library functions (Gorman, 2006). It was also highly recommended for its democratizing potential, certainly in parts of the world that do not have access to well-resourced libraries. In brokering between information and knowledge, Google Scholar was expected to be the reliable, neutral, and transparent (re)search tool the academic community had been waiting for—a kind of super-reference librarian that automatically extracts citations from reference lists and databases, and recognized scientific documents. Indeed, Google Scholar promises to be a service that helps you identify the most relevant research across the world of scholarly research by adopting the standards of scientists and librarians. As we can read in its manual:

Google Scholar aims to sort articles the way researchers do, weighing the full text of each article, the author, the publication in which the article appears, and how often the piece has been cited in other scholarly literature. The most relevant results will always appear on the first page.[3] [my emphasis]

In its stated aims and function, Google Scholar replicates some scientific core values (such as citation analysis and weighed evaluation) and assumes some of the precepts that guide librarians in their work (e.g., selection for relevance). Libraries and publishers, as traditional gatekeepers, have always explicated the values on which their search systems were based. Google Scholar introduced new (private and commercial) values, such as popularity and reputational ranking, and redefined old ones, such as citation analysis. However, these revamped values were never explicated and remain mostly invisible, hiding behind an overwhelmingly simple interface.

GOOGLE SCHOLAR AS INVISIBLE GATEKEEPER

A number of studies have compared Google Scholar's comprehensiveness to other (public and commercial) Web-based services, such as Metalib, Scopus, Web of Science, Ingenta, Muse, etc.[4] In general, these studies point to a few profound principles where Google Scholar's lack of public values is especially poignant, specifically citation analysis, transparancy of covered sources, and weighing or validating sources. At first sight, Google Scholar adopts one of the basic academic values—citation analysis—by letting algorithmic Web spiders create indexes to a vast web of academic materials. Like its parent engine, Google Scholar functions as a ranking system based on semantic links to a vast reservoir of sources that through their provenance might be considered academically sound. However, Google Scholar's algorithm works on the basis of *quantitative* citation analysis, a different process from the one scholars use in their protected academic universe where citations are also scored according to their relative status and weight in their specific professional disciplines.

Google Scholar is essentially a piece of social software whose efficacy is rooted in the activity of its users. Unlike library search engines, in Google Scholar sources are ranked on the basis of *popularity* rather than truth-value or relevance. In the Scholar context, there is no clear peer-review system or citation analysis system that publicly lays out its ranking principles; there are a number of algorithms—PageRank, named after its inventor Larry Page, being the most important one—that take the number of links and hits as the basic units of ranking, but whose exact working is a trade secret. PageRank is a quantitative rather than qualitative system: a source that is well linked to other sources and is often clicked on thus gains in ranking, regardless of the document's status, relevance, or value. As library scholar Margaret

Markland (2005, p. 25) observes, "Google equates 'linking to a page' as 'assigning importance,' but this definition of importance may not necessarily indicate quality." Due to the rising importance of search engines, academics have a vested interest in being cited, indexed, and linked through electronic databases. Through search engine optimization, the process of improving the visibility of a website or a Web page in search engines, researchers can actively improve their articles' findability and thus influence their ranking (Beel, Gipp, & Wilde, 2010).[5] Whether or not this is a legitimate method for researchers to engage in is open to discussion.

Another core value in the public library reference system is transparency in terms of its covered sources. First, they point at Google's incomplete and indeterminate coverage of source material. Despite the engine's crawl in a vast reservoir of published and unpublished materials, Google Scholar's coverage of scientific sources is still incomplete. To properly evaluate Google Scholar's scope, one would need a precise list of databases covered by the engine, but to date Google has not published a list of scientific journals crawled by its spiders. As Neuhaus, Neuhaus, Asher, and Wrede (2006) point out, Google Scholar has an extensive coverage of science and medical databases, open access databases, and single publisher databases, but it is rather weak in social science and humanities databases. Even if US researchers find the proprietary engine to be performing well in specific subject areas in comparison to other public library engines, they still note that a substantial portion of the citations provided by Google Scholar are incomplete (Walters, 2007; White, 2007). Moreover, Google Scholar shows a considerable time lag in citing newly published items and does not provide time stamps for its ranked results, so a researcher can never trace the "history" of a document (Hellsten, Leydesdorf, & Wouters, 2006). In short, users are unaware of how the engine's coverage is limited in terms of scope and time span. For students who fundamentally rely on the search engine for its comprehensive scope of covered sources, it is important to know how bias is already anchored in the selection of databases the engine crawls.

One could argue that Google Scholar covers much more sources than university libraries do in their Web databases, but here, again, the public value of sorting relevant and weighed items enters the equation. Alongside authorized copies of peer-reviewed published articles, Google Scholar also refers to various kinds of unofficial or gray sources, such as working papers, unpublished material, documents in preprint repositories, powerpoint presentations published on university websites, and lecture notes. When academics decide to publish on the Web articles that have not yet been peer reviewed, one could argue that research results become accessible and retrievable much sooner. However, as valuable as these sources may turn out to be, their uncertain status and undefined quality make it hard to gauge the documents' value, especially for inexperienced college students. In addition, sources are often undefined and, consequently, their publishing context gets lost in the presentation of the full text. Dubious hits will appear legitimate when shown within an interface branded as scholarly, and even if users are aware of the limitations, they could still be misled (Taylor, 2007). The indiscriminate ranking of sources on a page obscures the importance of the document's value based on its academic status. In other words, disclosure of the paper's status is entirely left to authors and its evaluation is entirely up to the user. The question is, of course, whether students can discern these differences of quality in listed documents.

As mentioned earlier, the engine ranks electronic sources found by its crawlers according to their popularity as a cited source. Popularity in the Google-universe has everything to do with quantity and very little with quality or relevance. To some extent, ranking academic sources through Google Scholar is like ranking celebrities: you get what most people voted for, or rather, clicked for.

The more a source is linked to, the higher it will sit in the ranking of a new query, whatever its value or relevance to a specific research question. Search engine scholarship is thus an *ecosystem of reputation* where popularity is ranked by an algorithm measuring the relative weight of sources as they are mentioned by random users.

Put simply, queries tend to reward sources already cited over sources that are less well connected; this "rich-get-richer" or "winner-takes-all" effect—frequently cited sources gain prominence at the expense of less connected sources—is a well-researched yet disputed phenomenon in search engines.[6] The bottom line is that search engines, in crawling references on specific topics, tend to favor groups of highly interlinked sites primarily published by visible (often institutional) sources. This "chunky" aspect of the Web is calcified by Google's PageRank technology (Halavais, 2009). Users who continuously trace the same sources by clicking on them unwittingly amplify the engine's privileging effect. In keeping with Evans's (2008) findings, several researchers have concluded that online searching funnels consensus and narrows the variety of sources and ideas (Bar-Ilan, 2008; Mikki, 2009).

Will Google Scholar's implied, invisible system of popularity ranking change our ideas about scholarly expertise? There is certainly nothing wrong with "reputational" ranking of sources per se. As Harvard law professor Cass R. Sunstein (2006) has shown, aggregated information of large numbers of searches generally provides accurate information. And yet, the system is vulnerable to bias and distortion: accuracy and relevance will increase when users are more knowledgeable about the issue or topic being searched, and will decrease when aggregated expert judgments suffer from systematic bias or error (Sunstein, 2006, p. 41). This general rule may also apply to Google Scholar as a specialized engine that is primarily used by people who share an interest in academic research. Obviously, the engine is intended to be used by experts or scholars, and it could be expected that the advanced expertise of its users will render it more intelligent over time. However, the variety of Google Scholar's users is as wide as the scope of documents it crawls. Just as the engine's ranking does not discriminate between published (peer reviewed) and non-published scholarly articles, the engine does not distinguish between established scholars and beginning students, or between scientists and lay persons, as users. The engine's motto, "Standing on the shoulders of giants," should therefore be taken with a grain of salt. While it is acceptable for students to stand on the shoulders of giants to learn a profession, it all changes when Google Scholar is functioning as a one-stop-shop on the road to scholarly knowledge.

Electronic library services are a great advancement in users' abilities to find and cite sources, but they are never simple mediators between data and knowledge. Few researchers have convincingly argued that electronic databases affect students' and scholars' search behavior and that interfaces influence the production of knowledge by steering the behavior of users (Introna & Nissenbaum, 2000; Van Couvering, 2007). One specific effect of online search activity, according to US sociologist James Evans (2008), is that research gets anchored less deeply into past and present scholarship. Paradoxically, as more journal issues are becoming available online, fewer journals and articles are being cited. He concludes that the online search, even if it is more efficient, accelerates consensus and narrows the range of findings and ideas on which academics can build their own research.

What holds for online resources in general applies to search engines in particular. Although Google Scholar is used far less than its parent-engine, Google's control over data and information from scholarly sources is amplified by the engine's ability to link up to other layers of data and databases (Hunter et al., 2009). But search engines filter out sources as a result of their customizing algorithms, thus narrowing the available scope of source for their individual users. Eli

Pariser (2011) has described this "filter bubble" as the personal ecosystem of information that is the effect of an invisible algorithmic editing of the Web by search engines. If two people type in the same keywords in Google, there is no guarantee that the ranked results will be the same on both computers. Personalization, filter bubbles, and click aggregation—mechanisms favored by engines like Google Scholar—may narrow rather than widen the availability of sources to individual academics, thus problematizing the public values of knowledge production.

So far, I have discussed how public library values, such as reliability, relevance, and transparency of rankings, are revamped in the technological context of Google Scholar; the invisible algorithmic structuring of these values requires a precise analysis of the mechanisms behind the engine's interface. Besides the platform's technology, its organization and political economy have to be examined in more detail, as Google's powerful position in the information retrieval market warrants extra vigilance. But before I address the drawbacks of having one proprietary engine as a preferred gateway to scientific knowledge construction, I would like to focus on the mutual shaping of engine technology and user behavior.

Google Scholar: Users and Usage

Google Search—and, by extension, Google Scholar—have come to predominate over all other electronic information services offered by libraries. There is little empirical or ethnographic research data yet to illustrate *how* students actually go about open searches, but surveys prove that students performing topic searches for scholarly papers overwhelmingly choose search engines, rather than library-offered research discovery networks, as their preferred starting point.[7] Students' search behavior shows a preference for speed and convenience at the expense of quality and weighed relevance (Markland, 2005, pp. 25-29). Although there are considerable differences in the ways people use search engines, inexperienced users can be expected to have a strong penchant for automated desktop queries, and generally resort to the most convenient tool.

Besides relying on the engine's functionality in terms of selecting sources, users also tend to accept Google's *ranking* at face value. Students with little research experience appear to have remarkable faith in Google's judgment when it comes to the engine's prioritizing of search results. An eye-tracking experiment performed by a multidisciplinary team of researchers revealed that college students trust the engine's ability to rank results by their relevance to the query (Pan et al., 2007). The research team deliberately manipulated abstracts, making them more or less relevant to the tasks, but the experiment showed that students tend to look primarily—or even exclusively—at the first 10 results displayed on the Google page; they click on results in higher positions rather than looking for the items most most relevant to their task. Especially when students are rather less familiar with the topic they are searching on, the potential for misguided trust is exacerbated by the non-egalitarian distribution of information on the result pages:

Combining users' proclivity to trust ranked results with Google's algorithm, increases the chances that those "already rich" by virtue of nepotism get filthy rich by virtue of robotic searchers. Smaller, less affluent, alternative sites are doubly punished by ranking algorithms and lethargic searchers. (Pan et al., 2007, p. 817)

Pan's test was executed in the context of Google's general search engine, but the page popularity mechanism works the same for Google Scholar. Students who trust Google Scholar as an arbiter of indexed and prioritized scientific information are likely to be equally uncritical in assessing and weighing sources' value. Trusting Google's engine as a reliable arbiter of knowledge sources seems to be a widespread default attitude among its users, as Pan et al. conclude. First, because people generally do not regard machines in their technical dimensions as manipulative tools, and second, because they have a blind trust in the people and companies designing and operating those tools. According to Pew researcher Deborah Fallows (2005, p. i), 68% of all users say that search engines are a fair and unbiased source of information. Even assuming that users of Google Scholar are more sophisticated than users of search engines in general, it is doubtful whether they are more knowledgeable about the concept of search engines and how they work.

Users' profound trust in the neutrality of the apparatus resounds in the assumption that search engines like Google Search are not in themselves regulative and they cannot be manipulated. This misconception is most obvious when it comes to search engines in general. While Google Search should be compared to the Yellow Pages rather than to a telephone directory, most users still do not recognize the engine's commercial intentions. Fallows (2005, p. ii) found that 62% of all search engine users are unaware of the distinction between paid and unpaid results, and only 18% can tell the difference between these two types. Manipulation of rankings via paid placement is an inherent part of the Google business strategy (Batelle, 2005) and the ability to distinguish between the two should be a compulsory part of information literacy training (Nicholson et al., 2006).

Google *has* to be able to manipulate its ranking mechanisms because the engine faces constant external manipulative actions, such as search optimization and click fraud. The company employs a number of engineers who are constantly fine-tuning its engine and recalibrating its ranked results, and yet they cannot always detect linking schemes in the G-universe. If Google finds out about click fraud or detects unauthorized optimization efforts, the company punishes the perpetrator by lowering its rank or removing it from the search results altogether.[8] However, it is not the manipulation that is problematic, it is the lack of transparency in how rankings are controlled that is at odds with public values. Google has a vested interest in pleasing its advertisers as well as its users. While Google engines are cemented in their user's trust in the reliability of its ranking systems, advertisers are paying the company on the basis of their rankings. When it comes to click fraud or search engine optimization, Google is prosecutor, lawyer, judge, jury, and appeal court at the same time.

In all fairness, the mechanisms of paid placements and ranking manipulation may be less pertinent to Google Scholar than to its parent engine because Google Scholar is not exactly part of a commercial context. And yet, since all Google engines are intricately connected, and because students tend to switch back and forth between Google Search and Google Scholar, the issue is also relevant to the role Google Scholar plays in scientific knowledge. The question of trust applies to the parent company as a whole, rather than to a single search engine service or platform. It is not an overstatement to say that we increasingly trust a single company to regulate the data needed for the production of scientific knowledge.

The Legal-Political Context of Google Scholar

Search engines, besides their prolific function as ranking tools, are also profiling machines. When talking about profiling machines, we commonly think of social networking sites such as Facebook or Twitter, but search engines are also powerful profiling tools by virtue of the metadata produced—often unwittingly—by their users. Every single search on the Internet leaves traces of its sender: keywords, activity log, date and time, search history, etc. All these data can easily be traced back to personal Internet addresses and thus to specific people. Even if they are not actually used to track Web behavior to specific users, these data can be aggregated to a level that allows for user *profiles*: typical features of people who

have shown similar search behavior. We are long used to the deployment of aggregated metadata in commercial contexts—for instance, through Amazon's automated message "Customers who bought this item, also bought …." Metadata are the backbone of all Google's search engines; through the provenance of aggregated profiling techniques, Google collects and connects endless streams of behavioral patterns and reconnects them in ways we can only begin to imagine. Every time a user performs a search through one of its engines (Search, Scholar, Images, Maps, News, YouTube, Orkut, etc.), Google gains information about our individual and collective search behavior. Its rich metadata collections, and particularly the aggregated profiles resulting from these data, are the company's most valuable asset vis-à-vis advertisers, marketers, and any other type of agency interested in users' potential interests, whether as consumers, employees, or voters. There are very few legal hurdles to the exploitation of metadata reaped from (free) searching, and most users are completely unaware of what the engine's metadata disclose about their identity or behavior.

It might be argued at this point that the perusal of metadata from Google Scholar is not commercially interesting and is therefore irrelevant to the argument laid out in this paper. Why would individual search behavior or even collective profiles of particular types of users (e.g., users in certain geographical areas, universities, subjects, disciplinary fields) be of interest to Google itself or to third parties, whether government or commercial agents? Academics searching for information usually work on the cutting edge of knowledge production and are therefore very interesting objects for individual and collective surveillance. Public library values require that they never disclose the interests of their clients to outsiders and that they protect every person's right to freedom of information. Search engines have never openly subscribed to these values and are still wrestling with the legal issues of confidentiality and privacy when it comes to the use of metadata—a large gray area that has not yet been fully explored in terms of its boundaries and limits. Even if search engine companies argue that they have no interest whatsoever in individual metadata records, it is clear that even anonymized logs of individual search data can identify people (Halavais, 2009). Legal battles with various governments over the right to access search data have led Google Inc. to acquiesce to specific demands made by regimes in countries with substantial user markets, such as China (Morozov, 2011). Even less regulated is the protection of metadata against the interests of *commercial* agencies for whom information about individual search behavior may be extremely valuable.

However important this type of personal privacy protection—including the vulnerability of stored metadata to malicious attacks by outsiders and unreliable insiders—it is not my main focus here. More pertinent to my argument is the power of search engines to steer *collective* profiling: collective profiles of users may eventually shape the production of knowledge, even if subtly and non-intentionally. Jonathan Poritz (2007) has eloquently explained this process as search engines creating "a network structure on the mind-map of the collective unconscious" (p. 11) He warns about the large unmapped legal and moral territory where issues of what he calls "collective privacy" are unregulated in the virtual bonanza of the Internet. Since collective privacy is even harder to define—and therefore harder to protect—than individual privacy, Poritz calls for vigilance in how search engines, and particularly the market leader, exploit instruments for the aggregation and interpretation of metadata to which they have exclusive access.

Collective profiling forms the basis of connective profiling: combining the results of several search platforms or databases to detect significant trends or patterns. Scientific ideas usually develop through associative thinking, the patterns of which can be traced back to groups of related, interlinked researchers. Search engines, in a way, are global associative memories of information sources;

they help trace and store metadata on its usage which may subsequently be analyzed to result in user profiles and be connected to other data collections or profiles. Hal Varian, one of Google's engineers, described his company's competitive edge as its ability for "nowcasting": by linking up data streams from various search platforms, such as data reaped from search queries of people looking for jobs, they can measure unemployment before government figures cite the official figures.[9] With regard to Google Scholar, for instance, tracking down the search behavior of (a group of) pharmaceutical researchers and connecting these aggregated data to trend analyses of virus dispersion or to search data for flu remedies may lead to a profitable form of nowcasting. Connective profiling can give insiders at search engine companies a considerable information advantage that may play well on stock markets. In fact, by allowing search engine companies to peruse and aggregate their search data, researchers unwittingly give away pieces of data, which, if intelligently combined, may lead to insights they could not possibly have achieved themselves.

I am not insinuating that search engine companies in general, or Google in particular, are currently abusing their privileged position in data mining to take advantage of individual researchers or groups generating data. What I am pointing at is a large normative and legal gray area where much is at stake that is currently unregulated. As Poritz proposes, legislation could be designed to prevent search engine companies and their employees from using aggregated search data for insider trading or to require full disclosure of these data in completely anonymized, aggregated form, in order to guarantee a level playing field where private search companies have no unfair advantage over public scholars who actually deliver most of the data. As it stands now, search engine companies have an unfair competitive edge over (public) researchers when it comes to the availability and accessibility of huge data collections, the assessment and interpretation of which are key to the production of knowledge.

INFORMATION LITERACY AND THE POLITICS OF KNOWLEDGE CREATION

In this chapter I have argued how Google Scholar is not a simple mediator but rather an active co-producer of academic knowledge. The popular search engine changed, implicitly and explicitly, traditional notions of scholarly expertise as well as public library values. Algorithmically produced connective intelligence has a real impact on the way in which sources are found and used. In the academic milieu, these socially based methods of information generation and retrieval enhance the "filter bubble" phenomenon. Engines like Google Scholar also make it difficult for novices—as well as experts—to separate materials that adhere to traditional academic standards from those that do not. In this final section of this chapter, I want to discuss how the technological unconsciousness of students and young scholars needs to be remedied not just by information literacy, but also by an enriched kind of information literacy that includes insights into the mechanisms and politics of knowledge production.[10] Now that the use of search engines in academic settings has become part of students' operative mindset, it is even more urgent to raise awareness of what these tools can do and how they work.

A number of librarians and library scholars have already responded to the growing dominance of search engines, particularly Google Search and Google Scholar, by emphasizing the importance of including proprietary engines in their instruction practices and websites. Explaining the differences between and limitations of various engines may ensure the effective use of resources by students and inexperienced scholars (Cathcart & Roberts, 2005; Ettinger, 2007; Schmidt, 2007). Fitting the tradition of teaching information literacy as a pedagogical skill (Grafstein, 2002), the antidote to students' ignorance is teaching them the technicalities of various search methods, including their benefits and drawbacks. Other scholars

regard e-literacy as an integral part of teaching information society, as they expand the definition of information literacy to include socio-technical aspects of search (Tuominen, Savolainen, & Talja, 2005; Wallis, 2005). Teaching the mechanics and technicalities of the advanced search is extremely important for students who need to be empowered in their quest for knowledge; the help of librarians in this process is essential, but the daunting task of educating students in information literacy cannot be limited to library and teaching professionals.

In addition to information literacy, I propose to widen the term to encompass a definition that goes well beyond pedagogical skills and teaching practices to include the economic, political, and socio-cultural dimensions of search engines (Crowley, 2005; Williams, 2007). Proprietary search engines substantially shape the road from raw data to scholarly knowledge while rendering essential processes of weighing, evaluating, and contextualizing data into black boxes. To turn information into knowledge, students must not only be socialized in the various stages of the process, they should also be enabled to critically analyze the tools that help construct knowledge. They need to understand how information works on all levels, including the more abstract levels of informational politics (Halavais, 2009; Rogers, 2005). Without a basic understanding of network architecture and the dynamics of network connections and their intersections, it is difficult to grasp the social, legal, cultural, and economic implications of search engines.

A more complete and profound comprehension of the underlying mechanisms of the search may raise students' critical awareness of their own agency. A preference for convenience has never been science's biggest enemy; naivety and indifference are arguably its biggest foes. As Nicholas Carr observes in his book on the world's circuited information: "We accept greater control in return for greater convenience. The spider's web is made to measure, and we're not unhappy inside it" (Carr, 2008b, p. 209). Unawareness of the implications of convenient yet black-boxed tools inevitably leads to more control by owners of search technologies over the production of knowledge. By combining social constructivist insights with insights into the legal and ideological structure of search engine dynamics in the teaching information literacy, we can equip students to face the complicated socio-technical systems their information world is made of. We are only at the early stages of a future in which the production of knowledge is increasingly automated, interlinked, and defined by search engines.

While Google is already the nerve center of our information society, we will soon be facing the emergence of intelligent systems that may well form the heart and mind of the information society. Information networks are the architectural grid of power distribution, as Castells (2009) argues, and search engines are important nodes in the construction and distribution of knowledge. In order to ensure future generations of critical and knowledgeable scholars, we need to teach information literacy enriched with analytical skills *and* critical judgment. The production of scientific knowledge is too important to leave to companies and intelligent machines.

CONCLUSION

From a company that carries "Do no evil" as its corporate mantra, one may expect more than a moral platitude when it comes to the construction and dissemination of academic knowledge. According to a recent Gartner report, "even if all Google-employees make good-faith attempts to follow through on the mandate to do no evil, the ability to execute is not assured" (Hunter et al., 2009, p. 37). Google assumes an enormous responsibility, so it should at least give insight into the basic mechanisms by which its tools execute selection and search and into the policies that guarantee certain basic values (such as quality and reliability) to its users. Google's reluctance

to disclose information on procedural policies, inclusion of sources, technical specifications of its algorithm, and policies on issues concerning security and privacy is a matter for concern. Transparency of procedures and methods for gathering sources are key factors for progress in the area of knowledge production.

Less than seven years after their arrival, search engines—Google Scholar most prominently among them—have imposed a layered technological network on what used to be a library-based system of indexing and referencing sources of knowledge, and have come to dominate user patterns of information search. Automated search systems developed by Google tap into public values scaffolding the library system and yet, when looking beneath the surface, core values such as transparency and openness are hard to find. The powerful technological network that increasingly filters access to (public) knowledge is itself rooted in obscure or simply unknown principles.

Manuel Castells (2009) defined this network strategy as "the ability to connect and ensure the cooperation of different networks by sharing common goals and combining resources, while fending off competition from other networks by setting up strategic cooperation" (p. 45). Search engines like Google Scholar constitute a nodal point of power, while the mechanism of knowledge production is effectively hidden in the coded mechanisms of the engine and in the unarticulated conventions of scholarly use, such as quality assessment and source presentation. Google, as a corporation deploying a large number of technological networks in a variety of subject areas—from geographical mapping and social networking to computational statistics—is a key player in the global distribution of communication power.

Castells (2009) refers to the tendency to connect various networks of communication as the "switching strategy," the "control of the connecting points between various strategic networks" (p. 46) As a prominent *switcher*, the company handles many specific interface systems that relate and connect a variety of user contexts that are all crucial to the formation of knowledge. It is through these switching processes enacted by actor-networks—networks that induce synergizing effects—that knowledge is constructed. Switchers are "made of networks of actors engaging in dynamic interfaces that are specifically operated in each process of connection" (Castells, 2009, p. 47). What is important here is not to identify concrete social actors who will use (or abuse) their powerful advanced position when it comes to data brokering, but to point out how the potential switching between different networks is a fundamental source of power in a global networked society. Manuel Castells urges that, in order to understand how power works, we need to "look [into] the *connections* between corporate communication networks, financial networks, cultural industrial networks, technology networks, and political networks" (Castells, 2009, p. 431, emphasis added). If we do not unravel ("unwire") how power works in a networked society, we cannot understand, neutralize, or counteract dominant forces of knowledge production.

Crucial to the "unwiring" of network activities is understanding the logic in which these processes are grounded. The "technological unconsciousness" (Beer, 2009) of most users exceeds their basic unawareness of the limited scope and manipulative ranking mechanisms governing their favourite search engine and their own search behavior. While search engines have profoundly redefined the meaning of some public library values, such as citation analysis and relevance, they also minimally subscribe to basic values such as neutrality and transparency. In addition, commercial search engines are conspicuously silent when it comes to policies of privacy and confidentiality protection. These values are extremely relevant when we turn the question "how do users benefit from Google?" into "how does Google benefit from its users?" The legal and political-economy contexts in which platforms mature are as important to unwire as the technological systems themselves.

REFERENCES

Bakkalbasi, N., Bauer, K., Glover, J., & Wang, L. (2006). Three options for citation tracking: Google Scholar, Scopus and Web of Science. *Biomedical Digital Libraries, 3*(7). Retrieved May 7, 2011, from http://www.bio-diglib.com/content/3/1/7

Bar-Ilan, J. (2007). Google bombing from a time perspective. *Journal of Computer-Mediated Communication, 12*, 910–938. doi:10.1111/j.1083-6101.2007.00356.x

Bar-Ilan, J. (2008). Which h-index? A comparison of WoS, Scopus and Google Scholar. *Scientometrics, 74*(2), 257–271. doi:10.1007/s11192-008-0216-y

Batelle, J. (2005). *The search. How Google and its rivals rewrote the rules of business and transformed our culture.* New York, NY: Penguin.

Beel, J. B. Gipp, Bela, & Wilde, E. (2010). Academic search engine optimization (ASEO): Optimizing scholarly literature for Google Scholar and Co. *Journal of Scholarly Publishing*, 176–190.

Beer, D. (2009). Power through the algorithm? Participatory web cultures and the technological unconscious. *New Media & Society, 11*(6), 985–1002. doi:10.1177/1461444809336551

Caldas, A., Schroeder, R., Mesch, G. S., & Dutton, W. H. (2008). Patterns of information search and access on the World Wide Web: Democratizing expertise or creating new hierarchies? *Journal of Computer-Mediated Communication, 13*, 769–793. doi:10.1111/j.1083-6101.2008.00419.x

Carr, N. (2008a). Is Google making us stupid? *The Atlantic Monthly*, July/August 2008. Retrieved May 7, 2011, from www.theatlantic.com/doc/print/200807/google

Carr, N. (2008b). *The big switch. Rewiring the world, from Edison to Google.* New York, NY: Norton.

Castells, M. (2009). *Communication power*. Oxford, UK: Oxford University Press.

Cathcart, R., & Roberts, A. (2005). Evaluating Google Scholar as a tool for information literacy. *Internet Reference Services Quarterly, 10*(3), 167–176. doi:10.1300/J136v10n03_15

Caufield, J. (2005). Where did Google get its value? *Libraries and the Academy, 5*(4), 555–572. doi:10.1353/pla.2005.0047

Crowley, B. (2005). *Spanning the theory-practice divide in library and information science*. Maryland: Scarecrow Press.

Ettinger, D. (2008). The triumph of expediency: The impact of Google Scholar on library instruction. *Journal of Library Administration, 46*(3), 65–72. doi:10.1300/J111v46n03_06

Evans, J. A. (2008). Electronic publication and the narrowing of science and scholarship. *Science, 321*(5887), 395–399. doi:10.1126/science.1150473

Fallows, D. (2005). *Search engine users* (Pew Internet and American Life Project). Retrieved May 7, 2011, from http://www.pewinternet.org/Reports/2005/Search-Engine-Users.aspx

Foucault, M., & Gordon, C. (Eds.). (1980). *Power/knowledge interviews: Selected and other writings 1972-1977*. New York, NY: Pantheon.

Gorman, G. E. (2006). Giving way to Google. *Online Information Review, 30*(2), 97–99. doi:10.1108/14684520610659148

Grafstein, A. (2002). A discipline-based approach to information literacy. *Journal of Academic Librarianship, 28*(4), 197–204. doi:10.1016/S0099-1333(02)00283-5

Halavais, A. (2009). *Search engine society*. Cambridge, MA: Polity Press.

Hargittai, E. (2004). Do you "Google"? Understanding search engine use beyond the hype. *First Monday, 9*(3). Retrieved May 7, 2011, from http://firstmonday.org/htbin/cgiwrap/bin/ojs/index.php/fm/article/view/1127/1047

Hargittai, E. (2007). The social, political, economic, and cultural dimensions of search engines: An introduction. *Journal of Computer-Mediated Communication, 12*, 769–777. doi:10.1111/j.1083-6101.2007.00349.x

Head, A. J., & Eisenberg, M. (2010). How today's college students use Wikipedia for course-related research. *First Monday, 15*(3). Retrieved May 7, 2011, from http://www.uic.edu/htbin/cgiwrap/bin/ojs/index.php/fm/article/view/2830/2476

Hellsten, I., Leydesdorff, L., & Wouters, P. (2006). Multiple presents: How search engines rewrite the past. *New Media & Society, 8*(6), 901–924. doi:10.1177/1461444806069648

Hijink, M. (2010, August 2). Google kan het heden tot in detail voorspellen. *NRC Handelsblad*, p. 9.

Hunter, R., De Lotto, R. J., Frank, A., Gassmann, B., Hallawell, A., & Heiser, J. ... Taylor, D. (2009) *What does Google know?* (Gartner Research Report G00158124). Retrieved from http://www.gartner.com/id=918012

Introna, L. D., & Nissenbaum, H. (2000). Shaping the Web: Why the politics of search engines matter. *The Information Society, 16*, 169–185. doi:10.1080/01972240050133634

Jacso, P. (2008). The pros and cons of computing the h-index using Google Scholar. *Online Information Review, 32*(3), 437–452. doi:10.1108/14684520810889718

Lohr, S. (2009, August 6). For today's graduate, just one word: Statistics. *The New York Times*, Technology section. Retrieved May 7, 2011, from http://www.nytimes.com/2009/08/06/technology/06stats.html

Markland, M. (2005). Does the student's love of the search engine mean that high quality online academic resources are being missed? *Performance Measurement and Metrics: The International Journal for Library and Information Services, 6*(1), 19–31. doi:10.1108/14678040510588562

Mikki, S. (2009). Google Scholar compared to Web of science: A literature review. *Nordic Journal of Information Literacy in Higher Education, 1*(1), 41–51.

Morozov, E. (2011). *The Net delusion: How not to liberate the world.* New York, NY: Penguin.

Neuhaus, C., Neuhaus, E., Asher, A., & Wrede, C. (2006). The depth and breadth of Google Scholar: An empirical study. *Libraries and the Academy, 6*(2), 127–141. doi:10.1353/pla.2006.0026

Nicholson, S., Sierra, T., Eseryel, U., Park, J., Barkow, P., Pozo, E., & Ward, J. (2006). How much of it is real? Analysis of paid placement in Web search engine results. *Journal of the American Society for Information Science American Society for Information Science, 57*(4), 448–461.

Nygren, E., Haya, G., & Widmark, W. (2006). Students experience of Metalib and Google Scholar. *Online Information Review, 31*(3), 365–375.

Online Computer Library Center. (2005). *College students' perceptions of libraries and information resources.* Dublin, OH: OCLC. Retrieved May 7, 2011, from http://www.oclc.org/reports/perceptionscollege.htm

Pan, B., Hembrooke, H., Joachims, T., Lorigo, L., Gay, G., & Granka, L. (2007). In Google we trust: Users' decisions on rank, position, and relevance. *Journal of Computer-Mediated Communication, 12*, 801–823. doi:10.1111/j.1083-6101.2007.00351.x

Pariser, E. (2011). *The filter bubble. What the Internet is hiding from you.* New York, NY: Penguin.

Poritz, J. (2007). Who searches the searchers? Community privacy in the age of monolithic search engines. *The Information Society, 23*(5), 383–389. doi:10.1080/01972240701572921

Rogers, R. (2005). *Information politics on the Web.* Cambridge, MA: The MIT Press.

Schmidt, J. (2007). Promoting library services in a Google world. *Library Management, 28*(6), 337–346. doi:10.1108/01435120710774477

Schroeder, R. (2007). Pointing users toward citation searching: Using Google Scholar and Web of Science. *Libraries and the Academy, 7*(2), 243–248. doi:10.1353/pla.2007.0022

Segal, D. (2010, February 12). The dirty little secrets of search. *The New York Times*, Business section. Retrieved May 7, 2011, from http://www.nytimes.com/2011/02/13/business/13search.html

Segev, E. (2008). Search engines and power: A politics of online (mis-)information. *Webology, 5*(2). Retrieved May 7, 2011, from http://www.webology.ir/2008/v5n2/a54.html

Sunstein, C. R. (2006). *Infotopia. How many minds produce knowledge.* Oxford, UK: Oxford University Press.

Taylor, S. (2007). Google Scholar—Friend or foe? *Interlending & Document Supply, 35*(1), 4–6. doi:10.1108/02641610710728122

Tuominen, K., Savolainen, R., & Talja, S. (2005). Information literacy as a sociotechnical practice. *The Library Quarterly, 75*(3), 329–345. doi:10.1086/497311

Van Couvering, E. (2007). Is relevance relevant? Market, science, and war: Discourse of search engine quality. *Journal of Computer-Mediated Communication, 12*. Retrieved May 8, 2011, from http://jcmc.indiana.edu/vol12/issue3/vancouvering.html

van Dijck, J. (2009). Users like you: Theorizing agency in user-generated content. *Media Culture & Society, 31*(1), 41–58. doi:10.1177/0163443708098245

Wallis, J. (2005). Cyberspace, information literacy and the information society. *Library Review, 54*(4), 218–222. doi:10.1108/00242530510593407

Walters, W. H. (2007). Google Scholar coverage of a multidisciplinary field. *Information Processing & Management, 43*(4), 1121–1132. doi:10.1016/j.ipm.2006.08.006

White, B. (2007). Examining the claims of Google Scholar as a serious information source. *New Zealand Library & Information Management Journal, 50*(1), 11–24.

Williams, G. (2007). Unclear on the context: Refocusing on information literacy's evaluative component in the age of Google. *Library Philosophy and Practice, 6*. Retrieved May 7, 2011, from http://www.encyclopedia.com/Library+Philosophy+and+Practice/publications.aspx?date=200706&pageNumber=1

ADDITIONAL READING

Cohen, N. S. (2008). The valorization of surveillance: Towards a political economy of Facebook. *Democratic Communiqué, 22*(1), 5–22.

Cowhey, P. F., & Aronson, J. D. (2009). *Transforming global information and communication markets: The political economy of innovation.* Cambridge, MA: The MIT Press.

Dahlberg, L. (2007). The Internet, deliberative democracy, and power: Radicalizing the public sphere. *International Journal of Media and Cultural Politics, 3*(1), 47–64. doi:10.1386/macp.3.1.47_1

Feenberg, A. (2009). Critical theory of communication technology: Introduction to the special section. *The Information Society, 25*(2), 77–83. doi:10.1080/01972240802701536

Fuchs, C. (2009). Information and communication technologies and society: A contribution to the critique of the political economy of the Internet. *European Journal of Communication, 24*, 69–87. doi:10.1177/0267323108098947

Gitelman, L. (2008). *Always already new: Media, history, and the data of culture.* Cambridge, MA: The MIT Press.

Milberry, K., & Anderson, S. (2009). Open sourcing our way to an online commons: Contesting corporate impermeability in the new media ecology. *The Journal of Communication Inquiry, 33*(4), 393–412. doi:10.1177/0196859909340349

Pariser, E. (2011). *The filter bubble. What the Internet is hiding from you.* New York, NY: Viking.

van Dijck, J. (2009). Users like you: Theorizing agency in user-generated content. *Media Culture & Society, 31*(1), 41–58. doi:10.1177/0163443708098245

KEY TERMS AND DEFINITIONS

Academic Publishing: The sub-field of publishing that distributes academic research and scholarship. Most academic work is published in journal article, book, or thesis form. Most scientific and scholarly journals, and many (although not all) academic and scholarly books go through some form of peer review or editorial refereeing to qualify texts for publication. The part of academic written output that is not formally published but merely printed up or posted is often called "gray literature."

Digital (or Electronic) Library: A library in which collections are stored in digital formats (as opposed to print, microform, or other media) and accessed by computers. The digital content may be stored locally, or accessed remotely via computer networks. A digital library is a type of information retrieval system.

Google Scholar: A freely accessible Web search engine that indexes the full text of scholarly literature across an array of publishing formats and disciplines. Released in November 2004, the Google Scholar index includes most peer-reviewed online journals by Europe and America's largest scholarly publishers.

Information Literacy: Narrowly defined, the ability to know when there is a need for information, and to be able to identify, locate, evaluate, and effectively use that information in the context of the issue or problem at hand. More broadly defined, a set of competencies that an informed citizen of an information society ought to possess to participate intelligently and actively in that society.

Political Economy: Different, but related, approaches to studying economic and political behaviors of people. The combination of economics with other fields allows the use of different, fundamental assumptions to challenge orthodox economic assumptions.

Search Engine Optimization: The process of improving the visibility of a website or Web page in search engines via organic search results. In general, the earlier (or higher ranked on the search results page) and more frequently a site appears in the search results list, the more visitors it will receive from the search engine's users.

Web Search Engines: Online tools and services to search for information on the World Wide Web and FTP servers. The search results are generally presented in a list of results often referred to as SERPS (search engine results pages). The information consists of Web pages, images, information, and other types of files.

ENDNOTES

[1] Head & Eisenberg (2010) found in a survey that the overwhelming majority of college students (95%) use Google search engines to start their course-related research. Only assigned course readings were listed as a more popular entry for starting research (97%). Wikipedia is listed as the 6th-highest source (85%) for information; librarians rank 14th (45%).

[2] See Head & Eisenberg (2010), who demonstrate from their survey that scholarly databases (EBSCO, ProQuest, JSTOR, etc) rank third in the resources students turn to for obtaining background on a topic, after Google and assigned course readings.

[3] See http://scholar.google.com/intl/en/scholar/about.html, accessed May 7, 2011. Emphasis in citation added by author.

[4] Mikki (2009) compares the free Web engine to Web of Science and concludes that Google Scholar performs poorly in terms of advanced information retrieval compared to scholarly databases. Schroeder (2007), comparing the same two tools, gives a comprehensive overview of studies comparing Google Scholar and Web of Science. In a comparative study of Google Scholar, Scopus, and Web of Science, Bakkalbasi, Bauer, Glover, and Wang (2006) conclude that each of these tools has strengths in specific disciplinary searches. A behavioral study comparing Metalib to Google Scholar (Nygren, Haya, & Widmark, 2006) shows students' preference for convenience leads them to Google Scholar as their first choice.

[5] Search engine optimization (SEO) refers to deliberate attempts to improve the visibility of a website or page in search engines via algorithmic results. If a page is ranked high in the result list, the more frequently it is visited and the more visitors it will attract.

SEO that targets academic search results is called academic SEO.

⁶ For a nuanced discussion of this "winner-takes-all" effect, see Caldas, Schroeder, Mesch, and Dutton (2008, pp. 770-772) who argue that the effect increases within a narrower area of search. Their webmetric analyses confirmed the "cliquishness" of the Web engine search.

⁷ In 2005, the Online Computer Library Center (OCLC) published a report stating that 89% of the college students surveyed begin their information searches with a search engine versus just 2% who begin with a university library website. Markland (2005) found that over 70% of students start with a general search engine, and Google is by far their favorite. Google's popularity dwarfs that of Yahoo!, MSNSearch, Gigablast, and Ask.com, all of which lag substantially behind the market leader. Estimates of what percentage of searches are performed through Google varies from 30% to 50% (Hargittai, 2004, 2007; Caldas, Schroeder, Mesch, & Dutton, 2008).

⁸ *New York Times* reporter David Segal (2010) discovered a large-scale click fraud scandal—a so-called "black hat" scheme involving one of Google's biggest customers, JC Penney. The department store's name showed up in the highest position when clicked in a score of different articles about topics ranging from dresses to furniture, a situation that lasted for months. After the *NYT* reporter had confronted Google about this scheme, Google (manually) adjusted the algorithm of its search engine in an attempt to redress it. Segal mused in his article, "Is it possible that Google was willing to countenance an extensive black-hat campaign because it helped one of its larger advertisers? It's the sort of question that European Union officials are now studying in an investigation of possible antitrust abuses by Google."

⁹ See an interview with Hal Varian—formerly professor of Economics at UC Berkely, and since 2007 employed by Google—in the Dutch newspaper *NRC Handelsblad* (Hijink, 2010). Varian directs Google's team of engineers working on perfecting the AdWords automated auction system.

¹⁰ Information literacy—generally considered the domain of librarians and library scholars—is defined by the American Library Association as "the lifelong ability to recognize the need for, to locate, evaluate and effectively use information." Digital information literacy (DIF) is regarded by the American Library Association as a subset of information literacy, defined as "the ability to find, evaluate and use digital information effectively, efficiently and ethically. DIF involves knowing how digital information is different from print information; having the skills to use specialized tools for finding digital information; and developing the dispositions needed in the digital information environment." See 21st Century Digital Information Fluency (DIF) project and model at <http://21cif.com> or Digital Information Literacy at http://wikieducator.org/Digital_information_literacy.

Chapter 9

Reviewing in the Age of Web 2.0:
What Does Web Culture Have to Offer to Scholarly Communication?

Lilian Landes
Bavarian State Library, Germany

ABSTRACT

With digitalization increasing, scholars' reading habits and communication methods are also changing, thus affecting the field of traditional reviewing in the humanities. The expert formulating a comprehensive review of a recently published work, will, in the medium term, see a scholarly community working together. In the age of Web 2.0, the disadvantages of a traditional book review, which usually does not allow for a reply or an open discussion, become apparent. This chapter describes (the preconditions for) these changes, as well as other issues in the current field of reviewing, that will eventually not only increase the speed of reviewing new publications in general, but will also, in compliance with the nature of this field, make it more focused on process and detail, more interdisciplinary, more flexible, and more international, thus adapting the model of "live" reviewing procedures as already established in the commercial book market.

INTRODUCTION

Leaving Reviewing 1.0[1]

Scholarly communication takes many forms. Though it may sound like a generalization, the speed of communication in the natural sciences tends to be faster than it is in the humanities.

Perhaps it can also be said that in the natural sciences there is more direct communication between scholars, because here developing research results within a group is traditionally common practice, and publication and communication are usually manifested through articles. This in itself ensures that colleagues tend to react to a publication more quickly than their counterparts in the humanities. The traditional book review is virtually unknown in the natural sciences where

DOI: 10.4018/978-1-4666-2178-7.ch009

the evaluation process is generally based on peer review, and practically always prior to publication. In contrast, in the humanities and social sciences the magnum opus—the qualifying text that is developed by a single scholar over several years, and then released, traditionally still via a publisher and in print—remains crucial. All in all, it is a rather cumbersome medium regarding publication and communication. At least within the European scholarly community, peer review does not take place prior to the publication of a monograph, but afterward. A newly released monograph often only attracts the attention of the author's colleagues because of a review published in a journal. According to Thomas Meyer, academic journals publishing book reviews

have established themselves as "guardians of quality" within a scholarly book market—monographs are still the common output format of scholarly research—because they not only ensure that minimum standards are maintained in publishing, but also shape the expectations and demands of readers and authors with their assessment and criticism. [My translation] (Meyer, 2011)[2]

In a similar way, Ylva Lindholm-Romantschuk describes the review itself as a "gatekeeper," since "[b]ooks represent intellectual innovations and are evaluated in terms of their value to the scholarly community. … A negative review may prevent the ideas in a book from reaching a wider audience" (Lindholm-Romantschuk, 1998: 41) and vice versa.

This shows that the process of reviewing in the humanities has to be clearly distinguished from reviewing procedures in the field of the natural sciences. Here, articles are often reviewed by anonymous peers prior to publication; in the humanities, this process takes place after the publication of (mostly) monographs, through the very distinctive text genre of the book review. In contrast to peer review, this can be called a "public evaluation of research" (Linholm-Romantschuk,

1998: 85). As a matter of course, the reviewer appears as an author, and the review is added to his or her list of publications.

Book reviewing emerged from a completely different scholarly tradition than peer reviewing. The processes for this form of review—such as finding suitable reviewers (who are increasingly often young scholars)—may begin one or two years after a text has been published, and are very different from the "advance" peer reviewing typical in the life sciences.[3] In Germany, some new approaches in open peer reviewing are found in in the humanities, such as the *Kunstgeschichte Open Peer Reviewed Journal* online.[4] However, the common practice of post-publication reviewing in the humanities is still dominant, and is therefore the focus of this chapter.

The journal editors act as the primary filter, as they explore the book market and actively contact reviewers about recent publications of interest. The reviewer then writes the review, usually pro bono. The time between a book being published and the writing, editing, printing and publication of a review of it can be as long as two years. Depending on how often the publication running the review appears, another year's delay may not be unusual.

The book review in the humanities is not just a crucial means of scholarly communication, but unlike other text genres, puts more emphasis on an accepted understanding of the term "expert" or "peer." Traditionally, the editors of review journals will ask scholars who are believed to be "experts" in a particular area of research to write a review of another scholar's recent publication of a text in that area. Here, "experts" are those who are considered capable of appropriately judging the methodology and results of a new monograph, as well as placing it in its scholarly context. The development of the Internet has revealed this traditional process to be slow, often rather monotonous and inflexible, and mired in a hierarchy. Communication between the reviewer and the author reviewed is impossible — unless it happens one to one without other scholars noticing it. Replies to a review published in a journal are extremely rare, difficult to relate to the review because of their delayed release (often a year later), and therefore frequently overlooked. In the age of the digital revolution, however, the image of the expert, the reviewer him- or herself, is changing. It is doubtful that in the medium and long term a journal's choice of a reviewer, writing and judging from an individual point of view, will meet the needs of a changing scholarly community which is also, and particularly, influenced by the Web 2.0 culture of participation.

The question I address here is whether the review as we know it can comply with the collaborative character, the shared expert knowledge, and the basic nature of the Internet. How would the field of reviewing have to transform itself to benefit from the potential offered by the Internet? To what extent can commercial platforms, such as Amazon, or social networks (e.g. Facebook, Twitter) be seen as exemplars? Which tools can help meet the specific needs of a scholarly book review?

BACKGROUND

Increasingly More, Increasingly Spread

The traditional field of reviewing is increasingly suffering from overabundance. A constantly growing number of new publications are reviewed by a group of scholars who are facing more pressure to publish their own work (William W. Savage [2009] speaks of "forced productivity"). This means that scholars want to see their work reviewed, but also have less time to read and review the lengthy works of their colleagues. More and more review journals are struggling to capture the attention of scholars who have to search for book reviews scattered across traditional print media and the Internet. Some smaller journals publish

their reviews online in addition to their print version, but they usually do this on their institute's home pages, which lacks visibility. Not only are the reviews difficult to find, the journal staff often struggle to amass the technical knowledge and manpower required for gathering the texts, tagging them with metadata, and ensuring their long-time storage in a way that they can be used by a researcher as an easily accessible work tool. All in all, the more traditional forms of review publication described above lead to confusion for the individual scholar who is trying to gain an overview of what is being published in his or her specific area of interest. Even the major traditional journals are increasingly becoming aware of this challenge. In the past, researchers would be aware of scheduled publication dates and would pull the most recent issues of acclaimed journals from a shelf in the university library in order to read through the review section, but a major transformation has already taken place, and the field of reviewing is lagging behind. Young academics, especially students, are increasingly limiting their sources of information to what can be Googled when trying to stay abreast of current developments within their discipline (meaning both reviews and conference reports).

Special scientific tools and search engines are also increasingly being used and demanded by scholars. It has become common knowledge that the citation rate of an electronically available text is significantly higher when compared to that of a text in print (Herb, 2010; Hajjem, Harnad, & Gingras, 2005). Google Books facilitates access to research documents, and especially primary literature in the public domain, to an extent that has substantially changed the everyday work of historians. Time and energy that used to be spent locating and obtaining relevant literature can now be used for analyzing and comparing it. It is obvious that this is also crucial for the reviewer. The significantly improved availability of basic and reference texts means that a recently published text that has to be reviewed can be placed against a background that facilitates differentiated assessment, compared to the use of only traditional (print) references. That the reviewers themselves want to be rewarded for their usually unpaid work with as much visibility as possible is self-evident. Unfortunately, Google Scholar does not list scholarly book reviews as a matter of principle. This could be a result of the review often being seen as a kind of "second-class" scientific literature (Linholm-Romantschuk, 1998: 37).

In light of these conditions, it is hardly surprising that online review journals in the humanities have been highly successful for years. A US survey in 2005 of historians publishing electronically suggested that as many as 16.5% were doing so, "and it was clear from comments that most of those publications were book reviews" (Dalton, 2009: 115). One might, for example, turn to the historical sciences in Germany, where two highly successful projects, the review journal *sehepunkte* and the information service *H-Soz-u-Kult*, were launched at a very early stage of online publishing. Every month they publish considerable (mostly triple digit) numbers of thematically specific historical reviews.

Due to rather short, or even open, release intervals, the process of publishing book reviews is shortened online, which means that the time between the publication of a book and its respective review is reduced. Furthermore, visibility on the Web is better than it is in print, due to tools enabling a full text search, enrichment with metadata, or the linking with central research tools relevant for the respective discipline. In the humanities, this can be achieved by linking the reviews to the respective book titles in the catalogues of the major scholarly libraries. Scholars need to be able to find the reviews while working on their own research questions, and ideally not having to depend on the release date of a traditional journal.

So although online review venues are enjoying an increase in popularity, it is still surprising that book reviews remain essentially the same but presented in a new medium. Instead of being printed, they are published in HTML. In this respect, the full potential of the Internet remains untapped (see Haber & Hodel, 2011). This is unfortunate because the potential of the Internet for reviews is significant: fast, flexible, and discourse-oriented forms of communication, typical of online exchanges, would highly benefit the development and nature of the book review, since it focuses on a post-release exchange about publications and is as recent and detailed as possible. Which place—and over the last couple of years, the incredible boom in social networks has shown this—could possibly be more convenient for facilitating scholarly communication?

Exchange is at the heart of social networks. Limiting oneself to sending or receiving comments and notifications goes against the basic character of such networks. For example, an institution that limits itself to sending information units is still acting as an instructing "expert" toward its audience. However, social media is kept alive through every actor's belief that the others are equal, which reflects a radically different idea of the "expert": in this case, expertise is jointly shaped by many single participants. This is the point related to the basic idea of a book review. An exchange process regarding the quality of a publication within the target audience is exactly what it should represent, and not primarily the (always subjective) judgment of an individual. One of the disadvantages of traditional reviewing is the fact that the comment is one-sided, with one reviewer talking and judging. Even when there is an exchange in traditional reviewing in the humanities (for instance, due to the reply of the author reviewed), the problem lies in the slow pace of the communication, owing to the distribution of the exchange across several issues of a journal.

REVIEWING EN ROUTE TO WEB 2.0

Using the Internet for reviewing, moving away from the result-oriented nature of the traditional "book review", and approaching the process-oriented nature of collective work—a defining feature of the Internet itself—means getting used to collaborative, shared scholarly work, and letting go of the idea of the one expert reviewer and doing research "behind closed doors." Scholarly progress within the various disciplines of the humanities is, in accordance with the natural sciences, increasingly linked to the idea of collaborative work and shared expertise. There is no longer anyone who seriously questions the growing significance of process-oriented scholarly practice, which is already becoming apparent in external research structures. Elements of the Web 2.0 mechanisms, such as those that have been established in commercial book markets for years, scarcely existed within the field of reviewing in the humanities until today (see Collins & Hide, 2010).

If one asks why, things become more obscure. In the humanities, terms such as "Web 2.0," "crowdsourcing," or "wisdom of the crowds" are associated with a greater decline in quality than in the natural sciences. Even the word "crowd" is already often perceived as a synonym for something non-scientific. The fact that a "scholarly crowd," and a group of interested non-professionals (especially in the field of history), who can also be taken seriously in terms of specific questions, exists, is often still ignored.[5] The same goes for the fact that the "scholarly crowd" can prove its special value when it becomes international.

A lack of internationalism is another problem for the current European reviewing tradition. Despite increasing digitalization of work tools, the field of history in Europe has thus far been limited to a national radius in terms of operation and perception. Although online publication would be highly suitable for going beyond national boundaries, and would circumvent the expensive distribution channels of printed review journals, many online review journals still mainly focus on new publications from their own country, or at least their language area.

"How can we benefit from the best of the Web 2.0 technologies while avoiding the worst?" Cathy Moran Hajo asked in 2009. "Do we want to turn our readers into collaborators? How would we do it?" (Hajo, 2009, paragraph 20). These are essential questions and should at least be touched upon.

THE POTENTIAL FOR COLLABORATIVE REVIEWING

How can the current barriers be overcome, and how can reviews benefit from the potential of the Internet? The answer is, by testing new tools that embrace the growing significance of "shared expertise," and that enable quality assurance and various generation needs, as well as a flexible international exchange regarding new publications.

Traditionally, the role of the reviewer is that of the (almost) unquestionable expert. In order to avoid "reviewing cartels", it is usually up to the editors of acclaimed journals to choose these experts in a way that frees the final product, the review, from any suspicion of favoritism. For several decades, this system enjoyed much trust and it is still practiced today. However, what has grown in the meantime is our demand for a more neutral examination of a text—regardless of whether it is applied to commercial or scholarly literature. This new demand is probably the result of the great significance that Web 2.0 related communication mechanisms on the Internet bear for the public and private perception of social issues. The essence of the Internet is to let the user exploit the existence of several opinions in order to form a central thread, which is not necessarily constituted by an objective, but possibly by an individual balancing of arguments emerging from the various aspects and fragments of crowd-based information and perspectives. For instance, the success of social bookmarks reflects that this attitude toward "professional information" has fundamentally changed. Traditionally, reading recommendations were given by traditional experts, as individual book reviews, or alternatively, as a review essay providing an overview of recent publications within a specific area of research, including an assessment of their quality. Whether the increasingly expanding Web culture is more democratic is subject for debate. However, there is no doubt that in the Web 2.0 environment skepticism about the expert appointed through self-proclamation or third-party promotion is growing. Likewise, there is an unquestionable growth of confidence in the ability of the masses to exchange recommendations, compare them, and, based upon the frequency of approvals, conclude to what extent the recommendation can be taken as objective. Attempting to achieve objectivity is traditionally a task for the editors of a journal, who knew the academic scene well enough so as not to ask a reviewer for his or her opinion if they knew that the reviewer had a prejudice against the author of the publication to be reviewed.

Another example is the scholarly blog culture, which has been spreading in France[6] for the last couple of years and is now much more accepted there than in Germany. The "new" experts, the "distributed experts" are increasingly willing to share their ideas with colleagues while working on their publications. The fear of taking possession of ideas is dismissed in the wake of the awareness that scholarship can benefit from early comments and discussions. The new perception of the expert goes hand in hand with a scholarship style of increasingly dividing work into smaller units that harmonizes well with comments or bookmarks from colleagues in various fields or even outside of academia. Dan Cohen, director of the Center for History and New Media at George Mason University, even suggests an "ethical imperative" to share scholarly information. "Engaging people in different disciplines and from outside academia has made his scholarship better" (Cohen, 2010, paragraph 26).

The evident development is that the user is taking up the role of the expert who chooses comments from a pool of opinions on offer that seem useful and justified for their own interests. In the case of a scholarly social Web culture, the user network consists of members from the academic expert community as well as others who may have a special interest in and knowledge of the subject but are not credentialed experts. However, it is still the case with scholarly or popular scientific blogs that the opinion of someone who is seen as a traditional expert will be rated higher than the comments of a layman. This is reinforced by the use of real names in scholarly discussions. Given the current situation, it seems doubtful whether the "pure model" of Web 2.0, meaning the democratic ideal of an interaction between professors, students and laymen who communicate equally through nicknames, will be able to establish itself in a scholarly environment over the coming years.

Since the beginning of 2010, the German Research Foundation has funded a pilot project that is creating a collaborative reviewing instrument for published writings in the field of European history. At the same time, it includes a control device for the sake of maintaining scholarly standards of quality regarding expert publications. The focus is only on works that have been published. The platform created for this was launched in January 2011 and is called recensio.net. It represents a joint project of the Bavarian State Library (BSB), Munich, the German Historical Institute, Paris (DHIP), and the Institute for European History (IEG), Mainz.

recensio.net is based on two fundamental ideas that combine traditional and innovative reviewing in one platform. The first pillar of the platform lets recensio.net act as an open access aggregator for traditional reviews, and a service provider for journals publishing reviews. Cooperating journals publish their reviews on recensio.net, in addition to their original place of publication. It is irrelevant whether this initial place of publication is online or in print. The editorial offices continue to work independently, and therefore recensio.net does not claim to be publishing exclusive review texts. The way they are published is kept highly flexible in order to respond to the needs of the cooperating journals. Usually the PDFs of the reviews are provided, thus presenting the user with the familiar layout of each journal. In contrast, online journals usually publish their texts in HTML. Also, each editorial office decides (if necessary, after consulting the respective publisher involved) whether a "moving wall," an embargo period, should be established between the original publication of the reviews in a journal and their upload to recensio.net.

Experience has shown that material that is bound by usage constraints is de facto more rarely consulted (and consequently less often cited and spread) than free material that can be linked and shared, regardless of whether it is peer reviewed or a result of shared knowledge. This is one reason why recensio.net is committed to the idea of open access. All content on the platform is freely available for the user at no charge. Each review can be downloaded as a PDF, including a citation notice. One can then continue to use it in accordance with the respective copyright rules. Long-term archival storage of the reviews is provided by the Bavarian State Library.

It is particularly important that the reviews be as easy as possible to find. All the reviews are searchable in full text, and are also tagged with precise metadata, which contains the names of the author and the reviewer and describes the reviewed work in detail, classifies it thematically (region, topic, and time), and enriches it with keywords. In 2012, all reviews will additionally be connected to the OPAC of the Bavarian State Library, which means that they will directly be linked to the title entry of the work reviewed. This will further increase their visibility, thus drawing the attention of "scholarly passersby" to them beyond Google. This also includes readers who normally would not have consulted the journal in which the review was originally published.

The interest of the journals in cooperating with recensio.net springs from the access to findability, indexing, and compiling of reviews on an international scale. Smaller journals in particular struggled to meet the increasing technical requirements for Web publications by themselves, especially the long-term archival storage and enrichment of content with metadata (subject and index headings, classifications according to place, time, and subject, etc.). Although initially it was thought that the platform would launch with about five cooperating journals, it already counted 18 when it went online in January 2011. Today it has 29 journals and expects more to join. recensio.net, in terms of the initial basic idea, is in this respect clearly acting as a "tool for gathering and orientation."

But what is more important for the issues discussed in this chapter is the second pillar of the platform, the question of "innovative reviewing." The Presentations page represents a major step toward Web 2.0 in that authors can upload to recensio.net presentations of already published works. The presentations are supposed to be short, specific summaries of the research results compiled in the publication presented. A limit of characters prevents too much self-promotion.

Next, the platform users, usually an academic audience, meaning scholars who themselves are mostly authors, become involved.

Early reception studies had already concluded that a recipient is at the same time always an actor. This is all the more evident within the field of digital culture, where the recipient is or may be a direct actor, rather than merely an indirect one. [My translation] (Schmale, 2010: 16)[7]

The increased merging of recipient and communicator, of producer and consumer, of author and reader on the Internet (with the role of the expert/peer constantly losing importance as it is merged into one) is allowed for on recensio.net by the possibility of other platform users leaving comments on presentations. A comment does not need to be a comprehensive review of an entire work, as used to be written by a peer hired by a journal, but can represent an opinion on a single aspect of the work. This lowers any inhibitions about becoming involved in reviewing in the first place (which, as outlined, is an increasing problem in view of the growing work pressure in everyday life at university) and also facilitates the possibility of looking beyond subject boundaries. For example, a political scientist may give an opinion about a certain aspect of historical work that is relevant to his or her area of study. In the case of traditional reviewing, the editors of a journal would have acted as a filter, and would have directly approached reviewers whom they considered to be appropriate for the topic. As a consequence, the professional contribution of the political scientist would have been lost, since he or she, as a non-member of the respective discipline, would not have been considered as a suitable peer for reviewing the work.[8]

The author of a presentation is automatically notified about an incoming comment by the platform system, so that he or she in turn can immediately become involved in a discourse with the person who left the comment. Ideally, this will lead to a "live review," with many peers practicing a process-related, granular, new way of writing about writings. Authors can present not only monographs, but also articles that have been published in edited volumes or journals. Furthermore, Internet resources for historians (databases, blogs, bibliographies, etc.) can also be presented and commented on. This is an important innovation for the humanities. Traditional reviewing has so far focused on book reviews and for the most part ignored the field of articles.

It will take time for this second pillar of the platform to become accepted. In order to facilitate this, authors are requested to name "reference authors"—colleagues whose work they have dealt with and cited in their publication—in the Web form used for creating the presentation. After the release of a presentation, these reference authors will be notified about the presentation on recensio.net, and about the possibility of directly

responding on the platform to the presented core statements. Thematically, the outline for the traditional reviews and the presentations is clearly defined by the platform's subtitle: review platform for European history. In the field of traditional reviews, recensio.net mostly cooperates with journals that have a mandate of going beyond national boundaries when it comes to choosing books and reviewers.

At the time of writing, recensio.net has been online for approximately a year. The success of the "classical" approach has gone beyond all expectations. However, when it comes to the innovative element of the platform, the commenting feature has rarely been used so far. This is a reflection of the status quo previously mentioned, the fact that scholarly reviewing is staying behind the modern possibilities of using the Internet and the development within the field of commercial reviewing. recensio.net is asking two new things from scholars at once: to present their work to a potentially global audience and at the same time to comment on other presentations at a professional level—voluntarily and in addition to the traditional reviewing process. The process of accepting and establishing this new form of reviewing will have to happen over a long period of time. The fact that presentations on an international scale have been uploaded right from the beginning can be seen as a good sign. The first step has been taken. For the time being, the motivation of platform users to not merely consume content, but also to actively comment, will remain a central aspect of testing the new reviewing tool.

The Europe-wide character of the platform is reflected in the choice of cooperating journals, as well as in the field of presentations and comments: recensio.net offers a complete trilingual navigation (English, German, and French). Traditional reviews are provided in the language in which they were originally published. When presenting and commenting, contributors can use any European language of their choice. Advanced searching can also filter search results by language.

What is the relationship between an approach as outlined here and the large amount of currently emerging book readers' sites, where laymen and experts both rate literature? Take Amazon, for instance, where reviews are mainly provided by laymen, or the success story LibraryThing, which combines one's personal management of literature with aspects of social bookmarking (see also Zotero, Mendeley, CiteULike). With regard to recensio.net, the main difference lies within the platform's basic concept, which pays attention to the special needs and the specific tradition of historical scholarship. European historians tend to remain a tightly-knit expert group in the sense that only historians comment on the work of other historians: the fact that laymen may indeed also leave comments on recensio.net is only accepted due to the existent monitoring responsibility assumed by the operators of recensio.net, an issue frequently touched upon in discussions at conferences. Securing an environment that "guarantees" quality is crucial for the target audience of the platform. This is where the second difference is rooted. The platform has a very narrow focus with regard to its content. This results from what has been mentioned so far, as well as from a very weak sense of interdisciplinary work to date. The openness for an exchange with other disciplines, with interested laymen, and also the flexibility of being able to view one's own writings as a snapshot, to allow for oneself the space necessary for corrections is all still in its infancy. Once a text is published, even if it is only a comment, it will be looked upon in Europe—and especially in Germany—as something carved in stone, which contradicts a classic Web 2.0 component, meaning a quick, fluid and mutually interactive way to exchange opinions. A third difference lies in the necessary methodical connection to the conventional medium of the book review, which the platforms mentioned – above all LibraryThing – do not offer. To bridge the gap between the online review and presentation to the "classical" or traditional book review (from the familiar journals, in their familiar layout, but with an easier access than in print) seems to be a convenient way to transfer the same text genre into the alternative new form of reviewing offered in parallel. An historian who is mostly still skeptical about the Internet, especially in its collaborative shape, can present and leave comments under his or her real name. He or she can perceive colleagues as colleagues, and laymen as laymen, always knowing that those comments that do not comply with the scholarly standards of the platform's operators will not be published in association with his or her name. This does not realize the original form of the Web 2.0 idea, but offers scholars the possibility of acquainting themselves with it to an extent that allows for their gradually shifting standards.

Questions for the Future

"Web 2.0 fits so perfectly with the way science works, it's not whether the transition will happen but how fast," says Chris Surridge, PLoS ONE (cited in Waldrop, 2008, paragraph 7), noting that what defines the collaborative Web also reflects what has always defined research: to acquire fragmented pieces of knowledge, to discuss them, to alter or to dismiss them, and to develop ideas based on several other fragments through dialogue. Print culture, which remains dominant in the humanities today, can only support these processes to a certain extent.

recensio.net is a pilot project, a test of how historical scholarship in Europe will adapt to the means predetermined by commercial Web applications at this point already, or in the future. In this respect, recensio.net is a test run focusing on a specific discipline and geographical region. So far, there seem to be no similar approaches in any other discipline, region, or linguistic area. This applies to the first pillar, which makes reviews from journals published in print and online accessible in Open Access. Many review journals generate their own reviews, which means that they choose books, request them from publishers, appoint reviewers and hire them, and then edit and publish the review. One might, for instance, consider the H-Net Reviews, which cooperate with one of the German examples mentioned earlier, *H-Soz-u-Kult*.[9] But recensio.net is explicitly not an independent journal, but a service provider for review journals, an open access aggregator for reviews. Ultimately, this service does not merely represent a supply of metadata for reviews from various journals, as is the case with *Historische Rezensionen* online.[10] Instead, it makes all reviews available for the user in full text, including both an optimized searchability function and long-time storage of the texts. With regard to the second pillar, there is, at least to my knowledge, no comparable approach that offers scholars the possibility of presenting already published works themselves, as well as a quality-assured environment for discussing these publications on the platform. Concepts for the combination of traditional Internet habits (facilitated access to traditionally published texts) and innovative use of the actual potential of Web-based communication are rare, and with regard to the text genre "scholarly book review," almost entirely non-existent.

Ideally, a European network of institutes and scholars from various disciplines would emerge, aimed at the development of such publication infrastructures, and responding to the current needs of scholarly (rather than scientific) practice. In this context, the changing relationship between author and reviewer, between layman and expert, and even the social conception of the intellectual[11] itself would have to be considered. How has the traditional perception of the intellectual as an expert for responding to social questions or judging publications been changed by the Web culture and the corresponding new forms of communication? Furthermore, the question arises whether this idea of the intellectual and the expert does not merely vary in different countries, but also among different disciplines. How can these differences benefit or complicate the development of international research and publication

environments? The actors' (consumer/producer) purposes are changing, merging, and becoming more transparent. To what extent will scholarly research be able to benefit from this transparency which, due to the adoption of Web 2.0 technologies, will ultimately also extend to include interested and knowledgeable laymen? What are the risks? Which means for balancing both are imaginable beyond those applied by recensio.net, and which experiences can be exchanged?

The necessity of considering these issues is obvious, since they are crucial for the future success of scholarly communication. The respective means will have to change due to the exponential digitalization of society and research.

One way to begin to answer these questions would be to look toward educating younger generations in the genre of the book review as a distinct text genre. Scholars usually begin to write reviews of scholarly books only after they have passed the first stage of qualification—for instance, their master's degree. This is the earliest point at which the editors of a journal or their doctorate supervisors consider them capable of formulating a qualified opinion about the work of their often older colleagues. Certain approaches are encouraged among younger scholars in order to arouse enthusiasm for critical reading and develop the self-confidence to voice their own opinion. In Germany, such an approach is represented by the Web portal Lesepunkte, which appeals to students aged 10–18 and focuses on novels and secondary literature in the field of history, which the children are encouraged to review. It would be desirable to establish similar initiatives in other countries.

But how can one prepare the young generation for the phrasing of comments in a scholarly environment? One could answer with a provocative question: is this even necessary? At school, in college, and in university, communication between learners is taking place in social networks to such an extent (albeit primarily still on a private level) that they are already familiar with how to formulate a message in a short, precise, and comprehensible manner, as well as how to keep the conversation going once the communicating partner responds. In this respect they are quite possibly far beyond older scholars, who regard the commenting feature with a mixture of skepticism and fear of contact. What remains for the younger generation to learn are the standards of a scholarly voicing of opinion. Teachers have to step up at this point by supporting initiatives like the one mentioned above, which familiarizes young people with traditional reviewing. University lecturers also have a part to play. Courses about digital writing are one option. Texts meant to be published online have to be written differently than those to be released in print: they need to be shorter, more fragmented, and more precise. This is especially important for reviews and the more informal comments in a scholarly context—those on recensio.net are supposed to constitute a "vivid review" in conjunction with other comments.

As mentioned earlier, the special feature of a review is the fact that the reviewer is usually someone whose work also gets reviewed, which means that everyone involved can relate to both positions. This offers good preconditions for presenting one's own writings, commenting on those of other scholars, and simultaneously searching for traditional book reviews on literature that is relevant for the individual's area of study. This reliance on searching represents a further challenge for teachers and lecturers: to develop a critical eye for books, to realize that not everything in print is necessarily good. At the same time, an important task for schools and universities is to teach students how to find and read reviews. This means teachers and lecturers must be aware of the most recent research tools. Of course, tools that list reviews that are available in open access are the most useful. What student will voluntarily pull a journal from a shelf in order to study the review for a book that is needed for a presentation?

CONCLUSION

Web 1.5

It is necessary to raise the question of how the Web 2.0 approach outlined in this article can be applied to scholarly reviewing, and to what extent the idea of a collaborative "peer crowd" can work in today's scholarly climate. After the launch of recensio.net, one of the major daily newspapers in Germany referred to the platform by using the term "Web 1.5," accordingly placing recensio.net somewhere between Web 1.0 and Web 2.0. The reason for this, as mentioned, is that incoming presentations and comments are monitored by the platform operators before they are released online. This is a procedure which, as shown, contradicts the "archetype" of Web 2.0, but at the same is the answer to a basic question: How "social" are the new scholarly networks, and how do they currently regulate themselves? Web 2.0 is based on the idea of self-regulation: 10 positive comments relativize one (possibly unjustified) that is negative. The size of the network and the frequency of comments are the preconditions for the functioning of this communicative mechanism. Both are not given when a new platform launches, especially in the case of a specialized scholarly one. recensio.net could offer a solution for a transition period: Monitoring for the sake of maintaining scholarly standards, as well as simply avoiding abuse while supervising user behavior, not least because the fear of a decline in quality and communicative standards in the field of online publication and communication is real among European scholars. The fact that the monitoring function in recensio.net has rarely been used thus far might be a significant detail.

The incentive for developing new methods and dealing with new technologies is very small for the established and institute-oriented people working with history. Due to a widely accepted and therefore self-stabilizing oblivion regarding methods and media, the majority of scholars reject the construction of new forms of history as a subject [My translation] (Sahle, 2008: 74).[12] At the same time, however, in contrast with other disciplines within the humanities, it is the historians who have created several successful portals, journals, repositories, blogs, and digitalization projects in the German-speaking world over the last couple of years.[13]

Ultimately, recensio.net's approach to reviews can also provide solutions for other disciplines. In the coming years, merging traditional and innovative approaches will be essential, as will tools that compile and create an overview (as a consequence of growing amounts of data). It will be essential to comprehend the changes that have already had an effect on work methods and communicative means, and that have already become second nature among the younger generation and will thus automatically also find their way into science in the medium term. That the omniscient expert will then become less important in comparison to the collaborative group seems to be certain. Work tools that simultaneously respond to the habits of the older generation and the needs of the following generation will have to be created, optimized, and shared over the coming years. One of the essential ways of maintaining this link in the field of humanities is the book review. Ensuring that its traditional forms can be accessed by young scholars and that more senior colleagues can take part in more social forms of reviewing enabled by the new technologies with minimal effort seems to be a promising approach.

Moran Hajo writes,

One thing that the Internet teaches is that trying something new, even if it fails, is in most cases better than waiting for the perfect opportunity to come along. ... Yes, we will trip up sometimes, and yes, we might get dirty. (Hajo, 2009)

This is a risk we should be willing to take if we want to develop new methods of publication for the future. However, Wolfgang Schmale remarks that "the precise time at which the essential *research* incentives will take place online, due to the internet having become the preferred place of publication and communication, cannot be predicted" [My translation] (Schmale, 2010: 51).[14] The same goes for the question of when the opinion of a single peer about a monograph will be regarded as too inflexible and limited in comparison to collaborative reviewing online. During the long transition period, both will coexist. It is the plea of this chapter that this coexistence should be turned into a process of cooperation.

REFERENCES

Cohen, P. (2010, August 23). Scholars test Web alternative to peer review. *New York Times*. Retrieved November 04, 2011, from http://www.nytimes.com/2010/08/24/arts/24peer.html

Collins, E., & Hide, B. (2010). Use and relevance of Web 2.0 resources for researchers. In T. Hedlund & Y. Tonta (Eds.). *Publishing in the networked world: Transforming the nature of communication, 14th International Conference on Electronic Publishing, 16-18 June 2010*. Helsinki, Finland: Hanken School of Economics. Retrieved June 8, 2011, from https://helda.helsinki.fi/handle/10227/599

Dalton, M. S. (2009). The publishing experiences of historians. In Greco, A. N. (Ed.), *The state of scholarly publishing. Challenges and opportunities* (pp. 107–146). New Brunswick, NJ: Transaction.

Haber, P., & Hodel, J. (2011). Geschichtswissenschaft und Web 2.0. Eine Dokumentation. [History and Web 2.0. A survey.] *The hist.net Working Paper Series, 2*. Retrieved February 12, 2011, from http://www.infoclio.ch/sites/default/files/standard_page/working_paper_geschichte_web2.0.pdf

Hajjem, C., Harnad, S., & Gingras, Y. (2005). *Ten-year cross-disciplinary comparison of the growth of open access and how it increases research citation impact*. Retrieved from http://eprints.ecs.soton.ac.uk/11688/1/ArticleIEEE.pdf

Hajo, C. M. (2009). Scholarly editing in a Web 2.0 world. *Documentary Editing, 31*, 92-103. Retrieved June 6, 2011, from http://aphdigital.org/people/cathy-moran-hajo/scholarly-editing-in-a-web-2-0-world/#_ftn1

Herb, U. (2010). Open Access, zitationsbasierte und nutzungsbasierte Impact Maße: Einige Befunde. [Open Access, citation- and user-related impact scales]. In *11th Proceedings of International Society for Knowledge Organization* (ISKO), German Chapter. Retrieved November 7, 2011, from http://eprints.rclis.org/handle/10760/14873#.TrebuHL0_1s

Linholm-Romantschuk, Y. (1998). *The flow of ideas within and among disciplines*. Westport, CT: Greenwood Press.

Meyer, T. (2011). Virtuelle Forschungsumgebungen in der Geschichtswissenschaft – Lösungsansätze und Perspektiven [Virtual research environments for history – approaches.]. *LIBREAS. Library Ideas, 7*(18). Retrieved June 9, 2011, from http://www.ib.hu-berlin.de/~libreas/libreas_neu/ausgabe18/texte/05meyer.htm

Nentwich, M., & König, R. (2010). Peer Review 2.0: Herausforderungen und Chancen der wissenschaftlichen Qualitätskontrolle im Zeitalter der Cyber-Wissenschaft. [Peer Review 2.0: Challanges and chances of scholarly quality monitoring in the age of cyber-science.] In Gasteiner, P., & Haber, P. (Eds.), *Digitale Arbeitstechniken für Geistes- und Kulturwissenschaften* [Digital work methods for the humanities and cultural sciences]. (pp. 143–163). Vienna, Austria: Böhlau.

Sahle, P. (2008). eScience history? In M.-L. Heckmann, J. Röhrkasten, & S. Jenks (Eds.), *Von Nowgorod bis London. Studien zu Handel, Wirtschaft und Gesellschaft im mittelalterlichen Europa. Festschrift für Stuart Jenks zum 60. Geburtstag* [From Novgorod to London. Studies on trade, economy and society in medieval Europe. Festschrift in honour of Stuart Jenk's 60th birthday] (pp. 63-74). Göttingen, Germany: V&R unipress.

Savage, W. W. (2009). Scribble, scribble, toil and trouble: Forced productivity in the modern university. In Greco, A. N. (Ed.), *The state of scholarly publishing: Challenges and opportunities* (pp. 1–7). New Brunswick, NJ: Transaction.

Schmale, W. (2010). *Digitale Geschichtswissenschaft*. Vienna, Austria: Böhlau.

Waldrop, M. M. (2008, January 9). Science 2.0: Great new tool, or great risk? Wikis, blogs and other collaborative Web technologies could usher in a new era of science. Or not. *Scientific American*. Retrieved June 8, 2011, from http://www.scientificamerican.com/article.cfm?id=science-2-point-0-great-new-tool-or-great-risk

ADDITIONAL READING

Borgman, C. L. (2010). Research data: Who will share what, with whom, when, and why? *China-North America Library Conference, Beijing*. Retrieved from http://works.bepress.com/borgman/238

Burgelman, J.-C., Osimo, D., & Bogdanowicz, M. (2010). Science 2.0 (change will happen …). *First Monday*, (July): 5. Retrieved from http://www.uic.edu/htbin/cgiwrap/bin/ojs/index.php/fm/article/view/2961/2573

Cassella, M. (2010). *Social peer-review e scienze umane, ovvero "della qualità nella Repubblica della scienza"* [Social peer-review and humanties] *JLIS.it., 1*(1), 111–132. doi: 10.4403/jlis-30

Cohen, P. (2010, November 16). Digital keys for unlocking the humanities' riches. *The New York Times*. Retrieved from http://www.nytimes.com/2010/11/17/arts/17digital.html?pagewanted=1

Farkas, M. G. (2009). *Social software in libraries. Building collaboration, communication, and community online.* Medford, NJ: Information Today.

Fisch, M., & Gscheidle, C. (2008). Mitmachnetz Web 2.0: Rege Beteiligung nur in Communitys. [Participation network Web 2.0: Active involvement only in communities.]. *Media Perspektiven, 7,* 356–364.

Fitzpatrick, K. (2007). CommentPress: New (social) structures for new (networked) texts. JEP. *Journal of Electronic Publishing, 10*(3). doi:10.3998/3336451.0010.305

Gehrke, G., & Gräßer, L. (2007). Neues Web, neue Kompetenz? [New web, new competence?] In Gehrke, G. (Ed.), *Web 2.0 – Schlagwort oder Megatrend? Fakten, Analysen, Prognosen* [Web 2.0 – catchword or super trend? Facts, analysis, predictions.]. (pp. 11–36). Dusseldorf, Germany: Kopaed.

Hartling, F. (2009). *Der digitale Autor. Autorschaft im Zeitalter des Internets* [The digital author. Authorship in the internet age.]. Bielefeld, Germany: Transcript.

Hedlund, T., & Tonta, Y. (Eds.). (2010). Publishing in the networked world: Transforming the nature of communication. *14th International Conference on Electronic Publishing,* 16-18 June 2010. Helsinki, Finland: Hanken School of Economics. Retrieved from https://helda.helsinki.fi/handle/10227/599

Hesse, H. A. (1998). *Experte, Laie, Dilettant. Über Nutzen und Grenzen von Fachwissen* [Expert, layman, amateur. On the potential and limits of expert knowledge.]. Opladen, Germany: Westdeutscher Verlag.

Libert, B., & Spector, J. (2008). *We are smarter than me: How to unleash the power of crowds in your business.* Upper Saddle River, NJ: Wharton School Pub.

Meckel, M. (2008). Aus Vielen wird das Eins gefunden – wie Web 2.0 unsere Kommunikation verändert. [Among many, the whole is found – how Web 2.0 is changing our communication.]. *Aus Politik und Zeitgeschichte, 39,* 17–23.

Nathenson, C. (2001). Electronic publishing and the future of humanities scholarship. *Trans: Internet-Zeitschrift für Kulturwissenschaften, 2001, 10.* Retrieved from http://www.inst.at/trans/10Nr/nathenson10.htm

Nentwich, M. (2003). *Cyberscience: Research in the age of the Internet.* Vienna, Austria: Austrian Academy of Sciences Press.

Pscheida, D. (2010). *Das Wikipedia-Universum. Wie das Internet unsere Wissenskultur verändert* [The Wikipedia universe. How the internet changes our culture of knowledge.]. Bielefeld, Germany: Transcript.

Siegfried, D., & Flieger, E. (2011). *World Wide Wissenschaft. Wie professionell Forschende im Internet arbeiten. Zusammenfassung der qualitativen und quantitativen Ergebnisse einer Untersuchung des ZBW – Leibniz-Informationszentrum Wirtschaft* [World Wide Science. How professional researchers work online. A summary of the qualitative and quantitative results of a study carried out by the ZBW – Leibniz Information Centre for Economics]. Bielefeld, Germany: Transcript. Retrieved from http://www.zbw.eu/presse/pressemitteilungen/docs/world_wide_wissenschaft_zbw_studie.pdf

Sprondel, W. M. (1979). "Experte" und "Laie". Zur Entwicklung von Typenbegriffen in der Wissenssoziologie. [Expert and layman. On the development of model terms in the social sciences.] In Sprondel, W., & Grathoff, R. (Eds.), *Alfred Schütz und die Idee des Alltags in den Sozialwissenschaften* [Alfred Schütz and the idea of everyday life in the social sciences.]. (pp. 140–154). Stuttgart, Germany: Enke.

Taraborelli, D. (2008). Soft peer review: Social software and distributed scientific evaluation. In *Proceedings of the 8th International Conference on the Design of Cooperative Systems* May 20th-23th, 2008, Carry-le-Rouet, France (pp. 99-110). Retrieved from http://coop.wineme.fb5.uni-siegen.de/?id=coop2008

Weingart, P. (2003). Experte ist jeder, alle sind Laien. [Everyone is an expert, everybody is a layman.] *Gegenworte, Zeitschrift für den Disput über Wissen, 11*, 58-61.

Young, J. R. (2006, July 28). Books 2.0: Scholars turn monographs into digital conversations. *Chronicle of Higher Education.* Retrieved from http://chronicle.com/article/Book-20/24367

KEY TERMS AND DEFINITIONS

Crowd: The term crowd denotes a phenomenon that can only be seen and related to as a whole, meaning the mass of Internet users who do not merely consume but also produce information online by providing several small contributions that form a constantly growing whole. Obviously, only a small percentage of all Internet users are involved in the reflection of specific questions, especially within the scholarly Web culture.

History: In this chapter, history refers to all historical disciplines.

Humanities: Humanities is a common academic category, including ancient history, history, languages, law, literature, philosophy, and theology. Especially with regard to the "new media," the English term has also established itself in other languages. In German, one speaks more and more of the eHumanities.

Open Access: The free and unrestricted access to research data, meaning either—databases, articles, reviews, and entire monographs. Especially in the humanities, where the monograph still plays a central role, there are intense debates about open access, since it challenges the common business models of scholarly publishers.

Peer: In this chapter, a peer is understood as a scholarly expert, usually in the field of traditional reviewing: the editors of a journal releasing reviews ask an expert to rate the methodology and scientific value of a new publication related to his or her specific area of research.

Platform: This means an Internet platform rooted in the humanities, a website that offers and/or compiles information, data, publications, or research tools in order to facilitate the work of individual scholars or scientific groups.

Review: In the given context, the term "review" refers to a text genre that is established within the humanities, its purpose being the rating of already published writings. Usually a scholar assigned by a journal rates a recently published monograph related to his or her individual area of research, with regard to its methodology and scientific value. The reviewer usually receives no payment for the review. However, it becomes part of his or her publication list.

Scholarly Communication: The subject-specific exchange between scholars. This can take place through various tools and media. For instance, traditional tools would be publications in journals or edited volumes, as well as book reviews in print journals. More recent ones include scholarly blogs or wikis, which allow for a quick and collaborative exchange among researchers.

Web 2.0: Web 2.0 is a now established term that points toward the development of communication forms on the Internet by differentiating collaborative formats (Web 2.0) from static ones

(Web 1.0). Web 2.0 refers to the active involvement of users of a website (blog, lexicon, database etc.) in generating its content.

ENDNOTES

1 am very much indebted to Christian Höschler who worked diligently and tirelessly on the linguistic editing of this article.

2 „[M]it der Herausbildung von Fachzeitschriften vor dem Hintergrund eines wissenschaftlichen Buchmarktes – Monographien sind nach wie vor das gängige Ergebnisformat wissenschaftlicher Forschung – haben Rezensionen das „Wächteramt der Qualitätssicherung" erlangt, indem sie nicht nur die Einhaltung von Mindeststandards bei Fachpublikationen kontrollieren, sondern vor allem mit Urteilen und Kritiken die Erwartungen und Ansprüche von Lesern und Autoren prägen."

3 See, for example, http://www.nature.com/nature/peerreview/debate/index.html

4 http://www.kunstgeschichte-ejournal.net/ See also the similar experiment undertaken by Shakespeare Quarterly (see Cohen, 2010).

5 A recent example of this was an expert chat on "Wikipedia meets history," organized by the German Gerda Henkel Foundation: http://www.lisa.gerda-henkel-stiftung.de/content.php?nav_id=2028&language=en [in German].

6 For instance, http://hypotheses.org/. See also: http://dhdhi.hypotheses.org/591.

7 „Schon die ältere Rezeptionsforschung hatte hervorgehoben, dass ein Rezipient immer auch Akteur ist. Dies gilt umso mehr im Feld der digitalen Kultur, wo der Rezipient nicht nur mittelbar, sondern unmittelbar Akteur ist bzw. sein kann."

8 On the significance of the commenting feature in an academic context, see the remarks on "New forms of the ex-post quality assurance" in Nentwich & König, 2010, pp. 147-148.

9 More examples can be found at http://www.acqweb.org/book_review

10 http://www.clio-online.de/hro

11 In March 2011, a conference on the changing role of the intellectual took place at the Institute for Advanced Study in the Humanities in Essen: "The public, media and politics – intellectual debates and science in the age of digital communication" (February 14–15, 2011), http://www.kwi-nrw.de/home/veranstaltung-360.html.

12 „Der Anreiz für die Entwicklung neuer Methoden und für die mühsame Auseinandersetzung mit neuen Technologien ist für das etablierte und institutionalisierte Personal der Geschichtsforschung äußerst gering. Aus einer weithin akzeptierten und damit sich selbst stabilisierenden Methoden- und Medienvergessenheit heraus verweigert sich der Großteil der Forschung dem Aufbau neuer Formen der Geschichtswissenschaft."

13 Just to name a few examples: historicum.net, sehepunkte, zeitenblicke, Clio-online, arthistoricum.net, infoclio.ch, arthistoricum.net, Archivalia, and weblog.hist.net.

14 „Der Zeitpunkt, von dem an die wesentlichen *Forschungs*impulse im Netz passieren, weil das Netz der von allen Mitgliedern des Systems der Geschichtswissenschaften bevorzugte Ort der Publikation und Kommunikation geworden ist, lässt sich nicht genau vorhersagen."

Chapter 10
The Effect of Social Software on Academic Libraries

Maria Cassella
University of Torino, Italy

Licia Calvi
NHTV University of Breda, The Netherlands

ABSTRACT

This chapter presents the results of a survey of Dutch and Italian academic libraries conducted to identify how academic libraries deal with the growing adoption of social media for professional purposes, and how they consider this adoption as the only possible way for them to reposition themselves among an audience that is more and more involved with social media. The results, surprisingly, show that although the interest and the need for such an adoption are felt rather strongly, the complete conversion to a library 2.0 is still not in reach. Many respondents, especially in the Dutch context, were interested in the outcome of this study to help them decide which direction they should take.

INTRODUCTION

Academic libraries are striving to reposition themselves in the digital environment and to redefine their role and expertise in a more complex informational context, where users have mostly become remote and where information retrieval and discovery tools have not improved library strategies to attract new users and to facilitate access to information. To advocate for, promote, and raise awareness of library collections and services, to win back former users and attract new ones,

academic libraries have been experimenting in the last years with several strategies: organizational changes (e.g., embedding the librarians' activity in academic departments to better support the research workflow), adoption of mobile technologies, and implementation of Web 2.0 tools.

Since 2005, manifold libraries have adopted different types of social software: wikis, blogs, and microblogging; social reference tools; sites that use RSS feeds to syndicate and broadcast content; widgets; virtual worlds; social bookmarking and social networking tools; and media sharing platforms have all been widely adopted and experimented with, with mixed results and

DOI: 10.4018/978-1-4666-2178-7.ch010

varied levels of uptake by users. However, since the beginning, RSS, blogs, wikis, and social networking platforms have been some of the libraries' favorite tools.

Among the social networking platforms, Facebook (FB) seems to be one of the most popular used so far. Several studies on the use of FB in academic libraries (Calvi, Cassella, & Nuijten, 2010; Charnigo & Barnett-Ellis, 2007; Ellison, 2007; Evans, 2006; Farkas, 2007; Hendrix, Chiarella, Hasman, Murphy, & Zafron, 2009; Powers, 2008) point to the changes that this adoption enforces on the library and how it affects the library's changing role. Charnigo and Barnett-Ellis (2007), for instance, indicate that for 54% of their interviewees FB is not useful for academic purposes; Hendrix et al. (2009) point out that only 12.5% of them have created and maintain a FB page; Calvi et al. (2010) outlined that what seems to be lacking is a well-defined and systematic strategy to attract and keep new users; Bietila, Bloechl, and Edwards (2009) support the idea that more research is needed before libraries and other academic institutions can become full (and appropriate) participants in spaces like Facebook.

Whatever strategy is followed—the so-called aggressive Friend and Feed approach (Ellison, 2007) or the simple promotion of the library's services on the library FB page, giving users the freedom to decide whether or not to become "fans" of that page— academic libraries and librarians have seen their role change. Their expertise is less recognized now than in the past and they need to redefine the way in which they can transfer their knowledge to their audience.

In this chapter, we intend to explore this issue further. In a previous paper (Calvi et al., 2010), we analyzed the FB pages of a selected number of academic libraries. Now we will present the results of a survey we conducted among library staff to verify how they envision the use of FB not just for marketing the library but also to re-qualify themselves as professionals.

WEB 2.0: DEFINITION AND FEATURES

To date there is no authoritative definition of Web 2.0, a term coined in 2004 in San Francisco during a brainstorming conference session between Tim O'Reilly and MediaLive International. In 2006 O'Reilly attempted to clarify the concept and to give a broad definition of what he meant by the neologism.

Web 2.0 is the business revolution in the computer industry caused by the move to the internet as platform, and an attempt to understand the rules for success on that new platform. Chief among those rules is this: Build applications that harness network effects to get better the more people use them. (This is what I've elsewhere called "harnessing collective intelligence".) (O'Reilly, 2006)

O'Reilly's definition shows us two of the most innovative features of Web 2.0 that help us to understand what Web 2.0 is. The first feature is the concept of the Web as a platform which essentially refers to the possibility of developing applications that run in a Web browser. As Web services need to be constantly updated, the concept underlying Web 2.0 is that every social tool and service is implemented in a beta environment. "Experimentation" is de facto the key word to characterize this "perpetual beta." The second feature of Web 2.0 is the use of the read/write tools that allow users to interact with the Net, to collaborate, to create and share content, and to build in a bottom-up approach to communities of practices.

O'Reilly also introduces the concept of "business revolution" in his definition. Being a platform that holds together huge communities of users and data on users, Web 2.0 is primarily a market that is different from, for example, the Semantic Web which, at the moment, still belongs to the sphere of pure academic research (Meschini, unpublished).

Although social software can be manifold—blogs, wikis, social networks, media-sharing platforms, and so on—they all share some characteristics:

1. **Ease of use and content sharing:** "Years ago, putting content on the Web was a job for tech-savvy individuals who were familiar with HTML and Web programming languages. With today's social software, anyone can add online content, including photos, text, audio and video" (Farkas, 2007). Although initially oriented to teens and young people, social software is becoming increasingly popular among adults and seniors. In social networks in particular, the rate of middle-aged and senior users is steadily increasing. According to CheckFacebook statistics, in September 2011 the social network platform had almost 800 million global users—155 million of whom live in the United States. An analysis of the age distribution of FB fans in the US shows that 23.8% of users are aged 25–34; 16.7% are aged 35–44; 12.4% are aged 45–54; and 7.9% are aged 55–64.

2. **Content Collaboration:** Social Web content is created collaboratively. People—friends, acquaintances, or even strangers—share their personal knowledge and add value to the available resources.[1] Wikis are the best example of successful user-generated joint content. As openly editable, collaboratively written tools, they capitalize on the so-called "wisdom of the crowds." In September 2011, for example, Wikipedia had more than 82,000 active contributors working on more than 19,000,000 articles in more than 270 languages. The Wikipedia English edition comprises almost 3,800,000 articles (Wikipedia English edition) and its popularity is increasing. Since 2001, Wikipedia's reputation and reliability have also grown. In December 2005, a comparative study on the accuracy of Wikipedia and the *Encyclopaedia Britannica* carried out by *Nature* found that the difference in accuracy was not significant: the average science entry in Wikipedia contained around four inaccuracies, and in *Britannica* about three (Giles, 2005).

3. **Conversations:** The social Web fosters conversations and conversations create knowledge as Gordon Pask's Conversation Theory explains (Pask, 1976). This theory, originating from Pask's cybernetics framework, shows how interactions lead to the "construction of knowledge." In the social Web, conversations occur in different forms and settings, synchronously (e.g., Instant Messaging software) or asynchronously (e.g., blogs), one-to-many (e.g., blogs), many-to-many (e.g., wikis), in leisure and professional spaces, and in mobile platforms. Forms of conversations could also be traced back in Web 1.0: newsletters, discussion lists, and forums are the best examples of Web 1.0 social tools. In libraries, catalogues are an example of a tool that communicates and interacts with users albeit in an automated and impersonal way. Whether Web 2.0 is only a "piece of jargon" or a revolutionary way to create and share collaborative contents and services differences is manifested in the scale of the conversations and in the level of participation and contribution. They are both much more diverse and extensive in Web 2.0 than in Web 1.0.

4. **Communities of Practice:** Communities of practice increase the value of a communication network: "social technologies benefit from one economy that awards value to the service as more people join the service" (Stutzman, 2006). Stutzman defines this condition as the "network effect." The network effect explains why communities of practice are the nourishment of the social Web, which exists only because people are using the same social tool. In Web 2.0, communities

are heterogeneous, have no boundaries, and are created bottom-up. There is no central authority and no hierarchy.

SOCIAL SOFTWARE IN LIBRARIES

Libraries are socially driven realities. Libraries run social spaces where people—students and researchers—meet and study. The physical academic library, for example, is a blended environment where the social and academic meet. Manifold academic libraries offer users space where students can meet and collaborate on school work; they offer coffee shops, WiFi access, and Information Commons. In these spaces, the line between the social and the academic blurs.

Partly to accomplish their social vocation, partly to reposition themselves in an increasingly complex environment, both physical and digital, where roles and functions need to be redefined and users are becoming more and more remote,[2] since 2005 libraries have been experimenting with different types of social software to win back former users and to attract new ones. Wikis, blogs, and microblogging; social reference tools; sites that use RSS feeds to syndicate and broadcast content; widgets; virtual worlds; social bookmarking and social networking tools; and media-sharing platforms have been widely adopted and experimented with despite the fact that users had, at the very beginning of Web 2.0, declared that they "did not see a role for the libraries in constructing social sites and most would not be very likely to contribute content, self-publish or join discussion groups if a library were to offer these services"(Online Computer Library Center, 2007).

Notwithstanding this, in February 2008 a survey carried out by the Association of Research Libraries revealed a wide adoption of Web 2.0 tools in academic libraries: 95% of the respondents used social software. Of those, 59 libraries provided user assistance via chat or instant messenger (94%), 54 used wikis (86%), 53 employed RSS to dissemi-

nate information to users (84%), 52 maintained blogs (82%), 45 used widgets such as MeeboMe (71%), 44 participated in social networking sites such as Facebook (70%), 35 had implemented tagging (55%), and 39 made use of media-sharing sites such as Flickr or YouTube (62%).

In 2005, Michael E. Casey coined the term "Library 2.0" in a post on his blog Library Crunch. According to Casey's definition (2005), Library 2.0 is a broad concept and does not refer uniquely to the adoption of social technologies in libraries and to the digital library setting/environment:

The heart of Library 2.0 is user-centered change. It is a model for library service that encourages constant and purposeful change, inviting user participation in the creation of both the physical and the virtual services they want, supported by consistently evaluating services. (Casey & Savastinuk, 2006)

This model for library service may be extremely complex to design as Web 2.0 tools are manifold, their scope is different, and the needs they answer are heterogeneous. Different social tools will have different effects on libraries and their users. Social OPAC, for example, revitalizes the catalogue and its resources, and RSS helps spread information and news. Blogs, wikis, and social networking platforms can be used as communication tools and to provide traditional services through new communication channels (e.g., Ask a Librarian). They help to update users on library themes and services and to create a wider sense of community around the library. They also tend to integrate the library activities in the users' social flow, giving rise to many privacy issues and concerns.

Social technologies adoption in libraries should be carefully evaluated as part of a more general communication strategy that integrates innovative communication channels and more traditional ones. The simple implementation of social software in a library is not a guarantee that users will use it.

RSS, Blogs, and Wikis in Libraries

RSS

Since the beginning, RSS, blogs, wikis, and social networking platforms have been among the favorite Library 2.0 tools. RSS, originally RDF Site Summary and more commonly dubbed Really Simple Syndication, are Web feed formats that users can subscribe to to receive information from their favorite sites. Libraries use them to tell users about new books and collections, to syndicate news from library newsletters, and to syndicate news and reporting summaries from the catalogue and from the e-collections (i.e., the e-journals and databases) subscribed to by digital libraries. The OhioLINK library consortium, for example, offers RSS feeds of the table of contents of any journal in its Electronic Journal Center to patrons of OhioLINK member libraries. RSS use in libraries can also be very interesting. Kim and Abbas, for example, write about the Knoxville Library at the University of Tennessee which has been using RSS functionality to offer patrons access to a rare digital copy of a Union soldier's Civil War diary (Kim & Abbas, 2010).

Blogs

The use of blogs in libraries is extremely versatile and almost limitless. They are used to share information about the libraries' upcoming events and services; to promote library collections; to create bibliographies, newsletters, or reviews; to share synopses and comments on books; to create forums; and to aggregate communities of users (e.g., children, adults, children and their parents, students). In big campuses, blogs are also an effective tool for library staff to communicate quickly and effectively—for example, sharing information and professional tips with other librarians. The Blogging Libraries Wiki[3] listed many public, academic, special, and school libraries blogs and provided examples of their scope, content, and use.

Meredith Farkas (2007) identifies three particular types of blogs managed by libraries:

- **Subject Blogs:** That offer news and information on a specific subject—for example, medicine, law, mathematics. The Georgia State University library,[4] for example, offers its users 34 blogs on various subjects ranging from economics to African-American studies to women's studies.
- **Reference Blogs:** That are similar in scope to the subject blogs but also contain a list of reference resources. These blogs replicate the function of a Virtual Reference Desk and the librarian plays the role of a filter to the informative resources. This type of blog is very useful for academic research communities that have very recently also begun to use massive reference management social tools such as Mendeley to share, comment on, and annotate bibliographies.
- **Blogs that Supplement Workshops:** This kind of blog helps disseminate information on events like workshops or conferences in real time. Additionally, blogs in libraries can also be used to support class work (e.g., information literacy classes) and offer students a tool for live comments and discussions in a classroom.

Wikis

Wikis have a big communicative potential for libraries. Successful wikis can become a great information resource for users and can help a library to create a sense of community among its patrons. Wikis in libraries can be grouped into three main categories:

1. Wikis fostering collaboration between libraries.
2. Wikis fostering collaboration between libraries and patrons.
3. Wikis for library staff.

An example of the first category is the Library Success[5] wiki which gathers great ideas and libraries' success stories. The School Library Association in Alaska publishes a wiki[6] of resources and documentation meaningful for the Alaska School librarians. The LIS wiki[7] is a space for collecting articles and general information about Library and Information Science. Wikis are also frequently used by libraries as a platform to discuss conference themes and to publish presentations and reports.

Wikis fostering collaboration between libraries and patrons flourish in public libraries. In manifold public libraries this type of wiki is used to get feedback and comments on books from users, to publish reviews, or to collect information on local social events. Worth citing, for example, is the Davis Wiki which collects information on local events, food, and stores in Davis (California).[8] Like blogs, wikis are an excellent tool for creating very rich subject guides and directories. Resources can be added by librarians and by patrons who also help manage the dead links.

Wikis are also widely used by internal library staff to communicate and share resources and documentation. According to Kai-Wah Chua (2009), 33% of wiki use in academic libraries is for work. There are manifold examples of wikis for libraries staff: the University of Minnesota libraries staff wiki is both a wiki for work and an information wiki on resources for librarians;[9] The University of Connecticut Libraries' Staff Wiki is a repository of Information Technology Services documents;[10] the Binghamton University Libraries use a wiki for the staff intranet.

Social Networks in Libraries

The impact of the social network is wide and long-lasting, and its success can be attributed to a variety of factors:

- Users of social network platforms believe in the idea that "people can be judged, for better or worse, by their friends and acquaintances" (Farkas, 2007). Social networks help people to succeed in life, love and business.
- Users are autonomous in managing their profiles.
- Social networks are extremely easy to use.

Typical uses of the social networks in academic libraries include the promotion of events, new collections, and services; communication between staff and users; and searching library catalogues and other information resources.

According to iLibrarian, Ellyssa Kroski's blog, the most popular applications and widgets used in libraries' Facebook pages are Books iRead; LibGuides librarian, a subject guide maker for libraries that lets the library display its guides in its Facebook profile and also provides a search of the library's catalogue; Librarian, a virtual service that provides links to books, scholarly sources, and reference resources which the community can add to and vote on; MyFlickr, Slideshare, University of Illinois at Urbana-Champaign Library Catalogue, del.ici.ous, JSTOR, and My Wikipedia.[11] The success of social networks is so impressive, that they have not even been touched by the privacy and copyright issues that have emerged recently and that represent one of the main problems in the digital environment and, more specifically, in the social Web.

To date, a few studies have explored the issue of privacy in social networks (Fernandez, 2009; Raynes-Goldie, 2010). Fernandez (2009) outlines that privacy concerns associated with Facebook must be balanced with the benefits of the platform. Librarians should have a full "understanding of how Facebook works and decide clearly what kind of presence they want to have within the framework it creates" (Fernandez, 2009). Raynes-Goldie (2010) draws the conclusion that social networks are changing the concept of privacy and that young people care about social privacy much more than they care about institutional privacy. However, the full implications for privacy in the age of Facebook and social media are still unknown, and libraries that adopt social tools should remain aware of this.

Facebook in Academic Libraries

Facebook (FB) is by far the most popular social network platform. Originally developed by Mark Zuckerberg, Dustin Moskovitz, and Chris Hughes in 2004 to provide Harvard students with a place where they could keep in contact with their classmates and, most importantly, share study-related information, Facebook "burst beyond its roots" by opening its membership to high school networks in 2005, and then to all Net users in 2007. The Facebook site opened to public registration late in 2006.[12]

In the last few years, Facebook has globally developed into one of the most prominent tools for social networking. The use of Facebook, and other social media, in libraries has been widely investigated (Bietila et al., 2009; Calvi et al., 2010; Charnigo & Barnett-Ellis, 2007; Ellison, 2007; Fernandez, 2009; Hendrix et al., 2009; Mack, Behler, Roberts, & Rimland, 2007; Miller & Jensen, 2007; Powers et al., 2008; Raynes-Goldie, 2010). In the literature on FB in academic libraries, many librarians express their concern about the use of social networking platforms in libraries. Charnigo and Barnett-Ellis (2007), for example, found that librarians were wary about the academic aspects of FB: 54% of the 126 librarians surveyed by the authors believed that FB did not serve an academic purpose; 12% were positive about the academic purpose of FB; and the remaining 34% were not sure what they felt. Marshall Breeding (2007), the director of Innovative Technology at Vanderbilt University, wrote about the enormous opportunities offered by adopting Web 2.0 tools in academic libraries. However, he also recognized that "the very nature of Facebook works against this scenario. The natural circle of Friends centers on one's peers [...] and it is unrealistic to think that

large numbers of undergraduate students would want to count librarians among their FB Friends" (Breeding, 2007).

In many instances academic librarians adopt FB pages for their libraries but are worried about the best way to approach students. Miller and Jensen (2007) advocate the aggressive "Friend and Feed" technique by which librarians "friend" as many students as possible. Powers, Schmidt, and Hill (2008) are more cautious about the practice of "friending" students. They suggest that a better approach is to recommend mentioning one's Facebook account in library instruction sessions and reference interviews and then letting the students find that account.

A few articles cited success stories about the use of social networking platforms in academic libraries. Beth Evans (2006), for example, created a Brooklyn College MySpace page. The library then used three employees to sift through MySpace profiles to find 4,000 Brooklyn College students, faculty, and graduates. Evans invited these affiliates to be the library's friends and seven months later the library had approximately 2,350 friends. Evans did not mention any downsides to the Brooklyn College Library MySpace experiment and indicated that it had been well received by its audience. Another success was the experiment led by Mack, Behler, Roberts, and Rimland (2007), who promoted their FB library page profile for the library reference service. During the fall of 2006, their librarians received 441 reference questions, 126 of which were collected through Facebook, 122 by email, and 112 by in-person consultations.

Hendrix, Chiarella, Hasman, Murphy, and Zafron (2009) also provided a different perspective on the use of FB in academic libraries. The authors used a survey to investigate health libraries' use of the popular social network. Of the 72 librarians who responded to the survey, 12.5% (9) maintained a Facebook page. Libraries used FB mainly "to market the library, push out announcements to library users, post photos, provide chat reference, and have a presence in the social network" (Hendrix et al., 2009). Librarians had a very positive attitude toward the future of their FB pages although its use was currently rather low.

Last year, the authors of this paper carried out a content analysis of 12 university libraries' Facebook pages (Calvi et al., 2010). Our goals in conducting this survey were:

- To assess whether FB pages could be an effective new tool for communicating and promoting academic library services;
- To assess whether FB pages could act as an outreach to students, both undergraduates and graduates, to ensure their loyalty to the library, or whether other solutions should be preferred (e.g., a personal librarian's profile);
- To assess what the most used sections and services of a FB academic library page were;
- To highlight the potentiality of FB as a new channel to implement value-added services for students (e.g., asynchronous quick reference, training courses, and tutorials);
- To verify whether there was any positive correlation between the use of FB library pages and the number of full-time, or full-time equivalent, students enrolled in a university or any other possible variables (e.g., a new library building, active libraries hosting events and exhibitions).

From our findings, we drew the following conclusions:

- There is no evidence that content delivery or service delivery—for example, reference assistance—have been improved by FB pages;
- FB is a space made for people, and the personal and the professional area seem to remain rather separate for FB users, but

FB pages help increase the communication with the students, provided that:
  - The use of Facebook and of other social tools in libraries is supported by a defined communication strategy;
  - Librarians are proactive and keep the wall alive by posting every day;
  - Librarians realize that Facebook is primarily a fun tool for users (FB library pages should contain a balance of fun and professional content to attract "fans" and to encourage them to interact with the library);
  - Facebook pages are fully integrated and interact with library websites and other library applications.

FACEBOOK LIBRARY PAGES FROM THE LIBRARIANS' POINT OF VIEW: QUALITATIVE SURVEY RESULTS

To complete the observational study we carried out in 2010 on library Facebook pages, we developed an open questionnaire consisting of questions and posted it on some Dutch forums for librarians (see Appendix)[13] and on AIB-CUR@LIST.CINECA. IT, the discussion list of Italian-speaking librarians, during the month of June 2011.

In our previous study (Calvi et al., 2010), we performed a content analysis of the FB profile of 12 British academic libraries, which we selected according to their number of students—having more or fewer than 10,000 students—and their overall profile—branch or generic libraries. We looked at the amount of traffic on their pages, measured by the number of posts on their walls and their date, in terms of how recent or outdated posts were. We got some interesting results (for details, see Calvi et al., 2010), although we found that they could not be generalized to the Italian or Dutch library context, in which we are currently involved, because of the different academic and librarian traditions they represented, together with a different target group attitude toward the use of academic libraries (for example, the British libraries are more learning centers than pure libraries, a concept that is only starting to develop in The Netherlands, with the library of the technical University of Delft being one of the most impressive examples of this evolution. UK libraries offer longer opening hours than libraries in the other two countries of reference and have a more open approach to experimenting with technology). The fact that relatively few Italian or Dutch libraries had created a profile on FB at the time of our previous study was for us a reason to make them the object of another study and to develop a completely different approach to characterize them. This is why we opted for a qualitative survey.

We received around 15 replies from the Dutch librarians' forums, although some were more an expression of general interest in the development of this field. In general, the feedback was enthusiastic. Respondents expressed high expectations for social media's future role in libraries, as well as great interest in the outcome of the current research, indicating that academic libraries believe in social media's potential but still do not know how to fully utilize that potential. We also received eight responses from the Italian AIB-CUR discussion list.

The qualitative nature of this research does not allow for a quantitative treatment of the results we collected, therefore we performed a sort of text mining.

In the following subsections, we will discuss and elaborate in detail on the replies we received. We have grouped them by:

- Librarians' perceptions of Web 2.0 in general, and its perceived benefits and bottlenecks
- Librarians' changing role and expertise
- Librarians' experience with FB

Web 2.0: The Librarians' Perspective

Most of the libraries in the study are still at the experimental stage with their use of social media. Their initial goal was to gain experience with them in order to evaluate the feasibility of a future and more in-depth and focused use of them. This would include the creation of a more innovative image for the library, the development of ad hoc advertisement campaigns for the library, and the building of a network to generate a recognized name for the library.

One option was to use students' favorite communication tool(s) to attract them, to speak their language, and to remove any barriers between them and the library. This, it was hoped, would improve relationships with students who use these applications. Staff knowledge about these applications (i.e., in terms of learning perspective), faster and easier communication channels, the possibility of interacting with potential (and not only real) users, the possibility of interacting with other software and platforms, the possibility of sharing library resources immediately, and adopting a less formal approach with their users are among the advantages envisaged by academic librarians. Facebook is regarded as a potentially useful tool that would allow librarians to communicate effectively with both users and other librarians.

Most of the libraries in our survey neither see nor foresee any disadvantage in the use of Web 2.0, apart from the time it costs them to use and learn it, and to keep the content on social platforms current and interesting for library customers. Some librarians, however, complained that they do not have enough time to cope with the increasing number of requests from their users, and, in particular, to verify all the information they provide them with, something that has become a more complex operation because of Web 2.0 tools. Others remarked that several Web 2.0 applications may be redundant, and time- and resource-consuming, and that often users seem to find it difficult to cope with a more informal relationship with the library, which remains an official institution within a larger academic body. One librarian stated that "With such a direct, non-mediated questioning, the risk of feeling awkward publicly is always present."

Librarians' Changing Role and Expertise

Librarians did not seem to have a clear idea about how to use FB as a way to keep their expertise up to date. This is due in part to their lack of expertise in using FB. Some, however, envisaged possible ways beyond FB to keep their expertise updated: they mentioned following relevant news sources on the Web, such as Mashable and The Next Web, reading computer magazines, and attending IT-related conferences to keep up relevant (personal or institutional) contacts, both via FB or other social software, like LinkedIn.

When it comes to defining a different role for librarians, many see themselves as having a shifting role, from information managers to information coaches. Because information is accessible everywhere and in every way, the task of the academic librarian is seen as becoming an art, some said—the art of collecting the right information at the right moment, from the right place, and for the right patron.

One librarian replied that "We (as academic librarians) have to be where our students are. Our profession is changing from content to connection." Another, however, remarked that "as an information specialist that graduated in 2010, I do not feel like a librarian in a changing environment." This response probably emphasizes the difference in expertise (and expectations) depending on the age category one belongs to: the younger generation of academic librarians is already part of this changing environment. For all librarians, though, the buzz word seems to be "experiment": they feel they have to use social media because their students do, even though they cannot accurately predict how this will unfold.

Despite this enthusiastic approach and positive attitude toward a profession that is perceived as less stable and more fluid, some librarians are questioning the added value of adopting social media and Web 2.0 tools compared to traditional services. Other new services need to be developed and performed as well: for instance, instructions in new media (e.g., (dis)advantages of new media, how to deal with them, etc.), so that the new academic librarian can develop the self-confidence that one needs to communicate and to use the media and opportunities with which they have always been familiar.

Some librarians define themselves as *Weblibrarians*, whereby the role of the library does not change in essence and FB simply offers a new way to communicate. As such, their role is not static but constantly changing, requiring the librarian to acquire new competences to remain up to date. As a guide to information, the academic librarian needs to be aware of the risks involved in information overload: quality not quantity needs to be the main focus when delivering information. One librarian also stressed that academic libraries must guarantee and support the use of quality products, both software and platforms, in general. So, librarians need to become not just guides through the information jungle, but also quality controllers to safeguard both their tasks and competencies and the successful accomplishment of students' activities.

In order to cope with these new challenges, most librarians stated that they stay informed by, for instance, reading the "right" magazines and Web content, following tweets and blogs by experts in their profession, getting to know their customers (i.e., the Web 2.0 students) better, trying out new things, and thinking about ways to implement these new things in their library. A major challenge for academic librarians is to focus on their customers: what do they do with social media? How can we (i.e., the academic librarians) meet them in the 2.0 world? The main expertise that is required from them comprises information literacy for both the students and the teachers. However, knowledge of the old tools does not have to be lost. In fact, it needs to be improved. And this can also be done by means of social media.

Many of the librarians we spoke to want advice on how to start using FB professionally. They seem to have no doubt that it is FB they need to master (see below) if they want to meet their students. However, they are not only (still) unprepared to face this challenge but also somehow scared (for themselves and for the library itself).

Librarians' Experience with FB: The Choice to be on FB

As mentioned previously, among all the available social platforms FB is the one that most libraries seem eventually to prefer. Not all academic libraries have a FB page or account, though, as our previous research (Calvi et al., 2010) pointed out. Moreover, whereas FB is the most popular social media platform, its usage can vary locally. So, for example, in The Netherlands, Hyves is a much more popular social site than Facebook.[14] Therefore, some academic libraries prefer to have a page on Hyves rather than on FB, although it is questionable whether this is the most appropriate choice and it is very much dependent on the libraries' target group. Some Dutch academic libraries do have a FB page, although not a full FB profile, which belongs to the institution they are affiliated with. Having a FB page gives libraries some internal and external visibility, allows more accessibility to their collection, and better positions the library as a member of the overall institution they belong to. Most of the Dutch libraries that responded to our questionnaire are still in the early stages of investigating the use of and investing in social media options.

Among the reasons why the academic libraries that contacted us had opened a FB account, most listed:

1. To communicate with their students; to inform them and to use their favorite social network to answer their questions;
2. To promote the library and its collections—some use FB pages to notify their users of new acquisitions or its services;
3. To use the FB chat facility as an "ask-a-librarian tool"—essentially to remove as many barriers as possible for users when interacting with the library staff.

What FB has to Offer to Academic Libraries

The choice to be on FB is motivated by the quality of the services and tools that FB has to offer academic libraries. The academic libraries that are currently on FB seem to favor the wall and the Events section. FB is also used to upload links, videos, and pictures with accompanying text. Some libraries, however, complained that they do not have many tools at their disposal for this purpose yet or that they do not yet properly use the ones they have. One library had integrated its catalog in its FB pages by using the Facebook Markup Language (FBML).

The situation described in the previous paragraph clearly points out that, in fact, only a limited number of FB tools and services are effectively used by the academic libraries in our survey. Part of the reason for this is the assumption that FB library pages are regarded as an institutional tool by students (see above), which therefore limits the scope and the possibilities of the activities they can perform. One librarian, for example, expressed concern that users may feel a non-peer relationship via FB pages, in that whoever writes on that page does it not as an individual but as an institution.

Additionally, one librarian remarked: "I would not underestimate the problem of posts getting lost among the loads on each library FB home." This statement does not, however, objectively reflect our experience. The numbers of fans that we have counted on library FB pages are too diverse to allow us to draw any general conclusion from them. The Dutch institutions with which we have been in contact, for example, have a very heterogeneous fan group when it comes to numbers: some have only 214 friends, some have 1,800. The Italian academic libraries that responded to our questionnaire counted between 12 and 600 fans. In both cases, the numbers differ significantly from the fan numbers we encountered in our previous analysis (Calvi et al., 2010). This discrepancy can again be ascribed to different traditions and approaches in the way libraries are perceived and used in the UK in comparison to (parts of) mainland Europe, in this case.

Despite the limited number of fans, the time spent on FB amounts to approximately 15–20 minutes per day for the Dutch libraries. The Italian academic libraries with which we had contact showed more diversity, spending between 5 minutes and 10 hours per day on FB. In both cases, however, the time is mainly used to check the news. Some libraries post once a week, spending about 30 minutes per week on FB. Very few libraries monitor and update their FB pages constantly.

Students are enthusiastic about the library being the first university-associated department to have an active presence on Facebook. After having seen the library on FB, some students have physically entered the library because they were attracted by the activities posted on the wall. Although no real change has been noticed in students' attitude, they seemed to appreciate this new communication channel. Being present on FB has reduced the distance between the library and its users, has made the library more visible and recognizable by students, and has made its name and task familiar. There is a sort of friendly loyalty developing: users click on the "Like" button because that is *their* library.

RECOMMENDATIONS

Web 2.0 tools are becoming widely adopted in academic libraries as they improve communication with users, but many issues need to be kept in mind to better exploit the communication potentialities of the Library 2.0:

- Librarians should learn how best to interact and communicate by using a social tool.
- Librarians should have a full understanding of the Web 2.0 platforms they choose to use. They need to develop new expertise and skills.
- Librarians' presence on the social Web should be active and effective. To best interact with users, "frequency is the king."
- Librarians should learn to balance both professional and personal issues in the Web 2.0 environment. Some users can be put off by the concept of institutional and may hesitate to interact with the library via social media.
- As the Web 2.0 is a beta environment and is constantly changing, libraries should experiment with the use of social tools but should also be ready to move on to the next tool or to the social networking platform if needed.

CONCLUSION

In this chapter, we have presented the results of a survey involving Dutch and Italian academic libraries on their changing expertise and profile in a fluid and moving environment where social media require them to adapt and to adopt different ways of communicating with their traditional audience while trying to attract new customers. The results, surprisingly, show that although the interest and the need for such an adoption are felt rather strongly, the complete conversion to a Library 2.0 is still not in sight. Many respondents, especially in the Dutch context, expressed an interest in the outcome of our study to help them decide which direction they should further develop.

REFERENCES

Bietila, D., Bloechl, C., & Edwards, E. (2009, March). *Beyond the buzz: Planning library Facebook initiatives grounded in user needs.* Paper presented at 14th Biannual Conference of the Association of College and Research Libraries. Retrieved from http://hdl.handle.net/1961/5136

Breeding, M. (2007). Librarians face online social networks. *Computers in Libraries, 27*(8), 30–33. Retrieved from http://www.librarytechnology.org/ltg-displaytext.pl?RC=12735

Calvi, L., Cassella, M., & Nuijten, K. (2010). Enhancing users' experience: A content analysis of 12 university libraries' Facebook profiles. In *Publishing in the networked world: Transforming the nature of communication- Proceedings of the 14th International Conference on Electronic Publishing (ElPub) 2010,* (pp. 258-269). Retrieved from http://elpub.scix.net/data/works/att/118_elpub2010.content.pdf

Casey, E. M., & Savastinuk, L. C. (September, 1, 2006). Service for the next-generation library. *Library Journal.* Retrieved from http://www.libraryjournal.com/article/CA6365200.html

Casey, M. E. (October, 21, 2005). Working toward a definition of Library 2.0. *LibraryCrunch.* Retrieved on from http://www.librarycrunch.com/2005/10/working_towards_a_definition_o.html

Charnigo, L., & Barnett-Ellis, P. (2007). Checking out Facebook.com: The impact of a digital trend on academic libraries. *Information Technology and Libraries, 26*(1), 23–34.

Ellison, N. (2007). *Facebook use on campus: A social capital perspective on social network site.* Paper presented at the ECAR Symposium, Boca Raton, FL, December 5–7, 2007.

Evans, B. (October, 15, 2006). Your Space or MySpace. *Library Journal.* Retrieved from http://www.libraryjournal.com/article/CA6375465.html

Farkas, M. (2007). *Social software in libraries: Building collaboration, communication, and community online.* Medford, NJ: Information Today.

Fernandez, P. (2009). Balancing outreach and privacy in Facebook: Five guiding decision points. *Library High Tech News, 26*(3). Retrieved from http://www.emeraldinsight.com/10.1108/07419050910979946

Giles, J. (2005, December). Internet encyclopaedias go head to head. *Nature, 438.* Retrieved from http://www.nature.com/nature/britannica/index.html doi:10.1038/438900a

Hendrix, D., Chiarella, D., Hasman, L., Murphy, S., & Zafron, M. L. (2009). Use of Facebook in academic health libraries. *Journal of the Medical Library Association, 97*(1), 44–47. Retrieved from http://www.ncbi.nlm.nih.gov/pmc/articles/PMC2605034/ doi:10.3163/1536-5050.97.1.008

Kai-Wah Chua, S. (2009). Using wikis in academic libraries. *Journal of Academic Librarianship, 35*(2), 170–176. doi:10.1016/j.acalib.2009.01.004

Kim, Y. M., & Abbas, J. (2010). Adoption of Library 2.0 functionalities by academic libraries and users: A knowledge management perspective. *Journal of Academic Librarianship, 36*(3), 211–218. doi:10.1016/j.acalib.2010.03.003

Mack, D., Behler, A., Roberts, B., & Rimland, E. (2007). Reaching students with Facebook: Data and best practices. *Electronic Journal of Academic and Special Librarianship, 8*(2). Retrieved from http://southernlibrarianship.icaap.org/content/v08n02/mack_d01.html

Meschini, F. (unpublished). *e-Content, tradizionale, semantico o 2.0? =* e-Content, traditional, semantic or 2.0? Retrieved from http://dspace.unitus.it/handle/2067/162

Miller, S. E., & Jensen, L. A. (2007). Connecting and communicating with students on Facebook. *Computers in Libraries, 27*(8), 18–29. Retrieved from http://www.infotoday.com/cilmag/sep07/index.shtml

O'Reilly, T. (2006, October). Web 2.0 compact definition: Trying again. *Radar.* Retrieved from http://radar.oreilly.com/archives/2006/12/web-20-compact.html

Online Computer Library Center. (2007). *Sharing, privacy and trust in our networked world.* Retrieved from http://www.oclc.org/reports/sharing/default.htm

Pask, G. (1976). *Conversation theory: Applications in education and epistemology.* New York, NY: Elsevier.

Powers, C., Schmidt, J., & Hill, C. (2008). Why can't we be friends? The MSU libraries find friends on Facebook. *Mississippi Libraries, 72*(1), 3–5.

Raynes-Goldie, K. (2010). Aliases, creeping, and wall cleaning: Understanding privacy in the age of Facebook. *First Monday, 15*(1). Retrieved from http://firstmonday.org/htbin/cgiwrap/bin/ojs/index.php/fm/article/view/2775/2432

Schonfeld, R. C., & Housewright, R. (2010). *Faculty survey 2009: Strategic insights for librarians, publishers, and societies.* Retrieved from http://www.ithaka.org/ithaka-s-r/research/faculty-surveys-2000-09/Faculty%20Study%202009.pdf

Stutzman, F. (2006, December). *Unit structures: The network effect multiplier, or Metcalfe's flaw.* Retrieved from http://chimprawk.blogspot.com/2006/07/network-effect-multiplier-or-metcalfes.html

ADDITIONAL READING

Alcock, J. (2009). Using Facebook pages to reach users: The experiences of Wolverhampton. *ALISS Quarterly, 4*(2), 2–6.

Badman, D. A., & Hartman, L. (2008). Developing current awareness services. *College & Research Libraries News, 69*(11), 670–672.

Bardyn, T. P. (2009). Library blogs: What's most important for success within the enterprise? *Computers in Libraries, 29*(6), 13–16.

Bejune, M., & Ronan, J. (2008). *Social software in libraries.* Washington, DC: ARL. Retrieved from http://www.arl.org/bm~doc/spec304web.pdf

Bradley, P. (2007). *How to use Web 2.0 in your library.* London, UK: Facet Publishing.

Casey, M., & Savastinuk, L. C. (2007). *Library 2.0: A guide to participatory library service.* Medford, NJ: Information Today.

Cvetkovic, M. (2009). Making Web 2.0 work. From 'librarian habilis to librarian sapiens'. *Computers in Libraries, 29*(9), 14–17.

Kroski, E. (2008). *Web 2.0 for librarians and information professionals.* New York, NY: Neil Schuman Publishers.

Meredith, F. (2007). *Building Academic Library 2.0 — Distance learning librarian Norwich University.* Northfield, A conference sponsored by the Librarians Association of the University of California. =2 November (Video.) Retrieved from http://it.youtube.com/watch?v=q_uOKFhoznI

Mitchell, E., & Kervin, G. (2008). Using open source social software as digital library interface. *D-Lib Magazine*, *14*(3/4). Retrieved from http://www.dlib.org/dlib/march08/mitchell/03mitchell.html doi:10.1045/march2008-mitchell

Sauers, M. P. (2006). *Blogging and RSS: A librarian's guide*. Medford, NJ: Information Today.

Schonfeld, R. C., & Housewright, R. (2010). *Faculty survey 2009: Strategic insights for librarians, publishers, and societies.* Retrieved from http://www.ithaka.org/ithaka-s-r/research/ faculty-surveys-2000-09/Faculty%20Study%202009.pdf

Widdows, K. (2009). In your Facebook, not in your face. *ALISS Quarterly*, *4*(2), 7–10.

KEY TERMS AND DEFINITIONS

Academic Libraries: Libraries belonging to institutions for higher education, like colleges and universities.

Web 2.0: The use of the internet as a tool to read/write and to allow users to interact, to collaborate, create and share content, and to build communities of practice in a bottom-up approach.

Social Media: Web 2.0 media application like Facebook or Twitter, that are used to connect to other people to socialize.

Facebook: One of the most well-known social media applications.

Facebook Library Pages: Pages developed by libraries on Facebook with the purpose of reaching a wider and younger audience.

Future Developments in Academic Libraries: The trends and developments that are taking place within academic libraries, especially when it concerns the use of new media in general and of social media in particular as an initiative to attract and engage a new audience.

ENDNOTES

[1] According to the economist Scott Page, a project is successful when heterogeneous competencies and skills are pulled together.

[2] A recent survey carried out in the United States in the academic environment by Ithaka S + R has revealed that faculty rely heavily on electronic resources but that the discovery of these resources does not go through the library:
"Although they [i.e., the faculty] may rely on resources licensed by the library, their pathway for discovery of these materials no longer goes through the library, except in a very technical sense; their access is only facilitated by the library 'behind the scenes'" (Schonfeld & Housewright, 2010).

[3] http://www.blogwithoutalibrary.net/links/index.php?title=Welcome_to_the_Blogging_Libraries_.Wiki

[4] http://homer.gsu.edu/blogs/library/

[5] http://www.libsuccess.org/index.php?title=Library_Success:_A_Best_Practices_Wiki

[6] http://akasl2.pbworks.com/w/page/1647193/FrontPage

[7] http://liswiki.org/wiki/Main_Page

[8] http://daviswiki.org/

[9] https://wiki.lib.umn.edu/

[10] http://wiki.lib.uconn.edu/index.php/Main_Page

[11] iLibrarian: http://oedb.org/blogs/ilibrarian/2007/top-ten-facebook-apps-for-librarians-part-three/

[12] Since 2006 Facebook has allowed institutional pages but it also encourages administrators of institutional pages to have a personal profile.

[13] http://nedbib.reuser.biz/; http://www.nvb-online.nl/http://www.loowi.org/ .

[14] Some examples can be found at http://nl-biblioblogs.pbworks.com/w/page/4573813/Facebook and, for Hyves, at http://nlbiblioblogs.pbworks.com/w/page/4573818/Hyves

APPENDIX

FB QUESTIONNAIRE FOR ACADEMIC LIBRARIANS

1. Why did your library decide to have a Facebook page?
2. What Facebook tools do you use most?
3. Why do you think some tools are not used?
4. Do you have fans? How many?
5. Generally speaking, what do you think are the advantages of using Web 2.0 applications in academic libraries?
6. What are the disadvantages?
7. How much of your daily working time do you spend on your library Facebook profile?
8. Can you trace/record any positive difference in the students' attitude toward the library since you decided to create a Facebook page for your library?
9. How do you see yourself as a librarian in this changing digital environment?
10. How do you redefine your role in this more complex informational context?
11. How do you redefine your expertise to keep up with the upcoming challenges in this changing informational environment?
12. In which way can FB be used to keep the expertise of the librarian within an academic library up-to date? Please list some concrete examples.
13. Any other comments?

Section 3
Reimagining Pedagogical Expertise

Chapter 11
Teaching Political Science Students to Find and Evaluate Information in the Social Media Flow

Megan Fitzgibbons
McGill University, Canada

ABSTRACT

The advent of social media necessitates new pedagogical approaches in the field of political science, specifically in relation to undergraduate students' critical thinking and information evaluation skills. Instead of seeking out traditional static pools of knowledge, researchers and researchers-in-training now interact with information in an amorphous stream of production and consumption. Socially created information is now firmly integrated in the basic subject matter of political science, as manifested in primary sources in the field, scholars' communication practices, and the emergence of collective and distributed expertise. Existing models of information evaluation competencies do not address these realities of participatory authorship and decentralized distribution of information. Thus, in order to educate "information-literate" students in political science, educators must foster an understanding of how information is produced and how to critically evaluate individual information sources in the context of academic tasks.

INTRODUCTION

On May 7, 2011, the *Guardian* newspaper in the United Kingdom printed an interview with a "heroine of the Syrian revolt": Amina Abdullah, purportedly a Syrian blogger. Praised as an outspoken, courageous activist who contributed to the protest movement through her blog, "A Gay Girl in Damascus," Amina developed a strong following around the world (Marsh, 2011) and demonstrated the power of Web 2.0 tools in furthering activism. Many were alarmed, then, when the *Guardian* reported one month later that Amina had been taken hostage, ostensibly by

DOI: 10.4018/978-1-4666-2178-7.ch011

Copyright © 2013, IGI Global. Copying or distributing in print or electronic forms without written permission of IGI Global is prohibited.

Syrian security forces (Hassan, 2011). Clearly, it would seem, dictatorial governments recognize and fear the power of social media. The saga took a different twist a few days later, however, when it was revealed that Amina and her blog were a hoax propagated by a middle-aged American PhD student living in Britain (Addley, 2011). The widely reported story became emblematic of social software's power not only to share information but also to deceive. Skills in evaluating information now more than ever underlie the ability to make sense of the world.

The discipline of political science is uniquely implicated in the rise of social media. The data that constitute fodder for study in the field are now highly diffuse. Primary materials pour out from sources ranging from politicians' tweets and blogs to documents "leaked" by Internet activists. Political action—from e-government to political protest—frequently takes place via networked conduits. Secondary sources, too, are no longer simply traditional research articles and professional commentary, as pundits of all stripes and academics alike spread their messages through websites and interactive media. Indeed, anyone with access to the relevant technology can be a content creator and thus a political actor. Therefore, instead of being able to rely on familiar pools where information collects, researchers and researchers-in-training now function in a constantly moving flow of information production and consumption (Boyd, 2010). In the complexity of this environment, it follows that skills in evaluating information are fundamental to the practice of political science.

The word "expert" is generally applied to someone who is a master of a particular technical skill or domain of knowledge. Expertise is often tied to recognized credentials as well as the means to publicly share knowledge, either through published work, via vetted media channels, or in classrooms and lectures. With regard to published information, then, expertise is linked to oversight and editorial review. The notion of

credibility is closely tied to expertise, as experts by definition are understood to be trustworthy. In the past, information had to come from particular channels in order to have the label of expertise applied. In the Web 2.0 environment, however, anyone with a piece of information to share can contribute to a larger "hive mind" of knowledge that can be accessed online.

This chapter explores connections between Web 2.0 tools and political science, as manifested in primary sources in the field, scholars' communication practices, and the emergence of collective and distributed expertise. Techniques and conceptual models for teaching information evaluation skills are then explored in light of the ubiquity of the information produced and disseminated through social, networked conduits. Analysis focuses on ways in which educators in political science can facilitate students' skills for evaluating information, which, in the flow of social media, is now an iterative, constant process that has changed the meaning of expertise. Educators must therefore more broadly educate students both in understanding how information is produced and how to critically evaluate individual information sources in the context of their academic tasks. Educators are no longer the only experts on whom students can, or indeed should, rely. The discussion primarily refers to the education of undergraduate university students, but the principles can apply to many student-teacher scenarios.

BACKGROUND

Goals of Political Science Education

Political science has been broadly defined as "the study of human behavior relating primarily to the operations of government, the state, and in principle other outcomes deemed important by actors" (Polsby, 2001). The ideas of power and conflict—among and within states—are also foundational themes. The field is complex, spanning a history that has seen the rise of normative, behavioralist, and post-behavioralist approaches (Gunnell, 2011) as well as splintering into a variety of sub-fields. Current research is increasingly interdisciplinary, with sociology, psychology, and communication studies contributing new frameworks for understanding how people and societies relate to each other and to governmental systems.

At the university level, students learn methodological and theoretical approaches to making sense of political phenomena, such as state formation, war, civil society, and electoral politics. As in other social sciences, courses are designed to introduce foundational thought in the field and encourage students to apply theories to explain events of the past and present while simultaneously developing an understanding of the field's unique methodologies of scholarship. They are also generally encouraged to foster a spirit of inquiry and question the phenomena that they observe in the world. In addition, the study of political science is sometimes seen as training for careers in politics (local, national, or international), diplomacy, public policy, international development, public administration, and law. Beyond the focus of "pure" academia, then, political science students are often exposed to practical dimensions of governments and develop transferable skills for employment in related fields.

Finally, the development of a civic sensibility is frequently seen to be an underlying goal of political science education. In an analysis of the links between democracy and political education in the United Kingdom, it has been argued that educators should increasingly value student-centered, constructivist, experiential learning approaches and seek out pedagogical methods that emphasize participation in the object of study (Sloam, 2008). Although academic political scientists are sometimes accused of detachment from the real-world workings of nations, the political science or governmental studies classroom is often singled out as a natural place to foster political engagement and rekindle the interest of generations that are perceived to be apathetic.

The study of the workings of governmental apparatus and of human behavior is fundamentally tied to the processes by which information is produced and communicated. Regardless of the ultimate goal or the sub-field of political science—methods, theory, comparative politics, domestic politics, international relations, or civic engagement—information is implicated in research and study. Educators, then, need to ask: what skills do students need in order to evaluate information in political science?

The Challenge of Critical Evaluation

The Internet is said to be a great democratizer in information dissemination, acting as an infinite conduit to information of all types. More than ever, information seekers access information via Web search engines and social networking sites, but the actual function and performance of these tools are not well understood by the general public. Indeed, reference librarians can testify that, anecdotally, it is common for people to believe that a given piece of information itself is actually *in*, rather than *retrieved by,* the search engine. Web search engines' results pages tend to obscure documents' types and origins from casual searchers. In the online environment, everything is seen through the vehicle of a Web browser, where visual cues as to documents' reliability and purpose are less marked.

There has been a lot of dialogue in recent years around the notion that today's young people are "wired" differently, with the label "Google" or "Net" generation often applied to describe their reliance on the Internet for information and communication. While the idea that "Google is making us stupid" (Carr, 2008) smacks of hyperbole, it is true that there have been significant shifts—over time—in how people access information for academic and personal purposes. One noteworthy aspect of this change is that information seekers, especially those who have had Internet access for their entire lives, often lack an understanding of the context of the information that they retrieve, as many types of material are undifferentiated when accessed through Web search engines (Rowlands, et al., 2008). The traditional experts on how to identify information types—professors and librarians—are no longer the sole intermediaries between students and the universe of information (Davis, 2003; Robinson & Schlegl, 2005). Web search tools now play a significant role in determining the information that students find.

Eli Pariser, self-described as an "Internet organizer and disorganizer," has become influential in raising awareness of the reality that many Internet services, including the powerhouses of Google, Facebook, Microsoft, Yahoo, and major news websites, manipulate Internet users' search experiences using invisible algorithms (Pariser, 2011). Rather than retrieving an objective picture of the vast range of the Web with a given search request, Internet users instead operate within invisible "filter bubbles," or personalized pockets of information that Web services shape based on users' past behavior. The manipulation is largely based on users' social network connections as well as geography and previous searches. For example, a person who comments frequently on left-wing discussion forums and has a large number of Facebook contacts who frequently share articles on left-leaning magazines' websites would likely retrieve documents that favorably portray a left-wing political candidate whose name was searched in a Web search engine. This has obvious implications for students when searching for politically charged information via their preferred Web search tools if they lack the skill or inclination to evaluate their results thoroughly. Giant Web service providers, Pariser argues, have become the new gatekeepers to information.

Researchers employed in institutions of higher education, the traditional experts in their fields, generally rely on tacit knowledge for critical thinking tasks and therefore often take the issue for granted (Randall & Kellian, 2009). Students lack experts' specialized mental models of how information is produced and organized, which means that they must employ more structured strategies for evaluating information. Countless authors in the fields of education and information studies have explored the difficulties that students currently face in critically evaluating the information, especially that which is found online. Models of information-seeking behavior that consider the entirety of students' research process are instructive for educators. In particular, new explorations of how students make judgments about authority can elucidate strategies for facilitating skill development in the social media world.

One particularly significant contribution, given its broad scope and multifaceted approach, is Project Information Literacy at the University of Washington. The ongoing study consists of a large body of nuanced data on students' information-seeking behavior, but one general conclusion thus far is that "research seems to be far more difficult to conduct in the digital age than it did in previous times" (Head & Eisenberg, 2009). This might be self-evident to anyone who has experienced the recent shifts in information paradigms, but it is a truth that should prompt educators to explicitly pursue the development of their students' abilities in finding and using information. These skills cannot be taken for granted.

Head and Eisenberg (2010) have found that students generally select fairly conservative paths to finding information by using course readings first, recognizing this as a useful first step for identifying appropriate materials. They also found that students often take a collaborative approach to evaluating information, with the majority seeking the opinions of friends and friends. Fewer than half reported seeking assistance from professors or librarians. Social software, of course, certainly enhances the ease with which acquaintances' opinions can be gathered.

In the area of critical evaluation, it has been found that students frequently show an awareness of the need to evaluate information found on the Internet and actively apply basic criteria to judge the currency and authorship of a given document

(Biddix, Chung, & Park, 2011; Head & Eisenberg, 2010; Meola, 2004; Metzger, Flanagin, & Zwarun, 2003). The problem, though, is that their skill sets are not necessarily strong enough to make sense of information that is created and distributed via social and networked channels. Randall and Kellian (2009), for example, found that although students recognize the need for authoritative sources, they have difficulty detecting bias. Head and Eisenberg (2010) likewise found that students had more difficultly in determining the credibility or "believability" of a resource found online than with the task of general evaluation (which includes judging the relevance and appropriateness of the source). Moreover, time pressures are a reality for students, leading them to privilege efficiency and accessibility over credibility in their information seeking (Biddix, et al., 2011).

Using a comparison of undergraduate political science students who completed a research training workshop with a control group, Dolowitz (2007) argues that students do in fact require training to understand the information landscape and to appropriately find, use, evaluate, and integrate print and digital resources in their writing assignments. Participants were presented with sets of resources that fell into a range of categories related to authority and accessibility: traditionally authoritative sources like subscription article indexes, newly free government data, social media like blogs and message forums, and tools for communicating with scholars (e.g., email). Students were not found to be particularly adept at understanding which tools were relevant for which purpose, as evidenced by their unsophisticated use of online research tools in particular, as well as their inability to differentiate academic information from other categories.

In an online environment where context is uncertain, credibility is often obscured. Therefore, students are required to go beyond the simple dichotomies of true/false and biased/unbiased information. They have to develop critical thinking skills that allow them to take into account the purpose and origin of texts. If students are to check

for authority—information that originates from an "expert"—what are they to do when the nature of expertise is undergoing change? Since the creation and dissemination of information via Web 2.0 channels is now integral to research in political science, students who are being educated in the discipline must understand, in a subject-specific way that differs from that of other disciplines, how information is produced, and be able to evaluate it critically. The point here is not that political science students are different from other undergraduates, but that their *discipline* and its resources require different evaluation techniques.

EVALUATING POLITICAL SCIENCE INFORMATION IN A WORLD OF CHANGING EXPERTISE

Social media are now integral to the study of political science, both as an object of study and as a conduit for information dissemination. The field of electoral politics is most directly connected to Web 2.0 communication issues, but the technologies are also relevant in international relations, comparative politics, and even political theory (e.g., in discussions of the democratization of information creation).

Three principle categories of information have been redefined by the rise of social media:

- Primary sources
- Professional scholarship
- Contributions based on collective and distributed expertise

It is not insignificant that the Internet has granted (and continues to grant) access to vastly greater quantities of information than ever before, increasing the body of information to be searched and studied. The evolutions represented in each of these categories must also be understood in the context of the general information explosion, which itself has the effect of obscuring information authority and expertise. As discussed, the information search experience is also intertwined with social media, as evidenced by Pariser's (2011) "filter bubbles."

Primary Sources: The "Data" of Political Science

Political scientists have always studied original source documents, such as leaders' speeches and writings, election counts, public opinion polls, official government statements, and so on. Now, however, the source, credibility, origin, and provenance of such documents are often dubious. In many countries, politicians' personal communications have a strong presence in the realm of Web 2.0, as can be evidenced by a Web search for a given politician's name. However, personal communications can be spoofed, are not necessarily preserved or organized for future study, and are disseminated on a wide range of disconnected platforms, making it difficult to collect the full body of data. We need new methodologies for analyzing these ephemeral documents and for examining the public's reactions to them. The format in which politicians disseminate information has also changed, with, for example, 140-character messages on Twitter and images on the photo-sharing website Flickr. It should be noted that social media give politicians and public figures vastly more control over the portrayal of their message. Web 2.0 tools can facilitate direct communication streams with the public that no longer need to be filtered or spun through mass media. For example, Japanese politicians have affirmed the use of alternative social channels such as the video-sharing site Nico Nico Douga for press conferences in order to bypass mass media interpretations and commentary (McCargo & Hyon-Suk, 2010; Nagata, 2011). National governments and international organizations also engage in communication via Web 2.0 tools. For example, the public and researchers alike can get information updates via the United Nation's

Facebook page. The relationship between these updates and other official communication channels is not necessarily explicit. Moreover, Facebook visitors can write their own posts on the UN's page and read other users' comments—adding a layer of commentary that is accessed directly alongside the primary source but usually does not identify the commentator. Numerical data are currently being produced and made available at astronomic rates, but the curator of the data is not always clear. The *Guardian* newspaper's World Government Data website is one of the many impressive tools to emerge in recent years that bring together datasets from disparate sources to be viewed and analyzed through one interface. While the source of the data is always noted, the question of reliability can be obscured if the *Guardian* is perceived to be the content provider. Interestingly, in addition to accessing data, users can comment on blog posts from the site's contributors, post links from the database directly into other social media sites, and even rate the quality of a given data set. Which begs the question: should users then trust the dataset with the highest user ratings? The Internet has also made possible the dissemination of previously inaccessible documents, some voluntarily released and some involuntarily. Recent years have seen a strong rise in transparency movements, which are dedicated to holding leaders and governments accountable for their action through the free sharing of information. While there are many players in the movement, the case of WikiLeaks has been the most dramatic in terms of implications for the nature of expertise in the study of politics. Founded by the now-notorious Julian Assange in 2006, WikiLeaks is a nonprofit media organization that collects highly sensitive and secret documents (in all formats including video) from anonymous sources and releases them—unfiltered—online. From there, the information is further distributed through a vast range of channels, such as mainstream news agencies, individuals' online social networks, and sites that mirror WikiLeaks' own content. The organization's name evokes a collaborative approach to collecting and disseminating information, but in fact, "expertise" in the provision of information is determined by WikiLeaks' leaders. Leaked documents have yielded groundbreaking data for analysis by researchers, including classified documents related to the US-led war in Iraq, private diplomatic cables with exchanges among leaders of several nations, and secretive international treaty negotiations (e.g., ACTA). The very existence of organizations like WikiLeaks has become an object of study, raising questions about the nature of government transparency and the ethics of Internet activism. It has been argued that with regard to the transparency movement, it both helps and hurts that we are living in a time of radical uncertainty about the "official" version of the truth. All kinds of "authoritative" claims made by leading public figures in recent years have turned out to be little more than thin air (Sifry, 2011, p. 16). The irony is, however, that the sources of the WikiLeaks information "dumps" themselves are kept anonymous, causing critics to doubt their authenticity. The WikiLeaks case represents a twofold truth for anyone seeking to evaluate authority in political science: official documents and statements cannot necessarily be trusted, and at the same time, the source and provenance of any primary document has to be questioned. In sum, networked dissemination of information has dramatically changed how political scientists and students access the primary data of their field, whether they are communications crafted by leaders and governments or information that is presented and curated collaboratively. More significantly, it has altered the criteria through which authenticity and expertise can be judged, as the source of the information itself now has a social dimension.

Professional Scholarship In the realm of secondary sources, academic experts are communicating outside of the usual information channels of the past. International relations scholars Carpenter and Drezner (2010) provide a useful survey of the use of Web 2.0 technologies in their field specifically, seeking to fill the "decided lack of scholarly discussion" (p. 256) on the profound impact of new media in teaching and research in the field. In the traditional world of academic publishing, scholars can engage in indirect discussion via letters to the editor, critical reviews of others' work, and citation. Now, however, discussions and works in progress are visible to the world. Informal conversations among scholars take place via blogs, microblogging services (e.g., Twitter), social networking sites (e.g., Academia.edu, Facebook, and LinkedIn), electronic mailing lists, and online discussion forums. Many widely read and trusted professional publications like *Foreign Policy*, the *Economist*, and *Foreign Affairs* include blog-style columns from regular contributors on which readers can freely comment. As in other fields, it has been argued that communication via social media furthers the research enterprise by enabling collaboration and exposing ideas to criticism before formal publication (Carpenter & Drezner, 2010). Moreover, transparency and open communication can circumvent some of the problematic practices of traditional peer review, where ghostwriting, plagiarism, nepotism, and falsified data can be uncovered, despite the near-sacredness of the institution. Academic communication now circumvents the traditional academic publishing model of peer review with the rise of social publishing sites and repositories like the Social Science Research Network (SSRN). Such services allow users to upload working papers, conference presentations, and versions of published articles for which they hold copyright, which readers can download, tag, and comment on. In addition, research groups make collaborative wikis available to the public, revealing their work and inviting commentary before publication. The popular search engine Google Scholar indexes this gray literature in addition to traditionally published materials. From the user's perspective, then, the search engine melds together works in many formats and stages of completion from writers who vary in their expertise: from graduate students' conference posters to master's theses to think-tank working papers to the most seminal journal articles ever published in the field. Information seeking has a social dimension as well. The notion of "scholarly impact" is also being redefined to include an individual's name recognition and level of participation in public dialogue (Smith, 2011). Many academics participate in social networks, and in addition to discussing issues, they use these channels to share information with others. Social networks are also a source of answers. Instead of seeking information independently, users frequently solicit book recommendations or advice on particular topics, trusting their network of contacts to provide a quick answer that is "good enough" for the purpose. Beyond personal contacts, there are also a number of Web 2.0 tools for sharing scholarly information. CiteULike and Mendeley, for example, are citation management programs that allow users to create profiles, share stored citations, and track the popularity of papers among other users. Many other services have features for generating recommendations for their users, such as the online retailer Amazon, which is well known for leveraging user data to promote further sales. Several tools take advantage of the idea in an academic setting—for example, the bX recommender service that many libraries use to recommend related articles to users.

Whether information is retrieved through personal or algorithmic social networks, the title of "expert" no longer belongs to a single individual. Collective intelligence has a real impact on which information sources are found and used. In the scholarly milieu, these socially based methods of information retrieval further the "filter bubble" phenomenon in which the information gatekeepers are now the Web services themselves (Pariser, 2011). For novices as well as experts, it can be difficult to separate the materials that adhere to the standards of the academic genre from those that constitute more informal communication or work in progress. At the same time, serious

scholars cannot ignore Web 2.0 dissemination of information if they want to stay abreast of trends and have an impact in their field.

Contributions Based on Collective and Distributed Expertise

Social media are frequently linked to meaningful political participation (e.g., Rheingold, 2008). Indeed, popular social software like YouTube, Twitter, and Facebook have been in the forefront of democratic action around the globe, including US labor strikes, the contested Iranian elections of 2009, and the Arab Spring revolutionary movements in 2011. Much scholarship has been dedicated to studying the impact of Web 2.0 technology in elections and social movements, with the general conclusion being that the tools are immensely powerful in communicating messages and mobilizing citizens (e.g., Attia, Aziz, Friedman, & Elhusseiny, 2011; Jaeger, Paquette, & Simmons, 2010; Schuff, Mandviwalla, Williams, & Wattal, 2010). Those who study politics must now often take into account social communication technologies as one of the factors that influence political behavior.

Web 2.0 tools have also increased lateral communication among voting publics, leading to the rise of "opinion leaders" in online environments. Scholars of network analysis,[1] which has a long tradition in communication studies and political science, pursue the question of how people determine expertise and trust in a social setting. The public often determines expertise according to perceived social position and knowledge (Ahn, Huckfeldt, Mayer, & Ryan, 2008; Huckfeldt, 2001; McClurg, 2006). In social networks, then, single voices can rise in prominence, based not on their credentials, but on their ability to use social software effectively in relation to the community's values. In some cases, the simple fact that information is accessible online is more important than the perceived expertise of the creator (Kaid & Postelnicu, 2006). Moreover, in today's media-saturated world, citizens tend to rely on mass media pundits, especially ones that fit their pre-formed views, in order to avoid information overload. A pundit's success, again, is determined by a public following, which can be made or broken by a social media presence. News reporting is becoming more and more participatory, with major networks across the globe inviting audiences to submit their own reports, photographs, comments, and videos to supplement or even replace the agency's content. It is common practice for news organizations to have Twitter accounts and Facebook pages both to push out information and also to invite commentary. Overall, this movement has changed the nature of expertise in news reporting, as the line between reporters and viewers is increasingly blurred. At the same time, as in the idea of "filter bubbles," user-driven content can lead people to be exposed only to what they want to see, rather than to a larger world of information that is encountered serendipitously or chosen by a gatekeeper. Moreover, the anonymity of participation in political action in a Web 2.0 environment allows hoaxes to be propagated quite easily, as in the case of the blogger "Amina."

Social models of knowledge creation are increasingly influential in the world of information in general, as typified by the Web 2.0 giant Wikipedia. Reference works like dictionaries and handbooks are by their very definition produced by experts for the benefit of non-experts. However, Wikipedia is entirely produced by volunteer contributors, whose expertise is self-defined. The idea, then, is that everyone can contribute in order to amass a broad and varied compendium of knowledge, which, according to the oft-quoted description, is "an idea that could never work in theory, only in practice" (Cohen, 2011). The value of every Wikipedia article must be taken on its own terms, evaluated in the context of the task at hand. For those studying political science, Wikipedia represents a source of factual information on broad and minute topics alike—especially those related to

current events—with the caveat that entries should be double-checked for accuracy. In addition, as with other Web 2.0 sources, Wikipedia provides evidence of popular conceptions of events and documents the issues that tend to mobilize participation in knowledge creation.

Societal relations, by definition, have an impact on political action, but in the world of Web 2.0, "society" spans geographic boundaries and creates conditions of anonymity that cannot exist in face-to-face communication. New experts who would not otherwise have a public voice can emerge. Content creators' views are accessible by all, but at the same time, but they are often mixed with traditionally published or otherwise vetted sources. The separation of categories of materials was more evident in the past, as "alternative" sources had to be specifically sought out. This amalgamation of material types necessitates careful examination of authorship and purpose before the information can be understood in its proper context.

In sum, Web 2.0 technologies and the rise of networked politics have changed 1) the nature of primary sources in political science, 2) the manner in which academic information is communicated, and 3) the ways in which secondary information and commentary are created and shared. The new, multifaceted networked channels through which political information is created and disseminated have broadened the field while increasing its complexity. It follows, then, that students likewise encounter difficulties in discerning expertise when faced with the task of evaluating information in the context of political science.

Information Literacy

Although the idea has been explored in many fields, the concept of "information literacy" has been championed by librarians over the past few decades. Information literacy can be defined as the ability to find, evaluate, and use information effectively (American Library Association, 1989). In the context of this paper, it should be emphasized that this definition includes an understanding of how information is produced and accessed. Traditionally, educators with a library background have tended to emphasize information-seeking aspects of information literacy—that is, the technical skills required for crafting a search strategy, navigating article indexes, and deciphering citations. However, the documents that buttress the theory of information literacy emphasize the full spectrum of information seeking and use.

Many organizations and individual institutions have developed standards for defining and measuring information literacy skills. The one most often cited is the Association of College and Research Libraries' (ACRL) Information Literacy Competency Standards for Higher Education, which consists of a system of overarching standards, performance indicators, and outcomes that act as evidence of information literacy skills. According to the five overarching standards, information literate students:

- Determine the extent of information needed
- Access the needed information effectively and efficiently
- Evaluate information and its sources critically
- Incorporate selected information into one's knowledge base
- Use information effectively to accomplish a specific purpose
- Understand the economic, legal, and social issues surrounding the use of information, and access and use information ethically and legally (Association of College and Research Libraries, 2000, "Information Literacy Defined").

Many institutions and individuals have adopted these standards to scaffold their information literacy education efforts. In addition, though, current theory in information literacy emphasizes the importance of the *disciplinary context* in students' successful development of the relevant competencies.

To this end, a document like the Political Science Research Competency Guidelines developed by the Law and Political Science Section of ACRL is quite useful in its elaboration of specific information literacy competencies via concrete and examples of specific competencies that students should develop in the context of the discipline (Association of College and Research Libraries, Law and Political Science Section, 2008). The ACRL document links the overarching standards with specific tasks that political science students might be required to complete, such as accessing demographic statistics from a government database, searching for articles in subject-specific indexes, or critiquing the methodology of public opinion surveys.

To take a broader example, the Quality Assurance Agency for Higher Education in the United Kingdom has created a set of "subject benchmarks" for the study of politics and international relations at the university level (Quality Assurance Agency for Higher Education, 2000). The document details learning outcomes that holders of undergraduate diplomas are expected to have reached. In addition to subject knowledge, graduates should develop skills in retrieving and critically evaluating political information and employ appropriate technologies for finding information and presenting their own ideas.

Information-literacy training based on competency standards has been widely applied in many institutions and research studies. The literature on political science education, too, testifies to several recent instances of this approach (Barberio, 2004; Dolowitz, 2007; Driver, Jette, & Lira, 2008; Marfleet & Dille, 2005; Olsen & Statham, 2005; Robinson & Schlegl, 2005; C. Stevens & Campbell, 2007; C. R. Stevens & Campbell, 2006, 2009; Thornton, 2006, 2008, 2010; Williams & Evans, 2008; Williams, Goodson, & Howard, 2006). However, a single-direction model of information creator/consumer is firmly ingrained in the codified approaches mentioned here. It is true that the ability to evaluate information underlies many of the competencies, for example in the indicators that refer to an understanding of the difference between "popular" and "scholarly" sources. In addition, the ability to select appropriate information for the task at hand is included. Students are meant to learn to recognize "authority," and the Law and Political Science Section of ACRL in particular advises that an information-literate student "consults with professors" and "consults with local experts on campus, in government, or in non-profit agencies" when faced with the task of validating information (2008, p. 10). In other words, traditional sources of authority are recommended. Traditional categories of information sources are emphasized, but the notions of dispersed, participatory authorship and revolutionary dissemination of primary information related to politics are not addressed. Further, social media are not mentioned in any of the standards related to accessing information. The exhortation to evaluate is there, but the task has new implications in a world in which expertise has been redefined by social media. In the current environment of socially shaped information flow, the standard categories of information do not necessarily apply. Moreover, the unique circumstances of political information must be taken into account when developing specific educational approaches.

Recommendations for Information Evaluation in Political Science

In order to further students' development of relevant information-literacy skills, competency standards must be brought to bear in a context-based, process-oriented manner that involves authentic situations and participatory learning. The old model of gatekeepers organizing information resources according to reliability and purpose no longer apply in the world of Web-based information retrieval, so students must develop strategies for dealing with information that is created and accessed through social channels. The competency standards' frameworks are generally broad enough to encompass new models of information dissemi-

nation, but the specific methods of teaching and assessing students' abilities need to be revisited in light of the importance of social information creation and retrieval.

Indeed, the approach of content-as-object in the information literacy standards does not take into account the complexities of information retrieval in the current age, when the actual channels of information themselves are implicated in how students conceptualize their learning (as argued by Whitworth, 2009). Moreover, the reliance on categorization of materials according to published format can be limiting, when, as has been argued, much of the subject of study involves the actual flow of information in addition to the final format. It is therefore recommended that educators abandon resource-centered training and focus instead on helping students to think critically in context (Head & Eisenberg, 2010).

Requiring students to cite a certain number of material types in their assignments is a common approach for furthering students' understanding of publishing and information dissemination. Robinson and Schlegl (2005) explore the effectiveness of this method, ultimately finding that providing grade incentives for citing certain material types is more effective than simply teaching students about the appropriateness of different types of information. Although they advise that professors *not* ban the use of the Internet, they note that students who are not graded on the inclusion of scholarly resources tend to rely more heavily on Web-based materials, to the possible neglect of more contextually suitable materials. However, they do not address the idea of information created collaboratively or through social media.

Explicit instruction on information types continues to be relevant, as beginning undergraduate students in particular do not necessarily understand the basic model of peer review and how a journal differs from a magazine. Despite the fact that they daily experience the sensation of information flowing around them, they should learn that certain types of information tend to collect in particular information resources. Dolowitz (2007) presents a training module designed to teach students to differentiate between different types of information sources, emphasizing heavily skills in categorizing information according to its purpose. Although the focus of the module was on identifying information types, it was significant that students were also taught to seek out individual experts and communicate via email, discussion groups, blogs, instant messaging, and Web conferencing. The implication here is that personal—as opposed to published—information has a real value for the research process. Pedagogy that eliminates discussion limits students' abilities to separate academic information from non-academic information and also their understanding of the larger process of scholarly communication. Exchanges through informal channels have long been an aspect of scholarly communication (e.g., letters to journals and conferences or colloquia), but until recently, this communication was not accessible to undergraduates. As researchers-in-training, it makes sense that students should become aware of informal professional discourse.

"Checklist" approaches to information evaluation are also quite common, as can be seen by examining nearly any instruction librarian's arsenal of information-literacy teaching tools.[2] These checklists generally require students to use external clues to evaluate the currency, purpose, authority, and validity of a source, with the aim of separating the proverbial wheat from the chaff. However, the checklist formula has come under criticism for its oversimplification of the evaluation task, guiding students toward binary judgments without prompting them to consider the larger context of the source (Dahl, 2009; Meola, 2004; Metzger, 2007). A more nuanced approach can be seen in evaluation tools that take a matrix approach.[3] A matrix-style worksheet requires students to rate an information source on a scale of appropriateness for their task according to the piece's authorship, approach, genre, and currency. Sources are evaluated according to a continuum of

factors that often require students to seek out additional contextual information about documents and their creators. Students have to consider, for example, if a given document is reliable vis-à-vis its factual basis, or whether it follows standards required for the academic genre, or why it might be effective as evidence to support their own argument.

Indeed, strategies that emphasize context over absolute judgments are more relevant when working with information found via social media. In this environment, it is crucial for students to understand how particular content came to be created and why this matters in terms of larger patterns of power relations and communication. Networked channels can lead to information that is politically charged by its very existence, and thus students must evaluate both the content and how it came to be created in the first place. Critical judgment is a process of iterative steps related to the task at hand. In political science, for example, the appropriateness of an article or website depends on whether primary evidence or secondary commentary is sought. The relative judgment might subsequently change as a result of further investigation, for example, if a student learns more about a particular political figure's bias or communication track record. Along these lines, exercises in comparing documents can be quite effective for helping students recognize differences in purpose and credibility (Meola, 2004).

The traditional annotated bibliography can also be a very useful instruction tool for context-focused evaluation if students are required to explain who wrote a document and why, and why it is therefore relevant for their task. Preparing students to understand the different types of evidence and argumentative strategies in their discipline also promotes critical evaluation skills (Fitzgerald & Baird, 2011). Activities that incorporate evaluation of methods can also promote a focus on the entire writing process rather than mechanical information retrieval skills.

Head and Eisenberg (2010) report that few students in their study employed Web 2.0 tools for managing their own coursework. As social networks are now the channels through which political information is created and disseminated, students should be given more opportunities to explore the tools critically and understand their implications for the study of politics beyond students' own personal use. Another important strategy is to create authentic environments in which students both find information and also produce information themselves. For example, course assignments can be designed around Wikipedia: students can create their own entries, correct errors in existing articles, critically evaluate articles' accuracy, and engage in discussion with other contributors (as proposed in Carpenter & Drezner, 2010). The evaluation lesson here is twofold. First, students experience firsthand how easily information can be created and distributed by non-experts (such as themselves), underlining the need for critical evaluation of any type of information. Second, it demonstrates how information creation can be collaborative and potentially empowering in a social or political sense. Furthermore, some would argue, students can learn the values of citizenship by participating in politics as content creators (Sloam, 2008).

User feedback and "peer review" are defining features of Web 2.0 services. The "experts" behind user-supplied information and product ratings can range from mechanical usage statistics, to information collected by site creators, to judgments made by user communities. From Amazon's rating system, to Facebook's famous "Like" button, to retweets on Twitter, user-driven assessments are valued to help Internet users identify trustworthy or valuable information. Students who likewise seek out this type of judgment aid for academic information might be drawn to tools like Google Scholar's "cited by" function and journal publishers' "most viewed" article lists. Such ratings can be quite useful for prompting new directions in research, but it is important to recognize that

there are limitations to the wisdom of the crowds. Students must understand that any given document should be evaluated on its own merit, regardless of how it was discovered in social channels.

One theme underlying all these recommendations is the value of inquiry-guided and participatory learning. Beginning with the influential 1998 report of the Boyer Commission on Educating Undergraduates in the Research University, there has been an ongoing movement in Europe and North America to better integrate research into undergraduate education. Beyond simply ingesting information and memorizing facts, the goal of this approach is for students to develop general and subject-specific skills for engaging in knowledge discovery, critical evaluation, and communication of ideas. For students to develop the skills needed to become researchers, they must mimic the research process of professionals. For political scientists, social media are an intrinsic part of this practice. Rather than being told that certain types of information are good or bad, students can go much farther in developing higher-order thinking skills when they experience the vagaries of the information environment firsthand. The reality is that today's students have always accessed information via the Internet and its complicated static and social flows of information (and presumably always will). Controlled classroom learning that focuses on the traditional roles of professors and librarians as information experts will not be transferrable to the world beyond the classroom. Thus, students are better served when educators assume the role of facilitators and guides that prompt them to question what they find and illustrate the implications of social communication channels for the enterprise of academia and political engagement in the world at large.

FUTURE RESEARCH DIRECTIONS

While many studies have examined students' and other groups' behavior in finding and evaluating information, more research is needed to investigate the effect, if any, of "filter bubbles" and Web 2.0 phenomena–like user ratings on young people's information behavior. It would likewise be interesting to investigate the same question among professional researchers, with comparisons made across disciplines.

Inquiry-based approaches to education have been widely discussed for many years, but more work is needed to assess their effectiveness in particular contexts, specifically in terms of information evaluation. Because the entrée to information-literacy skills development is so subject dependent, further work could focus on whether regional, national, and institutional differences affect how students evaluate information. Similarly, more systematic research on disciplinary differences in information use practices, especially with regard to Web 2.0 and the question of evaluation is needed.

In order to develop specific learning objects and lessons plans that foster skills in understanding expertise and evaluating information, new models for assessing credibility that take into account users' tasks and motivation beyond absolute judgments are needed (as recommended by Metzger, 2007).

Finally, more research is needed to investigate how experts in the field of political science themselves judge expertise. The academic profession is undergoing generational shifts, and it is important to better understand how social software will continue to shape academic communication in coming years. The next step, then, would be to compare this to how students evaluate information, and the gaps found therein could inform further pedagogical recommendations.

CONCLUSION

Students are now expected to differentiate between different types of expertise when they are seeking information, and sometimes even to participate in content creation themselves. Given the changing nature of expertise, evaluating information in the context of political science is a daunting task. Traditional gatekeepers to information are no longer relevant as the sole determinants of the information that students access. Dahl (2009) effectively summarizes the challenge of information-literacy training in a world of changing communication modes:

Applying narrow definitions of words such as "peer-reviewed", "scholarly" and "academic", and "expert" to the research task reinforces boundaries that are being pushed and, in some cases, eroded by the very people who engage in the task of scholarly investigation and communication (p. 159).

Expertise is defined by disciplinary context, ergo, information literacy has to be developed in the context of the subject, the task at hand, and the specific information resources required. This is not to say that the competencies are not transferrable, but the development of information literacy skills is most effectively approached via subject-based entry points. Social software and networked communication's integration with the study of politics—both in terms of the subject matter and methodology—has influenced the meaning of expertise and authority, demanding that subject-specific evaluation skills be taught in political science education.

In order to be successful, students must learn about the primary sources of political science—the data to be studied—and how this is more than ever the product of communication via social networks, which can empower citizens while simultaneously creating a false illusion of comprehensibility. They must also understand that academic communication happens via informal Web 2.0 channels in which traditional publishing models are only part of the picture. Finally, new experts now contribute commentary and data relevant to the study of politics, adding a further layer of complexity to the task of information evaluation. The solution to fostering students' development of these skills goes beyond the basic frameworks of information literacy competencies and binary checklists for evaluation. Students can explore the importance of information evaluation by experiencing first-hand the uncertainty of information overload. If they are given inquiry-based prompts instead of discrete tasks, they will be motivated to seek out wider ranges of sources that require more nuanced evaluation skills.

Political science education, like all disciplines, benefits from collaboration among different types of educators. As Meola (2004) points out, librarians cannot claim to be the sole experts in compiling a finite body of vetted information resources in today's information environment. However, they can advise learners and researchers on how information is produced and distributed, as well as the technical mechanics of information retrieval. They understand the theory and practice of information literacy and how holistic approaches should be taken to develop the fundamental skills of lifelong learning. University faculty are experts in their relative fields and are responsible for helping students learn the subject content of a course. As has been described, though, critical evaluation of information is not divorced from the subject matter itself.

With the guidance of librarians and professors, students can learn to use techniques like comparison and context-based judgments to evaluate how an information source was produced and why it may relevant for their purposes. As Whitworth (2009) argues, "the idea that all one needs to do to learn about something is to retrieve information that has already been created by others is actually no more than the old behaviourist approach to education reconstructed for the Internet age" (p. 103). For all their demonstration of information literacy competencies, students must still read, create knowledge, and communicate it to others in order to learn, and the task of distinguishing "expertise" must happen within this context.

REFERENCES

Addley, E. (2011, June 13). Gay girl in Damascus hoaxer acted out of vanity. *The Guardian.* Retrieved from http://www.guardian.co.uk/world/2011/jun/13/gay-girl-damascus-tom-macmaster

Ahn, T. K., Huckfeldt, R., Mayer, A. K., & Ryan, J. B. (2008, August). *Availability and the centrality of experts in the communication of political information.* Paper presented at the Annual Meeting of the American Political Science Association, Boston, MA.

American Library Association. (1989). *Presidential Committee on Information Literacy: Final report.* Retrieved June 16, 2011, from http://www.ala.org/ala/mgrps/divs/acrl/publications/whitepapers/presidential.cfm

Association of College and Research Libraries. (2000). *Information literacy competency standards for higher education.* Retrieved June 29, 2011, from http://www.ala.org/ala/mgrps/divs/acrl/standards/informationliteracycompetency.cfm

Association of College and Research Libraries. Law and Political Science Section. (2008). *Political science research competency guidelines.* Retrieved June 16, 2011, from http://www.acrl.org/ala/mgrps/divs/acrl/standards/PoliSciGuide.pdf

Attia, A. M., Aziz, N., Friedman, B., & Elhusseiny, M. F. (2011). Commentary: The impact of social networking tools on political change in Egypt's "revolution 2.0.". *Electronic Commerce Research and Applications, 10*(4), 369–374. doi:10.1016/j.elerap.2011.05.003

Barberio, R. P. (2004). The one-armed bandit syndrome: Overuse of the Internet in student research projects. *PS: Political Science & Politics, 37*(2), 307-311. doi: 10.1017.S1049096504004275

Biddix, J. P., Chung, C. J., & Park, H. W. (2011). Convenience or credibility? A study of college student online research behaviors. *The Internet and Higher Education, 14*(3), 175–182. doi:10.1016/j.iheduc.2011.01.003

Boyd, D. (2010). Streams of content, limited attention: The flow of information through social media. *EDUCAUSE Review, 45*(5), 26–36. Retrieved from http://www.educause.edu/EDUCAUSE+Review/EDUCAUSEReviewMagazineVolume45/StreamsofContentLimitedAttenti/213923

Boyer Commission on Educating Undergraduates in the Research University. S. S. Kenny, chair. (1998). *Reinventing undergraduate education: A blueprint for America's research universities.* Stony Brook, NY: State University of New York–Stony Brook.

Carpenter, C., & Drezner, D. W. (2010). International relations 2.0: The implications of new media for an old profession. *International Studies Perspectives, 11*(3), 255–272. doi:10.1111/j.1528-3585.2010.00407.x

Carr, N. (2008). Is Google making us stupid?: Why you can't read the way you used to. *Atlantic Monthly, 56*, Retrieved from http://www.theatlantic.com/magazine/archive/2008/07/is-google-making-us-stupid/6868/

Cohen, N. (2011, May 23). *Wikipedia.* Retrieved June 29, 2011, from http://topics.nytimes.com/top/news/business/companies/wikipedia/index.html

Dahl, C. (2009). Undergraduate research in the public domain: The evaluation of non-academic sources online. *RSR. Reference Services Review, 37*(2), 155–163. doi:10.1108/00907320910957198

Davis, P. M. (2003). Effect of the web on undergraduate citation behavior: Guiding student scholarship in a networked age. *portal. Libraries and the Academy, 3*(1), 41–51. doi:10.1353/pla.2003.0005

Dolowitz, D. P. (2007). The Big E: How electronic information can be fitted into the academic process. *Journal of Political Science Education, 3*(2), 177–190. doi:10.1080/15512160701338338

Driver, D., Jette, K., & Lira, L. (2008). Student learning identities: Developing a learning taxonomy for the political science classroom. *Journal of Political Science Education, 4*(1), 61–85. doi:10.1080/15512160701816135

Fitzgerald, J., & Baird, V. A. (2011). Taking a step back: Teaching critical thinking by distinguishing appropriate types of evidence. *PS: Political Science & Politics, 44*(3), 619–624. doi:10.1017/S1049096511000710

Gunnell, J. G. (2011). Political science, History of. In G. T. Kurian (Ed.), *The Encyclopedia of Political Science.* Retrieved from http://library.cqpress.com/

Hassan, N. (2011, June 7). Syrian blogger Amina Abdallah kidnapped by armed men. *The Guardian.* Retrieved from http://www.guardian.co.uk/world/2011/jun/07/syrian-blogger-amina-abdallah-kidnapped

Head, A. J., & Eisenberg, M. B. (2009). *Finding context: What today's college students say about conducting research in the digital age.* Retrieved from http://projectinfolit.org/pdfs/PIL_Progress-Report_2_2009.pdf

Head, A. J., & Eisenberg, M. B. (2010). *Truth be told: How college students evaluate and use information in the digital age.* Retrieved from http://projectinfolit.org/pdfs/PIL_Fall2010_Survey_FullReport1.pdf

Huckfeldt, R. (2001). The social communication of political expertise. *American Journal of Political Science, 45*(2), 425–438. doi:10.2307/2669350

Jaeger, P. T., Paquette, S., & Simmons, S. N. (2010). Information policy in national political campaigns: A comparison of the 2008 campaigns for President of the United States and Prime Minister of Canada. *Journal of Information Technology & Politics, 7*(1), 67–82. doi:10.1080/19331680903316700

Kaid, L. L., & Postelnicu, M. (2006). Credibility of political messages on the Internet: A comparison of blog sources. In Tremayne, M. (Ed.), *Blogging, citizenship, and the future of media* (pp. 149–164). New York, NY: Routledge.

Marfleet, B. G., & Dille, B. J. (2005). Information literacy and the undergraduate research methods curriculum. *Journal of Political Science Education, 1*(2), 175–190. doi:10.1080/15512160590961793

Marsh, K. (2011, May 7). A gay girl in Damascus becomes a heroine of the Syrian revolt. *The Guardian*. Retrieved from http://www.guardian.co.uk/world/2011/may/06/gay-girl-damascus-syria-blog

McCargo, D., & Hyon-Suk, L. (2010). Japan's political tsunami: What's media got to do with it? *The International Journal of Press/Politics, 15*(2), 236–245. doi:10.1177/1940161210361588

McClurg, S. D. (2006). The electoral relevance of political talk: Examining disagreement and expertise effects in social networks on political participation. *American Journal of Political Science, 50*(3), 737–754. doi:10.1111/j.1540-5907.2006.00213.x

Meola, M. (2004). Chucking the checklist: A contextual approach to teaching undergraduates website evaluation. *portal. Libraries and the Academy, 4*(3), 331–344. doi:10.1353/pla.2004.0055

Metzger, M. J. (2007). Making sense of credibility on the web: Models for evaluating online information and recommendations for future research. *Journal of the American Society for Information Science and Technology, 58*(13), 2078–2091. doi:10.1002/asi.20672

Metzger, M. J., Flanagin, A. J., & Zwarun, L. (2003). College student web use, perceptions of information credibility, and verification behavior. *Computers & Education, 41*(3), 271–290. doi:10.1016/S0360-1315(03)00049-6

Nagata, K. (2011, June 10). New media keep old media honest. *The Japan Times Online*. Retrieved from http://search.japantimes.co.jp/cgi-bin/nb20110610a1.html

Olsen, J., & Statham, A. (2005). Critical thinking in political science: Evidence from the introductory comparative politics course. *Journal of Political Science Education, 1*(3), 323–344. doi:10.1080/15512160500261186

Pariser, E. (2011). *The filter bubble: What the Internet is hiding from you*. New York, NY: Penguin Press.

Polsby, N. W. (2001). Political science: Overview. In Neil, J. S., & Paul, B. B. (Eds.), *International encyclopedia of the social & behavioral sciences* (pp. 11698–11701). Amsterdam, The Netherlands: Elsevier. doi:10.1016/B0-08-043076-7/01283-3

Quality Assurance Agency for Higher Education. (2000). *Subject benchmark statements: Politics and international relations*. Retrieved June 16, 2011, from http://www.qaa.ac.uk/Publications/InformationAndGuidance/Pages/Subject-benchmark-statement-Polictics-and-international-relations.aspx

Randall, M., & Kellian, C. (2009). How do you know that?: An investigation of student research practices in the digital age. *portal. Libraries and the Academy, 9*(1), 115–132. doi:10.1353/pla.0.0033

Rheingold, H. (2008). Using participatory media and public voice to encourage civic engagement. In Bennett, W. L. (Ed.), *Civic life online: Learning how digital media can engage youth*. (pp. 97–118).

Robinson, A. M., & Schlegl, K. (2005). Student use of the Internet for research projects: A problem? Our problem? What can we do about it? *PS: Political Science and Politics, 38*(2), 311–315.

Rowlands, I., Nicholas, D., Williams, P., Huntington, P., Fieldhouse, M., & Gunter, B. (2008). The Google generation: The information behaviour of the researcher of the future. *Aslib Proceedings, 60*(4), 290–310. doi:10.1108/00012530810887953

Schuff, D., Mandviwalla, M., Williams, C., & Wattal, S. (2010). Web 2.0 and politics: The 2008 U.S. presidential election and an e-politics research agenda. *Management Information Systems Quarterly, 34*(4), 669–688.

Sifry, M. L. (2011). *Wikileaks and the age of transparency*. Berkeley, CA: Counterpoint.

Sloam, J. (2008). Teaching democracy: The role of political science education. *British Journal of Politics and International Relations, 10*(3), 509–524. doi:10.1111/j.1467-856X.2008.00332.x

Smith, D. (2011, June 28). How do you solve a problem like clay shirky? Or, Silicon Valley discovers impact factor. Retrieved from http://scholarlykitchen.sspnet.org/2011/06/28/how-do-you-solve-a-problem-like-clay-shirky-or-silicon-valley-discovers-impact-factor/

Stevens, C., & Campbell, P. (2007). The politics of information literacy: Integrating information literacy into the political science curriculum. In Jacobson, T., & Mackey, T. (Eds.), *Information literacy collaborations that work* (pp. 123–146). New York, NY: Neal-Schuman.

Stevens, C. R., & Campbell, P. J. (2006). Collaborating to connect global citizenship, information literacy, and lifelong learning in the global studies classroom. *RSR. Reference Services Review, 34*(4), 536–556. doi:10.1108/00907320610716431

Stevens, C. R., & Campbell, P. J. (2009). Collaborating with librarians to develop lower division political science students' information literacy competencies. *Journal of Political Science Education, 4*(2), 225–252. doi:10.1080/15512160801998114

Thornton, S. (2006). Information literacy and the teaching of politics. *LATISS: Learning and Teaching in the Social Sciences, 3*(1), 29–45. doi:10.1386/ltss.3.1.29_1

Thornton, S. (2008). Pedagogy, politics and information literacy. *Politics, 28*(1), 50–56. doi:10.1111/j.1467-9256.2007.00310.x

Thornton, S. (2010). From "scuba diving" to "jet skiing"? Information behavior, political science, and the Google generation. *Journal of Political Science Education, 6*(4), 353–368. doi:10.1080/15512169.2010.518111

Whitworth, A. (2009). *Information obesity*. Oxford, UK: Chandos. doi:10.1533/9781780630045

Williams, M. H., & Evans, J. J. (2008). Factors in information literacy education. *Journal of Political Science Education, 4*(1), 116–130. doi:10.1080/15512160701816234

Williams, M. H., Goodson, K. A., & Howard, W. G. (2006). Weighing the research paper option: The difference that information literacy skills can make. *PS: Political Science & Politics, 39*(3), 513–519. doi:10.1017/S1049096506060793

ADDITIONAL READING

Andersen, J. (2006). The public sphere and discursive activities: Information literacy as sociopolitical skills. *The Journal of Documentation, 62*(2), 213–228. doi:10.1108/00220410610653307

Badke, W. (2010). How stupid is Google making us? *Online, 34*(6), 51–53.

Bos, A. L., & Schneider, M. C. (2009). Stepping around the brick wall: Overcoming student obstacles in methods courses. *PS: Political Science & Politics, 42*(2), 375–383. doi:10.1017/S1049096509090519

Boys, J. D., & Keating, M. F. (2009). The policy brief: Building practical and academic skills in international relations and political science. *Politics, 29*(3), 201–208. doi:10.1111/j.1467-9256.2009.01356.x

Davis, P. M. (2002). The effect of the web on undergraduate citation behavior: A 2000 update. *College & Research Libraries, 63*(1), 53–53.

Deardorff, M. D. (2005). Assessment through the grassroots: Assessing the department via student peer evaluation. *Journal of Political Science Education, 1*(1), 109–127. doi:10.1080/15512160590907649

Dillon, J., & McKeel, W. (2005). Political nihilism, alternative media and the 2004 presidential election. *SIMILE: Studies in Media & Information Literacy Education, 5*(2), 1–12. doi:10.3138/sim.5.2.003

Ernst, H. R., & Ernst, T. L. (2005). The promise and pitfalls of differentiated instruction for undergraduate political science courses: Student and instructor impressions of an unconventional teaching strategy. *Journal of Political Science Education, 1*(1), 39–59. doi:10.1080/15512160590907513

Forte, A. (2009). *Learning in public: Information literacy and participatory media.* Unpublished doctoral dissertation, Georgia Institute of Technology. Retrieved from http://hdl.handle.net/1853/29767

Foster, N. (2007). *Studying students: The undergraduate research project at the University of Rochester.* Chicago, IL: Association of College and Research Libraries.

Greenhow, C., & Robelia, B. (2009). Informal learning and identity formation in online social networks. *Learning, Media and Technology, 34*(2), 119–140. doi:10.1080/17439880902923580

Greer, C. F. (2005). How local television stations used the web to report the second anniversary of the 9/11 terrorist attacks. *SIMILE: Studies in Media & Information Literacy Education, 5*(3), 1–10. doi:10.3138/sim.5.3.002

Head, A. J., & Eisenberg, M. B. (2011). How college students use the web to conduct everyday life research. *First Monday, 16*(4). Retrieved from http://firstmonday.org/htbin/cgiwrap/bin/ojs/index.php/fm/article/view/3484/2857

Heaney, M. T., & McClurg, S. D. (2009). Social networks and American politics. *American Politics Research, 37*(5), 727–741. doi:10.1177/1532673X09337771

Huckfeldt, R. (2001). The social communication of political expertise. *American Journal of Political Science, 45*(2), 425–438. doi:10.2307/2669350

Ishiyama, J. (2002, August). *Participation in undergraduate research and the development of political science students.* Paper presented at the Annual Meeting of the American Political Science Association, Boston, MA.

Ishiyama, J., Breuning, M., & Lopez, L. (2006). A century of continuity and (little) change in the undergraduate political science curriculum. *The American Political Science Review, 100*(4), 659–665. doi:10.1017/S0003055406062551

Jenkins, H., Clinton, K., Purushotma, R., Robison, A. J., & Weigel, M. (2006). *Confronting the challenges of participatory culture: Media education for the 21st century.* Retrieved from http://digitallearning.macfound.org/site/c.enJLKQNlFiG/b.2029291/k.97E5/Occasional_Papers.htm

Livingstone, S. (2008). Internet literacy: Young people's negotiation of new online opportunities. In McPherson, T. (Ed.), *Digital youth, innovation, and the unexpected* (pp. 101–122). Cambridge, MA: MIT Press.

Marks, M. P. (2008). Fostering scholarly discussion and critical thinking in the political science classroom. *Journal of Political Science Education, 4*(2), 205–224. doi:10.1080/15512160801998080

Metzger, M. J., & Flanagin, A. J. (2011). *Credibility and digital media @ UCSB*. Retrieved June 16, 2011, from http://www.credibility.ucsb.edu/index.php

Omelicheva, M. Y. (2005). Self and peer evaluation in undergraduate education: Structuring conditions that maximize its promises and minimize the perils. *Journal of Political Science Education, 1*(2), 191–205. doi:10.1080/15512160590961784

Richey, S. (2009). Hierarchy in political discussion. *Political Communication, 26*(2), 137–152. doi:10.1080/10584600902851419

Rieh, S. Y., & Hilligoss, B. (2008). College students' credibility judgments in the information-seeking process. In McPherson, T. (Ed.), *Digital youth, innovation, and the unexpected* (pp. 49–72). Cambridge, MA: MIT Press.

Stevens, C. R., & Campbell, P. J. (2006). Collaborating to connect global citizenship, information literacy, and lifelong learning in the global studies classroom. *RSR. Reference Services Review, 34*(4), 536–556. doi:10.1108/00907320610716431

Teslik, L. H., & Schrage, E. (2009). *New media tools and public diplomacy*. Retrieved June 18, 2011, from http://www.cfr.org/public-diplomacy/new-media-tools-public-diplomacy/p19300

Thornton, S. (2009). Lessons from America: Teaching politics with the Google generation. *Enhancing Learning in the Social Sciences (ELiSS), 1*(2), 1-20. Retrieved from http://www.eliss.org.uk/PreviousIssues/Volume1Issue2/ViewArticle/tabid/72/itemid/68/pubtabid/242/repmodid/411/Default.aspx

Tremayne, M. (2006). *Blogging, citizenship, and the future of media*. New York, NY: Routledge.

Trudeau, R. H. (2005). Get them to read, get them to talk: Using discussion forums to enhance student learning. *Journal of Political Science Education, 1*(3), 289–322. doi:10.1080/15512160500261178

Warschauer, M., & Grimes, D. (2007). Audience, authorship, and artifact: The emergent semiotics of web 2.0. *Annual Review of Applied Linguistics, 27*, 1–23. doi:10.1017/S0267190508070013

Williams, V. C. (2006). Assuming identities, enhancing understanding: Applying active learning principles to research projects. *Journal of Political Science Education, 2*(2), 171–186. doi:10.1080/15512160600669015

Wilton, S., & Polkinghorne, S. (2010). Research is a verb: Exploring a new information literacy-embedded undergraduate research methods course. *Canadian Journal of Information and Library Science, 34*(4), 457–473.

KEY TERMS AND DEFINITIONS

Blog: A website used to quickly publish short texts, news, commentary, etc. Usually displayed in reverse chronological order. Often similar in content to a diary or newspaper column.

Filter Bubbles: A term coined by Eli Pariser to describe the limited pockets of information to which Internet users are exposed as a result of Web services' invisible algorithms that display information based on users' behavior.

Information Literacy: The skills required to find, evaluate, and use information effectively.

Microblog: Web services that allow users to post very short messages (usually one or two sentences), images, or videos that other users can view in real time. Twitter is the best-known microblogging service.

Political Science: A field of inquiry that focuses on systems of governments, power relations within and among nations, and human behavior in relation to these systems.

Primary Source: A text or recording (in any medium) that is studied as the data or evidence of an event or phenomenon. The designation of "primary" is relative to the purpose of study.

Social Media: Web-based applications that allow users to create and share content, often in a collaborative manner. Examples of social media include social networks, photo- and video-sharing websites, wikis, message forums, social bookmarking websites, blogs, and microblogging services. Also known as Web 2.0 technologies.

Social Networks: Websites that allow users to create profiles and form contacts with other users to communicate and share information in various media. Widely used social networks include Facebook, LinkedIn, Academia.edu, and MySpace.

Secondary Source: Commentary on or analysis of a text or event, usually involving interpretation of an original source, artifact, or observation.

ENDNOTES

[1]   For recent contributions, see the September 2009 special issue of *American Politics Research* (volume 3, number 5).

[2]   See, for example, the materials compiled in the DMOZ open project directory: http://www.dmoz.org/search?q=web+evaluation

[3]   See for example De Montfort University's Information Sources Matrix: http://www.library.dmu.ac.uk/Images/Selfstudy/ISEM-Leaflet.pdf

Chapter 12
The Net Generation and Changes in Knowledge Acquisition

Werner Beuschel
IBAW – Institute of Business Application Systems,
Brandenburg University of Applied Sciences, Germany

ABSTRACT

This chapter uses a methodological approach to investigate research and design knowledge acquisition in the context of social software applications, an area cluttered by an ever-growing number of applications and high expectations about the capabilities of a new generation of young users, the Net Generation. Its objectives are twofold: to provide a rational point of departure for developing a research and design framework and to exemplify it for the use of social software in higher education. The chapter scrutinizes popular assumptions about the Net Generation, basing the framework on the interdependency of user audience and technology. The results of a longitudinal exploratory study for the area of social software use in higher education are presented. The final part of the chapter discusses implications for the design of learning environments and a number of ideas for further research on knowledge acquisition within the social software context.

INTRODUCTION

Rarely has an innovative technology reached and engaged so many people in such a short time as social software. Since 1992, when the Internet, the World Wide Web, and the first browser came into being, young people in almost every country of the world have become increasingly connected to the Internet. According to figures from the Pew Internet & American Life Project study, 93% of young people are permanently online, while 75% use cell phones (Jones & Fox, 2009). Equally high numbers or growing rates are reported for the use of a large variety of social software, the latest wave of applications disseminated via the Internet.

Even more importantly, studies indicate that, for young people, using social software is not just

DOI: 10.4018/978-1-4666-2178-7.ch012

another activity during the day, alongside watching TV or talking on a cell phone. Web-based media seem to have become increasingly important in the lives of adolescents, constructing a new environment for social activities, communication, and cooperation (Roberts, Foehr, & Rideout, 2005).

In general we are still a long way away from being able to fully assess the ramifications of social software. Investigation of knowledge acquisition in the age of a networked society is a wide open field of research. Visionary predictions, industrial promises, and a host of well-publicized non-scientific stories about the use and abuse of social media abound.

Education, being part of the daily life of young people, is an important area of research. How this new technology will exert its influence when the current technology-savvy generation arrives at universities and other institutions of higher education is a question yet to be answered. While basic numbers, such as the use of cell phones or memberships in social networking systems, are regularly compiled, it is unclear how the phenomenon of constant connectivity will affect the knowledge acquisition of young people, if necessitated by education in general.

Social software use seems to begin at a very young age. Stories of Facebook accounts being opened by parents for their four-year-old children surface every so often. A major unknown factor is how young people carry their attitudes toward information handling into formal education. The overarching goal of this chapter is to outline a framework for research that provides an empirically supported basis for discussing social software in the context of users and knowledge acquisition.

In order to reason about educational systems, we need to look at the target groups, the generations entering the institutions. Thus, to clear the ground for the investigation regarding technology use and changing knowledge acquisition, a critical review is needed. Did technology really produce a completely new and different generation of learners? Do these changes reach deep enough that

we can speak of generational breaks? Shouldn't we rather look at empirical facts and ask about usage, time patterns, and preferences of students who actually use social software?

This framework is outlined in three steps: A review of the label and visionary assumptions about the "Net Generation" initiates the discussion. The next step presents results of an exploratory study in the field of higher education. Empirical facts on social software use by students provide an up-to-date insight into systems use, preferences, and concerns on the ground of an exploratory study. The final step in the chapter discusses issues of generalization and expansion of the framework as well as further research ideas.

BACKGROUND: GENERATIONAL CHANGES AND SOCIAL SOFTWARE

To fully appreciate the impressive changes in the human use of technology it may be helpful to be aware of the larger timeframe in which developments used to happen. In his article about the computer becoming an almost invisible, "ubiquitous" element of day-to-day life, Marc Weiser envisioned such an all-permeating wave of technology (Weiser, 1991). The wider perspective suggests a development period of several decades. While the 1990s were a time of technological shift toward networking, the following decade laid the groundwork for universal access.

Within this framework of investigation the target group of social software users and the available technology are essential variables. While both are basic elements, they are not fixed over time, but rather "moving targets" to a high degree. So if we aim at investigating how people—in our case students in tertiary education—cope with the challenges of acquiring, building, and disseminating information by using innovative technology we need to look at each element and at their evolving relationship and interaction.

The User Aspect: The "Net Generation"

Adventurous young people's unexpected and creative uses of networking technology led to their being defined as the "Net Generation," a term that is still popular. The label evoked the notion of a generational break, including far-reaching assumptions about the characteristics of a new generation of learners. For a critical assessment of its rationale and basis it is helpful to look back at the introduction of the term.

The fact of permanent connectedness to the Internet for an ever-growing share of young people was readily visible around 1995, a few years after browsers made the World Wide Web easily accessible. In line with viewing education as being influenced by technology, there is a long tradition of declaring the advent of new media a "revolution" (Oblinger & Rush, 1997). From this angle, the Net Generation was deemed to have completely different learning habits and attitudes—consequently leading to the demand for not only the adaptation of learning environments but also the creation of a new educational system in general.

The author Don Tapscott is usually credited with having coined the term Net Generation. Impressed by the ways in which young people used the networked technology early on, he criticized the educational system as being unsuited to the new technology. In contrast to the self-organized activities of network users he perceived the traditional teaching approach as " authoritarian, top-down, teacher-centered" (Tapscott, 1998: 129).

Tapscott gained his insights from a body of data collected from approximately 15,000 young network users in different countries (Tapscott, 1998). While the ethnographical method he used is certainly legitimate, the selection is necessarily biased as the only people included were already using a social network. No control group of non-networkers was set up. While the described find-ings themselves are novel and thought-provoking, the generalization of findings about the notion of generational characteristics is questionable.

The question behind the claim of a "new" generation has been at the center of a long, ongoing debate. It is the vision of a generation of young people who are always connected, communicating and socializing via networks and mobile devices. While the use of networked devices may be accepted as an obvious fact, the quick ascription of unique characteristics to this generation must be questioned. In our context of knowledge acquisition within educational institutions we need to assess the depth of those characteristics.

Another early proponent of the generational view, albeit from a promotional rather than scientific angle, was Marc Prensky.

Our students have changed radically. Today's students are no longer the people our educational system was designed to teach. Today's students have not just changed incrementally from those of the past, nor simply changed their slang, clothes, body adornments, or styles, as has happened between generations previously. A really big discontinuity has taken place. (Prensky, 2001:)

The discontinuity is expressed in the contrasting terms of Digital Natives vs. Digital Immigrants (Prensky, 2001), suggesting that there is a clear line to be drawn between both groups.

In the years that followed, proponents of the generational metaphor invented more labels, such as Netgeners, Generation @, and Generation Thumb. Despite many critical objections the metaphor still attracts new followers. Just recently a senior member of the Académie française invoked the storybook character Tom Thumb, whose name indicates that he is part of the new generation of touch-display users. "They no longer live in the same space" is the strong picture of the new generation the author evokes (Serres, 2011).

All these authors favor the idea of a deep generational break with the outstanding feature that young people would move through the networked world quite naturally by self-organization and mutual learning. Assuming these assumptions were correct, the logical answer to the research question of appropriate knowledge acquisition and learning environments would be clear: Simply follow the trail of activities of young people and provide sufficient means for self-organization and communication.

However, this easy way of designing new knowledge acquisition structures for young people by postulating the existence of a relatively coherent user community is not really borne out by broad data. While all these described observations may be credible, there are severe theoretical obstacles to subsuming them under one label. From this perspective, the assumptions and the style of conclusions of the Net Generation proponents have been called into question (Facer & Furlong, 2001; Schulmeister, 2008).

Critique of the Generational Focus

In a comprehensive literature review, the German scholar Schulmeister questions the Net Generation proponents' claims about user preferences and attitudes, searching for empirical rather than anecdotal evidence (Schulmeister, 2008). He shows that while there may be many indications of certain characteristics, the projection of those characteristics on a whole generation is not justified. His extensive review of scientific literature shows that no empirical study has yet succeeded in underscoring a generational transition on a broad scale. He also could not find proof for Prensky's much quoted claim that by using new media even the human brain adapts—at least not in the sense of generational characteristics unique to the Net Generation (Schulmeister, 2008, 77 f.).

Schulmeister also questions the terminology frequently used by the generational advocates. With reference to the term "singularity," which was used by Prensky to evoke the picture of a unique change, Schulmeister criticizes the arbitrary transfer of terms from one scientific field to another. In his critique he argues that those terms obscure the changes taking place, since they do not suggest any evolutionary development (Schulmeister, 2008: 17 f.).

The ill-founded dichotomy of digital natives versus digital immigrants, some critics point out, may also lead to wrong conclusions with respect to the objective of innovating our learning systems. "Ultimately hanging on to slogans like 'digital native' can lead to bad decision making" (Owen, 2004, quoted by Schulmeister, 2008: 12).

Another comprehensive discussion about the validity and proof of the generational metaphor and an extensive list of references is provided by way of a weblog from an international research project led by the Canadian researcher Bullen (see Bullen, Morgan, & Qayyum, 2011; Digital Learners, 2012). In a similar vein to the review study quoted above, Bullen notes the lack of empirical evidence in the Net Generation discussion and the problems of generalization: "One of the major problems with the digital native discourse is that it frames digital literacy in generational terms and portrays all people of a certain age as possessing a uniform set of digital technology skills" (Digital Learners, 2012).

Summarizing the discussion, three consequences can be stated with reference to the question of a foundation for the user element in the framework of knowledge acquisition:

- There is no target group that can be coherently described as Net Generation or Digital Natives.
- No single set of user characteristics can describe the target group.
- There is no simple, coherent answer to the quest for an appropriate structure of a knowledge acquisition environment, based on generational characteristics.

Schulmeister, in his critical review, arrives at the conclusion that adolescents' characteristics and motivations may better be explained by understanding them from the perspective of socialization, where media use is quite naturally embedded in efforts of building friendships and personal identity (Schulmeister, 2008: 91f.). To sum up, Schulmeister supports a statement from a Canadian study of the Media Awareness Network: "The Internet, for young people, is part of the pattern of their day integrated into their sense of place and time. The Internet just is" (Media Awareness Network, 2004: 8).

Schulmeister concludes his analysis with a number of statements:

- Media use is only one part of activities, albeit an intergral one.
- Traditional media (TV, video) usually still have priority.
- Time allocated to types of activity change over time.
- Prevalent functions are aimed at traditional media content (music, movies), while computer use is geared toward communication and contact.
- Media activities are means for social processes.
- Activities and age viewed together show the development of interests and attitudes.
- Media activities differ considerably according to ethnic and social background.
- Current media are perceived as natural, in the same way as "old" media were perceived by earlier generations.
- Existing computer competencies have not (yet) been transferred into learning on a wide scale by young people themselves.

(Schulmeister, 2008: 92f.).

Emergence of Group Characteristics as Focus

Summarizing the discussion allows some insights into the target group as an element of investigation. While for creating learning environments we may use observed capabilities of astute youngsters, such as learning by self-directed information gathering and sharing or peer-to-peer networking, we should avoid ascribing these preferences to all adolescents or students. As we may gather from the statements above, social software and media use by students should be viewed in the context of social experiences amassed on their way to becoming adults. This calls for the inclusion of guidance structures in the environments, making use of the potential of the available technology.

A side problem of the discussion is finding an appropriate label for the target groups. The advocates of the generational view use the term Net Generation; some critics favor Digital Learners instead (e.g., Bullen, 2008; Schulmeister, 2008). This term could equally evoke criticism, since learners are, of course, flesh-and-blood people, not digital avatars. However, a decision about the most appropriate term is not important for the purposes of this discussion, so we can leave the labeling question unanswered for now.

As noted earlier, there is no unique and coherent definition of the target group by generation that would allow the simple administration of consequences for educational environments. Instead, requirements may be as diverse as the profiles of any set of groups. For further refinement, the idea of a "didactic profile" for each group in question, matching user characteristics and information resources, may be considered (as proposed for mobile computing by Becking et al., 2009).

The argument to switch from generational characteristics to emergent profiles of interest and practice in describing target groups, as explained in the previous section, does not question the potential of social software in general. It does, however, alter expectations about how learning environments could be adapted to the needs of learners.

The Technology Aspect: Social Software and Web 2.0

Advances in Web-based technologies over the last two decades or so—often subsumed under the terms social software and Web 2.0—have triggered the development of systems and tools that foster many types of collaboration and learning in networks. Such tools also build a new basis for knowledge acquisition inside and outside of institutions. The next step in setting up the framework of investigation is therefore to ponder social software and Web 2.0 as the technological element, to look for experiences with it in the context of applications—especially learning—and to view it in relation to the target group.

Prerequisites

Both social software and Web 2.0 are mentioned frequently in popular and scientific writing, but they usually differ in definition and detail. Three core prerequisites of the technology are usually implied when the potential of social software or Web 2.0 is named (see O'Reilly, 2005):

- Connectivity of users via digital networking.
- Interactivity of user interfaces.
- Mobility of access devices.

Social software systems such as Facebook, youTube, Google+, Twitter, etc.; their use and abuse by users; and their market share and mutual business relationships are now the subject of many reports in the daily press. They are also sometimes referred to as social network systems. Large professional computer associations also influence the discussion by creating new umbrella terms. Social computing, for example, was proposed by IEEE (see Riedl, 2011). For the sake of

the present discussion, digital media and social media are seen as equivalent to social software.

The implementation of social software, which started around 1995, was sustained by ideas from the discussion surrounding the popular catchword Web 2.0, a term coined by Tim O'Reilly (2005) and sometimes used as an equivalent to social software. The main aspects with respect to the Internet as an enabling technology were:

- The Web should be understood as a general, all-connecting platform.
- User generated content is at its center.

The idea of a platform suggests allowing everybody to exchange not only data, but also information about ideas and services without immediate boundaries. The second point is that, in contrast to earlier stages of information technology, the input of data should preferably come from the users themselves, something that turned out to be the fulcrum of further developments. Examples of typical Web 2.0 tools are weblogs, wikis, chat forums, and podcasts.

The background of all social software and Web 2.0 applications is their enabling potential for social processes. This potential for collaboration via digital networks and organizing processes according to the users' own interests can be seen as a powerful force for redirecting educational environments, as advocated by various contributors to the public debate and the scientific discussion. Some examples are the works of the Net Generation advocates, as quoted earlier, where the idea of liberating education from rote learning and the authoritative administration of knowledge was part of the thrust (e.g., Tapscott, 2005). Authors advocating the Net Generation approach collected many examples of the creative use of networks; the potential was also discovered early on by authors commenting on the importance of digital media in education (e.g., Boyd, 2011b; Ito et al., 2009; Thomas & Brown, 2011). Prominent commentators on educational innovation—for example, John Seeley Brown—supported the creative aspect of the enabling process (see Thomas & Brown, 2011).

From the perspective of pedagogical approaches, constructivists also supported the importance and value of social interactions for building up common understanding and problem solving, thus embracing social software (for a discussion of constructivism in virtual learning environments see Beuschel, Gaiser, & Draheim, 2009).

These various lines of thought have obviously played together over the last two decades to help translate the ideas into learning environments. This has led to myriad actual configurations, where social software was added to or combined with existing environments. Only parts of these experiences can be reported, as probably every school, institute, or university—even on the teacher level—has experimented with such forms. A partial but systematic overview concerning projects on social software integration in the UK is presented by Schroeder, Minocha, and Schneider (2010).

Emerging Characteristics of Social Software

After about two decades of social software applications, a state-of-the-art review shows that they have been taken up in all aspects of life—business, education, and leisure activities—thus fulfilling the vision of ubiquitous computing (Weiser, 1995).

One of the important implications of social software use is the capability to transgress and permeate boundaries. As its application is not confined to specific areas it can overcome traditional boundaries, both organizational and structural, in a variety of ways.

"Digital media have escaped the boundaries of professional and formal practice, and the academic, governmental, and industry homes that initially fostered their development" (Davis, 2012).

Looking at the current state-of-the-art of applications some potential effects may be recognizable:

- Boundaries between inside and outside a company (e.g., customer relationships) are dissolved (Grudin, 2010).
- Boundaries of organizational hierarchies in companies are dissolved (Grudin, 2010).
- Boundaries of using social software in various states of one's personal life are dissolved—from school to university to professional work (Thomas & Brown, 2011).
- Boundaries of social software use inside or outside formal education are dissolved (Thomas & Brown, 2011).
- Boundaries between formal and informal learning are dissolved (Beuschel et al., 2009; Thomas & Brown, 2011).
- Boundaries barring access to information repositories are dissolved (Thomas & Brown, 2011).
- Boundaries of traditional forms of interest-guided communities are dissolved—from networks for non-government organizations with a continuous infrastructure to temporary and spontaneous forms, such as moblogging for fun activities or political interests.

Beyond organizational boundaries the discussion could certainly be continued into psychological fields of identity representation, mental and legal issues, human relationships, and so forth, which are not the focus of the present discussion (see Turkle, 1995).

A certain discontent among both lecturers and students rose up in the wake of discussions about appropriate learning environments. Social software and Web 2.0 tools were perceived as disruptive technologies, not fitting the environment or not sufficiently supporting the pedagogical process (Efimova & Fiedler, 2004). The integration of social software and Web 2.0 tools with existing environments were not regarded as sufficient (Fiedler & Pata, 2009). In other cases, specific Web 2.0 tools such as weblogs were perceived by some students as too demanding, creating tensions in the didactic process (Beuschel et al., 2010). The rising discontent may be due to other reasons that have not been sufficiently subjected to investigation and categorization to date.

Obviously a process of diversification of learning environments took place, although this is not yet seen as satisfying the need for preparing students not only for learning, but also for future tasks in work environments. A current critique points to the problem that the initial requirement of supporting self-organization may indeed be catering to some students, but overburdening others:

Personal learning environments put the onus on the learner to take responsibility, not only for their learning but also how they go about that learning and the tools that they use. Such self-determination and choice is ideal in a self-directed or informal learning scenario, but how can institutions provide such an experience for groups of learners? (Davis, 2012)

Davis's comment leads back to the critique of the generational view, which, as noted earlier, attributes outstanding characteristics of single learners to groups. If the current application of digital technology, social software included, is indeed not primarily an adolescent generation's problem, but part of the continuously ongoing cultural process of growing into adulthood, then the assumption of a coherent generation would mislead the redirection of learning environments. Simple trust in self-organization by learners would certainly satisfy an elite, but would fail to prepare many other learners to arrive at that stage. Observations of creative system uses may indeed help to create learning support. They just cannot be mandatory for all. With regard to social software, the goal then must be to bring the potential of social software in its emergent

character to fruition, by including features that allow students (and teachers) to select and adapt appropriate structures, both in general and at the personal level.

A FRAMEWORK FOR INVESTIGATING AND DESIGNING KNOWLEDGE ACQUISITION STRUCTURES

Target groups and social software technology were used as the cornerstones of the framework for investigating knowledge acquisition issues in higher education and that should also help guide design decisions—or at least help to learn from previous mistakes in setting up support structures.

The previous discussion assumed a perspective away from characterizing a target group via generational ascriptions. Instead, a view of group activities based on cultural and social contexts was favored. While the technology is new, the contexts of its use are time-tested: "The participation in social networks is a cultural technique, always well-kept by humankind, just transferred now into the virtual Web" (Schulmeister, 2008: 21, trans. by author).

Interdependency of Groups and Technology

Group activities and the technology a group uses should be viewed as being interdependent. The mutual influence can be exemplified by a thought experiment: If an interest-guided activity is carried out by an individual or group using social software, elements of text, pictures, or sound snippets would be uploaded to the system, directed toward a certain common interest of other potential users. If another technology or system comes up and seems to better represent their current interests, or is easier to use, then some people may decide to use the new technology and abandon the old one, while others remain loyal to the old technology.

To some degree, this switch seems to be happening with groups moving from using email or a mailing list to adopting a social network such as Facebook, or a microblogging tool like Twitter.

This example should also support the argument that there is no simple construction of a coherent generational target group, and certainly no design of an appropriate system from the start onward. Thus, guidelines for educational environments cannot be formulated as easily as it seemed in the beginning of the discourse. As arduous as it may seem, appropriate learning and knowledge acquisition structures would have to be based on insights obtained by empirical user studies. Trial and error, the diversity of social activities, and careful observation of emerging results would try to bring the potential of social software to fruition.

From this perspective, both elements—that is, user group and technology—are evolving through mutual adaption. They are not determined from start to end, and they are malleable by the expressions of user interest and adoption of new system features. Characteristic profiles may emerge after a while, when users interact with the system.

An analytical approach to the term "mobility" may provide another example for the value of developing a wider social and cultural understanding of users. Being mobile is usually described as the advantage of being independent from time and space restrictions and is often used to reason about the success of social software. As Schulmeister argues in his critical analysis of the generational assumption, it is not so much the mobility that is favored by users, but the gaining of control over the use of one's own time. This, he argues with reference to a study by Kvavik, should rather be seen as an element of human "convenience" (Kvavik, 2005; Schulmeister, 2008: 29 f.). Mobility from this perspective is simply the means to an end, not the end itself.

Examples of indirect influence, the way in which users influence and are influenced by attitudes toward social software, may serve as another way of finding out about malleability. Examples

could be seen on any of the well-known weblogs, which help to devise and shape opinions on Web issues. Danah Boyd's blog Apophenia is a rich source of opinionated discussions (Boyd, 2011a). For example, many contributors joined a discussion about the issue of mandatory requirements to identify oneself on the Web. In this case, the participation does not influence the tool itself, a weblog, in any way. But the expression and clarification of the user's points of view can be expected to influence Web policies in other contexts.

Implications for the Methodological Framework

Being based on social and technical aspects of a defined context of application, the theoretical approach here can be subsumed under the label of socio-technical frameworks. Such frameworks lay claim to providing a better understanding of how systems evolve from their interrelationship between user and technology. Here, embedding the interpretation of group or technology issues into the wider perspective of social and cultural prerequisites should help enhance our understanding of knowledge acquisition support, thus also giving guidance to further development decisions.

The approach of the framework for investigation is also in line with a body of research represented by the field of Social Informatics, which suggests "including the roles of information technology in social and organizational change, the uses of information technologies in social contexts, and the ways that the social organization of information technologies is influenced by social forces and social practices" (Social Informatics, 2011).

As the examples above should have indicated, explanations for the malleability of the technological underpinnings of social software could be sought in ever-widening contexts, becoming "richer" with every interpretational dimension. A recent proposal for directions of research presented similar arguments. In their recent book, Dourish and Bell outline an extended research methodology for ubiquitous computing, including issues of social media development (Dourish & Bell, 2011). The authors move beyond existing approaches and suggest a detailed ethnographic procedure. From their conception of the complexity of processes they argue for an extensive analysis, which should secure insights about social and cultural elements found during observation (Dourish & Bell, 2011). Their argument runs counter to the prevalent system of development methodology in software engineering, where abstracting from specific traits in the task is the main thrust (see Liskov, 2011).

This kind of analysis would serve the experience that social software is highly malleable in the process of user appropriation, since every user can contribute to adjusting and building his or her own environment. On the downside, a procedure as elaborate as this would require intensive, time-consuming efforts for any development or analytical process. For the present framework, an extended, contextual analysis would be an advantage.

The critical review of the two main elements, user and technology, in this chapter seeks to question current naive assumptions, thereby avoiding unproven visionary expectations as well as technology-deterministic views. Both elements need to be involved in an investigation of informational challenges, their mutual influences being the main focus. Users make choices, thereby influencing social software development and deployment. Social software, however, enables new forms of engagement of people. Those new forms may in turn lead to new structures of information, relevant for future knowledge acquisition.

Testing the Framework

The framework, although in its outline stage, will be used as guideline for an initial empirical investigation—an exploratory study on the use of social software by students in higher education.

The study should provide a better insight into the current state of usage. The results could in turn then help refine the framework and continue with the quest for insights into knowledge acquisition.

Applying the framework in a study suggests focusing on the two main elements of investigation. The user element is represented by university students; technology, as the other element, is represented by social software. The definition of social software is deliberately wide open, with the aim of not excluding any system or tool from the investigation.

EXPLORATORY STUDY ON SOCIAL SOFTWARE USE BY STUDENTS

Methodology

This section outlines and presents the results of an exploratory study. The study's initial purpose was to collect data on usage and attitudes of students using social software systems and Web 2.0 tools over an extended period of time. It serves to delineate the current state and development of social software use and reactions of students. Knowledge acquisition per se was not covered, but was incorporated via questions on the use of social networks (see Questionnaire in the Appendix).

Data were collected over the course of more than two years, from the cohort of the respective semester. German and foreign university students, attending classes that were part of a regular bachelor degree curriculum, participated.

Prior observations of courses over several years had already hinted that integrating social media into learning environments does not work by simply providing tools to students. Weblogs, for instance, need to be accompanied by motivation and guidance (Beuschel & Draheim, 2011). All positive claims about media, reflective and self-guided usage, and participation in public discussions should be viewed as references to enabling aspects, not as naturally occurring effects. Used in the classroom, social software and Web 2.0 features need to be employed within a learning environment to become viable. The potential of new media needs to be guided and developed. This basic understanding regards the application of technical systems as being embedded in social and cultural activities as explained in the framework rationale.

The observations initiated an exploratory study, which was repeated over several semesters with the respective cohort of the semester. The courses were part of the regular curriculum and were offered once a year. The main objectives of the study were to find out about use of social software, social media, and Web 2.0 tools. Important aspects of the study were estimated usage time, subjective attitudes, and expectations and fears toward social media.

Between 2008 and 2010, participants from four classes were asked to fill out the "Questionnaire on student usage and attitudes toward Web 2.0" developed by the author (see Appendix). Thus, each round of the study was geared toward different cohorts of students, although they did have similar backgrounds and course requirements (see Table 1).

Fifteen question areas focused on the variety of social media usage and student characteristics. Class size ranged from 8 to 13 for the elective courses, which ran in three consecutive years. The

mandatory course in 2010 had 70 students, all in their first year at the university. Altogether, 95 students participated in the study. In addition to filling out the questionnaire, course participants were also involved in subsequent discussions in class, while some participants were also interviewed.

Results

The following figures present results from the evaluation of the set of questionnaires. The various question areas, each with subsections, focused on the variety of Web 2.0 tools, the frequency of their use, special sites, business experiences, perceived added value, and individual student data like gender, age, nationality, and study status. Multiple entries in the questionnaire fields were possible in specified cases. Percentage figures in the tables relate to the number of participants in each course. Due to space restrictions, only the most salient results of the 15 question areas, Q1 to Q15, are presented here, in particular the type of social software used by students (Figure 1) and the type of social network system (SNS) used (Figure 2). The two areas are discussed in greater detail below.

The following list presents an overview of the subjects and results of the 15 question areas:

Table 1. Overview of courses and number of participating students

Term: Course Topic Position in the Curriculum	Students enrolled	Students participating in the study
Summer 2008: "Web2.0" Elective course, 4. semester	12	12
Summer 2009: "Web2.0" Elective course, 4. semester	13	13
Summer 2010: "Web 2.0" Elective course, 4. Semester	08	08
Winter 2009-10: "Intro. to Bus. Informatics" Mandatory course, 1. semester	70	62
Overall: Summer 2008 until Winter 2009/10	103	95

Figure 1. Social software used by students

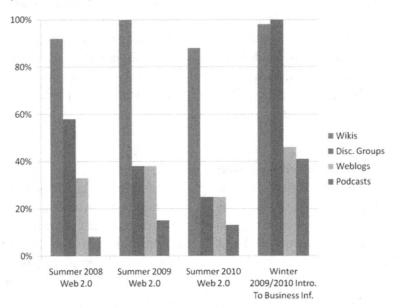

Figure 2. Social network systems used by students

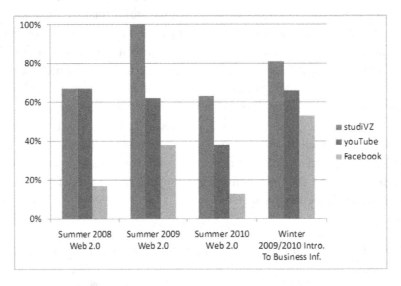

- Question area 1 (Q1) focused on the type of social software used by participating students (see Figure 1 and discussion below). The four tools named most often were wikis, discussion groups, weblogs, and podcasts.
- Q2 concentrated on the type of social network system used by the students (see Figure 2 and discussion below). The three front-runners were the German system studiVZ, which is similar to Facebook, in first place, with youTube in second place and Facebook in third place.
- Social network systems not denoted in Figure 2 were named less frequently. MySpace, XING, Twitter, and Jappy were all chosen more than once.

- Q3 asked specifically for the use of auction and recommender systems.
- Q4 asked which shopping and price comparison systems the students used. The systems eBay and Amazon were strong leaders here, named consistently in all groups.
- Information-gathering systems were the focus of Q5, with Wikipedia as the strong leader.
- Q6 was a supplementary question in case any systems were overlooked in previous sections. It asked which additional Web 2.0 systems were used. Answers did not result in additional insights; they rather showed that—for the students—there is only a vague distinction between Web 2.0 systems and other application systems with Web 2.0-like extensions, like instant messaging or document management systems.
- Results for Q7 and Q8 both refer to the detailed use of weblogs. According to the results, the vast majority of students neither maintain a blog nor intend to establish one. Reading others' entries is the most frequent activity, if any is named at all.
- With regard to the growing use of Web 2.0 tools in business systems—Q9—the participants had few encounters to report. Only a few students named wikis, forums, or intranets in the context of business applications. This is probably due to the lack of professional experience.
- Q10 investigated the frequency with which specified Web 2.0 functions were used. "Voting" was most common, followed by "identity management." Other Web 2.0 functions were rarely named; in order of frequency the following showed up: "backtracking," "tagclouds," and "moblogging."
- Q11 asked for personal added value when using Web 2.0 systems. "Information gathering/exchanging/sharing" was by far the most prevalent entry, followed at some distance by "social contact/staying or getting

in touch" with people. A few entries mentioned "enhanced personal profile," "solution finder," and "fun."
- Q12 referred to the use of Web 2.0 tools for personal information management in learning or individual activities, allowing open answers. Among the entries were "learning management systems" and "Wikipedia."
- Q13 asked for an assessment of perceived dangers when using a social network system. Surprisingly, a large portion of assessments rated danger as "medium" or "high."
- Q14 allowed open answers on personal experiences with Web 2.0, which may have been perceived as "good" or "bad." No previous definition or distinction was given, items were just collected. There was no clear majority for any reply. On the plus side, "sharing information" and "finding friends" were named several times; "fun," "learning," and "courtship" were mentioned once each. On the negative side, "identity theft," "unreliable information," "online mobbing," and "spam" were mentioned, but without indicating a particular trend.
- Q15 solicited personal data from the participating students. Based on the entries, the student body can be described as being relatively uniform: almost all students were aged 18–25 and were studying for a bachelor degree. Foreign students, almost all from Africa or Asia, made up about 20% of the student body in the questionnaire.

DISCUSSION AND IMPLICATIONS

Discussion

All the participants in the study were enrolled in the Business Informatics curriculum at a medium-sized university in Germany. Thus, the average knowledge profile of participants regarding social software, especially as regards technical knowledge, is certainly higher than that of an average person of the same age. Conclusions drawn from the study would hold for students of technical subjects, and not necessarily for all groups of young people. As the use of digital systems is an integral part of the curriculum here, any generalizations to groups in other areas of study should be made with care. The two question areas Q1 and Q2 are discussed in greater detail.

The steady and high rates of wiki applications in this case, shown in Figure 1, can be explained by the fact that wikis were a regular part of other courses offered in the curriculum (e.g., database courses), so students were familiar with them. The second place for the use of discussion groups could also be attributed to their frequent use in various classes. When the topic was raised in class it appeared that many students participated over some time in extracurricular discussions on the Web. This should be explored in further studies with the aim of supporting emergent knowledge acquisition structures. As the results show, most students use weblogs in a passive way—that is, by reading rather than writing them—if they use them at all. This result mirrors those of earlier studies (Beuschel & Draheim, 2011). The growing use of podcasts is interesting, although audio elements are not frequently produced by lecturers in this environment. Again, the relationship to knowledge acquisition should be explored in more detail.

The two-year longitudinal evaluation brought to light the high degree of multiple social network memberships shown in Figure 2, with an emphasis unsurprisingly on a specific social network. When students were asked about this, their explanations were fairly predictable: the choice of which network to join is influenced by the bulk of their friends already being there. Thus, German students prefer the German network StudiVZ, a system very similar to Facebook, although independent of it. Foreign students of Asian descent usually preferred Facebook "to connect with friends back home." The strong growth rate of

Facebook members, frequently reported in the press and supposedly sitting at 800 million in early 2012, can also be recognized in the study on a small scale. Frequently named reasons for using social networks, such as finding friends and connecting to other people (see Q11 and Q14), are by and large in accordance with comparable studies (see Schulmeister, 2008).

Pedagogical Implications

The discussion about the demand for appropriate learning environments, for students in tertiary education in this case, may yield some—albeit preliminary—insights. As the framework of research suggests, the focus should be on the two main elements and their interdependency: emerging characteristics of user groups and social software technology. The insights should be viewed with some caution, considering the limited database employed.

Looking at the issue of emerging groups, in our case it turns out that working groups formed by students tend to be fairly stable not only during the course itself, but also over the course of the curriculum. This may be due to the fact that many courses allow or even demand the formation of groups of two to five individuals for jointly solving homework assignments. Thus, the same students often work together over several semesters. This has obvious advantages for ease of cooperation within a group while the course lasts, but it also limits the range of experiences with different people. This seemed to be particularly true for different ethnicities—in our case, students from Africa or Asia—who tended to remain with students from the same nationality, as did the Germans. Social software could help to permeate this boundary. As a task, the instructor organized a forum-like text chat, requiring all students in the course to take part during a certain time period.

As the evaluation of questionnaire items and subsequent discussions with the students suggest, students deliberately use any source they can find on the Web for the task at hand, simply by referring to familiar search engines like Google. The selection seems to be arbitrary, and is sometimes influenced by peer knowledge. The Asian students mentioned using sources from their peers, German students from theirs. They do not seem to develop, over time, any sophistication in their search routines. One group of students expressed concern about the sometimes questionable quality of items found on the Web, while others gladly accepted whatever they found.

Pedagogical implications for knowledge acquisition support:

- Learning environments should provide students with guidance and help for the acquisition of high-quality knowledge via social software on the Web.
- The process of searching and selecting items as part of student knowledge acquisition on the Web—for example, for solving a homework task—should be accompanied and guided by the lecturer so as to enhance quality.
- Lecturers should provide or organize structures and examples for the use of social software in the selection of knowledge elements.
- Lecturers should address insecurities, fears, and negative experiences of students if the potential of social software is to be exploited to the full.

General Implications for Supporting Knowledge Acquisition with Social Software

The discussion in this section proposes some specific research issues with expectations about current phenomena that could drastically influence learning. In terms of research, these issues merit closer inspection with a view to helping to prepare and clarify future approaches to knowledge acquisition. They are not necessarily connected

with educational contexts and are by no means exhaustive.

The following issues should be considered in any analysis or design effort in relation to knowledge acquisition based on social software:

- **Users already know:** Children are familiar with networks and social software from an early age. It is not unusual for 10-year-olds to own a cell phone and to be a member of a social network. Thus, if they enter tertiary education, usually at age 18, the all-round use of network devices is a fact of life. Schools and universities can no longer ignore these preconditions, as any consideration for quick information dispersion in an institution may show.
  - ○ **Consequence:** A research approach must carefully consider preconditions of knowledge.
- **The device is not important any more:** The arrangement of hardware and software and its representation in a device—for instance, a specific cell phone—is no longer important. Software can be engrained into hardware chips and hardware can be simulated via software. What the future device will look like and how future access will happen, currently often via laptop or mobile phone, is difficult to predict.
  - ○ **Consequence:** An investigation should consider not only devices but the greater infrastructure of dissemination.
- **Knowledge is fluid:** Knowledge in former times could be considered as stable, at least for some time and to some degree, and was drawn from time-tested repositories like libraries. Knowledge derived from social software applications may depend on the process of creation itself. As an example, the categorization of certain archeological finds could be achieved via a network of interested laymen all over the

world. Within this open network a process of crowdsourcing starts in order to include the "wisdom of many" (Surowiecki, 2005). The results depend, of course, on the characteristics of the participating individuals, their number, and their method of cooperation. Thus, the restrictions and preconditions of the new knowledge produced and disseminated may not be clear to outsiders who make use of the data.

- Consequence: The type and quality of knowledge creation should be subject to consideration in a research setting.

- **If it's not there, users can build it themselves:** Social software and Web 2.0 tools allow users to quickly create individual structures in a computer or the privately owned part of a network by including special widgets in a browser, including apps or using mashup functionality. When looking at student workspaces in the study, it seems that this type of self-organized knowledge creation could gain momentum. The intertwinement of given structures and self-built structures makes it difficult to follow a straight line when observing changes, as it used to be previously with a given software program in a specific environment. A recent example is the self-organized way in which students represent their institution on websites to other students (see, for example, Pidaparthy, 2011).

  - Consequence: A research setting should carefully consider the subject area and the stability of its nature over time, selecting a specific investigative method. The method of "action-oriented research," where researchers are not neutral observers but help users define their needs, might be considered. The opposite method—sheer observation of computer-supported activities without questioning the us-

ers—can lead to false interpretations of intentions.

- **It takes time:** Experience gained in research areas related to social software—for instance, human-computer interaction and computer-supported cooperative work—has alerted us to the fact that technological innovation that involves organizational transitions or group effort can take much more time than expected. The adoption of tools for communication and collaboration means encountering many "hurdles and other new challenges," from which we should try to recognize patterns for solutions (Grudin, 2011).

  - Consequence: Research in social software should factor in the time for transitions and look at contextual settings rather than devices.

FUTURE RESEARCH DIRECTIONS

In this chapter, the suggestions for further research are geared toward the application of social software in education. The results of this exploratory study can only be interpreted as indicators, since the number of participants was limited.

With reference to the research framework developed above, it may help to check on the context of learning. Research results should be interpreted with reference to the wider intention of the framework, which is intended to help answer questions of analysis and design for appropriate learning environments. Based on the framework outlined earlier, the following list can be used to observe the wider context of analysis and design:

- Analysis of emergent characteristics of the basic elements, users, and social software technology.
- Analysis of their interdependency.
- Design indications for the handling of information for knowledge acquisition.

- Design indications for appropriate support of students with knowledge acquisition tasks.
- Design indications for learning environments that incorporate knowledge acquisition structures.

The exploratory study needs to be followed up by in-depth investigations and reinforced by further studies. In order to be able to better generalize the results of investigations, the following expansion of research subjects is suggested (their sequence not being incidental, but suggesting a growing scope of attention):

- Expanding the scope of studies to include students at other universities—which would also allow for comparative results.
- Expanding the scope of studies to online curricula, to amass comparative results for face-to-face versus online education.
- Tailoring the investigation toward specific tasks and connected knowledge acquisition activities.
- Tailoring the investigation of tasks and knowledge acquisition toward the shifting line between formal and informal learning.
- Expanding the scope of studies to an overarching view of social software in primary, secondary, and tertiary education.
- Expanding the scope of studies to an overarching view of social software by including university students and young people who have just joined the workforce.

When we look at the current discussion about social networks and social media, stories about use and abuse abound. There is also already a vast body of research on social networks, social media, and tools with Web 2.0 characteristics. A compilation of social network investigations contains over 450 items to date (see Boyd, 2011b). What seems lacking is a categorization of research approaches and subjects that allow a quick search and comparison in terms of a unifying matrix of research interests.

CONCLUSION

The use of social software for knowledge acquisition is a research area in a vast, rapidly evolving field. This chapter began by reflecting on prerequisites of the area and aimed at developing an appropriate research framework that could help identify issues of knowledge acquisition in learning environments.

Since the context surrounding the target audience of students is replete with high expectations, the basic elements of the framework—students as users and the field of social software technology—are scrutinized first. This leads to the critical review of the frequently claimed existence of a Net Generation. Instead of ascribing fixed characteristics to user groups and social software, the research framework proposes a perspective of emergent characteristics. This socio-technical view is based on a mutual relationship whereby users exert influence over social software and social software influences the choices of users.

An exploratory two-year study of students using social software exemplifies the research approach. The study reveals social software use by students on a small scale, investigating their expectations and concerns. Its main results show high degrees of membership in social networking sites and the use of multiple Web 2.0 tools for the purpose of information and communication. The data also provide insights into the students' expectations of the added value of social software as well as the perceived risks of sharing personal information on the Web.

A discussion of the study's results leads to further methodological considerations. On this basis, some implications for the design of learning environments with social software are stated and issues for further investigation are suggested. The discussion concludes with ideas about substantiating the research framework and extending the scope of investigation for knowledge acquisition with social software.

REFERENCES

Becking, D., Betermieux, S., Bomsdorf, B., Feldmann, B., Heuel, E., Langer, P., & Schlageter, P. (2004). Didactic profiling: Supporting the mobile learner. *World Conference on E-learning in Corporate, Government, Health and Higher Education, Association for the Advancement of Computers in Education* (pp. 1760–1767).

Beuschel, W., & Draheim, S. (2011). Integrating social media in tertiary education: Experiences and predicaments. *Proceedings of the DigitalWorld 2011. Third International Conference on Mobile, Hybrid, and On-line Learning (eL&mL 2011)*, (pp. 76-81). Gosier/Guadeloupe, France. Retrieved January 10, 2012, from www.thinkmind.org/index.php?view=article&articleid=el ml_2011_4_30_50082

Beuschel, W., Gaiser, B., & Draheim, S. (2009). Informal communication in virtual learning environments. In Rogers, P., Berg, G. A., Howard, C., Boettcher, J., Justice, L., & Schenk, K. (Eds.), *Encyclopedia of distance learning* (2nd ed., *Vol. II*, pp. 1164–1168). Hershey, MA: IGI Global. doi:10.4018/978-1-60566-198-8.ch166

Boyd, D. (2011a). *"Real names" policies are an abuse of power.* Retrieved October 20, 2011, from www.zephoria.org/thoughts/archives/2011/08/04/real-names.html

Boyd, D. (2011b). *Bibliography of research on social network sites.* Retrieved January 10, 2012, from www.danah.org/researchBibs/sns.php

Bullen, M., Morgan, T., & Qayyum, A. (2011). Digital learners in higher education: Generation is not the issue. *Canadian Journal of Learning Technology, 37*(1). Retrieved January 10, 2012, from www.cjlt.ca/index.php/cjlt/article/view/550/298

Davis, H. (2012). *Institutional personal learning environments—Paradise or paradox?* Keynote Lecture 3. Retrieved January 12, 2012, from www.csedu.org/KeynoteSpeakers.aspx

Digital Learners in Higher Education. (2012). Retrieved January 10, 2012, from http://digital-learners.wordpress.com/tools-resources/

Dourish, P., & Bell, G. (2011). *Divining a digital future – Mess and mythology in ubiquitous computing.* Cambridge, MA: The MIT Press.

Efimova, L., & Fiedler, S. (2004): Learning webs: Learning in weblog networks. In P. Kommers, P. Isaias, & M. B. Nunes (Eds.), *Proceedings of the IADIS International Conference Web Based Communities* (pp. 490-494). Lisbon, Portugal: IADIS Press.

Facer, K., & Furlong, R. (2001). Beyond the myth of the "Cyberkid": Young people at the margins of the information revolution. *Journal of Youth Studies, 4*(4), 451–469. doi:10.1080/13676260120101905

Fiedler, S., & Pata, K. (2009). Distributed learning environments and social software: In search for a framework of design. In Hatzipanagos, S., & Warburton, S. (Eds.), *Handbook of research on social software and developing community ontologies* (pp. 145–158). Hershey, PA: IGI Global. doi:10.4018/978-1-60566-208-4.ch011

Grudin, J. (2011). *Enterprise uses of social media.* Retrieved September 28, 2011, from rkcsi.indiana.edu/Speakers/SpeakerFiles/2011/J_Grudin.pdf

Ito, M., Baumer, S., Bittanti, M., Boyd, D., Cody, R., & Herr-Stephenson, B. (2009). *Hanging out, messing around, geeking out: Kids living and learning with new media. MacArthur Foundation Series on Digital Media and Learning.* Cambridge, MA: The MIT Press.

Jones, S., & Fox, S. (2009). *Generations online.* Pew Internet & American Life Project. Retrieved January 10, 2012, from www.pewinternet.org

Kvavik, R. (2005). Convenience, communications, and control: How students use technology. In Oblinger, D., & Oblinger, J. L. (Eds.), *Educating the Net generation*. Boulder, CO: Educause.

Liskov, B. (2011). *The power of abstraction*. Retrieved January 10, 2012, from http://www.stanford.edu/class/ee380/Abstracts/110420.html

Media Awareness Network. (2004, February). *Young Canadians in a wired world- Phase II: Focus groups*. Retrieved January 10, 2012, from www.media-awareness.ca/english/special_initiatives/surveys/phase_two/index.cfm

O'Reilly, T. (2005). *What is Web 2.0?* Retrieved September 28, 2011, from www.oreilly.de/artikel/web20.html

Oblinger, D., & Rush, S. C. (Eds.). (1997). *The learning revolution. The challenge of information technology in the academy*. Bolton, MA: Anker Publishing Company.

Owen, M. (2004). *The myth of the digital native*. Retrieved January 10, 2012, from www.futurelab.org.uk/resources/publications_reports_articles/web_articles/Web_Article561

Pidaparthy, U. (2011). *How colleges use, misuse social media to reach students*. Retrieved January 08, 2012, from www.cnn.com/2011/10/20/tech/social-media/universities-social-media/index.html?hpt=hp_bn6

Prensky, M. (2001). Digital natives, digital immigrants. *Horizon*, *9*(5), 1–6. doi:10.1108/10748120110424816

Riedl, J. (2011). The promise and peril of social computing. *IEEE Computer*, January, 93-95.

Roberts, D. F., Foehr, U. G., & Rideout, V. (2005). *Generation M: Media in the lives of 8–18-year-olds*. The Kaiser Family Foundation.

Schroeder, A., Minocha, S., & Schneider, C. (2010). The strengths, weaknesses, opportunities and threats of using social software in higher and further education teaching and learning. *Journal of Computer Assisted Learning*, *26*, 159–174. doi:10.1111/j.1365-2729.2010.00347.x

Schulmeister, R. (2008). *Gibt es eine "Net Generation"?* Manuscript in preparation. Retrieved February 25, 2012, from www.zhw.uni-hamburg.de/pdfs/Schulmeister_Netzgeneration.pdf

Serres, M. (2011). *Tom Thumb – New challenges of education*. Retrieved January 10, 2012, from penseesdunfrancaisenhongrie.over-blog.com/article-discours-de-michel-serres-sur-l-enseignement-86546463.html

Social Informatics. (2012). Retrieved January 10, 2012, from rkcsi.indiana.edu/

Surowiecki, J. (2005). *The wisdom of crowds*. New York, NY: First Anchor Books.

Tapscott, D. (1998). *Growing up digital: The rise of the Net Generation*. New York, NY: McGraw Hill.

Thomas, D., & Brown, J. S. (2011). *A new culture of learning: Cultivating the imagination for a world of constant change*. PA: Breinigsville.

Weiser, M. (1991). The computer for the twenty-first century. *Scientific American*, *265*(3), 94–104. doi:10.1038/scientificamerican0991-94

ADDITIONAL READING

Allen, J. P. (2010). Knowledge sharing successes in Web 2.0 communities. *IEEE Technology & Society, 29*(1).

Anderson, S., & Mohan, K. (2011). Social networking in knowledge management. *IT Professional, 13*(4), 24–28. doi:10.1109/MITP.2011.68

Benkler, Y. (2011). *The penguin and the Leviathan: The triumph of cooperation over self-interest.* New York, NY: Crown Business.

Bergqvist, T., Hudson, B., Lithner, J., & Lindwall, K. (2008). *Podcasting in school.* Paper presented at the Sixth Research Seminar of the Swedish Society for Research in Mathematics Education (MADIF 6), Stockholm, January 29–30, 2008.

Bergström, P., & Lindwall, K. (2008). Teaching and learning podcasting through blogging. *Tidskrift för lärarutbildning och forskning, 3–4,* 13-34.

Boyd, D. (2011). *Pew Research confirms that youth care about their reputation.* Retrieved February 10, 2012, from www.zephoria.org/thoughts/archives/2010/05/26/pew-research-confirms-that-youth-care-about-their-reputation.html

Brown, J. S., & Duguid, P. (2000). *The social life of information.* Boston, MA: Harvard Business School Press.

Bush, V. (1945). As we may think. *The Atlantic.* Retrieved January 10, 2012, from www.theatlantic.com/doc/194507/bush/

Carr, N. (2008). Is Google making us stupid? *Atlantic (Boston, Mass.), 302*(1), 56–63.

Collins, A., & Halverson, R. (2009). *Rethinking in the age of technology.* New York, NY: Teachers College Press.

Conklin, J. (2005). *Dialogue mapping: Building shared understanding of wicked problems.* Hoboken, NJ: Wiley.

Costello, T. (2011). Social networking: Guest editor's introduction. *IEEE Computing Now.* Retrieved January 10, 2012, from www.computer.org/portal/web/computingnow/archive/august2011

de Bono, E. (2005). *The six value medals.* London, UK: Random House.

de Paula, R., & Fischer, G. (2005). Knowledge management: Why learning from the past is not enough! In Davis, J., Subrahmanian, E., & Westerberg, A. (Eds.), *Knowledge management: Organizational and technological dimensions* (pp. 21–54). Heidelberg, Germany: Physica Verlag.

Fischer, G. (2011). Understanding, fostering, and supporting cultures of participation. *Interactions (New York, N.Y.), 18*(3), 42–53. doi:10.1145/1962438.1962450

Fischer, G., & Ostwald, J. (2001). Knowledge management: Problems, promises, realities, and challenges. *IEEE Intelligent Systems, 16*(1), 60–72. doi:10.1109/5254.912386

Geddes, S. (2004). Mobile learning in the 21st century: Benefit for learners. *The Knowledge Tree: An e-Journal of Learning Innovation.*

Kirkpatrick, D. (2010). The Facebook effect. The inside story of the company that is connecting the world. New York, NY.

Lee, M., & Chan, A. (2007). Pervasive, lifestyle-integrated mobile learning for distance learners: An analysis and unexpected results from a podcasting study. *Open Learning: The Journal of Open and Distance Learning, 22*(3), 201–218.

Media Awareness Network. (2005). *Young Canadians in a wired world- Phase II: Student survey.* November. Retrieved January 10, 2012, from www.media-awareness.ca/english/special_initiatives/surveys/phase_two/index.cfm

Mørch, A. I., & Skaanes, M. A. (2010). Design and use of an integrated work and learning system: Information seeking as critical function. In Ludvigsen, S., Lund, A., Rasmussen, I., & Säljö, R. (Eds.), *Learning across sites: New tools, infrastructures and practices* (pp. 138–155). London, UK: Routledge.

Nardi, B. A., Schiano, D. J., & Gumbrecht, M. (2004). Blogging as social activity, or, would you let 900 million people read your diary? *Proceedings of CSCW'04, ACM, 6*(3), 222-231.

Prensky, M. (2005). Engage me or enrage me. *EDUCAUSE Review, 40*, 61–64.

Prensky, M. (2009). H. Sapiens digital: From digital immigrants and digital natives to digital wisdom. *Innovate, 5*(3), 1–8.

Quinn, C. (2000). *mLearning: Mobile, wireless, in-your-pocket learning.* Retrieved January 10, 2012, from http://www.linezine.com/2.1/features/cqmmwiyp.htm

Rushkoff, D. (2010). *Program or be programmed. Ten commands for the digital age.* New York, NY: OR Books.

Selwyn, N. (2007). "Screw blackboard... do it on Facebook!": an investigation of students' educational use of Facebook. Poke 1.0 – Facebook social research symposium. University of London, November 15. Retrieved January 10, 2012, from www.scribd.com/doc/513958/Facebook-seminar-paper-Selwyn

Siemens, G. (2005). *Connectivism: A learning theory for the digital age.* Retrieved January 10, 2012, from www.elearnspace.org/Articles/connectivism.htm

Stahl, G. (2006). *Group cognition: Computer support for building collaborative knowledge.* Cambridge, MA: The MIT Press.

Tuomi-Gröhn, T., & Engeström, Y. (2003). *Between school and work: New perspectives on transfer and boundary crossing.* Amsterdam, The Netherlands: Pergamon.

Turkle, S. (1995). *Life on the screen: Identity in the age of the Internet.* New York, NY: Simon and Schuster.

Vodanovich, S., Sundaram, D., & Myers, D. (2010). Digital natives and ubiquitous information systems. *Information Systems Research, 21*(4), 711–723. doi:10.1287/isre.1100.0324

KEY TERMS AND DEFINITIONS

Apps: Small software programs to be used on mobile devices, available on the Web, with specialized functions for day-to-day purposes, like looking up bus schedules or city maps.

Crowdsourcing: A group activity whereby individuals, institutions, or companies—not necessarily experts—work together to answer a question or perform a task.

Informal Learning: Learning that is neither institutionally planned nor functionally defined, but is opportunistic and spontaneous. It can take place within or outside of institutionally planned education.

Knowledge Acquisition: The computer-supported process of purposefully collecting or creating information that can be used in knowledge-relevant tasks or human activities.

Mashups: Web-based programs that can combine results from two or more software sources on the Web to produce and provide new information.

Microblogging: Using a Web-based program to disseminate information to other user group members. Similar to weblogging, but with limited character entries. One example is Twitter.

Moblogging: An activity, started by an individual or group, to assemble a number of Web users by any social network system to announce and carry out spontaneous events.

Social Network System: Web-based social software system, with an emphasis on providing support for building a virtual community of people with similar interests.

Social Software: Collective term for Web-based systems supporting one or several of the following activities: personal representation, interest-based communication and interaction, virtual community building. Prominent examples are Facebook, Flickr, Google+, LinkedIn, youTube.

Web 2.0: Refers to innovative Web-based systems or tools for interaction and communication, and stresses the role of user contributions on Web-based platforms. Some examples of tools are weblogs, wikis, chats, and podcasts; email is sometimes included as an early example.

APPENDIX: QUESTIONNAIRE ON STUDENT USAGE AND ATTITUDES TOWARD WEB 2.0

QUESTIONNAIRE ON STUDENT USAGE AND ATTITUDES TOWARD WEB 2.0

-Administrative field, do not enter-

Please answer the following questions. It will take approximately 20 minutes.

Privacy assurance: the questionnaire is strictly anonymous; no personal answers will be identified or distributed.

You may fill out open questions in English or German.
If boxes are given, please check exactly one box.

1) How often do you use tools with Web 2.0 aspects? Please check the appropriate field.

- Discussion groups/Forums/Chats

frequently (every day)	sometimes (every week)	rarely (once in a while)	never

- Weblogs

frequently (every day)	sometimes (every week)	rarely (once in a while)	never

- Wikis

frequently (every day)	sometimes (every week)	rarely (once in a while)	never

- Podcasts

frequently (every day)	sometimes (every week)	rarely (once in a while)	never

- Other, please name: _____

    _____

    _____

    _____

2) In which Social Networking Systems do you participate?
- ☐ Facebook
- ☐ MySpace
- ☐ studiVZ
- ☐ XING
- ☐ youTube
- ☐ Second Life
- ☐ Twitter
- ☐ Chatroulette
- ☐ other: _____
  _____
  _____
  _____
  _____

2a) If you do, what is your main motivation or usage interest?
_____
_____
_____

2b) If you do, how much time do you spend per day with your Social Networking Systems?

Much more than 1 hour	about 1 hour	a few minutes	just occasionally

2c) What is your best/worst experience with participating in a Social Networking System?
_____
_____
_____

3) Which Auction or Recommender Systems do you use?
- ☐ Ebay
- ☐ Others:

_____
_____
_____
_____
_____

4) Which Shopping and Price Comparison Systems do you use?
- ☐ Amazon
- ☐ epinions
- ☐ Others:

_____
_____
_____
_____
_____

5) Which Web 2.0 systems do you use for information gathering?

- ☐ Wikipedia
- ☐ Wikimedia
- ☐ Others:_____

_____
_____
_____

6) Which other Web 2.0-systems do you use?

_____
_____
_____

7) Do you maintain a personal Weblog?
- ☐ Yes
- ☐ No

7a) If yes, what is the motivation for your Weblog?

_____
_____

7b) If no, do you intend to create a Weblog?
- ☐ Yes, for the purpose of _____
- ☐ No

8) With regard to Weblogs,
- do you write contributions?

frequently (every day)	sometimes (every week)	rarely (once in a while)	never

- do you write comments to other contributions?

frequently (every day)	sometimes (every week)	rarely (once in a while)	never

- do you read other's entries?

frequently (every day)	sometimes (every week)	rarely (once in a while)	never

Please check exactly one box.

9) Have you ever used Web 2.0 functions as part of a **business system**, e.g. a Weblog of a big company? Please describe the context and application briefly.

_____
_____
_____
_____
_____

10) Which features of Web 2.0 systems have you used so far?

    ☐ Tagging
    ☐ Moblogging
    ☐ Syndication (Feeds)
    ☐ Backtracking
    ☐ Tagclouds
    ☐ Voting/Polls
    ☐ Personal Identity Management/Identity Representation

Others:
    ☐ _____
    ☐ _____
    ☐ _____

11) What is your personal added value when you use Web 2.0 systems? Please refer to examples.
Most important value of using Web 2.0:

        _____
        _____
Further important values: _____
        _____

12) Do you use Web 2.0-tools to organize your personal interests in learning and knowledge management? Please refer to examples.

_____
_____
_____

13) If you use Social Networking Systems please rate the level of danger(s) you perceive in terms of privacy (Datenschutz), online security and so on. Please add a reason.

Low danger   _____
        _____

Medium danger_____

        _____

High danger   _____
        _____

14) Have you had any special experiences - good or bad – with Web 2.0? Please describe.

_____

_____

_____

15) Please fill in some personal information:
- ☐ Female
- ☐ Male

Nationality
- ☐ German student
- ☐ Foreign student

Age range:
18-20
21-25
26-30
Over 30

Next educational degree to be acquired: _____

THANK YOU VERY MUCH!

< Contact information >

Chapter 13
Faculty and Undergraduate Perceptions of Expertise within Social Media

Mary J. Snyder Broussard
Lycoming College, USA

Rebecca A. Wilson
Susquehanna University, USA

Janet McNeil Hurlbert
Lycoming College, USA

Alison S. Gregory
Lycoming College, USA

ABSTRACT

Social media applications like wikis, blogs, and comments on online news feeds emphasize user participation, encouraging ongoing revision by volunteer expertise. Surveying undergraduate students and teaching faculty at two small liberal arts institutions enabled the researchers to examine how both students and faculty view this new expertise, and how appropriate each group sees this expertise for completing undergraduate research. The results show that students are using social media extensively for preliminary research and educational videos, with Wikipedia and YouTube being the most popular sites for this purpose. Students and faculty continue to value advanced degrees, publications, and experience as the most important indicators of expertise. Students and faculty agree that users must always question the accuracy of information on social media sites, but faculties are not satisfied with students' ability to evaluate such information.

INTRODUCTION

Academic libraries and librarians have long been the gatekeepers of expert information. Through books and journals, they offered content that had undergone multiple stages of evaluation in the form of editing and peer review. Moreover, budget limitations forced further pre-consumer evaluation, where collection development librarians selected from the information sources available on the market and chose those best suited to their patrons' needs within the financial constraints. The

DOI: 10.4018/978-1-4666-2178-7.ch013

smaller the institutional budget, the more vetted the information readily available to users of that library. Similarly, information literacy programs had the straightforward task of assisting students in defining the differences between scholarly publications (thus scholarly information) and the more general books and magazines that they were apt to find in the public library or newsstand. However, as the Web became commonly available, the definition of "publisher" began to change.

At first, any provider of online information at least needed the technological skills and equipment to post the information and the user needed persistence to find it. Today, those barriers have been removed. The new generation of Web applications allows for—and encourages—interaction, user participation, and almost instant collaboration. Publishers of information do not need knowledge of coding languages such as HTML, and their information is easy to find through search engines like Google. Social media have not only drastically changed the nature and timing of information available to students, but also allow for ongoing revision. Vehicles such as Wikipedia, although sometimes disparaged by academics, indicate a new collaborative style of presenting information from volunteers not restricted by formal editing or publishing schedules.

Some traditional information sources are beginning to recognize the value of the new information contained in social media. The LexisNexis Academic database includes the full text of selected blogs, Britannica Online has been working on wiki-like features, and *Choice* book reviewers occasionally compare the coverage of new reference books to the corresponding entries in Wikipedia. *The Cambridge Handbook of Expertise and Expert Performance* (Ericsson, Charness, Hoffman, & Feltovich, 2006) defines "expertise" with a citation from Wikipedia, arguably lending credence to the nascent idea of socially constructed knowledge as legitimate authority—a trend likely to continue. Present educators of undergraduates must produce students who have the ability to utilize and assess an ever-widening array of information sources from an ever-widening array of "experts."

Roger McHaney (2011) says we are near the "tipping point" with social media, referring to a book of that title by Malcolm Gladwell (2000). He states that "when a critical mass of 20 percent of teachers uses the new technologies favored by tech-savvy millennials, an irreversible tipping point will occur" (McHaney, 2011, p. 3). Already, 93% of young adults (ages 18–29) are going online, according to a recent national Pew report, and 72% of them are using social media (Lenhart, Purcell, Smith, & Zickhur, 2010). A report published by the Centre for Information Behaviour and Evaluation of Research (CIBER) surveyed more than 2,000 researchers from 215 countries on how they use social media in their research process. They found that 79.7% of survey participants use social media for research (CIBER, 2010). Moran, Seaman, and Tinti-Kane (2011) surveyed "teaching faculty from across all of higher education" (p. 5) and found that more than 75% had used a social media site in the past month, 78% use social media for professional (non-teaching) use, and approximately 66% have used social media sites in their classrooms.

For the past decade, the general attitude of academia has been to disregard social media and to simply instruct students to avoid social media sites for class assignments. However, students' use of social media has become so pervasive that it is past time to reconsider our position. In this chapter, we present the results of a survey given to undergraduate students and faculty at two small liberal arts institutions. The survey assessed how students and faculty viewed this information through social media, how they defined an expert, and how appropriate they regarded the content for completing undergraduate research. The results show that students are already using social media for class assignments, with or without their professor's blessing. This demonstrates the increased need for new information literacy skills to prepare our students for life after college.

BACKGROUND

Social media allow users to connect, to socialize, and to share what they know. While older generations that grew up with one-way media might not buy into the new technologies, younger generations assume media are broken if they cannot interact with them (Shirky, 2008). The Internet allows for collaborative projects on an unprecedented scale. Whereas previous information sources required a great deal of work from a small number of experts, projects such as Wikipedia are a metaphorical piggy bank of knowledge; millions of ordinary Internet users put just a small amount of their "cognitive surplus" (Shirky, 2008) into the same place to make the most comprehensive encyclopedia humanity has ever known. This democratization of media is changing how students interact with information.

Much thought has been given in the literature to the teaching impact of social media. Fine arts and humanities professors are taking advantage of YouTube (Desmet, 2009); collaborative projects such as Hands-On Universe and Bugscope give students worldwide access to equipment such as high-powered telescopes and scanning electron microscopes that they otherwise could not afford (Brown & Adler, 2008); YouTubeEDU and iTunesU enable students and hobbyists alike to watch and to listen to lectures from world-renowned scholars (Gilroy, 2010); students are sometimes required to post their work on public blogs and to comment on each other's work (Brown & Adler, 2008); and professors are designing assignments where students enhance the coverage and accuracy in a source like Wikipedia rather than simply disparaging its contents (Chandler & Gregory, 2010).

In addition to the practical articles on social media in education, there is a growing body of literature on the theoretical learning benefits that social media offer students. Maloney (2007, n.p.) states that the uses of social media "mirror much of what we know to be good models of learning, in that they are collaborative and encourage participation by the user." Brown and Adler (2008) argue that students now have the opportunity to not only "learn about" content in a field, but also to "learn to be" practitioners in the field, starting out with "legitimate peripheral participation" (p. 19) and moving into the center of the field with increasingly demanding tasks as their skills improve. Deitering and Gronemyer (2011) discuss the advantage of using social media in library instruction. Professors often forget how entrenched they are in their discipline's community of practice, which remains foreign to their students. Observing and participating in online knowledge communities within an academic discipline allows students to observe how their personal experiences intersect with the existing scholarly research.

Anderson (2004) coined the term "long tail" to describe the wider range of specialty products that online retailers like Amazon can provide to geographically diverse niche markets. Just as online retailers have "broken the tyranny of physical space" (Anderson, 2004, n.p.) for media consumers, the Internet has opened up the "long tail" to researchers. Social media enable people with niche interests to find each other, whether they are wiccans or optical physicists, and to participate in conversations relevant to their field of interest (Brown & Adler, 2008; Shirky, 2008). Furthermore, these scholarly discussions used to be closed off, limited to conversations between small groups and those attending conferences. Now these discussions are transparent, available for other scholars and students to see. These "dialogs become searchable, browsable resources that students can use to see the debates, the arguments, and the intellectual energy beneath the surface of polished, published, scholarly work" (Deitering &

Gronemyer, 2011, p. 490). Encouraging students to view these dialogues, composed of arguments and differences in opinion, can help them realize that knowledge does not consist of absolute truths with a right side and a wrong side. Rather, knowledge is the culmination of these dialogues that continue to shift and change as new works are published and new academics participate.

Most discussions of social media in the academic literature address the questionable quality of the information involved, particularly with Wikipedia. Andrew Keen is probably the best-known social media critic. In the Introduction to his book *The Cult of the Amateur*, Keen says that social media's participants are monkeys "creating an endless digital forest of mediocrity" (2007, p. 3). *The Quill* published an article reporting the results of five "expert" analyses of five Wikipedia articles ranging from Harry Potter to a mathematical theory. While the experts found few factual errors, they did find that the writing quality varied greatly. Problems observed included assertions not proved, symbols not adequately explained for those new to the field, bias, missing citations, and the topic being not well represented in general (How does Wikipedia measure up?, 2008). *Nature's* often cited article found that the accuracy of 42 science articles in Wikipedia was comparable to that of *Britannica* (Giles, 2005). Berinstein (2006) feels that each of these two encyclopedias has its place, and applauds Wikipedia for its evolving efforts to promote quality. She concludes, "managing [volunteers] is like herding cats. But, like cats, these volunteers manage themselves pretty well" (n.p.).

In response to the questionability of anyone being able to add content to sites such as Wikipedia, efforts have been made to create similar sites where only verified experts could contribute. One such effort was Nupedia, which required peer review and produced almost nothing (Berinstein, 2006). Traditional models of peer review clearly do not translate well into the world of social media. Indeed, as more and more academics embrace the

positive qualities of social media, we are likely to see new types of publication. One media professor had her students create YouTube critiques on YouTube because she "felt that her students needed to participate in this new medium [YouTube] in order to critique it" (Parry, 2011, n.p.). The videos were later "published" as part of her precedent-setting, free "video book" published by The MIT Press. New softwares are being developed to support publications that straddle traditional publication and social media, with major academic publishers and societies backing these new types of publications (Parry, 2011).

McHaney (2011) says that we have reached "a new digital shoreline" (p. xvii). He presents a convincing case that higher education must recognize the millennial generation as different from previous ones, and that we must reconstruct our idea of teaching, or "fade away" (p. 3). The current generation of college students is accustomed to unprecedented customization. They are bringing their "toys" (p. 36) into the classroom in creative ways, such as taking collaborative notes on Facebook, capturing digital pictures of class materials, chatting virtually about class content with classmates, and live-streaming lectures for friends unable to attend class. Informal learning through social media is a way of life for these students, and while professors do not have to teach them "on their terms" (p. 48), we cannot continue to ignore the effects of these technologies on students. McHaney feels that this is an excellent opportunity to rethink how instructors in higher education teach, and how careful integration of technologies based on sound pedagogies and learning theories can enhance student learning and create the lifelong learning skills our students will need to succeed in the future.

Rheingold (2010) takes this a step further by embracing the use of these technologies on the condition that professors develop five interconnected literacies specific to social media. The first social media literacy is Attention. With so many sources fighting for students' attention, they must learn how to direct and divide their attention appropriately. The second literacy is Participation; students do not necessarily already know how to be responsible participants in social media and what kinds of participation are most useful to others. The third literacy is Collaboration; students need to be taught how to collaborate virtually and physically. The fourth literacy is Network Awareness. This includes a broad understanding of how social media operate, and also focuses on narrower issues such as privacy concerns. The final literacy is Critical Consumption, also known as "crap detection" (a reference to a quote by Ernest Hemingway). Students need to be taught how to evaluate the reliability of the information they consume. Rheingold believes there is more at stake than just an individual's education, and that civilization's very freedom is threatened by a lack of skill in these new literacies (Rheingold, 2009).

Student researchers leaving the safer world of traditional library resources must consider a new meaning for the word "expertise." Traditional indicators of an academic expert include formal education, affiliation with a reliable institution, experience, and authorship of books and articles, particularly those that are peer reviewed and frequently cited. With the exception of experience, these indicators are often reasonably objective and easily identifiable. In contrast, social media allow collective authoring by people who may not have the academic credentials to which we are accustomed in academia. How do these traditional criteria for expertise align with the potentially evolving definition of an expert in the world of Web 2.0? Despite the vast quantity of literature that discusses these new resources and their practical and theoretical uses in the classroom, little has been done to acknowledge the changing nature of expertise and how this might affect scholarly research.

Our study focused on how students and faculty regard this new collective intelligence, what uses they make of it, and how valid they see it as a component of undergraduate research. Small

colleges and universities with an emphasis on undergraduate education make an ideal setting for such an initial study because these institutions encourage strong relationships between students and professors. These relationships with professors, in addition to a culture of information literacy programs led by the libraries at such institutions, give participants a foundation for their responses to such a survey.

Students and faculty at two small Pennsylvania institutions dedicated to undergraduate education were surveyed about the acceptability of information from social media for research assignments. We knew of individual professors who were using social media in the classroom and felt that our students were beginning to use Web 2.0 applications for more than social purposes, but we wanted to document these perceptions. Survey site A, with a student body of 1,400, and survey site B, with a student body of 2,100, both offer a liberal arts education.

METHODOLOGY

After securing Institutional Review Board approvals at both institutions, the researchers conducted two surveys at each institution, one for students and one for faculty (see Appendices for full surveys). The surveys focused on the social media sites used, how they are used for research projects, and individual definitions of an "expert." The two surveys were parallel, but not identical. As an incentive to participate, respondents of each group had the opportunity to submit their email addresses to be entered into a raffle for gift certificates for their respective campus cafés. Surveys were completely anonymous and email addresses were kept separate from survey data.

For students, the survey was conducted on each campus in classes within the humanities (six classes), social sciences (five classes), sciences (five classes), business (four classes), and the arts (six classes). Class sizes varied and students were not necessarily majors in those disciplines. Because the survey was given in class and most classrooms did not have computers, the students completed a paper survey and their answers were later transferred into SurveyMonkey (a Web-based survey tool). A total of 540 students participated in the survey. Students' class levels from each school were relatively balanced with 25.6% freshmen, 28% sophomores, 23.3% juniors, and 23% seniors. While there were more female respondents (58.9%) than male respondents (41.1%), this reflects the overall student body of each campus and higher education as a whole.

An email request for faculty survey participants went to all faculty at each institution. Faculty respondents completed the survey directly in SurveyMonkey. A total of 114 faculty responded to the survey, with nearly identical levels of participation at both survey sites. This represents 59% of the faculty full-time equivalent (FTE) at survey site A and 40% of the faculty FTE at survey site B. The experience level of faculty was varied, with approximately half (50.9%) having taught for 15 years or less, and the rest having more than 16 years of teaching experience. For faculty, there were slightly more male respondents (52.6%) than female respondents (47.4%), again reflecting the make-up of the faculty on both campuses.

Statistical analyses were completed using SAS version 9.1 (SAS Institute, 2008). Chi square analyses were completed to determine possible frequency differences in responses. The significance level for all analyses was set at $p < .05$. The survey allowed participants to respond to more than one choice for most questions, so percentages in the results often do not add up to 100%.

We expected younger (N=32) and older (N=82) faculty to have different attitudes, and chose to divide the two groups at 10 years of experience. The logic was that those who had taught for fewer than 10 years would have begun teaching when social media sites such as Wikipedia and MySpace/ Facebook were emerging or had already entered into our mainstream culture.

Students' academic majors were grouped into five broad categories: social sciences (N=164), fine arts (N=91), humanities (N=84), business (N=84), and math and sciences (N=104). If more than one major was indicated, only the first was used in this study. Undeclared students or respondents who left this question blank (N=13) were removed from comparisons among majors. Communications students and faculty were tallied as fine arts because of the heavy art and commercial design components in the courses on both campuses. We looked at faculty divided by disciplines, but sample sizes were not large enough to draw meaningful conclusions.

Six focus groups were conducted to supplement the data from the survey. Three focus groups were held on each campus, for a total of 31 participants. The focus groups comprised freshmen (N=8), sophomores (N=9), juniors (N=11), and seniors (N=3), and the participants represented a wide variety of academic majors. There were 13 male (41.9%) and 18 female (58.1%) participants. Of these, seven had also completed the survey. (See Appendix A and Appendix B for the survey questions.)

Student Results

Student use of social media is unquestionably pervasive (see Figure 1). Not surprisingly, the sites that students use most are Facebook (95.7%), YouTube (88%), and Wikipedia (71.7%). A vast majority of students not only use these sites, they use them often. Three-quarters of the students surveyed view these applications multiple times each day. When asked whether they used these sites to find information for research projects, over half (57.4%) admit to such use, even though only 2% felt that professors (universally) accept this information (another 39.1% indicated that it depended on the professor, and 35.2% indicated it depended on the source).

While Facebook is the most popular social media tool, Wikipedia is by far the most popular

Figure 1. What social media sites do students use for class projects?

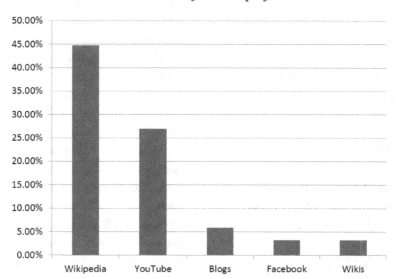

social media tool *for research*. Slightly more than 90% of student respondents reported using it as a quick reference for leisure purposes. A similar question asked if students used Wikipedia; 71.7% responded in the affirmative. More than half (52.4%) of students report using Wikipedia as a starting place for research projects, 39.8% follow the references at the ends of articles, and 7% would cite Wikipedia at the end of a research paper.

Students are evidently evaluating the information they find online. When asked how they judge the accuracy of information from sources such as Wikipedia or YouTube, 79.6% of students reported checking or comparing the information to other sources; however, 40.7% also admitted to relying on their own judgment. A majority of students (63.9%) reported that they do not trust the information in comments at the end of news articles. Students have more confidence in the suitability of online articles and books by scholars (94.4%) and in websites ending in .edu, .org., or .gov (86.1%), and 54.8% consider content identified by Google Scholar to be acceptable.

Students are using social media for class assignments in creative ways. In survey comments

and focus groups, a number of students indicated that they have used Facebook as a way to gather original research. With very little effort, they can post links or use the polls feature in Facebook to survey all their online friends. While this is not a random sample, it may be quite acceptable if they are trying to learn the opinions of college students. One student had posted a humorous clip on his or her Facebook wall and then looked at his or her peers' reactions to the clip to gather opinions about it. Since many students have hundreds of online friends, this may be an easier way to collect a large sample size for their projects than was ever practical with paper surveys.

Several trends emerged while comparing the class levels to one another. Students increasingly use social media applications for research as they progress through college. Freshmen are the least likely—only 47.8%—to use these Web 2.0 applications for research, and this gradually increases to 66.9% of seniors using these applications. Alarmingly, the percentage of students who say they trust content found anywhere on the Internet by using Google also gradually increases from 5.8% as freshmen to 14.5% as seniors. This should give us pause. One possible explanation might be that freshmen are more cautious about using non-traditional sources when they first enter college for fear of reprisal, but then become more comfortable doing so as they experiment with using such information and discover that faculty accept it. This might be worth exploring in future focus groups.

Faculty Results

A higher percentage of students than faculty use the six major social media sites listed in the survey, with the exception of blogs (Figure 2). However, many faculty of all ages are using social media sites. Like students, faculty primarily use Face-book (64%), YouTube (58.8%), and Wikipedia (54.4%). As expected, higher percentages of younger faculty (those teaching for less than 10 years) reported using five of the six social media tools on the survey and younger and older faculty were nearly equal in Wikipedia use (Figure 3). Frequency of use among faculty varied greatly. About 25% of faculty indicated heavy use at several times a day, another 25% use these sources

a few times a week, and another 25% use them a few times a month.

Students were correct in assuming that few faculty would accept information in a research paper from a social media source; only 1.8% of faculty say they would accept such information. However, just as students said much depended on the individual professor for this question, many professors (41.2%) also said it depended on the situation or assignment. When asked to elaborate, many faculty mentioned allowing students to use such sources for preliminary research followed by more credible sources. They also allowed their use for informal assignments, creative or non-traditional assignments, and class discussions; students were allowed to use primary source videos such as interviews and advertisements, scientific animations or demonstrations, and blogs written by recognized experts, and they could also gather opinions and document social behavior. While it is not surprising that so few professors allow the use of social media sources on student research assignments, it is surprising that nearly half of the faculty (46.5%) said that they use these

Figure 2. Comparison of faculty and student use of social media

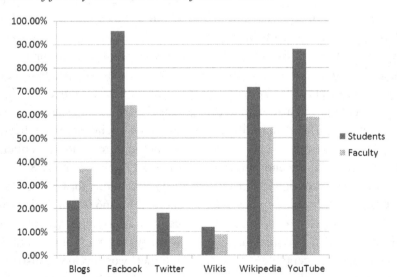

Figure 3. Faculty social media use by age

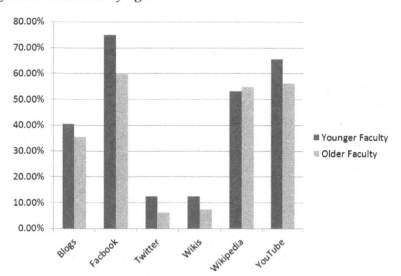

applications for their own research. This difference may be explained by the results of another question on the faculty survey, where only two faculty members (1.8%) agreed that students were capable of judging the validity of information on a social media source. Clearly, faculty members have little confidence in students' ability to evaluate information and have greater trust in their own judgment.

Currently, very few professors at the two schools surveyed are using social media in the classroom. Only 17 faculty members (14.9%) say they have designed assignments where students used social media tools under their supervision. While this is not a large number, it is more than we expected and we suspect that this number will grow in the future. These assignments have included requiring students to create original YouTube videos, wikis, and blog entries to report research progress. In addition, faculty post examples of their teaching materials online. Perhaps more enlightening are the instructions faculty give to students regarding the use of social media sources for research papers. Some faculty respondents (30.7%) say that they suggest Wikipedia as a starting place to begin research. Thirty respondents

(26.3%) said that students can responsibly put information from social media applications into context through class discussions, 35.1% require students to confirm the validity of information from such sources, and another 21.9% require students to check the references of the author. This may indicate that social media applications and evaluation skills are being discussed in a small but significant number of undergraduate classrooms.

Expertise in Social Media

Students and faculty offer remarkably similar definitions of an "expert" (Figure 4). Both groups continue to emphasize advanced degrees, experience, and publications, though it is surprising that students (90.7%) seem to value the advanced degree more than faculty do (75.4%). This difference is statistically significant with $\chi^2(1, N=654)=20.57$, $p<.001$. When faculty are compared by number of years teaching, newer faculty appear to value the degree more than older faculty do, though this difference is not quite statistically significant $\chi^2(1, N=114)=1.93$, $p>.05$. In both groups, very few interpreted extensive reading as a hobby, or following blogs and posting opinions as signs of

Figure 4. Indicators of scholarly expertise

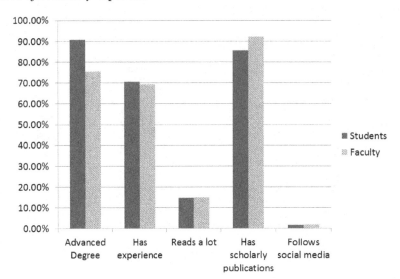

expertise. These results indicate that despite the changing media, they do not see the information from sources like Wikipedia as coming from "experts."

The survey offered only five suggestions for indicators of an expert, but the comments and focus groups provided additional indicators. Students value an author's educational affiliation with a prestigious university, and value traditional publications more than online ones. When looking at online publications, students evaluate the sponsoring agency as an indicator of author expertise. While only seven faculty members provided additional comments about experts, nearly all the faculty comments address the subjectivity of *any* indicator of an expert. One stressed the need for critical evaluation of all sources and authors, and added that peer-reviewed scholarly publications have "already been through some sort of filtering process." This subjectivity and the subsequent frustration were echoed in the student focus groups; students realized that authors can fake credentials, and that not all degrees and publications are equal. Students also lamented that in some fields like art, all expertise is subjective, and that in fields such as history, the same facts can elicit different, arguably valid opinions.

The focus group participants acknowledged the importance of using sources written by "experts" but they struggle to identify meaningful expertise.

While there is some indication in the literature that some professors nationally are improving Wikipedia by contributing to it (Chandler & Gregory, 2010; Grathwohl, 2011), few of the professors in our study are. Slightly more than 5% of faculty reported having contributed to Wikipedia as a volunteer, while 7.4% of students reported contributing to Wikipedia either as a volunteer (5.3%) or as part of a class project (3.3%; several students answered positively to both parts of this question). When this is combined with the comments on how faculty and students use social media sites such as Wikipedia and YouTube for research, it appears that our sample uses social media more as consumers than as active participants. Facebook appears to be an exception to this observation, though it is not often used for research. This merits further exploration in future studies.

Among students and faculty alike, there were many concerns about the issue of quality control. Some see the technologies developing to ensure the availability of more credible information while others see our society lowering its standards and surrendering to students' supposed apathy toward high-quality, scholarly information. Surprisingly, many students as well as faculty see traditional media and social media combining into new forms, such as scholarly collaborations to create peer-reviewed, open-access publications that are timelier and more affordable, and that allow authors to retain the copyright. Many others focused on social media's ability to facilitate communication and collaboration among scholars. A few mentioned the "softening" of the lines between scholarly and popular opinions, but a number of respondents mentioned the need to move forward and look at the future of knowledge in a new way just as we have come to accept updated methods of access such as online databases. As one faculty responder stated, "The 'great conversation' shifts its locus, and we're all able to participate."

DISCUSSION

Several overarching themes were shared by students and faculty alike, both in the comments and in the student focus groups. The first is that different academic disciplines use different types of information and communication sources. Many students and faculty showed specific uses for sites such as YouTube, which were particularly useful for the performing arts and for history for original video footage of historic events or interviews with eyewitnesses. One religion professor cited the emotional bias of biblical information on the Internet as the reason he/she forbids its use by students. Furthermore, indicators of expertise vary by discipline. One philosophy major in a focus group quipped that the criteria for being an expert in his field were that you had to be "(1) dead and (2) persecuted."

A second theme was that of social media as a means of communication. Throughout the survey comments and focus groups, faculty and students stressed social media sites as communication tools. While using social media primarily for social purposes, they might learn about news stories that their friends or professors have shared on Facebook. One professor said that he/she uses it to correspond with fellow scholars, but stressed that these correspondences complement rather than replace traditional connections and publications. Some students said that it is easier to communicate with their professors through Facebook than by email.

The final overarching theme is that of evaluation, which is fundamentally tangled in any discussion of the use of social media sources for undergraduate research. Readers have always had to evaluate the accuracy of the information they encounter, but now the medium is changing. As stated in our introduction, students used to have a limited amount of information available at their academic libraries. Small academic libraries with limited budgets provided limited choices. Students only had to evaluate the difference between a scholarly source versus a popular source, and whether a book or an article was more appropriate to their information needs. As technology changed, information became more accessible. Online databases made finding scholarly articles infinitely easier. Online journal packages brought a much larger variety of full-text scholarly journals to libraries at a more affordable price. In addition, the volume of information on the Web, regardless of quality, has exploded and continues to grow exponentially as it becomes continually easier for anyone to publish. Experts and amateurs alike collaborate to develop information. These collaborations produce conversations that lead to new concepts and ways of viewing the world without official peer review or publishing. While these casual scholarly conversations have always existed among intellectuals, the ease of publishing on the Internet has made the conversation more transparent, more accessible, and more participatory than ever before. Today's students, drowning in information, can easily be overwhelmed by this excess, which has also made the need for evaluation more important than ever before.

Although students and faculty agree that there is a new future for information, it raises many doubts for those who consider the implications carefully. While there is some legitimate assumption of accuracy in the information provided in the books and journals at an academic library, the information provided through social media applications increasingly places the burden of evaluation on the consumer. This affects faculty and students differently. Our results show that faculty members are more confident about using social media for their own research than they are about allowing students to use it. This is understandable, as faculty members are familiar with the scholarly discussions in their disciplines, which give them a larger framework for assessment of new information. In contrast, students have a smaller framework in which to incorporate and appraise new information. When traditional characteristics of expertise such as advanced degrees and traditional publications are weakened, students may not have the tools to adequately assess or take advantage of the transparent scholarly dialogues on the Internet.

Our results indicate that students are indeed selective in their choice of research-appropriate information, but faculty members do not seem satisfied with their evaluation skills. With little background knowledge, students cannot easily evaluate how the information in a source fits into the broader scholarly dialogue, which is often what experienced scholars would do. They must resort to relying on the stated objective qualifications of an author. Even in this case, they place more importance on degrees from some universities than others, without knowing anything about the individual programs from which those degrees come. Furthermore, if no such information is given, they place an alarming amount of trust in websites based purely on .edu or .org domain names. It is safe to conclude that they do think about the qualifications of an expert when selecting their resources, but their conclusions are often based on superficial evidence because they do not

have the depth of knowledge necessary for more meaningful analysis.

Although some faculty simply dismiss the information in sources such as Wikipedia and prohibit its use in student papers (just as they dismissed the Internet as a whole when it was new), our results show that many faculty see these new technologies as an opportunity to change knowledge. On the one hand, students take direction from their individual faculty members in what they *admit* they use for research papers (in the form of formal citations). On the other hand, just as they used to resort to information in general encyclopedias in the past, they will use social media sources regardless of their professors' directions—quietly and without citation. Instead, some professors seem to be opening up to another option that validates the legitimate uses that social media can provide. Faculty can help students develop the evaluation skills needed to discern good information in these sources and use them to explore the scholarly debates within their field.

While the teaching of information evaluation has long been seen as a role that academic librarians fill, teaching faculty may need to become stronger partners in this area. It was evident that the use of social media sources for research varies greatly from one academic discipline to another. Taking full advantage of the benefits that social media offer undergraduate students for research purposes requires subject knowledge that librarians may not have. However, this is also an advantage. With years of experience in their fields, professors forget how foreign the non-experts (their students) find the accepted jargon and practices within their fields. Librarians who understand research and the creation of scholarly knowledge in a broad sense, but are not practitioners in a particular academic discipline, can help bridge the gap between the experts (professors) and the novices (students). This offers an opportunity for librarians to work with faculty to teach the new information literacy skills required by these Web 2.0 applications.

It is clear from the overall results of this study that at the present time, those faculty and students who value the role social media play in undergraduate research see it as augmenting rather than replacing traditional publications and relationships. Scholars meet each other at conferences and continue their correspondence through Facebook. Both well-known scholars and new professors seeking tenure and promotion continue to publish in scholarly, peer-reviewed journals, yet sometimes post the results of their current research on blogs long before it is publishable in traditional venues. Professors have access to teaching materials on YouTube that undeniably enhance their own explanations. Students can effortlessly poll hundreds of online friends for a class project. They have access to millions of documentaries and interviews at their fingertips. They can quickly browse five Wikipedia articles to choose a topic for their research paper before committing themselves to research in books and articles. Clearly, there is a place in undergraduate research for social media alongside scholarly books and articles.

FUTURE RESEARCH DIRECTIONS

The present study only provides a preliminary picture of a change in the transmission of knowledge. One direction would include administering the survey to a larger population. Despite the fact that our two institutions are similar in many ways, the data gathered from each population was not identical. As opinions are likely to be influenced by the unique campus culture of each institution, we cannot claim that the same survey would yield matching results at other institutions. Our results only address the attitudes of undergraduates and faculty, but do not address those of graduate students or those of an institution heavily invested in research.

Another direction for future research would be to follow student and faculty attitudes as they

change over time. As faculty become more acquainted with the social media applications that their undergraduates are using, it is expected that some will begin to restructure their assignments to guide students through a new way of exploring research. We expect students' use of social media for research to grow in the future, and perhaps their contributions to grow as well.

Including additional social media options such as Google Docs, Skype, and Slideshare on the survey would likely change the responses, particularly among faculty. Our study primarily focused on how social media are being used for undergraduate research and only asked superficial questions about faculty uses for their own research. While CIBER's faculty survey (2010) is enlightening, more detailed use on how faculty use social media for research would be helpful.

The study generated much data, not all of it pertaining to our focused research questions. For example, the comments on the faculty survey regarding whether or not new knowledge is being created through social media are enough for a separate study. Another future study could focus on the increasing popularity of YouTube as a research resource. Wikipedia is likely to remain a dominant "go-to" source for quick information access, but we were surprised at how many respondents were using YouTube for research. One focus group participant noted that YouTube is "like a visual wiki" where one can quickly find information better suited to auditory and visual learners. YouTube may someday become a commonplace research starting point.

CONCLUSION

Current college students are past the tipping point when it comes to using social media. They are no longer using it just to socialize; they are using it to find background information, communicate with their professors, and gather original data. This information is adding content to their assignments and research papers, with or without citations, and with or without faculty approval. They are evaluating sources and looking for "expert" information, but do not necessarily have sufficient skills to do so.

Our results show that many faculty members are also using social media for personal and professional purposes. However, unlike those in Moran, Seaman, and Tinti-Kane's (2011) study, few of our professors are making use of social media in the classroom. Advocates of social media in the classroom, like McHaney (2011) and Rheingold (2010), stress that while students use social media for information purposes, they are not necessarily literate in these networks. If professors are not using these nearly ubiquitous tools in the classroom, students are not developing the necessarily literacies. It is past time for higher education to rethink its stance on social media and incorporate it into our students' education, teaching them Rheingold's (2010) five literacies to promote responsible use and promote lifelong learning.

We are not suggesting incorporating technology for technology's sake. This is an opportunity to rethink how we teach and engage students with the literacies necessary for today's world. It is an opportunity to combine evaluation skills of "good" and "bad" resources online with an introduction to an evaluation of the scholarly dialogue where many "good" sources never reach absolute agreement. This scholarly dialogue used to be either spread over many articles and books (making it difficult for students to assess the bigger picture), or held behind closed doors at conferences and personal communications among scholars. Now these dialogues are appearing on blogs, wikis, Facebook walls, and discussion boards. Regardless of the intended audience, students can see these debates and new findings in real time and in smaller, more manageable pieces. This offers exciting opportunities that allow students to observe the scholarly dialogue and to participate in it as novice scholars themselves. Furthermore,

when these discussions are opened to a broader audience, more participants will contribute, leading to new conclusions and innovative directions for research, thereby pushing the boundaries of knowledge.

Faculty and librarians worry about how undergraduates will be able to reach valid conclusions regarding the authenticity of such sources when the students are constantly overloaded with information. The knowledge that incorporates experiences is even more difficult to fold into the undergraduate learning environment, especially if it represents ongoing discussion in which ultimate certainty is never reached. These challenges will not disappear, but will instead become the future fabric of a liberal arts education.

REFERENCES

Anderson, C. (2004). The long tail. *Wired, 12*(10). Retrieved June 28, 2011, from http://www.wired.com/wired/archive/12.10/tail.html

Berinstein, P. (2006). Wikipedia and Britannica. *Searcher, 14*(3), 16–26.

Brown, J. S., & Adler, R. P. (2008). Minds on fire: Open education, the long tail, and learning 2.0. *EDUCASE Review, 43*(1), 16–32.

Chandler, C. J., & Gregory, A. S. (2010). Sleeping with the enemy: Wikipedia in the college classroom. *The History Teacher, 43*(2), 247–257.

CIBER. (2010). *Social media and research workflow*. Retrieved July 5, 2011 from http://www.ucl.ac.uk/infostudies/research/ciber/social-media-report.pdf

Deitering, A., & Gronemyer, K. (2011). Beyond peer-reviewed articles: Using blogs to enrich students' understanding of scholarly work. *portal: Libraries and the Academy, 11*(1), 489–503.

Desmet, C. (2009). Teaching Shakespeare with YouTube. *English Journal, 99*(1), 65–70.

Ericsson, K. A., Charness, N., Hoffman, R. R., & Feltovich, P. J. (Eds.). (2006). *Cambridge handbook of expertise and expert performance.* New York, NY: Cambridge University Press. doi:10.1017/CBO9780511816796

Giles, J. (2005). Internet encyclopaedias go head to head. *Nature, 438*(7070), 900–901. doi:10.1038/438900a

Gilroy, M. (2010). Higher education migrates to YouTube and social networks. *Education Digest: Essential Readings Condensed for Quick Review, 75*(7), 18–22.

Gladwell, M. (2000). *The tipping point: How little things can make a big difference.* Boston, MA: Little, Brown.

Grathwohl, C. (2011, January 7). Wikipedia comes of age. *Chronicle of Higher Education.* Retrieved September 22, 2011, from http://chronicle.com/article/article-content/125899/

How does Wikipedia measure up? (2008). *The Quill, 96*(9), 16-19.

Keen, A. (2007). *The cult of the amateur: How today's Internet is killing our culture.* New York, NY: Doubleday.

Lenhart, A., Purcell, K., Smith, A., & Zickuhr, K. (2010). Social media & mobile internet use among teens and young adults. *Pew Internet & American Life Project.* Retrieved September 22, 2011, from http://www.pewinternet.org/~/media//Files/Reports/2010/PIP_Social_Media_and_Young_Adults_Report_Final_with_toplines.pdf

Maloney, E. J. (2007). What Web 2.0 can teach us about learning. *Chronicle of Higher Education, 53*(18). Retrieved June 28, 2011, from http://chronicle.com

McHaney, R. (2011). *The new digital shoreline: How Web 2.0 and Millennials are revolutionizing higher education.* Sterling, VA: Stylus Publishing, LCC.

Moran, M., Seaman, J., & Tinti-Kane, H. (2011). *Teaching, learning, and sharing: How today's higher education faculty use social media.* Retrieved September 12, 2011, from http://www.babson.edu/Academics/Documents/babson-survey-research-group/teaching-learning-and-sharing.pdf

Parry, M. (2011, February 20). Free "video book" from MIT Press challenges limits of scholarship. *Chronicle of Higher Education.* Retrieved September 17, 2011, from http://chronicle.com/article/Free-Video-Book-From/126427

Rheingold, H. (2009). Crap detection 101. *SFGate.* Retrieved September 22, 2011, from http://blog.sfgate.com/rheingold/2009/06/30/crap-detection-101/

Rheingold, H. (2010). Attention, and other 21st-century social media literacies. *EDUCAUSE Review, 45*(5), 14–24.

SAS Institute. (2008). *SAS* (version 9.1) .

Shirky, C. (2008). *Here comes everybody.* Presentation at Web 2.0 Expo, April 22–25 in San Francisco. Retrieved June 28, 2011, from http://www.blip.tv/file/855937

ADDITIONAL READING

Bassford, M., & Ivins, J. (2010). Encouraging formative peer review via social networking sites. *British Journal of Educational Technology, 41*(5), E67–E69. doi:10.1111/j.1467-8535.2009.00936.x

Baytiyeh, H., & Pfaffman, J. (2010). Volunteers in Wikipedia: Why the community matters. *Journal of Educational Technology & Society, 13*(2), 128–140.

Callanan, L. (2004). Defining expertise in the interdisciplinary classroom. *Pedagogy: Critical Approaches to Teaching Literature, Language, Composition, and Culture, 4*(3), 385–399. doi:10.1215/15314200-4-3-385

Cheuk, B. (2007). Social networking analysis: Its application to facilitate knowledge transfer. *Business Information Review, 24*(3), 170–176. doi:10.1177/0266382107081612

Collis, B., & Moonen, J. (2008). Web 2.0 tools and processes in higher education: Quality perspectives. *Educational Media International, 45*(2), 93–106. doi:10.1080/09523980802107179

Golian-Lui, L. M. (2011). Social networking: Strategic use and effective policies in higher education. *Library Issues, 31*(3).

Greenhow, C. (2009). Social scholarship: Applying social networking technologies to research practices. *Knowledge Quest, 37*(4), 42–47.

Gruber, T. (2008). Collective knowledge systems: Where the Social Web meets the Semantic Web. *Web Semantics: Science. Services and Agents on the World Wide Web, 6*(1), 4–13. doi:10.1016/j.websem.2007.11.011

Raban, D. R., & Rafaeli, S. (2007). Investigating ownership and the willingness to share information online. *Computers in Human Behavior, 23*(5), 2367–2382. doi:10.1016/j.chb.2006.03.013

Shachaf, P. (2009). The paradox of expertise: Is the Wikipedia reference desk as good as your library? *The Journal of Documentation, 65*(6), 977–996. doi:10.1108/00220410910998951

Shirky, C. (2008). *Here comes everybody: The power of organizing without organizations*. New York, NY: Penguin Press.

KEY TERMS AND DEFINITIONS

Knowledge Creation: The act of constructing new understanding by gathering, reviewing, and assimilating material from a number of sources, undertaken by scholars or experts in a field or discipline.

Peer Review: A process in academic publishing where an author's manuscript must be reviewed and approved by at least one specialist in that discipline before being published.

Social Media: Online technologies that allow users to communicate and collaborate.

Social Networking: One example of social media that focuses on the social relationships of its participants.

User-Generated Content: Material created and posted online, often developed in collaborative or aggregate ways, by many individual users of social media in a wide variety of media forms.

Web 2.0: A term to describe the second generation of Web technologies that allow Web users to easily participate and create content, not just view static information posted by others.

APPENDIX A: FACULTY SURVEY

SOCIAL NETWORKING AND ACADEMIC RESEARCH

These questions are about social networking applications. Common ones used by college students and some faculty are Facebook, Wikipedia, and YouTube. We generally think of social networking as online activities that we use outside of the classroom. The overall definition of social networking focuses on building relationships via computers among people with common interests who want to share information. This survey focuses on the new information that these applications may make available to us, and the possibility that the information could be used with your own research or for undergraduate research.

1. How many years have you been teaching?
_____ 1–3
_____ 4–6
_____ 7–9
_____ 10–12
_____ 12–15
_____ More than 16

2. I teach at _____ School A _____ School B

3. Mark the social networking applications that you use:
_____ Blogs
_____ Facebook
_____ Twitter
_____ Wikis
_____ Wikipedia
_____ YouTube
Others: (please specify) _____

4. How often do you use these applications or others like them?
_____ several times a day
_____ once a day
_____ a few times a week
_____ a few times a month
_____ never

5. Do you believe that information on social networking applications like Wikipedia or YouTube is a new way of creating knowledge that has never been available for scholarly research under the traditional publication model?
_____ yes
_____ no
Explain: _____

6. Do you accept information on student research papers that comes from these social networking sources?
_____ yes
_____ no
_____ depends on the particular assignment
_____ depends on the particular social networking application

Please give some examples of acceptable applications:
_____

7. Do you ever use these social networking applications or others like them to find information for your own research?
_____ yes
_____ no

8. Online articles (for example, articles on CNN.com) are often followed by comments added by other readers. Check all the statements that are true for you:
_____ I read these comments.
_____ I add to these comments.
_____ I would consider using some of the information in these comments for my own research.
_____ I accept information from these comments as cited works on students' research papers.
_____ I do not trust the information in these comments.

9. Consider your use of Wikipedia: Check all the statements that are true for you:

_____ I use Wikipedia as a quick reference for leisure purposes- - biography, quick facts.

_____ I suggest Wikipedia to students as a place for students to begin research.

_____ I use Wikipedia instead of an encyclopedia.

_____ I use Wikipedia because it represents a diverse group of volunteers offering information.

_____ I follow the references at the ends of articles in Wikipedia for my own research.

_____ I have contributed to information in Wikipedia as a volunteer.

_____ I do not use Wikipedia.

10. What instructions do you give to students about using information from social networking sources for research papers or class assignments? Check all that apply:

_____ Through class discussions, students are able to put such information in an appropriate context and use the material in a responsible manner.

_____ Students are required to properly cite information from these sources.

_____ Students are required to verify or confirm validity of such information in a second source.

_____ Students are required to check references of the author/content-owner.

_____ I believe students can determine the reliability/validity of online information using their own judgment.

_____ I encourage students to be creative when using social networking sources and have no restrictions.

_____ I believe students can judge whether a social source is reputable or not.

_____ As a class, my students and I participate in creating content for social sites such as:

_____

_____ No instructions are given; students use their own discretion or I open a discussion about questionable material on a class assignment.

_____ Students may not use information from social sites as research in my courses.

Other comments:_____

_____

11. How would you define an "expert" who can give "expert information?" Check all that apply.

_____ Someone who studied in a subject area and obtained an advanced degree from a university

_____ Someone who has a lot of experience in a particular field or subject area

_____ Someone who reads a lot about a subject and considers it a special interest or hobby

_____ Someone who has done scholarly research on a particular topic which has been published in a peer-reviewed journal or edited book

_____ Someone who follows wikis or blogs and posts their opinions about a topic

Other comments about what an expert is:

_____

12. Have you assigned/allowed your students to share or create information for classes under your supervision using blogs, wikis, Facebook, YouTube, or similar social networking applications?

_____yes _____no

If yes, in which course(s) or subject area? _____

13. If you were to predict the future, would you anticipate that more scholarly and expert material will appear in social networking applications on the Web? Please comment:

_____

_____

APPENDIX B: STUDENT SURVEY

SOCIAL NETWORKING AND ACADEMIC RESEARCH

These questions are about social networking applications. Common ones used by college students are Facebook, Wikipedia, and YouTube. We generally think of social networking as online activities that students use outside of the classroom. The overall definition of social networking focuses on building relationships via computers among people with common interests who want to share information. This survey focuses on the new information that these applications may make available to us, and the possibility that the information could be used for your own research or for undergraduate research in general.

1. Tell us a little about yourself:
Academic level: _____ Freshman _____ Sophomore _____ Junior _____ Senior
Gender: _____ Male _____ Female
Major: _____
I attend _____ School A _____ School B

2. Mark the social media applications that you read/contribute to: (Check all that apply)
_____ Blogs
_____ Facebook
_____ Twitter
_____ Wikis
_____ Wikipedia
_____ YouTube

3. How often do you read/contribute to these applications or others like them?
_____ Several times a day
_____ Once a day
_____ A few times a week
_____ A few times a month
_____ Never

4. Do you ever utilize these social networking applications or others like them to find information for research projects?
_____ Yes
_____ No
If "Yes", which ones? _____

5. Do you believe that your professors accept information that comes from these social networking sources?
_____ Yes
_____ No
_____ Depends on the individual professor
_____ Depends on the source

6. How can you tell if information found on applications such as Wikipedia or YouTube is accurate and conveys knowledge? Check all that apply:
_____ I trust what is on the Web.
_____ I check/compare the information to other sources.
_____ I verify the author(s) credentials.
_____ I use my own judgment depending on each situation.
_____ Other (Please specify):_____

7. Online articles (for example, articles on CNN.com) are often followed by comments added by other readers. Check all the statements that are true for you:
_____ I read these comments.
_____ I add to these comments.
_____ I would consider using some of the information in these comments for a research project.
_____ I would cite these comments in a research paper.
_____ I do not trust the information in these comments.

8. Which of the following statements applies to your use of Wikipedia: Check all that are true for you:

_____ I use Wikipedia as a quick reference for leisure purposes- - biography, quick facts

_____ I use Wikipedia as a place to start a research project.

_____ I use Wikipedia instead of an encyclopedia.

_____ I use Wikipedia because it represents diverse group of volunteers offering information.

_____ I follow the references at the ends of articles in Wikipedia.

_____ I always cite Wikipedia if I use it for a college research project.

_____ I have contributed to information in Wikipedia as a volunteer.

_____ I have contributed to information in Wikipedia as part of a course assignment.

9. From which online sources do you believe your professor would accept research as being "legitimate" or "expert?" Check all that apply:

_____ Web sites/content found anywhere on the Internet using Google or similar search tools

_____ Web sites/content with edu, .org, .gov, or similar non-commercial domain

_____ Online books/articles/ content written by scholars in a specialized subject area

_____ Any books/articles/content found on the Web

_____ Content/information found through Google Scholar

_____ Content/information found at social networking sites written by a community of volunteers using the site, e.g. Wikipedia, blogs, wikis, Facebook, etc

_____ Content/information found at *certain* social networking sites.

Other: (Please specify) _____

10. How would you define an "expert" who can give "expert information?" Check all that apply:

_____ Someone who studied in a subject area and obtained an advanced degree from a university

_____ Someone who has a lot of experience in a particular field or subject area

_____ Someone who reads a lot about a subject and considers it a special interest or hobby

_____ Someone who has conducted scholarly research on a particular topic and had their work published

_____ Someone who follows wikis or blogs and posts their opinions about a topic

Other (Please specify):

_____

11. Have you shared or created information for classes under the supervision of your faculty member using blogs, wikis, Facebook, YouTube, or similar social networking applications?

_____ Yes _____ No

12. If you were to predict the future, would you anticipate that more scholarly and expert material will appear in social networking applications on the Web? Please comment:

_____

_____

Chapter 14

Textperts:
Utilizing Students' Skills in the Teaching of Writing

Abigail A. Grant
Indiana University of Pennsylvania, USA

ABSTRACT

Text messaging has many similarities to poetry or short prose writing. Instructors typically discount text messaging as a distraction in the classroom, but this chapter includes a review of the positive aspects of implementing the genre of text messaging in the composition classroom as a means of teaching writing. Using a community of practice approach, this chapter looks at the technologically savvy generation of college students in today's classrooms and attempts to capitalize, educationally, on the writing skills that students already possess. Next, it explores both the theoretical and practical implementations of this genre into the composition classroom with careful consideration of the positive and negative impacts of this, before examining the transition from student text messaging to the writing of other, longer genres. Although this chapter's focus is on the teaching of writing, the information can be considered to be interdisciplinary.

INTRODUCTION

I do want to argue that teachers of composition need to pay attention to, and come to value, the multiple ways in which students compose and communicate meaning, the exciting hybrid, multimodal texts they create—in both non-digital and digital environments—to meet their own needs in a changing world. We need to better understand the importance that students attach to composing, exchanging, and interpreting new different kinds of texts that help them make sense of their experiences and lives—songs and lyrics, videos, written essays illustrated with images, personal web pages that includes sound clips. We need to learn from their motivated efforts to communicate with each other, for themselves and for others, often in resistance to the world we have created for them. We need to respect the rhetorical sovereignty of young people from different backgrounds,

DOI: 10.4018/978-1-4666-2178-7.ch014

communities, colors, and cultures, to observe and understand the rhetorical choices they are making, and to offer them new ways of making meaning, new choices, new ways accomplishing their goals. – Cynthia Selfe (2009)

As Web 2.0 technologies become more mainstream and part of students' everyday lives, we, as instructors, have to consider the implications of these technologies on student learning and the possibilities that they may hold for instruction. Text messaging, in particular, has become a part of students' everyday lives; something that they will not even put away for the duration of a 50-minute class. Despite the criticism that texting in the classroom usually garners from many faculty members, I believe that understanding and accepting text messaging as an effective means of communication is a great step toward developing the technological relationship between students and teachers. By incorporating text messaging into classrooms, instructors are welcoming a skill set that college-aged students value tremendously. Text messaging makes the students the experts in technology, and in this case, in writing in a format they know very well. For too long, text messaging has been looked upon as a mode of writing unsuited for academic purposes. It may not be the ideal type of writing that composition instructors are looking for, but it is its own unique genre of writing and students, as experts of this genre, should be praised for their writing developments and efforts. Cynthia Selfe (1999) has rallied for an understanding of technological literacy and its role in the composition classroom. According to Selfe, *technological literacy* is defined as "a complex set of socially and culturally situated values, practices, and skills involved in operating linguistically within the context of electronic environments, including reading, writing, and communicating" (p. 11). This chapter considers text messaging as a growing social software in and outside of the classroom, and, as with all Web 2.0 technologies, not something that can be ignored

for its communicative opportunities. The most positive effect of utilizing text messaging in the classroom is that bestowing agency on students as "textperts"—technological experts in text messaging writing skills—may result in an increase in student interest in writing, and. Using texting as an instruction tool in the classroom can also provide an opportunity to discuss the rights and responsibilities of digital citizenship. Although this chapter will focus on the role that texting can play in the composition classroom, the suggestions I make may be adapted and applied productively across different disciplines.

BACKGROUND

Cynthia Selfe's (2009) words quoted at the beginning of this chapter serve as a starting point for considering text messaging as a community of practice in which sometimes the students are experts and the instructors are novices. Selfe argues that instructors should take the unique opportunities that various demographics of students offer in regards to teaching and learning composition. In my experience with composition students, these opportunities would include striving to understand their preferred modes of communication and writing, and using that as a starting ground for other types of writing. One of the key elements of Selfe's argument is *respect*: having respect for our students' abilities, capabilities, and rhetorical interests. Banning text messaging based on our own assumptions about that technology does a great disservice to our students.

Utilization of text messaging for composition studies is still relatively new. Mahatanankoon and O'Sullivan (2008) discuss the concerns of computer anxiety as it applies to text messaging: "[a]lthough text messaging use has grown dramatically in recent years, this means of communication … are still unfamiliar to the many newer adopters and as such is potentially anxiety provoking" (p. 980). Since Mahatanankoon and O'Sullivan wrote their article in 2008, text messaging usage has grown exponentially, especially among the college-aged students of our classrooms (Crystal, 2008, p. 90).

Other scholars, such as Boettcher and Conrad (2010), identify text messaging as an effective means of communication, as "good nearly synchronous tools that faculty can use to be available for quick information checks, for example, before an assignment is due" (p. 59). In this situation, the authors are referring to allowing text messaging between students and the instructors in an online setting for, as they call it, "quick information checks." Boettcher and Conrad also consider the effectiveness of peer communication via text messaging for group assignments and course collaboration. I recently started considering texting as a form of writing in light of Sweeny's (2010) assertion that "[t]eens use technology for creative and collaborative communication and experiment with different applications to express their own personalities. Their use is tied to socializing and obtaining feedback from others" (p. 124). As an instructor in the composition classroom, my goal is to provide students with the motivation and agency to "play" with their writing and develop their writer's voice, without neglecting the communicative voices that they have already developed through technologies such as text messaging and Facebook. Willigham (2009) maintains that in order for students to compile knowledge, they need to be able to connect a lesson to something with which they are familiar. He claims that "[k]nowledge is more important [than imagination], because it is a perquisite for imagination, or at least for the sort of imagination that leads to problem solving, decision making, and creativity" (p. 46). Therefore, as instructors, we need to ensure that students have the opportunity to exercise their creativity by nurturing the skills that they already have and use. Contextualizing a writing assignment within a familiar technological framework allows for greater student agency and creativity.

Seeking and soliciting feedback from others is one of the most important parts of the writing process, typically found in an environment known as the writers' workshop. Though this is typical for creative writing courses, it is often neglected in other types of classes, including the traditional composition classroom. Text messaging can thus be a way to solicit "User participation in the form of writing feedback, suggestions, and ideas generated by other writers" (Sweeny, 2010, p. 125). This is a way to have students invest in their own writing in a manner that is comfortable to them because the technology is familiar. According to Choi and Ho (2002), this implication of technology allows users to utilize their experience and creates agency in students related to their technological capabilities. Therefore, texting allows students to assume agency over their own writing, something that may have a broadening and positive impact on the rest of their education.

According to Frey, Fisher, and Gonzalez (2010), "Encouraging students to use current technology—to power up—allows them to interact with the curriculum and with one another in ways that teachers of the past could only have hoped for" (p. 112). Just because an instructor is be wary of new technologies does not mean that it is not an acceptable or preferred practice for student learning. With regard to writing, text messaging could allow for the collaboration, learning, and productivity necessary for ensuring student success. O'Connell (2010) discusses text messaging as a mode of communication that avoids direct face-to-face contact, an aspect of text messaging that many users enjoy. The isolation of text messaging parallels many of the writing tasks assigned in composition classes in which students are expected to work independently to create a draft. By utilizing a technology that students already use in their everyday lives, the learning potential is realized: students can write in a mode they like while practicing the skills relevant to the traditional writing process.

Students want to write and enjoy doing it every day. They just do not seem to be very keen on writing in the genres that their instructors typically require. They text message, Tweet, Facebook, note, email, list, save, and edit. Although these processes may not be in the form of research papers, they should not be discredited. I have witnessed my undergraduate students discussing word choices in text messages, peer reviewing their messages, and having extensive conversations about the connotation of text messages they both receive and send. These mini-composition lessons are conducted both in groups and alone and strengthen their understanding and conveyance of ideas in various genres. Therefore, students are already familiar with many of the processes of the first-year composition course; they are just not accustomed to the terminology of the discipline. By recognizing students as experts in these writing and editing processes, we welcome them into this community of scholarship based on their familiarity with the processes rather than isolate them based on what they do not know (Grant, 2011).

Texting in the Classroom and Digital Citizenship

An interdisciplinary consideration of the use of text messaging for educational purposes is Sweeny's identification of an opportunity for students learning about "digital citizenship." She defines "digital citizenship" as an "understand[ing of] human, cultural, and societal issues related to technology and practicing legal and ethical behavior in digital environments" (p. 123). Digital citizenship can also be defined as an individual taking steps to become an invested member of a digital or technological community. This may come in the form of classroom involvement, a business relationship, or general technological involvement with society (social networking). With the face of technology and society rapidly changing, it seems in the best interest of students to prepare them for these rapid changes and to teach them to be responsible citizens of this digital age.

Traditions and social norms shift as technology continues to be a part of everyday life. For example, Crystal (2008) shares an anecdote concerning a Filipino woman attending a funeral who "was not surprised when at the wake for a friend's father she saw people bowing their heads and gazing toward folded hands ... 'People were actually sitting there and texting ... Filipinos don't see it as rude anymore'" (p. 95). This may be an extreme case of the social changes unfolding in the digital age, but it calls attention to a glaring pedagogical need: instructors need to be equipped to help students navigate their appropriate place in society today without ignoring the technology. This situation also demonstrates the impact of digital citizenship on our traditional or mainstream culture: social protocol regarding technology and communication is rapidly changing to incorporate communicative methods including text messaging. Instructors may need to discuss with students the etiquette of using texting in different social situations, but should also consider adding text messaging into their repertoire of increasingly socially acceptable correspondence.

One of the goals of acquiring a sense of digital citizenship is to "exhibit a positive attitude toward using technology that supports collaboration, learning, and productivity" (Sweeny, 2010, p. 123). Text messaging is not a technological advance that is going to fade away in the near future; its popularity is constantly growing. Therefore, instructors need to nurture a more positive attitude and need to be more willing to accept and utilize technology such as text messaging in the classroom.

Reframing Instructors' Anxieties about Texting in the Classroom

Most instructors worry that, if given the chance to text in class, students will pay attention to their phones and not pay attention to the classroom or writing activities. In my experience, *they already do*. Embracing the genre of texting and the unique opportunities it offers in terms of writing can detract from the "taboo" nature of texting in class and make it a technology and genre that is encouraged. Rather than *deny a behavior*, I believe that we should *encourage their writing*. Sweeney (2010) echoes this in her rationale for incorporating new literacies: "Teachers may be concerned about the way some students write using these different ICTs [information and communication technologies], imaging the potential negative impact on their students' academic writing, but this interest can be an instructional advantage" (p. 121). Selfe (2009) and the thematic development of the field of "computers and writing" have become accustomed to the consideration of moving the idea of writing *off* of the page and, now, even away from traditional word processing. A move from the PowerPoint type of presentation to a Prezi presentation serves as an example of a transition to a non-linear, multimodal technology utilized for writing and presenting. The 2012 call for papers for the Computers and Writing conference asks for scholars to consider multimodality in a variety of manners and to question the ways in which we have previously described "writing" and "composition" (North Carolina State University, 2011). Therefore, text messaging has inherent composition instructional capabilities such as brainstorming, following the writing process, editing for clarity and word limitation, eliminating wordiness, and clarification of the expected outcome of a text, but the instructors' biases about writing may prohibit such opportunities.

Instructors may also believe that text messaging diminishes the writing and spelling abilities of students because of the use of shorthand and abbreviations, oftentimes made-up abbreviations. According to Wood, Jackson, Hart, Plester, and Wilde (2011), who conducted a study dealing with the effects of text messaging on 9- and 10-year-old children's reading abilities, spelling, and phonological processing skills, "the results indicated that "within the mobile phone group, there was evidence that use of text abbreviations was positively related to gains in literacy skills." The conclusions also show "that text messaging does not adversely affect the development of

literacy skills within this age group, and that the children's use of textisms when text messaging is positively related to improvement in literacy skills, especially spelling" (p. 28). Although this study refers to a younger demographic, many of its findings are transferable to the demographic of current college undergraduates considering a greater opportunity for their affiliation as "digital natives" (Prensky, 2001). Much of the current demographic of first-year composition students have had cell phones since they were tweens. Taking into account the level of digital citizenship of our individual students is a necessary step toward understanding their capabilities with writing and technology in general. If we have students who are willing, able, and prefer to write utilizing multimodal technologies, why should we stop them because of our uncertainty or unwillingness? Though we should not assume that all of our students are digital natives, instructors should take advantage of the opportunities these technologies present (Amicucci, 2011).

Recent research on the effects of literacy skills on college-aged students who used text messaging conducted by Drouin (2011) found that there are "significant, *positive* relationships between text messaging frequency and literacy skills (spelling and reading fluency)" (p. 67). In these findings, Drouin points out that there may be a miscommunication between instructors and students. Drouin's study was based on 152 college students at a midsize university who were tested for grammar, literacy ability, and textese fluency and frequency. The author then analyzed the data comparing texting frequency to grammatical and literacy abilities to determine a possible correlation, which indicated a positive relationship, as described above.

A study on SMS conducted by Shafie, Azida, and Osman (2010) was concerned with the possible negative ramifications of text messaging on students' writing and spelling abilities. One of the research conclusions from this study, however, indicates that "students know the different style of language to be used during formal and informal situations. This ability to switch and use the language accordingly enables young people to use proper English and texted English appropriately" (p. 30). I will explain ways in which text messaging can be utilized in the classroom, taking into consideration the particular constraints of the genre, later in this chapter.

Texting and Multitasking as Instructional Assets

Current research argues both sides of the multitasking argument: multitasking has dramatically negative effects on individuals' cognitive abilities *or* multitasking is reprogramming the ways in which today's students think and operate, which may not be a bad thing in itself. Baron (2008) takes the middle ground of this argument in asking, "Is multitasking with communication technologies necessarily detrimental to cognitive performance? The answer may reflect the extent to which people think of themselves as doing multitasking" (p. 39). Baron argues that multitasking comes naturally to students as they are used to working with computers which are "naturally multitasking devices" (p. 39). Integrating text messaging into the classroom can be viewed on the positive end of the multitasking spectrum. Student text messaging will be twofold: they will satisfy their innate *want* to send text messages only in the context of a class assignment and will work on their writing at the same time. As outlined in "Utilizing Texting in the Classroom," below, there are a number of ways for an instructor to choose to integrate text messaging into classroom discussion or writing activities, some of which involve students multitasking. For instance, students could be asked to participate in a texting poll on a subject question in the duration of a course period.

The detriment, as identified by Baron, is that multitasking is a skill that escapes the capacity of comfort in anyone other than teenagers and young adults. However, Baron does point out that many activities that older adults perform—such as driving a car—constitute multitasking. This, as with any other form of multitasking, is a skill that develops with practice and over a period of time: "in learning to drive a car, the ability to look three places at once develops with experience" (p. 39). Though older adults may need to practice newer technologies in order to gain a sense of comfort in their abilities when it comes to using technology, our students are already much more tech-savvy and, therefore, more comfortable with their multitasking abilities. We may be doing our students a disservice in writing off the abilities they have acquired thorough their use of technology and text messaging, especially when we consider that "42 percent of teenage cellphone users boast the ability to text while blindfolded" (p. 1051). This statistic may be taken as empowering in terms of the potential it offers to instructors to harness students' aptitudes for instructional purposes. As an instructor, I would be thrilled to know that students are working on my class assignments outside the classroom, even if they are combining them with other activities.

And even the definition of multitasking is under debate. Researchers at Stanford University working with the concept of multitasking have made a distinction between multitasking and what they consider to be "media multitasking," a specific kind of multitasking that is popular among youth and includes texting, checking email, or listening to television or music while doing other things (Ballagas, 2010, p. 1). These researchers coined that term following several studies that demonstrated disjointed results in youths' abilities to multitask as compared with their ability to multitask with social media devices. Ballagas argues that media multitasking is not the same as traditional multitasking where the focus is on "switching attention back and forth" (p. 1). Media multitasking, he argues, is "about directing attention in a new way," something that is becoming more of a way of life for those invested in multimodal communications rather than a distraction from a preferred location (p. 1). This research demonstrates that students who are media multitasking in class (texting and writing a draft of a paper) are not necessarily breaking their attention from the task at hand; the influence of media has made this a more fluid transition while simultaneously accomplishing two tasks. Research is beginning to show that young adults are comfortable with the process of media multitasking and that the process of doing multiple things at once in the context of technology is becoming a mainstream expectation in American society.

Utilizing Texting in the Classroom

Depending on how the instructor utilizes text messaging in the classroom, students may have to use their cell phones during a class period. Perhaps not all students will have cell phones, and some students will be distracted by others using their phones and dislike the activity. To alleviate such concerns, having a democratic classroom discussion at the beginning of the course will create a framework for text messaging in the classroom, and give students an opportunity to voice their ideas, concerns, and questions.

There are multiple ways in which text messaging *can* be used in the classroom, all of which rely on the 160-character limit. For instance, use text messaging as a means to demonstrate its connections to poetry, including significance of word choice and punctuation. Students can be given a short poem, such as William Carlos Williams's "This Is Just to Say," and be asked to adapt it into text message form or write their own piece in a similar fashion. Having to work within such a strict character limit, students learn that they need to choose their words, punctuation, ideas, transitions, and connections very carefully. Instructors could use this opportunity to discuss the effects of punctuation or rhymes on meaning in poetry. If an instructor wanted to allow students to use their cell phones in the classroom, students could draft this assignment on their phones. If an

instructor is not comfortable allowing the use of cell phones, students may write their ideas and drafts on a piece of paper, while keeping track of character limits (including spaces and punctuations). Working within a limited character set such as the one afforded by a text message is also an effective means of practicing proofreading and editing skills. If students have difficulties with wordiness in their writing, text messaging provides a definitive character limit as a starting ground for producing quality poetry and prose.

Instructors can also use text messaging as a means to discuss characterizations of genre. For instance, what are the characteristics of a text message? Of a poem? How are these similar? How are these different? What are audience considerations of text messages, poems, emails, research papers, and other genres? For instructors who may be less comfortable with the use of cell phones in class, now is the time to discuss that characteristic of text messaging. What are the positives and negatives of each and any of these forms of communications? At a recent conference presentation on using text messaging to teach composition, participants questioned the appropriateness of using cell phones or text messaging as a means of classroom engagement. Some argued that allowing text messaging in the classroom would be a disservice to students for when they enter the workforce. Other participants countered this claim by arguing that most work environments are relatively cell-phone friendly. This type of discussion is easily transferable to the undergraduate composition classroom in order to discuss appropriateness of genre in given contexts, which is also a discussion about the rights and responsibilities of digital citizenship. Students could be divided by majors or career interests and asked to brainstorm the appropriateness of cell phone usage or text messaging in their career paths. From there, they could discuss other genres of writing that are used in their careers and the similarities and differences of the genres.

Text messaging can be used as a building block to writing longer prose. This can be done as a step-by-step process beginning with text messaging as poetry and then moving into complete sentences, then paragraphs, and so forth. Or, an instructor could use text messaging to demonstrate the similarities of and differences between the type of language that is typically used in text messaging, "textese," and the language of complete sentences and academic writing. These exercises may take the form of mini lessons, such as drafting cause and effect text messages, compare and contrast text messages, or descriptions, or writing succinct thesis statements.

Text messaging also presents a potential for communicating in larger lecture courses via question and response. Cheung (2008) "demonstrates how mobile phone text messaging can be used to overcome the limitations of pencil-and-paper experiments without incurring the costs of full computerization" (p. 51). For instance, websites such as Poll Everywhere (2011) allow instructors or meeting organizers to allow audience interactions through text-messaging polls. Perhaps at the beginning of a class period, an instructor could pose a question to the class with a variety of options posted on Poll Everywhere. At a certain time or throughout the class, students have the opportunity to text their response to a predetermined Poll Everywhere number that would report on the instructors' computer screen or on a projected screen, if available. This is a way in which all students can take an active approach to their course and be involved in a classroom environment that is traditionally isolating. By working within the comfort level of the students, instructors allow for greater student investment in coursework and in their own learning. This also creates agency for students who may be confident about their ability to answer or their knowledge of a subject but are apprehensive about speaking in front of their classmates.

Regardless of what methods the instructor uses to incorporate text messaging into the classroom, the importance of using text messaging as a mode of writing is that it allows students to feel in control of their writing. By affording them the title of "expert" of a particular genre, students will feel that they are capable of completing a number of writing tasks. In considering students as experts, instructors need to work with their individual classes to negotiate the ways in which technology can be utilized most effectively for each group of students.

FUTURE RESEARCH DIRECTIONS

Much research still remains to be conducted in the area of text messaging as a means to teach composition and to be incorporated into instruction in other disciplines. This is an emerging area of study, especially in conjunction with other technologies with similar character limits, such as Twitter. Baseline studies need to be conducted in order to assess students' willingness and interest in using their personal technologies as an extension of the writing classrooms. Will they see it as a fun activity that expands their academic experience or will they view it as an infringement upon their personal technological territory?

Empirical studies need to be conducted in classrooms that utilize text messaging and also those that do not in order to examine the effectiveness of such a technology in a writing class. As with many specific technologies, instructors are just now beginning to explore the opportunities that these technologies have to offer for composition students. Therefore, the more qualitative, quantitative, and rhetorical research conducted on any and all of these technologies the greater our understanding of the possibilities and instructional effectiveness of these technologies. Additional studies outside of the classroom, such as that of Maher et al. (2010), need to be examined to allow us to consider the impact of text messaging as a form of communication, which will also help facilitate additional discussion of students as experts and the capabilities that status affords students in their classroom environments.

CONCLUSION

Although instructors, myself included, may be apprehensive about the incorporation of a technological aspect such as text messaging to learning, there are positive effects from such a decision. By embracing text messaging as a possible classroom technology, instructors will likely find an increased interest in writing, greater awareness of digital literacy, and a productive way to deal with multitasking in the classroom. By allowing students to incorporate the skills that they already possess into the composition classroom, and validating their previous knowledge about technology, instructors acknowledge their students' position as experts in this technology and so encourage them to take greater responsibility over their writing skills. As technology continues to develop, so will the abilities, capabilities, and expectations of students. Instructors need to stay abreast of these advances to best meet changing student needs. Text messaging is just one of the technological modes that have a significant following among present-day students and may have implications on the ways in which students want to learn in the future. Though there may still be pros and cons to the implementation of these technologies, instructors may find it rewarding to explore this opportunity to provide technologically-savvy youth with writing projects that stimulate and build upon the literacy skills that they already possess.

REFERENCES

Amicucci, A. N. (2011, May). *They aren't all digital natives: Dismantling myths about students' relationships with technology.* Research presented at the meeting of Computers and Writing, Ann Arbor.

Ballagas, R. (2010). *"Media multitasking" is not always multitasking.* Nokia Research Center. Retrieved March 4, 2011, from www.stanford.edu/group/multitasking/memos/Ballegas_Multitasking_Memo.pdf.

Baron, N. (2008). *Always on: Language in an online and mobile world.* Oxford, UK: Oxford University Press.

Boettcher, J. V., & Conrad, R. (2010). *The online teaching survival guide: Simple and practical pedagogical tips.* San Francisco, CA: Jossey-Bass.

Cheung, S. L. (2008). Using mobile phone messaging as a response medium in classroom experiments. *The Journal of Economic Education,* (Winter): 51–67. doi:10.3200/JECE.39.1.51-67

Choi, C. C., & Ho, H. (2002). Exploring new literacies in online peer-learning environments. *Reading Online, 6*(1). Retrieved from www.readingonline.org/newliteracies/lit_index.asp?HREF=choi/index.html

Crystal, D. (2008). *Txting: The gr8 db8.* Oxford, UK: Oxford University Press.

Drouin, M. A. (2011). College students' text messaging, use of textese and literacy skills. *Journal of Computer Assisted Learning, 27,* 67–75. doi:10.1111/j.1365-2729.2010.00399.x

Frey, N., Fisher, D., & Gonzalez, A. (2010). *Literacy 2.0: Reading and writing in 21st century classrooms.* Bloomington, IN: Solution Tree Press.

Grant, A. A. (2011, May). *Embracing the inevitable: Utilizing student text messaging to teach composition.* Research presented at the meeting of Computers and Writing, Ann Arbor.

Mahatanankoon, P., & O'Sullivan, P. (2008). Attitude toward mobile text messaging: An expectancy-based perspective. *Journal of Computer-Mediated Communication, 13,* 973–992. doi:10.1111/j.1083-6101.2008.00427.x

North Carolina State University. (2011). *Archi-texture: Composing and constructing in digital space*. Retrieved October 1, 2011, from http://chasslamp.chass.ncsu.edu/~cw2012/cfp

O'Connell, M. (2010). "To text or not to text": Reticence and the utilization of short message services. *Human Communication, 13*(2), 87–102.

Poll Everywhere. (2011). *Poll Everywhere: Instant audience feedback*. Retrieved October 5, 2011, from http://www.polleverywhere.com

Prensky, M. (2001). Digital natives, digital immigrants. *Horizon, 9*(5), 1–6. doi:10.1108/10748120110424816

Selfe, C. (1999). *Technology and literacy in the twenty-first century: The importance of paying attention*. Carbondale, IL: Southern Illinois University Press.

Selfe, C. (2009). Aurality and multimodal composing. *College Composition and Communication, 60*(4), 616–663.

Shafie, L. A., Azida, N., & Osman, N. (2010). SMS language and college writing: The language of the college texters. *International Journal of Emerging Technologies in Learning, 5*(1), 26–31.

Sweeny, S. M. (2010). Writing for the instant messaging and text messaging generation: Using new literacies to support writing instruction. *Journal of Adolescent & Adult Literacy, 52*(2), 121–130. doi:10.1598/JAAL.54.2.4

Willigham, D. T. (2009). *Why don't students like school?* San Francisco, CA: Jossey-Bass.

Wood, C., Jackson, E., Hart, L., Plester, B., & Wilde, L. (2011). The effect of text messaging on 9- and 10-year-old children's reading, spelling, and phonological processing skills. *Journal of Computer Assisted Learning, 27*, 28–36. doi:10.1111/j.1365-2729.2010.00398.x

ADDITIONAL READING

Coe, J. E. L., & Oakhill, J. V. (2011). "txtN is ez f u no h2 rd": The relation between reading ability and text-messaging behavior. *Journal of Computer Assisted Learning, 27*(1), 4–17. doi:10.1111/j.1365-2729.2010.00404.x

Cooke, A. (2008). Type. Send. Communicate: Text and instant messaging within the workforce and its effects on management. Paper presented at the meeting of the National Communication Association.

Figliola, P. M. (2009). Text and multimedia messaging: Emerging issues for Congress: RL34632. *Congressional Research Service: Report, 2009*, 1–16.

Haggan, M. (2007). Text messaging in Kuwait: Is the medium the message? *Journal of Cross-Cultural and Interlanguage Communication, 26*(4), 427–449. doi:10.1515/MULTI.2007.020

Hanson, T. L., Drumheller, K., & Mallard, J. (2011). Cell phones, text messaging, and Facebook: Competing time demands of today's college students. *College Teaching, 59*(1), 23–30. doi:10.1080/87567555.2010.489078

Hawisher, G., LeBlanc, P., Moran, C., & Selfe, C. L. (1996). *Computers and the teaching of writing in American higher education, 1979-1994: A history*. Norwood, NJ: Ablex Publishing Corporation. doi:10.2307/358464

Holtgraves, T. (2011). Text messaging, personality, and the social context. *Journal of Research in Personality, 45*(1), 92–99. doi:10.1016/j.jrp.2010.11.015

Jones, G. M., & Schieffelin, B. B. (2009). Talking text and talking back: "My BFF Jill" from boob tube to YouTube. *Journal of Computer-Mediated Communication, 14*, 1050–1079. doi:10.1111/j.1083-6101.2009.01481.x

Kemp, N., & Bushnell, C. (2011). Children's text messaging: Abbreviations, input methods, and links with literacy. *Journal of Computer Assisted Learning, 27*(1), 18–27. doi:10.1111/j.1365-2729.2010.00400.x

Kennedy, S. (2010). More text, less talk. *Information Today, 27*(11), 15–17.

Kreiner, D. S. (2011). Knowledge of text message abbreviations as a predictor of spelling ability. *Perceptual and Motor Skills, 112*(1), 295–309. doi:10.2466/13.28.PMS.112.1.295-309

Lee, C. (2010). Learning "new" text-making practices online: From instant messaging to Facebooking. *International Journal of Learning, 16*(12), 111–124.

Ling, R. (2005). Mobile communications vis-à-vis: Teen emancipation, peer group integration, and deviance. In Harper, R., Palen, L., & Taylor, A. (Eds.), *The inside text: Social, cultural, and design perspectives on SMS* (pp. 175–193). Netherlands: Springer. doi:10.1007/1-4020-3060-6_10

Maher, J. E., Pranian, K., Drach, L., Rumptz, M., Casciato, C., & Guernsey, J. (2010). Using text messaging to contact difficult-to-reach study participants. *American Journal of Public Health, 100*(6), 969–969. doi:10.2105/AJPH.2009.188391

Maher, M. (2007). You've got messages: Modern technology recruiting through text-messaging and the intrusiveness of Facebook. *Texas Review of Entertainment & Sports Law, 8*(1), 125.

Nolan, C., Quinn, S., & MacCobb, S. (2011). Use of text messaging in a mental health service for university students. *Occupational Therapy in Mental Health, 27*(2), 103–125. doi:10.1080/0164212X.2011.565702

Pettigrew, J. (2009). Text messaging and connectedness with close interpersonal relationships. *Marriage & Family Review, 45*(6-8), 697–716. doi:10.1080/01494920903224269

Powell, D., & Dixon, M. (2011). Does SMS text messaging help or harm adults' knowledge of standard spelling? *Journal of Computer Assisted Learning, 27*(1), 58–66. doi:10.1111/j.1365-2729.2010.00403.x

Reid, F. J. M., & Reid, D. J. (2010). The expressive and conversational affordances of mobile messaging. *Behaviour & Information Technology, 29*(1), 3–22. doi:10.1080/01449290701497079

Richardson, J., & Lenarcic, J. (2008). Text messaging as a catalyst for mobile student administration: The "trigger" experience. *International Journal of Emerging Technologies & Society, 6*(2), 140–155.

Riley, W., Obermayer, J., & Jean-Mary, J. (2008). Internet and mobile-phone text messaging intervention for college smokers. *Journal of American College Health, 57*(2), 245–248. doi:10.3200/JACH.57.2.245-248

Shuter, R., & Chattopadhyay, S. (2010). Emerging interpersonal norms of text messaging in India and the United States. *Journal of Intercultural Communication Research, 39*(2), 123–147. doi:10.1080/17475759.2010.526319

Thomas, K., & Orthober, C. (2011). Using text messaging in the secondary classroom. *American Secondary Education, 39*(2), 55–76.

Thompson, L., & Cupples, J. (2008). Seen and not heard?: Text messaging and digital sociality. *Social & Cultural Geography, 9*(1), 95–108. doi:10.1080/14649360701789634

Thurlow, C. (2003). *Generation txt? The sociolinguistics of young people's text-messaging*. Retrieved June 15, 2011, from http://faculty.washington.edu/thurlow/research/papers/Thurlow&Brown(2003). htm.

Varnhagen, C. K., McFall, G. P., Pugh, N., Routledge, L., Sumida-MacDonald, H., & Kwong, T. E. (2010). lol: new language and spelling in instant messaging. *Reading and Writing, 23*(6), 719–733. doi:10.1007/s11145-009-9181-y

Wei-F., Wang, F., & Ken, Y. (2010). Students' silent messages: Can teacher verbal and nonverbal immediacy moderate student use of text messaging in class? *Communication Education, 59*(4), 475–496. doi:10.1080/03634523.2010.496092

Weimer, K. (2010). Text messaging the reference desk: Using upside wireless' SMS-to-email to extend reference service. *The Reference Librarian, 51*(2), 108–123. doi:10.1080/02763870903579729

KEYWORDS

Asynchronous Learning: Typically used to refer to a type of online learning not conducted in real time.

Character: Letters, symbols, punctuation, and spaces that take up space in a text message.

Character Limit: The total amount of characters allotted for a certain type of technology. For text messaging, this is typically 160 characters.

SMS: Acronym for Short Messaging System; a brief manner (in the case of text messaging, 160-character limit) of communication via Web or phone.

Synchronous Learning: Typically used to refer to a type of online learning conducted in real time. Face-to-face classroom learning is also synchronous.

Technological Literacy: The ability to successfully communicate with others using the linguistic qualities of technologies including computers, cell phones, etc.

Textese: A specific language used by texters in text messaging, often consisting of abbreviations and acronyms.

Textpert: Combination of "texter" and "expert," used to indicate an individual with high proficiency and interest in texting.

Txt: An abbreviation for "text," often used while texting.

Chapter 15

Working toward Expert Status:
Love to Hear Students Go Tweet, Tweet, Tweet

Tamara Girardi
Indiana University of Pennsylvania, USA

ABSTRACT

Twitter represents a virtual, global classroom of collective intelligence and an epistemological shift in which the "experts" in the exchange are not necessarily the traditional teachers. The experts on Twitter are those who share information of value and do so often, a definition that could and should include students engaging the medium for academic purposes. As an academic tool, Twitter offers students the opportunity to engage in a wider discourse than the classroom environment and to gain confidence in their knowledge and potential "expert" status. Furthermore, the nature of Twitter closely aligns with Tapscott's (2009) identified norms for the Net Generation, which includes current high school and college-aged students. The eight norms—freedom, customization, scrutiny, integrity, collaboration, entertainment, speed, and innovation—provide an appropriate theoretical framework for a curriculum-related question such as: What is the value of implementing Twitter into classroom instruction?

INTRODUCTION

You've felt it; I've felt it. Change has become central to life in the 21st century. Sometimes the speed of this change is overwhelming, especially in a world where the Internet places so much information right at our fingertips ... The pace of this change will be limited only by our ability to manage it. Our students will encounter even more rapid change when they graduate, especially in the information they will require to perform effectively in the workplace. Thus, the ability to read and write becomes even more important to our children's future than it was to ours. Rapid change will be increasingly a part of their lives, and we need to begin now to prepare them. (Leu, 2001: paras. 1 & 2)

DOI: 10.4018/978-1-4666-2178-7.ch015

Recently, I served as the official Twit (someone who uses Twitter—also known as a Twitterer) at a conference for published and aspiring authors of fiction. The role required my fingers to be glued to my netbook keyboard so that when an author, literary agent, or other publishing professional shared some wise kernel of information I could launch that message into the Twittersphere in 140 characters or fewer. Inevitably, an attendee would ask the question that Twitter enthusiasts often hear: "Why in the world would I use Twitter?" A discussion ensued in which I defended Twitter's value as a Web 2.0 technology that engages authors, agents, editors, and readers in publishing discussions, a discourse in which this particular skeptic wished to take part. Such interaction offers writers unique opportunities to share insights and be judged by the value of those insights rather than solely on some designation of expert status. With Twitter, the emphasis is not placed on who you are but on what you say. In other words, the experts are not necessarily those with impressive degrees and decades of experience (although they are not omitted from the list of Twitter experts). A Twitter expert is a Twitterer who shares valuable information with others and does so often; they are judged by what they say online and not by their résumé offline. Such a power structure is often very different from that in face-to-face experiences, including traditional classrooms where teachers are considered the experts. Furthermore, by limiting all users to 140 characters, Twitter encourages an additional balance of power compared to power structures in traditional classrooms where teachers have historically possessed the prerogative to lecture throughout the entire class period or perhaps grant portions of time to hear a few student voices.

Even instructors with the best intentions of fostering student interaction and mining student voices in the classroom face limitations such as time, student confidence, and opportunity. Twitter is a tool that classroom teachers can embrace to better engage student voices and to encourage students to value their own opinions and those of their classmates. To that end, this chapter will 1) explain the basics and benefits of using Twitter; 2) illustrate how Twitter embraces Net Generation (current high school and college) students as experts who contribute to rather than simply absorb knowledge; 3) offer examples of how Twitter has been successfully implemented in classrooms; 4) troubleshoot potential challenges for classroom use; and 5) consider what the future of a Twitter-friendly classroom might mean for students and educators.

BACKGROUND

Although Twitter is grossly underutilized in classroom instruction, it remains one of the many Web 2.0 technologies transforming the ways in which Internet users communicate and gain knowledge. Just three years ago, only 24% of Americans kept a profile page on a social networking site; the most recent data from 2010 showed a participation rate of 48%. The greatest popularity lies with Americans aged 12–17 years, 18–24 years, and 25–34 years at 78%, 77%, and 65%, respectively (Webster, 2010: 12). This means that many of these Americans are in their school years (elementary through post-secondary), a fact that leads instructors to question what collaborative technologies could mean for the classroom. "Just as advances in computing and telecommunications have improved medicine, finance, manufacturing, and numerous other sectors of society, these changes are reshaping education—transforming what we learn, how we acquire knowledge, and how our schools function" (Dede, 2000: 171). Some experts believe technology is changing more than our industries, including education. More specifically, scholars believe technology has actually changed the ways the current generation of students process information (Carr, 2010; Prensky, 2001).

Valuing the Tool

Approximately 90 million Americans are "on" Twitter (Savage, 2011), and the site boasts nearly 200 million users worldwide. Each day about 370,000 new users sign up (Miller & Bilton, 2010). The majority of users (33%) are aged 25–34 years, and female users (53%) outnumber male users (47%) (Webster, 2010: 22).

The website first prompted users with the question: What are you doing? Often users responded by detailing mundane daily tasks and experiences. As a result, critics have argued that the site's inane ramblings are of no consequential value (Lyons, 2009; McFedries, 2007; Popkin, 2007; Stephenson, 2011).

Twitter is stupid ...Why do we think we're so important that we believe other people want to know about what we're having for lunch, how bored we are at work, or the state of inebriation we happen to be in at this very moment in time? (Popkin, 2007: paras. 11 & 13).

It is certainly fair to say that some users tweet about lunch, boredom, and drunkenness, but it is also fair to say that Twitter is what you make of it. A few minutes of exploration will show anyone new to the site that Twitter is a lively discourse where users share links to interesting and entertaining articles and videos on the Web. The site is very social and can also be used for educational purposes.

Twitter users have been the breaking news source for historic moments such as US Airways Flight 1549 landing on the Hudson River in 2009 and the Navy Seals invading Osama bin Laden's compound in 2011. In fact, in the hours following bin Laden's death, Twitter boasted an incredible 3,400 tweets per second as the world looked to the site for news about and reactions to the momentous historical event (Copeland, 2011). As far as the Twitterverse is concerned, Web 2.0 technologies offer "a new golden age of access and participation," not "a new dark age of mediocrity and narcissism" (Carr, 2010: 2). Researchers are beginning to agree.

Twitter has ... evolved into a complex information-dissemination platform, especially during situations of mass convergence ... It was only a matter of time before the research community turned to it as a rich source of social, commercial, marketing and political information. (Gayo-Avello, 2011: 121)

Yet the implementation of Twitter follows on a decades-old debate about technology in the classroom. According to Selfe (1999):

Technology literacy—meaning computer skills and the ability to use computers and other technology to improve learning, productivity, and performance—has become as fundamental to a person's ability to navigate through society as traditional skills like reading, writing, and arithmetic. (3)

While technology is undeniably part of our students' lives as Selfe suggests, researchers have urged educators to be sensitive to the concept of the digital divide, a separation between those who cannot afford technology and those who can (Cuban 2001; Gunkel, 2003; Jenkins, with Purushotma, Clinton, Weigel, & Robison, 2009; Mitchell, 1995; Virilio, 1997). In fact, former President Clinton launched the Technology Literacy Challenge in 1996, pushing for a society whose youth is technologically literate. As technology use has increased in the classroom, researchers and critics have discouraged educators' rush to adopt technology without fully understanding its value (Brende, 2004; Cope & Kalantzis, 2007; Mauriello & Pagnucci, 2003; Postman, 1992). The primary concern here is to insure that technology tools are enhancing our intentions rather than guiding our pedagogy, which is why understanding our audience of students and the tools available (two goals considered in this chapter) is imperative.

The Net Generation: A Theoretical Framework

In the $4 million research study, "The Net Generation: A strategic investigation," Tapscott (2009) termed the generation born between 1977 and 1997 the Net Generation and discovered that these young people approach life with eight "norms" – "distinctive attitudinal and behavioral characteristics that differentiate this generation from their baby-boom parents and other generations" (74). The norms are freedom, customization, scrutiny, integrity, collaboration, entertainment, speed, and innovation. Since they combine to create a picture of the students in our classrooms, they provide an appropriate theoretical framework for curricula questions in this chapter and in general, questions such as: What is the value of implementing Twitter into classroom instruction? In addition to the insight into our classroom pedagogies that Tapscott's discovery offers, the norms also answer some questions about why our current educational system is not working for some students. For instance, Net Geners, as Tapscott refers to them, prefer the freedom of choice and the freedom to move around, both physically and between different concepts and ideas. They operate personal devices such as iPods and cell phones that are customized to their exact needs. Contrary to what many professors believe, these young people have also developed the ability to scrutinize information from the many sources they encounter online every day. Furthermore, Tapscott found that the generation cares "about integrity—being honest, considerate, transparent, and abiding by their commitments" (82). They are natural collaborators, often working and sharing with others online, and natural players, combining work and play whenever possible. They are the generation of fast-paced lifestyles, instant response, multitasking, and constant innovation. Together, these norms paint a picture of our students that is quite different from the roles traditional educational paradigms assign them in our classrooms. Outdated pedagogies rely on the lecture-based banking model which Freire (1970) criticized due to its lack of student freedom, customization, collaboration, and innovation. Likewise, the banking model discourages scrutiny; rather, it expects students to listen, learn, and regurgitate in tests without challenging or validating the knowledge espoused. Even more updated pedagogies designed around well-meaning intentions of encouraging student agency, such as those emphasizing the social construction of knowledge (Dewey, 1916; Vygotsky, 1978) and collaborative learning (Bruffee, 1993; Kuhn, 1970), may fail to meet the norms of Net Generation students. Collaborative assignments appear on syllabi year after year without customization to new groups of students or the freedom for those students to innovate the assignments on their own. In other words, our educational system not only ignores those skills in which our students may claim expert status, but is also holding onto an outdated view of the student and what he or she can do.

The Net Geners have grown up digital and they're living in the twenty-first century, but the education system in many places is lagging at least 100 years behind. The model of education that still prevails today was designed for the Industrial Age. It revolves around the teacher who delivers a one-size-fits-all, one-way lecture. The student, working alone, is expected to absorb the content delivered by the teacher. This might have been good for the mass production economy, but it doesn't deliver for challenges of the digital economy, or for the Net Gen mind. (Tapscott, 2009: 122)

In other words, the goal is to see our students as "knowledge producers" rather than "knowledge consumers" (Cope & Kalantzis, 2007; McLoughlin & Lee, 2010).

Twitter's design provides an opportunity for students to find their voices and identify as knowledge producers. The medium is an excellent one for this purpose as the "experts" on Twitter are not defined by the length of their résumés. Experts have credibility, and their opinions are highly valued as a result. With Twitter, credibility is earned by dissemination of frequent and valuable (useful, educational, or interesting) tweets. With technology in general, our students already possess credibility; connecting them with Twitter and encouraging them to share content about topics they know and love is a good way to build their credibility with this particular technology and to transfer the role of expert from the teacher to a collective of experts that includes both the teacher and the students.

Twitter Fridays, Films, and Role-Play

Monica Rankin's US history students at the University of Texas at Dallas showed the value of Web 2.0 technology's strongest attribute—its engagement of millions of voices, so different from the traditional classroom setting where only a few students carry the discussion. Rankin's spring 2009 class was a traditional lecture-style, 90-student, auditorium-based learning experience that placed her in the expert role as lecturer and limited class discussion to those students who felt most comfortable speaking in such an environment. However, Rankin decided to transform that environment every Friday by discussing an assigned reading via Twitter. Students brought laptop computers or smart phones to class to tweet, and the graduate assistant projected the Twitterstream onto the screen at the front of the auditorium and typed in any handwritten tweets from students who did not have the technology to participate.

The result was a more engaged discussion in which all the students—not only the few who had time to speak during the limited class period—participated (Miners, 2009; Rankin, 2009). Another benefit was realized when Rankin had to miss class for a conference presentation. That Friday, she participated remotely by logging in to Twitter from her hotel room and becoming part of the discussion that her graduate assistant was leading back in the Dallas classroom. Likewise, students who missed class due to illness could still participate in the Friday discussions.

Educators and researchers at the University of Minnesota, Twin Cities, offer another case where Twitter was successfully implemented to increase student engagement. Reyerson, Mummey, and Higdon (2011) aimed to transform a 30-year-old Medieval Cities of Europe course with the help of technology. A team comprising the instructor, a graduate student reader/grader, an undergraduate, and two educational technology consultants transformed the 80-student classroom from a lecture-based environment to one that relied on the technology of clickers to poll students, Twitter to respond to films, a map exercise, and group presentations. The "particular goal" in using Twitter was to "limit 'lights out, heads down' disengagement during in-class films" (Reyerson, Mummey, & Higdon, 2011: 354). To prepare the students, the instructor posted an instructional video on using Twitter on Moodle and provided a list of questions for students to consider while watching the films and tweeting. For example, in response to David Macaulay's film *Cathedral*, students received the following prompts:

- Why would a medieval city invest the kind of financial resources, labor power, and political capital that it took to build a cathedral when there were so many other needs?
- The film employs both a traditional documentary style and an animated fictional story. What are the advantages and disadvantages of these methods? How does the animation in particular affect your reception of the film as a teaching tool? (357)

The exercise yielded hundreds of tweets with the first two films alone. By creating a word cloud collage of the most common themes, students were able to gain a sense of the classroom community's response to the films. At the end of the semester "a number of students" endorsed the simultaneous use of Twitter while watching films in the class (Reyerson et al., 2011: 359).

Another example of Twitter engagement in the classroom comes from a research group composed of students and faculty from Indiana University's learning Sciences Program and administrators and English teachers from several high schools in southeast Indiana. The group's goal was to implement new media literacies in the classroom with the following learning objectives: 1) ability to write about and talk about characters and characterization in sophisticated ways, 2) ability to identify and negotiate norms of written participation in a range of technology-driven communities" (McWilliams, Hickey & Hines, 2011: 238). The researchers believed in the importance of technology in the classroom, but also admitted to the challenges "in developing pedagogical approaches that can be personally engaging and socially meaningful" (239). The teachers chose to utilize Twitter as part of a unit featuring Arthur Miller's play *The Crucible* because of its "dynamic online community" (239). While many English classes have the students take on character roles and read a play aloud in class, this unit coupled that traditional element with encouraging those same students to also tweet in the voices of their assigned characters. To accomplish this, the students developed Twitter handles and uploaded profile photos appropriate to their characters and tweeted during the in-class reading of the play.

In the beginning we helped students identify key moments that might lead a character to respond via Twitter; later in the unit, students took over this responsibility as they began to see the role that this backchanneling tool could play. (240)

Furthermore, students began interacting with each other, suggesting when other students might have something to say in their characters' voices.

All three of these examples have Tapscott's (2009) norms in common. Students watching the medieval films and acting out *The Crucible* were free to move from the real-time concepts (the film and the reading of the play) to the dynamic online community of Twitter. The high school students in the third case were able to personalize their Twitter profiles to correspond with their characters. All three classrooms featured innovation and collaboration with one of the fastest-paced Web 2.0 technologies currently in use. Students were expected to customize the assignment to their course's academic expectations and scrutinize their peers' tweets before responding. In addition, these examples all feature opportunities for the students involved to become experts with the confidence and credibility to share something valuable. Students in each of the situations proved hesitant at first, but their interest and expertise, both with Twitter and their respective course material, increased enough to encourage the researchers and educators in each case that implementing the technology was worthwhile.

Suggested Practices

1. Join the Twitterverse

It's hard to know whether all this tweeting adds up to anything significant. Of course, much the same was once said of blogs; now it's well-accepted that a well-written blog post can be just as influential as a newspaper op-ed. Twitter offers a nonstop stream of views, ideas, opinions, and emotions; get yourself in the flow or be left behind. (Petrelli, 2011: 90)

As Petrelli suggests, the most effective way for educators to implement Twitter in their pedagogy effectively is to engage the tool long before they ask their students to. "A teacher does not need to be an expert Twitter user ... in order to bring these types of activities into the classroom, but she does need to be able to provide both organizing and thematic support" (McWilliams, Hickey, Hines, Connor, & Bishop, 2011: 243). To gain an understanding that would allow for such support, instructors need not spend endless hours tweeting; they can begin by following other educators, researchers, writers, corporations, or news outlets—any Twitterers whose profiles and tweets may be related to the course the instructors teach. Watching and observing the interaction on Twitter is a perfectly acceptable first step. However, in order to truly understand the value and limitations of the tool, educators should move beyond observations to interactions when they feel comfortable enough to do so.

2. Look to what Others Have Done

Although the literature on Twitter use for educational purposes is limited, there are certainly several examples in recent publications. For example, seniors at University Laboratory High School in Illinois participated in a less traditional literary discussion of Dante's *Inferno* via Twitter. The "Twitter in Hell" assignment charged students with the challenge of writing tweets "describing each level in hell as if they were Dante writing to his beloved Beatrice" (Barack, 2009: 14). Business professor Elaine Young used Twitter with her students at Champlain College in Vermont to foster connections between students and business professionals in the community. Students consulted with local companies on the value of various social networking sites in promoting their products, and even after Young's marketing course ended, she said her students' Twitter accounts maintained active (Miners, 2009). An instructor with the Auburn University Harrison School of Pharmacy implemented Twitter in a pharmacy management course to encourage interaction among the students who attended the course via two different campuses (Fox & Varadarajan, 2011). In addressing the question "Does microblogging help teacher education students develop self-reflective practices?" a researcher from the University of Waikato in New Zealand found "Twitter chronologically logged participants'

reflective thinking during a school practicum, reduced isolation and supported a sense of community" (Wright, 2010: 263). There are also the aforementioned examples from the University of Texas at Dallas (Miners, 2009; Rankin, 2009), the University of Minnesota, Twin Cities (Reyerson et al., 2011), and southeast Indiana high schools (McWilliams, Hickey & Hines, 2011).

A second resource to mine involves other social networking sites. For example, a Florida teacher launched an "Around the World with 80 Schools" project by creating a page on the social network Ning (Davis, 2010). Three hundred teachers from around the world signed up, and the teacher proceeded to set up meetings between her class and classes around the world using Skype. She assigned her students roles to document the interaction, locate the other classes' location on a map, fact check the information received, and tweet about the interaction live. When her students were learning about orcas, she connected with a class in a part of British Columbia "where whale watching is a common pasttime" (15). In this one example, the class used technologies such as Ning, Google, Skype, and Twitter.

However, viable ideas should not be limited to academia. In the spring of 2010, a blogger named Neiman Fellow, at Harvard University, and a contributing editor of *Wired,* Jeff Howe, posted "I have a dream. An idea. A maybe great notion. As Augie March might say, 'I got a scheme.' What If everyone on Twitter read the same book at the same time?" (Howe, 2010: 54). The Twitterverse responded, and when Howe "didn't try to impose [his] own rules on it, [his] scheme metamorphosed into a movement" (54). His idea sparked a discussion among thousands of strangers all reading the same work of literature, Neil Gaiman's *American Gods.*

Howe's innovation and particular expertise sparked the reading revolution, but the expertise of those who participated should also be noted. They shared "insights, questions, and commentary in the machine gun bursts that are Twitter's native form" (Howe, 2010: 54). Discussions like the one spawned by Howe are very frequent on Twitter; they represent good opportunities to engage students in a discourse wider than the classroom. An instructor need only do a little digging to find them.

3. Be Creative

However, locating examples of Twitter usage is not enough. Educators must be willing to experiment with other instructors' success and apply similar ideas to their own course content and students. For example, *Public Relations Tactics* published a Twitter interview with @prsarahevans who moderates #journchat for journalists and public relations professionals. The interview was conducted via Twitter, so the questions and answers were limited to 140 characters although some answers consisted of a string of responses. Educators might borrow this example and assign students a task of searching Twitter for someone such as, for example, Sarah Evans (a US country singer and songwriter) to interview. Composition teachers might encourage students to include the interview responses in an upcoming essay or presentation. Sociology professors might assign students a research project to ask one question over Twitter and analyze the responses. Art history teachers may require students to interview a museum employee about an artwork of the students' choice housed in the museum. Literature teachers may use the interview tactic as a way to dig deeper into the characters of a particular story, play, or novel, and assign students a task of interviewing each other "in character." Public relations or journalism students could set up an interview with a school administrator, local politician, or the homecoming queen and promote the interview to members of the community encouraging them to join in and ask questions as well. These are all examples modified from one idea—conducting an interview via Twitter. Instructors may truly embrace Net Generation norms and introduce their students to Twitter before allowing the class

to brainstorm ways they might use the tool to enhance their education.

4. Honor School and Student Policies

Just as Net Gen students prefer a little more freedom in their academic lives, so do many educators, particularly at the high school level. While incorporating Twitter into a traditional course unit may sound attractive, educators would be wise to consider any restrictions their institutions place on use of social media in the classroom.

Before allowing students to create and post written content online, teachers need to check the school or district acceptable use policy to ensure that the use of these tools will not be violating any terms of the policy. Besides specific prohibitions related to the tools, there may also be restrictions on posting students' work. And teachers working with students younger than 13 need to read the terms of services for the tools they propose to use to make sure they will not be violating these guidelines. (Brooks-Young, 2010: 72)

According to Brooks-Young, use of social media is banned in the majority of US school districts. If schools do grant permission, it is also important to request student permission as well. In Rankin's (2009) Twitter experiment, she made Twitter engagement optional for students. Twitter is a public forum, so all her students' tweets are accessible by anyone with a Twitter account. Furthermore, the Library of Congress files all tweets for safekeeping, so her classroom discussions would become part of that archive as well. According to Rankin, fewer than 15 of her 90 students chose to handwrite their comments rather than creating a public profile and tweeting online.

5. Anticipate Challenges

Before beginning a unit that utilizes Twitter, educators should realize that although nearly 80%

of teens (Tapscott, 2009) are using social media sites, there is no telling which sites a particular group of students is using—unless teachers ask. Regardless, there will likely be a need for some instruction on the tool itself. Students may have heard of Twitter, but are unable to use it. They may have heard the myths that Twitter is for useless chatter about where people are or what they are doing. There may be some stereotypes and unrealistic expectations to break down before true learning can begin.

Educators could spend one class period covering signing on to Twitter and learning the basics. I have organized workshops for writers doing exactly this, and the workshops are conducted in an hour. When writers walk in, they know nothing about Twitter. When they leave, they are signed on, sending tweets, and following others' tweets. During the workshops, I often have Twitter helpers around the room, facilitating the workshop tasks. Recruiting former or current students with Twitter experience may ensure that the one hour you have to familiarize all your students with the site is used to its full potential.

Another potential challenge with Twitter is the 140-character limit (which can be manipulated into 180 characters by some non-Twitter applications). Skeptics often challenge what value audiences can gain from a limit of 140 characters. However, Carr's (2010) revelation of his own limited attention span and the suggestion that our brains have been programmed to think less linearly suggest that such a limited, fragmented discussion (which Twitter provides) might be what Internet users are actually programmed to welcome. In her Twitter Experiment, Rankin (2009) revealed that although students were limited by 140 characters, in some cases it encouraged them to cut the fluff out of their comments, something they would not have been forced to do otherwise. Thus, Twitter use is quite the lesson in rhetoric, albeit brief rhetoric. A well-designed assignment can be enhanced by Twitter's character limitations rather than hampered by them.

FUTURE RESEARCH DIRECTIONS

Empirical research on Twitter is limited. At the present time, most of the discussions on Twitter in the classroom are informal reflections of practice. Such insight is indeed valuable, yet structured research must be done to make any real claims about Twitter's place in the classroom. For instance, researchers could look at school districts' and parents' thoughts about and expectations of incorporating a technology that exposes students to a very public audience the world over. Researchers could look at what schools (both secondary and post-secondary) are using Twitter and how; they could design empirical studies to evaluate the ways students respond to Twitter in school and whether using it increases learning or retention of material. In the spirit of this text's central claim, the role of the "expert" in Twitter discourse could be further analyzed. While there are certainly areas of the site, such as the character limit, that create equality among users, there are other instances, such as the number of followers, where power and expertise are clear factors. Findings on how Twitter envisions the "expert" could further enlighten class discussions and usage of the tool. Finally, as was the case with Young's business students (Miners, 2009), researchers could study whether use of Twitter in the classroom continues once the semester ends.

It should also be noted, however, that research such as this takes time, and the potential flaw with Web 2.0 technologies is that time is often limited. The social network of the moment may not be in use a few years from now. Furthermore, designers make frequent changes to sites such as Twitter, and those changes could make current research studies and claims obsolete. Because of this, reflective practice may be educators' greatest asset in understanding and implementing Web 2.0 technologies. Furthermore, educators should find innovative ways—such as utilizing Twitter, blogs, websites, or writing scholarly articles—to share their reflective practice of new technologies. In other words, if more teachers shared their Twitter experiences in the ways the educators discussed in this chapter have, other educators may feel more comfortable implementing new technologies such as Twitter.

CONCLUSION

In his essay "A New Culture of Teaching for the 21st Century," Wiske (2002) proposes three challenges for teachers when considering implementation of a new technology in the classroom. "First, the technology must afford significant educational advantage … Second, the technology must be readily affordable, networked, and portable … Third, technology alone does not change school practice" (70). In response to these challenges, the Web 2.0 technology of Twitter excels. First, Twitter is a resource that allows for collaboration and discussion, either by students identifying themselves or by allowing them anonymity, which could perhaps lead to freer discussions. Furthermore, the site creates an atmosphere of exchanged knowledge which students can observe or participate in. Second, the technology is accessible in several ways. Students may access it through school computers, home computers, library computers, video gaming systems such as Xbox or Playstation 3, or cellular phones and other portable devices such as iPads or iPods. While many of these technologies are expensive and therefore some students may not have access to them, there are ways for all students to be connected and to participate in a Twitter exchange. Finally, the recommendations here are not that Twitter alone will, or should, change practice. Teachers must understand the tool and then use innovation and creativity to apply it to the classroom. The discussion of Dante's *Inferno* was a great example of such creativity. Likewise, in the spirit of truly changing practice and getting students more involved, as Net Generation norms suggest they would like to be, teachers could engage students in a dialogue to discover their ideas for Twitter exchanges. Again, this is another way in which technology redefines the students as experts, empowering them with the confidence in their abilities to gain and share knowledge. Yes, there are many challenges to implementing and adjusting to technology. When Rankin brought Twitter into her history classroom once a week, she knew it would be "messy, but messy doesn't necessarily mean that it's going to be bad" (Smith, 2009).

Relinquishing control and taking chances are not simple feats for educators; however, the advantages of Web 2.0 technologies such as Twitter are too numerous to ignore.

Emerging interactive media are aiding the development of richer curricula, better teaching strategies, more effective organizational structures, stronger links between schools and society, and the empowerment of disenfranchised learners. Researchers and educators who foster the dissemination of best practices are creating virtual communities of practice to empower reform in schooling. Furthermore, new interactive media promise to give all students and teachers the opportunity to learn complex concepts and skills. (Dede, 2002: 171)

Twitter provides students with a way to connect to the wealth of information that is the Internet through word-of-mouth advertising from people they trust and feel similar to. The limit of 140-character updates is more of a challenge than a detriment, encouraging students to engage their creativity to share in the discussion, while at the same time allowing them to gain a sense of confidence and potentially acquire a particular form of expertise in the Twitter world.

REFERENCES

Barack, L. (2009, April). Twittering Dante: New models for student writing in the digital age. *School Library Journal*, 14–15.

Brende, E. (2004). *Better off: Flipping the switch on technology.* New York, NY: Harper Perennial.

Brooks-Young, S. (2010). *Digital-age literacy for teachers: Applying technology standards to everyday practice.* Thousand Oaks, CA: SAGE.

Bruffee, K. (1993). *Collaborative learning: Higher education, interdependence, and the authority of knowledge.* Baltimore, MD: Johns Hopkins University Press. doi:10.2307/358879

Carr, N. (2010). *The shallows: What the Internet is doing to our brains.* New York, NY: Norton.

Cope, B., & Kalantzis, M. (2007). New media, new learning. *The International Journal of Learning, 14*(1), 75–79.

Copeland, R. (2011). Tweet all about it. *Metro, 169,* 96-100.

Cuban, L. (2001). *Oversold and underused: Computers in the classroom.* Cambridge, MA: Harvard University Press.

Davis, M. R. (2010, November). Social networking goes to school. *Education Digest,* 14–19.

Dede, C. (2002). A new century demands new ways of learning. In Gordon, D. T. (Ed.), *The digital classroom: How technology is changing the way we teach and learn* (pp. 171–174). Cambridge, MA: Harvard Education Letter.

Dewey, J. (1916). *Democracy and education: An introduction to the philosophy of education.* New York, NY: Macmillan.

Fox, B. I., & Varadarajan, R. (2011). Technology in pharmacy education: Use of Twitter to encourage interaction in a multi-campus pharmacy management course. *Academic Journal of Pharmaceutical Education, 75*(5), 1–8.

Freire, P. (1970). *Pedagogy of the oppressed.* New York, NY: Continuum.

Gayo-Avello, D. (2011). Don't turn social media into another "literary digest" poll. *Communications of the ACM, 54*(10), 121–128. doi:10.1145/2001269.2001297

Gunkel, D. J. (2003). Second thoughts: Towards a critique of the digital divide. *New Media & Society, 5,* 499–522. doi:10.1177/146144480354003

Howe, J. (2010, May 17). What if?: An attempt to bring one book to the online masses. *Publishers Weekly, 54.*

Interview with @prsarahevans. (2011, April). *Public Relations Tactics, 13.*

Jenkins, H. (with Purushotma, R., Clinton, K., Weigel, M., & Robison, A. J. (2009). *Confronting the challenges of participatory culture: Media education for the 21st century.* Cambridge, MA: MIT Press.

Kuhn, T. (1970). *The structure of scientific revolutions* (2nd ed.). Chicago, IL: University of Chicago Press.

Leu, D. J. Jr. (2001, March). Internet project: Preparing students for new literacies in a global village. *The Reading Teacher, 54*(6). Retrieved from http://www.readingonline.org/electronic/elec_index.asp?HREF=/electronic/RT/3-01_Column/index.html

Lyons, D. (2009). Don't Tweet on me. *Newsweek, 154*(13), 31.

Mauriello, N., & Pagnucci, G. S. (2003). Balancing acts: Tightrope walking above an ever changing (Inter)Net. In Takayoshi, P., & Huot, B. (Eds.), *Teaching writing with computers. An introduction* (pp. 79–91). Boston, MA: Houghton Mifflin Company.

McFedries, T. (2007). Technically speaking: All a-twitter. *IEEE Spectrum, 44*(10), 84. doi:10.1109/MSPEC.2007.4337670

McLoughlin, C., & Lee, M. J. W. (2010). Personalized and self regulated learning in the Web 2.0 era: International exemplars of innovative pedagogy using social software. *Australasian Journal of Educational Technology, 26*(1), 28–43.

McWilliams, J., Hickey, D. T., & Hines, M. B. (2011). Using collaborative writing tools for literary analysis: Twitter, fan fiction and *The Crucible* in the secondary English classroom. *Journal of Media Literacy Education, 2*(3), 238–245.

Miller, C., & Bilton, N. (2010, October 31). Why Twitter's C.E.O. demoted himself. *New York Times,* p. 1.

Miners, Z. (2009, June 2). Twitter goes to college. *US News & World Report.* Retrieved from http://usnews.com/articles/education/2009/06/02/twitter-goes-to-college_print.htm

Mitchell, W. J. (1995). *City of bits: Space, place and the Infobahn.* Cambridge, MA: The MIT Press.

Petrilli, M. J. (2011). All a-Twitter about education: Improving our schools in 140 characters or less. *Education Next, 11*(4), 90–91.

Popkin, H. A. S. (2007). *Twitter nation: Nobody cares what you're doing.* Technotica on MSNBC.com. Retrieved from http://www.msnbc.msn.com/id/18445274/

Postman, N. (1992). *Technopoly: The surrender of culture to technology.* New York, NY: Vintage Books.

Prensky, M. (2001). Digital natives, Digital immigrants, part II: Do they really think differently? *Horizon, 9*(6). Retrieved from http://marcprensky.com/writing/Prensky%20-%20Digital%20Natives,%20Digital%20Immigrants%20-%20Part2.pdf doi:10.1108/10748120110424843

Rankin, M. (2009). *Some general comments on the "Twitter Experiment" by Monica Rankin (UT Dallas).* Monica Rankin's Home Page. Retrieved from http://www.utdallas.edu/~mrankin/usweb/twitterconclusions.htm

Reyerson, K., Mummey, K., & Higdon, J. (2011). Medieval cities of Europe: Click, tweet, map, and present. *The History Teacher, 44*(3), 353–367.

Savage, N. (2011, March). Twitter as medium and message. *Communications of the ACM, 54*(3), 18–20. doi:10.1145/1897852.1897860

Selfe, C. (1999). *Technology and literacy in the twenty-first century: The importance of paying attention.* Urbana, IL: NCTE.

Smith, K. (2009). *The Twitter experiment: Twitter in the classroom.* Retrieved from http://www.youtube.com/watch?v=6WPVWDkF7U8

Stephenson, G. (2011). I don't get Twitter. *Our Schools/Our Selves, 20*(3), 197-200.

Tapscott, D. (2009). *Grown up digital: How the Net Generation is changing your world.* New York, NY: McGraw Hill.

Virilio, P. (1997). *Open sky.* London, UK: Verso.

Vygotsky, L. (1978). *Mind in society.* Cambridge, MA: Harvard University Press.

Webster, T. (2010). *Twitter usage in America: 2010.* The Edison Research/Arbitron Internet and Multimedia Study.

Wiske, S. (2002). A new culture of teaching for the 21st century. In Gordon, D. T. (Ed.), *The digital classroom: How technology is changing the way we teach and learn* (pp. 69–77). Cambridge, MA: Harvard Education Letter.

Wright, N. (2010, November). Twittering in teacher education: reflecting on practicum experiences. *Open Learning, 25*(3), 259–265. doi:10.1080/02680513.2010.512102

ADDITIONAL READING

Alexander, B. (2006). Web 2.0: A new wave of innovation for teaching and learning? *EDUCAUSE Review, 41,* 32–44. Retrieved from http://www.educause.edu/ir/library/pdf/ERM0621.pdf

Anderson, P. (2007). *What is Web 2.0? Ideas, technologies and implications for education, JISC Report.* Retrieved from http://www.jisc.ac.uk/media/documents/techwatch/tsw0701b.pdf

Anderson, S. (2011, October). The Twitter toolbox for educators. *Teacher Librarian, 39*(1), 27–30.

Arafeh, S., Levin, D., Rainie, L., & Lenhart, A. (2002). *The digital disconnect: The widening gap between Internet-savvy students and their schools.* Pew Internet Life Project. Retrieved from http://www.pewinternet.org/Reports/2002/The-Digital-Disconnect-The-widening-gap-between-Internetsavvy-students-and-their-schools.aspx

Bennett, S., Maton, K., & Kervin, L. (2008). The "digital natives" debate: A critical review of the evidence. *British Journal of Educational Technology, 39*(5), 775–786. doi:10.1111/j.1467-8535.2007.00793.x

Browning, L., Gerlich, R., & Westermann, L. (2011). The new HD classroom: A "hyper diverse" approach to engaging with students. *Journal of Instructional Pedagogies, 51*-10.

Clark, J. E. (2010). The digital imperative: Making the case for a 21st-century pedagogy. *Computers and Composition, 27*, 27–35. doi:10.1016/j.compcom.2009.12.004

De Boor, T., & Kramer Halpern, L. (2007). *Creating & connecting: Research and guidelines on online social—and education—networking.* National School Boards Association. Retrieved from http://www.nsba.org/site/docs/41400/41340.pdf

Enda, J. (2011, October/November). Campaign coverage in the time of Twitter: How technology has transformed reporting on presidential politics. *American Journalism Review,* 14-21.

Galagan, P. (2009, March). Twitter as a learning tool. Really: Savvy trainers are using microblogging to foster informal learning and meet like-minded peers. *Training + Development,* 28-31.

Gardner, H. (2000/2002). Can technology exploit our many ways of knowing? In Gordon, D. T. (Ed.), *The digital classroom: How technology is changing the way we teach and learn* (pp. 32–35). Cambridge, MA: Harvard Education Letter.

Guhlin, M. (2008). The Twitter experience: Exploring professional learning networks. *TechEdge,* 15-17.

Hawisher, G. E., & Selfe, C. L. (Eds.). (1997). *Literacy, technology, and society: Confronting the issues.* Upper Saddle River, NJ: Prentice Hall.

Hawisher, G. E., & Selfe, C. L. (Eds.). (1999). *Passions, pedagogies, and 21st century technologies.* Logan, UT: Utah State University Press.

Hawisher, G. E., & Selfe, C. L. (Eds.). (2000). *Global literacies and the world-wide web.* New York, NY: Routledge.

Hemmi, A., Bayne, S., & Land, R. (2009). The appropriation and repurposing of social technologies in higher education. *Journal of Computer Assisted Learning, 25*, 19–30. doi:10.1111/j.1365-2729.2008.00306.x

Hennessy, S., Deaney, R., & Ruthven, K. (2005). Emerging teacher strategies for mediating "technology-integrated instructional conversations": A socio-cultural perspective. *Curriculum Journal, 16*(3), 265–292. doi:10.1080/09585170500256487

Jones, M., & Soho, S. (2009). *Everything Twitter: From novice to expert.* New York, NY: Soho Publishing.

Kodrich, K., & Laituri, M. (2011). Making a connection: Social media's key role in the Haiti earthquake. *Journal of Communication and Computer, 8*, 624–627.

Laferrière, T., Lamon, M., & Chan, C. K. K. (2006). Emerging e-trends and models in teacher education and professional development. *Teaching Education, 17*(1), 75–90. doi:10.1080/10476210500528087

Laitsch, D. (Ed.). (2003). The effects of computers on student writing: What the research tells us. *ASCD Research Brief, 1*(7). Retrieved from http://www.ascd.org/publications/researchbrief/v1n07/toc.aspx

Lenhart, A., Arafeh, S., Smith, A., & Rankin Macgill, A. (2008). *Writing, technology, and teens.* Pew Internet & American Life Project. Retrieved from http://www.pewinternet.org/~/media//Files/Reports/2008/PIP_Writing_Report_FINAL3.pdf

Lenhart, A., Madden, M., Rankin Macgill, A., & Smith, A. (2007). *Teens and social media.* Pew Internet & American Life Project. Retrieved from http://www.pewinternet.org/~/media//Files/Reports/2007/PIP_Teens_Social_Media_Final.pdf

Lew, A. (2011). *Web 2.0 teaching tools.* Retrieved from http://www.schoollibraryjournal.com/article/CA6640877.html

McFedries, P. (2010). *Twitter tips, tricks, and tweets* (2nd ed.). Indianapolis, IN: Wiley Publishing. doi:10.1002/9781118257791

McLoughlin, C., & Lee, M. J. W. (2008). Future learning landscapes: Transforming pedagogy through social software. *Innovate: Journal of Online Education, 4*(5). Retrieved from http://innovateonline.info/?view=article&id=539

Miller, E. (2002). Technology is not just a tool. In Gordon, D. T. (Ed.), *The digital classroom: How technology is changing the way we teach and learn* (pp. 30–31). Cambridge, MA: Harvard Education Letter.

Morris, T. (2009). *All a Twitter: A personal and professional guide to social networking with Twitter.* Canada: Pearson.

Pogue, D. (2009). *The world according to Twitter.* New York, NY: Workman Publishing.

Pongsajapan, R. A. (2009). *Liminal entities: Identity, governance, and organizations on Twitter.* Unpublished dissertation, Georgetown University, Washington, DC.

Prensky, M. (2008). The role of technology in teaching and the classroom. *Educational Technology.* Retrieved from http://marcprensky.com/writing/Prensky The_Role_of_Technology-ET-11-12-08.pdf

Rybalko, S., & Seltzer, T. (2010). Dialogic communication in 140 characters or less: How Fortune 500 companies engage stakeholders using Twitter. *Public Relations Review, 36,* 336–341. doi:10.1016/j.pubrev.2010.08.004

Yancey, K. B. (2009). *Writing in the 21st century: A report from the National Council of Teachers of English.* Retrieved from http://www.ncte.org/library/NCTEFiles/Press/Yancey_final.pdf

KEY TERMS AND DEFINITIONS

Follow: Twitter's version of "friending" someone; allows tweets by the person followed to appear in the follower's Twitterstream.

Handle: A person's Twitter name; begins with the @ symbol.

Hashtag (#): A Twitter file folder; any tweet that includes a particular hashtag will be filed in a searchable Twitterstream for all Twitter users to access.

Twapper Keeper: An independent application that archives all tweets with a particular hashtag.

Tweet: The 140-character message a twit or tweeter sends via Twitter.

Tweeter: A person who uses Twitter.

Twit: A person who uses Twitter.

Twittersphere: The nation of Twitter users and enthusiasts.

Twitterstream: A twit's homepage that lists all tweets from his or her followers.

Section 4
Case Studies of Collective or Decentralized Expertise

Chapter 16
Professional ICT Knowledge, Epistemic Standards, and Social Epistemology

Frederik Truyen
University of Leuven, Belgium

Filip Buekens
Tilburg University, The Netherlands

ABSTRACT

Several co-evolving trends have impacted expectations of professional workers' quality of knowledge. The abundance of information shared through the Internet, the ever-increasing specialization of tasks, the possibility of immediately accessible information through social networks, the participation of stakeholders in the social web, and the increased requirements for separation of duty in a corporate context have contributed to a situation where the current 'knowledge worker' is not expected to have the same level of readily available knowledge as before. This chapter describes this phenomenon in detail with a case study from ICT-expert jobs. It shows that an ICT manager can no longer overlook the work of collaborators, just by virtue of being the smartest employee around. He/she will increasingly rely on organizational procedures and professional standards to assess whether the right people - with the right competencies for the job – are at his/her disposal. After describing the specifics of professional knowledge for ICT experts and the role of social software plays in this, the chapter focuses on the epistemological aspects of ICT expertise. The authors discuss current strands of reliabilistic accounts for knowledge in relation to expertise. They show that besides reliability, it is accuracy that is needed in order to perform as an expert.

INTRODUCTION

Accuracy is a thoroughly social concept. In discussing "interactive expertise", the social constraints on knowledge are explored further, in direct relation to the social networks that are facilitated by social software and web 2.0 technolo-

gies. In fact, as advocated in connectivism, acting as part of a strong knowledge network allows for adaptation to current knowledge needs.

Once a theoretical framework has been set up, we will look into aspects of knowledge acquisition, dissemination and consolidation made possible by social software and web 2.0: track while scan, information filtering, information re-use, open source and crowd sourcing.

DOI: 10.4018/978-1-4666-2178-7.ch016

In this chapter, we will discuss how the requirements for professional expert knowledge have evolved through the Internet and its technologies. We will show how the role of social software not only impacts the way knowledge is created and disseminated, but also what an individual is expected to know in order to be considered an expert in the field. We will focus on examples of ICT (information and communications technology) experts, as they are easily recognized as such in society and have a close link to the technology discussed.

The Internet in general, and social software in particular, has an obvious impact on how ICT workers collaborate. This comes as no surprise. But changing ways of collaborating, in the end, also means changing expectations of co-workers' knowledge. When one builds a social network around a particular domain of knowledge, one comes to trust certain people for their knowledge. Building such a reliable network helps to forge a stable working environment. It helps to vet decisions and diminish uncertainties. In this chapter, we propose that the requirement for accuracy is a central and underestimated aspect when assessing expert knowledge. This requirement helps us understand why the ICT profession evolved in the way that it did, and why social software and web 2.0 have emerged as a natural environment for ICT knowledge acquisition, dissemination and consolidation.

The Knowledge of ICT Professionals

In what follows, we will look into the professional knowledge of ICT workers in small to large teams, typically SME's (small and medium enterprises) whose core business isn't ICT. The examples we have in mind are primarily the systems support people - like system administrators (sysadmins) - who are responsible for the company network, its servers, its main application hosting and in many cases, providing support for the users of its infrastructure.

While the ICT profession has a solid basis in mathematics in general and computer science in particular, the cases that we examine demonstrate how a large amount of the expert knowledge required is acquired through trial and error, and through a reliance on so-called "best practices". The trial-and-error methodology - inherent in designing ICT solutions - makes for loose selection criteria, many solutions for the same problem, a lack of convincing arguments and the distinct feeling amongst customers that they are dealing with an immature business.

It also means that supervision is hard to accomplish: an ICT-manager is often in charge of several specialized domain teams, the members of which have more in-depth knowledge than the manager himself. Whereas the team leader is typically a *primus inter pares*, the manager supervising the team leaders is neither a primus (he/she doesn't have the specialty of the teams) nor an equal: his/her way of dealing with ICT is on a more functionally abstract, organizational level. This leads us to a first, important observation, viz. that supervision of expert teams is only partially based upon individual knowledge. Merely knowing more about the same subject is not the sufficient condition of being a qualified ICT manager.

Supervision of ICT is then managed through several possible mechanisms:

- The implementation of ICT management standards such as COBIT (www.isaca.org/Knowledge-Center/COBIT) or ITIL (www.itil-officialsite.com), which provide general frameworks that ensure one is prepared for all possible risks – this is mainly the case in larger organizations;
- Certification or accreditation of ICT professionals, for certain roles;
- Auditing, both internal and external;
- Consultation;
- Peer assessment;
- In service training.

The ICT manager must make sure that his/her collaborators prove that their knowledge is up-to-date and that they have acquired their opinions through acceptable channels, such as training, the consultation of peers, reading professional literature, conforming to audit reports, and implementing accepted standards. While the average ICT professional enjoys exceptionally high levels of knowledge, this knowledge is:

- For a large part not what he/she has learned in college;
- Mostly insufficient to perform the job without additional information;
- Elusive to his/her supervisors;
- Often incoherent and poorly underpinned.

ICT professionals have coped with this situation by adopting social software and web 2.0 technologies, to share experiences and get required knowledge on demand (Andres & Akan, 2010; Andres & Shipps, 2010; Al-Taitoon et.al., 2003). These tools encompass:

- Blogs, mostly to testify about day-to-day experiences and to share expert opinions;
- Wikis, in most cases to build structured documentation;
- Tweets, as a kind of background chatter, to stay current on what is happening at conferences or in projects;
- Forums, which are still the number one source for detailed knowledge on software installation issues;
- Feeds, which can be used as alert lists, and which make it possible to easily follow a multitude of online sources;
- Specialized bibliographical and technical online databases (many have disappeared in favor of Wikipedia);
- Instant messaging tools to chat.

Hendriks (1999) discusses how the motivation for sharing knowledge is stimulated by technol-ogy; van de Hooff e.a. (2003) highlights the link with knowledge communities; and Owen-Smith & Powell (2004), Lin (2007), Chang & Harrington (2007), Björk & Magnussen (2009) and Boshuizen & Geurts (2009) provide in-depth studies of how this relates to innovation capability.

Apart from the more traditional sources of information - like scientific journal articles, library collections, conferences, scientific organization reports, ICT company documentation and websites - a lot of informal, public sources are available and take a more prominent role, due to their findability through Google and other search engines (Battelle 2005; Morville 2005). To many, Google itself has become an expert-on-demand, always readily available (Lu & Yuan 2011). Through clever use of social software, a junior ICT professional will be able to rapidly become part of a network, know how to identify trusted sources, and find ways to get the knowledge he/she needs on time. For a typical helpdesk operator this involves knowledge of specialized websites. *Tweakers.net* or *Slashdot.org* are very popular, just like magazines such as *C&T*. For an ICT professional, a lot of knowledge is stored on computers, in the 'cloud', and on diverse electronic devices, so that it is easily retrievable when needed, as if it were an extension of the mind itself (an idea advanced by Clark & Chalmers in 1998). These technology-enhanced, online knowledge sources simultaneously allow for and support the increased mobility of the ICT workforce, which in its turn has an impact on work practices (Kakihara 2003). It also means the classical library is rapidly transforming itself into a collection of web services (see Schiltz et.al., 2007 and Holmberg et.al., 2009).

Social network sites improve on printed media through their speed (which is very relevant for e.g. computer security) and interactivity. This has led more hardware and software vendors to abandon printed documentation of their products, and instead, offer the necessary information online. There are those who do want to have printed materials, and for whom a flourishing secondary market now offers expensive handbooks.

When a system administrator performs a Linux installation, in most cases his/her foreknowledge will not be sufficient. It is very likely that the software distribution contains new packages that differ from the previous installation, which may or may not create incompatibilities with existing software. So the likelihood that the system administrator will need up-to-date knowledge during the installation process is very high. To be able to perform these tasks in a routine manner, a typical sysadmin will not only read specialized magazines, but will monitor various news feeds and forums, to be rapidly aware of what is to be expected. When unforeseen situations arise, a quick search on the net will often give useful clues, but it is not uncommon to initiate an internet chat session, with colleagues who cope with similar problems.

The ICT Expert

Let us have a closer look into the example of the typical sysadmin, responsible for a small- to-medium sized ICT infrastructure. This includes servers, PC workstations, laptops, and a network (with routers, switches, an internet access point, and maybe some wireless access points). Mostly, his/her task will consist of designing network architecture, planning the cabling, making order requests for the acquisition of servers, installing those servers, installing management software for them, organizing workstation deployment, rolling out software on PC's, performing upgrades and maintenance, and examining security. These are quite versatile jobs, and most SME's do not have many qualified personnel to do this: if the system administrator is not working alone, it will often only be in a team of two or three, with one senior member.

In most cases, a bachelor degree in Applied Informatics is required (see Hagan, 2004). The curriculum consists of a sizable portion of math,

theoretical courses stemming from computer science, some information management courses, an apprenticeship and practical seminars. Students following these curricula have a quite specific profile. It is not uncommon that their hobbies are also related to computing, or computer gaming (Guzman & Stanton 2009). A substantial portion of the knowledge they need on the job stems from informal learning at home or at sideline jobs. They usually have a home network, routers and more than one PC.

Although their highest level of schooling is, generally speaking, a bachelor's degree, most of them are perceived as "experts". This has to do with the relatively rare availability of people with this profile (Lovegrove & Round 2005), and the fact that, in today's society, their knowledge has become increasingly relevant (Moleke et.al., 2003). A typical "computer geek" will be regarded as someone with very detailed, reliable knowledge, who is very confident in what he/she is doing and who is very literate in it. There is a lot of literature about the relation between "geek" or "nerd" and "ICT professional" largely centering on gender aspects, since it is perceived that the geek image might deter young women from joining the profession (see for e.g., Young, 2003; Pau et.al., 2005; Crump et.al., 2007; Varma, 2007; Hunter, 2009). The role these ICT savvy people take up, whether at work or at home, is clearly that of an expert: they are often asked for advice on what ICT equipment to buy, how to install software, how to protect against viruses and malware and so on. They would also give consultations on how to set up a home network and could give valuable advice to smaller businesses about how to run a website.

Informal, On-the-Job Learned Knowledge

It is important to note a few striking aspects about what ICT experts tend to know. First, the bulk of their knowledge is only remotely related to their university-level studies. Despite their comprehensive study of math, the 'rule of three' is what they will most often use. A lot of mathematical concepts like matrices are very present in ICT, but they have been operationalized, and it is perfectly possible to grasp them for the purposes of ICT (e.g. filling an array with values) without active knowledge of the mathematical theory involved. Logic reasoning and analytical skills are of course required, and are part of the psycho-technical tests that candidates have to take for an ICT job. But one can have the analytical prowess without having a deep mathematical insight.

Second, the knowledge they need to perform their day-to-day professional duties is very close to the knowledge they build up informally, through their hobby. Third, their "expert knowledge" is quite different from the scientific knowledge that they have been given in formal education: much of it is 'know how' rather than propositional knowledge, it is ill-structured, not systematic, has come about through trial-and-error, rather than through deductive reasoning or organized experimental methodology. And finally, while what they know helps them to make decisions with amazing certainty, it is difficult for them to make explicit the implicit know-how on the basis of which they make such decisions. And even though this knowledge is very detailed, it is not quite theoretically elaborate. To give one example: in job interviews, such experts often have difficulties spelling out and correctly explaining the full name of an ICT acronym. It is not uncommon to find a system administrator capable of building small databases, which perform quite well, to support his/her work but who, on the other hand, would fail to list rather introductory knowledge on database theory.

The failure to academically ground crucial knowledge, and the need to rightfully acknowledge the place of importance that informal, learned on-the-job knowledge holds, makes it necessary to define both common standards of reference and social accreditation mechanisms, in order to vali-

date the acquired competencies (see Theoharidou & Gritzalis 2007 as an example in the domain of computer security).

The Social Network

How can knowledge that is badly needed and highly regarded have such murky academic credentials? This has to do with several factors. One obvious reason is the volatility and ever-evolving nature of these technological domains. It is, for a systems engineer, very rare to order the same server hardware more than once. It suffices that a few months elapse, and the vendor will have already updated his/her catalogue and/or made technical changes. There is a very rapid obsolescence cycle in such hardware. The validity of the knowledge one acquires will often expire, and sooner rather than later. But an even more important factor is that there is simply too much knowledge generated on the fly, in particular work situations, for all of it to be captured by the formal education system. ICT is typically a field that offers generic solutions that have to be customized for a wide variety of application domains.

So how do ICT professionals cope with this problem? It is here that developments in Internet and web technology in general, and social software in particular, come into play. In fact, a typical sysadmin will use an array of tools to get the required information on time, on demand.

Suppose a new server needs to be installed. Chances are some of the hardware drivers must be adjusted. This means that during installation, new parameters have to be implemented and/or modified. It is likely the sysadmin will opt for:

- A Google search;
- A scan on a website that hosts drivers;
- Consulting a forum, about the type of hardware or the flavor of Linux that is being installed;
- Consulting a wiki ;

• Starting a chat session with some other expert, who might already have the required experience.

The fact that an ICT expert is using multimode communications to fill in daily knowledge gaps does not mean that his/her knowledge is just based on hearsay. In fact, the ICT expert develops metacognitive skills to assess the validity of his/her sources (Schiltz et.al., 2007). He/she will know which blogs to read, where to find documentation online, which peers to chat with. Strongly embedded in his/her community of practice (see Wenger, 1998), he/she manages to form reliable judgments on the issues at hand, even if his/her classical schoolbook knowledge on the field proves to be unimpressive.

Today's expertise in ICT doesn't stand on its own. Its credibility not only depends on the classical, formal education that is based on scientific research. The expertise is socially acquired by the ICT professional, in the way that he/she interacts with his/her social environment, by being connected to the right people (e.g. through LinkedIn), by reading the right forums and blogs, and by being appreciated by his/her peers. Nordan et.al. (2008) discuss how digital social networks help ICT professionals to develop conceptual, contextual and operational knowledge.

It is important to note, however, that this social network goes far beyond his/her peers. Ideally, the network involves representative stakeholders in the knowledge domain. An ICT expert working on systems for the visually impaired will often find himself involved in websites of the social organizations for this group. This kind of social network allows for ICT developments to directly get in touch with the stakeholders involved (Von Konsky, 2008).

Individual Expertise, Mainstream Solutions

Suppose you ask an ICT expert how to implement a wireless security solution. As it happens, he/she has made a particular setup long before a mainstream app has been launched, and still uses it because it matches 90% of the required performance criteria. But do we want him/her to recommend the same solution to us? As an expert, he/she still ought to recommend the mainstream solution, or at least mention it and explain why it has become so popular, instead of bluntly proposing to do it with his/her own solution. We expect that experts are on top of what is happening in their field, and can argue why they hold dissenting opinions or propose uncommon solutions in particular cases.

There is more to being an expert than know-how. It is equally important to know how a problem is solved in a *standard* or *generally accepted* way and what the standard solutions are. Of course, precisely because one is an expert, one can also find ad hoc solutions when mainstream solutions are not available. However, resilience by ICT professionals in adopting mainstream solutions when they become available remains a problem. That is why an ICT manager will usually want a survey of existing alternatives and propose a methodology in which different aspects of the solutions under consideration are compared. ICT people with seniority tend to have a better overview of the different aspects of an ICT problem. For example, one might want to consider interoperability, user-friendliness, existing experience base, financial aspects, and security when developing an ICT solution.

So, although the expertise of an ICT professional is a very personal matter, stemming from a lot of informal and on-the-job learning, there is a need for a second opinion, and for social corroboration of the acquired insights, in order to avoid idiosyncratic solutions that are not scalable.

Given the way much of the individual expertise comes about - highly linked to personal motivation, learned informally on-the-job, through the buildup of a knowledge network, and the need to keep all this in line with mainstream, scalable solutions - it is very important that organizations like SME's develop a strategy to capture this knowledge and consolidate it into the organization (see Huysman & Derksen, 1998; Huysman & De Wit, 2002 and 2004; Orlikowski, 2002; Ikujiro et.al., 2006).

In today's knowledge networks, expectations about the justification of knowledge have changed dramatically. We expect the knowledge worker to "prove" that he/she is 'in the know' by demonstrating the validity of the network that helps him to make his/her decisions. This means that, apart from standard demands like proving that you have followed updater or specialization courses, we also require that the knowledge worker self-certifies himself by showing: that he/she actively participates in networks highly regarded by his/her peers; that he/she explains and is able to validate the sources of his/her information; and that he/she can show that experts with similar competencies would come to similar decisions, based on standard criteria.

Alvin Goldman (2001) holds that cognitive expertise should be defined in 'veritistic' (i.e. truth-linked) terms: "Experts in a given domain …have more beliefs (or higher degrees of belief) in true propositions and/or fewer beliefs in false propositions within that domain than most other people (or better: than the vast majority of people) do" (Goldman, 2001, p. 91). "An expert… in domain D is someone who possesses an extensive fund of knowledge (true belief) and a set of skills or methods for apt and successful deployment of this knowledge to new questions in the domain." (Idem, p. 92) Goldman's reliabilistic account of knowledge stems from the simple observation that in most cases, the expert knows more truths about the subject than other people. The latter is not deemed a coincidence, but is supposed to rely on the fact that the expert is using reliable

methods to come to his/her assessments. Methods are reliable when they yield the same predictions in the same circumstances. The Internet, the web, and even more so web 2.0 (see O'Reilly, 2005) and social software have hugely contributed to the self-organization of expertise in the ICT context, where participants in forum discussions have found each other online, exchanged ideas and insights, and gradually built expertise networks where one knows who should be called an expert (see e.g. Björk & Magnusson 2009).

The social capital these experts acquire has multiple sources: authoritative relations to the subject matter at hand, e.g. when someone is the lead programmer of a given open source software suite, or just the way someone interacts on the forums, his/her 'karma' so to say (See Huysman & Wulf, 2004; Chiu, Hsu & Wang, 2006). There is something 'tribal' to it: a novice gets aggregated in a group and acquires some authority through time, if his/her statements prove reliable.

This means that ICT managers who hire ICT experts often scan the web to find blog posts and forum contributions to evaluate candidates. In many branches of technical ICT, such as systems engineering, operating systems or security, it is commonly known who are the "best of the best" when it comes to a particular piece of software or hardware.

However, the reliabilistic account of expert knowledge as formulated by Alvin Goldman does not fully capture the way knowledge works in our case of the ICT professional. First of all, claiming that the expert is the one who knows more about a subject matter is only part of what is the case. To be an expert, it does not suffice to know a lot about the subject. It is much more important to know the *right* propositions, i.e. those that matter in the context and fit the non-epistemic goals that are operative in the context. Amateurs know plenty of details on the subject of their hobby, e.g. astronomy, but they are not capable of functioning as a professional astronomer due to the fact that they both lack insight in what would be accurate knowledge and are incapable of seeing how it all fits together. The expert must not only be reliable, but also able to acquire and implement the right kind of knowledge. What he knows must be sufficiently accurate. In what follows, we will further develop the concept of accurate knowledge and explore how social software and web 2.0 bring a lot to the table to help filter the accurate truths in professional communication.

The Expert is Accurate

A lot of technically proficient people can make their PC work, and know a plethora of petty facts about computing. Some add to this a formal education in ICT, but this doesn't make them experts yet. They become experts when they manage to formulate what they know in such a way that their consultation makes sense for others to consult them. By offering in-depth knowledge to other professionals in an easily understandable way, one's expertise becomes appreciated by colleagues. This doesn't make each expert into an academic for that matter. The focus of professional expertise remains, rather, making the right judgments in the field, while on the job. An academic on the contrary can take more distance from particular situations and develop a more abstract view on the matter. Nevertheless, expertise does require adaptation to the right level of accuracy.

What do we mean by accuracy? A lot of statements are true, but not narrow enough to "hit the target" in all circumstances. For example, suppose my wife asks whether a glass on the table contains water. If I taste it and say yes, the statement "yes, it is water", is true and perfectly justified. I am a trustworthy informer when I would make this claim, and my wife has good reasons to believe me. However, if an apprentice in a laboratory asks whether the fluid in a glass is water, simply tasting is not really enough. A more elaborate way to determine the nature of a substance is required in the social context of a lab. I will also be required to make a more accurate statement: "this fluid is H_2O".

Seeking and receiving accurate information is an easily recognizable phenomenon. Consider Paul Grice's famous example in *Logic and Conversation*: A is planning with B an itinerary for a holiday in France. Both know that A wants to see his/her friend C, if doing so would not involve too great a prolongation of the journey.

A: Where does C live?
B: Somewhere in the South of France.

B's answer is, as he/she very well knows, not informative enough to meet A's needs. This infringement on the *Maxim of Quantity* ('Make your contribution as informative as is required for the current purposes of the conversation') can only be explained by the supposition that B is aware that to be more informative would be to say something that infringed upon the *Maxim of Quality*, ('Don't say what you lack adequate evidence for'), so B implicates that he/she does not know in which town C lives (Grice 1989, p. 34).

Grice's abductive explanation assumes it is commonly known, among the conversants, what would constitute an accurate answer to the question at this particular stage of the conversation. Although what B says is true, a more informative answer would infringe on the second maxim of Quality, which explains why B's contribution implicates that he/she does not know where C lives, *given* the standard of accurateness operative in the conversation. The example illustrates how the ulterior purpose of the exchange determines what will count as an *accurate* (and not just *true*) answer. If A and B were to discuss C's secret whereabouts on a need-to-know basis, B's answer could have been accurate enough. The operative standards of accuracy are therefore a function of what one needs to know in order to succeed in realizing non-epistemic projects: where to go on holiday, how to build a plane that should transport 520 passengers at least 8000 miles, etc. Merely telling and acquiring truths would be a parody of an epistemically fruitful conversation. Note that standards need not be *shared*: I can provide accurate information given that I know *your* epistemic purposes, even though I don't share them. Why invest costly epistemic efforts in irrelevant subjects just because the epistemic actions yield true beliefs (Grimm 2008, p. 731)? And given an interest in a subject matter, it is not just true but accurate beliefs we aim at. The additional, imposed constraint of accuracy de-trivializes the search for truth. (I know that Paris is more than 1 mile away from where I'm currently writing, but that inaccurate truth doesn't help me when planning the itinerary.)

Unlike accuracy, truth does not admit of degrees. If statements *S* and *S'* both express true propositions, one cannot be *more* true than the other while *S* can be more accurate than *S'* in the same context (Unger, 1974 and 1975, but compare Elgin, 2004; see Braun & Sider 2006, and Smith, 2008 for dissent). J. L. Austin famously held that 'true' and 'false' indicate "... a general dimension of being a right or proper thing to say, as opposed to a wrong thing, in these circumstances" (Austin 1962, p. 145). 'France is hexagonal' is in some contexts an accurate description of France's shape, but how can this be if the proposition expressed is literally false? And it must surely be false that a proposition is true *because* it was the proper thing to say.

What will count as an accurate truth is not determined by the subject matter that one's epistemic actions are directed toward, for the world cannot itself determine what will count as an accurate statement about it. Considerations that influence the setting of the operative standards and their attainability in the context of inquiry are informed by what motivates us to form a view about a topic or subject matter (visiting C in France, reaching Paris given the amount of fuel in the tank, building an instrument that satisfies specific safety requirements, …), and to select those outputs of one's epistemic actions that are accurate enough to serve those goals. 'Wanting to know the truth about what happened' implies that *accurate* truths about the events are being sought,

and the operative standard in this case may simply be set by the relevant Yes/No-question ('Did the bomb explode?'). The context of a question often contains good indications of what will count as an accurate answer to it. 'How many apples are there in this bag?' 'Less than 2000' will be a true but inaccurate answer. The exact number of apples in the bag, given a normal counting method, in this case sets the standard.

Accuracy and Reliability

In measurement theory, *accuracy* indicates the degree of proximity of a measured or calculated quantity to its reference value, sometimes misleadingly referred to as the 'true value', for no measurement is absolutely accurate. Its measurement-theoretical counterpart is *precision*, *i.e.* the degree to which a series of measurements or calculations have similar outcomes. Only in the context of a particular representative structure - the Fahrenheit scale for example - does the number 80 (an entity in the representing domain) represent some property of an object (its temperature). The smooth curvature of (graphed) data is an illustrative comparison: each data point on a curve is supposed to represent an independently ascertained truth, but the actual data rarely fall precisely on the curve (Elgin 2004).

Precision refers to the similarity of a series of measurement results, while accuracy is obtained insofar as a token result is close enough to an independently fixed value (the standard). Reliable methods need not yield accurate results. You could have a very precise measurement under a systematic bias, causing your results to be generally "off the mark". The overall precision of a series of results depends on its reproducibility within the laboratory and in other contexts. Many reliabilist accounts of knowledge capture the epistemological counterpart of precision – the reliability of process types that yield knowledge. In his tracking account of knowledge, Robert Nozick (1981) operates by tracking connections with the fact believed: (i) if *p* were not true, the agent wouldn't believe that *p*, and (ii) if *p* were true (under circumstances slightly differing from those actually obtaining), he/she would (still) believe that *p*. Once it is acknowledged that knowledge is true belief, acquired via reliable methods, the question of what the method is supposedly reliable for arises: producing a true belief in exactly those circumstances, producing a true belief in circumstances much like those actually obtaining, producing a true belief in all the circumstances likely enough to be worth considering, or producing a true belief in all possible circumstances (Craig 1999, p. 54)? Like *precision* (its measurement-theoretic counterpart), reliability is characterized by a *pattern*. But however reliable the process, token outcomes may still be inaccurate. Suppose that B is a very reliable informant with respect to C's country-wise whereabouts (in the reliabilist sense): in the actual world and in many nearby possible worlds, he/she has true beliefs about C's location – France or England. Yet it doesn't follow that he/she can give the information required by those who seek C's *exact* location in France or England. Alternatively, B may have come to know C's exact location in France, but only accidentally (he/she overheard a conversation about C). He/she will then provide accurate information based on an unreliable method. Note that accuracy requires public and attainable standards, while the workings of reliable processes are, on most versions of reliabilism, not directly accessible to agents. One can be very reliable at a cognitive task with little or no understanding of what makes one reliable. Our grasp of the belief-forming mechanisms may be largely tacit (Matthews 2007, p. 118).

Craig (1999) speaks of 'indicator properties' as those which an inquirer seeks to identify in an informant, as a guide to his or her truth-telling ability (p. 135). Our account suggests further indicator properties for experts: their ability to set appropriate standards of accuracy and to deliver on those standards. Ernest Sosa's analogy of the archer and her target (Sosa, 2003) can be particu-

larly helpful here: accuracy is to hit the point, and as she practices, she hits closer to the target and her accuracy improves. When her shots are tightly clustered, they are precise, and the archer becomes more reliable. Hitting the intended target involves compensating for whatever is causing her precision to veer from the target – she is trying to map actual precision to the public standard of accuracy (hitting the point, or whatever area she decides will be the target). Similarly, in inquiry we seek reliable agents who provide us with truths that satisfy the operative standards of accuracy. What counts as accurate information cannot be cashed out in terms of the truths an expert reliably detects. That would be like drawing a circle around arrows on a board and then to claim that the target was hit. It would also be a mistake to set standards too wide because it would turn any reliable method into one that yields accurate results (hitting the dartboard is easy). Those who set overambitious standards may overestimate the reliability of their methods. Practical goals, standards for accuracy, the reliability of one's epistemic methods in view of these goals and the operative standards set in view of these goals are interacting in practical epistemic rationality.

Accuracy is inherently conversational: it has to do with the attunement of one's epistemic methods to expectations set by non-epistemic goals. When I'm talking to my neighbor and say my house is 2 meters away from the street, my statement is true but not accurate enough for the water company who will need a more precise measurement. Standards of accuracy can shift from context to context.

Adding the notion of accuracy to the reliabilistic account of knowledge helps to build a theory that is much more apt to explain how professional knowledge works in the information age, and also takes into account the importance that multimode communications technologies so typically exemplified by social software and web 2.0 applications have taken in our knowledge creation networks. Without the constant attunement of standards of accuracy to the practical goals we are pursuing, we would end up with abstract and empty knowledge claims, and would no longer be able to sift essential insights from random facts.

Whereas the classical web, by greatly facilitating the spread of information, had the inherent drawback that this information, being largely decontextualized, could land in the hands of the wrong person at the wrong moment, or could be completely misunderstood or applied in the wrong circumstances, web 2.0 techniques embed information in a community of practice where the right statements are filtered out, and where the interpretative context is supported by online expert users.

Interactional Expertise

Harry Collins has highlighted the importance of informal knowledge, acquired in on-the-job learning (Collins, 2010). Tacit knowledge is the unspoken knowledge that you share with others on the job, and ensures that you speak a common "language" with those you collaborate with. Typically, it is what builds communities of practice. To the outsider, it may seem that the "language" ICT professionals share between each other is hermetic and not accessible. It does involve a lot of tacit knowledge, the threshold of which you have to pass in order to access the "inner circle".

But the knowledge we are talking about is only in partially tacit. It is not the knowledge that everyone should possess, to be able to participate. The knowledge we are hinting at, which is pulled from the internet on demand, is exactly the kind of knowledge that makes these ICT professionals "experts" and regarded as "being in the know". Yet they often do not master all details by heart, and often fail to grasp deeper models that could help explain their knowledge. So, it is evident that the requirements put on their ability to justify themselves have severely changed.

Collins and Evans distinguish several layers of specialist expertise (Collins & Evans, 2007).

Besides ubiquitous tacit knowledge, they discern contributory and interactional expertise: "over the last half-century, the most important transformation in the way expertise has been understood is a move away from seeing knowledge and ability as quasi logical or mathematical and toward a more wisdom-based or competence-based model"(Collins & Evans 2007, p. 23).

In order to better situate the work of Collins & Evans, we should first refer to the five stages of building contributory expertise described by Dreyfus and Dreyfus (1986). At the first stage we find the novice. The novice tries to follow rules by the book and is not very well adapted to changing conditions. In the second stage, that of the advanced beginner, more context-specific adaptation takes place. At the level of competence, in stage 3, the application of rules has become intuitive, and a large variety of situational indications are recognized and adapted to. One becomes proficient, at the fourth stage, when one is able to approach the whole problem in a holistic manner. In this scheme, expertise fully occurs at stage 5, with intuitive recognition of whole contexts and fluid performance.

The problem with this model, according to Collins and Evans, is that it looks at expertise in an individualistic way, and doesn't account for social negotiation (Collins & Evans, 2007, p. 26). This is an important point for the topic we are looking into right now. While a computer could learn to ride a bicycle (by giving the right inputs to keep the bicycle balanced), it would already be a lot harder to imagine a computer driving a bike through traffic. The social conventions that are proper to the group of participants in traffic require a lot of "understanding". So, while it can be argued that our brain does not actually perform the same complex calculations that are necessary for a computer to keep the bike balanced, it is more important to recognize that our brain does quite different things: it anticipates traffic. The latter is dependent on social understanding. Apart from adding the social perspective to contributory expertise, Collins and Evans introduce a notion with farther reaching implications: the notion of interactional expertise. Interactional expertise is expertise that is framed in the language of the specialization, and in the absence of practiced expertise (Collins & Evans 2007, p. 28).

Of course the ICT professionals we are looking into in this study are contributive experts, but when they – as is increasingly the case – document themselves through the web and social software, with information from other experts that explore areas that they themselves are less acquainted with, they fit the notion of interactional expertise very well: it sits in between practice-based knowledge and "academic" knowledge from books. It is the knowledge acquired by engaging with a social network that relates to practice. Conversely, we can argue that the notion of interactive expertise is precisely what is needed to describe the kind of expertise that we so often find with ICT professionals. The reason has to do with the very nature of the ICT profession itself. ICT technology supports a wide variety of human activities, and implementing an ICT solution involves understanding the social processes behind these activities. This means that in the analysis phase, many conversations will take place with domain specialists – contributive experts in their field – to detail the logic behind the practice, which needs to be supported by an ICT solution. A typical ICT business consultant or analyst will need to be able to acquire the vocabulary and core concepts of the domain he/she is working for. This means, e.g., understanding a lot of basic principles and accountant terminology when developing accounting software.

Sometimes, when large, transformational solutions have to be deployed, senior analysts will lead the startup phases of ICT projects. Sometimes, as is the case at Leuven University, a specialized function is created for this: in the case of Leuven University it is called an "information architect". But many, if not most ICT jobs, involve this balance between contributory expertise in the

strict ICT domain and interactional expertise in a serviced domain.

Of course, a developer working for years on accountant software will master a good deal of the language of accounting, without being an accountant. The ability to absorb the language of the domains supported by ICT is a differential skill, which often determines whether one will progress to higher, more organizational ICT functions, or contrarily develop a more technically oriented career that emphasizes the core contributive ICT expertise. Although the latter certainly can give access to highly remunerated jobs – technical expertise is high in demand - the former offers easier access to management functions, due to its broader scope and reliance on social skills.

A second reason why interactional expertise is so important to ICT functions is specialization. In fact, ICT, modular by nature, evolves in a multitude of directions. This makes it virtually impossible to be a "Jack of all trades", and to keep on top of every technical aspect related to the ICT solutions that one has to deploy. Web security is quite a different domain from, say, storage solutions or digital imaging. But more often than not, an ICT solution integrates these different functionalities into one networked whole. This inevitably implies teamwork and attunement with expert ICT colleagues. Even when someone is an expert in one of the core ICT domains, mastering the language(s) of the other expert(s) that make a contribution to the solution, will still be necessary. This requires interactional expertise.

Given the importance of the social network in interactional expertise, it comes as no surprise that social software is playing an increasingly vital role in the practical acquisition of those skill sets. Forums and blogs, and increasingly, *Twitter* and highly "socialized" websites like *Slashdot,* make it possible to stay current with the vocabulary and concepts of adjacent ICT domains.

This innovative notion of interactive knowledge also comes close to what is discussed in Georges Siemens' book *Knowing Knowledge*

(Siemens 2006). Connectivism, a theory advanced by George Siemens (Siemens 2004 and 2006) and Stephen Downes (2008) is an epistemic theory that stresses the fact that a lot of our current knowledge comes about because we are part of all these new technological networks. It sees knowledge not as a static collection such as in a library, but highlights its intricate relationship with learning and communication: "knowing and learning are today defined by connections. Connectivism is the assertion that learning is primarily a network forming process" (Siemens, 2006, p. 15).

For a discussion of connectivism see Kop & Hill (2008) and Guder (2010). Similar views, on the importance of networks for in knowledge, have been developed for another audience and with another main focus by Manuel Castells (1996), David Weinberger (2002 and 2007), and Yochai Benkler (2006).

Knowing Knowledge is targeted at a broad audience, aiming to help organizations in adapting their structure, so as to cope with the knowledge demands of the future. Even though the lack of technical finesse will leave professional philosophers unsatisfied, it is a good read that offers some compelling views on how important being connected and being part of a network is for the creation of knowledge. Knowledge is not seen as static, but fluid, with important roles for co-creation, dissemination, communication, personalization and - last but not least - implementation (Siemens 2006, p. 6). Siemens posits that "knowledge has changed; from categorization and hierarchies, to networks and ecologies." He points out that "this changes everything and emphasizes the need to change the spaces and structures of our organizations." (Siemens, 2006, p. v).

The ICT profession is a good example of this change: ICT professionals only partially rely on their academic training to do their work: the vast majority of what they must know to perform is learned on the job, by interacting with a robust network of information suppliers, whether those are websites, forums, chat rooms or interpersonal networks. Meta-cognition of these networks' validity is as important as a good understanding of the basic principles of ICT. Reliance on such networks allows ICT workers and teams to specialize without losing view on the larger picture.

Specialization and Separation of Duty

As mentioned earlier, specialization also means that a typical ICT manager is no longer a *primus inter pares*: his/her subordinates will often have more accurate knowledge. An example is a manager for information security, who can have someone on his/her team for Identity and Authentication Management (IAM). The latter's task is so complex that the IAM manager will almost naturally develop in-depth knowledge, which would be otherwise unavailable to his/her team leader. Supervision will consist in placing a demand on the subordinate to demonstrate competence in his/her field by regularly attending conferences and seminars on IAM, by proving membership in interest groups on this topic, and eventually, by requesting an external audit on a regular basis.

A similar evolution stems from the Sarbanes-Oxley (SOX) Act and similar legislation to implement separation of duty in business processes (Weil & Ross 2004). This legislation has a huge impact on accountancy systems and their more generic ICT support systems: in essence, it amounts to ICT support people no longer having all administrative rights to the systems they maintain; in purpose, it is a preventative measure against the implementation of unverified computer software in an accounting system, which would allow fraudulent schemes. The whole idea is that no one should be able to slip rogue software code into an accountancy software suite: those who vet the software to be included in a new release must be different from those who develop it and from those that draft the requirements. Of course, this means that much more information needs to be made explicit, and there is an increased demand for information exchange between developers and other ICT staff. It also means that no single individual has complete oversight of the system; the "knowledge" of how the system eventually works is collectively, rather than individually, held. This also implies that no single programmer involved in such a project can full justify of what he/she presumes to know. In the wake of the implementation of SOX, elaborate IT governance models have been developed to enhance the control of organizations over their ICT solutions and ICT workforce (an example of this is CoBIT 4.1).

This is a typical example of how increased specialization, exponential knowledge growth and security concerns cumulatively propel us to a point where there is more information than can be known by any professional alone in order to maintain oversight. This means that social organization is required to share the burden and minimize the risks. In these cases, web 2.0 applications fit very well, allowing for the capture of knowledge flow and keeping a trace of the knowledge built up in practice. Many companies have developed internal wiki's for sharing workplace knowledge, or keep daily blogs to inform employees of new procedures. In digital knowledge networks professionals can take up the role of experts vis-à-vis other professionals, who do not have the same specialization (Nordan et.al., 2008). This is what we would like to call the "knowledge circle": professional knowledge acquired on the job becomes the expert knowledge that is delivered to others. The key to these kinds of networks is that people take responsibility for a part of the knowledge domain: in essence, their message is: "Trust me, I'll sort that out". In this way other workers can concentrate on their part of the to-be-acquired knowledge and be confident there won't be any loose ends.

Track while Scan

Today's ICT professional should then, what we would call - using terminology from air combat

radars - "track while scan": while constantly scanning in a wide swath, for information throughout a social network about anything even remotely related to his/her field of expertise, the expert would zoom in and track specialized topics, which others trust him to follow. He/she would then report back to the community on his/her knowledge - e.g. how to implement certificates to safely retrieve emails on a smart phone - by discussing this in forums, posting on blogs, or documenting it on a wiki.

What is particularly striking when conducting job interviews with ICT professionals is the lack of precision and readily supplied knowledge on generic computing issues, compared to their very detailed knowledge in other areas. People with excellent programming skills can often be in doubt about the answers to simple questions, like whether HTTP is a Transmission or a Transfer protocol, or wouldn't know that JSON stands for Javascript Object Notation even though they make web applications using the technology.

Their high level of accuracy is compensatory for their lack of general knowledge: they actually have a very consistent and elaborate grasp of the HTTP protocol and how it works, and have no trouble implementing JSON solutions in a web project.

Is this a mere difference between "knowing how" and "knowing that?" Although this is an attractive expression, it doesn't seem to be the best account of the issue at hand. Of course, for a large part the expertise of an ICT job consists in "knowing how". Many of the skills acquired "on the job" are built on trial-and-error experience and are not systematized. But that doesn't mean this knowledge would be purely casuistic. Proof of this is how ICT professionals typically excel at solving and confronting new, unforeseen problems. Their understanding of the "mechanics of ICT" suggests that they have an above average ability to problem solve and to anticipate what will happen, even though their operating context is in constant evolution. They will prove to be very reliable in determining the truth of important statements about their field, while being less reliable on less relevant issues. Their expertise resides in their accuracy. In this way we feel Alvin Goldman's reliabilistic rendering of professional knowledge is not entirely complete.

Information Filtering

Compared to broadcast media, the Internet's multimode communications allow a more individualized approach that brings accurate information to the right person. For this to happen, the internet in its current web 2.0 form is organized in such a way that the internet agents (communities, bots, computer programs, scripts, other users) work together to filter out the desired information. Specific to the ICT field, one of the better examples is *Tweakers.net*, a state-of-the-art website with advanced forums, blogs, Q&A, sophisticated profile management and the possibility of fine-tuning the selection and frequency of the information retrieved. The "Tweaker Gallery", showing member activity, and the "Expert Panels," are especially innovative.

The expectations towards professional knowledge have been profoundly influenced by these technological developments. Whereas before, a trained expert was expected to know a sizable portion of his/her field by heart as ready knowledge, today, that would be a futile if not impossible undertaking: the knowledge is there, on demand, in the network, and it is the expert's duty to be able to retrieve it when needed.

This means much more emphasis is put on metacognitive skills, such as knowledge about reliable sources, trusted informants, and relevant aspects. It is also important to know the right procedures and accepted methodologies for assessing information and using it. Today's professional is capable of identifying his/her training needs and where he/she can obtain it, invoking external audits or consultation, reading the right professional

magazines, online blogs or scientific journals and utilizing direct chat lines with people in the know.

Information Re-Use, MASHUPs, Re-Packaging, and Translation

Of increasing importance is the skill of translating information into knowledge, at the right level of accuracy that is needed for the task. A math paper can become the basis of a small script to perform a complex indexing action. Information from multiple and diverse sources has to be compiled in a power-point presentation and report to describe a new ICT policy. In many ways, the re-packaging and re-use of information, to build adequate knowledge in a particular setting, is the professional norm.

As mentioned earlier, an expert is someone who knows the expected level of accuracy required by higher stakes, has views on how we could improve accuracy levels on the one hand, and more importantly, is able to choose an appropriately lower level of accuracy, to communicate information to non-experts.

Only with the latter skills can expert knowledge be passed through to other professionals in the knowledge network.

This way, a knowledge circle is formed where the expert translates knowledge into more accessible information for other professionals, and who in their turn build new expert knowledge which is adapted to their professional field. This way there can be a feedback loop, leading to an upward spiral of ever-increasing levels of accuracy. The real strength of social software is that it allows for an easy, endless recombination of knowledge chunks into new 'mashups', accessible to new user groups in other disciplines and for hitherto unforeseen applications (Hey, 2010). Good examples of mashups are *Google NGram* (ngrams.googlelabs.com) and *Yahoo Pipes* (pipes.yahoo.com).

Open Source and Crowdsourcing

To make knowledge dissemination on the web viable, it is necessary to adopt an open attitude towards sharing (Brown & Duguid, 2002; Brown et.al,. 2008). From very early on, open source software and open licensing models have driven the internet to provide common knowledge resources to ICT professionals. The importance of openly available knowledge, as we find it today on *Wikipedia* and as it is often provided under a GPL, GNU or Creative Commons licensing model, cannot be overestimated. Available through a simple Google search, such knowledge, or, in more elaborate forms, scripts or even complete software solutions through *Sourceforge*, can be discovered by people working in very different domains of expertise, so that insights spread beyond one's own field of competence. This increasingly popular way of rapid development ensures that unexpected, out-of-the-box solutions can emerge. Information sharing on the web has taken a decisive step with social software, since now these open resources are not simply distributed on the web, but shared in an interactive way so that anyone can contribute.

Crowdsourcing takes this idea even further: in this case, projects rely on the wisdom and contribution of the crowds, by inviting internet users to participate in designs, decisions, and visions for the project (See Hudson-Smith et.al., 2009; Doan & Halevy, 2011). Robson and Rew (2010) discuss how the idea of crowd sourcing is used even in unexpected contexts, such as surgical oncology, by relying on group knowledge to make difficult decisions. Similar research has been done by Samantha Adams on health service improvements (Adams, 2011).

CONCLUSION

In this chapter, we had a thorough look into how ICT professionals perform their work as experts.

We have pointed out that the ICT community has found innovative ways to share knowledge collaboratively, using social software and other web technologies. We have also tried to link this up with current literature on learning and social epistemology, and shown how our expectations towards the knowledge of experts are changing.

ICT expert knowledge is distributed in a knowledge network, supported by Internet technologies, so that it can be delivered on demand. The ICT expert has the meta-cognitive skills to position him or herself in this network, to assess the quality of his/her informants and to make an adequate judgment in increasingly specific situations. On the other hand, the expert's opinions and advice should be scalable to mainstream demands, and should be measured against industry standards. This way, the ICT expert is both reliable and accurate. His/her judgments have a responsibility to a specific knowledge domain that he/she has endorsed. Social networks, and in particular the social software solutions in support of those, capture these responsibilities, to make them transparent and explicit. The separation of duties is also an allocation of duties, in a virtualized workforce. Today's recipes - such as open source, and crowd sourcing - are typical examples of how acquiring and sustaining knowledge has become a collective task in the context of ICT professionals.

REFERENCES

Adams, S. A. (2011). Sourcing the crowd for health services improvement. *Social Science & Medicine, 72*, 1069–1076. doi:10.1016/j.socscimed.2011.02.001

Al-Taitoon, A., Sörensen, C., & Gibson, D. (2003). Modern professionals and their tools: ICT supporting organizational flexibility and control. *Proceedings of 11th European Conference of Information Systems*. Retrieved from http://is2.lse.ac.uk/asp/aspecis/20030147.pdf

Andres, H. P., & Akan, O. H. (2010). Assessing team learning in technology-mediated collaboration: An experimental Study. *Journal of Educational Technology Systems*, *38*(4), 473–487. doi:10.2190/ET.38.4.g

Andres, H. P., & Shipps, B. P. (2010). Team learning in technology-mediated distributed teams. *Journal of Information Systems Education*, *21*(2), 213–221.

Austin, J. L. (1962). *How to do things with words*. Oxford, UK: University Press.

Battelle, J. (2005). *The search: How Google and its rivals rewrote the rules of business and transformed our culture*. New York, NY: Penguin.

Benkler, Y. (2006). *The wealth of networks: How social production transforms markets and freedom*. New Haven, CT: Yale University Press.

Björk, J., & Magnusson, M. (2009). Where do good innovation ideas come from? Exploring the influence of network connectivity on innovation idea quality. *Journal of Product Innovation Management*, *26*(6), 662–670. doi:10.1111/j.1540-5885.2009.00691.x

Boshuizen, J., & Geurts, P. (2009). Regional social networks as conduits for knowledge spillovers: Explaining performance of high-tech firms. *Tijdschrift voor Economische en Sociale Geografie*, *100*(2), 183–197. doi:10.1111/j.1467-9663.2009.00528.x

Braun, D., & Sider, T. (2006). Vague, so untrue. *Noûs (Detroit, Mich.)*, *41*, 133–156. doi:10.1111/j.1468-0068.2007.00641.x

Brown, J. S., & Duguid, P. (2002). *The social life of information*. Harvard Business Press.

Castells, M. (1996). *The rise of the network society. The information age: Economy, society and culture* (*Vol. 1*). Oxford: Blackwell.

Chang, M. H., & Harrington, J. E. Jr. (2007). Innovators, imitators, and the evolving architecture of problem-solving networks. *Organization Science*, *18*(4), 648–666. doi:10.1287/orsc.1060.0245

Chiu, C.-M., Hsu, M.-H., & Wang, E. T. G. (2006). Understanding knowledge sharing in virtual communities: An integration of social capital and social cognitive theories. *Decision Support Systems*, *42*(3), 1872–1888. doi:10.1016/j.dss.2006.04.001

Collins, H. (2010). *Tacit knowledge*. University of Chicago Press.

Collins, H., & Evans, R. (2007). *Rethinking expertise*. University of Chicago Press.

Craig, E. (1999). *Knowledge and the state of nature*. Oxford, UK: Clarendon Press. doi:10.1093/0198238797.001.0001

Crump, B. J., Logan, K. A., & McIlroy, A. (2007). Does gender still matter? A study of the views of women in the ICT industry in New Zealand. *Gender, Work and Organization*, *14*(4), 349–370. doi:10.1111/j.1468-0432.2007.00348.x

Doan, A., Ramakrishnan, R., & Halevy, A. Y. (2011). Crowdsourcing systems on the World-Wide Web. *Communications of the ACM*, *54*(4), 86–96. doi:10.1145/1924421.1924442

Downes, S. (2008). How do you know? *Theoretical foundations of distance education online course*. September 1, 2008. Retrieved from http://orgunx. anadolu.edu.tr/etanit.asp?oy=2006&dn=001&dk =UZE501&dl=01&dg=&yy=1&br=5506010100 &tc=26710713580>

Dreyfus, H. L., & Dreyfus, S. E. (1986). *Mind over machine: the power of human intuition and expertise in the age of the computer*. Oxford, UK: Basil Blackwell.

Elgin, C. Z. (2004). True enough. *Philosophical Issues*, *14*, 113–131. doi:10.1111/j.1533-6077.2004.00023.x

Goldman, A. I. (1999). *Knowledge in a social world*. New York, NY: Oxford University Press. doi:10.1093/0198238207.001.0001

Goldman, A. I. (2001). Experts: Which ones should you trust? *Philosophy and Phenomenological Research, 63*(1), 85–110. doi:10.1111/j.1933-1592.2001.tb00093.x

Grice, P. (1989). *Studies in the way of words*. Boston, MA: Harvard University Press.

Guder, C. (2010). Patrons and pedagogy: A look at the theory of connectivism. *Public Services Quarterly, 6*(1), 36–42. doi:10.1080/15228950903523728

Guzman, I. R., & Stanton, J. M. (2009). IT occupational culture: The cultural fit and commitment of new information technologists. *Information Technology & People, 22*(2), 157–187. doi:10.1108/09593840910962212

Hagan, D. (2004). Employer satisfaction with ICT graduates. *Proceedings of the Sixth Conference on Australasian Computing Education,* Vol. 30, (pp. 119–123).

Hendriks, P. (1999). Why share knowledge? The influence of ICT on the motivation for knowledge sharing. *Knowledge and Process Management, 6*(2), 91–100. doi:10.1002/(SICI)1099-1441(199906)6:2<91::AID-KPM54>3.0.CO;2-M

Holmberg, K., Huvila, I., Kronqvist-Berg, M., & Widén-Wulff, G. (2009). What is library 2.0? *The Journal of Documentation, 65*(4), 668–681. doi:10.1108/00220410910970294

Hudson-Smith, A., Batty, M., Crooks, A., & Milton, R. (2009). Mapping for the masses: Accessing web 2.0 through crowdsourcing. *Social Science Computer Review, 27*(4), 524–538. doi:10.1177/0894439309332299

Hunter, A. (2009). High-tech rascality: Asperger's syndrome, hackers, geeks, and personality types in the ICT industry. *Editorial: Closing the income gap with Australia*, 39.

Huysman, M., & de Wit, D. (2002). *Knowledge sharing in practice*. Springer.

Huysman, M., & de Wit, D. (2004). Practices of managing knowledge sharing: Towards a second wave of knowledge management. *Knowledge and Process Management, 11*(2), 81–92. doi:10.1002/kpm.192

Huysman, M., & Derksen, F. (1998). Learning from the environment: Exploring the relationship between organizational learning, knowledge management and information/communication technology. *AMCIS 1998 Proceedings*, (p. 200).

Huysman, M., & Wulf, V. (2004). *Social capital and information technology*. MIT Press.

Ikujiro, N., von Krogh, G., & Voelpel, S. (2006). Organizational knowledge creation theory: Evolutionary paths and future advances. *Organization Studies, 27*(8), 1179–1208. doi:10.1177/0170840606066312

Kakihara, M. (2003). *Emerging work practices of ICT-enabled mobile professionals*. Unpublished doctoral dissertation, University of London, UK.

Kop, R., & Hill, A. (2008). Connectivism: Learning theory of the future or vestige of the past? *International Review of Research in Open and Distance Learning, 9*(3), 1–13.

Lin, H.-F. (2007). Knowledge sharing and firm innovation capability: An empirical study. *International Journal of Manpower, 28*(3/4), 315–332. doi:10.1108/01437720710755272

Lovegrove, G., & Round, A. (2005). *IT professionals in education: Increasing the supply*. Report from the north-east regional meeting, November 2005. Retrieved from http://www.bcs.org/upload/pdf/itprofnewcastle.pdf

Lu, L., & Yuan, Y. C. (2011). Shall I Google it or ask the competent villain down the hall? The moderating role of information need in information source selection. *Journal of the American Society for Information Science and Technology, 62*(1), 133–145. doi:10.1002/asi.21449

Matthews, R. J. (2007). *The measure of mind: Propositional attitudes and their attribution.* Oxford, UK: Oxford University Press.

Moleke, P., Paterson, A., & Roodt, J. (2003). *ICT and associated professionals. Human resources development review 2003: Education, employment and skills in South Africa* (pp. 634–659). Cape Town, South Africa: HSRC Press.

Morville, P. (2005) *Ambient findability.* Cambridge, MA: O'Reilly Publishing.

Nordan, N. A. M., Abidin, A. I. Z., Mahmood, A. K., & Arshad, N. I. (2008). Digital social networks: Examining the knowledge characteristics. *World Academy of Science. Engineering and Technology, 45,* 248–254.

O'Reilly, T. (2005) *What is Web 2.0? – Design patterns and business models for the next generation of software.* Retrieved from http://www.oreillynet.com/pub/a/oreilly/tim/news/2005/09/30/what-is-web-20.html

Orlikowski, W. J. (2002). Knowing in practice: Enacting a collective capability in distributed organizing. *Organization Science, 13*(3), 249–273. doi:10.1287/orsc.13.3.249.2776

Owen-Smith, J., & Powell, W. W. (2004). Knowledge networks as channels and conduits: The effects of spillovers in the Boston biotechnology community. *Organization Science, 15*(1), 5–21. doi:10.1287/orsc.1030.0054

Pau, R., Argles, D., White, S., & Lovegrove, G. (2005). *Computer geek versus computer chic: IT career and IT education.* 6th International Women into Computing Conference, Greenwich, UK. Retrieved from http://eprints.ecs.soton.ac.uk/id/eprint/10840

Robson, N., & Rew, D. (2010). Collective wisdom and decision making in surgical oncology. *European Journal of Surgical Oncology, 36*(3), 230–236. doi:10.1016/j.ejso.2010.01.002

Schiltz, M., Truyen, F., & Coppens, H. (2007). Cutting the trees of knowledge: Social software, information architecture and their epistemic consequences. *Thesis Eleven, 89,* 94-114.

Siemens, G. (2004). *Connectivism: A learning theory for the Digital* Age. Retrieved from http://www.elearnspace.org/Articles/connectivism.htm

Siemens, G. (November 12, 2006). *Connectivism: Learning theory or pastime for the self-amused?* Retrieved from http://www.elearnspace.org/Articles/connectivism_self-amused.htm

Smith, N. J. J. (2008). *Vagueness and degrees of truth.* Oxford, UK: Oxford University Press. doi:10.1093/acprof:oso/9780199233007.001.0001

Sosa, E. (2003). The place of truth in epistemology. In DePaul, M., & Zagzebski, L. (Eds.), *Intellectual virtue: Perspectives from ethics and epistemology.* Oxford, UK: Oxford University Press.

Theoharidou, M., & Gritzalis, D. (2007). Common body of knowledge for information security. *Security & Privacy, 5*(2), 64–67. doi:10.1109/MSP.2007.32

Unger, P. (1975). *Ignorance.* Oxford, UK: Oxford University Press.

Van den Hooff, B., Elving, W., Meeuwsen, J. M., & Dumoulin, C. (2003). Knowledge sharing in knowledge communities. In Huysman, M., Wenger, E., & Wulf, V. (Eds.), *Communities and technologies* (pp. 119–141). Deventer, The Netherlands: Kluwer, B.V.

Varma, R. (2007). Women in computing: The role of geek culture. *Science as Culture, 16*(4), 359. doi:10.1080/09505430701706707

Von Konsky, B. (2008). Defining the ICT profession: A partnership of stakeholders. *Proceedings of the 21st Annual NACCQ Conference,* (pp. 4–7).

Weinberger, D. (2002). *Small pieces loosely joined: A unified theory of the Web.* New York, NY: Basic Books.

Weinberger, D. (2007). *Everything is miscellaneous: The power of the new digital disorder.* New York, Ny: Henry Holt and Company.

Young, J. (2003). The extent to which information communication technology careers fulfill the career ideals of girls. *Australasian Journal of Information Systems, 10*(2), 115–125.

ADDITIONAL READING

Brown, J. S., & Adler, R/ P. (2008). Minds on fire: Open education, the long tail, and learning 2.0. *EDUCAUSE Review, 43*(1), 16–32.

Clark, A., & Chalmers, D. J. (1998). The extended mind. *Analysis, 58*, 10–23. doi:10.1093/analys/58.1.7

Foley, R. (2001). *Intellectual trust in ourselves and others.* Cambridge, UK: Cambridge University Press. doi:10.1017/CBO9780511498923

Giere, R. (2006). *Scientific perspectivism.* Chicago, IL: University of Chicago Press.

Goldman, A. (1986). *Epistemology and cognition.* Cambridge, MA: Harvard University Press.

Goldman, A. (1999). *Knowledge in a social world.* New York, NY: Oxford University Press. doi:10.1093/0198238207.001.0001

Goldman, A. (2009). Social epistemology: Theory and applications. *Epistemology. Royal Institute of Philosophy, 64*(Supplement), 1–18. doi:10.1017/S1358246109000022

Goldman, A. I. (2004). *Pathways to knowledge: Private and public.* Oxford: Oxford University Press.

Grimm, S. (2008). Epistemic goals and epistemic values. *Philosophy and Phenomenological Research, 77*(3), 725–744. doi:10.1111/j.1933-1592.2008.00217.x

Hempel, C. (1965). *Aspects of scientific explanation and other essays in the philosophy of science.* New York, NY: Free Press.

Hey, T. (2010). The next scientific revolution. *Harvard Business Review, 88*(11), 56–63.

Kusch, M. (2002). *Knowledge by agreement.* Oxford, UK: Clarendon Press. doi:10.1093/0199251223.001.0001

Kusch, M. (2009). Testimony and the value of knowledge. In Haddock, A., Millard, A., & Pritchard, D. H. (Eds.), *Epistemic value* (pp. 60–95). Oxford, UK: Oxford University Press. doi:10.1093/acprof:oso/9780199231188.003.0004

Kvanvig, J. (1992). *The intellectual virtues and the life of the mind: On the place of the virtues in epistemology.* Savage, MD: Rowan and Littlefield.

Matthews, R. J. (2007). *The measure of mind: Propositional attitudes and their attribution.* Oxford, UK: Oxford University Press.

Nozick, R. (1981). *Philosophical explanations.* Cambridge, UK: Harvard University Press.

Richard, M. (2008). *When truth gives out.* Oxford, UK: Oxford University Press. doi:10.1093/acprof:oso/9780199239955.001.0001

Scheffler, I. (2009). *Worlds of truth: A philosophy of knowledge.* New York, NY: Oxford University Press. doi:10.1002/9781444310948

Stalnaker, R. (1974). Pragmatic presupposition. In Munitz, M., & Unger, P. (Eds.), *Semantics and philosophy.* New York, NY: New York University Press.

Suarez, M. (2003). Scientific representation: Against similarity and isomorphism. *International Studies in the Philosophy of Science, 17*, 225–244. doi:10.1080/0269859032000169442

Teller, P. (2011). Two models of truth. *Analysis, 71*(3), 465–472. doi:10.1093/analys/anr049

Unger, P. (1974). Truth. In Munitz, M. K., & Unger, P. (Eds.), *Semantics and philosophy: Studies in contemporary philosophy* (pp. 257–290). New York, NY: New York University Press.

Unger, P. (1975). *Ignorance: The case for skepticism*. Oxford, UK: Oxford University Press.

Van Fraassen, B. (2008). *Scientific representation*. Oxford, UK: Oxford University Press. doi:10.1093/acprof:oso/9780199278220.001.0001

Weil, P., & Ross, J. (2004). *ICT governance: How top performers manage ICT decision rights for superior results*. Cambridge, MA: Harvard Business School Press.

Wenger, E. (1998). *Communities of practice: Learning, meaning, and identity*. Cambridge, UK: Cambridge University Press.

Williams, B. (1985). *Ethics and the limits of philosophy*. London, UK: Fontana.

Williams, B. (2002). *Truth and truthfulness*. Princeton, NJ: Princeton University Press.

KEY TERMS AND DEFINITIONS

Accuracy: Is a quality of beliefs that signifies how and to what extent a true belief fits an external, pragmatically defined standard.

Connectivism: Is a theory of learning that stresses the networked nature of knowledge. Knowledge is not an property of the individual but something that comes about in social networks. Even though not technically elaborated enough to function in the epistemological debates, the theory is very popular in e-learning circles, and is a follow-up to socio-constructivism. It presents itself as a learning theory for the digital age.

ICT Expert: In this paper we use this term rather broadly as a person who is regarded contextually as an expert in ICT. This is often the Systems Administrator in a Small to Medium Business context.

Informal Learning: A wide variety of learning that occurs outside of formal education, such as language acquisition, but also on-the-job learned skills and socially acquired knowledge in a community of practice.

Interactional Expertise: A notion coined by Collins & Evans, describing a particular form of expertise which differs from what is commonly considered contributory expertise, which is also deeply laden with tacit knowledge. Interactional expertise is expertise in the language of the specialism without expertise in the practice of the field.

Precision: Is a measurement-theoretic notion that reflects the precise degree to which a series of measurement outcomes have similar outcomes.

Reliabilism: Is a theory about what turns true beliefs into knowledge. It argues that the right cognitive processes that enable us to form a belief must be reliable for a true belief to count as knowledge.

Separation of Duty: Is an increasingly important notion in corporate control and IT governance, where one organizes labor in such a way that more than one person is required to fulfill a particular task. The aim is to prevent fraud and reduce error probability. Separation of Duty is an important strategy to comply with the Sarbanes-Oxley Public Company Accounting Reform and Investor Protection Act. It implies that IT solutions for accountancy provide strict rules to make sure a single person cannot perform a complete financial transaction.

Social Epistemology: Studies the social dimension of knowledge, such as acquisition of knowledge through testimony, and the social and cultural forces influencing the production and dissemination of knowledge.

Tacit Knowledge: Knowledge that you master, but have difficulties to explain or make explicit. A very typical example is the ability to speak a language. Many experts-in-the-field hold knowledge acquired on-the-job which is difficult to transmit in schoolbook format.

Chapter 17
Decentralized Expertise:
The Evolution of Community Forums in Technical Support

Steven Ovadia
LaGuardia Community College, USA

ABSTRACT

This chapter discusses the authority structures found within the community support forums of open and closed source operating systems (Linux, Windows, and OS X), demonstrating how, because of these forums, technical expertise is shifting away from the organizations responsible for creating these systems and into the community using them. One might expect this kind of migration within Linux communities, where in theory anyone can contribute to the code of the project, but it is also being seen in closed source projects, where only certain people, usually employees, have access to the underlying code that controls the operating system. In these situations, expertise is becoming decentralized despite the fact that members of the support community sometimes lack access to the code behind these operating systems.

INTRODUCTION

The moment one buys a personal computer, the countdown begins to the moment when the computer will fail in some way. It is one of the inevitabilities of computer ownership.

Once a computer fails, if the user cannot resolve the issue herself, she will try to find someone who can help. It sounds like a relatively simple prospect, but as anyone who has tried to repair a computer will tell you, determining the problem is often quite challenging. Is the issue related to hardware or software? Or is there another variable, like a wireless router or the Internet connection? According to a Pew Internet & American Life Project report, 29% of surveyed users whose computers had failed in the past year had contacted user support for help, while the same percentage had tried to fixed the problem themselves (Horrigan, 2008, p. 6). It is not surprising that some telecommunication companies are considering offering technical support as an add-on service (Gubbins, 2009, p. 34).

DOI: 10.4018/978-1-4666-2178-7.ch017

The even split between users who seek formal support and those who try to repair their computers themselves is significant as it also represents a split in authority structures. For some users, vendors represent authority. For these kinds of users, because the vendor made the product, the vendor is responsible for repairing the product. Other users try to fix their own product because they do not trust the expertise of the vendor, because they feel they can resolve the issue on their own, or because the vendor could not help them to their satisfaction.

As more online support forums are becoming available, many users are becoming less dependent on the centralized expertise of a vendor and are coming to rely on the decentralized expertise of a community of users. This shift is quite visible in the support forums associated with various operating systems. These forums allow users of all skill levels to post support questions to a community at large, possibly bypassing formal support channels (although, as we shall see, some vendors do provide formal support within these community areas). This type of community-driven technical support would be much more challenging to implement without the aid of the Internet.

Finding formal, centralized support for Windows is relatively straightforward, once one understands who to contact for help. Although the operating system is produced by Microsoft, Microsoft directs users to contact the computer manufacturer for assistance with the operating system.[1] It does, however, provide phone, email, and chat support to customers who purchase Windows separately from their computer.

Apple users have a less complicated path to follow for help. All Apple hardware and software have a one-year warranty and up to 90 days of technical support via telephone.[2] That warranty can be extended if a customer purchases AppleCare, Apple's technical support package. Apple users without AppleCare can also purchase customized support.

Linux is an open source operating system based on the Unix operating system. As an open source project, Linux is developed collaboratively, with people from around the world contributing code, time, and energy to the project. Linux is freely available for anyone who wants it and most contributors are volunteers. Unlike OS X and Windows, it is not a commercial product, although some vendors have created commercial versions of Linux.

Its open source status means that most Linux users have no formal technical support options. Some Linux providers offer an enterprise solution for businesses, but the average home user looking to install Linux on a personal machine is pretty much left to her own devices (although there are vendors who sell hardware with Linux distributions already installed and who provide varying levels of technical support).

Open source refers to software that is developed using publicly available source code:

There are three dimensions to the concept of "open source" as it applies to computing. First, open source is a philosophy about computing and sharing programming code to improve the quality of computing. The term "open source" also refers to a wide array of operating systems and applications that have been developed under this philosophy, and, finally, it represents a general approach to the treatment of intellectual property, usually in reference to licensing software or related documentation. (Tomer, 2002, p. 155)

Users seeking technical support usually visit forums based upon their Linux distribution (a distribution is a more specific version of the Linux operating system), so an Ubuntu distribution user who cannot connect to the Internet on his Dell laptop would probably start his research with a search of the Ubuntu forums.[3] Even if a user does not know he wants to search a forum, forums tend to come up high in Google searches for Linux distributions and problems. At time of writing, a

Google search for "Ubuntu no volume" has its top two results from forum sites, with Google giving users the option to pull more results from forums. Closed source operating systems like OS X and Windows also have forums, though, and while users might not be aware of them, they too often come up in Google searches. For instance, as of this writing, a Google search for "can't open explorer" leads users to the Microsoft-hosted support forums. So even if a user is not aware of a specific forum or an operating system, it seems general Internet searching can often direct him to one.

Different forums have different procedures, processes, and cultures. But the common functionality is that users can post questions about the operating system and other users will attempt to answer the question. Some forums are a mix of employees and users; others are all volunteers.

These decentralized, community-based forums are changing the structures of expertise and authority. Where operating system support was once purely the domain of the vendors who produced them (or, in the case of Microsoft, the hardware companies who installed them), now we see technical support expertise distributed out into the community of users. Vendors might have authority in the creation of some of these operating systems, but their users—users with no formal affiliation to the organization responsible for these operating systems—might demonstrate greater expertise in repairing and understanding them.

Where once users had to turn to formal, company-sponsored experts for operating system technical support, now users have the option of turning to experts working independently of the company or organization producing the operating system. While in the past operating system support was solely in the hands of company-sponsored experts, now many users not affiliated with a company have enough expertise to offer support to other users on various issues.

In this chapter I will examine the support forums of closed source and open source operating systems (Windows, OS X, and Linux), investigat-

ing the authority structures within those forums and demonstrating how technical support expertise for these projects is moving away from the entities responsible for the creation of the software (a centralized model) and into the community of users (a decentralized model). Where operating system technical support expertise was once limited to those creating the operating system, now expertise is more an issue of who can provide the correct solution to a given technical challenge in a given moment.

BACKGROUND

The literature exploring the dynamics of operating system support in forums is sparse. Lakhani and von Hippel (2003) looked at online support in open source projects (specifically, the Apache server software project), and found that users helped other users for a variety of reasons, including reputation enhancement and to learn more about the project (p. 940). Knuppel (2000) investigated Linux newsgroups as communities of practice and found that most Linux newsgroup messages were users giving their opinion, followed by users giving orientation (p. 24). A study by Ahmed, Campbell, Jaffar, and Capretz (2009) explored the role of online forums in open source software support, and found that the forums are crucial to identifying software defects (p. 178).

Many researchers have also explored the social dynamics of open source communities. Chopra and Dexter's (2008) comprehensive overview of free and open source software touches on just about all the social components of these communities; others who have explored this world include Toral, Martinez-Torres, Barrero, and Cortes (2009); Xu, Jones, and Shao (2009); and Zhao (1999).

There have also been more specific studies of the Debian community. Debian is a Linux distribution (and the one on which Ubuntu is based). Mateos-Garcia and Steinmueller's (2008) research was not directed specifically to the issue of support,

297

but did discuss the authority structures that exist within the project (p. 337). The authors reported that, despite Debian's established governance structure, technical decision making was sometimes too decentralized, delaying development of the distribution (p. 342). While decentralized technical support might have some advantages, according to this case study of Debian, decentralized development is not always advantageous. Coleman and Hill (2005) do not discuss support forums explicitly, but do explore the ethical volunteerism that is a part of the Debian community culture (p. 275). Obviously, this volunteerism will have an impact on support forums in the future in some way, since very few people are paid to participate in those kinds of support channels.

There is also a body of work on online question and answer sites, of which support forums could be considered a subset. Shah, Oh, and Oh (2009) divided online question and answer sites into three categories: digital reference services, expert services, and social question and answer sites (p. 205). The authors defined a digital reference service as one where librarians answer questions as opposed to an expert service, which features some sort of specialized non-librarian expert answering questions (p. 206). Finally, they defined a social question and answer site as one where anyone within the community can answer a question.

These forums represent an interesting space. Because forums are often used for question and answer purposes, they might be considered a type of question and answer site. Contextualizing the forum using Shah, Oh, and Oh's three categories of question and answer sites is not simple, though. Just about all forums are social question and answer sites to some extent, since anyone can attempt to answer any questions. But there is also a degree of expertise within these forums. Some people answering questions might have formal ties to the operating system with which they are helping but others might be experts simply because they know a lot about a product, despite having no role in the development of the project.

However, Shah, Oh, and Oh (2009) provide a relatively broad definition of expert services that can apply to understanding expertise in the forums: "Expert services are question asking and answering services offered by various types of commercial and noncommercial organizations other than libraries, including professional societies and organizations, schools, corporations, and even individuals in specific subject domains" (p. 206). This definition would apply to someone with formal developer-based ties to a project, as well as to someone who is merely proficient in using a particular operating system. This study is also relevant to the current context in that it discusses how a tool like the ability to rate answers can help users understand the quality of answers given in these forums (p. 206). In expert forums that allow user ratings, expertise is not just a matter of a respondent's personal belief in her expertise, but also quantifiable matter, based upon the ratings of other users. Users cannot view and assess expertise in the same way as in most traditional, centralized support channels, like telephone support. Ratings can make expertise easier to assess. When expertise is easier for end-users to assess, it is easier to decentralize, since users do not have to depend upon a centralized authority to confer expertise.

Users posting questions about their computers online is nothing new. Howard Rheingold (2000) discusses it in his book, *The Virtual Community*. He quotes Dan Ben-Horin, founder of the CompuMentor project:

The CompuMentor project began four and a half years ago when I couldn't get my new 24-pin printer to print envelopes without smudging. I had just started logging onto the WELL, so I posted my printer question in the IBM conference. The answers I received were not only informal but also profuse, open-hearted, full-spirited. The proverbial thought balloon instantly appeared. These computerites on the WELL wanted to share their skills...

...My own learning had really commenced when my next-door neighbor expressed a willingness to help me whenever I needed him. And I needed him frequently. Now, here on the WELL was a whole community of helpful electronic next-door neighbors. (pp. 277-78)

Given that *The Virtual Community* was originally published in 1993, we see Ben-Horin discussing a period of time in the late 1980s. It is worth pointing out that WELL was an early dial-in bulletin board system featuring forums that pre-dated the rise of the World Wide Web. So it seems that very early on, users latched onto the idea of asking questions and having peers, as opposed to vendors, answer their questions. Ben-Horin uses the metaphor of helpful neighbors when talking about getting computer help from a forum, which presumably differs from going through an official technical support channel, where one might not have that same kind of experience. While the people helping Ben-Horin were not necessarily credentialed experts or official vendor representatives, he still accepted their advice because it was authoritative enough for his purposes.

Lankes (2008) explores this distinction, juxtaposing authority against reliability:

Reliability commonly refers to something or someone perceived as dependable and consistent in quality. If you have a reliable car, it is one that runs well over time. Reliability to the scientist is simply the consistency of data, such that the same treatment (e.g., questions, experiments, or applications) yields the same result over time. If an authority approach is exemplified by believing that a given news anchor will give a credible answer, then switching from news station to news station looking for commonalities in the same story exemplifies a reliability approach. (p. 109)

Forum users seem to trust the reliability of the forums, if not the necessarily the authority of the individual respondent. This kind of trust in

answers found in certain forums is not surprising, given the number of open source projects that use forums as a communication mechanism and as a form of technical support (Ahmed et al., 2009, p.174). Linux is an open source project, so it has a conceptual framework that would involve forums as a support channel.

EXPERTISE AND AUTHORITY WITHIN SUPPORT FORUMS

Ubuntu Forums

Because Linux is a freely available operating system, it's difficult to tell how popular one distribution is as opposed to another. There are no sales numbers to indicate what people are buying. Anecdotally, however, it seems that Ubuntu is one of the more popular Linux distributions, if not the most popular.

The Ubuntu project is an open source project sponsored by Canonical, a private company. Despite being privately owned, the project has its own governance structure (Bacon, 2009, p.247). Support forums are a part of the Ubuntu governance and are overseen by a forum council. The council has a few responsibilities:

- Encourage all forum members to follow the Forum Code of Conduct, and abide by the Ubuntu Code of Conduct.
- Appointing or recalling administrators, moderators and forums staff or determining criteria by which they are appointed.
- Resolving disputes between forums staff and moderators as per the existing dispute resolution system and forums guidelines.
- With advice, feedback, and help from the forums staff, maintaining and enforcing the Forums Guidelines and associated infrastructure (e.g., the resolution center).[4]

In addition to the council, there are also forum moderators, who are users who have been granted an elevated status within the forums. Their names appear in red and their role is to help users get their questions answered.

Despite this formal structure, the format of the forums is relatively simple: users of all skill levels post questions about Ubuntu and other users answer them. One question might have a few different answers, so the user must decide which answer is best. The best answer might originate from someone on the forum council, or someone closely associated with the Ubuntu project, but that is not a given.

The forum actually reinforces the idea that correct answers can come from anyone by not giving much information about the expertise of the answerer. The site will indicate how many times a user has posted, but that is all. There is no reputation ranking metric. Users are not required to list their expertise or credentials anywhere in their user profile.

Consider how different this process is from typical technical support. Rather than contacting a company and being delegated to an expert, or at least someone one hopes is an expert, in the Ubuntu community, users must instead ask each other for help (although, like Apple, Ubuntu does offer fee-based support in a service that seems more for corporate users than personal ones).

In some ways, Ubuntu is deferring to its users in how to support their own product. This might be for financial reasons, as it is cheaper to use volunteers than to pay support technicians. But this model of operation also aligns with Ubuntu's status as an open source product (as Linux is by definition).

Because open source software often does not yield much financial reward, it is frequently built by volunteer communities. These communities depend upon other community members to report bugs in software—and to fix them. As Ahmed et al. (2009) reported that a high volume of messages in an online forum correlated positively with open, or unresolved, bug reports (p. 177), meaning that the forums were successfully being used to document bugs, which were then claimed for repair by developers on the project.

Open source projects, like Linux, have a history of users reporting problems to the community at large. Traditionally, the reporting has been about bugs. This form of reporting easily evolves into the current scenario where users report all kinds of problems with software. In the case of Linux forums, we see users reporting problems that might not be the fault of the software, but instead could be user error or the fault of hardware.

This evolution is visible in the Ubuntu Forums, where the forums are not used for bug reporting (Ubuntu has a separate site for reporting and tracking bugs), but instead are used purely for issues of user support. The two community elements of the bug reporting paradigm are still present: one part of the community reports a problem while another part of the community attempts to fix it. But rather than reporting and fixing problems in the software, the Ubuntu forums are for reporting and fixing problems with the usage of the software itself, wherever the problem might actually lie. It is a subtle but important difference.

This movement of message forums from a bug reporting tool to a support tool does not affect the authority structures of open source projects. In fact, it reinforces their decentralized authority structure. With proprietary operating systems, only certain people have permission to make changes to code. Programmers with that access, who work for the company selling the software, have more authority than programmers without that access. But with an open source operating system, like Linux, anyone can submit changes to the code, thus giving anyone with technical skill an authority that does not hinge on employment status. The decentralized authority to submit changes to enhance code would also extend to the decentralized authority to provide support for that very same code.

Within the Ubuntu Forums, expertise is a quality unrelated to employment or project contributor status. Even in the Ubuntu Forums, a forum moderator might provide answers with less authority than a knowledgeable community member who is not formally recognized by the Ubuntu governance. For users trying to solve problems, the important thing is they trust the reliability of the forums as a whole, even if an answer comes from someone with no formal affiliation with Ubuntu or Canonical.

Ask Ubuntu

Ubuntu Forums represents just one community of one operating system. Ask Ubuntu[5] is another community where users can post support requests that are answered by their peers.

Ask Ubuntu does not have an official relationship with Canonical, the company behind Ubuntu. It is an independent site that is part of a network of technology-focused question and answer sites, where users post questions and other users answer them, making for a support model even more decentralized than the one seen in the Ubuntu Forums.

Ask Ubuntu uses a complex algorithm that gives users certain privileges as they increase their reputation score. In addition to reputation, all users can vote on specific answers, indicating whether each answer is useful. Finally, someone who has posted a question can mark a response as the best answer. These answer assessment tools could be why some users might post a question there rather than in the Ubuntu Forums. The ability to accrue points might also make some users more inclined to answer questions in Ask Ubuntu, rather than the Ubuntu Forums.

Like the Ubuntu Forums, Ask Ubuntu is moderated by community members. Unlike the Ubuntu Forums, where moderators are selected by figures within the Ubuntu governance power structure, within the Ask Ubuntu site, moderators are voted in by the community. Community members and the elected moderators might have no formal connection to Canonical or Ubuntu.

This structure, while possibly complicated and challenging for some new users, allows users to assess authority using a number of metrics. For instance, most users might give more weight to answers from users with a higher reputation score, since the reputation score should indicate some degree of expertise. However, by allowing users to vote on each individual answer, someone with a lower reputation score but a high in-question rating for a particular answer might become more authoritative within the context of an answer to a single question. That is because the in-question answer rating is quantifying expertise in a very specific context—the answer to a single question. Other users might know more about the various parts of Ubuntu as a whole, and thus have high reputation scores, but if their expertise does not include the answer to a particular question, another, less expert user, who knows that one piece of information, might actually have the best answer. Finally, a questioner marking an answer as the best answer might send a message to users researching their own Ubuntu challenges. The best answer mark usually indicates that the answer worked for the asker, and so is an endorsement of sorts. This is context-based authority that might not carry over from answer to answer.

Writing on relevance and credibility in the context of new media, Benkler (2006) points out that both relevance and credibility depend on the extent to which users trust a given piece of information and find it useful. Forum users want a credible, correct answer, but even if there is no centralized authority structure to help establish credibility, they will be inclined to trust an answer that relates to their problem and helps them resolve it.

Chen, Ho, and Kim (2010) closely examined Google Answers, Google's now defunct question and answer site that allowed users to set prices for answers. In their examination of the Google Answers service, they found that "answerers with high reputations are seen as spending more time [crafting answers to questions] and producing higher quality answers" (p. 660). Ask Ubuntu's reputation tracking makes it easier for users to assess reputation, but raises the question of whether users with higher reputations have answers perceived as better because the answer is better or because their reputation leads users to interpret the answer as better.

Either way, again we see authority moving away from the creators of the software (although there's nothing that prohibits Ubuntu developers from participating in the Ask Ubuntu forums), and becoming decentralized into a larger community of users. Where a phone call or email to technical support requires the person being helped to trust in the expertise of the person helping them, based upon the fact that the person is employed by the software creator and thus seems to have an institutionally vested form of authority, within Ask Ubuntu, the person asking or researching a question can use a number of different metrics to assess the authority of the person answering the question, or, perhaps even more helpfully, the reliability of a given answer.

The organization of the Ask Ubuntu forums allows for an authority based on the reputation of a person answering a question, although there is always the possibility of a person with a high reputation having their answer corrected by someone with a lower one. This contributes to the reliability of the forum as a whole.

Microsoft Answers

As with the two Ubuntu forums discussed earlier, answers.microsoft.com, users can answer other users on the official Windows support forums.[6] They can also indicate if a particular post was helpful.

What's interesting about Answers, though, is its heavy presence of Microsoft support personnel (a user's status is indicated next to her name in the question thread). The structure of the forums,

while not precluding a non-Microsoft–employed user from answering questions about Windows, is Microsoft-centric.

Community Moderators

These are volunteers who are here to help the community, answer questions, and work to keep the community healthy and fun. Community moderators are members of the community, not Microsoft employees. People who make extraordinary contributions to the community may be asked to be community moderators.

Support Engineers

Support engineers are experts who are engaged [by] Microsoft to answer your questions.

Forum Moderators

Forum moderators are experts engaged [by] Microsoft to mark the best answers, manage abuse, and maintain community health.

Forum Owners

These are Microsoft employees in charge of a particular forum. Forum owners are ultimately responsible for the health of the forum.

MVPs

Most Valuable Professionals are independent experts who are offered a close connection with people at Microsoft. They can often answer the most challenging questions.

Microsoft Employees

Microsoft employees participating in the forums have a badge that says Microsoft. These community members may work in the forums, or they may be general employees participating by asking or answering questions.

Content Creators

Content Creators are community members who have consistently contributed excellent content to the forums. Their posts are often marked as answers.

Content Curators

Content Curators are community members who have consistently identified good, helpful content on the forums. Many of the posts they've voted as helpful end up being voted "most helpful" or being marked as answers.

Site Sheriffs

Site Sheriffs are community members who have consistently identified and reported cases of abuse on the forums.[7]

We see that while non-Microsoft–affiliated personnel can certainly contribute and enhance their reputation through well-regarded, well-received answers, the forums have a decidedly Microsoft focus that is not seen in Canonical's Ubuntu Forums or Apple's support forums. While the Microsoft forums have the look and feel of a decentralized support space, reviewing these forum member titles reveals many Microsoft personnel participating in various capacities, making the forum more like publicly viewable traditional technical support than community-driven decentralized support. While users are free to help each other, Microsoft creates an environment where Microsoft-affiliated personnel can also assist users.

There are many possible reasons for this heavier presence of Microsoft-affiliated personnel within the forums. Microsoft is a large company and can probably better afford to deploy personnel to its forums. Because Windows is a closed source product, only Microsoft-affiliated personnel have access to how it works at the code level. That can make it difficult for non-Microsoft employees to answer and address certain types of questions.

Within the Microsoft-controlled forums, the authority structure could give more power to Microsoft-affiliated contributors, because in many ways they are best equipped to answer many questions. Non-Microsoft–affiliated users can answer questions and become authoritative, but it seems a challenging prospect. When a user is confronted with two answers, one from a user who has accrued reputation points in the Answers forum and one who has a clearly listed Microsoft affiliation, which one will be more trusted?

Answering that question would require further study of forum users, but the very fact that it is a question to ponder says much about authority structures within the Microsoft Answers forum. Microsoft allows for the possibility of decentralized expertise while also providing traditional expertise based on company credentials.

Apple Support Communities

Like Microsoft, Apple also has operating system support forums on its site[8] where users can post questions and other users will answer them. Like the Ask Ubuntu forums and Microsoft Answers, users can accrue points based on the quality of their answers. In theory, points correlate with answer quality.

Unlike MicrosoftAnswers, Apple Support Community does not indicate affiliations, except for forum moderators, sometimes called Community Hosts or Community Mods. One cannot tell if someone answering a question is related to Apple or another member of the community. Apple employees were once identified as such in the forums, but that is no longer the case.[9] Like Microsoft Answers and Ask Ubuntu, the Apple discussion area is point-based, with users earning points for either correct answers (10 points) or helpful answers (5 points). As users accrue points, they earn privileges on the site, although Apple does not outline what those privileges are.

Answers flagged as correct (by the asker), are immediately moved to the top of the thread, in addition to being indicated as correct in the order in which the answer was posted.

The choice to move correct answers to the top of threads and out of context is interesting in that it places a focus on the correct answer, or the answer that has been identified as being correct, but it takes away the conversation that might surround an answer. Within the realm of online technical support, this conversation may include things like exceptions to a correct answer or another approach that is equally correct. A questioner indicating that someone has posted the correct answer means the answer worked for the questioner but it does not necessarily mean the answer will work for all users. Pulling an answer out of context and directly linking it to the answer could prevent other users from discovering alternative answers.

One reason for this approach might be because Apple has tight integration between its software and hardware (the support community is broadly organized by software type and hardware type—it does not get more specific than that, the way both the official Microsoft and Ubuntu forums do). The Macintosh OS X operating system is only available on Apple hardware, meaning the hardware and software have been optimized to work with each other. In theory, this should mean fewer technical issues than a user might see with Windows and Linux, which have to work across a multitude of hardware configurations. Despite Apple's tight integration of hardware and software, though, the board represents a more decentralized approach to technical support, with users supporting users, rather than Apple-affiliated personnel supporting users.

MacRumors Forums

Another popular site for getting Macintosh OS X support, as well as sharing feedback on the operating system itself, is the MacRumors Forums.[10]

The forums area is a sub-area of the popular MacRumors site[11] where many Apple enthusiasts go to for news about Apple products.

The MacRumors forums are geared more toward discussion of Apple and Apple-related issues, but there is a support component to it. It uses the same discussion board software as the Ubuntu Forums and has a lot of the same functionality. Users are easily identified by the date they joined the forums and by a user title that is based on the number of posts they have made. A newbie has fewer than 30 posts, while a G5 has at least 30,000 posts. In theory, this helps users get a sense of who is experienced and who is new, although there is not necessarily a correlation between the number of posts made by a user and the accuracy of their responses.

MacRumors is a completely separate entity from Apple. It is a site run by enthusiasts but not anyone officially affiliated with Apple. This forum is another example of a decentralized authority structure when it comes to user support. It is certainly possible for Apple employees to interact with users on the forums, but there is no way to identify these employees. Authority within the MacRumors support forums is therefore based entirely on the authority of the answers, not on any publicly viewable affiliation or reputation metric.

DISCUSSION

Technical support has long been an issue of expertise. Software creators are assumed to have authority and expertise because they created the software. But two factors are changing that assumption. One is that closed source software vendors, like Apple and Microsoft, have embraced online support forums and are allowing its users to help each other. While the specifics of the authority structure vary between forums, for the most part, it's a fairly straightforward issue of users asking questions and then deciding who best answered them. Vendors, to a certain extent, are deferring to the decentralized expertise of their users, allowing them the chance to answer questions previously reserved for formal, centralized technical support.

Both Microsoft Answers and Ubuntu Forums have hybrid support forum structures that provide expertise both from within their respective projects and also external to those projects. With Ubuntu (and Linux in general), the difference between internal and external expertise is a bit more complex, since, in theory, anyone can enter a project at any time. For a project like Windows, becoming a member of their team is less straightforward, involving an entire hiring process.

Interestingly, Apple's support forum structure is entirely community-based, with no publicly acknowledged Apple employees participating, although it is possible that employees monitor the Apple-hosted forums to make sure damaging misinformation is not being shared. And the MacRumors forum expertise would be even further decentralized, as there is no formal relationship between those forums and Apple.

While one could argue that the presence of Microsoft-affiliated personnel within their support forums shifts expertise away from the community and back to the vendor, there seems to be an opportunity for non-Microsoft–employed forum participants to cultivate their own reputation. Of course, a major challenge for non-Microsoft–employed forum participants is that they do not have access to the Windows source code the way many Microsoft employees do.

Even without access to the code, as is the case with both the Windows and OS X operating system codes, the model for technical support is starting to decentralize. It is no longer necessarily a case of users needing to approach software creators for technical support. Now users also have the option of bypassing the software creator and working with a decentralized community of users. While vendors have an economic interest in keeping the code behind their operating systems private and centralized, there does not seem to be the same impetus to centralize technical support, creating the opportunity for users to support each other.

The second factor in this changing attitude toward technical support is the rise in popularity of open source software. Because anyone can contribute to open source projects and because the code is available to anyone who wishes to see it, technical support expertise lies in what is probably a bigger pool of users. There is not just the expertise of anyone who has formally contributed to the project, but there is also the expertise of the volunteer-based community that has seen or understands the underlying operating system code. As Benkler and Nissenbaum (2006) point out, open source projects are driven by unpaid help:

The [open source] effort is sustained by a combination of volunteerism and good will, technology, some law—mostly licensing like the GNU Public License that governs most free software development—and a good bit of self-serving participation. But all these factors result in a model of production that avoids traditional price mechanism or firm managers in organizing production or motivating its participants. (p. 396)

Open source communities thrive on the community helping to grow the product, and technical support is a way to help projects (by actually helping users of said software).

Operating system-level technical support is moving from centralized experts knowledgeable in all parts of the system to a decentralized community, where a given member might be knowledgeable about only one aspect of the operating system, but is knowledgeable enough to help other users fix that one thing.

FUTURE RESEARCH DIRECTIONS

Future researchers might consider examining answer accuracy by user affiliation. It might be interesting to see if users with formal ties to projects have more accurate answers than non-formally affiliated users do. It might also be interesting to track user perceptions of these answers. Are answers from someone publicly affiliated with a project seen as more authoritative than those from someone with no visible affiliation?

Another direction to explore is the accuracy of the answers provided in these community forums. Do people formally affiliated with a project tend to provide more accurate answers than those who are unaffiliated? Do these community-driven forums give accurate advice? How does the accuracy percentage compare with typical one-to-one formal technical support?

It also might be interesting to examine how problems and challenges reported on the forums make their way into formal bug reports. Do the various software developers monitor the forums to see where users are facing challenges? How many of the technical support requests posted in forums are actually software defects? The various support forums represent an interesting data set. If software developers were to consider users reliable and/or authoritative to a certain extent, they might see the support requests as potential software bugs that might be repairable. But that would probably mean that developers would have to assume users are asking for help because they do not know how to use software, or are using it incorrectly, as well as that their problem might be related to the software itself.

Tracking this sort of movement might be complex, but comparing forum posts to bug reports might help investigate if there is a correlation between end-user issues reported on the forums and user issues filed as bug reports (this would not be possible for Windows and OS X, which do not have publicly viewable bug tracking reports). Although it might be more complicated to track, it would be interesting to see if user-reported issues with software are addressed in future software releases and to what extent.

Future researchers might also explore the content of the forums, categorizing the types of questions asked for each operating system, and seeing if any patterns emerge in terms of who answers each type of question, and if the answers are consistently reliable.

CONCLUSION

Supporting an operating system can be a challenging task for users of all technical skill levels. In the past, users trying to fix their computers had little choice but to work with the vendor behind an operating system (or, in the case of Windows users, to interface with the hardware vendor), or to hire a third party to help troubleshoot their computer problems.

However, the rise of both official and unaffiliated community forums gives users the chance to help each other. Proprietary, closed source operating systems are adapting the decentralized support techniques of the open source world and are deferring to the expertise of their users, even when those users have no formal ties to a project. For closed source software creators, this is a huge conceptual shift. In essence, they are taking full responsibility for the creation of their operating system, developing all of their code in-house, but in terms of supporting that code, they are allowing for the possibility that users can support their software without even having access to the underlying code.

There are many possible reasons for this new view of community-based technical support. It could be because it is less expensive than a formal, centralized technical support channel. It could be a way of preventing users from visiting third-party sites for technical support. Whatever the reason, Microsoft and Apple are in a position to offer this kind of community support because of the expertise found in their user communities.

Regardless of whether a user is using OS X, Windows, or Linux, all users now have access to technical support communities beyond whatever is offered by the entities responsible for the production of the operating systems. Expertise and authority now rest in these communities. For open source projects, like Ubuntu, expertise and authority have always resided, to a certain extent, in a decentralized community of users, but for closed source projects like Mac OS X and Windows, this represents a significant shift in the role users assume in using their operating systems.

REFERENCES

Ahmed, F., Campbell, P., Jaffar, A., & Capretz, L. (2009). Defects in open source software: The role of online forums. *Proceedings of World Academy of Science: Engineering & Technology, 52*, 174–178.

Bacon, J. (2009). *The art of community: Building the new age of participation*. Sebastopol, CA: O'Reilly Media.

Benkler, Y. (2006). *The wealth of networks*. New Haven, CT: Yale University Press.

Benkler, Y., & Nissenbaum, H. (2006). Commons-based peer production and virtue. *Journal of Political Philosophy, 14*(4), 394–419. doi:10.1111/j.1467-9760.2006.00235.x

Chen, Y., Ho, T.-H., & Kim, Y.-M. (2010). Knowledge market design: A field experiment at Google Answers. *Journal of Public Economic Theory, 12*(4), 641–664. doi:10.1111/j.1467-9779.2010.01468.x

Chopra, S., & Dexter, S. (2008). *Decoding liberation: The promise of free and open source software*. New York, NY: Routledge.

Coleman, E. G., & Hill, B. (2004). The social production of ethics in Debian and free software communities: Anthropological lessons for vocational ethics. In Koch, S. (Ed.), *Free/open source software development* (pp. 273–295). Hershey, PA: Idea Group Publishing. doi:10.4018/978-1-59140-369-2.ch013

Gubbins, E. (2009, December 22). Move over, geek squad. *Telephony*, 34-36.

Horrigan, J., & Jones, S. (2008). *When technology fails*. Washington, DC: Pew Internet and American Life Project. Retrieved September 21, 2011, from http://www.pewinternet.org/~/media//Files/Reports/2008/PIP_Tech_Failure.pdf.pdf

Knuppel, M. (2000). *A characterization of the Linux community of practice using Linux newsgroups and Bales' Interaction Process Analysis*. Unpublished Master's thesis, University of North Carolina at Chapel Hill.

Lakhani, K. R., & von Hippel, E. (2003). How open source software works: "Free" user-to-user assistance. *Research Policy, 32*(6), 923–943. doi:10.1016/S0048-7333(02)00095-1

Lankes, R. D. (2007). Trusting the internet: New approaches to credibility tools. In Metzberger, M. J., & Flanagin, A. J. (Eds.), *Digital media, youth, and credibility* (pp. 101–121). Cambridge, MA: The MIT Press.

Mateos-Garcia, J., & Steinmueller, W. E. (2008). The institutions of open source software: Examining the Debian community. *Information Economics and Policy, 20*(4), 333–344. doi:10.1016/j.infoecopol.2008.06.001

Rheingold, H. (2000). *The virtual community: Homesteading on the electronic frontier*. Cambridge, MA: The MIT Press.

Shah, C., Oh, S., & Oh, J. S. (2009). Research agenda for social Q&A. *Library & Information Science Research, 31*(4), 205–209. doi:10.1016/j.lisr.2009.07.006

Tomer, C. (2002). Open source. *Computer Sciences, 3*, 155–158. New York, NY: Macmillan Reference USA.

Toral, S. L., Martínez-Torres, M. R., Barrero, F., & Cortés, F. (2009). An empirical study of the driving forces behind online communities. *Internet Research, 19*(4), 378–392. doi:10.1108/10662240910981353

Xu, B., Jones, D. R., & Shao, B. (2009). Volunteers' involvement in online community based software development. *Information & Management, 46*(3), 151–158. doi:10.1016/j.im.2008.12.005

Zhao, H. (1999). *A qualitative study of the linux open source community.* Unpublished Master's thesis, University of North Carolina at Chapel Hill.

ADDITIONAL READING

Antweiler, W., & Frank, M. Z. (2004). Is all that talk just noise? The information content of internet stock message boards. *The Journal of Finance, 59*(3), 1259–1294. doi:10.1111/j.1540-6261.2004.00662.x

Barcellini, F., Detienne, F. A., Burkhardt, J.-M., & Sack, W. (2008). A socio-cognitive analysis of online design discussions in an open source software community. *Interacting with Computers, 20*(1), 141–165. doi:10.1016/j.intcom.2007.10.004

Baytiyeh, H., & Pfaffman, J. (2010). Open source software: A community of altruists. *Computers in Human Behavior, 26*(6), 1345–1354. doi:10.1016/j.chb.2010.04.008

Bekkers, V. (2004). Virtual policy communities and responsive governance: Redesigning on-line debates. *Information Polity: The International Journal of Government & Democracy in the Information Age, 9*(3/4), 193–203.

Casaló, L. V., Flavián, C., & Guinaliu, M. (2010). Relationship quality, community promotion and brand loyalty in virtual communities: Evidence from free software communities. *International Journal of Information Management, 30*(4), 357–367. doi:10.1016/j.ijinfomgt.2010.01.004

Chopra, S., & Dexter, S. (2008). *Decoding liberation: The promise of free and open source software.* New York, NY: Routledge.

Crowston, K., Li, Q., Wei, K., Eseryel, U. Y., & Howison, J. (2007). Self-organization of teams for free/libre open source software development. *Information and Software Technology, 49*(6), 564–575. doi:10.1016/j.infsof.2007.02.004

da Cunha, J. V., & Orlikowski, W. J. (2008). Performing catharsis: The use of online discussion forums in organizational change. *Information and Organization, 18*(2), 132–156. doi:10.1016/j.infoandorg.2008.02.001

Desouza, C. (2004). A framework for analyzing and understanding online communities. *Interacting with Computers, 16*(3), 579–610. doi:10.1016/j.intcom.2003.12.006

Di Gangi, P. M., & Wasko, M. (2009). Steal my idea! Organizational adoption of user innovations from a user innovation community: A case study of Dell IdeaStorm. *Decision Support Systems, 48*(1), 303–312. doi:10.1016/j.dss.2009.04.004

Evans, B. M., Kairam, S., & Pirolli, P. (2010). Do your friends make you smarter? An analysis of social strategies in online information seeking. *Information Processing & Management, 46*(6), 679–692. doi:10.1016/j.ipm.2009.12.001

Flanagin, A. J., & Metzger, M. J. (2007). The role of site features, user attributes, and information verification behaviors on the perceived credibility of web-based information. *New Media & Society, 9*(2), 319–342. doi:10.1177/1461444807075015

Krieger, B. L. (2003). Making internet communities work: Reflections on an unusual business model. *The Data Base for Advances in Information Systems*, *34*(2), 50–59. doi:10.1145/784580.784587

Kwok, J. S. H., & Gao, S. (2004). Knowledge sharing community in P2P network: A study of motivational perspective. *Journal of Knowledge Management*, *8*(1), 94–102. doi:10.1108/13673270410523934

Lee, H. (2005). Implosion, virtuality, and interaction in an internet discussion group. *Information Communication and Society*, *8*(1), 47–63. doi:10.1080/13691180500066862

Martínez-Torres, M. R., Toral, S. L., Barrero, F., & Cortés, F. (2010). The role of internet in the development of future software projects. *Internet Research*, *20*(1), 72–86. doi:10.1108/10662241011020842

Metzberger, M. J., & Flanagin, A. J. (Eds.). (2009). *Digital media, youth, and credibility*. Cambridge, MA: The MIT Press.

O'Mahony, S. (2003). Guarding the commons: How community managed software projects protect their work. *Research Policy*, *32*(7), 1179–1198. doi:10.1016/S0048-7333(03)00048-9

Searls, D. (2003). Linux for suits: Original and ultimate communities. *Linux Journal*, *107*, 50.

Shirky, C. (2008). *Here comes everybody*. New York, NY: Penguin Press.

Sowe, S. K., Stamelos, I., & Angelis, L. (2008). Understanding knowledge sharing activities in free/open source software projects: An empirical study. *Journal of Systems and Software*, *81*(3), 431–446. doi:10.1016/j.jss.2007.03.086

Swift, M., Balkin, D. B., & Matusik, S. F. (2010). Goal orientations and the motivation to share knowledge. *Journal of Knowledge Management*, *14*(3), 378–393. doi:10.1108/13673271011050111

Toral, S. L., Martinez-Torres, M. R., & Barrero, F. (2010). Analysis of virtual communities supporting OSS projects using social network analysis. *Information and Software Technology*, *52*(3), 296–303. doi:10.1016/j.infsof.2009.10.007

von Krogh, G., & Spaeth, S. (2007). The open source software phenomenon: Characteristics that promote research. *The Journal of Strategic Information Systems*, *16*(3), 236–253. doi:10.1016/j.jsis.2007.06.001

Vujovic, S., & Ulhoi, J. P. (2006). An organizational perspective on free and open source software development. In J. B. Bitzer & P. J. H. Schroder (Eds.), *The economics of open source software development* (pp. 185-205). Amsterdam, The Netherlands: Elsevier. Retrieved September 21, 2011, from www.sciencedirect.com/

Walther, J. B. (2007). Selective self-presentation in computer-mediated communication: Hyperpersonal dimensions of technology, language, and cognition. *Computers in Human Behavior*, *23*(5), 2538–2557. doi:10.1016/j.chb.2006.05.002

KEY TERMS AND DEFINITIONS

Community Forum: An online environment where users can post questions and statements and other users within the community can respond.

Kernel: The part of the operating system interacting with hardware.

Linux: A collaboratively developed open source operating system, where anyone can contribute and distribute code. Linux is based on the Linux kernel which is based on UNIX.

Moderator: A forum user with additional administrative powers and responsibilities, such as the ability to delete other users' comments and to ban users from posting. Moderators also often help to steer conversations and guide new users.

Open Source: Software projects where anyone with the desire and technical skill can contribute and where the underlying source code must always be publicly available for anyone to use or modify.

Operating System: The software layer between computer hardware and its programs. Examples include Windows, OS X, and Linux.

Question and Answer Sites: Sites where users can post questions and other users will answer them. Where community forums might include statements and opinion sharing in addition to questions and answers, question and answer sites are specifically for the purpose of answering questions.

Software Bug: An error in the coding of software that can usually only be resolved by fixing the software at its code level.

UNIX: An operating system developed by AT&T that was one of the first to be usable across different hardware configurations.

ENDNOTES

1   http://windows.microsoft.com/en-US/windows/help/contact-support
2   http://www.apple.com/support/products/
3   www.ubuntuforums.org
4   https://wiki.ubuntu.com/ForumCouncil
5   www.askubuntu.com
6   http://answers.microsoft.com/en-us
7   http://answers.microsoft.com/en-us/Page/faq#faqWhosWho1
8   https://discussions.apple.com/
9   https://discussions.apple.com/message/15045852#15045852
10   http://forums.macrumors.com
11   http://www.macrumors.com

Chapter 18
Interaction and Expertise in an Appalachian Music Archive

Emily Clark
The University of Texas at Austin School of Information, USA

ABSTRACT

In the world of archives, Web 2.0 means more than wider and easier access to digital surrogates of archival objects. Newly developing Web 2.0 applications provide multiple possibilities for contextualizing archival objects through the contributions of many users, rather than a few established experts, marking a shift in archival practice and the role of the expert archivist. For many archival objects with origins in collaborative and popular cultural traditions, a context for online access that invites collaboration and challenges the authority of the expert is particularly conducive to helping users make sense of the archival objects. While this may lead to tensions between innovation and tradition in archival practice, user-contributed knowledge and multiple interpretations of documents can be incorporated as a complement to institutional records, rather than a replacement for traditional methods of description and classification. The purpose of this chapter is to describe recent developments in interactive and collaborative online archives that challenge and enhance traditional ideas about archival expertise. For one Appalachian folk song collection in particular, a community of expertise, ownership, and collaboration may help to keep unique recordings in continued use as part of a living, and still-evolving, musical tradition.

INTRODUCTION

The nature and goals of archives are in flux. Technology is changing how the user finds information about historical documents and how the user interacts with the archival object itself. The traditionally distinct goals of archives, museums,

and libraries are converging as Web 2.0 applications lead to the possibility, and even expectation, of universal, open, and easy access to cultural and historical objects.

Archivists are beginning to experiment with the possibilities afforded by Web 2.0, incorporating user interaction and contribution into websites displaying archival materials, while also trying to retain longstanding principles of archival prac-

DOI: 10.4018/978-1-4666-2178-7.ch018

tice. One manifestation of the tension between innovation and tradition in the archive is the question of authority and expertise. As archives become open to user contribution in organizing, describing, and making sense of historical documents, established experts are no longer the sole interpreters and designators of context and meaning. Though user-contributed knowledge may present a challenge to the expertise of the archivist and the authority of the institutional record, cultural memory institutions may include multiple interpretations of archival documents to complement and enhance traditional methods of archival practice. In this chapter, after discussing recent studies and experiments in participatory and interactive archives as well as a particular lacuna in the area of archives of music, I will explain how a reconfiguration of archival tradition in the Web 2.0 environment may serve to provide better access for diverse audiences, incorporating different kinds of expertise to highlight different facets and meanings of objects in the archive. By examining in particular a collection of Appalachian folk song recordings, I will show that music archives are a particularly interesting and appropriate arena in which to challenge traditional notions of the archive and archival practice and to explore new ways of serving diverse users in the Web 2.0 environment, in this case fostering a community of appreciation, knowledge, and expertise around a collection of objects with historical, cultural, and artistic value.

Web 2.0 and the Memory Institution

Records are always in the process of being made ... "their" stories are never ending... and the stories of those who are conventionally called records creators, records managers, archivists, users and so on are (shifting, intermingling) parts of bigger stories understandable only in the ever-changing broader contexts of society. (Duff & Harris, 2002, p. 265)

While archives, museums, and libraries are often grouped together as information organizations or memory institutions, they have traditionally fulfilled different societal functions, evidenced by differing practices of organization and documentation. Libraries, traditionally, are primarily concerned with providing access to individual objects, while museums strive to educate by transmitting historical narratives about periods in art and history. The goal of an archive is to reveal collections of objects or documents as evidence of human activity, such as the functioning of an organization or the course of an individual's life, carefully arranged and described by the archivist for use by researchers.

Technology has brought the goals and challenges of these distinct memory institutions closer together. In the Web 2.0 environment, the focus has shifted toward providing universal access to documents and objects of all kinds, in all kinds of institutions. Rare and fragile archival material in digital form can circulate as widely as a library e-book, leaving behind the constraints of its carefully curated context as well as its vulnerability to damage. At the same time, however, Given and McTavish (2010) write, "Not everyone favors this shift to the digital landscape ... [some argue] that the materiality of collections is being lost as information is homogenized and simplified for public consumption" (p. 9). Digital objects can easily be extracted from curated context and become filtered by a user's search constraints. For the archivist, providing contextual information that is permanently attached to objects or their digital surrogates, to be consumed along with the object, is a new challenge; so too is the goal of guiding the public toward original archival objects, when much of the information to be gleaned from them can just as (or more) easily be consumed in a pre-digested from somewhere on the Internet. Decontextualization and oversimplification of archive and museum collections is a threat as user filtering separates digital materials from their institutionally assigned meanings and contexts and leaves the user solely responsible for making sense of culturally and historically meaningful objects.

However, innovations afforded by Web 2.0 can lead to new shades of complexity in understanding cultural and historical collections. Cameron (2008) writes about the democratization of the object as the Internet transforms the relationships among institutions, collections, and communities. Collections of all types have long stood as stable markers for meanings, categories, and values assigned by an academic community of curatorial experts for museum visitors to "read and use ... in certain ways" (p. 229). Cameron describes a shift where collection items, long interpreted as simple "facts" of symbolic significance, become complex matters of human concern and interest in a networked environment. Cameron writes, "The complexities of objects, their lived realities, their use and consumption are seen as problems to be removed by classification, although this is changing" (p. 235). Aspects of use and consumption—the realm of the public, as opposed to elite interpretations of symbolic value—are surfacing as significant properties of historical and cultural objects, to be preserved along with the objects themselves. Meaning-making in the memory institution shifts from a closed system, under the jurisdiction of experts in classification and symbolism, to a system democratically open to relationality, unpredictability, ambiguity, and emergence (Cameron, 2008).

One way to democratize the memory institution and shift toward a new kind of expertise is to incorporate social media and Web 2.0 applications into Web-accessible collections. Russo, Watkins, Kelly, and Chan (2008) write about museum integration of social media as an "ideal opportunity ... to build online communities of interest around authentic cultural information" (p. 21). The traditional one-to-many model of communication establishes the authority of the expert; social media provide the possibility of many-to-many communication, where "curatorial knowledge acts as a hub around which an

online community of interest can build" (p. 23). The museum can use its authority to "maintain a cultural dialogue with its audiences in real time ... providing audiences with a voice, allowing them to participate in cultural debate" (p. 24) rather than to assert the interpretations of institutional experts. The result is the museum as a social and collaborative site "in which knowledge, memory, and history are examined, rather than ... where cultural authority is asserted" (p. 22).

As archives, museums, and libraries converge into encompassing institutions of cultural heritage with digital capabilities for broad access and new kinds of user interaction and participation, it is prudent to briefly examine the term that has been coined for these new bodies: *memory institutions*. Dempsey (1999) writes,

Collections [of memory institutions] contain the memory of peoples, communities, institutions, individuals, the scientific and cultural heritage, and the products throughout time of our imagination, craft and learning. They join us to our ancestors and are our legacy to future generations.

A parsing of the term raises the question: who determines "our" legacy of memory? Individual and collective memories are subjective, fallible, and constructed. When we, as a society, entrust an institution with the presentation and preservation of memory, are we asking for an authoritative, expert-constructed, unified account of history to assist and correct our fallible personal memories? Or are we asking the institution to incorporate individual and collective voices, subjective and fallible as they may be, into institutional memory?

Archives in Web 2.0

The perspective of the archivist, distinct from those of other memory institution professionals in museums and libraries, is linked to the fundamental concepts and practices that comprise the archival tradition. The archivist evaluates the archival object or document as evidence of some activity that produced it. This evidential information—about the individual, organization, or cultural group and circumstances that produced the document—determines its value, which remains bound up in its relationship with other documents in the corpus. To establish intellectual control over a document is to reach an understanding of what the document is, where it came from, how and why it was produced, and how it fits in with the rest of the record. To establish physical control is to physically organize documents in such a way that specific items can be found and retrieved as needed, while remaining parts of the whole. The role of the archivist is to establish both intellectual and physical control over the holdings of a repository, fitting items into organizational and descriptive structures that convey the original order of the documents' creation—and thus the evidential meaning of the documents—to future users. This process, of arranging and describing records according to their original order so that evidential value is apparent to future users of the archive, has been established as the expertise of the archivist (O'Toole & Cox, 2006).

An important concept for archival practice is provenance, which is a guiding principle in the task of arranging: the *creator* of a document determines its evidential meaning. An archivist generally keeps all documents produced by a single source (individual, organization, or institution) together so that they provide context for one another in natural groupings based on how and why they were created. In an archive, the archivist aims to determine the original order in which documents were created, and to maintain it and convey it to the user through archival arrangement (O'Toole & Cox, 2006). Arrangement according to provenance is said to reveal the "forces, activities, and functions" that produce records (Fox & Wilkerson, 1998, p. 6).

Provenance, the context of creation, is one kind of context that enters into the process of making sense and meaning of archival documents or objects. But often, for researchers or other users of

archival materials, context of *use* is important as well, as documents may transfer hands and hold different symbolic or actual meanings in different circumstances. Wexelblat and Maes (1999) label this kind of information about an object's ongoing life of use "interaction history": "the records of the interactions of people and objects" (p. 270). On physical objects, these "records" might be visible signs of use, such as dog-eared pages in a book. An object with such historical traces can be called "history-rich" (p. 270).

While archival expertise in arranging and describing focuses on the context of creation, users of archives may be interested in the interaction history of an archival object—the evidential value not just of the object itself, but of its different uses over time by people other than its creator, even extending to subsequent generations or unintended user groups. Duff and Harris (2002) ask, "What do archivists mean by the terms 'text' and 'context'? … Does the making of a record, ultimately, have a beginning and an ending?" (p. 265). With many objects now in digital form—both original objects and archival surrogates—the interaction history or "biography" (Kopytoff, 1986) of an object beyond its creation—its interactions and recontextualizations that may provide evidential meaning to the future researcher—no longer leaves permanent and visible traces, but must be deliberately recorded and (often tenuously) linked or attached to the object by digital means (Wexelblat & Maes, 1999).

As archives become more open to interaction in the digital age, they are still characterized by established principles of archival practice. Evans (2007) suggests that a more networked model of the archive is merely

Are-articulation of archival principles, refreshed and presented to meet the realities of the information economy and the technological and social climate of the twenty-first century … Archivists cannot collect everything and they cannot treat all collections at the same level. Nor can they operate in isolation. (pp. 388-389)

Evans warns against the archivist playing the role of "Keeper of the Ancient Writings ... good at saving information, but not effective at retrieving and revealing it" (p. 388), which, indeed, is counter to the archivist's fundamental goal of making information available to future researchers as evidence of the past and present. The holdings and work of archives are "a common and public good," not "the protected property of an institution" (p. 394). The meeting of archives and Web 2.0 marks a shift in perspective, not a change in principles.

In exploring the potentialities presented by this perspective shift, some notable articles in archival studies discuss the incorporation of user participation into the archivist's primary activities: appraisal (Shilton & Srinivasan, 2007), arrangement and description (Shilton & Srinivasan, 2007; Duff & Harris, 2002), and creating finding aids for collections (Duff & Harris, 2002; Krause & Yakel, 2007).

Shilton and Srinivasan write, "We believe that traditional practices of appraisal, arrangement, and description can be rearticulated as participatory, community-oriented processes" (p. 87). The act of appraisal, or selecting what to include in archival holdings and what to reject as valueless, can also be described as the act of "asserting chosen narratives as truth" (p. 88), thereby determining what documents comprise the archival record that will endure to inform future generations. Duff and Harris (2002) posit that the archivist may be labeled a "storyteller" who weaves narratives of description, connecting archival documents to tell the story of a time, place, and culture (p. 265). Archival description "is a way of constructing knowledge through processes of inscription, mediation, and narration ... In describing records, archivists are working with context, continually locating it, constructing it, figuring and refiguring it" (pp. 275-276).

A finding aid is a digital or paper document that provides the primary mode of access for a researcher in the archives by laying out the contents of a collection according to the arrangement the archivist has determined for it. Duff and Harris (2002) describe finding aids as "predominantly static objects which describe a pre-existing order centred on one predominant provenance" (p. 272). The traditional, static finding aid cannot accommodate the multiple contexts and signifying roles that many archival objects inhabit throughout their histories of existence.

Krause and Yakel (2007) hold that the finding aid, as the main point of contact between the work of the archivist and that of the researcher, would be enhanced by the dynamic and interactive capabilities afforded by a Web 2.0 environment. They write, "Enabling direct and indirect interaction among visitors and archivists, collaborative filtering, and other Web 2.0 features might make archival materials more accessible and enrich the traditional finding aid" (p. 282). In their endeavor to create an interactive finding aid for an archival collection of paper documents and photos, they incorporate category browsing, searching, bookmarks, comments, and "footprints" of previous users' navigation paths to try to enhance users' "ability to make meaningful use" of the static archival description provided in the traditional finding aid. Users can effectively help each other navigate the collection through the comments and footprints they leave behind (p. 288). Even further, Krause and Yakel would consider future incorporation of tagging and ranking of materials, as well as user annotation of the finding aid itself (p. 312).

Social Navigation of Digital Image Collections

Notably, the leading projects in incorporating Web 2.0 technologies to elicit the help of the masses in identification and contextualization have to date occurred primarily in digital image collections. The Library of Congress, Smithsonian, and National Library of Australia have all participated in exploratory studies of user tagging of digital images using the photo-hosting site Flickr (Springer et al., 2008; Kalfatovic, Kapsalis, Spiess, Van Camp, & Edson, 2008; Clayton, Morris, Venkatesha, & Whitton, 2008). Users added their own descriptive or identifying terms to individual images, and could comment on them as well. All three institutions found that the exploratory endeavors resulted in increased access to and interest in collections items, as well as the creation of valuable descriptive information; all three project reports discuss the possibility of future incorporation of user-generated tags into institutional classification systems. Matusiak (2006) writes, "Social classification does not have to be seen as an alternative or replacement of traditional indexing, but rather as an enhancement. These two approaches can supplement each other" (p. 295). In the report sponsored by the National Library of Australia, Clayton et al. (2008) write, "User tagging allows us, as the custodians of national collections, to: interpret collections more broadly; balance technical description with common language; engage and create communities from afar; and give the public a sense of ownership of our collections" (p. 24). In the Library of Congress report, Springer et al. (2008) conclude that the project:

Has allowed the Library to encourage discovery of historical material ... increase learning and stimulate an educational interest in history ... stimulate communication, not just between members of the public and the Library, but also with each other ... tap into the expertise in communities of interest ... and elicit contributions

Why have image collections been particularly good sites for experiments with participatory indexing? Matusiak (2006) gives a list of ways in which "the complexity and richness of visual medium" presents "challenges to concept-based indexing," which may also be read as a list of reasons why engaging users in participatory indexing can be beneficial. I quote the list verbatim here:

- Images are rich and often contain information useful to researchers from many disciplines.
- Image is often used for a purpose not anticipated by the original creator.
- The same image can mean different things to different people.
- Images can have several layers of meaning from specific to more abstract.
- Unlike text document, image does not contain information about its authorship. (Matusiak, 2006, p. 285)

Later, she adds that there is often "difficulty in mapping a user's mental model of what a picture is about with the indexer's mental model" (p. 286).

The experiments with participatory indexing described above occurred in the context of museum collections, rather than archives. While the archive presents a body of related documents as a meaningful entity rather than a collection of individually interesting items, it is more in line with the goals of museums and libraries, concerned with providing item-level access, to ask users to evaluate, identify, and contextualize individual objects such as photographs. As digital networks allow users to consider archival objects outside of a traditional archival context, though, could non-traditional indexing and description at the item level, viable through mass participation, increase the range of uses and meaning for archival material as well?

Authority and Expertise in the Web 2.0 Archive

Calls to open traditional archival practice to user or community participation may be read as a challenge to the authority and expertise of the archivist; in the literature, issues of *power* and *voice* are recurring themes. Karp (1992) writes, "Sources of power are derived from the capacity of cultural institutions to classify and define peoples and societies. This is the power to represent: to reproduce structures of belief and experience through which cultural differences are understood" (pp. 1-2). Shilton and Srinivasan (2007) assert that archives of material arranged, described, and presented according to traditional principles of the field in static classification structures omit the perspectives, interpretations, and historical narratives of marginalized communities. Duff and Harris (2002) write,

Acknowledging one type of provenance, one act of creation, or one method of describing, will fail to capture the rich complexities of the records in our care ... There always have been and always will be many provenances, multiple voices, hundreds of relationships, multiple layers of context, all needing to be documented ... We need to create holes that allow in the voices of our users (pp. 274-279)

With the power to create "holes" and allow multiple, non-expert voices to enter archival practice, the archivist has the ability to empower individuals and communities and improve the accuracy of the historical record. "By broadening their traditional tools to actively engage marginalized communities in the preservation process, archivists can preserve local knowledge and create representative, empowered archives" (Shilton & Srinivasan, 2007, p. 87). Duff and Harris (2002) further assert that the archivist has a duty to "re-imagine" archival descriptive standards as "instruments for calling the future in through a challenging of the instinct merely to replicate existing power relations" (p. 266).

Incorporating multiple voices, especially through direct user and community input, may be seen to challenge the archivist's authoritative and expert arrangement and description of archival materials and, through it, of history. Yakel (2006) suggests that this may be why archives have been slow to incorporate participatory features afforded by Web 2.0: research in archives is traditionally "a one-way conversation, with the archives

providing information," and conceptualizing the user as "co-creator" is "foreign to archivists" (p. 160). Interactive archival websites have "ceded some control over these core archival functions to their visitors ... reimagining the ways in which researchers can interact with the archival record and with fellow travelers in the virtual archives" (p. 163).

Shilton and Srinivasan (2007) write, "It is through ... dialogue with diverse images, accounts, descriptions, and so on that others can begin to construct a meaningful understanding of [archival] objects" (p. 677). Archivists have the power to decide which accounts and descriptions of the past and present are made available to future publics. Through training in the archival field, the professional archivist develops expertise in the task of deciding which narratives are "truth," and in processes of arrangement and description that involve an "inevitable reframing" of chosen narratives (p. 88). The archivist then constructs a finding aid, which, although a culturally and individually constructed object reflecting the values of a perspective determined by time and place, is not an object *of* study per se, but an object that *guides* study and interpretation of archival materials (Duff & Harris, 2002, p. 272).

Srinivasan, Boast, Becvar, and Furner (2009) hold that the goal of a successfully engaging participatory archive would not be to expel notions of expertise altogether, but to "reconnect objects with diverse expert accounts" and "revive objects as agents within an ongoing exploratory dialog" (p. 667). "A set of foundational expert voices" can "help orient the objects" (p. 671) for ongoing, user-participatory conversation and interpretation. The model Srinivasan et al. propose, of an interactive Web 2.0 archive, redefines the expertise of the archivist by placing it alongside other, varied expert interpretations of the objects in a deliberate and careful process of recontextualization.

Incorporating multiple voices into processes of arrangement and description necessitates a rejection not of expertise itself or of the archivist as expert, but of the notion that expertise must be singular and exclusive. When Shilton and Srinivasan (2007) engage marginalized communities in the appraisal of cultural objects, the result is not a questioning of the archivist as expert, but a redefinition of the archivist as *an* expert, alongside cultural-insider experts who can provide additional, equally valuable perspectives on particular archival objects. In the second half of this chapter, I will describe another project, concerning archival content from the domain of popular/populist America, that exemplifies the potential benefits for archives of Web 2.0 affordances, user participation, item-level description and access, and a concept of expertise reconfigured to include a whole community of different perspectives.

INTERACTION AND EXPERTISE IN AN APPALACHIAN MUSIC ARCHIVE

Considering Music Archives

While scholars in archival studies are beginning to study two-way interactions between users and archives, and archivists are launching experiments involving user and community participation in archival processes, there are some areas of archives that have to date been largely overlooked in terms of interactive and participatory potential. Recorded music collections are one of these areas.

Music recordings in archives have long been a challenge in terms of preservation and access, which is perhaps why music collections have not yet been sites for experimentation with new technologies. The International Association of Music Libraries' working group on the Access to Music Archives Project notes "the complexity of music archives regarding their locations, formats, provenance, and access."[1] Music recordings, captured in many different formats from wax cylinders to born-digital files and each requiring special equipment and software for playback, are often tucked away, a few here and there, within larger manuscript collections and are sometimes ignored altogether due to lack of time, equipment, or expertise. Digitization of music collections is both time-sensitive (due to deteriorating or obsolete media) and complex compared to paper documentation. Archives that can make paper-based collections available may not have the time or resources to deal with other media, and much remains buried.

Music in archives also raises issues—especially as collections are increasingly digitized and networked—about the ability of traditional archival goals and practices to adequately provide access to objects that may be individually interesting to users. According to traditional archival practice, musical objects in archives would be interpreted as any other document is: as part of a body of evidence of the activities of its creator. While a musical recording or score may contribute to historical evidence, I would argue that this kind of work could also be valuable on its own, and should be made individually accessible. Digital and networked archives open up the possibility for the discovery of individually valuable objects (including visual and verbal art as well). There can be a diversity of value and meaning in an expressive work, not just concerning the life of its creator but also an understanding of artistic or political movements, as well as potential for inspiration, reinterpretation, and personal emotional connection. This diversity of value and meaning could present an opportunity to experiment with the incorporation of different kinds of contextualization, description, and expertise into the archive (for example, of musicians, musicologists, and fans).

This mode of consideration at the individual-object level—a mode facilitated by Internet searching and filtering practices, where user-entered criteria lead to ever more refined and decontextualized search results—diverges from the traditional archival practice of considering the object or document primarily as part of a body of evidence, and in this strict sense, a collection that allows description and access at this level might no longer be considered an archive. Imagining the possibilities for indexing at the item level, though, may reveal the potential of the redefined archive to better serve users with diverse interests in its contents.

Musical archival objects may have different meanings for different people. Matusiak's (2006) list of traits that make photo collections particularly challenging for traditional indexing, and therefore particularly apt for participatory indexing, may also be read to reflect the complexity of musical objects in archives. Music transcends discipline in its value; while musicologists and ethnomusicologists may study recordings for particular information, so may historians and cultural theorists of all types, gleaning different kinds of information from the same objects. Music may be "used" for "a purpose not anticipated by the original creator" (p. 285): for example, an activist or political song may also be enjoyed solely for its aesthetic appeal, just as a song written to be aesthetically appealing may later be adopted as a call to activism of some sort. One song "can mean different things to different people," and can have "several layers of meaning from specific to more abstract" (p. 285); for example, a particular Woody Guthrie song can be "about" a stroll down a highway, the beauty of a country, a call to social and environmental responsibility, and the inauguration of Obama as US president, all at the same time. An expert indexer's conception of what a song is about does not necessarily correspond with what any given listener perceives at any given time. Also, similar to a photograph, a recording does not necessarily offer up straightforward information about its authorship, which means that many historical recordings are of mysterious origin. This sort of puzzle often cannot be solved through indexing expertise, but only through tracking down any living individual who may still hold the requisite knowledge. (From the realm of audiovisual media archives, where individual objects of interest or artistic merit raise similar issues of access and indexing, Lost Films[2] provides an example of

an innovative site where users can contribute personal knowledge to help identify missing or unidentified historical films.)

By involving different groups of users in the indexing process, the participatory archive can address and emphasize different aspects of its holdings. The historical-musicologist-as-indexer may interpret the piece in the context of a developing artistic movement or period. The ethnomusicologist-as-indexer might explain the cultural significance of a particular recording. Listeners-as-indexers could reveal the varied emotional effects of a work on different audiences. These are all different significances of a piece that may have value to the users of the archive.

Musical recordings in archives thus raise complex issues of evaluation, interpretation, and access. For these reasons, music collections may be seen by some as dangerous grounds for experimentation in the digital realm. Instead, we can interpret these problems as signifying a particularly compelling and appropriate arena in which to challenge traditional notions of the archive and archival practice and explore new ways of serving diverse users in the Web 2.0 environment. The following case study of an Appalachian song collection is an example of the Web 2.0 archive, challenging traditional notions of archival description and expertise. Music has often served a function of bringing people together into communities, both historically and in contemporary times, and music archives are rife with potential for bringing people together, through the Web, into communities of knowledge and use.

The Bascom Lamar Lunsford Collection at Columbia University

In 1935, Appalachian lawyer, folklorist, and performing musician Bascom Lamar Lunsford traveled from his native North Carolina to Columbia University and, over a span of several days, recorded more than 315 songs, folktales, dance calls, and anecdotal reflections onto 79 twelve-inch aluminum discs. These recordings comprise a "memory collection" of material Lunsford had collected over decades of travel, communicating and collaborating with musicians and common people all over the region. Throughout the recordings, Lunsford frequently credits individual people who taught him his songs (for example, the song "Edward" is performed "as sung by Mrs. D.W. Townsend in Bat Cave, North Carolina"). His performance on these recordings is apparently from memory, including such statements of provenance.

In his spoken introduction to the collection, Lunsford states, "[These records] are not to be used for commercial purposes." A decade before his invitation to record at Columbia University, Lunsford founded the Mountain Dance and Folk Festival in Asheville, North Carolina, "as a means for people to share and understand the beauty and dignity of the Southern Appalachian music and dance traditions that have been handed down through generations in Western North Carolina ... for education and entertainment."[3] Lunsford's legacy of appreciation for the Appalachian folk tradition, his rejection of commercialism, and his commitment to sharing the musical knowledge of common people (and giving them credit for it, too!) led to the belief that his memory collection would be prime grounds for experimentation with methods of digital access that challenge traditional modes of archival representation and promote continued access to and diverse interpretations of the songs themselves. In spring 2011, as a master's student at the University of Texas at Austin School of Information, I had the opportunity to work with Columbia professor of ethnomusicology Aaron Fox and Lunsford archivist Jennie Halperin and to assist in making plans for an interactive, accessible website via which the general public can listen to, download, and participate in a community of knowledge based around the Lunsford memory collection recordings. (At the time of writing the information architecture of the site is being developed while we wait for grant funding to complete an archival-quality redigitization of the aluminum discs.)

Lunsford's descendants, who were consulted in the planning of the Web archive, and who, in a sense, are also the stewards of his work and legacy, have expressed a specific concern about releasing the song collection into the digital domain: it is important to the family that Lunsford's work is made "very accessible to the common man," explained one family member by email. The Web archive should not be a research tool created for the sole benefit of outside scholars; rather, to open up the archive to multiple voices and uses would be to convey the respect Lunsford had for the authority of the common person as he collected different versions of songs and unique styles of performance and brought them back to Columbia University and the greater world.

The primary goal of those working with the Lunsford collection is to provide access to an invaluable cultural and historical resource. Since Lunsford made very few commercial recordings, he is a somewhat "lost" figure of the Appalachian folk tradition, though the recordings that do exist widely are held in high esteem by scholars and folk musicians. (A search on YouTube reveals that his songs are quite frequently covered and reinterpreted by known and amateur musicians alike.) Making a sizable collection of largely unheard Lunsford recordings available—and, moreover, easily accessible—to the public will likely be a notable development in the Appalachian folk world. Unknown songs, unusual versions of known songs, and Lunsford's anecdotal introductions and interludes that provide a unique context for the songs all present historical documentation that defies homogeneous interpretations of songs that are now part of the folk music canon; this collection conveys the personal nature and diverse interpretations of canonical songs that make the Appalachian folk tradition unique.

Within the broad goal of providing access, the Lunsford memory collection presents a prime opportunity for experimentation with Web 2.0 applications, user participation, and the redefinition of archival expertise. Lunsford's aesthetic and his music-collecting and music-sharing practices are centered on the common man, and do not pay homage to any kind of single, authoritative expert voice. The experts here are "Mrs. D.W. Townsend in Bat Cave, North Carolina" and the other "common" women and men who shared their musical knowledge with Lunsford, permitting it to be recorded in his notes and in his memory. Accordingly, the goal of the archive is not just to provide access to the songs, but also to provide a forum for sharing individual interpretations and developing multidimensional, community-based meanings for the songs. The Lunsford memory collection website will draw contextualizing expertise from the "common man [and woman]."

The Lunsford recordings are archival objects, but the Lunsford memory collection website is a departure from the traditional archival practice of providing a description of a creator's whole body of documents grouped together. Lunsford's personal papers are held elsewhere, and while these recordings may contribute to the evidence of Lunsford's activities as a song collector and performer, the individual songs also have much historical and cultural value of their own. In a strict and traditional sense, by extracting the songs from other contextualizing documents (as well as their physical carriers) and interpreting them one by one, this digital collection is no longer a traditional archive. The Lunsford memory collection website presents a reconfigured conception of an archive of music, where each song is not merely evidence of a past event, but is valued for its continuing expressive life as it is further heard, interpreted, and performed.

The Bascom Lamar Lunsford Collection in Web 2.0: Envisioning the Site and its Use

For this project to be meaningful to all kind of archives with a variety of funding situations, it was important to choose an open-source content management system that is widely available for free. The Lunsford site is being constructed using CollectiveAccess, "a highly configurable cataloguing tool and web-based application for museums, archives, and digital collections."[4] CollectiveAccess is available for free download[5] under the GNU Public License, a license that permits access to open-source material. CollectiveAccess was also chosen for its ease of use, needing "little to no custom programming."[6] It supports a wide variety of media formats including audio media; allows interactions and participation such as commenting, tagging, and uploading; and has advanced capabilities such as geospatial mapping of data.

The capabilities of this widely available Web 2.0 content management system serve as the basis for envisioning a website for the Lunsford collection that will encourage interaction and invite contribution, and as a result place the task of contextualizing the Lunsford songs, with regards to both historical and contemporary significance, in the hands of the virtual general public, rather than the professional archivist alone. This public could include experts in Appalachian history, musicology, and performance, but it will not be limited to "experts" of any kind; rather, a community-based expertise developed through the contributions of many diverse voices would be the ideal result. This will be fostered through the features listed and explained below.

First, the 315 songs will be available for free download. Typically in a music archive, online media is only available by streaming, and often the user of the archive has to be physically present in the reading room of the archive to gain access to the materials on an individual basis, in a controlled setting. This is often done in an effort to respect copyright restrictions that prohibit copying and distribution of the materials. For music recordings especially, once they are digitized it can be difficult to control illegal copying and distribution, and archivists must go to lengths to adhere to these legal responsibilities.

For the Lunsford collection, conveying a sense of shared ownership of the songs is fundamental to the site; they are held by an institution, but they also belong to "the common man [and woman]." The first step in fostering reinterpretations and new personal memories of the songs is to let them be "owned" by many. Resolving copyright issues takes work, and is not always possible, but in this case, through ongoing negotiations with Lunsford's descendants and the multiple institutions who can claim rights to his material legacy, it has become an attainable goal to release the recordings for free download under a Creative Commons ShareAlike license that allows use and/or modification of a work, as long as it is attributed to the original source and not used for commercial purposes.[7]

In order to download, users will register for the site and log in, an unobtrusive process by which the administrators of the site can gather very basic information about users, including an estimated number of people interested in the site. Registering will also allow the user to provide a brief, one- or two-sentence "biography" where she or he can summarize her or his interest in the Lunsford collection, or provide any other information she or he desires to share with other visitors.

Anyone can view the entire site without logging in. Each of the 315 songs will have a page with information about the song: basic cataloging information provided by the archive, as well as any additions contributed by visitors to the site.

Logged-in visitors to the site can "comment" or "contribute" through each song's page. A comment could be, for example, some historical information about the song; identification of an individual credited on the track; or a personal reflection or anecdote about the song. While it may seem that

a task of any kind of archive is to collect and preserve factual information rather than personal reflections, Lunsford's recordings themselves are rich with instances that exemplify the historical, context-imbuing value found in the anecdote; for example, before playing the song "Shout Lullie," Lunsford recounts, "It's always been a delight of mine to go high into the mountains and spend the night with the mountaineer in the mountain cabin, his little mud-doppled happy home, take down the old tackhead banjo, and sing 'Shout Lullie.'" Lunsford's reflection here is personal, drawing the listener in to imagine this experience; and it raises questions of historical fact as well: what exactly is a tackhead banjo, and what is the significance of his mention of it here?

I found the answer to this question in a post on a musical instrument artisans' online forum, LuthierBuilt.net: a tackhead banjo is a fretless form of the instrument, invented in the 1800s, and was associated with musicians who could not afford professionally crafted banjos, as it could be made at home with minimal materials including the tacks used to attach the head to the hoop.[8] Contributors to this kind of online forum may also be some of the same people who would be interested in sharing comments and historical facts on the Lunsford site. Through these sorts of contributions—both the historically factual and the reflectively personal—each song will be given a context pieced together from a community of knowledge, which may draw from the expertise of musical instrument artisans, musicians, music appreciators, Appalachian scholars, Appalachian residents, or anyone else with an interest in Lunsford's songs or life. For a collection of 315 songs, sourcing this information from many people with diverse personal and professional expertise will create a vastly more thorough and potentially more meaningful context for the songs than could possibly be given by a single or small number of professional archivists.

A visitor may also "contribute" to a song's page, adding chords, lyrics, or even a new version of a Lunsford song. Chords and lyrics of songs of all genres are often shared through online forums, and sometimes multiple, divergent versions of the same song exist and can be considered legitimate (or can instigate interesting debate about which is the "correct" version). Allowing multiple users to contribute chords and lyrics is an invitation for multiple valid interpretations. This is consistent with the tradition from which Lunsford's songs arise: for Appalachian folk music, and folk in general, different musicians' versions of songs sometimes diverge greatly from previous versions, and there is not necessarily one correct, authoritative, or "original" version. Often, folk songs are so old that an original instance of a song cannot be identified. This is another likely reason why Lunsford credits individuals on the recordings in his memory collection: one person's version of a song may be so distinct as to deserve authorship credit, even though the song is considered traditional or anonymous. Here, unique variants are legitimate versions, and Lunsford records them in his canon, to share with the world as representative of the tradition.

This, too, is a motivation behind allowing users to upload or link to their own versions of songs in the collection, which will subsequently be displayed on a geospatial map on each song's page. New versions of old songs will assist in providing a contemporary context for listeners to understand the songs and their meanings, and to understand how folk songs develop. The map for each song will show where Lunsford "found" it (information he announces on many of the recorded tracks, and which may also be found in his personal papers), and will situate it alongside historical and contemporary instances of the song, each placed in its own geographic locale, creating a map that gives a sense of the song's development across time and space.

A look at YouTube may help in imagining further what the comments and contributions sections might look like for a specific song. Song

number 173 on Lunsford's aluminum discs is called "Old Stepstone." On YouTube, the first several results for a search for "Old Stepstone" are versions of the same song by contemporary artists, both known and amateur. The first video shows established "freak folk" musician Bonnie "Prince" Billy performing the song on solo guitar in a recording studio. The information given by the YouTube poster calls the song "Goodbye Dear Old Stepstone" and credits Lunsford as the composer. The second and third results are two amateur "bedroom musician" videos by young males on guitars, both of whom also call the song "Goodbye Dear Old Stepstone." One credits Lunsford as composer, while the other credits Bonnie "Prince" Billy, clearly having heard Billy's cover of the song and assumed the performer to be the composer as well (as often happens with traditional songs). The fourth video shows internationally known Swedish folk musician Kristian Matsson, who performs widely under the moniker The Tallest Man on Earth, walking the streets of Sydney, Australia, and playing the song on guitar while being filmed for a French music blog. This video calls the song "Stepstone" and the attribution reads "traditional, after Bascom Lamar Lunsford." More video results show versions on solo ukulele, by a bluegrass ensemble, and by numerous people who give credit to other composers, including Woody Guthrie, who has also recorded the song.

The page for "Old Stepstone" on the Lunsford website could link to the performances of all these participants, both known and amateur, placing the links on a geospatial map that would show how the song has traveled from Appalachia to recording studios and bedrooms all over the US, as well as Australia and beyond. Conversations that take place in YouTube comments on these videos—such as debate over whether the song was composed by Woody Guthrie or existed long before Guthrie's time—could occupy the comments section of the page. This participatory, engaging dialogue, illustrated by musical examples from around the country and world, would provide a context for visitors to the site who could be coming across the song, or music of the Appalachian tradition, for the first time.

The array of contemporary performances convey two important qualities of the folk music tradition: folk songs are available for anyone to reclaim, reinterpret, and share with others; and along the path of multiple reinterpretations, authorship credit often becomes lost or confused. Even a folk music expert may be incorrect when identifying an original composer or other facts about a folk song's often complex, multi-pronged development over time. The Lunsford site will provide a forum for dialogue, where multiple opinions and interpretations of a song's history and meaning can be voiced and can remain connected with the song for future visitors to peruse: the dialogue becomes a part of the archive. This participatory development of knowledge—engaging musicians, historians, and casual music-appreciators alike—results in a new kind of expertise that is apt for a collection of origin-ambiguous, oft-appropriated songs from the folk tradition. Well-known contemporary folk musicians, amateur guitarists, Guthrie devotees, and other folk fans are all experts at finding meaning and beauty in music. The historical significance, contemporary cultural significance, and personal meaning identified by all these potential participants are contributions toward a community of expertise surrounding the Lunsford recordings.

This kind of interactive archive does not necessitate a rejection of traditional notions of academic expertise in the archival setting. To return to the ideas of Srinivasan et al. (2009) quoted earlier in this chapter, eliciting contributions from some established experts—"a set of foundational expert voices" (p. 671)—will serve to spark dialogue and give the archive an interdisciplinary grounding. Scholars in cultural studies, Appalachian studies, and musicology will be asked to contribute prefaces to the collection, as well as to participate in discussion about the songs. Placed alongside

the comments and interpretations of members of the general public—experts of a different kind—scholarly expertise will be reconfigured as one element of a community of expertise, and will serve to add to the diversity of interpretations of the archival material.

Thus, aside from providing access to and interpretations of the resources in its holdings, an archive can serve to build a community of interest and knowledge, reconfiguring traditional notions of archival expertise. In a traditional physical archive, one might dog-ear the page of a book or even pencil an annotation on a paper finding aid. In the digital realm, aided by Web 2.0 software, visitors can leave their interaction traces in a non-damaging, constructive, and communicative way. For website visitors, interaction traces establish awareness of and common ground with other users and can serve to cultivate social interaction and dialogue (Lee, Danis, Miller, & Yung, 2001, pp. 2-3). The interaction histories of digital objects, evident through the comments and contributions left for future visitors to see, reflect and encourage the continued use of materials in an archive and create connections between the visitors who experience, interpret, and continue to use them.

For traditional notions of expertise in an archive, this represents not a rejection but a reconfiguration. In a Web 2.0 environment, it is possible for multiple interpretations to be voiced simultaneously, with equal legitimacy. Alongside the voice of the archivist, which emerges as she appraises, processes, and determines the best mode of access to the materials, the interpretations of experts across relevant disciplines, as well as those of other visitors with academic or personal interest in the materials, can be present for users of the archive to take into account. The result is a community of expertise that brings together knowledge, experience, and interpretations from diverse voices and multiple facets of society. For the Lunsford collection, this may result in a deeper understanding of folk tradition, Appalachian ideas of expertise, and the history of Lunsford's songs and methods of collecting. It may also lead to widespread, continued use of the collection, for both scholarly and personal purposes, by all sorts of people.

FUTURE RESEARCH DIRECTIONS

The Bascom Lamar Lunsford memory collection is one example of the use of Web 2.0 features to challenge and redefine notions of expertise that have been foundational to longstanding archival practice. Other research and experiments in interactive archives are ongoing and widespread (e.g., Krause & Yakel, 2007; Shilton & Srinivasan, 2007; Yakel, 2006; case studies from Daines & Nimer, 2009; and websites such as Lost Films), and scholars in archival studies are continuing to imagine and examine further possibilities for participatory archival practices.

While scholars in the field research and theorize, it is also important for professional archivists to experiment with real collections, putting the principles and ideas into action. Transparency of archival practice, in general, is a related area of research and an important area for experimentation in archives. A colophon, or statement of the archivist's approach in appraising and processing a collection, can provide a starting point for dialogue between the user and the archivist, even in traditional, physical archives with paper finding aids (Krause & Yakel, 2007, p. 290). Archivists also share their methods of opening up the archive by publishing papers about their experiments. This kind of transparency removes some of the mystique of the "Keepers of the Ancient Writings," redefining archival expertise as subjective, interpretive, and fallible, and calling for users of archives to reflect critically on traditional archival practices.

This does not mean that archivists, or training in traditional archival practice, are unnecessary in a Web 2.0 environment. Archivists are needed to envision, allow, and facilitate increased participation and interaction in archives, and to determine

when and how these can be utilized appropriately. Archivists may find their professional roles changing and developing in the Web 2.0 environment, but the profession will continue to be relevant and necessary. It is the duty of the archivist to creatively explore the facets of the job, finding the best ways to utilize developing technological resources to contextualize and recontextualize collections, helping the public make meaningful use of cultural and historical resources long into the future.

In taking on this challenge, archivists should not shy away from particularly challenging collections or types of media. While collections of recorded music have long been challenging to archivists with respect to preservation and access, the example of the Bascom Lamar Lunsford collection may show that complicated media such as recorded music can prove to be particularly interesting and rewarding cases for experimentation.

In the future, archivists will likely continue to become more comfortable with a reconfigured conception of archival expertise. Embracing Web 2.0 technology and user participation will become a requirement of the profession. While the professional archivist will continue to be necessary for the stewardship of cultural and historical documents and artifacts, current trends suggest that an increasing number of cultural memory institutions will also invite user contribution and multiple voices into the lasting cultural and historical record.

CONCLUSION

As archivists begin to experiment with possibilities for user contribution and participation afforded by Web 2.0, issues of authority and expertise in the archive are facing an inevitable redefinition. Facts, reflections, and interpretations from the general public can enhance, challenge, or even replace the context assigned by expert archivists for the collections under their stewardship. As exemplified by the Bascom Lamar Lunsford memory collection, for archival objects produced by a popular musical tradition, participatory archival practices afford opportunities to present collections in the context of multiple voices, diverse interpretations, and a collaborative community of ownership and expertise. For online collections of archival materials of many different formats and traditions, additional multiple perspectives and interpretations can enhance the meaning of the traditional institutional record.

As interactive archives become more common, thoughtful investigation of interactive tools is required. The contemporary archivist can creatively use the potentialities of the Web 2.0 environment to better convey the cultural context of archival material, to engage users in a deeper and more personal way, and to foster participation in the creation of knowledge around archival material. Documents and artifacts in archives represent the knowledge, practices, lives, cultures, and legacy of all of humanity. Web 2.0 technologies provide new ways for archivists to approach their tasks with this in mind, thoughtfully and creatively incorporating the experiences and expertise of all types of people into contextualizing and interpreting archival holdings. Through further study and experimentation, archival expertise can be redefined not as understanding the meaning of archival material per se, but as understanding the deeply complex and meaningful interactions between users, archives, and archival objects.

REFERENCES

Cameron, F. R. (2008). Object-oriented democracies: Conceptualising museum collections in networks. *Museum Management and Curatorship*, *23*(3), 229–243. doi:10.1080/09647770802233807

Clayton, S., Morris, S., Venkatesha, A., & Whitton, H. (2008). *User tagging of online cultural heritage items: A project report for the 2008 Cultural Management Development Program.* Unpublished report, Australia.

Daines, J. G., & Nimer, C. L. (2009). *The interactive archivist: Case studies in utilizing Web 2.0 to improve the archival experience.* Retrieved from http://interactivearchivist.archivists.org

Dempsey, L. (1999). Scientific, industrial, and cultural heritage: A shared approach. *Ariadne*, *22*, •••. Retrieved from http://www.ariadne.ac.uk/issue22/Dempsey

Duff, W. M., & Harris, V. (2002). Stories and names: Archival description as narrating records and constructing meanings. *Archival Science, 2*, 263–285. doi:10.1007/BF02435625

Evans, M. J. (2007). Archives of the people, by the people, for the people. *The American Archivist*, *70*(2), 387–400.

Fox, M. J., & Wilkerson, P. L. (1998). *Introduction to archival organization and description: Access to cultural heritage.* Santa Monica, CA: Getty Information Institute.

Given, L., & McTavish, L. (2010). What's old is new again: The reconvergence of libraries, archives, and museums in the digital age. *The Library Quarterly, 80*(1), 7–32. doi:10.1086/648461

Kalfatovic, M. R., Kapsalis, E., Spiess, K. P., Van Camp, A., & Edson, M. (2008). Smithsonian Team Flickr: A library, archives, and museums collaboration in Web 2.0 space. *Archival Science, 8*, 267–277. doi:10.1007/s10502-009-9089-y

Karp, I. (1992). Introduction: Museums and communities: The politics of public culture. In Karp, I., Kreamer, C. M., & Levine, S. D. (Eds.), *Museums and communities: The politics of public culture* (pp. 1–18). Washington, DC: Smithsonian Institution Press.

Kopytoff, I. (1986). The cultural biography of things: Commoditization as process. In Appadurai, A. (Ed.), *The social life of things: Commodities in cultural perspective* (pp. 64–92). Cambridge, MA: Cambridge University Press.

Krause, M. G., & Yakel, E. (2007). Interaction in virtual archives: The Polar Bear Expedition Digital Collections next generation finding aid. *The American Archivist, 70*(2), 282–314.

Lee, A., Danis, C., Miller, T., & Jung, Y. (2001). Fostering social interaction in online spaces. In M. Hirose (Ed.), *INTERACT '01: Proceedings of the Eighth IFIP Conference on Human-Computer Interaction* (pp. 59-66). Amsterdam, The Netherlands: IOS Press.

Matusiak, K. K. (2006). Towards user-centered indexing in digital image collections. *OCLC Systems & Services: International Digital Library Perspectives, 22*(4), 283–298.

O'Toole, J., & Cox, R. (2006). *Understanding archives and manuscripts*. Chicago, IL: Society of American Archivists.

Russo, A., Watkins, J., Kelly, L., & Chan, S. (2008, January). Participatory communication with social media. *Curator, 51*(1), 21–31. doi:10.1111/j.2151-6952.2008.tb00292.x

Shilton, K., & Srinivasan, R. (2007). Participatory appraisal and arrangement for multicultural archival collections. *Archivaria, 63*, 87–101.

Springer, M., Dulabahn, B., Michel, P., Natanson, B., Reser, D., Woodward, D., & Zinkham, H. (2008, October). *For the common good: The Library of Congress Flickr pilot project*. Washington, DC: Library of Congress.

Srinivasan, R., Boast, R., Becvar, K. M., & Furner, J. (2009). Blobgects: Digital museum catalogs and diverse user communities. *Journal of the American Society for Information Science and Technology, 60*(4), 666–678. doi:10.1002/asi.21027

Wexelblat, A., & Maes, P. (1999). Footprints: History-rich tools for information foraging. In *Proceedings of the SIGCHI Conference on Human Factors in Computing Systems: The CHI Is the Limit* (pp. 270-277). New York, NY: ACM Press.

Yakel, E. (2006). Inviting the user into the virtual archives. *OCLC Systems & Services: International Digital Library Perspectives, 22*(3), 159–163.

ADDITIONAL READING

Appadurai, A. (2003). Archive and aspiration. In J. Brouwer & A. Mulder (Eds.), *Information is alive: Art and theory on archiving and retrieving data* (pp. 14-25). Rotterdam, The Netherlands: NAi Publishers.

Brothman, B. (1991). Orders of value: Probing the theoretical terms of archival practice. *Archivaria, 32*, 78–100.

Brown, R. (1991). The value of "narrativity" in the appraisal of historical documents: Foundation for a theory of archival hermeneutics. *Archivaria, 32*, 152–156.

Buckland, M. K. (1977). What is a "document"? *Journal of the American Society for Information Science American Society for Information Science, 48*(9), 804–809. doi:10.1002/(SICI)1097-4571(199709)48:9<804::AID-ASI5>3.0.CO;2-V

Cameron, D. (1971). The museum, a temple or the forum. *Curator, 14*(1), 11–24. doi:10.1111/j.2151-6952.1971.tb00416.x

Cook, T. (1992). Mind over matter: Towards a new theory of archival appraisal. In Craig, B. (Ed.), *The archival imagination: Essays in honour of Hugh A. Taylor* (pp. 38–70). Ottawa, ON: Association of Canadian Archivists.

Cook, T. (2001). Archival science and postmodernism: New formulations for old concepts. *Archival Science, 1*(1), 3–24. doi:10.1007/BF02435636

Cook, T., & Schwartz, J. M. (Eds.). (2002). Archives, records, and power. *Archival Science*, *2*(1-4).

Crane, S. (1997). Memory, distortion, and history in the museum. *History and Theory*, *3*(4), 44–63. doi:10.1111/0018-2656.00030

Craven, L. (Ed.). (2008). *What are archives? Cultural and theoretical perspectives: A reader.* Burlington, VT: Ashgate.

Curtis, N. G. (2006). Universal museums, museum objects, and repatriation: The tangled lives of things. *Museum Management and Curatorship*, *21*, 117–121.

Derrida, J. (1995). *Archive fever: A Freudian impression* (Prenowitz, E., Trans.). Chicago, IL: University of Chicago Press.

Dunbar, A. W. (2006). Introducing critical race theory to archival discourse: Getting the conversation started. *Archival Science*, *6*(1), 109–129. doi:10.1007/s10502-006-9022-6

Duranti, L. (2001). The impact of digital technology on archival science. *Archival Science*, *1*(1), 39–55. doi:10.1007/BF02435638

Foucault, M. (1971/1992). *The archaeology of knowledge and the discourse on language.* New York, NY: Pantheon.

Gilliland-Swetland, A. J. (2000). *Enduring paradigm, new opportunities: The value of the archival perspective in the digital environment.* Council on Library and Information Resources.

Grossman, R. (2006, October). *Our expectations about archives: Archival theory through a community informatics lens.* Paper presented at meeting of the Community Informatics Research Network, Prato, Italy.

Ham, F. G. (1975). The archival edge. *The American Archivist*, *38*(1), 5–13.

Hamilton, C., Harris, V., Taylor, J., Pickover, M., Reid, G., & Saleh, R. (2002). *Refiguring the archive.* Dordrecht, The Netherlands: Kluwer Academic Publishers. doi:10.1007/978-94-010-0570-8

International Association of Music Libraries, Archives and Documentation Centres. *Access to Music Archives working group: Project development.* (n.d.). Retrieved from http://www.iaml.info/activities/projects/access_to_music_archives/development

Johnston, I. (2001). Whose history is it anyway? *Journal of the Society of Archivists*, *22*(2), 213–229. doi:10.1080/00379810120081154

Latour, B. (1986). Visualization and cognition: Thinking with eyes and hands. *Knowledge in Society*, *6*, 1–40.

Light, M., & Hyry, T. (2002). Colophons and annotations: New directions for the finding aid. *The American Archivist*, *65*(2), 216–230.

Mackenzie, A. (1997). The mortality of the virtual: Real-time, archive and dead-time in information networks. *Convergence: The International Journal of Research into New Media Technologies*, *3*(2), 59–71. doi:10.1177/135485659700300208

Manoff, M. (2004). Theories of the archive from across the disciplines. *Portal: Libraries and the Academy*, *4*(1), 9–25. doi:10.1353/pla.2004.0015

Pitti, D. V., & Duff, W. M. (Eds.). (2001). *Encoded archival description on the Internet.* Binghamton, NY: The Haworth Information Press.

Reilly, T. (2005). *From provenance to practice: Archival theory and return to community.* Paper presented at meeting of the First Nations, First Thoughts Conference, Edinburgh, Scotland.

Ridener, J. (2009). *From polders to postmodernism: A concise history of archival theory.* Duluth, MN: Litwin.

Roe, K. (2005). *Arranging and describing archives and manuscripts.* Chicago, IL: Society of American Archivists.

Schellenberg, T. R. (1956). *Modern archives: Principles and techniques.* Chicago, IL: University of Chicago Press.

Schwartz, J. (1995). "We make our tools and our tools make us": Lessons from photographs for the practice, politics, and poetics of diplomatics. *Archivaria, 40,* 40–74.

Still, A., & Velody, I. (Eds.). (1998). The archive. *History of the Human Sciences, 11*(4).

Taylor, H. (1987-88). Transformation in the archives: Technological adjustment or paradigm shift? *Archivaria, 25,* 12–28.

Taylor, H. (1988). "My very act and deed": Some reflections on the role of textual records in the conduct of affairs. *The American Archivist, 51*(4), 456–469.

Trofanenko, B. (2006). Interrupting the gaze: On reconsidering authority in the museum. *Journal of Curriculum Studies, 38*(1), 49–65. doi:10.1080/00220270500038511

Yakel, E. (2003). Impact of Internet-based discovery tools on use and users of archives. *Comma: International Journal on Archives, 2-3,* 191–200.

KEY TERMS AND DEFINITIONS

Appraisal: The process of determining which documents or artifacts to add to archival holdings, typically determined by an archivist's evaluation of evidentiary or representative value.

Archive: A cultural memory institution primarily concerned with presenting documents and artifacts as part of the cultural and historical record and as evidence of human activity.

Finding Aid: A document that serves as the primary access point for a researcher in the archives by listing the contents of a collection in an order determined by the archivist.

Interaction History: An object's ongoing use by people, often evidenced by semi-permanent or permanent marks of use (such as a dog-eared page in a book).

Intellectual Control: An understanding of what a document is, where it came from, how and why it was produced, and how it fits into the cultural and historical record.

Library: A cultural memory institution primarily concerned with providing patrons with access to individual objects.

Museum: A cultural memory institution primarily concerned with educating visitors and encouraging appreciation of culture and history.

Original Order: A principle of archival arrangement, which holds that arranging documents in the same order in which they were created most accurately reveals their evidential meaning.

Provenance: A principle of archival arrangement, which holds that the creator of a document determines the evidential meaning of the document.

ENDNOTES

[1] http://www.iaml.info/activities/projects/access_to_music_archives

[2] http://www.lost-films.eu

[3] http://www.folkheritage.org/75thannua.htm

[4] http://www.collectiveaccess.org/about/overview

[5] http://www.collectiveaccess.org

[6] http://www.collectiveaccess.org/about/overview

[7] http://www.creativecommons.org

[8] http://www.luthierbuilt.net

Chapter 19
Rethinking Expertise in the Web 2.0 Era:
Lessons Learned from Project Durian

Ilias Karasavvidis
University of Thessaly, Greece

ABSTRACT

Social software facilitates the linking of people in unprecedented ways and leads to new knowledge creation and application practices. Even though expertise remains an important constituent of these practices, there is a knowledge gap in the literature regarding its role. This chapter was written with the aim of filling this gap by using Project Durian as a case study. Project Durian presented a unique opportunity to study expertise as mediated by social software because it involved both social software and various layers, forms, and configurations of expertise. In this chapter, data from Project Durian are used to examine the outsourcing of tasks and the role that social software played in that outsourcing. Data analysis indicated that, in the hybrid practice that was established, expertise was spatio-temporally distributed, involved individuals with a broad range of skills, facilitated the crossing of disciplinary boundaries, and was renegotiated. The implications of these findings for expertise in the Web 2.0 era are discussed.

INTRODUCTION

This chapter is an exploration of the novel practices of expertise in the light of social software, using Project Durian as a case study. Project Durian (*Sintel*, 2011) was initiated in 2009 by the Blender Foundation (Blender Foundation, 2011), the organization behind Blender[1], a 3D content creation suite. As a Free and Open Source Software (FOSS) activist and a committed Blender advocate, I had been closely following Project Durian from its beginning. However, because the natural foci for the Blender community were (a) the software and (b) the movie, it did not occur to me at the time that I was actually participating in a massive, groundbreaking crowdsourcing practice revolving around social software. It was only after the project had ended that I began to reflect

DOI: 10.4018/978-1-4666-2178-7.ch019

on it, explicitly thinking about Durian in terms of expertise and social software. This chapter is a first attempt at exploring the relation between social software and expertise in the context of Project Durian.

As Blender is FOSS, its history and development can be fully understood only in the context of the free software movement. Consequently, Project Durian will be introduced against a FOSS and open content backdrop.

Free and Open Source Software

The term FOSS denotes software that is characterized by four kinds of freedom as defined in the licenses through which the software is distributed. These four fundamental freedoms grant users the right to run, copy, distribute, study, change, and improve the software (Free Software Foundation, n.d.; McGowan, 2005). What these freedoms mean in practice is that the end user can obtain the software without cost, has an unlimited number of licenses, may use the software for any purpose, may study and improve it, and may redistribute the improvements to the community so that others can also benefit. FOSS offers many advantages over proprietary software, including, but not limited to, reliability, security, performance, stability, cost, escape from vendor lock-up, and scalability (Chopra & Dexter, 2008).

What is unique about FOSS is the underlying production model, which has two distinctive features. First, the source code is produced using a peer-to-peer development model that is public and collaborative in nature. Unlike proprietary software development which is highly centralized, open source software development is not. Raymond (2001) compared it to a bazaar. Second, the vast majority of open source software developers are volunteers, which means that for the most part they are not paid for their contributions and write code in their spare time.

While FOSS initially emerged as a model for software development, it has gradually evolved

into a phenomenon with far-reaching effects (Raymond, 2001; Lessig, 2005; O'Reilly, 2005a). The collaborative ideas and principles that underlie the development of FOSS can be applied to any type of collaboration that focuses on any kind of work or content (Schweik, 2007). The FOSS movement has affected many other areas of human activity, content creation being one of the most pertinent for the purposes of this chapter. More specifically, thanks to Creative Commons licenses (Creative Commons, n.d.), nowadays users can create and share digital content legally. Such licenses allow the distribution of copyrighted digital content in a reasonable way. For example, users can use a photograph released under a Creative Commons Attribution license to create a derivative work at no charge provided they give credit to the individual who created the original photograph (Creative Commons, n.d.; Lessig, 2004).

Project Durian: An Historical Account

Located in Amsterdam, The Netherlands, the Blender Foundation is a non-profit organization that coordinates the development of Blender. More specifically, the Blender Foundation maintains and improves the source code of Blender; establishes services for the users and developers of Blender; establishes funding for the development of Blender; and provides individual artists and small teams with a complete free and open source 3D-creation pipeline. In addition to coordinating software development, the Blender Foundation also organizes open projects. These projects usually have two main targets: a development, software-related target and a creative target. The open movie projects are the means by which the Blender Foundation realizes these targets.

Since 2006, the Blender Foundation has successfully created five open projects: Orange (2006, produced the 3D animated movie *Elephant's Dream*), Peach (2007–08, produced the 3D animated movie *Big Buck Bunny*), Apricot

(2008, produced the open game Yo Frankie!), and Durian (2009–10, produced the 3D animated movie *Sintel*). These projects are open in that the final product, be it a movie or a game, is released under an open license. More specifically, each final product is available under a Creative Commons Attribution (A) license which means that everyone is free to publish, redistribute, reuse, or re-create it. At the same time, the Blender Foundation releases the actual production files. These files serve both as educational materials, so that users can study how the production team crafted everything, and as means for re-creating the final products or modifying them to create a derivative work. In fact, these production files serve functionally the same purpose.

Due to its commitment to FOSS, the Blender Foundation uses only FOSS applications for these open projects. As there are no licensing fees or royalties involved, the funding for the Blender Foundation open projects comes from pre-sale campaigns of project DVDs, workshops, sales of educational and training materials such as books and video-tutorials, subsidies, donations, and corporate sponsoring. While later projects have attracted considerable funding through sponsorships, the Blender user-base has been a constant source of income for the open projects through the successful CD or DVD pre-sales model. This means that users purchase the DVD containing both the finished product and the production files, thereby helping the Blender Foundation fund the project in advance. When the project is completed the users receive the DVD by snail mail. The Blender Foundation acknowledges the contributions of its users: every Blender user who purchases the DVD online through the pre-sales option is name mentioned in the main film credit scroll.

The third open movie, *Sintel* (2011), is a short film about a girl named Sintel and a baby dragon named Scales. Sintel finds a baby dragon (Scales) with an injured wing and forms a close emotional bond with it as she helps it recover from its injury. When Scales recovers and is able to fly again,

it is caught by an adult dragon and taken away from Sintel. She decides to rescue her friend and embarks on a long quest, facing all sorts of difficulties (she has to fight beasts, warriors, and natural elements) along the way. Eventually, Sintel ends up in Dragon Lands and finds a baby and an adult dragon in a cave. She believes the baby dragon to be Scales and approaches it. However, the baby dragon flees, alerting the adult dragon which then attacks Sintel. In the fight that follows the adult dragon knocks Sintel out but for some reason does not kill her instantly. This gives Sintel the opportunity to rise and slay the adult dragon. Having inflicted a fatal strike, Sintel recognizes the scar on the adult dragon's wing. Then she realizes that the adult dragon that she has just killed is actually an adult Scales. Crushed with sorrow, Sintel leaves the scene, unaware that she is being followed by the baby dragon.

In line with the rationale behind open movie targets, Project Durian aimed to develop Blender further by making *Sintel* (Blender Foundation & Levy, 2010a), a project with both artistic and technical goals. Regarding the former, the plan was to make a 3D animated short film to showcase Blender's capabilities. The technical goal was to evolve Blender 2.4 series into 2.5 by doing a complete code rewrite and graphical user interface (GUI) redesign. Movie funding was provided by sponsors (mostly corporations such as DivX), DVD pre-sales, Blender store sales, and donations.

The initial Durian team comprised four members who were in charge of the pre-processing: Ton Roosendaal (producer), Colin Levy (director), Martin Lodewijk (script concept), and David Revoy (concept artist). The team made a public call for participants (Roosendaal, 2009a; 2009b) and 150 community members submitted portfolios. Four applicants were eventually selected and the initial core team was formed. This team comprised three software developers, five 3D artists, a concept artist, a movie director, and a producer. Because of this selection process, the initial Durian core team represented one of the two greatest assortments of Blender experts ever assembled in one place. (The other being the annual Blender Conference in Amsterdam, which is attended by hundreds of users from all over the world.) One would expect that creating an animated short movie over a period of eight months would not be much of a challenge for such a team of experts, but the Durian core team faced three problems that made their task a very difficult one.

First, when the team was assembled in Amsterdam there was neither a movie script nor any real story, except that the movie would be about a dragon and a girl named Sintel. It took six months to get to the final script (Next Pixel & Blender Foundation, 2010). Second, Blender was not ready. From a technical standpoint, the Blender version (2.5x) to be used in making the movie was at a pre-alpha stage. While this may seem paradoxical, it should be borne in mind that one of the main objectives in making the movie was to develop the software further. Bugs, crashes, and missing features all created many challenges, particularly in the initial phases of the project (Next Pixel & Blender Foundation, 2010). Third, while the initial idea was to make a seven-minute film, in the course of the project the length of the movie almost doubled to 12 minutes 24 seconds, plus credits lasting 2 minutes 24 seconds. The initial core team realized that to tell the story well more shots were needed and this translated to needing more time to complete the project. It turned out that the human resources allocated for the task were not enough to finish the movie in the allotted time frame. Both the producer (Next Pixel & Blender Foundation, 2010) and the film director (Levy, 2009) shared this with the community. The dilemma the production team faced was a grave one: cut the film down or get help.

The Durian core team comprised 18 members. The six-minute animated movie *Day & Night* (Reher & Newton, 2010), which was also released in 2010, involved a staff of 84. It should be noted that *Day & Night* was produced by Pixar, a top, Academy Award-winning computer animation

studio in Hollywood. Comparing the number of staff involved without also factoring in differences in budget, equipment, facilities, hardware, software, and overall experience in making animated movies, for example, is not fair, but it does help underline the Blender Foundation's troubles.

The Blender Foundation addressed the problem in two ways. First, more artists were hired to work on the project; eventually the initial core team doubled and became the final core team (hereafter referred to as the Durian core team). Between December 2009 and April 2010, eight more members (all artists) joined the core team to work full-time at the Amsterdam studio and the project completion deadline was extended twice. However, the extra resources turned out to be insufficient because the film length had also increased and more shots were added. The initial core team was so far behind schedule that when most of the new team members arrived they were surprised to see that the movie was in its initial, and not final, stages (Next Pixel & Blender Foundation, 2010).

Second, the Blender Foundation turned to outsourcing in two ways. It assigned two professional 3D animation studios that had an exclusive FOSS production pipeline, Licuadora Studio (Argentina) and Hand Turkey Studios (United States), the task of completing a few movie shots. It also turned to crowdsourcing, involving the global Blender community in the making of the movie. This distribution of human resources—and subsequently expertise—is depicted in Figure 1.

Project Durian marked the first time that the Blender Foundation had turned to outsourcing, both to professionals (i.e., the experts working for the two 3D animation studios) and to the Blender community at large. While turning to professional artists (with whom the Durian core team had strong bonds because of past collaborations) is an established practice, relegating certain tasks to the Blender community meant venturing into completely uncharted territory and made Project Durian a unique case of distributed expertise. Even though certain historical precedents

Figure 1. Outsourcing: The distribution of human resources in Project Durian

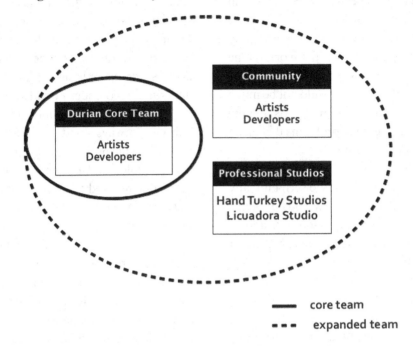

such as Wikipedia and GoldCorp Inc. (Tapscott & Williams, 2006) are successful examples of crowdsourcing and expertise pooling, they have not been investigated with a focus on expertise. As the collective intelligence of the community is one of the critical determinants of successful community contributions, understanding expertise pooling is a precondition for understanding community outsourcing in cases like Project Durian.

Expertise Studies

Since the pioneering work in chess in the second half of the 20th century (e.g., de Groot, 1978; Simon & Chase, 1973), expertise studies have proliferated. Consequently, expertise is one of the most rapidly expanding areas in cognitive psychology. Expertise has different meanings depending on the historical period within which it is examined (Ericsson & Smith, 2002) and it has been investigated in many different domains. Nowadays, there is an extensive knowledge base on expertise, its nature, development, distinctive properties, and mechanisms (see, for example,

Ericsson & Smith, 2002; Ericsson, 2003; Feltovich, Prietula & Ericsson, 2006; Chi, 2006; Ericsson, 2009). The main approach of expertise studies is to analyze exceptional performance under standardized conditions to determine the performance components that make it superior (Ericsson & Smith, 2002). This usually involves either expert-novice comparisons or extended analyses of individual experts (Ericsson & Smith, 2002; Chi, 2006).

The literature findings in the domain of expertise show that, compared to novices, experts excel in many ways. They generate best solutions, detect deep task features, have qualitatively different problem representations, have more accurate self-monitoring, are more able to select appropriate strategies, and perform with minimal cognitive effort (Chi, 2006). Expertise is also limited in its scope, however, and does not transfer to other domains. Finally, expertise involves functional, abstracted representations, automation, reflection, and adaptation (Feltovich, Prietula & Ericsson, 2006). While it was initially assumed that experience could account for the development of expertise, it was eventually discovered that the complex representations and mechanisms that mediate expert performance could not be accounted for by mere experience and that a great deal of deliberate practice is required (Feltovich et al., 2006; Ericsson, 2009). Despite these important advances in understanding expertise, it has been stressed that our knowledge of how expertise works in complex domains is incomplete (Ericsson & Smith, 2002). Research evidence suggests that the mechanisms mediating expert performance are very complex (Ericsson, 2003).

Influenced by cognitive psychology approaches to expertise, this body of research is characterized by an interest in the development of expertise in individuals. After all, an expert is an individual with an exceptional skill set in any domain, be it intellectual or physical. This emphasis is clearly reflected in Ericsson & Smith's (2002) definition of expertise: "the study of expertise seeks to understand and account for what distinguishes outstanding individuals in a domain from less outstanding individuals in that domain, as well as from people in general" (pp. 517-18) (emphasis added). This focus on individuals is understandable given that the general aim of psychology as a science is to determine invariant processes and attributes of individuals that could be generalized to predict human behavior. However, this conceptualization has two main limitations.

The first limitation is related to the shift of focus from individuals and individual expertise to groups and expertise in teams. Working environments and work conditions have changed drastically as jobs have become more demanding. In the contemporary workplace, problems are often ambiguous, ill-defined, and loosely structured. As a rule, work environments have become dynamic and complex, and require experts from different domains. Organizations have attempted to address these new demanding complexities through the creation and management of expert teams (Salas, Rosen, Burke, Goodwin, & Fiore, 2006). In fact, the work by Salas et al. (2006) is among the few that focus on teams of experts instead of individual experts. However, their review is based on the literature on teams in general as opposed to expert teams. It should be noted that a team of experts might be a different entity compared to a team of non-experts or a team of any combination of experts and non-experts. Not only do Salas et al. (2006) fail to acknowledge this as a limitation of their literature review, they also argue that such a multidisciplinary approach has the advantage of combining the literature on team studies and the literature on expertise. While their review makes an important contribution in that it highlights the conditions under which expert teams are known to perform best, whether or not this review is sufficient for understanding expert teams remains inconclusive. For example, if we take Project Durian as our point of reference, it is questionable whether the conclusions drawn by Salas et al. about how expert teams function best can be applied to Project Durian for two reasons. First, in Project Durian the community, one of the main constituents of expertise, was characterized by a very wide range of expertise, literally ranging from novices to experts. Second, while all the members of one of the teams (the Durian core team) worked together at the same studio in Amsterdam for several months, the community members were situated all over the world and made asynchronous contributions.

The second limitation is related to the role of technology in mediating expertise. In an era of rapid technological developments, new, technology-mediated knowledge creation and application practices have emerged. A defining feature of many contemporary practices is that expert knowledge and skill are mediated by social software, the software used to support the process of social networking (i.e., the act of creating networks of relationships between people [Burkhardt, 2009]). Social software tools have many affordances: collaborative information discovery and sharing; content creation; connectivity and social rapport; and knowledge and information aggregation and content modification (Lee & McLoughlin, 2010). Such affordances allow communication between, collaboration between, and sharing of users at an unprecedented scale, thereby enabling new practices and new forms of practices. What is particularly interesting about social software is the pivotal role that users play. As social networks are based on an architecture of participation, new models of production and consumption emerge, such as crowdsourcing and wikinomics (Surowiecki, 2004; Tapscott & Williams, 2006). The underlying principle behind such models is that the pooling of resources through user participation and sharing leads to collective intelligence (O'Reilly, 2005b). This entails the harnessing of the intelligence of groups of people to enable greater productivity than is ever possible when individuals work in isolation (Gregg, 2010). The added value of social software is that it links people and helps them leverage their existing relationships (Burkhardt, 2009). Consequently, certain tasks can be performed not just by skilled individuals working at the same place and time but also by groups of skilled individuals who might be spatially and temporally distributed. In this sense, social software facilitates the creation of online Communities of Practice (CoP) (Lee & McLoughlin, 2010; Chatti & Jarke, 2010).

Despite the fact that the importance of social software is being increasingly recognized, the crucial role that it can play in facilitating expertise has not yet been explored. The overwhelming majority of studies in the area of expertise have placed no emphasis on social software tools, and researchers with a clearer focus on expert teams—such as Salas et al. (2006)—have not investigated the role and function of social software in how expert teams perform. In a complex socio-technical practice such as Project Durian, it is questionable whether the conclusions of Salas et al. apply. This is because in Project Durian, community outsourcing involved social software to such an extent that it would have been inconceivable without it.

Focus of the Study

To shed light on the impact of social software on expertise, the outsourcing of tasks by the Durian core team to the Blender community and the role social software played are analyzed below. More specifically, the following research questions are addressed:

- Which tasks were outsourced to the Blender community?
- Which software applications mediated outsourcing and how?
- What was the response of the Blender community?
- What are the implications for social software–mediated outsourcing of expertise?

METHOD

Data Collection and Analysis

All texts that were publicly available in all major online spaces mediating the communication of the Durian core team with the community were used as data sources. These texts were multimodal, including written and oral speech, static images, and videos. More specifically, the main data sources were the *Sintel* documentary, the Durian blog, and the Blenderartists.org news and discussion forum.

To determine the nature of community contributions in terms of expertise, our main unit of analysis was the help event. A help event was defined as any explicit call for help by the Durian core team or any unsolicited help offered by the Blender community. Using a bottom-up approach, all the data sources were initially processed to categorize help events in very rough categories regarding help calls by the core team and help offers by the Blender community. After this first pass of the whole data set, the process was iterated several times, aggregating the help calls whenever possible and triangulating help events by drawing on different data sets (e.g., examining all occurrences of a specific help event on the Durian blog and in the *Sintel* documentary).

When all help events were identified, they were further categorized along four main dimensions. The first dimension involved the type of help sought. Two main help types were identified: advice and artifacts, differentiated by the essence of the input requested. Advice was of a conceptual nature and referred to feedback, critique, and technical suggestions. Artifacts referred to more material (i.e., non-discursive) types of input, such as 3D models, textures, and animation cycles. The second dimension, help specifics, elucidated the specific help topic involved. The third dimension, help initiation, distinguished between events in which help was asked by the Durian team and events in which unsolicited help was offered by the Blender community. The last dimension, social software, referred to the software types that were involved in every help event. As this data analysis approach is qualitative in nature, Atlas.ti[2] was the software used for data coding and analysis.

RESULTS

The Mediation of Outsourcing: Social Software

As social software laid the foundations for community outsourcing, the research questions will be approached in an inverse order. Thus, we will begin by reviewing the social software tools that were used in Project Durian. This will provide sufficient background information against which the help events can be subsequently examined.

Outsourcing part of the work to either the two professional animation studios or the community required the appropriate networking infrastructure and software tools. Social software mediated the interaction and communication between the Durian core team on the one hand and the professional studios and the Blender community on the other. Given the orientation of this chapter, we will focus exclusively on the exchanges between the core team and the Blender community. The communication and collaboration of the Durian core team and the community took place in many different online spaces. While each online space

Table 1. Software used for the project

Purpose	Social Software Type	Function	Examples
communication	blog	asynchronous threaded discussions	http://www.sintel.org/
			http://twitter.com/#!/BlenderDurian/
	IRC	real-time coaching by and discussion with Durianders	#Blenderdurian on FreeNode Network
	forum	asynchronous threaded discussions	http://www.Blenderartists.org/forum/
	wiki	asset planning and management for the community sprints	http://wiki.blender.org/index.php/Org:Institute/Open_projects/Durian
	video streaming	asynchronous communication	http://www.youtube.com/user/BlenderFoundation
			http://vimeo.com/user2228390
file sharing	file sharing	sharing of assets (particularly 3D models)	http://www.blendswap.com/
		sharing of experimental Blender versions	http://graphicall.org/

Table 2. Overview of help events

n	Help Event (H)	Type of Help	Help Specifics	Help Initiation	Social Software Mediating Help Events
1	guardians	advice	artistic suggestions	Duran Core Team	blog
2	first community sprint	artifacts	models, textures	Duran Core Team	blog, IRC, Blender wiki, Blendswap, Video Channels (YouTube, Vimeo)
3	second community sprint	artifacts	models, animation cycles	Duran Core Team	blog, IRC, Blender wiki, Blendswap, Video Channels (YouTube, Vimeo), forum (Blenderartists.org)
4	minisprint	artifacts	models, textures	Duran Core Team	blog, blendswap
5	logo design	artifacts	text graphic	Duran Core Team	blog, blendswap
6	static renders	advice	artistic suggestions	Community	blog, blenderartists, file sharing hosts
7	movie trailer	advice	artistic suggestions	Community	blog, blenderartists, file sharing hosts
8	DPX to 35 mm film	advice	technical suggestions	Duran Core Team	blog
9	video encoding	advice	technical suggestions	Duran Core Team	blog

met different needs, they all mediated the core team-community interaction, facilitated collaboration, and enabled the pooling of expertise. It should be emphasized that, depending on the task, these social software tools were usually employed in various combinations. An overview of the social software tools used, and their use in Project Durian is given in Table 1.

As can be seen in Table 2, two general types of social software tools were used, communication and file sharing.

Communication

The blog was the most prominent and frequently used social software tool employed in Project Durian. It was the primary means of communication between the core team and the Blender community. All kinds of project-related news and updates were posted on the blog. The team members blogged frequently (there was at least one post per week) and followed the comments posted by the community members, responding whenever needed. Sometimes the user comments included questions that could not be answered by the core team member who made the original post so other core team members would take over and

contribute to the discussions. Usually, each core team member would respond to all comments and remarks made by the community in his or her respective area of expertise (e.g., animation or compositing). When more than one Durian core member was in charge of a specific area, any of these members could be involved in responding. The Blender community responded to every single blog post made throughout the project. All blog posts were read by community members and in some posts there were more than a hundred community comments. In addition to blogging, the Durian core team also used microblogging in an attempt to provide more frequent, daily news and production updates to the Blender community.

Although a few Blender Internet Relay Chat (IRC) channels had been established before Project Durian commenced, a new channel was set up for the purposes of the movie. Technically speaking, IRC has been around for too long to qualify as social software, but it was used on two occasions in conjunction with other social software applications and so it is included in this review. The IRC channel represented the only synchronous case of online communication for Project Durian.

The news and discussion forum on Blenderartists.org was also frequently used throughout the project. As community members could not create new posts on the Durian blog to initiate a discussion or raise an issue, they turned to the Blenderartists.org fora. Blenderartists.org is the timeless classic online space for Blender. It is the host of the most active and vibrant online Blender community with thousands of members. Several threads were created in the course of the project, either by the community or by the Durian core team members themselves.

The Blender wiki was also used for the three community sprints held between February and April 2010. It is interesting to note that the use of the wiki was more the result of necessity than the product of deliberate design by the Durian core team.

Several blog posts included videos (e.g., project news and updates, sprint messages, production moments, samples of work produced, instructions). These embedded videos were hosted in the official Blender Foundation channels of the two most popular streaming video hosts, YouTube and Vimeo. As a rule, the community responded both to the blog posts in which videos were embedded and to the respective videos posted on the official YouTube or Vimeo Blender Foundation channels.

File Sharing

In addition to communication tools, outsourcing frequently required the exchange and sharing of digital data. While many file hosts were used throughout the project, two hosts stand out, Blendswap.com and Graphicall.org. For the purposes of the first Durian sprint (see below), the community needed a system for submitting models, and obtaining reviews, criticisms, and approvals by the core team. Blendswap was a file hosting site that had launched at that time and focused exclusively on the sharing of 3D models among the Blender community. File hosting was also facilitated by Graphicall.org, a site focusing on the sharing of user-compiled experimental builds of Blender. These builds incorporated the

latest tools and features coded by the developers. It should be noted that at times of rapid development—such as the period covering Project Durian—a stable version might take months to release while experimental builds (i.e., non-stable builds) are available daily. This made Graphicall. org a very appealing option to the Blender community members for using the latest features that the Blender developers had coded.

Community Outsourcing: An Analysis of All Help Events

Figure 2 shows the Project Durian timeline and Table 2 gives an overview of all help events.

All help events took place between February and October 2010. Their approximate dates can be determined in the project timeline in Figure 2. Each help event is analyzed below along the four main dimensions outlined above.

H1: Guardians. In two successive blog posts the core team released static renders (i.e., still images) of the four guardians and requested community input (Dansie, 2010a; 2010b). These were the first posts to explicitly request community feedback and critiques. Ben Dansie (2010b) explained the reasoning behind the release of the guardian renders: "At this point we are unleashing them a bit to see how far the community can help us bring them visually." One of the Durian core team members even provided specific directions as to the kind of feedback that the team found desirable, namely detailed comments as opposed to general remarks. Several community members criticized how the four guardians looked and the critiques were often quite harsh, highlighting important problems such as the wax skin look. For the most part, the criticisms were directed at some of the artistic choices. In addressing some of the community comments in the follow-up blog post, art director David Revoy explicitly stated that *Sintel* is an open movie and users should feel free to post top-notch concept art for the guardians. He even went so far as to argue that "If the team

Figure 2. Project Durian timeline

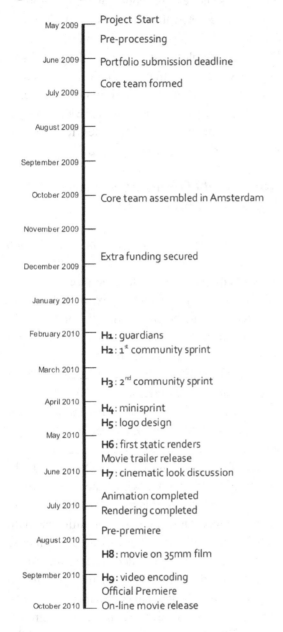

May 2009	Project Start
	Pre-processing
June 2009	Portfolio submission deadline
	Core team formed
July 2009	
August 2009	
September 2009	
October 2009	Core team assembled in Amsterdam
November 2009	
December 2009	Extra funding secured
January 2010	
February 2010	H1: guardians
	H2: 1st community sprint
March 2010	H3: 2nd community sprint
April 2010	H4: minisprint
	H5: logo design
May 2010	H6: first static renders
	Movie trailer release
June 2010	H7: cinematic look discussion
	Animation completed
July 2010	Rendering completed
	Pre-premiere
August 2010	H8: movie on 35mm film
September 2010	H9: video encoding
	Official Premiere
October 2010	On-line movie release

feel it's better, there will be no problem to use them" (Revoy, 2010a). Several comments later on the same thread, he even challenged another community member by saying, "If you think you got better thinking on the guardian design, please share it" (Revoy, 2010b). These are a few examples of a dialogue that developed between the Durian core team and community members who were interested in contributing to the project. As these exchanges suggest, for this help event the Durian core team took the suggestions the community made very seriously, and tried to build on them and to combine them with the concept art the art director had already produced.

H2: First Community Sprint. The first community sprint was an interactive online event that lasted a few hours and involved a shared, real-time collaboration between the core team and the community. It was held on February 20, 2010, and focused on modeling and texturing. The core team needed props for the city scenes as these were the most complex and detailed ones in the movie (Levy, 2010b). The core team planned to create an IRC channel and to invite people to pick one of the assets and start modeling and texturing it, posting their progress online as they went along. The core team would then provide real-time critique and suggestions for improving the models. However, the overwhelming community response made it impossible for the team to handle so many submissions, monitor the progress, and provide feedback (Guillemette, 2010). To address this problem the core team turned to the Blender wiki: they added a list of all the models needed and the community members were allowed to choose whatever they wanted to model. The community sprint was a "stellar success," exceeding the core team's expectations for participation and quality output (Levy, 2010c). In fact, on one occasion more than 300 people participated simultaneously. The models the Durian core team eventually selected from the many that were submitted to Blendswap.com were used in the production of *Sintel* and the contributors got a special mention in the film credits. To acknowledge the extent of community participation and contributions, film director Colin Levy confessed in a thank-you video to the community that "I am not too anxious about the movie getting done any more" (Levy, 2010c). This is a clear indication that the Blender community was dependable in the Durian core team's struggle against time.

H3: Second Community Sprint. The second community sprint was a two-part sprint, focusing on extras and animations of extras, and was held on March 27, 2010. As the director said in the blog post announcement, "We need tons of background characters!" (Levy, 2010d). The core team explained that they had a market scene but there was nothing there but Sintel and a dragon. As the team put it in the corresponding post-video address, "despite the team continually growing we still don't have time [to work on the extras]" (Blender Foundation, 2010). While in the first community sprint no specific details were given regarding the assets, the core team provided specific instructions (concept art) for the second sprint (Levy, 2010e). Because of the complexity of the second task assigned to the community, the second sprint was to last slightly longer so the participants could upload their finished animated models to Blendswap within a few days. Once again, the community sprint was very successful in terms of both participation and quality of output. Much like the first community sprint, the models and animation cycles submitted to Blendswap. com by the community members were screened by two Durian core team members who selected the most appropriate ones and integrated them with the rest of the movie assets. The contributors of the models that were selected to be used in the movie also received a special mention in the film credits.

H4: Minisprint. The third community sprint was a smaller-scale event compared to the previous two sprints, which is why the director called it a "minisprint." As he put it in the Durian blog post announcement,

We're stretched to the limit and we need to get a crucial prop for the film modeled and textured: Sintel's backpack. Instead of figuring out who on the team can spare a half a day to work on this, we thought we'd just open it up to the community! (Levy, 2010f)

Once again, the community responded to the call, created 3D models, and uploaded them to Blendswap.com. Following the established tradition, core team members selected the most appropriate model and acknowledged the community contributor in the film credits.

H5: Text Logo Design. In April 2010 there was a call for a good quality text logo for the film (Roosendaal, 2010a). The high quality of the numerous submissions was acknowledged by the core team (Roosendaal, 2010b).

H6: First Movie Renders. Shortly before releasing the trailer, the core team posted a few movie stills on the Durian blog (Maeter, 2010). The community's criticism of these renders was very harsh and highlighted a multitude of problems (e.g., hair, lightning, focus, framing, and overall cinematic look). In less than four days this blog post received more than 150 community responses. Senior Blender community members (i.e., those with thousands of posts on Blenderartists.org) offered harsh criticism and questioned some of the artistic and technical choices the core team had made. In their reaction to the community comments, the core team members said that they were aware of the problems but the severe time pressures made fixing them difficult (Boubred, 2010). Thus, the Durian core team acknowledged the limitations of the work they had produced and legitimized the issues the community had raised.

What is particularly interesting about this help event is that the Durian core team did not explicitly ask for critiques, as the release of the trailer was imminent and those stills were simply sneak peeks of what was to follow. This is the first indication of the Blender community taking the initiative and making detailed suggestions without explicitly being asked to do so. This initiative is what makes this help event markedly different from the previous ones.

H7: Cinematic Look. The movie trailer (Blender Foundation & Levy, 2010b) was released four days after the release of the first static renders (Roosendaal, 2010c). Notwithstanding minor points of criticism, the community response to the trailer on the blog post announcement, on the corresponding thread on Blenderartists.org news forum, and on the Blender Foundation video channels was, generally speaking, very positive. Much like the sixth help event, what sets this event apart is community initiation. More specifically, some community members took the initiative and provided feedback to the Durian core team on how to improve the movie. A new thread was started on the Blenderartists.org news forum to propose improvements to the cinematic look of the trailer (jason7, 2010). Many issues were raised in the thread but eventually the discussion centered on color correction. Several community members actively participated in the discussion, either by posting some color-corrected stills (images) from the movie trailer or by providing feedback on the stills fellow community members had posted. After the first few posts, the thread turned into a meta-discussion about the usefulness of the thread; some users strongly argued that the Blender team did not need the thread while others insisted that the posters meant well and that the thread would actually be very productive and helpful to the Durian team should they need to consult it. William Reynish and Beorn Leonard, the two Durian core team members who participated in the discussions, explicitly stated that the Durian team does look at such threads, that the thread was interesting, and that some of the proposed color-corrections were not bad. Overall, they argued that the discussion was worth having. Beorn Leonard acknowledged that the community proposals did have a point because the core team did not have time to do color grading for consistency and mood. Moreover, he engaged in dialogue with the Blender community regarding the proposed corrections to certain stills from the movie trailer. For example, his feedback to one community member noted that the proposed correction did not convey the actual scene details properly. To give an indication of how important this thread was for the community, it should be noted that it was by far the most popular one on

Blenderartists.org in May 2010, attracting more than 1,200 views and receiving 122 responses from the community.

H8: DPX to 35 mm film. In this call for help the producer asked community members who had experience with the Digital Picture eXchange (DPX) file format to film conversion pipeline for suggestions (Roosendaal, 2010d). The producer responded to several informative posts, ultimately taking into consideration the suggestions made by the community.

H9: Encoding. In the last help event, the Durian core team requested assistance with encoding the movie in various video formats (Leonard, 2010). In the blog post, core team member Beorn Leonard explicitly acknowledged that he had volunteered for this task but was no expert in video encoding. The core team had decided to crop (remove the outer parts) and letterbox (transferring from a wide-screen aspect ratio to standard width video format while preserving the original aspect ratio) the 2K (2048 x 1536 pixels) version of the movie and this led to a heated debate between the movie producer and a few community members who did not agree with the decision. After an exchange of several messages, the core team agreed to scale the original 2K renders (from 2048 pixels to 1920 pixels) without cropping and letterboxing. This represents one of the most interesting moments in the help events because the Blender community arguments and persistence led the core team to reconsider their initial decision. This is a prime example of how the community changed one of the decisions the core team had already taken.

DISCUSSION

As was argued in the Introduction, expertise studies have focused on expertise in individuals and not on expertise in teams, especially in teams made up of individuals distributed across space and time. Moreover, former approaches to expertise have largely ignored the role of technology, especially how social software might affect notions and practices of expertise. Contemporary work practices, however, are increasingly being characterized by the creation and management of expert teams to meet the demanding work conditions. At the same time, technology and social software are increasingly being used for the pooling of expertise in teams. Project Durian was used as our case study because it was characterized by both expertise pooling and social software use. In this section I will discuss the main findings of how social software affected community outsourcing in Project Durian.

Distribution of Expertise

Social software facilitated the spatio-temporal distribution of expertise. While having a group of experts working on a shared task is not uncommon these days, engaging experts from all over the world to work on a shared task the way Project Durian did is still novel. While the Durian team members (the core team) were all located in Amsterdam and worked at the same time, the Blender community (the expanded team) was located all over the world and contributed asynchronously. The Blender Foundation's contribution was to establish a new hybrid practice that had a real, conventional layer (Durian core team), and an online, virtual layer (expanded team from around the globe). In this hybrid practice, the online part was spatio-temporally dispersed. It is obvious that establishing a hybrid expert team would have been practically impossible without social software. It has been noted that one of the affordances of social software is that it helps create online communities (Lee & McLoughlin, 2010; Chatti & Jarke, 2010). While many social software-based CoPs have only an online presence (e.g., Wikipedia), the Blender Foundation created a hybrid community, comprising real and virtual parts. What Project Durian suggests is that in novel socio-technical settings, expertise can take on new forms (e.g., spatio-temporal, hybrid) that have been rather

uncommon to date. For example, this distribution of expertise is not found in any of the conditions Salas et al. (2006) report as conducive to making expert teams work best, but it was essential for the success of Project Durian and is increasingly becoming a constituent of many novel practices.

Pooling of Expertise

The Durian core team outsourced certain tasks to the community. It should be emphasized that these tasks were not trivial ones as they required high levels of expertise. The final outcome was the result of the pooling of the expertise of the Durian core team, and the Blender community. The resulting expertise pool was greater than the expertise of either contributing party in isolation (O'Reilly, 2005b; Weiss, 2005). Project Durian suggests that in the Web 2.0 era, expertise should be examined not only as a property of individuals—as is typically the case with expertise studies—but also as a property that can be attributed to both individuals and teams that are spatio-temporally distributed. The role social software played in realizing this was fundamental as it helped reconfigure expertise from an individualistic dimension to a more social one of a distributed nature. Although former studies (e.g., Salas et al., 2006) have implied this pooling of expertise, owing to the hybrid nature of the distribution of expertise discussed above, Project Durian suggests that a new type of expertise pooling is possible, and that this type of expertise can be defined and understood only in relation to social software.

Range of Expertise

The architecture of participation upon which social software is based invites everyone to contribute regardless of their skill. By definition, it does not exclude anyone from participating, even a complete novice. The prototypical example of involving users from a wide range of expertise is Wikipedia, an online encyclopedia whose participation structure enables everyone to contribute. Despite its limitations, Wikipedia stands out as the most successful example of worldwide collaboration among experts and novices to produce a general-purpose information site. Project Durian employed a similar strategy, enabling every community member to make a contribution.

However, the expertise of the Durian core team members and the Blender community members was not on a par. After all, not every community member had a stunning enough portfolio to be eligible for the Durian team. This does not mean that the Blender community was exclusively made up of non-experts. Several community members were more than skilled enough to be eligible for the Durian team but they could not meet some of the specific project requirements (e.g., live and work in Amsterdam for a period of 6–8 months) due to other work engagements, family, and other commitments. The new, hybrid, spatio-temporally distributed practice the Blender Foundation created involved not only experts but also users falling into a wide range of expertise. The added value of such an approach is that all contributions count, regardless of the expertise of the contributors.

On the one hand, only the best contributions will survive because there are two main filtering mechanisms in place. First, the community itself can select the best or more fitting contributions to the goal. For example, in selecting the text logo for *Sintel*, the community voted on what they deemed the most fitting logo. Second, the Durian core team that was in charge of the whole project has the last word. In the aforementioned text logo example, two of the core team members took the community vote into consideration but ultimately they made the final decision. In other similar cases, such as Sintel's backpack, the core team had the freedom to combine ("frankenstein" as the director put it) the contributions of various community members to create a final result that would have been impossible without those contributions. On the other hand, an open participation structure

such as Project Durian involving hundreds of users leads to a broad diversity of expert opinion. In fact, the potential of a large community such as the Blender community with various levels of expertise lies precisely in this diversification.

Even though involving a group of individuals with various levels of skill might seem potentially problematic, the findings of expertise studies suggest otherwise. More specifically, the literature indicates that experts also suffer important limitations. For example, because of the way they represent problems, sometimes experts tend to overlook surface details or are more prone to bias than novices are (Chi, 2006). If such behaviors are likely with experts, then the practice established by Project Durian, which involves individuals of various levels of expertise, might safeguard against such a likelihood.

Boundary Crossing

Making an animated 3D short movie is a very complex task and requires different forms of expertise in many domains. For example, making *Sintel* called for many different types of experts in areas such as modeling, texturing, lightning, rigging, animating, compositing, and rendering. The social software–mediated practice established by the Blender Foundation allowed not only the harnessing of the expertise of many individuals but also the harnessing of the expertise of individuals skilled in many different domains. For example, the community made decisive contributions in many areas (see help events on guardians, look, community sprints, video encoding, and DPX to film). When task demands in terms of disciplinary complexity are at a crossroads, social software might enable the crossing of the barriers of different domains. The literature on expertise suggests that its major limitation is that it is domain-bound and does not transfer to other domains (Chi, 2006; Feltovich et al., 2006). What Project Durian suggests is that the crossing of boundaries of different domains of expertise is possible on an impressively massive scale. Thus, by linking experts from different areas of expertise, social software enables what might be called collective multi-expertise—that is, new configurations of expertise involving experts from different domains who might be spatio-temporally distributed. Overall, project Durian suggests that the limitations pertaining to the domain-specificity of expertise might be overcome. Historically, this has been reported in the past by others but on a different scale (see, for example, the case of GoldCorp Inc., presented by Tapscott & Williams, 2006).

Renegotiating Expertise

Because of the open participation structures, questioning expert reasoning and performance is more likely in social software–based expertise practices compared to more typical, hierarchically structured traditional practices. This kind of questioning is fully compatible with the long-established tradition in FOSS which is open and democratic in nature. The issue of who has the authority (i.e., expertise) to make suggestions and proposals to the Durian core team emerged on a number of occasions (e.g., community feedback to the static renders on the Durian blog, discussion about cinematic look on Blenderartists.org news forum). For instance, in the thread on the cinematic look on Blenderartists.org many community members questioned the validity of the thread arguing that "the Durian team knows better." However, other community members strongly objected to such an interpretation, stating that the thread did have a valid purpose, which was to provide constructive suggestions to the Durian core team. Interestingly enough, the aforementioned debate about the cinematic look was resolved by two Durian core team members who joined in to validate the discussions and legitimize the concerns of the community (jason7, 2010). Generally speaking, the Blender community often had long discussions about whether or not their feedback and critiques were relevant to the Durian core team. The debates

about who "knows better" essentially hint at how expertise is questioned in such environments. Even though the expertise of the Durian core team was never questioned or disputed by the Blender community, not all the decisions made by the core team were optimal or error-free ones. The open participation structure of Project Durian made it possible for the Blender community to highlight problematic or sub-optimal choices the core team made. This openness led to meta-discussions about the usefulness of such discussions which are less likely to occur in formal, more hierarchically structured environments.

The questioning of expertise that characterized Project Durian might remedy overconfidence, one of the important limitations of expertise (Chi, 2006). In such an open environment, there are multiple checks of the same material (tasks, artifacts, etc.) both on a local level, by the Durian core team, and on a broader level, by the Blender community. Having such large numbers of experts with various expertise levels entails having more eyes looking at the same problem. According to Linus's Law,[3] if a large beta-tester and co-developer community is committed to developing a piece of software, it is highly likely that every software bug will be detected and fixed (Raymond, 2001). In the long run, the openness of social software-based practices might promote an attitude that could ultimately facilitate critical review and reflection.

We learned from Project Durian that social software was essential in four main respects. First, social software provided the means to redistribute expertise not only from individuals to teams but also from teams working at the same place and time to teams collaborating across space and time. The role that social software played in this redistribution was crucial. It helped create online spaces in which both the core team (working at the same space-time) and the community (geographically scattered at a global level and asynchronously) worked together to produce an outcome which was the result of expertise pooling of all those involved. Second, social software facilitated the contribution of individuals with various levels of expertise. As the range of expertise involved novices and experts alike, the contributions of the Blender community varied considerably in terms of quality. A diverse community is more likely to produce an output that has high added value. Social software enabled the Durian core team to harness the expertise of the Blender community. Third, social software enabled the participation of individuals of various expertise levels from many different domains. In the case of Project Durian, social software helped with boundary crossing on a massive scale as experts from many different domains were assembled. Fourth, social software helped establish a practice in which expert reasoning and performance were questioned and renegotiated. By definition, social software is characterized by open participation structures which are democratic in nature. On several occasions, this participation structure facilitated a dialogue (a) between the Durian core team and the Blender community and (b) among the Blender community members themselves.

In light of the above, new forms and configurations of expertise might not be fully accounted for by traditional approaches to expertise. New practices are characterized by the distribution of expertise across space and time; the creation of a wide pool of expertise which is greater than the expertise of any individual in isolation; the overcoming of expert bias because many experts with varying levels of expertise are involved; the transcending of disciplinary boundaries within which expertise is typically confined; and the questioning of expertise due to the open, participatory structures. Consequently, established models of expertise are both incompatible with and insufficient for studying novel socio-technical settings such as Project Durian.

IMPLICATIONS

The Blender Foundation had no former experience in using the expertise of its user base in the open projects it had undertaken. While the Durian core team wanted to engage the community, there was no clear plan set in the beginning. The core team anticipated some user participation but its members were quite overwhelmed by the community response and the willingness to contribute. It is clear that the Durian core team improvised because they did not know how to harness all the user excitement and interest in participating. Many community members wanted to help out, and to get a piece of the action and their moment of fame by receiving an honorable mention in the film credits. Once the Durian core team was convinced that the quality of the community input would be very high, outsourcing certain tasks to the community emerged as a very appealing option. The key to the team's successful expertise pooling was its responsive and flexible approach toward community suggestions. Essentially, the community steered the Durian core team in a certain direction. "Let us be more than your critics and advisers. Let us be your fellow artists!" (Losee, 2010) read one community member post on the Durian blog. The openness and willingness to experiment allowed the Durian core team to guide and structure the community input.

The Blender Foundation did not have a clear engagement plan at the outset, but for future crowdsourcing of social software–mediated projects, it is clear that special attention should be given to planning. Given a large, diverse, enthusiastic, and committed user community, any plan should have at least four major dimensions.

First, it should have a specific outline of community engagement, specifying ways to harness the collective expertise of the face-to-face community and the virtual community. While the Durian core team planned to engage the Blender community in the making of *Sintel*, there seemed to be no clear strategy as to how to achieve that.

Second, the plan should also have an outline of the specific social software tools to be used and the ways in which these tools are going to be used to harness the expertise of the community. The analysis of Project Durian indicates that there were no specific plans regarding software tools and that they were chosen as the Durian core team went along (e.g., initially the team planned to provide real-time feedback through IRC but the overwhelming community response urged them to consider other options such as a wiki).

Third, a clear task engagement plan is also required. In the case of Project Durian almost all the outsourcing seemed to be more impromptu than planned. While it might not be feasible to plan everything down to the smallest detail, it seems reasonable to plan which tasks to outsource, when, and how. Both short- and long-term planning seem to be important for facilitating community engagement. For example, in Project Durian the calls for help were not always announced in advance, which served the needs of the Durian core team more than those of the Blender community. Failure to check the Durian blog daily could have led to missed opportunities for participation. Moreover, the lifetime of help events was a few days at best. This means that community engagement could not be maximized. The scale of the tasks being outsourced is also an issue worth considering in some detail. For example, in contrast to other successful outsourcing examples—such as GoldCorp Inc. which outsourced everything—due to its design the Durian core team chose to outsource only small-scale tasks which were of a modular nature and, in principle, could be completed without interfering with the rest of the project. Depending on the nature of the tasks being outsourced, it might be worth exploring opening up tasks of a larger scale. After all, historical precedents such as Wikipedia or GoldCorp Inc. (Tapscott & Williams, 2006) suggest that collective undertakings of this type which outsource core tasks on a massive scale are successful.

Finally, the timing of the outsourcing might also be of critical importance. If the core team is seeking a wide diversity of opinion, then outsourcing tasks early on might help significantly because of great diversification of the community. For example, when the Durian core team requested community help with the look of the guardians, many community members made important suggestions that could not be pursued because the concept artist had already set the overall look and, therefore, few deviations were visually possible. However, if many decisions have already been made the community might have less freedom. Achieving the correct balance between these two approaches requires a lot of experimentation.

The last dimension in terms of planning is related to clear evaluation mechanisms and procedures. In the case of Project Durian, some of the community contributions (artifacts) were evaluated by the core team only while others (feedback) were evaluated (i.e., discussed) by the community as well as the core team. Although leadership is definitely required to coordinate such large-scale projects, future projects might benefit from filtering the community input by the community itself as much as by the organization or team which is coordinating the outsourcing.

CONCLUSION

In recent years rapid technological developments have led to the emergence of new knowledge creation and application practices. Owing to the fact that it links people in unprecedented ways, social software is an important constituent of such practices. To date, what these profound changes mean for expertise has not been systematically explored, and there is a knowledge gap regarding expertise in these new social software–mediated practices. The aim of this chapter was to fill this gap by examining Project Durian which involved both experts and social software. Project Durian essentially harnessed the collective expertise of both the core team and the Blender community. As my analysis indicated, the Blender Foundation established a hybrid practice in which expertise was spatio-temporally distributed. Moreover, the expertise came from individuals with a broad range of skills and not only traditional experts. The pooling of expertise from experts in many different domains was found to facilitate the boundary crossing of various disciplines. Finally, the open participation structures resulted in challenging and renegotiating expertise. Paradoxically, some of my findings regarding expertise in Project Durian might help overcome some of the limitations that characterize conventional, individualistic approaches to expertise. As I hope I have demonstrated, the new practices that social software facilitates create a new socio-technical landscape in which the traditional notion of expertise needs to be re-examined. As new forms and configurations of expertise entail new practices of expertise in novel settings, more research is required in this area, especially regarding social software–mediated expertise in teams.

ACKNOWLEDGMENT

I express my sincere gratitude to both the Durian core team and the enthusiastic Blender on-line community for unintentionally providing me with an in-depth course in new forms of social software-mediated expertise pooling. This has been a truly extraordinary experience. I would also like to thank the editor of this volume and two anonymous reviewers for helping me distance myself from project Durian and put it into perspective. Finally, many thanks are due to my wife and son for putting up with many of my obsessions for so long.

REFERENCES

Blender Foundation. (2010, March 24). *Durian Project: "Extras" modeling & animation sprint.* Retrieved from http://www.youtube.com/watch?v=6jeJ-Ta5UQc

Blender Foundation. (2011). Retrieved June 15, 2011, from http://www.blender.org/blenderorg/blender-foundation/

Blender Foundation (Producer) & Levy. C. (Director). (2010a). *Sintel.* Retrieved from http://www.youtube.com/watch?v=eRsGyueVLvQ

Blender Foundation (Producer) & Levy. C. (Director). (2010b). *Sintel Trailer, Durian Open Movie Project.* Retrieved from http://www.youtube.com/watch?v=HOfdboHvshg

Boubred, A. (2010, May 13). *Reaction from the team.* Retrieved from http://www.sintel.org/news/reaction-from-the-team/

Burkhardt, P. (2009). Social software trends in business: Introduction. In Deans, C. P. (Ed.), *Social software and Web 2.0 technology trends* (pp. 1–16). New York, NY: Information Science Reference.

Chatti, M. A., & Jarke, M. (2010). Social software for bottom-up knowledge networking and community building. In Lytras, M., Tennyson, R., & de Pablos, P. O. (Eds.), *Knowledge networks: The social software perspective* (pp. 17–27). New York, NY: Information Science Reference.

Chi, M. T. H. (2006). Two approaches to the study of experts' characteristics. In Ericsson, K. A., Charness, N., Feltovich, P. J., & Hoffman, R. R. (Eds.), *The Cambridge handbook of expertise and expert performance* (pp. 21–30). Cambridge, UK: Cambridge University Press. doi:10.1017/CBO9780511816796.002

Chopra, S., & Dexter, S. D. (2008). *Decoding liberation: The promise of free and open source Software.* London, UK: Routledge.

Creative Commons. (n.d.). *About the licenses*. Retrieved from http://creativecommons.org/licenses/

Dansie, B. (2010a, February 5). *Guardians*. Retrieved from http://www.sintel.org/news/guardians/

Dansie, B. (2010b, February 7). *Guardians – Community help*. Retrieved from http://www.sintel.org/news/guardians-community-help/

de Groot, A. (1978). *Thought and choice in chess*. The Hague, The Netherlands: Mouton.

Ericsson, K. A. (2003). The search for general abilities and basic capacities. Theoretical implications from the modiðability and complexity of mechanisms mediating expert performance. In Sternberg, R. J., & Grigorenko, E. L. (Eds.), *The psychology of abilities, competencies, and expertise* (pp. 93–125). Cambridge, UK: Cambridge University Press. doi:10.1017/CBO9780511615801.006

Ericsson, K. A. (2009). Enhancing the development of professional performance: Implications from the study of deliberate practice. In Ericsson, K. A. (Ed.), *Development of professional expertise. Toward measurement of expert performance and design of optimal learning environments* (pp. 405–431). Cambridge, UK: Cambridge University Press. doi:10.1017/CBO9780511609817.022

Ericsson, K. A., & Smith, J. (2002). Prospects and limits of the empirical study of expertise: An introduction. In Levitin, D. J. (Ed.), *Foundations of cognitive psychology. Core readings* (pp. 517–550). Cambridge, MA: The MIT Press.

Feltovich, P. J., Prietula, M. J., & Ericsson, K. A. (2006). Studies of expertise from psychological perspectives. In Ericsson, K. A., Charness, N., Feltovich, P. J., & Hoffman, R. R. (Eds.), *The Cambridge handbook of expertise and expert performance* (pp. 41–67). Cambridge, UK: Cambridge University Press. doi:10.1017/CBO9780511816796.004

Free Software Foundation. (n.d.). *The free software definition*. Retrieved from http://www.gnu.org/philosophy/free-sw.html

Gregg, D. (2010). Designing for collective intelligence. *Communications of the ACM, 53*(4), 134–138. doi:10.1145/1721654.1721691

Guillemette, J.-S. (2010, February 17). *Blender 2.5 Alpha 1 and more info on the sprint!* Retrieved from http://www.sintel.org/news/blender-2-5-alpha-1-and-more-info-on-the-sprint/

jason 7. (2010, May 15). *Sintel trailer color correction tests (big images)*. Retrieved from http://blenderartists.org/forum/showthread.php?187115-sintel-trailer-color-correction-tests-%28big-images%29

Lee, M. J. W., & McLoughlin, C. (2010). Social software as tools for pedagogical transformation: Enabling personalization, creative production, and participatory learning. In Lambropoulos, N., & Romero, M. (Eds.), *Educational social software for context-aware learning: Collaborative methods and human interaction* (pp. 1–22). New York, NY: Information Science Reference.

Leonard, B. (2010, September 18). *Encoding issues – A call for help*. Retrieved from http://www.sintel.org/news/3622/

Lessig, L. (2004). *Free culture: How big media uses technology and the law to lock down culture and control creativity*. New York, NY: Penguin.

Lessig, L. (2005). Open code and open societies. In Feller, J., Fitzgerald, B., Hissam, S. A., & Lakhani, K. R. (Eds.), *Perspectives on free and open source software* (pp. 349–360). Cambridge, MA: The MIT Press.

Levy, C. (2009, October 8). *Directorial address 01*. Retrieved from http://www.sintel.org/news/directorial-address-01/

Levy, S. (2010b, February 16). *Community modeling sprint!* Retrieved from http://www.sintel.org/news/community-modeling-sprint/

Levy, S. (2010c, February 21). *Modeling sprint—A stellar success!* Retrieved from http://www.sintel. org/news/modeling-sprint-a-stellar-success/

Levy, S. (2010d, March 25). *Community sprint: Background characters!* Retrieved from http:// www.sintel.org/news/community-sprint-back-ground-characters/

Levy, S. (2010e, March 27). *Background character sprint: Details* Retrieved from http://www.sintel. org/production/background-character-sprint-details/

Levy, S. (2010f, April 12). *Make us a backpack!* Retrieved from http://www.sintel.org/production/ make-us-a-backpack/

Losee, R. (2010). Comment-6572. In B. Dansie, (2010b, February 7). *Guardians – Community help.* Retrieved from http://www.sintel.org/news/ guardians-community-help/

Maeter, S. (2010, May 9). *F12's.* Retrieved from http://www.sintel.org/news/f12s/

McGowan, D. (2005). Legal aspects of free and open source software. In Feller, J., Fitzgerald, B., Hissam, S. A., & Lakhani, K. R. (Eds.), *Perspectives on free and open source software* (pp. 361–391). Cambridge, MA: The MIT Press.

Next Pixel (Producer) & Blender Foundation. (Producer). (2010). *Sintel making of/documentary* Retrieved from http://www.youtube.com/ watch?v=IN6w6GnN-Ic

O'Reilly, T. (2005a). The open source paradigm shift. In Feller, J., Fitzgerald, B., Hissam, S. A., & Lakhani, K. R. (Eds.), *Perspectives on free and open source software* (pp. 461–481). Cambridge, MA: The MIT Press.

O'Reilly, T. (2005b). *What is Web 2.0: Design patterns and business models for the next generation of software.* Retrieved March 20, 2009, from http://www.oreillynet.com/pub/a/oreilly/ tim/news/2005/09/30/what-is-web-20.html

Raymond, E. S. (2001). *The cathedral and the bazaar: Musings on Linux and open source by an accidental revolutionary.* Sebastopol, CA: O'Reilly & Associates.

Reher, K. (Producer), & Newton, T. (Director). (2010). *Day & Night.* Pixar. Retrieved from http:// www.youtube.com/watch?v=VpN0vwgVBZk

Revoy, D. (2010a). Comment-6699. In B. Dansie, (2010b, February 7). *Guardians—Community help.* Retrieved from http://www.sintel.org/news/ guardians-community-help/

Revoy, D. (2010b). Comment-6722. In B. Dansie, (2010b, February 7). *Guardians—Community help.* Retrieved from http://www.sintel.org/news/ guardians-community-help/

Roosendaal, T. (2009a, May 5). *Call for participation.* Retrieved from http://www.sintel.org/ applications/

Roosendaal, T. (2009b, May 5). *Durian Project announcement.* Retrieved from http://www.sintel. org/news/durian-project-announcement/

Roosendaal, T. (2010a, April 21). *Logo / identity design.* Retrieved from http://www.sintel.org/ news/logo-identity-design/

Roosendaal, T. (2010b, April 27). *Logo part 2.* Retrieved from http://www.sintel.org/production/ logo-part-2/

Roosendaal, T. (2010c, May 13). *Sintel trailer!* Retrieved from http://www.sintel.org/news/ sintel-teaser/

Roosendaal, T. (2010d, August 24). *Get Blender graphics on 35mm film.* Retrieved from http:// www.sintel.org/news/get-blender-graphics-on-35mm-film/

Salas, E., Rosen, M. A., Burke, C. S., Goodwin, G. F., & Fiore, S. M. (2006). The making of a dream team: When expert teams do best. In Ericsson, K. A., Charness, N., Feltovich, P. J., & Hoffman, R. R. (Eds.), *The Cambridge handbook of expertise and expert performance* (pp. 439–453). Cambridge, UK: Cambridge University Press. doi:10.1017/CBO9780511816796.025

Schweik, C. M. (2007). Free/open source software as a framework for establishing commons in science. In Hess, C., & Ostrom, E. (Eds.), *Understanding knowledge as a commons: From theory to practice* (pp. 277–309). Cambridge, MA: The MIT Press.

Simon, H. A., & Chase, W. G. (1973). Skill in chess. *American Scientist, 61*, 394–403.

Sintel. (2011). Retrieved June 15, 2011, from http://www.sintel.org/

Surowiecki, J. (2004). *The wisdom of crowds: Why the many are smarter than the few and how collective wisdom shapes business, economies, societies and nations*. Anchor.

Tapscott, D., & Williams, A. D. (2006). *Wikinomics: How mass collaboration changes everything*. New York, NY: Penguin.

Weiss, A. (2005). The power of collective intelligence. *netWorker, 9*(3), 16–23. doi:10.1145/1086762.1086763

ADDITIONAL READING

Ackerman, M., Pipek, V., & Wulf, V. (2003). *Sharing expertise: Beyond knowledge management*. Cambridge, MA: The MIT Press.

Coleman, D., & Levine, S. (2008). *Collaboration 2.0: Technology and best practices for successful collaboration in a Web 2.0 world*. Silicon Valley, CA: Happy About.

Cook, N. (2008). *Enterprise 2.0: How social software will change the future of work*. Surrey, UK: Gower Publishing.

Cooper, D., DiBona, C., & Stone, M. (Eds.). (2005). *Open sources 2.0: The continuing evolution*. Sebastopol, CA: O'Reilly.

DiBona, C., & Ockman, S. (Eds.). (1999). *Open sources: Voices from the open source revolution*. Sebastopol, CA: O'Reilly.

Dumova, T., & Fiordo, R. (Eds.). (2010). *Handbook of research on social interaction technologies and collaboration software: Concepts and trends*. New York, NY: Information Science Reference.

Ericsson, K. A. (Ed.). (1996). *The road to excellence: Acquisition of expert performance in the arts and sciences, sports and games*. Hillsdale, NJ: LEA.

Furht, B. (Ed.). (2010). *Handbook of social network technologies and applications*. New York, NY: Springer. doi:10.1007/978-1-4419-7142-5

Howe, J. (2008). *Crowdsourcing: Why the power of the crowd is driving the future of business*. New York, NY: Crown Publishing.

Lessig, L. (2006). *Code, version 2.0*. New York, NY: Basic Books.

Ludvigsen, S., Lund, A., Rasmussen, I., & Säljö, R. (Eds.). (2011). *Learning across sites. New tools, infrastructures and practices*. New York, NY: Routledge.

Moody, G. (2002). *Rebel code: Linux and the open source revolution*. Boston, MA: Basic Books.

Stallman, R. M. (2002). *Free software, free society: Selected essays of Richard M. Stallman*. Boston, MA: GNU Press.

KEY TERMS AND DEFINITIONS

Blender: The leading free and open source 3D graphics suite available for all major operating systems under the GNU General Public License. While Blender was initially developed as a proprietary software, in 2002 its source code was released. Blender is developed by the community and only two full-time developers at the Blender Foundation. Blender's feature list is extensive and includes 3D modeling, shading, animation, rigging, rendering, physics simulations, compositing, video editing, and interactive 3D applications. As blenderheads (Blender users) love to say, Blender is a project by the Blender community for the Blender community.

Blendswap.com: A file hosting site that allows Blender artists to share 3D models freely under Creative Commons licenses. Blender community members can find quality user-submitted 3D models on the site, which was launched in early 2010 and rose to public prominence after the modeling sprints organized by the Durian core team. Nowadays it is the most popular site for users to exchange Blender models in the form of .blend files.

Collective Intelligence: A form of intelligence that emerges from the collaboration of (and competition between) individuals working in groups. *Collective intelligence* characterizes group decision making and problem solving in many disciplines (e.g., biology). Owing to the writings of O'Reilly (definition of Web 2.0) and Tapscott & Williams (2006), the term became very popular circa 2004 as a defining feature of Web 2.0. Examples of collective, Net-enabled intelligence include the GNU/Linux operating system (software-wise) and Wikipedia (content-wise). Blender 3D is itself an example of peer-production software.

Expertise: The characteristics (knowledge or skills) that distinguish outstanding individuals in a given domain from less outstanding individuals in that domain. Some domains have objective criteria for identifying experts, while others do not. Expertise studies have examined how expertise is developed by either comparing the performances of novices and experts or by analyzing the performances of experts. Research suggests that experts differ from novices in many ways, including performing a task with minimal cognitive effort, detecting deep task features, and having qualitatively different task representations. Contemporary research suggests that exceptional performance is the result of many years of deliberate practice.

GraphicAll.org: A community-run file hosting site for building and hosting user-compiled experimental builds of Blender. It started in 2005 with an exclusive focus on sharing Blender builds but today allows building and sharing other open source software graphics projects such as Inkscape and Gimp. Since 2005 it has been the definitive online space for obtaining Blender SVN builds with the latest coded tools and functions.

Outsourcing/Crowdsourcing: A process in which a company contracts out a (typically non-core) service to another company. In the Web 2.0 era outsourcing has evolved into crowdsourcing: companies try to take advantage of the talent, expertise, and creativity of a large, undefined group of people, a crowd. One of the first documented cases of Internet-mediated crowdsourcing is GoldCorp, detailed by Tapscott & Williams their 2006 text, *Wikinomics*.

Sintel: The fourth Blender Foundation project, following *Elephant's Dream*, *Big Buck Bunny*, and *Yo Frankie!* As with the previous Blender Foundation open movie projects, *Sintel* was expected to showcase Blender's capabilities and develop Blender further. The creation of the film was coordinated by the Blender Foundation, with funding from donations, commercial sponsors, and pre-sales of the film's DVDs. The DVDs included both the final film and the complete production data set under Creative Commons Attribution License.

Social Software: A category of software systems that facilitate the process of social networking. Social networking denotes the act of creating networks of relationships between people. The term *social software* refers to all the applications that allow the communication and collaboration between users. While the software itself does not perform social networking per se, it does help connect users, thereby helping them leverage their relationships.

Web 2.0: Considered by many to be a very nebulous concept. Generally speaking it refers to the second generation of the World Wide Web in which the Web is being transformed from a medium to a platform. O'Reilly, who initially coined the term to describe technological evolutions circa 2004, provided a prototypical definition that included seven core principles. However, the inventor of the Web, Berners Lee, objected to the definition proposed by O'Reilly. Today, the term *Web 2.0* is typically used interchangeably with the term *social software*, which adds to the confusion surrounding the definition of the concept. Web 2.0 is a technology concept and denotes the combination of a range of existing technologies (such as HTML, CSS, XML, AJAX) to enable users to produce, consume, and remix data from multiple sources. One of the most highlighted of Web 2.0's features is the architecture of participation which allows users to add value to the application they use. Examples of Web 2.0 tools are blogs, wikis, social bookmarking, RSS feeds, and folksonomies.

ENDNOTES

[1] Version 2.58a. http://www.blender.org/

[2] Version 6.2. http://www.atlasti.com/

[3] Linus Torvalds is the software engineer who initiated the development of the Linux operating system

Compilation of References

About. (2011). From Wikipedia. Retrieved July 06, 2011, from http://en.Wikipedia.org/w/index.php?title=Wikipedia:About&oldid=437810305

Adams, S. A. (2011). Sourcing the crowd for health services improvement. *Social Science & Medicine, 72,* 1069–1076. doi:10.1016/j.socscimed.2011.02.001

Addley, E. (2011, June 13). Gay girl in Damascus hoaxer acted out of vanity. *The Guardian.* Retrieved from http://www.guardian.co.uk/world/2011/jun/13/gay-girl-damascus-tom-macmaster

Adler, B. T., & de Alfaro, L. (2006). *A content- driven reputation system for the Wikipedia* (Technical Report No. ucsv-06-18). Santa Cruz, CA: University of California, Santa Cruz. Retrieved from http://works.bepress.com/luca_de_alfaro/3

Adler, B. T., de Alfaro, L., Pye, I., & Raman, V. (2008). *Measuring author contributions to the Wikipedia* (Technical Report No. UCSC-SOE-08-08). Santa Cruz, CA: University of California, Santa Cruz.

Administrators. (2012). From Wikipedia. Retrieved January 26, 2012, from http://en.wikipedia.org/wiki/Wikipedia:Administrators

Agichtein, E., Castillo, C., Donato, D., Gionis, A., & Mishne, G. (2008). Finding high-quality content in social media. *WSDM '08 Proceedings of the International Conference on Web Search and Web Data Mining.*

Ahmed, F., Campbell, P., Jaffar, A., & Capretz, L. (2009). Defects in open source software: The role of online forums. *Proceedings of World Academy of Science: Engineering & Technology, 52,* 174–178.

Ahn, T. K., Huckfeldt, R., Mayer, A. K., & Ryan, J. B. (2008, August). *Availability and the centrality of experts in the communication of political information.* Paper presented at the Annual Meeting of the American Political Science Association, Boston, MA.

Alexa. (n.d.). *Alexa top 500 global sites.* Retrieved from http://www.alexa.com/topsites

Alfalab. (2011). Retrieved July 13, 2011, from http://alfalab.ehumanities.nl/

Al-Taitoon, A., Sörensen, C., & Gibson, D. (2003). Modern professionals and their tools: ICT supporting organizational flexibility and control. *Proceedings of 11th European Conference of Information Systems.* Retrieved from http://is2.lse.ac.uk/asp/aspecis/20030147.pdf

Althusser, L. (1970). Ideology and ideological state apparatuses. In L. Althusser (Ed.), *Lenin and philosophy and other essays.* Retrieved from http://www.marxists.org/reference/archive/althusser/1970/ideology.htm

American Library Association. (1989). *Presidential Committee on Information Literacy: Final report.* Retrieved June 16, 2011, from http://www.ala.org/ala/mgrps/divs/acrl/publications/whitepapers/presidential.cfm

Amicucci, A. N. (2011, May). *They aren't all digital natives: Dismantling myths about students' relationships with technology.* Research presented at the meeting of Computers and Writing, Ann Arbor.

Amirault, R. J., & Visser, Y. L. (2009). The university in periods of technological change: A historically grounded perspective. *Journal of Computing in Higher Education, 21*(1), 62–79. doi:10.1007/s12528-009-9016-5

354

Amundsen, C., Winer, L., & Gandell, T. (2004). Designing teaching for student learning. In Saroyan, A., & Amundsen, C. (Eds.), *Rethinking teaching in higher education: From a course design workshop to a faculty development framework* (pp. 71–93). Sterling, VA: Stylus Publishing, LLC.

Anderson, C. (2004). The long tail. *Wired, 12*(10). Retrieved June 28, 2011, from http://www.wired.com/wired/archive/12.10/tail.html

Anderson, C. (2008, June 23). The end of theory: The data deluge makes the scientific method obsolete. *Wired* [Online edition]. Retrieved June 25, 2011, from http://www.wired.com/science/discoveries/magazine/16-07/pb_theory

Anderson, P. (2007). What is Web 2.0? Ideas, technologies and implications for education. *JISC Technology and Standards Watch*. Bristol, UK: JISC. Retrieved July 13, 2011, from http://www.jisc.ac.uk/media/documents/techwatch/tsw0701b.pdf

Andres, H. P., & Akan, O. H. (2010). Assessing team learning in technology-mediated collaboration: An experimental Study. *Journal of Educational Technology Systems, 38*(4), 473–487. doi:10.2190/ET.38.4.g

Andres, H. P., & Shipps, B. P. (2010). Team learning in technology-mediated distributed teams. *Journal of Information Systems Education, 21*(2), 213–221.

Angwin, J., & Fowler, G. A. (2009). Volunteers log off as Wikipedia ages. *Wall Street Journal—Eastern Edition, 254*(123), A1-A17. Retrieved from http://search.ebscohost.com.proxy.iwu.edu/login.aspx?direct=true&db=nfh&AN=45358947&site=eds-live&scope=site

Antonijevic, S., & Beaulieu, A. (2010). *Crossing the unexpected: Benefits and challenges of scholarly collaboration in a humanities lab*. HASTAC 2010: Grand Challenges and Global Innovations Conference, April 15, 2010. Retrieved October 10, 2011, from http://www.ichass.illinois.edu/hastac2010/HASTAC_2010/Presentations/Entries/2010/4/15_Crossing_the_Unexpected__Benefits_and_Challenges_of_Scholarly_Collaboration_in_a_Humanities_Labs.html

Armstrong, R., Waters, E., Roberts, H., Oliver, S., & Popay, J. (2006). The role and theoretical evolution of knowledge translation and exchange in public health. *Journal of Public Health, 28*(4), 384–389. doi:10.1093/pubmed/fdl072

Asaravala, A. (2004). *Warnings: Blogs can be infectious*. Wired News.

Ashton, J., & Newman, L. (2006). An unfinished symphony: 21st century teacher education using knowledge creating heutagogies. *British Journal of Educational Technology, 37*(6), 825–840. doi:10.1111/j.1467-8535.2006.00662.x

Association of American Colleges and Universities. (2002). *Greater expectations: A new vision for learning as a nation goes to college* [Electronic version]. Washington, DC: Author. Retrieved July 2, 2007, from http://www.greaterexpectations.org

Association of College and Research Libraries. (2000). *Information literacy competency standards for higher education*. Retrieved June 29, 2011, from http://www.ala.org/ala/mgrps/divs/acrl/standards/informationliteracycompetency.cfm

Association of College and Research Libraries. Law and Political Science Section. (2008). *Political science research competency guidelines*. Retrieved June 16, 2011, from http://www.acrl.org/ala/mgrps/divs/acrl/standards/PoliSciGuide.pdf

Attia, A. M., Aziz, N., Friedman, B., & Elhusseiny, M. F. (2011). Commentary: The impact of social networking tools on political change in Egypt's "revolution 2.0.". *Electronic Commerce Research and Applications, 10*(4), 369–374. doi:10.1016/j.elerap.2011.05.003

Austin, J. L. (1962). *How to do things with words*. Oxford, UK: University Press.

Ayers, P., Matthews, C., & Yates, B. (2008). *How Wikipedia works: And how you can be a part of it*. San Francisco, CA: No Starch Press.

Bacon, J. (2009). *The art of community: Building the new age of participation*. Sebastopol, CA: O'Reilly Media.

Badke, W. (2008, January). If everything is miscellaneous [Review of the book *Everything is miscellaneous*]. *Online, 32*(1), 48–50.

Bakhtin, M. M. (1981). *The dialogic imagination: Four essays* (Holquist, M., Trans.). Austin, TX: University of Texas Press.

Bakkalbasi, N., Bauer, K., Glover, J., & Wang, L. (2006). Three options for citation tracking: Google Scholar, Scopus and Web of Science. *Biomedical Digital Libraries, 3*(7). Retrieved May 7, 2011, from http://www.bio-diglib.com/content/3/1/7

Ballagas, R. (2010). *"Media multitasking" is not always multitasking*. Nokia Research Center. Retrieved March 4, 2011, from www.stanford.edu/group/multitasking/memos/Ballegas_ Multitasking_Memo.pdf.

Barack, L. (2009, April). Twittering Dante: New models for student writing in the digital age. *School Library Journal*, 14–15.

Barberio, R. P. (2004). The one-armed bandit syndrome: Overuse of the Internet in student research projects. *PS: Political Science & Politics, 37*(2), 307-311. doi: 10.1017.S1049096504004275

Bar-Ilan, J. (2007). Google bombing from a time perspective. *Journal of Computer-Mediated Communication, 12*, 910–938. doi:10.1111/j.1083-6101.2007.00356.x

Bar-Ilan, J. (2008). Which h-index? A comparison of WoS, Scopus and Google Scholar. *Scientometrics, 74*(2), 257–271. doi:10.1007/s11192-008-0216-y

Baron, N. (2008). *Always on: Language in an online and mobile world*. Oxford, UK: Oxford University Press.

Barthes, R. (2006). From work to text. In Hale, D. J. (Ed.), *The novel: An anthology of criticism and theory, 1900-2000* (pp. 235–241). Malden, MA: Blackwell.

Batelle, J. (2005). *The search. How Google and its rivals rewrote the rules of business and transformed our culture*. New York, NY: Penguin.

Battelle, J. (2005). *The search: How Google and its rivals rewrote the rules of business and transformed our culture*. New York, NY: Penguin.

Baum, E. B. (2004). *What is thought?* Cambridge, MA: The MIT Press.

Beaulieu, A., de Rijcke, S., & van Heur, B. (2012). Authority and expertise in new sites of knowledge production. In Wouters, P., Beaulieu, A., Scharnhorst, A., & Wyatt, S. (Eds.), *Virtual knowledge*. Cambridge, MA: The MIT Press.

Beaulieu, A., & Wouters, P. (2009). E-research as intervention. In Jankowski, N. (Ed.), *e-Research: Transformations in scholarly practice* (pp. 54–69). New York, NY: Routledge.

Becking, D., Betermieux, S., Bomsdorf, B., Feldmann, B., Heuel, E., Langer, P., & Schlageter, P. (2004). Didactic profiling: Supporting the mobile learner. *World Conference on E-learning in Corporate, Government, Health and Higher Education, Association for the Advancement of Computers in Education* (pp. 1760–1767).

Beel, J. B. Gipp, Bela, & Wilde, E. (2010). Academic search engine optimization (ASEO): Optimizing scholarly literature for Google Scholar and Co. *Journal of Scholarly Publishing*, 176–190.

Beer, D. (2009). Power through the algorithm? Participatory web cultures and the technological unconscious. *New Media & Society, 11*(6), 985–1002. doi:10.1177/1461444809336551

Begley, S. (2011, March 7). I can't think! *Newsweek, 157*(10), 28-33.

Bellow, S. (2001). *Ravelstein*. New York, NY: Penguin.

Benjamin, R., & Wigand, R. (1995). Electronic markets and virtual value chains on the information highway. *Sloan Management Review*, (Winter): 62–72.

Benkler, Y. (2006). *The wealth of networks*. New Haven, CT: Yale University Press.

Benkler, Y. (2006). *The wealth of networks: How social production transforms markets and freedom*. New Haven, CT: Yale University Press.

Benkler, Y., & Nissenbaum, H. (2006). Commons-based peer production and virtue. *Journal of Political Philosophy, 14*(4), 394–419. doi:10.1111/j.1467-9760.2006.00235.x

Bennet, S., Maton, K., & Kervin, L. (2008). The 'digital natives' debate: A critical review of the evidence. *British Journal of Educational Technology, 39*(5), 775–786. doi:10.1111/j.1467-8535.2007.00793.x

Berinstein, P. (2006). Wikipedia and *Britannica. Searcher, 14*(3), 16–26.

Beuschel, W., & Draheim, S. (2011). Integrating social media in tertiary education: Experiences and predicaments. *Proceedings of the DigitalWorld 2011. Third International Conference on Mobile, Hybrid, and On-line Learning (eL&mL 2011)*, (pp. 76-81). Gosier/Guadeloupe, France. Retrieved January 10, 2012, from www.thinkmind.org/index.php?view=article&articleid=elml_2011_4_30_50082

Beuschel, W., Gaiser, B., & Draheim, S. (2009). Informal communication in virtual learning environments. In Rogers, P., Berg, G. A., Howard, C., Boettcher, J., Justice, L., & Schenk, K. (Eds.), *Encyclopedia of distance learning* (2nd ed., *Vol. II*, pp. 1164–1168). Hershey, MA: IGI Global. doi:10.4018/978-1-60566-198-8.ch166

Biddix, J. P., Chung, C. J., & Park, H. W. (2011). Convenience or credibility? A study of college student online research behaviors. *The Internet and Higher Education, 14*(3), 175–182. doi:10.1016/j.iheduc.2011.01.003

Bietila, D., Bloechl, C., & Edwards, E. (2009, March). *Beyond the buzz: Planning library Facebook initiatives grounded in user needs.* Paper presented at 14th Biannual Conference of the Association of College and Research Libraries. Retrieved from http://hdl.handle.net/1961/5136

Björk, J., & Magnusson, M. (2009). Where do good innovation ideas come from? Exploring the influence of network connectivity on innovation idea quality. *Journal of Product Innovation Management, 26*(6), 662–670. doi:10.1111/j.1540-5885.2009.00691.x

Blair, A. (2010). *Too much to know: Managing scholarly information before the modern age.* New Haven, CT: Yale University Press.

Blender Foundation (Producer) & Levy. C. (Director). (2010a). *Sintel.* [Video]. Retrieved from http://www.youtube.com/watch?v=eRsGyueVLvQ

Blender Foundation (Producer) & Levy. C. (Director). (2010b). *Sintel Trailer, Durian Open Movie Project.* [Video]. Retrieved from http://www.youtube.com/watch?v=HOfdboHvshg

Blender Foundation. (2010, March 24). *Durian Project: "Extras" modeling & animation sprint.* [Video file]. Retrieved from http://www.youtube.com/watch?v=6jeJ-Ta5UQc

Blender Foundation. (2011). Retrieved June 15, 2011, from http://www.blender.org/blenderorg/blender-foundation/

Bloland, H. G. (2005). Whatever happened to postmodernism in higher education? No requiem in the new millennium. *The Journal of Higher Education, 76*(2), 121–150. doi:10.1353/jhe.2005.0010

Boettcher, J. V., & Conrad, R. (2010). *The online teaching survival guide: Simple and practical pedagogical tips.* San Francisco, CA: Jossey-Bass.

Bomis. (2011). Retrieved July 06, 2011, from http://en.Bomis.org/wiki?title=Bomis&oldid=100773755

Boshuizen, J., & Geurts, P. (2009). Regional social networks as conduits for knowledge spillovers: Explaining performance of high-tech firms. *Tijdschrift voor Economische en Sociale Geografie, 100*(2), 183–197. doi:10.1111/j.1467-9663.2009.00528.x

Boubred, A. (2010, May 13). *Reaction from the team.* [Video file]. Retrieved from http://www.sintel.org/news/reaction-from-the-team/

Boyd, D. (2011a). *"Real names" policies are an abuse of power.* Retrieved October 20, 2011, from www.zephoria.org/thoughts/archives/2011/08/04/real-names.html

Boyd, D. (2011b). *Bibliography of research on social network sites.* Retrieved January 10, 2012, from www.danah.org/researchBibs/sns.php

Boyd, D. (2010). Streams of content, limited attention: The flow of information through social media. *EDUCAUSE Review, 45*(5), 26–36. Retrieved from http://www.educause.edu/EDUCAUSE+Review/EDUCAUSEReviewMagazineVolume45/StreamsofContentLimitedAttenti/213923

Boyd, D., & Ellison, N. (2007). Social network sites: Definition, history, and scholarship. *Journal of Computer-Mediated Communication, 13*(1). Retrieved from http://jcmc.indiana.edu/vol13/issue1/boyd.ellison.html. doi:10.1111/j.1083-6101.2007.00393.x

Boyer Commission on Educating Undergraduates in the Research University. S. S. Kenny, chair. (1998). *Reinventing undergraduate education: A blueprint for America's research universities*. Stony Brook, NY: State University of New York–Stony Brook.

Boyer, E. L. (1990). *Scholarship reconsidered*. Princeton, NJ: Carnegie Foundation for the Advancement of Teaching.

Braun, D., & Sider, T. (2006). Vague, so untrue. *Noûs (Detroit, Mich.)*, *41*, 133–156. doi:10.1111/j.1468-0068.2007.00641.x

Breeding, M. (2007). Librarians face online social networks. *Computers in Libraries*, *27*(8), 30–33. Retrieved from http://www.librarytechnology.org/ltg-displaytext.pl?RC=12735

Brende, E. (2004). *Better off: Flipping the switch on technology*. New York, NY: Harper Perennial.

BritannicaStore.com. (2010). Retrieved July 06, 2011, from http://www.britannicastore.com/The-Encyclopaedia-Britannica-2010-Copyright/invt/printset10

Brooks-Young, S. (2010). *Digital-age literacy for teachers: Applying technology standards to everyday practice*. Thousand Oaks, CA: SAGE.

Brown, J. S., & Adler, R. P. (2008). Minds on fire: Open education, the long tail, and learning 2.0. *EDUCASE Review*, *43*(1), 16–32.

Brown, J. S., & Duguid, P. (2002). *The social life of information*. Boston, MA: Harvard Business School Press.

Bruffee, K. (1993). *Collaborative learning: Higher education, interdependence, and the authority of knowledge*. Baltimore, MD: Johns Hopkins University Press. doi:10.2307/358879

Bruns, A. (2008). *Blogs, Wikipedia, Second Life, and beyond: From production to produsage*. Peter Lang Publishing.

Bukatman, S. (1993). *Terminal identity: The virtual subject in postmodern science fiction*. Durham, NC: Duke University Press.

Bullen, M., Morgan, T., & Qayyum, A. (2011). Digital learners in higher education: Generation is not the issue. *Canadian Journal of Learning Technology*, *37*(1). Retrieved January 10, 2012, from www.cjlt.ca/index.php/cjlt/article/view/550/298

Bullen, M., Morgan, T., & Qayyum, A. (2011). Digital learners in higher education: Generation is not the issue. *Canadian Journal of Learning and Technology*, *37*(1), 1–24.

Burkhardt, P. (2009). Social software trends in business: Introduction. In Deans, C. P. (Ed.), *Social software and Web 2.0 technology trends* (pp. 1–16). New York, NY: Information Science Reference.

Caldas, A., Schroeder, R., Mesch, G. S., & Dutton, W. H. (2008). Patterns of information search and access on the World Wide Web: Democratizing expertise or creating new hierarchies? *Journal of Computer-Mediated Communication*, *13*, 769–793. doi:10.1111/j.1083-6101.2008.00419.x

Calvi, L., Cassella, M., & Nuijten, K. (2010). Enhancing users' experience: A content analysis of 12 university libraries' Facebook profiles. In *Publishing in the networked world: Transforming the nature of communication- Proceedings of the 14th International Conference on Electronic Publishing (ElPub) 2010*, (pp. 258-269). Retrieved from http://elpub.scix.net/data/works/att/118_elpub2010.content.pdf

Cameron, F. R. (2008). Object-oriented democracies: Conceptualising museum collections in networks. *Museum Management and Curatorship*, *23*(3), 229–243. doi:10.1080/09647770802233807

Canadian Institute for Health Research. (2004). *Knowledge translation strategy: Niche and focus 2005– 2009*. Ottawa, Canada: Canadian Institute of Health Research.

Carpenter, C., & Drezner, D. W. (2010). International relations 2.0: The implications of new media for an old profession. *International Studies Perspectives*, *11*(3), 255–272. doi:10.1111/j.1528-3585.2010.00407.x

Carr, N. (2008). Is Google making us stupid?: Why you can't read the way you used to. *Atlantic Monthly*, *56*, Retrieved from http://www.theatlantic.com/magazine/archive/2008/07/is-google-making-us-stupid/6868/

Carr, N. (2008b). *The big switch. Rewiring the world, from Edison to Google*. New York, NY: Norton.

Carr, N. (2010). *The shallows: What the Internet is doing to our brains*. New York, NY: Norton.

Casey, E. M., & Savastinuk, L. C. (September, 1, 2006). Service for the next-generation library. *Library Journal*. Retrieved from http://www.libraryjournal.com/article/CA6365200.html

Casey, M. E. (October, 21, 2005). Working toward a definition of Library 2.0. *LibraryCrunch*. Retrieved on from http://www.librarycrunch.com/2005/10/working_towards_a_definition_o.html

Castells, M. (1996). *The rise of the network society. The information age: Economy, society and culture* (*Vol. 1*). Oxford: Blackwell.

Castells, M. (2009). *Communication power*. Oxford, UK: Oxford University Press.

Cathcart, R., & Roberts, A. (2005). Evaluating Google Scholar as a tool for information literacy. *Internet Reference Services Quarterly, 10*(3), 167–176. doi:10.1300/J136v10n03_15

Caufield, J. (2005). Where did Google get its value? *Libraries and the Academy, 5*(4), 555–572. doi:10.1353/pla.2005.0047

Chandler, C. J., & Gregory, A. S. (2010). Sleeping with the enemy: Wikipedia in the college classroom. *The History Teacher, 43*(2), 247–257.

Chang, M. H., & Harrington, J. E. Jr. (2007). Innovators, imitators, and the evolving architecture of problem-solving networks. *Organization Science, 18*(4), 648–666. doi:10.1287/orsc.1060.0245

Charnigo, L., & Barnett-Ellis, P. (2007). Checking out Facebook.com: The impact of a digital trend on academic libraries. *Information Technology and Libraries, 26*(1), 23–34.

Chatti, M. A., & Jarke, M. (2010). Social software for bottom-up knowledge networking and community building. In Lytras, M., Tennyson, R., & de Pablos, P. O. (Eds.), *Knowledge networks: The social software perspective* (pp. 17–27). New York, NY: Information Science Reference.

Chen, Y., Ho, T.-H., & Kim, Y.-M. (2010). Knowledge market design: A field experiment at Google Answers. *Journal of Public Economic Theory, 12*(4), 641–664. doi:10.1111/j.1467-9779.2010.01468.x

Chesney, T. (2006). An empirical examination of Wikipedia's credibility. *First Monday, 11*(11).

Cheung, C. M. K., & Thadani, D. R., (2010). The state of electronic word-of-mouth research: A literature analysis. *PACIS 2010 Proceedings, Paper 151*.

Cheung, S. L. (2008). Using mobile phone messaging as a response medium in classroom experiments. *The Journal of Economic Education*, (Winter): 51–67. doi:10.3200/JECE.39.1.51-67

Chi, E. H., Pirolli, P., & Lam, S. K. (2007). Aspects of augmented social cognition: Social information foraging and social search. *Proceedings of the 2nd International Conference on Online Communities and Social Computing* (pp. 60-69). Beijing, China: Springer-Verlag.

Chi, M. T. H. (2006). Two approaches to the study of experts' characteristics. In Ericsson, A. K., Charness, N., Feltovich, P. J., & Hoffman, R. R. (Eds.), *The Cambridge handbook of expertise and expert performance* (pp. 21–30). New York, NY: Cambridge University Press. doi:10.1017/CBO9780511816796.002

Ching, Y.-H., & Hsu, Y.-C. (2011). Design-grounded assessment: A framework and a case study of Web 2.0 practices in higher education. *Australasian Journal of Educational Technology, 27*(5), 781–797.

Chiu, C.-M., Hsu, M.-H., & Wang, E. T. G. (2006). Understanding knowledge sharing in virtual communities: An integration of social capital and social cognitive theories. *Decision Support Systems, 42*(3), 1872–1888. doi:10.1016/j.dss.2006.04.001

Cho, H., Gay, G., Davidson, B., & Ingraffea, A. (2007). Social networks, communication styles, and learning performance in a CSCL community. *Computers & Education, 49*, 309–329. doi:10.1016/j.compedu.2005.07.003

Choi, C. C., & Ho, H. (2002). Exploring new literacies in online peer-learning environments. *Reading Online, 6*(1). Retrieved from www.readingonline.org/newliteracies/lit_index.asp?HREF=choi/index.html

Chopra, S., & Dexter, S. D. (2008). *Decoding liberation: The promise of free and open source Software*. London, UK: Routledge.

CIBER. (2010). *Social media and research workflow*. Retrieved July 5, 2011 from http://www.ucl.ac.uk/infostudies/research/ciber/social-media-report.pdf

Clayton, S., Morris, S., Venkatesha, A., & Whitton, H. (2008). *User tagging of online cultural heritage items: A project report for the 2008 Cultural Management Development Program*. Unpublished report, Australia.

Cluley, G. (2011, June 7). Facebook changes privacy settings for millions of users: Facial recognition is enabled. *Naked Security*. Retrieved June 25, 2011, from http://nakedsecurity.sophos.com/2011/06/07/facebook-privacy-settings-facial-recognition-enabled

Cobo Romaní, C., & Moravec, J. W. (2011). *Aprendizaje invisible. Hacia una nueva ecología de la educación*. Barcelona, Spain: Col·lecció Transmedia XXI. Laboratori de Mitjans Interactius/Publicacions i Edicions de la Universitat de Barcelona.

Cobo Romaní, C., & Pardo Kuklinski, H. (2007). *Planeta Web 2.0. Inteligencia colectiva o medios fast food*. Barcelona, Spain: GRID, Universitat de Vic/Flacso México.

Cohen, N. (2011, May 23). *Wikipedia*. Retrieved June 29, 2011, from http://topics.nytimes.com/top/news/business/companies/wikipedia/index.html

Cohen, P. (2010, August 23). Scholars test Web alternative to peer review. *New York Times*. Retrieved November 04, 2011, from http://www.nytimes.com/2010/08/24/arts/24peer.html

Coleman, E. G., & Hill, B. (2004). The social production of ethics in Debian and free software communities: Anthropological lessons for vocational ethics. In Koch, S. (Ed.), *Free/open source software development* (pp. 273–295). Hershey, PA: Idea Group Publishing. doi:10.4018/978-1-59140-369-2.ch013

Collins, E., & Hide, B. (2010). Use and relevance of Web 2.0 resources for researchers. In T. Hedlund & Y. Tonta (Eds.). *Publishing in the networked world: Transforming the nature of communication, 14th International Conference on Electronic Publishing, 16-18 June 2010*. Helsinki, Finland: Hanken School of Economics. Retrieved June 8, 2011, from https://helda.helsinki.fi/handle/10227/599

Collins, A., & Halverson, R. (2009). *Rethinking education in the age of technology: The digital revolution and schooling in America*. New York, NY: Teachers College Press.

Collins, H. (2010). *Tacit knowledge*. University of Chicago Press.

Collins, H., & Evans, R. (2007). *Rethinking expertise*. University of Chicago Press.

Conole, G., & Culver, J. (2010). The design of cloudworks: Applying social networking practice to foster the exchange of learning and teaching ideas and designs. *Computers & Education, 54*(3), 679–692. doi:10.1016/j.compedu.2009.09.013

Contributing to Wikipedia. (2011). From Wikipedia. Retrieved June 14, 2011, from http://en.Wikipedia.org/wiki/Wikipedia:Contributing_to_Wikipedia

Cope, B., & Kalantzis, M. (2007). New media, new learning. *The International Journal of Learning, 14*(1), 75–79.

Copeland, R. (2011). Tweet all about it. *Metro, 169*, 96-100.

Costa, G. J. M., & Silva, N. S. A. (2010). Knowledge versus content in e-learning: A philosophical discussion. *Information Systems Frontiers, 12*(4), 399–413. doi:10.1007/s10796-009-9200-1

Craig, E. (1999). *Knowledge and the state of nature*. Oxford, UK: Clarendon Press. doi:10.1093/0198238797.001.0001

Creative Commons. (n.d.). *About the licenses*. Retrieved from http://creativecommons.org/licenses/

Creswell, J. W. (2007). *Qualitative inquiry & research design: Choosing among five approaches*. Thousand Oaks, CA: Sage Publications.

Crowley, B. (2005). *Spanning the theory-practice divide in library and information science*. Maryland: Scarecrow Press.

Crump, B. J., Logan, K. A., & McIlroy, A. (2007). Does gender still matter? A study of the views of women in the ICT industry in New Zealand. *Gender, Work and Organization, 14*(4), 349–370. doi:10.1111/j.1468-0432.2007.00348.x

Crystal, D. (2008). *Txting: The gr8 db8*. Oxford, UK: Oxford University Press.

Cuban, L. (2001). *Oversold and underused: Computers in the classroom*. Cambridge, MA: Harvard University Press.

Dahl, C. (2009). Undergraduate research in the public domain: The evaluation of non-academic sources online. *RSR. Reference Services Review, 37*(2), 155–163. doi:10.1108/00907320910957198

Daines, J. G., & Nimer, C. L. (2009). *The interactive archivist: Case studies in utilizing Web 2.0 to improve the archival experience*. Retrieved from http://interactivearchivist.archivists.org

Dalton, M. S. (2009). The publishing experiences of historians. In Greco, A. N. (Ed.), *The state of scholarly publishing. Challenges and opportunities* (pp. 107–146). New Brunswick, NJ: Transaction.

Dansie, B. (2010a, February 5). *Guardians*. [Web log message]. Retrieved from http://www.sintel.org/news/guardians/

Davis, H. (2012). *Institutional personal learning environments—Paradise or paradox?* Keynote Lecture 3. Retrieved January 12, 2012, from www.csedu.org/KeynoteSpeakers.aspx

Davis, M. R. (2010, November). Social networking goes to school. *Education Digest*, 14–19.

Davis, P. M. (2003). Effect of the web on undergraduate citation behavior: Guiding student scholarship in a networked age. *portal. Libraries and the Academy, 3*(1), 41–51. doi:10.1353/pla.2003.0005

de Groot, A. (1978). *Thought and choice in chess*. The Hague, The Netherlands: Mouton.

de Rijcke, S., & Beaulieu, A. (2011). Image as interface: Consequences for users of museum knowledge. *Library Trends, Special Issue on Involving Users in the Co-Construction of Digital Knowledge in Libraries, Archives, and Museums, 59*(3), 664–685.

Dede, C. (2002). A new century demands new ways of learning. In Gordon, D. T. (Ed.), *The digital classroom: How technology is changing the way we teach and learn* (pp. 171–174). Cambridge, MA: Harvard Education Letter.

Deitering, A., & Gronemyer, K. (2011). Beyond peer-reviewed articles: Using blogs to enrich students' understanding of scholarly work. *portal. Libraries and the Academy, 11*(1), 489–503.

Dempsey, L. (1999). Scientific, industrial, and cultural heritage: A shared approach. *Ariadne, 22,* •••. Retrieved from http://www.ariadne.ac.uk/issue22/Dempsey

Denecke, K., & Nejdl, W. (2009). How valuable is medical social media data? Content analysis of the medical web. *Information Sciences, 179,* 1870–1880. doi:10.1016/j.ins.2009.01.025

Deresiewicz, W. (2011, May 23). Faulty towers: The crisis in higher education. *The Nation* [Electronic version]. Retrieved June 24, 2011, from http://www.thenation.com/article/160410/faulty-towers-crisis-higher-education

Desmet, C. (2009). Teaching Shakespeare with YouTube. *English Journal, 99*(1), 65–70.

Dewey, J. (1916). *Democracy and education: An introduction to the philosophy of education*. New York, NY: Macmillan.

Digital Learners in Higher Education. (2012). [Weblog]. Retrieved January 10, 2012, from http://digitallearners.wordpress.com/tools-resources/

Dillenbourg, P., & Jermann, P. (2007). Designing integrative scripts. In F. Fischer, H. Mandl, J. Haake, & I. Kollar (Eds.), *Scripting computer-supported collaborative learning – Cognitive, computational, and educational perspectives,* (pp. 275-301), Computer-Supported Collaborative Learning Series. New York, NY: Springer.

Dillenbourg, P., & Jermann, P. (2010). Technology for classroom orchestration. In M. S. Kline & I. M. Saleh (Eds.), *New science of learning: Cognition, computers, and collaboration in education* (pp. 525-552). New York, NY: Springer Science+Business Media.

Dillenbourg, P., & Hong, F. (2008). The mechanics of CSCL macro scripts. *International Journal of Computer-Supported Collaborative Learning, 3*(1), 5–23. doi:10.1007/s11412-007-9033-1

Doan, A., Ramakrishnan, R., & Halevy, A. Y. (2011). Crowdsourcing systems on the World-Wide Web. *Communications of the ACM, 54*(4), 86–96. doi:10.1145/1924421.1924442

Dobbins, M., Robeson, P., Ciliska, D., Hanna, S., Cameron, R., & O'Mara, L. (2009). A description of a knowledge broker role implemented as part of a randomized controlled trial evaluating three knowledge translation strategies. *Implementation Science; IS*, *4*(1), 23. doi:10.1186/1748-5908-4-23

Doctorow, C. (2006). *On "Digital Maoism: The hazards of the new online collectivism" by Jaron Lanier*. Retrieved June 14, 2011, from http://www.edge.org/discourse/digital_maoism.html

Dokoupil, T. (2008). *Revenge of the experts*. Retrieved June 06, 2011, from http://www.newsweek.com/2008/03/05/revenge-of-the-experts.html

Dolowitz, D. P. (2007). The Big E: How electronic information can be fitted into the academic process. *Journal of Political Science Education*, *3*(2), 177–190. doi:10.1080/15512160701338338

Dourish, P., & Bell, G. (2011). *Divining a digital future – Mess and mythology in ubiquitous computing*. Cambridge, MA: The MIT Press.

Downes, S. (2006). *Learning networks and connective knowledge*. Retrieved from http://it.coe.uga.edu/itforum/paper92/paper92.htlm

Downes, S. (2008). How do you know? *Theoretical foundations of distance education online course*. September 1, 2008. Retrieved from http://orgunx.anadolu.edu.tr/etanit.asp?oy=2006&dn=001&dk=UZE501&dl=01&dg=&yy=1&br=5506010100&tc=26710713580>

Downes, S. (2008). *Introducing edupunk*. Retrieved from http://www.downes.ca/cgi-bin/page.cgi?post=44760

Dreyfus, H. L., & Dreyfus, S. E. (1986). *Mind over machine: the power of human intuition and expertise in the age of the computer*. Oxford, UK: Basil Blackwell.

Driver, D., Jette, K., & Lira, L. (2008). Student learning identities: Developing a learning taxonomy for the political science classroom. *Journal of Political Science Education*, *4*(1), 61–85. doi:10.1080/15512160701816135

Dron, J. (2007). Designing the undesignable: Social software and control. *Journal of Educational Technology & Society*, *10*(3), 60–71.

Drouin, M. A. (2011). College students' text messaging, use of textese and literacy skills. *Journal of Computer Assisted Learning*, *27*, 67–75. doi:10.1111/j.1365-2729.2010.00399.x

Drucker, P. F. (1959). *Landmarks of tomorrow*. New York, NY: Harper.

Duff, W. M., & Harris, V. (2002). Stories and names: Archival description as narrating records and constructing meanings. *Archival Science*, *2*, 263–285. doi:10.1007/BF02435625

Efimova, L., & Fiedler, S. (2004): Learning webs: Learning in weblog networks. In P. Kommers, P. Isaias, & M. B. Nunes (Eds.), *Proceedings of the IADIS International Conference Web Based Communities* (pp. 490-494). Lisbon, Portugal: IADIS Press.

Elgin, C. Z. (2004). True enough. *Philosophical Issues*, *14*, 113–131. doi:10.1111/j.1533-6077.2004.00023.x

Ellison, N. (2007). *Facebook use on campus: A social capital perspective on social network site*. Paper presented at the ECAR Symposium, Boca Raton, FL, December 5–7, 2007.

Encyclopedia of Life. (2011). *Help build EOL*. Retrieved July 06, 2011, from http://www.eol.org/content/page/help_build_eol

Epstein, S. (1996). *Impure science: AIDS, activism, and the politics of knowledge*. Berkeley, CA: University of California Press.

Ericsson, K. A. (2003). The search for general abilities and basic capacities. Theoretical implications from the modiðability and complexity of mechanisms mediating expert performance. In Sternberg, R. J., & Grigorenko, E. L. (Eds.), *The psychology of abilities, competencies, and expertise* (pp. 93–125). Cambridge, UK: Cambridge University Press. doi:10.1017/CBO9780511615801.006

Ericsson, K. A. (2006). *The Cambridge handbook of expertise and expert performance*. Cambridge, UK: Cambridge University Press. doi:10.1017/CBO9780511816796

Ericsson, K. A. (2009). Enhancing the development of professional performance: Implications from the study of deliberate practice. In Ericsson, K. A. (Ed.), *Development of professional expertise. Toward measurement of expert performance and design of optimal learning environments* (pp. 405–431). Cambridge, UK: Cambridge University Press. doi:10.1017/CBO9780511609817.022

Ericsson, K. A., Charness, N., Hoffman, R. R., & Feltovich, P. J. (Eds.). (2006). *Cambridge handbook of expertise and expert performance*. New York, NY: Cambridge University Press. doi:10.1017/CBO9780511816796

Ericsson, K. A., & Smith, J. (2002). Prospects and limits of the empirical study of expertise: An introduction. In Levitin, D. J. (Ed.), *Foundations of cognitive psychology. Core readings* (pp. 517–550). Cambridge, MA: The MIT Press.

Ericsson, K., & Smith, J. (1991). *Toward a general theory of expertise: Prospects and limits*. New York, NY: Cambridge University Press.

Errors in the Encyclopedia Britannica that Have Been Corrected in Wikipedia. (2011). From Wikipedia. Retrieved July 6, 2011, from http://en.Wikipedia.org/wiki/Wikipedia:Errors_in_the_Encyclop%C3%A6dia_Britannica_that_have_been_corrected_in_Wikipedia

Ettinger, D. (2008). The triumph of expediency: The impact of Google Scholar on library instruction. *Journal of Library Administration*, *46*(3), 65–72. doi:10.1300/J111v46n03_06

Evans, B. (October, 15, 2006). Your Space or MySpace. *Library Journal.* Retrieved from http://www.libraryjournal.com/article/CA6375465.html

Evans, J. A. (2008). Electronic publication and the narrowing of science and scholarship. *Science*, *321*(5887), 395–399. doi:10.1126/science.1150473

Evans, M. J. (2007). Archives of the people, by the people, for the people. *The American Archivist*, *70*(2), 387–400.

Expert. (2011). In the *Oxford English Dictionary Online*. Retrieved September 19, 2011, from http://www.oed.com/view/Entry/66551?rskey=hpFQT6&result=1

Eysenbach, G. (2008). Credibility of health information and digital media: New perspectives and implications for youth. In Metzger, M. J., & Flanagin, A. J. (Eds.), *Digital media, youth, and credibility* (pp. 123–154). Cambridge, MA: The MIT Press.

Eysenbach, G., & Jadad, A. (2001). Evidence-based patient choice and consumer health informatics in the internet age. *Journal of Medical Internet Research*, *3*(2). doi:10.2196/jmir.3.2.e19

Eysenbach, G., & Köhler, C. (2002). How do consumers search for and appraise health information on the world wide web? Qualitative study using focus groups, usability tests, and in-depth interviews. *British Medical Journal*, *324*(7337), 573–577. doi:10.1136/bmj.324.7337.573

Facebook. (2011). *Statistics|Facebook.* Retrieved June 11, 2011, from http://www.facebook.com/press/info.php?statistics

Facer, K., & Furlong, R. (2001). Beyond the myth of the "Cyberkid": Young people at the margins of the information revolution. *Journal of Youth Studies*, *4*(4), 451–469. doi:10.1080/13676260120101905

Fallows, D. (2005). *Search engine users* (Pew Internet and American Life Project). Retrieved May 7, 2011, from http://www.pewinternet.org/Reports/2005/Search-Engine-Users.aspx

Farkas, M. (2007). *Social software in libraries: Building collaboration, communication, and community online*. Medford, NJ: Information Today.

Feltovich, P. J., Prietula, M. J., & Ericsson, K. A. (2006). Studies of expertise from psychological perspectives. In Ericsson, K. A., Charness, N., Feltovich, P. J., & Hoffman, R. R. (Eds.), *The Cambridge handbook of expertise and expert performance* (pp. 41–67). Cambridge, UK: Cambridge University Press. doi:10.1017/CBO9780511816796.004

Fernandez, P. (2009). Balancing outreach and privacy in Facebook: Five guiding decision points. *Library High Tech News, 26*(3). Retrieved from http://www.emeraldinsight.com/10.1108/07419050910979946

Fiedler, S., & Pata, K. (2009). Distributed learning environments and social software: In search for a framework of design. In Hatzipanagos, S., & Warburton, S. (Eds.), *Handbook of research on social software and developing community ontologies* (pp. 145–158). Hershey, PA: IGI Global. doi:10.4018/978-1-60566-208-4.ch011

Fisher, W. R. (1984). Narration as human communication paradigm: The case of public moral argument. *Communication Monographs, 51*, 1–22. doi:10.1080/03637758409390180

Fitzgerald, J., & Baird, V. A. (2011). Taking a step back: Teaching critical thinking by distinguishing appropriate types of evidence. *PS: Political Science & Politics, 44*(3), 619–624. doi:10.1017/S1049096511000710

Five Pillars. (2011). From Wikipedia. Retrieved July 06, 2011, from http://en.Wikipedia.org/w/index.php?title=Wikipedia:Five_pillars&oldid=437188511

Flanagin, A. J., Metzger, M. J., Pure, R., & Markov, A. (2011). User-generated ratings and the evaluation of credibility and product quality in ecommerce transactions. *Proceedings of the 44th Hawaii International Conference on Systems Science.*

Flanagin, A. J., & Metzger, M. J. (2000). Perceptions of Internet information credibility. *Journalism & Mass Communication Quarterly, 77*(3), 515–540. doi:10.1177/107769900007700304

Flanagin, A. J., & Metzger, M. J. (2007). The role of site features, user attributes, and information verification behaviors on the perceived credibility of web-based information. *New Media & Society, 9*(2), 319–342. doi:10.1177/1461444807075015

Flanagin, A. J., & Metzger, M. J. (2008). The credibility of volunteered geographic information. *GeoJournal, 72*(3), 137–148. doi:10.1007/s10708-008-9188-y

Fogg, B. J., Marshall, J., Laraki, O., Osipovich, A., Varma, C., & Fang, N. ... Treinen, M. (2001). What makes Web sites credible? A report on a large quantitative study. *Proceedings of the SIGCHI Conference on Human Factors in Computing Systems* (pp. 61-68). Seattle, WA: ACM.

Foucault, M., & Gordon, C. (Eds.). (1980). *Power/knowledge interviews: Selected and other writings 1972-1977.* New York, NY: Pantheon.

Fourie, I. (1999). Should we take disintermediation seriously? *The Electronic Library, 17*(1), 9–16. doi:10.1108/02640479910329400

Fox, B. I., & Varadarajan, R. (2011). Technology in pharmacy education: Use of Twitter to encourage interaction in a multi-campus pharmacy management course. *Academic Journal of Pharmaceutical Education, 75*(5), 1–8.

Fox, M. J., & Wilkerson, P. L. (1998). *Introduction to archival organization and description: Access to cultural heritage.* Santa Monica, CA: Getty Information Institute.

Free Software Foundation. (n.d.). *The free software definition.* Retrieved from http://www.gnu.org/philosophy/free-sw.html

Freire, P. (1970). *Pedagogy of the oppressed.* New York, NY: Continuum.

Frey, N., Fisher, D., & Gonzalez, A. (2010). *Literacy 2.0: Reading and writing in 21st century classrooms.* Bloomington, IN: Solution Tree Press.

Gant, S. (2007). *We're all journalists now: The transformation of the press and reshaping of the law in the Internet age.* New York, NY: Free Press.

Garcia, L. M., & Roblin, N. P. (2008). Innovation, research, and professional development in higher education: Learning from our own experience. *Teaching and Teacher Education, 24*, 104–116. doi:10.1016/j.tate.2007.03.007

Garrison, D. R., & Vaughan, N. D. (2009). *Blended learning in higher education: Framework, principles, and guidelines.* San Fransisco, CA: Jossey-Bass.

Gayo-Avello, D. (2011). Don't turn social media into another "literary digest" poll. *Communications of the ACM, 54*(10), 121–128. doi:10.1145/2001269.2001297

Gibbons, M., Limoges, C., Nowotny, H., Schwartzman, S., Scott, P., & Trow, M. (1994). *The new production of knowledge: The dynamics of science and research in contemporary societies.* London, UK: Sage.

Gibson, W. (1984). *Neuromancer.* New York, NY: Ace Books.

Giles, J. (2005). Internet encyclopaedias go head to head. *Nature, 438*(7070), 900–901. doi:10.1038/438900a

Giles, J. (2005, December). Internet encyclopaedias go head to head. *Nature, 438*. Retrieved from http://www.nature.com/nature/britannica/index.htmldoi:10.1038/438900a

Gilmour, D. (2004). *We the media: Grassroots journalism by the people, for the people*. Sebastopol, CA: O'Reilly Media.

Gilroy, M. (2010). Higher education migrates to YouTube and social networks. *Education Digest: Essential Readings Condensed for Quick Review, 75*(7), 18–22.

Given, L., & McTavish, L. (2010). What's old is new again: The reconvergence of libraries, archives, and museums in the digital age. *The Library Quarterly, 80*(1), 7–32. doi:10.1086/648461

Gladwell, M. (2000). *The tipping point: How little things can make a big difference*. Boston, MA: Little, Brown.

Glott, R., Schmidt, P., & Ghosh, R. (2010). *Wikipedia survey: Overview of results*. United Nations University. Retrieved from http://www.wikipediastudy.org/docs/Wikipedia_Overview_15March2010-FINAL.pdf

Goldman, A. I. (1999). *Knowledge in a social world*. New York, NY: Oxford University Press. doi:10.1093/0198238207.001.0001

Goldman, A. I. (2001). Experts: Which ones should you trust? *Philosophy and Phenomenological Research, 63*(1), 85–110. doi:10.1111/j.1933-1592.2001.tb00093.x

Gorman, G. E. (2006). Giving way to Google. *Online Information Review, 30*(2), 97–99. doi:10.1108/14684520610659148

Grafstein, A. (2002). A discipline-based approach to information literacy. *Journal of Academic Librarianship, 28*(4), 197–204. doi:10.1016/S0099-1333(02)00283-5

Graham, I. D., Logan, J., Harrison, M., Straus, S., Tetroe, J., Caswell, W., & Robinson, N. (2006). Lost in knowledge translation: Time for a map? *The Journal of Continuing Education in the Health Professions, 26*, 13–24. doi:10.1002/chp.47

Grant, A. A. (2011, May). *Embracing the inevitable: Utilizing student text messaging to teach composition*. Research presented at the meeting of Computers and Writing, Ann Arbor.

Grathwohl, C. (2011, January 7). Wikipedia comes of age. *Chronicle of Higher Education*. Retrieved September 22, 2011, from http://chronicle.com/article/article-content/125899/

Gregg, D. (2010). Designing for collective intelligence. *Communications of the ACM, 53*(4), 134–138. doi:10.1145/1721654.1721691

Grice, P. (1989). *Studies in the way of words*. Boston, MA: Harvard University Press.

Grudin, J. (2011). *Enterprise uses of social media*. Retrieved September 28, 2011, from rkcsi.indiana.edu/Speakers/SpeakerFiles/2011/J_Grudin.pdf

Gubbins, E. (2009, December 22). Move over, geek squad. *Telephony*, 34-36.

Guder, C. (2010). Patrons and pedagogy: A look at the theory of connectivism. *Public Services Quarterly, 6*(1), 36–42. doi:10.1080/15228950903523728

Guillemette, J.-S. (2010, February 17). *Blender 2.5 Alpha 1 and more info on the sprint!* [Web log message]. Retrieved from http://www.sintel.org/news/blender-2-5-alpha-1-and-more-info-on-the-sprint/

Gunkel, D. J. (2003). Second thoughts: Towards a critique of the digital divide. *New Media & Society, 5*, 499–522. doi:10.1177/146144480354003

Gunnell, J. G. (2011). Political science, History of. In G. T. Kurian (Ed.), *The Encyclopedia of Political Science*. Retrieved from http://library.cqpress.com/

Guzman, I. R., & Stanton, J. M. (2009). IT occupational culture: The cultural fit and commitment of new information technologists. *Information Technology & People, 22*(2), 157–187. doi:10.1108/09593840910962212

Haake, J. M., & Pfister, H.-R. (2010). Scripting a distance-learning university course: Do students benefit from net-based scripted collaboration? *International Journal of Computer-Supported Collaborative Learning, 5*(2), 191–210. doi:10.1007/s11412-010-9083-7

Haber, P., & Hodel, J. (2011). Geschichtswissenschaft und Web 2.0. Eine Dokumentation.[History and Web 2.0. A survey.] *The hist.net Working Paper Series, 2.* Retrieved February 12, 2011, from http://www.infoclio.ch/sites/default/files/standard_page/working_paper_geschichte_web2.0.pdf

Hagan, D. (2004). Employer satisfaction with ICT graduates. *Proceedings of the Sixth Conference on Australasian Computing Education,* Vol. 30, (pp. 119–123).

Hajjem, C., Harnad, S., & Gingras, Y. (2005). *Ten-year cross-disciplinary comparison of the growth of open access and how it increases research citation impact.* Retrieved from http://eprints.ecs.soton.ac.uk/11688/1/ArticleIEEE.pdf

Hajo, C. M. (2009). Scholarly editing in a Web 2.0 world. *Documentary Editing, 31,* 92-103. Retrieved June 6, 2011, from http://aphdigital.org/people/cathy-moran-hajo/scholarly-editing-in-a-web-2-0-world/#_ftn1

Halavais, A. (2009). *Search engine society.* Cambridge, MA: Polity Press.

Halic, O., Lee, D., Paulus, T., & Spence, M. (2010). To blog or not to blog: Student perceptions of blog effectiveness for learning in a college-level course. *The Internet and Higher Education, 13*(4), 206–213. doi:10.1016/j.iheduc.2010.04.001

Hall, S. (1992). Cultural identity and diaspora. In Rutherford, J. (Ed.), *Identity: Community, culture, difference.* London, UK: Sage.

Hand, M. (2008). *Making digital cultures: Access, interactivity and authenticity.* Aldershot, UK: Ashgate.

Hanrahan, M. (2007). Plagiarism, instruction, blogs. In Roberts, T. (Ed.), *Student plagiarism in an online world: Problems and solutions* (pp. 183–193). Hershey, PA: IGI. doi:10.4018/978-1-59904-801-7.ch012

Haraway, D. J. (1991). *Simians, cyborgs, and women: The reinvention of nature.* New York, NY: Routledge.

Hargadon, A., & Sutton, R. I. (2000). Building an innovation factory. *Harvard Business Review, 78*(3), 157–166.

Hargittai, E. (2004). Do you "Google"? Understanding search engine use beyond the hype. *First Monday, 9*(3). Retrieved May 7, 2011, from http://firstmonday.org/htbin/cgiwrap/bin/ojs/index.php/fm/article/view/1127/1047

Hargittai, E. (2007). The social, political, economic, and cultural dimensions of search engines: An introduction. *Journal of Computer-Mediated Communication, 12,* 769–777. doi:10.1111/j.1083-6101.2007.00349.x

Hase, S., & Kenyon, C. (2007). Heutagogy: A child of complexity theory. *Complexity: An International Journal of Complexity and Education, 4,* 111-118. Retrieved October 15, 2011, from http://issuu.com/gfbertini/docs/heutagogy_-_a_child_of_complexity_theory.

Hassan, N. (2011, June 7). Syrian blogger Amina Abdallah kidnapped by armed men. *The Guardian.* Retrieved from http://www.guardian.co.uk/world/2011/jun/07/syrian-blogger-amina-abdallah-kidnapped

Hayles, N. K. (1999). *How we became posthuman: Virtual bodies in cybernetics, literature, and informatics.* Chicago, IL: The University of Chicago Press.

Hayles, N. K. (2002). Material metaphors, technotexts, and media-specific analysis. In Hayles, N. K. (Ed.), *Writing machines* (pp. 18–33). Cambridge, MA: Mediawork, The MIT Press.

Hayles, N. K. (2011). How we think: Transforming power and digital technologies. In Berry, D. (Ed.), *Understanding the digital humanities.* London, UK: Palgrave.

Head, A. J., & Eisenberg, M. (2010). How today's college students use Wikipedia for course-related research. *First Monday, 15*(3). Retrieved May 7, 2011, from http://www.uic.edu/htbin/cgiwrap/bin/ojs/index.php/fm/article/view/2830/2476

Head, A. J., & Eisenberg, M. B. (2009). *Finding context: What today's college students say about conducting research in the digital age.* Retrieved from http://projectinfolit.org/pdfs/PIL_ProgressReport_2_2009.pdf

Head, A. J., & Eisenberg, M. B. (2010). *Truth be told: How college students evaluate and use information in the digital age.* Retrieved from http://projectinfolit.org/pdfs/PIL_Fall2010_Survey_FullReport1.pdf

Hellsten, I., Leydesdorff, L., & Wouters, P. (2006). Multiple presents: How search engines rewrite the past. *New Media & Society, 8*(6), 901–924. doi:10.1177/1461444806069648

Hendriks, P. (1999). Why share knowledge? The influence of ICT on the motivation for knowledge sharing. *Knowledge and Process Management, 6*(2), 91–100. doi:10.1002/(SICI)1099-1441(199906)6:2<91::AID-KPM54>3.0.CO;2-M

Hendrix, D., Chiarella, D., Hasman, L., Murphy, S., & Zafron, M. L. (2009). Use of Facebook in academic health libraries. *Journal of the Medical Library Association, 97*(1), 44–47. Retrieved from http://www.ncbi.nlm.nih.gov/pmc/articles/PMC2605034/doi:10.3163/1536-5050.97.1.008

Hennessy, S., Ruthven, K., & Brindley, S. (2005). Teacher perspectives on integrating ICT into subject teaching: Commitment, constraints, caution, and change. *Journal of Curriculum Studies, 37*(2), 155–192. doi:10.1080/0022027032000276961

Herb, U. (2010). Open Access, zitationsbasierte und nutzungsbasierte Impact Maße: Einige Befunde. [Open Access, citation- and user-related impact scales]. In *11th Proceedings of International Society for Knowledge Organization* (ISKO), German Chapter. Retrieved November 7, 2011, from http://eprints.rclis.org/handle/10760/14873#.TrebuHL0_1s

Hijink, M. (2010, August 2). Google kan het heden tot in detail voorspellen. *NRC Handelsblad*, p. 9.

Hilligoss, B., & Rieh, S. Y. (2008). Developing a unifying framework of credibility assessment: Construct, heuristics, and interaction in context. *Information Processing & Management, 44*(4), 1467–1484. doi:10.1016/j.ipm.2007.10.001

History of Wikipedia. (2011). From Wikipedia. Retrieved June 14, 2011, from http://en.Wikipedia.org/wiki/History_of_Wikipedia

Hoffman, D., Novak, T., & Chatterjee, P. (1995). Commercial scenarios for the Web: Opportunities and challenges. *Journal of Computer-Mediated Communication, 1*(3). Retrieved from http://jcmc.indiana.edu/vol1/issue3/hoffman.html

Holmberg, K., Huvila, I., Kronqvist-Berg, M., & Widén-Wulff, G. (2009). What is library 2.0? *The Journal of Documentation, 65*(4), 668–681. doi:10.1108/00220410910970294

Homan, J. M. (1996). Disintermediation and education. *Bulletin of the Medical Library Association, 84*(4), 589–590.

Hong, T. (2006). The influence of structural and message features on Web site credibility. *Journal of the American Society for Information Science and Technology, 57*(1), 114–127. doi:10.1002/asi.20258

Horrigan, J., & Jones, S. (2008). *When technology fails.* Washington, DC: Pew Internet and American Life Project. Retrieved September 21, 2011, from http://www.pewinternet.org/~/media//Files/Reports/2008/PIP_Tech_Failure.pdf.pdf

Hovland, C. I., Janis, I. L., & Kelley, J. J. (1953). *Communication and persuasion.* New Haven, CT: Yale University Press.

Hovland, C. I., & Weiss, W. (1951). The influence of source credibility on communication effectiveness. *Public Opinion Quarterly, 15*, 635–650. doi:10.1086/266350

How does Wikipedia measure up? (2008). *The Quill, 96*(9), 16-19.

Howe, J. (2006). *Crowdsourcing: A definition.* Retrieved July 06, 2011, from http://crowdsourcing.typepad.com/cs/2006/06/crowdsourcing_a.html

Howe, J. (2010, May 17). What if?: An attempt to bring one book to the online masses. *Publishers Weekly, 54.*

Howe, J. (2008). *Crowdsourcing: Why the future of the crowd is driving the future of business.* New York, NY: Crown Business Publishing.

Huckfeldt, R. (2001). The social communication of political expertise. *American Journal of Political Science, 45*(2), 425–438. doi:10.2307/2669350

Hudson-Smith, A., Batty, M., Crooks, A., & Milton, R. (2009). Mapping for the masses: Accessing web 2.0 through crowdsourcing. *Social Science Computer Review, 27*(4), 524–538. doi:10.1177/0894439309332299

Hughes, J. E., & Narayan, R. (2009). Collaboration and learning with Wikis in higher classrooms. *Journal of Interactive Online Learning, 8*(1), 63–77.

Hunter, A. (2009). High-tech rascality: Asperger's syndrome, hackers, geeks, and personality types in the ICT industry. *Editorial: Closing the income gap with Australia*, 39.

Hunter, R., De Lotto, R. J., Frank, A., Gassmann, B., Hallawell, A., & Heiser, J. … Taylor, D. (2009) *What does Google know?* (Gartner Research Report G00158124). Retrieved from http://www.gartner.com/id=918012

Huygens. (2011). Retrieved July 13, 2011, from http://www.huygens.knaw.nl

Huysman, M., & Derksen, F. (1998). Learning from the environment: Exploring the relationship between organizational learning, knowledge management and information/communication technology. *AMCIS 1998 Proceedings*, (p. 200).

Huysman, M., & de Wit, D. (2002). *Knowledge sharing in practice*. Springer.

Huysman, M., & de Wit, D. (2004). Practices of managing knowledge sharing: Towards a second wave of knowledge management. *Knowledge and Process Management, 11*(2), 81–92. doi:10.1002/kpm.192

Huysman, M., & Wulf, V. (2004). *Social capital and information technology*. MIT Press.

Hyde, M., & Mitra, A. (2000). On the ethics of creating a face in cyberspace: The case of a university. In Berdayes, V., & Murphy, J. (Eds.), *Computers, human interaction and organizations* (pp. 161–188). New York, NY: Praeger.

Ikujiro, N., von Krogh, G., & Voelpel, S. (2006). Organizational knowledge creation theory: Evolutionary paths and future advances. *Organization Studies, 27*(8), 1179–1208. doi:10.1177/0170840606066312

Interview with @prsarahevans. (2011, April). *Public Relations Tactics, 13*.

Introna, L. D., & Nissenbaum, H. (2000). Shaping the Web: Why the politics of search engines matter. *The Information Society, 16*, 169–185. doi:10.1080/01972240050133634

Ito, M., Baumer, S., Bittanti, M., Boyd, D., Cody, R., & Herr-Stephenson, B. (2009). *Hanging out, messing around, geeking out: Kids living and learning with new media. MacArthur Foundation Series on Digital Media and Learning*. Cambridge, MA: The MIT Press.

Jacobson, N., Butterill, D., & Goering, P. (2003). Development of a framework for knowledge translation: Understanding user context. *Journal of Health Services Research & Policy, 8*, 94–99. doi:10.1258/135581903321466067

Jacobson, N., Butterill, D., & Goering, P. (2004). Organizational factors that influence university-based researchers' engagement in knowledge transfer activities. *Science Communication, 25*(3), 246. doi:10.1177/1075547003262038

Jacso, P. (2008). The pros and cons of computing the h-index using Google Scholar. *Online Information Review, 32*(3), 437–452. doi:10.1108/14684520810889718

Jaeger, P. T., Paquette, S., & Simmons, S. N. (2010). Information policy in national political campaigns: A comparison of the 2008 campaigns for President of the United States and Prime Minister of Canada. *Journal of Information Technology & Politics, 7*(1), 67–82. doi:10.1080/19331680903316700

Jankowski, N. (Ed.). (2009). *e-Research: Transformations in scholarly practice*. New York, NY: Routledge.

Jarvis, J. (2009). *What would Google do?* New York, NY: Collins Business.

jason 7. (2010, May 15). *Sintel trailer color correction tests (big images)*. [Online forum post]. Retrieved from http://blenderartists.org/forum/showthread.php?187115-sintel-trailer-color-correction-tests-%28big-images%29

Javanmardi, S., & Lopes, C. (2010). Statistical measure of quality in Wikipedia. *Proceedings of the First Workshop on Social Media Analytics*, Washington, DC (p. 132). doi:10.1145/1964858.1964876

Jenkins, H. (with Purushotma, R., Clinton, K., Weigel, M., & Robison, A. J. (2009). *Confronting the challenges of participatory culture: Media education for the 21st century*. Cambridge, MA: MIT Press.

Jenkins, H. (2006). *Convergence culture: Where old and new media collide*. New York, NY: New York University Press.

Johnson, K. (2007). Collectivism vs. individualism in a wiki world: Librarians respond to Jaron Lanier's essay "Digital Maoism: The hazards of the new online collectivism.". *Serials Review, 33*(1), 45–53. doi:10.1016/j.serrev.2006.11.002

Johnson, M., & Liber, O. (2008). The personal learning environment and the human condition: From theory to teaching practice. *Interactive Learning Environments, 16*(1), 3–15. doi:10.1080/10494820701772652

Johnston, R. (1998). The university of the future: Boyer revisited. *Higher Education, 36*, 253–272. doi:10.1023/A:1003264528930

Jones, S., & Fox, S. (2009). *Generations online.* Pew Internet & American Life Project. Retrieved January 10, 2012, from www.pewinternet.org

Jones, C., Ramanau, R., Cross, S., & Healing, G. (2010). Net generation or digital natives: Is there a distinct new generation entering university? *Computers & Education, 54*(3), 722–732. doi:10.1016/j.compedu.2009.09.022

Kahneman, D., Slovic, P., & Tversky, A. (Eds.). (1982). *Judgment under uncertainty: Heuristics and biases.* Cambridge, UK: Cambridge University Press.

Kaid, L. L., & Postelnicu, M. (2006). Credibility of political messages on the Internet: A comparison of blog sources. In Tremayne, M. (Ed.), *Blogging, citizenship, and the future of media* (pp. 149–164). New York, NY: Routledge.

Kai-Wah Chua, S. (2009). Using wikis in academic libraries. *Journal of Academic Librarianship, 35*(2), 170–176. doi:10.1016/j.acalib.2009.01.004

Kakihara, M. (2003). *Emerging work practices of ICT-enabled mobile professionals.* Unpublished doctoral dissertation, University of London, UK.

Kalfatovic, M. R., Kapsalis, E., Spiess, K. P., Van Camp, A., & Edson, M. (2008). Smithsonian Team Flickr: A library, archives, and museums collaboration in Web 2.0 space. *Archival Science, 8*, 267–277. doi:10.1007/s10502-009-9089-y

Kaltenbrunner, W., & Wouters, P. (2010). E-research and methodological innovation in Dutch literary studies. *First Monday, 15*(6). Retrieved July 13, 2011, from http://firstmonday.org/htbin/cgiwrap/bin/ojs/index.php/fm/article/view/3078

Kanalley, C. (January 27, 2011). Egypt's Internet shut down, according to reports. *The Huffington Post.* Retrieved from http://www.huffingtonpost.com/2011/01/27/egypt-internet-goes-down-_n_815156.html

Karp, I. (1992). Introduction: Museums and communities: The politics of public culture. In Karp, I., Kreamer, C. M., & Levine, S. D. (Eds.), *Museums and communities: The politics of public culture* (pp. 1–18). Washington, DC: Smithsonian Institution Press.

Kazepides, T. (2010). *Education as dialogue: Its prerequisites and its elements.* Montreal, Canada: McGill-Queens University Press.

Keen, A. (2008). *Web 1.0 + web 2.0 = web 3.0.* Retrieved July 6, 2011, from http://andrewkeen.typepad.com/the_great_seduction/2008/04/web-10-web-20-w.html

Keen, A. (2007). *Cult of the amateur: How today's Internet is killing our culture and assaulting our economy.* Great Britain: Doubleday/Currency.

Keen, A. (2007). *The cult of the amateur: How today's Internet is killing our culture.* New York, NY: Doubleday.

Keller, J. (2011, January 23). Colleges search for their place in the booming mobile web. *The Chronicle of Higher Education* [Electronic version]. Retrieved June 26, 2011, from http://chronicle.com/article/colleges-search-for-their/126016

Kelly, K. (2010). *What technology wants.* New York, NY: Viking.

Kim, Y. M., & Abbas, J. (2010). Adoption of Library 2.0 functionalities by academic libraries and users: A knowledge management perspective. *Journal of Academic Librarianship, 36*(3), 211–218. doi:10.1016/j.acalib.2010.03.003

King, A. (2007). Scripting collaborative learning processes: A cognitive perspective. In Fischer, F., Kollar, I., Mandl, H., & Haake, J. M. (Eds.), *Scripting computer-supported collaborative learning* (pp. 13–37). New York, NY: Springer. doi:10.1007/978-0-387-36949-5_2

Kittur, A., Chi, E. H., Pendleton, B. A., Suh, B., & Mytko-wicz, T. (2007). Power of the few vs. wisdom of the crowd: Wikipedia and the rise of the bourgeoisie. *Proceedings of the 25th International Conference on Human Factors in Computing Systems*.

Klein, K. E. (2008). *Demystifying Web 2.0: Richard J. Goossen shows how entrepreneurs can make the most of Web 2.0*. Retrieved from http://www.businessweek.com/smallbiz/content/jun2008/sb20080616_188170.htm

Knuppel, M. (2000). *A characterization of the Linux community of practice using Linux newsgroups and Bales' Interaction Process Analysis*. Unpublished Master's thesis, University of North Carolina at Chapel Hill.

Kogan, H. (1958). *The great EB: The story of the Encyclopaedia Britannica*. University of Chicago Press.

Kop, R., & Hill, A. (2008). Connectivism: Learning theory of the future or vestige of the past? *International Review of Research in Open and Distance Learning, 9*(3), 1–13.

Kopytoff, I. (1986). The cultural biography of things: Commoditization as process. In Appadurai, A. (Ed.), *The social life of things: Commodities in cultural perspective* (pp. 64–92). Cambridge, MA: Cambridge University Press.

Krause, M. G., & Yakel, E. (2007). Interaction in virtual archives: The Polar Bear Expedition Digital Collections next generation finding aid. *The American Archivist, 70*(2), 282–314.

Kuhn, T. (1970). *The structure of scientific revolutions* (2nd ed.). Chicago, IL: University of Chicago Press.

Kvavik, R. (2005). Convenience, communications, and control: How students use technology. In Oblinger, D., & Oblinger, J. L. (Eds.), *Educating the Net generation*. Boulder, CO: Educause.

Lakhani, K. R., & von Hippel, E. (2003). How open source software works: "Free" user-to-user assistance. *Research Policy, 32*(6), 923–943. doi:10.1016/S0048-7333(02)00095-1

Lamb, B. (2005). *C-SPAN Q&A, Jimmy Wales*. Retrieved June 20, 2011, from http://www.q-and-a.org/Transcript/?ProgramID=1042

Lang, E., Wyer, P., & Haynes, R. Brian. (2007). Knowledge translation: Closing the evidence-to-practice gap. *Annals of Emergency Medicine, 49*(3), 355–363. doi:10.1016/j.annemergmed.2006.08.022

Lanier, J. (2006). *Digital Maoism: The hazards of the new online collectivism*. Retrieved July 6, 2011, from http://www.edge.org/3rd_culture/lanier06/lanier06_index.html

Lanier, J. (2010a, September 15). Does the digital classroom enfeeble the mind? *The New York Times*, p. MM32.

Lanier, J. (2010). *You are not a gadget*. New York, NY: Knopf.

Lanier, J. (2010b). *You are not a gadget: A manifesto*. New York, NY: Alfred A. Knopf.

Lankes, R. D. (2007). Trusting the internet: New approaches to credibility tools. In Metzberger, M. J., & Flanagin, A. J. (Eds.), *Digital media, youth, and credibility* (pp. 101–121). Cambridge, MA: The MIT Press.

Lankes, R. D. (2008). Trusting the Internet: New approaches to credibility tools. In Metzger, M. J., & Flanagin, A. J. (Eds.), *Digital media, youth, and credibility* (pp. 101–122). Cambridge, MA: The MIT Press.

Laouris, Y., Underwood, G., Laouri, R., & Christakis, A. (2010). Structured dialogue embedded within emerging technologies. In G. Veletsianos (Ed.), *Emerging technologies in distance education* (pp. 153-173). Athabasca, Canada: Athabasca University Press. Retrieved February 28, 2011, from http://www.aupress.ca/index.php/books/120177

Laurillard, D. (2002). *Rethinking university teaching: A conversational framework for the effective use of learning technologies*. New York, NY: RoutledgeFalmer. doi:10.4324/9780203304846

Lee, A., Danis, C., Miller, T., & Jung, Y. (2001). Fostering social interaction in online spaces. In M. Hirose (Ed.), *INTERACT '01: Proceedings of the Eighth IFIP Conference on Human-Computer Interaction* (pp. 59-66). Amsterdam, The Netherlands: IOS·Press.

Lee, M. J. W., & McLoughlin, C. (2010). Social software as tools for pedagogical transformation: Enabling personalization, creative production, and participatory learning. In Lambropoulos, N., & Romero, M. (Eds.), *Educational social software for context-aware learning: Collaborative methods and human interaction* (pp. 1–22). New York, NY: Information Science Reference.

Lenhart, A. (January 14, 2009). Social networks grow: Friending Mom and Dad. *Pew Internet & American Life Project.* Retrieved from http://pewresearch.org/pubs/1079/social-networks-grow

Lenhart, A., Purcell, K., Smith, A., & Zickuhr, K. (2010). Social media & mobile internet use among teens and young adults. *Pew Internet & American Life Project.* Retrieved September 22, 2011, from http://www.pewinternet.org/~/media//Files/Reports/2010/PIP_Social_Media_and_Young_Adults_Report_Final_with_toplines.pdf

Leonard, B. (2010, September 18). *Encoding issues – A call for help.* [Web log message]. Retrieved from http://www.sintel.org/news/3622/

Lepore, E., & Van Gulick, R. (Eds.). (1991). *John Searle and his critics*. Oxford, UK: Blackwell.

Lessig, L. (2004). *Free culture: How big media uses technology and the law to lock down culture and control creativity*. New York, NY: Penguin.

Lessig, L. (2005). Open code and open societies. In Feller, J., Fitzgerald, B., Hissam, S. A., & Lakhani, K. R. (Eds.), *Perspectives on free and open source software* (pp. 349–360). Cambridge, MA: The MIT Press.

Leu, D. J. Jr. (2001, March). Internet project: Preparing students for new literacies in a global village [Exploring Literacy on the Internet department]. *The Reading Teacher, 54*(6). Retrieved from http://www.readingonline.org/electronic/elec_index.asp?HREF=/electronic/RT/3-01_Column/index.html

Levy, C. (2009, October 8). *Directorial address 01* [Video file]. Retrieved from http://www.sintel.org/news/directorial-address-01/

Levy, S. (2010b, February 16). *Community modeling sprint!* [Web log message]. Retrieved from http://www.sintel.org/news/community-modeling-sprint/

Levy, S. (2010c, February 21). *Modeling sprint—A stellar success!* [Web log message]. Retrieved from http://www.sintel.org/news/modeling-sprint-a-stellar-success/

Levy, S. (2010d, March 25). *Community sprint: Background characters!* [Web log message]. Retrieved from http://www.sintel.org/news/community-sprint-background-characters/

Levy, S. (2010e, March 27). *Background character sprint: Details* [Web log message]. Retrieved from http://www.sintel.org/production/background-character-sprint-details/

Levy, S. (2010f, April 12). *Make us a backpack!* [Web log message]. Retrieved from http://www.sintel.org/production/make-us-a-backpack/

Levy, P. (1997). *Collective intelligence: Mankind's emerging world in cyberspace*. New York, NY: Basic Books.

Lih, A. (2009). *The Wikipedia revolution: How a bunch of nobodies created the world's greatest encyclopedia*. New York, NY: Hyperion.

Lin, H.-F. (2007). Knowledge sharing and firm innovation capability: An empirical study. *International Journal of Manpower, 28*(3/4), 315–332. doi:10.1108/01437720710755272

Linholm-Romantschuk, Y. (1998). *The flow of ideas within and among disciplines*. Westport, CT: Greenwood Press.

Lipka, S. (2009, May 1). Colleges using technology to recruit students try to hang on to the conversation. *The Chronicle of Higher Education* [Electronic version]. Retrieved June 1, 2011, from http://chronicle.com/article/colleges-using-technology-to/117193

Liskov, B. (2011). *The power of abstraction*. Retrieved January 10, 2012, from http://www.stanford.edu/class/ee380/Abstracts/110420.html

Lohr, S. (2009, August 6). For today's graduate, just one word: Statistics. *The New York Times*, Technology section. Retrieved May 7, 2011, from http://www.nytimes.com/2009/08/06/technology/06stats.html

Losee, R. (2010). Comment-6572. In B. Dansie, (2010b, February 7). *Guardians – Community help.* [Comment on Web log message]. Retrieved from http://www.sintel.org/news/guardians-community-help/

Lovegrove, G., & Round, A. (2005). *IT professionals in education: Increasing the supply.* Report from the north-east regional meeting, November 2005. Retrieved from http://www.bcs.org/upload/pdf/itprofnewcastle.pdf

Lu, L., & Yuan, Y. C. (2011). Shall I Google it or ask the competent villain down the hall? The moderating role of information need in information source selection. *Journal of the American Society for Information Science and Technology, 62*(1), 133–145. doi:10.1002/asi.21449

Lyons, D. (2009). Don't Tweet on me. *Newsweek, 154*(13), 31.

Lyons, W. (1995). *Approaches to intentionality.* Oxford, UK: Clarendon Press.

Mack, D., Behler, A., Roberts, B., & Rimland, E. (2007). Reaching students with Facebook: Data and best practices. *Electronic Journal of Academic and Special Librarianship, 8*(2). Retrieved from http://southernlibrarianship.icaap.org/content/v08n02/mack_d01.html

Mackiewicz, J. (2007). *Reviewer bias and credibility in online reviews.* Paper presented at the Association for Business Communication Annual Convention.

Madden, M., & Fox, S. (2006). *Riding the waves of "Web 2.0."* Retrieved from http://pewresearch.org/pubs/71/riding-the-waves-of-web-20

Maeter, S. (2010, May 9). *F12's.* [Web log message]. Retrieved from http://www.sintel.org/news/f12s/

Magnus, P. D. (2008). Early response to false claims in Wikipedia. *First Monday, 13*(9). Retrieved from http://search.ebscohost.com.proxy.iwu.edu/login.aspx?direct=true&db=edsref&AN=IDBEEJCC&site=eds-live&scope=site

Mahatanankoon, P., & O'Sullivan, P. (2008). Attitude toward mobile text messaging: An expectancy-based perspective. *Journal of Computer-Mediated Communication, 13,* 973–992. doi:10.1111/j.1083-6101.2008.00427.x

Maloney, E. J. (2007). What Web 2.0 can teach us about learning. *Chronicle of Higher Education, 53*(18). Retrieved June 28, 2011, from http://chronicle.com

Marfleet, B. G., & Dille, B. J. (2005). Information literacy and the undergraduate research methods curriculum. *Journal of Political Science Education, 1*(2), 175–190. doi:10.1080/15512160590961793

Margaryan, A., Littlejohn, A., & Vojt, G. (2011). Are digital natives a myth or reality? University students' use of digital technologies. *Computers & Education, 56*(2), 429–440. doi:10.1016/j.compedu.2010.09.004

Markland, M. (2005). Does the student's love of the search engine mean that high quality online academic resources are being missed? *Performance Measurement and Metrics: The International Journal for Library and Information Services, 6*(1), 19–31. doi:10.1108/14678040510588562

Marsh, K. (2011, May 7). A gay girl in Damascus becomes a heroine of the Syrian revolt. *The Guardian.* Retrieved from http://www.guardian.co.uk/world/2011/may/06/gay-girl-damascus-syria-blog

Martin, B. (1998). *Information liberation: Challenging the corruptions of information power.* London, UK: Freedom Press.

Mateos-Garcia, J., & Steinmueller, W. E. (2008). The institutions of open source software: Examining the Debian community. *Information Economics and Policy, 20*(4), 333–344. doi:10.1016/j.infoecopol.2008.06.001

Matthews, R. J. (2007). *The measure of mind: Propositional attitudes and their attribution.* Oxford, UK: Oxford University Press.

Matusiak, K. K. (2006). Towards user-centered indexing in digital image collections. *OCLC Systems & Services: International Digital Library Perspectives, 22*(4), 283–298.

Mauriello, N., & Pagnucci, G. S. (2003). Balancing acts: Tightrope walking above an ever changing (Inter)Net. In Takayoshi, P., & Huot, B. (Eds.), *Teaching writing with computers. An introduction* (pp. 79–91). Boston, MA: Houghton Mifflin Company.

McCargo, D., & Hyon-Suk, L. (2010). Japan's political tsunami: What's media got to do with it? *The International Journal of Press/Politics, 15*(2), 236–245. doi:10.1177/1940161210361588

McClurg, S. D. (2006). The electoral relevance of political talk: Examining disagreement and expertise effects in social networks on political participation. *American Journal of Political Science, 50*(3), 737–754. doi:10.1111/j.1540-5907.2006.00213.x

McFedries, T. (2007). Technically speaking: All a-twitter. *IEEE Spectrum, 44*(10), 84. doi:10.1109/MSPEC.2007.4337670

McGann, J. J. (2001). *Radiant textuality: Literature after the World Wide Web*. New York, NY: Palgrave.

McGowan, D. (2005). Legal aspects of free and open source software. In Feller, J., Fitzgerald, B., Hissam, S. A., & Lakhani, K. R. (Eds.), *Perspectives on free and open source software* (pp. 361–391). Cambridge, MA: The MIT Press.

McHaney, R. (2011). *The new digital shoreline: How Web 2.0 and Millennials are revolutionizing higher education*. Sterling, VA: Stylus Publishing, LCC.

McLoughlin, C., & Lee, M. J. W. (2010). Personalized and self regulated learning in the Web 2.0 era: International exemplars of innovative pedagogy using social software. *Australasian Journal of Educational Technology, 26*(1), 28–43.

McLuhan, M., & Fiore, Q. (2005). *The medium is the massage*. Berkeley, CA: Gingko Press. (Original work published 1967)

McWilliams, J., Hickey, D. T., & Hines, M. B. (2011). Using collaborative writing tools for literary analysis: Twitter, fan fiction and *The Crucible* in the secondary English classroom. *Journal of Media Literacy Education, 2*(3), 238–245.

Media Awareness Network. (2004, February). *Young Canadians in a wired world- Phase II: Focus groups*. Retrieved January 10, 2012, from www.media-awareness.ca/english/special_initiatives/surveys/phase_two/index.cfm

Meola, M. (2004). Chucking the checklist: A contextual approach to teaching undergraduates web-site evaluation. *portal. Libraries and the Academy, 4*(3), 331–344. doi:10.1353/pla.2004.0055

Meschini, F. (unpublished). *e-Content, tradizionale, semantico o 2.0?* = e-Content, traditional, semantic or 2.0? Retrieved from http://dspace.unitus.it/handle/2067/162

Metzger, M. J. (2007). Making sense of credibility on the web: Models for evaluating online information and recommendations for future research. *Journal of the American Society for Information Science and Technology, 58*(13), 2078–2091. doi:10.1002/asi.20672

Metzger, M. J., Flanagin, A. J., Eyal, K., Lemus, D. R., & McCann, R. (2003). Bringing the concept of credibility into the 21st century: Integrating perspectives on source, message, and media credibility in the contemporary media environment. *Communication Yearbook, 27*, 293–335. doi:10.1207/s15567419cy2701_10

Metzger, M. J., Flanagin, A. J., & Medders, R. (2010). Social and heuristic approaches to credibility evaluation online. *The Journal of Communication, 60*(3), 413–439. doi:10.1111/j.1460-2466.2010.01488.x

Metzger, M. J., Flanagin, A. J., & Zwarun, L. (2003). College student web use, perceptions of information credibility, and verification behavior. *Computers & Education, 41*(3), 271–290. doi:10.1016/S0360-1315(03)00049-6

Meyer, T. (2011). Virtuelle Forschungsumgebungen in der Geschichtswissenschaft – Lösungsansätze und Perspektiven [Virtual research environments for history –approaches.]. *LIBREAS. Library Ideas, 7*(18). Retrieved June 9, 2011, from http://www.ib.hu-berlin.de/~libreas/libreas_neu/ausgabe18/texte/05meyer.htm

Michalski, J. (1995). People are the killer app. *Forbes ASAP*, June 5, 120-122.

Mikki, S. (2009). Google Scholar compared to Web of science: A literature review. *Nordic Journal of Information Literacy in Higher Education, 1*(1), 41–51.

Miller, C., & Bilton, N. (2010, October 31). Why Twitter's C.E.O. demoted himself. *New York Times*, p. 1.

Miller, S. E., & Jensen, L. A. (2007). Connecting and communicating with students on Facebook. *Computers in Libraries, 27*(8), 18–29. Retrieved from http://www.infotoday.com/cilmag/sep07/index.shtml

Miners, Z. (2009, June 2). Twitter goes to college. *US News & World Report*. Retrieved from http://usnews.com/articles/education/2009/06/02/twitter-goes-to-college_print.htm

Mitchell, W. J. (1995). *City of bits: Space, place and the Infobahn*. Cambridge, MA: The MIT Press.

Mitra, A. (2002). Trust, authenticity and discursive power in cyberspace. *Communications of the ACM*, *45*(3), 27–29. doi:10.1145/504729.504748

Mitra, A., & Schwartz, R. L. (2001). From cyber space to cybernetic space: Rethinking the relationship between real and virtual spaces. *Journal of Computer-Mediated Communication*, *7*(1). Retrieved from http://jcmc.indiana.edu/vol7/issue1/mitra.html.

Moleke, P., Paterson, A., & Roodt, J. (2003). *ICT and associated professionals. Human resources development review 2003: Education, employment and skills in South Africa* (pp. 634–659). Cape Town, South Africa: HSRC Press.

Molenda, M. (1997). Historical and philosophical foundations of instructional design: A North American view. In Tennyson, R., Schott, F., Seel, N., & Dijkstra, S. (Eds.), *Instructional design: International perspectives* (pp. 41–53). Lawrence Erlbaum Associates.

Moore, M. G. (2007). Web 2.0: Does it really matter? *American Journal of Distance Education*, *21*(4), 177–183. doi:10.1080/08923640701595183

Moran, M., Seaman, J., & Tinti-Kane, H. (2011). *Teaching, learning, and sharing: How today's higher education faculty use social media*. Retrieved September 12, 2011, from http://www.babson.edu/Academics/Documents/babson-survey-research-group/teaching-learning-and-sharing.pdf

Morozov, E. (2011). *The Net delusion: How not to liberate the world*. New York, NY: Penguin.

Morozov, E. (2011, March 24). E-salvation [Review of the book *What technology wants*]. *New Republic (New York, N.Y.)*, *242*(4), 28–31.

Morville, P. (2005) *Ambient findability*. Cambridge, MA: O'Reilly Publishing.

Nagata, K. (2011, June 10). New media keep old media honest. *The Japan Times Online*. Retrieved from http://search.japantimes.co.jp/cgi-bin/nb20110610a1.html

Nardi, B., Whittaker, S., & Schwartz, H. (2002). NetWorks and their activity in intensional networks. *Computer Supported Cooperative Work*, *11*(1), 205–242. doi:10.1023/A:1015241914483

National Research Council. (2000). *How people learn: Brain, mind, experience, and school*. Washington, DC: National Academy Press.

Negroponte, N. (1997). Re-intermediated. *Wired*, 5.09.

Nelson, T. (1987). *Computer lib/Dream machines* (Rev. ed.). Redmond, WA: Tempus Books of Microsoft Press. (Original work published 1974)

Nentwich, M., & König, R. (2010). Peer Review 2.0: Herausforderungen und Chancen der wissenschaftlichen Qualitätskontrolle im Zeitalter der Cyber-Wissenschaft. [Peer Review 2.0: Challanges and chances of scholarly quality monitoring in the age of cyber-science.] In Gasteiner, P., & Haber, P. (Eds.), *Digitale Arbeitstechniken für Geistes- und Kulturwissenschaften* [Digital work methods for the humanities and cultural sciences]. (pp. 143–163). Vienna, Austria: Böhlau.

Neuhaus, C., Neuhaus, E., Asher, A., & Wrede, C. (2006). The depth and breadth of Google Scholar: An empirical study. *Libraries and the Academy*, *6*(2), 127–141. doi:10.1353/pla.2006.0026

New Media Consortium & EDUCAUSE Learning Initiative. (2007). *The horizon report: 2007 edition*. Austin, TX: The New Media Consortium.

Next Pixel (Producer) & Blender Foundation. (Producer). (2010). *Sintel making of/documentary* [Video]. Retrieved from http://www.youtube.com/watch?v=IN6w6GnN-Ic

Nicholson, S., Sierra, T., Eseryel, U., Park, J., Barkow, P., Pozo, E., & Ward, J. (2006). How much of it is real? Analysis of paid placement in Web search engine results. *Journal of the American Society for Information Science American Society for Information Science*, *57*(4), 448–461.

Nordan, N. A. M., Abidin, A. I. Z., Mahmood, A. K., & Arshad, N. I. (2008). Digital social networks: Examining the knowledge characteristics. *World Academy of Science. Engineering and Technology*, *45*, 248–254.

North Carolina State University. (2011). *Architexture: Composing and constructing in digital space*. Retrieved October 1, 2011, from http://chasslamp.chass.ncsu.edu/~cw2012/cfp

Nowotny, H., Scott, P., & Gibbons, M. (2003). Introduction: Mode 2' revisited: The new production of knowledge. *Minerva*, *41*(3), 179–194. doi:10.1023/A:1025505528250

Nupedia. (2011). From Wikipedia. Retrieved 06/07, 2011, from http://en.Wikipedia.org/w/index.php?title=Nupedia&oldid=434451549

Nygren, E., Haya, G., & Widmark, W. (2006). Students experience of Metalib and Google Scholar. *Online Information Review, 31*(3), 365–375.

O'Connell, M. (2010). "To text or not to text": Reticence and the utilization of short message services. *Human Communication, 13*(2), 87–102.

O'Keefe, D. J. (2002). *Persuasion: Theory & research.* Thousand Oaks, CA: Sage Publications, Inc.

O'Neill, D. K., Asgari, M., & Dong, Y. R. (2011). Trade-offs between perceptions of success and planned outcomes in an online mentoring program. *Mentoring & Tutoring: Partnership in Learning, 19*(1), 45–63. doi:10.1080/13611267.2011.543570

O'Reilly, T. (2005). *What is Web 2.0: Design patterns and business models for the next generation of software.* Retrieved from http://oreilly.com/web2/archive/what-is-web-20.html

O'Reilly, T. (2005a). The open source paradigm shift. In Feller, J., Fitzgerald, B., Hissam, S. A., & Lakhani, K. R. (Eds.), *Perspectives on free and open source software* (pp. 461–481). Cambridge, MA: The MIT Press.

O'Toole, J., & Cox, R. (2006). *Understanding archives and manuscripts.* Chicago, IL: Society of American Archivists.

Oblinger, D., & Rush, S. C. (Eds.). (1997). *The learning revolution. The challenge of information technology in the academy.* Bolton, MA: Anker Publishing Company.

Olsen, J., & Statham, A. (2005). Critical thinking in political science: Evidence from the introductory comparative politics course. *Journal of Political Science Education, 1*(3), 323–344. doi:10.1080/15512160500261186

Online Computer Library Center. (2005). *College students' perceptions of libraries and information resources.* Dublin, OH: OCLC. Retrieved May 7, 2011, from http://www.oclc.org/reports/perceptionscollege.htm

Online Computer Library Center. (2007). *Sharing, privacy and trust in our networked world.* Retrieved from http://www.oclc.org/reports/sharing/default.htm

Open Access Directory. (2011). Retrieved July 06, 2011, from http://oad.simmons.edu/oadwiki/Main_Page

Open Source Software. (2011). From Wikipedia. Retrieved July 06, 2011, from http://en.Wikipedia.org/w/index.php?title=Open_source&oldid=438039561

O'Reilly, T. (2006, October). Web 2.0 compact definition: Trying again. *Radar.* Retrieved from http://radar.oreilly.com/archives/2006/12/web-20-compact.html

Orlikowski, W. J. (2002). Knowing in practice: Enacting a collective capability in distributed organizing. *Organization Science, 13*(3), 249–273. doi:10.1287/orsc.13.3.249.2776

Owen, M. (2004). *The myth of the digital native.* Retrieved January 10, 2012, from www.futurelab.org.uk/resources/publications_reports_articles/web_articles/Web_Article561

Owen-Smith, J., & Powell, W. W. (2004). Knowledge networks as channels and conduits: The effects of spillovers in the Boston biotechnology community. *Organization Science, 15*(1), 5–21. doi:10.1287/orsc.1030.0054

Pan, B., Hembrooke, H., Joachims, T., Lorigo, L., Gay, G., & Granka, L. (2007). In Google we trust: Users' decisions on rank, position, and relevance. *Journal of Computer-Mediated Communication, 12*, 801–823. doi:10.1111/j.1083-6101.2007.00351.x

Pardo Kuklinski, H. (2010). *Geekonomia. Un radar para producir en el postdigitalismo.* Barcelona, Spain: LMI/Publicacions i Edicions de la Universitat de Barcelona.

Pariser, E. (2011). *The filter bubble. What the Internet is hiding from you.* New York, NY: Penguin.

Parry, M. (2011, February 20). Free "video book" from MIT Press challenges limits of scholarship. *Chronicle of Higher Education.* Retrieved September 17, 2011, from http://chronicle.com/article/Free-Video-Book-From/126427

Pask, G. (1976). *Conversation theory: Applications in education and epistemology.* New York, NY: Elsevier.

Pau, R., Argles, D., White, S., & Lovegrove, G. (2005). *Computer geek versus computer chic: IT career and IT education*. 6th International Women into Computing Conference, Greenwich, UK. Retrieved from http://eprints.ecs.soton.ac.uk/id/eprint/10840

Paulson, S. (2011, June 19). Does Islam stand against science? *The Chronicle of Higher Education* [Electronic version]. Retrieved June 27, 2011, from http://chronicle.com/article/does-Islam-stand-against/127924

Paulus, T. M., Payne, R. L., & Jahns, L. (2009). "Am I making sense here?": What blogging reveals about undergraduate student understanding. *Journal of Interactive Online Learning, 8*(1), 1–22.

Pawlowski, S., & Robey, D. (2004). Bridging user organizations: Knowledge brokering and the work of information technology professionals. *Management Information Systems Quarterly, 28*, 645–672.

Penny, C., & Bolton, D. (2010). Evaluating the outcomes of an eMentoring program. *Journal of Educational Technology Systems, 39*(1), 17–30. doi:10.2190/ET.39.1.c

Pershing, B. (2009). *Kennedy, Byrd the latest victims of Wikipedia errors*. Retrieved June 27, 2011, from http://voices.washingtonpost.com/capitol-briefing/2009/01/kennedy_the_latest_victim_of_w.html

Petrilli, M. J. (2011). All a-Twitter about education: Improving our schools in 140 characters or less. *Education Next, 11*(4), 90–91.

Pidaparthy, U. (2011). *How colleges use, misuse social media to reach students*. Retrieved January 08, 2012, from www.cnn.com/2011/10/20/tech/social-media/universities-social-media/index.html?hpt=hp_bn6

Pidduck, A. B. (2010). Electronic social networks, teaching, and learning. In W. A. Wright, M. Wilson, & D. MacIssac (Eds.), *Collected essays on learning and teaching, Volume III* (pp. 106-111). STHLE Society for Teaching and Learning in Higher Education/SAPES Société pour l'avancement de la pédogie dans l'enseignement superior. Retrieved February 4, 2011, from http://apps.medialab.uwindsor.ca/ctl/CELT/vol3/CELT18.pdf.

Poe, M. (2006). The hive. *Atlantic Monthly, 298*(2), 86. Retrieved from http://search.ebscohost.com.proxy.iwu.edu/login.aspx?direct=true&db=aph&AN=21796182&site=eds-live&scope=site

Pogatchnik, S. (2009). Student hoaxes world's media on Wikipedia. Retrieved June 29, 2011, from http://www.msnbc.msn.com/id/30699302/ns/technology_and_science-tech_and_gadgets/t/student-hoaxes-worlds-media-Wikipedia/

Poll Everywhere. (2011). *Poll Everywhere: Instant audience feedback*. Retrieved October 5, 2011, from http://www.polleverywhere.com

Polsby, N. W. (2001). Political science: Overview. In Neil, J. S., & Paul, B. B. (Eds.), *International encyclopedia of the social & behavioral sciences* (pp. 11698–11701). Amsterdam, The Netherlands: Elsevier. doi:10.1016/B0-08-043076-7/01283-3

Popkin, H. A. S. (2007). *Twitter nation: Nobody cares what you're doing*. Technotica on MSNBC.com. Retrieved from http://www.msnbc.msn.com/id/18445274/

Poritz, J. (2007). Who searches the searchers? Community privacy in the age of monolithic search engines. *The Information Society, 23*(5), 383–389. doi:10.1080/01972240701572921

Postman, N. (1992). *Technopoly: The surrender of culture to technology*. New York, NY: Vintage Books.

Powers, C., Schmidt, J., & Hill, C. (2008). Why can't we be friends? The MSU libraries find friends on Facebook. *Mississippi Libraries, 72*(1), 3–5.

Prensky, M. (2001). Digital natives, Digital immigrants, part II: Do they really think differently? *Horizon, 9*(6). Retrieved from http://marcprensky.com/writing/Prensky%20-%20Digital%20Natives,%20Digital%20Immigrants%20-%20Part2.pdf-doi:10.1108/10748120110424843

Presner, T. (2010). *Digital humanities 2.0: A report on knowledge*. Retrieved July 13, 2011, from http://cnx.org/content/m34246/latest/

Procter, R., Williams, R., Stewart, J., Poschen, M., & Snee, H. (1926). Voss, A., & Asgari-Tarhi, M. (2010). Adoption and use of Web 2.0 in scholarly communications. *Philosophical Transactions of the Royal Society A, Theme Issue: e-Science: Past. Present and Future II, 368,* 4039–4056. doi:doi:10.1098/rsta.2010.0155

Qderth. (2011, June 10). *Rebecca Black: Friday* (official video). Retrieved June 27, 2011, from http://www.youtube.com/watch?v=9u9-AdPAOy0

Quality Assurance Agency for Higher Education. (2000). *Subject benchmark statements: Politics and international relations.* Retrieved June 16, 2011, from http://www.qaa.ac.uk/Publications/InformationAndGuidance/Pages/Subject-benchmark-statement-Polictics-and-international-relations.aspx

Rains, S. A., & Karmikel, C. D. (2009). Health information-seeking and perceptions of website credibility: Examining Web-use orientation, message characteristics, and structural features of websites. *Computers in Human Behavior, 25*(2), 544–553. doi:10.1016/j.chb.2008.11.005

Randall, M., & Kellian, C. (2009). How do you know that?: An investigation of student research practices in the digital age. *portal. Libraries and the Academy, 9*(1), 115–132. doi:10.1353/pla.0.0033

Rankin, M. (2009). *Some general comments on the "Twitter Experiment" by Monica Rankin (UT Dallas).* Monica Rankin's Home Page. Retrieved from http://www.utdallas.edu/~mrankin/usweb/twitterconclusions.htm

Ravenscroft, A. (2011). Dialogue and connectivism: A new approach to understanding and promoting dialogue-rich networked learning. *International Review of Research in Open and Distance Learning, 12*(3), 139–160.

Raymond, E. (1999). The cathedral and the bazaar. *Knowledge, Technology & Policy, 12*(3), 23. Retrieved from http://search.ebscohost.com.proxy.iwu.edu/login.aspx?direct=true&db=ehh&AN=6128761&site=eds-live&scope=sitedoi:10.1007/s12130-999-1026-0

Raymond, E. S. (2001). *The cathedral and the bazaar: Musings on Linux and open source by an accidental revolutionary.* Sebastopol, CA: O'Reilly & Associates.

Raynes-Goldie, K. (2010). Aliases, creeping, and wall cleaning: Understanding privacy in the age of Facebook. *First Monday, 15*(1). Retrieved from http://firstmonday.org/htbin/cgiwrap/bin/ojs/index.php/fm/article/view/2775/2432

Read, B. (2006). Can Wikipedia ever make the grade? *The Chronicle of Higher Education, 53*(10), A31–A36. Retrieved from http://search.ebscohost.com.proxy.iwu.edu/login.aspx?direct=true&db=ehh&AN=22984124&site=eds-live&scope=site

Rector, L. H. (2008). Comparison of Wikipedia and other encyclopedias for accuracy, breadth, and depth in historical articles. *RSR. Reference Services Review, 36*(1), 7. Retrieved from http://search.ebscohost.com.proxy.iwu.edu/login.aspx?direct=true&db=eda&AN=32895218&site=eds-live&scope=sitedoi:10.1108/00907320810851998

Reher, K. (Producer), & Newton, T. (Director). (2010). *Day & Night* [Short Animation]. Pixar. Retrieved from http://www.youtube.com/watch?v=VpN0vwgVBZk

Revoy, D. (2010a). Comment-6699. In B. Dansie, (2010b, February 7). *Guardians—Community help.* [Comment on Web log message]. Retrieved from http://www.sintel.org/news/guardians-community-help/

Revoy, D. (2010b). Comment-6722. In B. Dansie, (2010b, February 7). *Guardians—Community help.* [Comment on Web log message]. Retrieved from http://www.sintel.org/news/guardians-community-help/

Reyerson, K., Mummey, K., & Higdon, J. (2011). Medieval cities of Europe: Click, tweet, map, and present. *The History Teacher, 44*(3), 353–367.

Rheingold, H. (2009). Crap detection 101. *SFGate.* Retrieved September 22, 2011, from http://blog.sfgate.com/rheingold/2009/06/30/crap-detection-101/

Rheingold, H. (2000). *The virtual community: Homesteading on the electronic frontier.* Cambridge, MA: The MIT Press.

Rheingold, H. (2008). Using participatory media and public voice to encourage civic engagement. In Bennett, W. L. (Ed.), *Civic life online: Learning how digital media can engage youth* [PDF version]. (pp. 97–118).

Rheingold, H. (2010). Attention, and other 21st-century social media literacies. *EDUCAUSE Review, 45*(5), 14–24.

Rhoten, D., Racine, L., & Wang, P. (2009). *Designing for learning in the 21st century* (Working paper). Retrieved from http://startl.org/about/the-future-of-learning/

Riedl, J. (2011). The promise and peril of social computing. *IEEE Computer*, January, 93-95.

Rieh, S. Y., & Belkin, N. J. (1998). Understanding judgment of information quality and cognitive authority in the WWW. *Proceedings of the 61st Annual Meeting of the American Society for Information Science* (Vol. 35, pp. 279-289).

RIN (Research Information Network). (2010). *If you build it, will they come? How researchers perceive and use Web 2.0*. Retrieved July 13, 2011, from http://www.rin.ac.uk/our-work/communicating-and-disseminating-research/use-and-relevance-Web-20-researchers

Rinaldo, S. B., Tapp, S., & Laverie, D. A. (2011). Learning by Tweeting: Using Twitter as a pedagogical tool. *Journal of Marketing Education*, *33*(2), 193–203. doi:10.1177/0273475311410852

Roberts, D. F., Foehr, U. G., & Rideout, V. (2005). *Generation M: Media in the lives of 8–18-year-olds*. The Kaiser Family Foundation.

Roberts, C. (2010). Correlations among variables in message and messenger credibility scales. *The American Behavioral Scientist*, *54*(1), 43–56. doi:10.1177/0002764210376310

Robinson, A. M., & Schlegl, K. (2005). Student use of the Internet for research projects: A problem? Our problem? What can we do about it? *PS: Political Science and Politics*, *38*(2), 311–315.

Robson, N., & Rew, D. (2010). Collective wisdom and decision making in surgical oncology. [EJSO]. *European Journal of Surgical Oncology*, *36*(3), 230–236. doi:10.1016/j.ejso.2010.01.002

Rogers, R. (2005). *Information politics on the Web*. Cambridge, MA: The MIT Press.

Roosendaal, T. (2009a, May 5). *Call for participation* [Web log message]. Retrieved from http://www.sintel.org/applications/

Roosendaal, T. (2009b, May 5). *Durian Project announcement* [Web log message]. Retrieved from http://www.sintel.org/news/durian-project-announcement/

Roosendaal, T. (2010a, April 21). *Logo / identity design* [Web log message]. Retrieved from http://www.sintel.org/news/logo-identity-design/

Roosendaal, T. (2010b, April 27). *Logo part 2* [Web log message]. Retrieved from http://www.sintel.org/production/logo-part-2/

Roosendaal, T. (2010c, May 13). *Sintel trailer!* [Web log message]. Retrieved from http://www.sintel.org/news/sintel-teaser/

Roosendaal, T. (2010d, August 24). *Get Blender graphics on 35mm film* [Web log message]. Retrieved from http://www.sintel.org/news/get-blender-graphics-on-35mm-film/

Rosen, R. R. (September 3, 2011). So, was Facebook responsible for the Arab Spring after all? *The Atlantic Online*. Retrieved from http://www.theatlantic.com/technology/archive/2011/09/so-was-facebook-responsible-for-the-arab-spring-after-all/244314/

Rowlands, I., Nicholas, D., Williams, P., Huntington, P., Fieldhouse, M., & Gunter, B. (2008). The Google generation: The information behaviour of the researcher of the future. *Aslib Proceedings*, *60*(4), 290–310. doi:10.1108/00012530810887953

Rushkoff, D. (2010). *Program or be programmed: Ten commands for a digital age*. New York, NY: OR Books.

Russo, A., Watkins, J., Kelly, L., & Chan, S. (2008, January). Participatory communication with social media. *Curator*, *51*(1), 21–31. doi:10.1111/j.2151-6952.2008.tb00292.x

Ruth, A., & Houghton, L. (2009). The wiki way of learning. *Australasian Journal of Educational Technology*, *25*(2), 135–152.

Sahle, P. (2008). eScience history? In M.-L. Heckmann, J. Röhrkasten, & S. Jenks (Eds.), *Von Nowgorod bis London. Studien zu Handel, Wirtschaft und Gesellschaft im mittelalterlichen Europa. Festschrift für Stuart Jenks zum 60. Geburtstag* [From Novgorod to London. Studies on trade, economy and society in medieval Europe. Festschrift in honour of Stuart Jenk's 60th birthday] (pp. 63-74). Göttingen, Germany: V&R unipress.

Salas, E., Rosen, M. A., Burke, C. S., Goodwin, G. F., & Fiore, S. M. (2006). The making of a dream team: When expert teams do best. In Ericsson, K. A., Charness, N., Feltovich, P. J., & Hoffman, R. R. (Eds.), *The Cambridge handbook of expertise and expert performance* (pp. 439–453). Cambridge, UK: Cambridge University Press. doi:10.1017/CBO9780511816796.025

Sanger, L. M. (2006). *Why make room for experts in Web 2.0?* Retrieved June 14, 2011, from http://www.Bomis.org/roomforexperts.html

Sanger, L. M. (2007). *Who says we know? On the new politics of knowledge.* Retrieved June 14, 2011, from http://edge.org/conversation/who-says-we-know-on-the-new-politics-of-knowledge

Sanger, L. M. (2009). The fate of expertise after "Wikipedia." *Episteme: A Journal of Social Epistemology, 6*(1), 52-73. Retrieved from http://search.ebscohost.com.proxy.iwu.edu/login.aspx?direct=true&db=phl&AN=PHL2133300&site=eds-live&scope=site

Sarkar, M. B., Butler, B., & Steinfield, C. (1995). Intermediaries and cybermediaries: A continuing role for mediating players in the electronic marketplace. *Journal of Computer-Mediated Communication, I*(3). Retrieved from http://jcmc.indiana.edu/vol1/issue3/sarkar.html

SAS Institute. (2008). *SAS* (version 9.1) [software].

Savage, N. (2011, March). Twitter as medium and message. *Communications of the ACM, 54*(3), 18–20. doi:10.1145/1897852.1897860

Savage, W. W. (2009). Scribble, scribble, toil and trouble: Forced productivity in the modern university. In Greco, A. N. (Ed.), *The state of scholarly publishing: Challenges and opportunities* (pp. 1–7). New Brunswick, NJ: Transaction.

Scanfeld, D., Scanfeld, V., & Larson, E. L. (2010). Dissemination of health information through social networks: Twitter and antibiotics. *American Journal of Infection Control, 38*, 182–188. doi:10.1016/j.ajic.2009.11.004

Schiff, S. (2006). Know it all: Can Wikipedia conquer expertise? *New Yorker (New York, N.Y.), 82*(23), 36–43. Retrieved from http://search.ebscohost.com.proxy.iwu.edu/login.aspx?direct=true&db=mzh&AN=2006534151&site=eds-live&scope=site

Schiltz, M., Truyen, F., & Coppens, H. (2007). Cutting the trees of knowledge: Social software, information architecture and their epistemic consequences. *Thesis Eleven, 89*, 94-114.

Schmale, W. (2010). *Digitale Geschichtswissenschaft* [Digital history]. Vienna, Austria: Böhlau.

Schmidt, J. (2007). Promoting library services in a Google world. *Library Management, 28*(6), 337–346. doi:10.1108/01435120710774477

Schonfeld, R. C., & Housewright, R. (2010). *Faculty survey 2009: Strategic insights for librarians, publishers, and societies.* Retrieved from http://www.ithaka.org/ithaka-s-r/research/faculty-surveys-2000-09/Faculty%20Study%202009.pdf

Schreibman, S., Siemens, R., & Unsworth, J. (2001). *A companion to digital humanities.* London, UK: Blackwell.

Schroeder, A., Minocha, S., & Schneider, C. (2010). The strengths, weaknesses, opportunities and threats of using social software in higher and further education teaching and learning. *Journal of Computer Assisted Learning, 26*, 159–174. doi:10.1111/j.1365-2729.2010.00347.x

Schroeder, R. (2007). Pointing users toward citation searching: Using Google Scholar and Web of Science. *Libraries and the Academy, 7*(2), 243–248. doi:10.1353/pla.2007.0022

Schuff, D., Mandviwalla, M., Williams, C., & Wattal, S. (2010). Web 2.0 and politics: The 2008 U.S. presidential election and an e-politics research agenda. *Management Information Systems Quarterly, 34*(4), 669–688.

Schulmeister, R. (2008). *Gibt es eine "Net Generation"?* Manuscript in preparation. Retrieved February 25, 2012, from www.zhw.uni-hamburg.de/pdfs/Schulmeister_Netzgeneration.pdf

Schweiger, W. (2000). Experience or image? A survey on the credibility of the world wide web in Germany in comparison to other media. *European Journal of Communication, 15*, 37–59. doi:10.1177/0267323100015001002

Schweik, C. M. (2007). Free/open source software as a framework for establishing commons in science. In Hess, C., & Ostrom, E. (Eds.), *Understanding knowledge as a commons: From theory to practice* (pp. 277–309). Cambridge, MA: The MIT Press.

Scolari, C. A. (2008). *Hipermediaciones. Elementos para una teoría de la comunicación digital interactiva.* Barcelona, Spain: Gedisa.

Scolari, C. A. (2009). Mapping conversations about new media: The theoretical field of digital communication. *New Media & Society, 11,* 943–964. doi:10.1177/1461444809336513

Searle, J. (1983). *Intentionality: An essay in the philosophy of mind.* Cambridge, UK: Cambridge University Press. doi:10.1017/CBO9781139173452

Secretary of Education's Commission on the Future of Higher Education. (2006). *A test of leadership: Charting the future of U.S. higher education.* Washington, DC: U.S. Department of Education, Education Publications Center.

Segal, D. (2010, February 12). The dirty little secrets of search. *The New York Times,* Business section. Retrieved May 7, 2011, from http://www.nytimes.com/2011/02/13/business/13search.html

Segev, E. (2008). Search engines and power: A politics of online (mis-)information. *Webology, 5*(2). Retrieved May 7, 2011, from http://www.webology.ir/2008/v5n2/a54.html

Selfe, C. (1999). *Technology and literacy in the twenty-first century: The importance of paying attention.* Carbondale, IL: Southern Illinois University Press.

Selfe, C. (2009). Aurality and multimodal composing. *College Composition and Communication, 60*(4), 616–663.

Serres, M. (2011). *Tom Thumb – New challenges of education.* Retrieved January 10, 2012, from pensees-dunfrancaisenhongrie.over-blog.com/article-discours-de-michel-serres-sur-l-enseignement-86546463.html

Shafie, L. A., Azida, N., & Osman, N. (2010). SMS language and college writing: The language of the college texters. *International Journal of Emerging Technologies in Learning, 5*(1), 26–31.

Shah, C., Oh, S., & Oh, J. S. (2009). Research agenda for social Q&A. *Library & Information Science Research, 31*(4), 205–209. doi:10.1016/j.lisr.2009.07.006

Shilton, K., & Srinivasan, R. (2007). Participatory appraisal and arrangement for multicultural archival collections. *Archivaria, 63,* 87–101.

Shirky, C. (2008). *Here comes everybody: The power of organizing without organizations.* New York, NY: Penguin Books.

Shirky, C. (2010). *Cognitive surplus: Creativity and generosity in a connected age.* New York, NY: Penguin.

Siegel, L. (2008). *Against the machine: Being human in the age of the electronic mob.* New York, NY: Spiegel and Grau.

Siemens, G. (2004). *Connectivism: A learning theory for the Digital Age.* Retrieved from http://www.elearnspace.org/Articles/connectivism.htm

Siemens, G. (November 12, 2006). *Connectivism: Learning theory or pastime for the self-amused?* Retrieved from http://www.elearnspace.org/Articles/connectivism_self-amused.htm

Sifry, M. L. (2011). *Wikileaks and the age of transparency.* Berkeley, CA: Counterpoint.

Silver, D. (2000). Looking backwards, looking forward: Cyberculture studies 1990-2000. In D. Gauntlett, D. (Ed.), *Web studies: Rewiring media studies for the digital age* (1st ed.). London, UK: Arnold. Retrieved from http://www.com.washington.edu/rccs/intro.asp

Simon, H. A., & Chase, W. G. (1973). Skill in chess. *American Scientist, 61,* 394–403.

Sintel. (2011). Retrieved June 15, 2011, from http://www.sintel.org/

Sloam, J. (2008). Teaching democracy: The role of political science education. *British Journal of Politics and International Relations, 10*(3), 509–524. doi:10.1111/j.1467-856X.2008.00332.x

Smith, D. (2011, June 28). How do you solve a problem like clay shirky? Or, Silicon Valley discovers impact factor. Retrieved from http://scholarlykitchen.sspnet.org/2011/06/28/how-do-you-solve-a-problem-like-clay-shirky-or-silicon-valley-discovers-impact-factor/

Smith, K. (2009). *The Twitter experiment: Twitter in the classroom.* Retrieved from http://www.youtube.com/watch?v=6WPVWDkF7U8

Smith, N. J. J. (2008). *Vagueness and degrees of truth.* Oxford, UK: Oxford University Press. doi:10.1093/acprof:oso/9780199233007.001.0001

Social Informatics. (2012). Retrieved January 10, 2012, from rkcsi.indiana.edu/

Sosa, E. (2003). The place of truth in epistemology. In DePaul, M., & Zagzebski, L. (Eds.), *Intellectual virtue: Perspectives from ethics and epistemology.* Oxford, UK: Oxford University Press.

South, S. R. (2010). Making the move from shouting to listening to public action: A student perspective on millennials and dialogue. *Journal of Public Deliberation,* 6(1), 1–10.

Springer, M., Dulabahn, B., Michel, P., Natanson, B., Reser, D., Woodward, D., & Zinkham, H. (2008, October). *For the common good: The Library of Congress Flickr pilot project.* Washington, DC: Library of Congress.

Srinivasan, R., Boast, R., Becvar, K. M., & Furner, J. (2009). Blobgects: Digital museum catalogs and diverse user communities. *Journal of the American Society for Information Science and Technology,* 60(4), 666–678. doi:10.1002/asi.21027

Statistics. (2011). From Wikipedia. Retrieved 07/06, 2011, from http://en.Wikipedia.org/wiki/Special:Statistics

Stephenson, G. (2011). I don't get Twitter. *Our Schools/Our Selves,* 20(3), 197-200.

Stevens, C. R., & Campbell, P. J. (2006). Collaborating to connect global citizenship, information literacy, and lifelong learning in the global studies classroom. *RSR. Reference Services Review,* 34(4), 536–556. doi:10.1108/00907320610716431

Stevens, C. R., & Campbell, P. J. (2009). Collaborating with librarians to develop lower division political science students' information literacy competencies. *Journal of Political Science Education,* 4(2), 225–252. doi:10.1080/15512160801998114

Stevens, C., & Campbell, P. (2007). The politics of information literacy: Integrating information literacy into the political science curriculum. In Jacobson, T., & Mackey, T. (Eds.), *Information literacy collaborations that work* (pp. 123–146). New York, NY: Neal-Schuman.

Straus, S., Tetroe, J., & Graham, I. (2009a). Defining knowledge translation. *Canadian Medical Association Journal,* 181, 165–168. doi:10.1503/cmaj.081229

Straus, S., Tetroe, J., & Graham, I. (2009b). *Knowledge translation in health care: Moving from evidence to practice.* Chichester, UK: John Wiley and Sons. doi:10.1002/9781444311747

Stross, R. (2006). Anonymous source is not the same as open source. *New York Times (Late City Edition),* 155, 5. Retrieved from http://search.ebscohost.com.proxy.iwu.edu/login.aspx?direct=true&db=eda&AN=20642306&site=eds-live&scope=site

Stutzman, F. (2006, December). *Unit structures: The network effect multiplier, or Metcalfe's flaw.* Retrieved from http://chimprawk.blogspot.com/2006/07/network-effect-multiplier-or-metcalfes.html

Sudsawad, P. (2007). *Knowledge translation: Introduction to models, strategies and measures.* Austin, TX: Southwest Educational Development Laboratory, National Center for the Dissemination of Disability Research.

Suh, B., Convertino, G., Chi, E., & Pirolli, P. (2009). The singularity is not near: Slowing growth of Wikipedia. *WikiSym '09 Proceedings of the 5th International Symposium on Wikis and Open Collaboration,* Orlando, Florida. doi:10.1145/1641309.1641322

Sunstein, C. R. (2006). *Infotopia. How many minds produce knowledge.* Oxford, UK: Oxford University Press.

Sunstein, C. R. (2006). *Infotopia: How many minds produce knowledge.* New York, NY: Oxford University Press.

SURF. (2011). Retrieved July 13, 2011, from http://www.surf.nl

Surowiecki, J. (2004). *The wisdom of crowds: Why the many are smarter than the few and how collective wisdom shapes business, economies, societies and nations.* Anchor.

Sweeny, S. M. (2010). Writing for the instant messaging and text messaging generation: Using new literacies to support writing instruction. *Journal of Adolescent & Adult Literacy,* 52(2), 121–130. doi:10.1598/JAAL.54.2.4

Sweetser, K. D. (2007). Blog bias: Reports, inferences, and judgments of credentialed bloggers at the 2004 nominating conventions. *Public Relations Review*, *33*(4), 424–428. doi:10.1016/j.pubrev.2007.08.012

Tamarkin, M. & The 2010 EDUCAUSE Evolving Technologies Committee. (2010, November). December). You 3.0: The most important evolving technology. *EDUCAUSE Review*, *45*(6), 30–44.

Tapscott, D. (1998). *Growing up digital: The rise of the Net Generation*. New York, NY: McGraw Hill.

Tapscott, D. (2009). *Grown up digital: How the Net Generation is changing your world*. New York, NY: McGraw Hill.

Tapscott, D., & Williams, A. D. (2006). *Wikinomics: How mass collaboration changes everything*. New York, NY: Penguin.

Taraborelli, D. (2008). How the Web is changing the way we trust. *Proceeding of the 2008 Conference on Current Issues in Computing and Philosophy* (pp. 194-204). IOS Press.

Taylor, S. (2007). Google Scholar—Friend or foe? *Interlending & Document Supply*, *35*(1), 4–6. doi:10.1108/02641610710728122

Teeuwen, M. in collaboration with Brouwer, T., Stancefield Eastwood, B., Garrison, M., Guillaumin, J., Lozovsky, N., ... Sroczynski, A. (2010). *Carolingian scholarship and Martianus Capella: The oldest commentary tradition*. Retrieved July 13, 2011, from http://martianus.huygensinstituut.knaw.nl

Theoharidou, M., & Gritzalis, D. (2007). Common body of knowledge for information security. *Security & Privacy*, *5*(2), 64–67. doi:10.1109/MSP.2007.32

Thomas, D., & Brown, J. S. (2011). *A new culture of learning: Cultivating the imagination for a world of constant change*. PA: Breinigsville.

Thompson-Canino, J., Cotton, R., & Torneo, E. (2009). *Picking cotton: Our memoir of injustice and redemption*. New York, NY: St. Martin's Press.

Thornton, S. (2006). Information literacy and the teaching of politics. *LATISS: Learning and Teaching in the Social Sciences*, *3*(1), 29–45. doi:10.1386/ltss.3.1.29_1

Thornton, S. (2008). Pedagogy, politics and information literacy. *Politics*, *28*(1), 50–56. doi:10.1111/j.1467-9256.2007.00310.x

Thornton, S. (2010). From "scuba diving" to "jet skiing"? Information behavior, political science, and the Google generation. *Journal of Political Science Education*, *6*(4), 353–368. doi:10.1080/15512169.2010.518111

Tierney, J. (2011, April 26). A generation's vanity, heard through lyrics. *The New York Times*, p. D1.

Toffler, A. (1980). *The third wave: Democratization in the late twentieth century*. New York, NY: Bantam Books.

Tomer, C. (2002). Open source. [New York, NY: Macmillan Reference USA.]. *Computer Sciences*, *3*, 155–158.

Top Sites in the United States. (2011). From Alexa. Retrieved June 20, 2011, from http://www.alexa.com/topsites/countries/US

Toral, S. L., Martínez-Torres, M. R., Barrero, F., & Cortés, F. (2009). An empirical study of the driving forces behind online communities. *Internet Research*, *19*(4), 378–392. doi:10.1108/10662240910981353

Tucker, R. (2010, May 27). Disintermediation: The disruption to come for Education 2.0. *Reading About Leading*. Retrieved from http://www.readingaboutleading.com/?p=767

Tuominen, K., Savolainen, R., & Talja, S. (2005). Information literacy as a sociotechnical practice. *The Library Quarterly*, *75*(3), 329–345. doi:10.1086/497311

Turing, A. M. (1950). Computing machinery and intelligence. *Mind*, *59*(236), 433–460. doi:10.1093/mind/LIX.236.433

Turkle, S. (1984). *The second self: Computers and the human spirit*. New York, NY: Simon and Schuster. doi:10.1177/089443938600400229

Turkle, S. (2011). *Alone together: Why we expect more from technology and less from each other*. New York, NY: Basic Books.

Twitter. (2011). *Twitter is the best way to discover what's new in your world*. Retrieved June 23, 2011, from http://www.twitter.com/about

Unger, P. (1975). *Ignorance*. Oxford, UK: Oxford University Press.

Usher, N. (2010). Goodbye to the news: How out-of-work journalists assess enduring news values and the new media landscape. *New Media & Society*, *12*(6), 911–928. doi:10.1177/1461444809350899

Van Couvering, E. (2007). Is relevance relevant? Market, science, and war: Discourse of search engine quality. *Journal of Computer-Mediated Communication, 12*. Retrieved May 8, 2011, from http://jcmc.indiana.edu/vol12/issue3/vancouvering.html

Van den Hooff, B., Elving, W., Meeuwsen, J. M., & Dumoulin, C. (2003). Knowledge sharing in knowledge communities. In Huysman, M., Wenger, E., & Wulf, V. (Eds.), *Communities and technologies* (pp. 119–141). Deventer, The Netherlands: Kluwer, B.V.

van Dijck, J. (2009). Users like you: Theorizing agency in user-generated content. *Media Culture & Society*, *31*(1), 41–58. doi:10.1177/0163443708098245

Van Doren, C. (1962). The idea of an encyclopedia. *The American Behavioral Scientist*, *6*(1), 23. Retrieved from http://search.ebscohost.com.proxy.iwu.edu/login.aspx?direct=true&db=eda&AN=53228037&site=eds-live&scope=sitedoi:10.1177/000276426200600105

van Zundert, J., & Boot, P. (2011). The digital edition 2.0: Services, not resources. *Bibliothek und Wissenschaft*, *44*(2011), 141-152.

van Zundert, J., Zeldenrust, D., & Beaulieu, A. (2009). Alfalab. Construction and deconstruction of a digital humanities experiment. *Proceeding of the IEEE e-Science Conference*, December 9-11, 2009 (pp. 1-5). Oxford, UK. Retrieved October 8, 2011, from http://alfalablog.huygensinstituut.nl/wp-content/bestanden/2010/10/Alfalab-paper-Oxford-2009.pdf

van Zundert, J., Antonijevic, S., Beaulieu, A., van Dalen-Oskam, K., Zeldenrust, D., & Andrews, T. (2011). Cultures of formalization: Towards an encounter between humanities and computing. In Berry, D. (Ed.), *Understanding the digital humanities*. London, UK: Palgrave.

Varma, R. (2007). Women in computing: The role of geek culture. *Science as Culture*, *16*(4), 359. doi:10.1080/09505430701706707

Viégas, F. B., Wattenberg, M., Kriss, J., & van Ham, F. (2007). Talk before you type: Coordination in Wikipedia. *Proceedings of the 40th Annual Hawaii International Conference on System Sciences* (HICSS'07), (p. 78a). doi:10.1109/HICSS.2007.511

Virilio, P. (1997). *Open sky*. London, UK: Verso.

Von Konsky, B. (2008). Defining the ICT profession: A partnership of stakeholders. *Proceedings of the 21st Annual NACCQ Conference*, (pp. 4–7).

von Schiller, J. C. F. (2004). *On the aesthetical education of man* (R. Snell, Trans.). New York, NY: Dover. (Republication of Schiller, F. (1954). *On the aesthetical education of man* (R. Snell, Trans.). New Haven: Yale University Press. (Original work published in 1794-1795)

Vygotsky, L. (1978). *Mind in society*. Cambridge, MA: Harvard University Press.

Waldrop, M. M. (2008, January 9). Science 2.0: Great new tool, or great risk? Wikis, blogs and other collaborative Web technologies could usher in a new era of science. Or not. *Scientific American*. Retrieved June 8, 2011, from http://www.scientificamerican.com/article.cfm?id=science-2-point-0-great-new-tool-or-great-risk

Wallis, J. (2005). Cyberspace, information literacy and the information society. *Library Review*, *54*(4), 218–222. doi:10.1108/00242530510593407

Walters, W. H. (2007). Google Scholar coverage of a multidisciplinary field. *Information Processing & Management*, *43*(4), 1121–1132. doi:10.1016/j.ipm.2006.08.006

Warnick, B. (2004). Online ethos: Source credibility in an "authorless" environment. *The American Behavioral Scientist*, *48*(2), 256–265. doi:10.1177/0002764204267273

Webster, T. (2010). *Twitter usage in America: 2010*. The Edison Research/Arbitron Internet and Multimedia Study.

Weinberger, D. (2007). *Everything is miscellaneous: The power of the new digital disorder*. New York, Ny: Henry Holt and Company.

Weinberger, A., Ertl, B., Fischer, F., & Mandl, H. (2005). Epistemic and social scripts in computer-supported collaborative learning. *Instructional Science*, *33*(1), 1–30. doi:10.1007/s11251-004-2322-4

Weinberger, D. (2002). *Small pieces loosely joined: A unified theory of the Web*. New York, NY: Basic Books.

Weinberger, D. (2007). *Everything is miscellaneous: The power of the new digital disorder*. New York, NY: Times Books.

Weiner, R. (2011, June 6). Fight brews over Sarah Palin on Paul Revere Wikipedia page. *The Washington Post* [Electronic version]. Retrieved June 27, 2011, from http://www.washingtonpost.com/blogs/the-fix/post/sarah-palin-fans-fight-over-paul-revere-wikipedia-page/2011/06/06/AGxtzHKH_blog.html

Weiser, M. (1991). The computer for the twenty-first century. *Scientific American, 265*(3), 94–104. doi:10.1038/scientificamerican0991-94

Weiss, A. (2005). The power of collective intelligence. *netWorker, 9*(3), 16–23. doi:10.1145/1086762.1086763

Weller, M. (2011). A pedagogy of abundance. *Spanish Journal of Pedagogy, 249*, 223–236.

Wexelblat, A., & Maes, P. (1999). Footprints: History-rich tools for information foraging. In *Proceedings of the SIGCHI Conference on Human Factors in Computing Systems: The CHI Is the Limit* (pp. 270-277). New York, NY: ACM Press.

White, B. (2007). Examining the claims of Google Scholar as a serious information source. *New Zealand Library & Information Management Journal, 50*(1), 11–24.

Whitworth, A. (2009). *Information obesity*. Oxford, UK: Chandos. doi:10.1533/9781780630045

Wikipedians. (2012). From Wikipedia. Retrieved January 26, 2012, from http://en.wikipedia.org/wiki/Wikipedia:Wikipedians#cite_note-0

Williams, G. (2007). Unclear on the context: Refocusing on information literacy's evaluative component in the age of Google. *Library Philosophy and Practice, 6*. Retrieved May 7, 2011, from http://www.encyclopedia.com/Library+Philosophy+and+Practice/publications.aspx?date=200706&pageNumber=1

Williams, M. H., & Evans, J. J. (2008). Factors in information literacy education. *Journal of Political Science Education, 4*(1), 116–130. doi:10.1080/15512160701816234

Williams, M. H., Goodson, K. A., & Howard, W. G. (2006). Weighing the research paper option: The difference that information literacy skills can make. *PS: Political Science & Politics, 39*(3), 513–519. doi:10.1017/S1049096506060793

Willigham, D. T. (2009). *Why don't students like school?* San Francisco, CA: Jossey-Bass.

Wilson, P. (1983). *Second-hand knowledge: An inquiry into cognitive authority*. Westport, CT: Greenwood Press.

Winchester, S. (1998). *The professor and the madman: A tale of murder, insanity, and the making of the Oxford English Dictionary* (1st ed.). New York, NY: HarperCollins.

Winchester, S. (2003). *The meaning of everything: The story of the Oxford English Dictionary*. New York, NY: Oxford University Press.

Wise, A., & Duffy, T. M. (2008). Designing online conversations to engage local practice: Implications of a knowledge-building framework. In R. Luppicini (Ed.), *Handbook of conversation design for instructional applications* (pp. 177-200). Hershey, PA: Information Science Reference (Idea Group Inc.).

Wise, A. F., & O'Neill, D. K. (2009). Beyond "more" versus "less": A reframing of the debate on instructional guidance. In Tobias, S., & Duffy, T. M. (Eds.), *Constructivist instruction: Success or failure?* (pp. 82–105). New York, NY: Routledge, Taylor and Francis.

Wiske, S. (2002). A new culture of teaching for the 21st century. In Gordon, D. T. (Ed.), *The digital classroom: How technology is changing the way we teach and learn* (pp. 69–77). Cambridge, MA: Harvard Education Letter.

Wood, C., Jackson, E., Hart, L., Plester, B., & Wilde, L. (2011). The effect of text messaging on 9- and 10-year-old children's reading, spelling, and phonological processing skills. *Journal of Computer Assisted Learning, 27*, 28–36. doi:10.1111/j.1365-2729.2010.00398.x

Wouters, P., & Beaulieu, A. (2006). Imagining e-science beyond computation. In Hine, C. (Ed.), *New infrastructures for knowledge production: Understanding e-science* (pp. 48–70). Hershey, PA: Idea Group. doi:10.4018/978-1-59140-717-1.ch003

Wouters, P., & Beaulieu, A. (2007). Critical accountability: Dilemmas for interventionist studies of e-science. *Journal of Computer-Mediated Communication, 12*(2). doi:10.1111/j.1083-6101.2007.00339.x

Wright, N. (2010, November). Twittering in teacher education: reflecting on practicum experiences. *Open Learning, 25*(3), 259–265. doi:10.1080/02680513.2010.512102

Xu, B., Jones, D. R., & Shao, B. (2009). Volunteers' involvement in online community based software development. *Information & Management, 46*(3), 151–158. doi:10.1016/j.im.2008.12.005

Yakel, E. (2006). Inviting the user into the virtual archives. *OCLC Systems & Services: International Digital Library Perspectives, 22*(3), 159–163.

Young, J. (2003). The extent to which information communication technology careers fulfill the career ideals of girls. *Australasian Journal of Information Systems, 10*(2), 115–125.

Yueng, C. A., Noll, M. G., Meinel, C., Gibbens, N., & Shadbolt, N. (2011). Measuring expertise in online communities. *Intelligent Systems, IEEE, 26*(1), 26–32. doi:10.1109/MIS.2011.18

Zhao, H. (1999). *A qualitative study of the linux open source community.* Unpublished Master's thesis, University of North Carolina at Chapel Hill.

About the Contributors

Tatjana Takševa studied Literature and Linguistics at the University of Belgrade, Former Yugoslavia, and the Humanities at York University, Canada. She holds an M.A. and a Ph.D. from the University of Toronto, Canada. Currently, she is Associate Professor at the Department of English at Saint Mary's University, Canada, where she teaches courses in literature and culture. In addition to having published a monograph on 17th century reading habits in the manuscript medium and models of literary knowledge dissemination, as well as scholarly articles on literary subjects, she is the author of numerous articles and book chapters on ICT, pedagogy, cross-cultural communication and the digital humanities. Her research interests are focused on how different media in historical contexts affect human cognition, as well as cultural models of knowledge creation and dissemination.

* * *

Cheryl Amundsen is Director of the Institute for the Study of Teaching and Learning in the Disciplines and Associate Professor in the Faculty of Education at Simon Fraser University, British Columbia, Canada. She has a long-standing interest in academic development and her research has focused on how academics develop pedagogical knowledge in relationship to their subject matter and the thinking underlying instructional decisions. More recently, she has ventured beyond the focus on classroom teaching to look at the pedagogy of doctoral education and identity development of early career academics (doctoral students, postdocs, and pre-tenure faculty).

Anne Beaulieu is project manager of the Groningen Energy and Sustainability Programme. She joined the University of Groningen following several years as senior research fellow at the Royal Netherlands Academy of Arts and Sciences (KNAW), where she also acted as deputy programme leader of the Virtual Knowledge Studio for the Humanities and Social Sciences between 2005 and 2010. Before that, she investigated the development of neuroimaging and cognitive neuroscience, (PhD University of Amsterdam 2000). In 1999, she was appointed Lecturer in Science, Culture and Communication, in Bath, UK. A dominant theme in Beaulieu's work is the importance of interfaces for the creation and circulation of knowledge. Past research projects at the KNAW in the area of e-science and e-research focused on data-sharing, on knowledge networks, and on visualisation and visual knowledge. Beaulieu has also done extensive work in the field of digital humanities, on new (ethnographic) research methods and on ethics in e-research.

Werner Beuschel is Professor of Information Management in Brandenburg, Germany, where he started the Business Informatics curriculum at Brandenburg University of Applied Sciences in 1993. He received his Diploma and Ph.D. in Computer Science from the Technical University Berlin. Dr. Beuschel has been involved in CSCL (Computer Supported Cooperative Learning) activities for many years. He was a co-organizer of the Virtual University of Applied Sciences in Germany, which is offering online-curricula since 2001. He worked as a lecturer and was a visiting researcher at the University of California, Irvine, where he is affiliated with the CRADL Lab at the Bren School of Information and Computer Sciences. His current research interests include Web-based learning environments, digital support of creative design phases, and social media in higher education.

Filip Buekens (1959) holds a PhD in philosophy and is Associate Professor at Tilburg University (Tilburg Center for Logic and Philosophy of Language) and Professor of Philosophy at the University of Leuven (Belgium). He is currently working on social ontology, applying John Searle's theory of institutions to religious and anthropological phenomena. His published work also includes articles on the conflict between the scientific and the manifest image, theories of truth and accuracy, and semantics.

Licia Calvi is a Senior Lecturer at NHTV Breda University of Applied Sciences (The Netherlands), where she teaches Interactivity and Interaction Design and Media Theory in the Master of Media Innovation. She is Senior Researcher at ICEMER, the International Centre for Experimental Media Effect Research at NHTV where she is responsible for the Casual Medialab as part of the international project on "Biometric Design for Casual Games" she is coordinating since 2010. Her current research interests are in the field of culture and heritage, digital libraries, new media, interaction design and interactivity, interactive art. She is a member of the editorial board of the *International Journal of E-learning, of Social and Humanistic Computing,* and *of Technology Enhanced Learning.*

Maria Cassella is Librarian Coordinator at the University of Turin, as well as the Coordinator of the National University and Research Committee of the Italian Libraries Association. She is author or co-author of many scholarly articles, chapters and books published in Italian and in English. Her current research interests are in the fields of digital libraries, open access, scholarly communication, statistics and evaluation, mobile applications. Since 2008 Maria Cassella is part of the working group of the Wiki OA Italia, the Italian wiki on open access. Since 2009 she has been member of the IFLA Standing Committee on Statistics and Evaluation. She is in the editorial board of the *Italian Journal of Library and Information Science.*

Emily Clark holds a Master of Science in Information Studies from the School of Information at the University of Texas at Austin with a focus in audio and digital media archives, and a Bachelor of Arts in Ethnomusicology from Oberlin College. She is particularly interested in investigating the use of audio, video, and other media as pedagogical tools for cross-cultural learning and communication. Other academic interests include field recordings, oral history, human rights archives, and intellectual property law in regards to traditional cultural and artistic expression. Emily currently volunteers as a consultant in the archives of a number of non-profit organizations in Chicago, acting on her belief that a lack of government or corporate resources should not prevent an institution from maintaining, developing, and sharing its material culture and history.

Cristóbal Cobo Romaní is a research fellow at the Oxford Internet Institute - University of Oxford. He coordinates research on innovation and knowledge transference, learning and future Internet: KNetworks or SESERV (FP7, European Commission). Hi research has been acknowledged as Distinguished by the British Council of Economic and Social Research (ESRC), and he received his PhD "cum laudem" in Communication Sciences at Universitat Autònoma de Barcelona. He is the co-author of *Invisible Learning* (2011). He has been a speaker in 15 countries (+ 2 TEDx).

Laurie Craig Phipps is a continuing faculty member in the department of Business Quantitative Methods at Kwantlen Polytechnic University. He is also currently a PhD student in Educational Technology & Learning Design at Simon Fraser University. His major research interest is the role of dialogue for learning within fully online or 'blended' courses in higher education. Other interests include the use of technology in higher education and the role of faculty in promoting learning with and through technology.

Karina van Dalen-Oskam is head of the Department of Literary Studies / Textual Scholarship at the Huygens Institute for the History of the Netherlands, a research institute of the Royal Netherlands Academy of Arts and Sciences (KNAW). She is a literary scholar in the discipline of digital and computational humanities, focusing on stylistic analysis of Medieval Dutch texts and Modern Dutch and English fiction. One of the stylistic elements she analyzes is proper names in modern novels, which she approaches with methods inspired by computational linguistics. She is project leader of eLaborate and of The Riddle of Literary Quality, in which she collaborates with researchers of the Fryske Akademy and the Institute for Logic, Language and Computation of the University of Amsterdam.

José van Dijck is a Professor of Comparative Media Studies at the University of Amsterdam. She has a PhD in Comparative Literature from the University of California, San Diego (UCSD) and previously taught at the Universities of Groningen and Maastricht. Her visiting appointments include MIT, UC Santa Cruz, Concordia University Montreal and University of Technology, Sydney. Her work covers a wide range of topics in media theory, media technologies, cultural memory, social media, television and culture. She is the author/editor of over one hundred articles and eight books, including *Manufacturing Babies and Public Consent: Debating the New Reproductive Technologies* (New York University Press, 1995); *ImagEnation: Popular Images of Genetics* (New York University Press, 1998); *The Transparent Body: A Cultural Analysis of Medical Imaging* (Seattle: University of Washington Press, 2005); and *Mediated Memories in the Digital Age* (Stanford University Press 2007).

Megan Fitzgibbons is currently a Liaison Librarian at McGill University, where she works with the department of Political Science, the department of Educational Counselling and Psychology, and the School of Continuing Studies language programs to meet students' and faculty members' learning and research needs through many facets of library services. Her research interests include learner-centered approaches to teaching, embedded librarianship, Web 2.0 tools for information management, information literacy, and library outreach to diverse populations. She completed her Master of Library and Information Studies degree at Dalhousie University in Halifax, Nova Scotia.

Andrew Flanagin (Ph.D., Annenberg School for Communication, University of Southern California) is a Professor in the Department of Communication at the University of California at Santa Barbara, where he also serves as the Director of the Center for Information Technology and Society. His research focuses on the ways in which information and communication technologies structure and extend human interaction, with particular emphasis on the processes of organizing and information evaluation and sharing.

Tamara Girardi is a PhD candidate at Indiana University of Pennsylvania where she is writing her dissertation "It *Can* Be Acquired and Learned: Building a Writer-Centered Pedagogical Approach to Creative Writing." She has presented workshops on engaging Twitter as a means of networking with other published authors and publishing professionals such as literary agents and editors for Pittsburgh area writers' groups and conferences. With a Master of Letters in Creative Writing from the University of St. Andrews in Scotland, she writes young adult fiction that features on fantastical and paranormal elements. She teaches composition courses at Westmoreland County Community College.

Abigail Grant is currently finishing her PhD in Composition and TESOL at Indiana University of Pennsylvania where she is writing a dissertation on teacher training for online instructors. She is also working as an English Instructor at College of the Albemarle in Elizabeth City, North Carolina. Grant also serves as an adjunct instructor for Everest College of Phoenix online and the University of Phoenix. Her research interests are online pedagogy, technology in first-year writing courses, and the relationship of mutuality and technology.

Alison S. Gregory is an Assistant Professor and Instructional Services Librarian at Lycoming College in Williamsport, PA. In addition to teaching undergraduate research and information skills, she coordinates the library's extensive outreach events for students, faculty and staff. Alison earned her Bachelor of Arts degree in history from Lycoming College and her Master of Science in Library Science from Clarion University of Pennsylvania. Her research interests include the role of faculty-librarian collaboration in the development of undergraduate research and the use of problem-based learning and other active learning pedagogies in information literacy instruction.

Ethan Hartsell (M.A. University of California, Santa Barbara) received his Master's Degree in Communication from University of California, Santa Barbara in 2011. He studies media effects, social media, and credibility, and has published work on kids and Internet use, news media bias, and selective exposure.

Ilias Karasavvidis is a Lecturer on Information and Communication Technologies (ICT) in Education in the Department of Preschool Education at the University of Thessaly, Greece. He is the head of the ICT Research Unit of the Natural Sciences and Technologies Lab in the same Department. He holds an honors degree in Teacher Education from the University of Crete and a PhD in Educational Technology from the University of Twente. His current research interests include learning with ICT and more specifically Web 2.0, digital games, and digital media applications in teaching and learning.

Lilian Landes studied Art History and Archaeology at the Universities of Marburg and Munich. In Munich she received the Doctor's degree with a dissertation about social genre painting in Germany in the 1840s. She joined the Centre for Electronic Publishing at the Bavarian State Library in 2008 after having worked four years at the University of Munich (Collaborative Research Centre "Early Modern Period"). At the BSB she has been a member of the academic editorial team of perspectivia.net. Since 2010 she has been co-ordinating the recensio.net project (review platform for European History). Furthermore she works on themes like open access, academic publishing, and scientific Web 2.0 culture.

Michael Mangus (B.S., University of Pittsburgh) is a graduate student in the Department of Communication at UC Santa Barbara. His research investigates the mechanisms that support dynamic social processes -- such as coordination, cooperation, and trust -- in mediated contexts. Michael holds a B.S. in Information Science from the University of Pittsburgh.

Alex Markov (B.A., Northwestern University; M.A., University of California, Santa Barbara) is a Doctoral student in the Department of Communication at the University of California, Santa Barbara. Alex's research focuses on how people evaluate the credibility of information online, with an emphasis on social and cognitive processes.

Miriam Metzger (Ph.D., Annenberg School for Communication, University of Southern California) is an Associate Professor in the Department of Communication at the University of California at Santa Barbara. Her interests lie at the intersection of media, information technology, and trust, centering on how information technology alters our understandings of credibility, privacy, and the processes of media effects.

Ananda Mitra (PhD, University of Illinois) teaches the relationship among human communication, society, culture, and the new digital technologies at Wake Forest University. He has published ten books including his most recent book, *Alien Technology: Coping with Modern Mysteries* (SAGE, 2011), where he argues that most people are increasingly alienated from the tools they use leading to a variety of challenges in everyday life. Professor Mitra is also the inventor of the idea of "narbs" that suggests that digital social media have offered individuals an opportunity to create tiny narrative bits that produce the digital identity of a person. In addition to his work with new technologies, culture, and society, Dr. Mitra also leads students in a summer course in India where the students are offered an immersive learning experience in various parts of India.

Janet McNeil Hurlbert is Associate Dean and Director of Library Services at Lycoming College, Williamsport, Pennsylvania. Her Bachelor of Arts degree in history and Master in Library Science degree are both from the University of Denver. Prior work experience includes reference positions at Iowa State University and Virginia Commonwealth University where she also became the head of collection management. Hurlbert edited the book *Defining Relevancy: Managing the New Academic Library*, published by Libraries Unlimited (Greenwood Press), as well as authoring numerous book chapters and articles in professional and teaching journals. She has presented at numerous conferences including the Annual Lilly Conference, Miami University, the LOEX Conference, the annual American Library Association Conference, and the Association of College and Research Libraries Conference. Hurlbert has coordinated several LSTA grants to support the Lycoming County Women's History Digital Collection.

Steven Ovadia is Associate Professor/Web Services Librarian at LaGuardia Community College (City University of New York). He frequently writes about how users interact with information in online contexts. He is the Internet Connection columnist for *Behavioral & Social Sciences Librarian*, and his work has been published in *Journal of Academic Librarianship*, *Library Philosophy and Practice*, and *Journal of Web Librarianship*. He has an MLIS from Palmer School of Library and Information Science and an MA in Applied Social Research from Queens College (City University of New York).

Hugo Pardo Kuklinski is a member of Imagine.CC, member of the Interactive Media Lab (LMI), Universitat de Barcelona, and Full Professor of Department of Digital Communication, Universitat de Vic in Barcelona. He holds a PhD in Audiovisual Communication from the Universitat Autònoma de Barcelona. He has been Visiting Professor at Stanford Human-Computer Interaction Group, Stanford University, USA (2007/09). He is the author of *Geekonomía. Un radar para producir en el postdigitalismo* (2010) and *Planeta Web 2.0. Inteligencia colectiva o medios fast food* (2007).

Rebecca Pure (M.A., University of California at Santa Barbara) is a Doctoral candidate in the Department of Communication at the University of California at Santa Barbara, and has completed an external emphasis in Technology and Society. Rebekah's research focuses on how Internet users manage their uncertainty online regarding information credibility, online aggression, and privacy.

Mary J. Snyder Broussard is an Assistant Professor and Instructional Services Librarian at Lycoming College in Williamsport, PA. Mary received her Master of Library Science degree from Indiana University. She teaches library research strategies to undergraduate students, coordinates reference services, and maintains the library Web site. Her research interests include educational games in libraries, social media and other Web technologies, and the central role of academic libraries in preventing plagiarism. She is a heavy user of many popular social media sites and maintains a blog on educational games in libraries.

Frederik Truyen (1961) is Associate Professor at the Faculty of Arts, University of Leuven in Belgium since 1997, where he teaches Information Science and Online Publishing. He holds a PhD in Philosophy (Logic) since 1991, based on a study of Gottlob Frege's Theory on Object and Concept. He has been Coordinator ICT for Humanities and Social Sciences at Leuven University since 2006 and Head of ICT Services at the Faculty of Arts KU Leuven since 1989. He has been in charge of Digital Humanities at the Institute for Cultural Studies. He is active in the area of ICT at several levels of the University, mostly related to Web technology and E-Learning. He currently chairs the ICT Council for Humanities and Social Sciences, and is involved in many projects on Open Educational Resources. He publishes on E-Learning, ICT Education, and Epistemology.

Carlos Alberto Scolari (Argentina, 1963) holds a PhD in Applied Linguistics and Language of Communication from the Catholic University of Milan. He is currently Associate Professor at the Universitat Pompeu Fabra (Barcelona) where he teaches Methods of Message Analysis and Message Analysis in Interactive Media. Between 2004-2006 he was coordinator of the Ibero-American Network of Digital Communication (ALFA Program). He is the author of *Hipermediaciones. Elementos para una teoría de la comunicación digital interactiva* (2008) and *Hacer click. Hacia una socio-semiótica de las interacciones digitales* (2004) among other titles.

Christopher Sweet is the Information Literacy Librarian at The Ames Library (Illinois Wesleyan University, Bloomington, IL). He graduated with a B.A. from Augustana College (Rock Island, IL) and a MS degree from Graduate Studies in Library and Information Science program at the University of Illinois (Urbana-Champaign). Christopher's background includes a wide range of experience in archives, public libraries and community colleges. His current research interests include information literacy pedagogy, the impact of new media on information, and service learning. He is also active in campus and community environmental causes.

Christopher Watts is Director of the Newell Center for Arts Technology and Associate Professor of Music at St. Lawrence University in Canton, New York. A teacher, composer, and media artist, Watts holds the Doctor of Musical Arts degree from the University of Cincinnati. In classes, composition, performance, and writing, Watts explores the relationships among people and the technologies they use. He teaches courses in music technology, composition, digital media art, programming, and physics/perception of music. Recent creative work includes fixed-media pieces as well as live-interactive performances. Watts has published articles on the role of technology in higher education—especially in liberal education and as a vehicle for collaboration—and given numerous conference presentations on related topics.

Rebecca A. Wilson is Associate Professor and Associate Director of the Blough-Weis Library at Susquehanna University in Selinsgrove, PA. She earned her Master's of Library Science at Florida State University, and her Doctorate of Education at Penn State University. Earlier research focused on students' use of the Internet for course-related research, an interest that led into her current research on students and their use of social media. In her former position at Penn State, Dr. Wilson participated in the NEH-funded United States Newspaper Program for the State of Pennsylvania, a project designed to locate, catalog and preserve historic newspapers across the country. She currently oversees the internal operations of the Library at Susquehanna University.

Alyssa Wise is Assistant Professor of Education at Simon Fraser University in Vancouver, Canada, associated with the Educational Technology & Learning Design Program. Taking a constructivist perspective on learning, she is interested in the tensions and overlap between current "consumer" and "community" models of interaction in online spaces. Her research examines the design, use, and evaluation of online learning environments with an emphasis on experiences that foster a dynamic interplay between individuals' trajectories of understanding and groups' collective development of ideas. In her current work she is focusing on learning in the context of asynchronous online discussions, investigating how learners "listen" to others' comments, take on different conversational roles, and engage in argumentation and knowledge construction practices.

Joris J. van Zundert is a Researcher and Developer in the field of computational humanities at the Huygens Institute for the History of The Netherlands, a research institute of The Netherlands Royal Academy of Arts and Sciences (KNAW). As a researcher and developer he is interested in the applications and capabilities of digital algorithms for historic and literary analysis. As a Project Manager Joris van Zundert headed several IT infrastructure projects in the humanities domain. He is also Chair of the European 'Interedition' project aimed at furthering interoperability and collaboration in digital humanities tool building. Joris van Zundert studied Dutch literature and linguistics at the University of Utrecht (The Netherlands) and specialized in historical literature. In 2005 he was appointed scientific researcher at the Huygens Institute. In 2006 he became Head of the 'Digital Humanities Software R&D Team' of the same institute.

Index